THE JOHN HARVARD LIBRARY

Bernard Bailyn
Editor-in-Chief

THE JOHN HARVARD LIBRARY

THE WORKS OF
JAMES WILSON

Edited by Robert Green McCloskey

IN TWO VOLUMES

VOLUME I

THE BELKNAP PRESS OF
HARVARD UNIVERSITY PRESS
CAMBRIDGE, MASSACHUSETTS

1967

John Harvard Library books are edited
at the Charles Warren Center for Studies
in American History, Harvard University.

Library of Congress Catalog Card Number 67-14344

Printed in the United States of America

CONTENTS

INTRODUCTION BY ROBERT GREEN MC CLOSKEY   I

A NOTE ON THE TEXT   49

THE WORKS OF JAMES WILSON   53

BIBLIOGRAPHICAL GLOSSARY   849

INDEX   857

INTRODUCTION

Introduction

I

ON February 17, 1964, Mr. Justice Black held for the Supreme Court that the Constitution requires congressional districts to be, as nearly as practicable, equal; and cited as authority for this revelation three sentences uttered by Mr. Justice James Wilson in 1791.[1] If we permit ourselves the convenient fancy that the shades of the dead contemplate the affairs of the living,[2] it is easy to guess what Wilson's reaction might have been. He would surely have been gratified as men naturally are when they see their principles ultimately vindicated, and the specific mention of his name would have pleased him, for "the love of honest and well earned fame is deeply rooted in honest and susceptible minds."[3] This mention might also have surprised him a little, because although he yearned to be remembered by a "just and grateful country,"[4] that country has managed to forget him pretty thoroughly for the better part of two centuries. But if he were surprised to be given credit for the constitutional inno-

---

[1] *Wesberry v. Sanders*, 376 U.S. 1, 17 (1964). The sentences were: "[A]ll elections ought to be equal. Elections are equal, when a given number of citizens, in one part of the state, choose as many representatives, as are chosen by the same number of citizens, in any other part of the state. In this manner, the proportion of representatives and of the constituents will remain invariably the same." *The Works of James Wilson* (John Harvard Library Edition), p. 406. (Cited hereafter as JHL *Works*.) Mr. Chief Justice Warren cited the same passage in the state reapportionment case, *Reynolds v. Sims*, 377 U.S. 533, 564 n. 41 (1964). The choice of Wilson for historical support was not fortuitous. He unquestionably did believe in what is now called the principle of "one man, one vote"; and he seems to be the *only* important founding father who expressed himself unequivocally to this effect. It is also tolerably plain from the chapter cited by Black that Wilson thought the Constitution should be interpreted as embodying the principle. For he says that the Constitution rests "on the great democratical principle of a representation of the people," and that this principle "necessarily draws along with it the consideration of another principle equally great — the principle of free and equal elections." JHL *Works*, p. 402. On the other hand, Black's further citations — to King, Madison, and Steele in the ratification debates — provide much more doubtful support for his argument. King and Madison were pretty clearly talking about the power of *Congress* to regulate apportionment; and the words of Steele must be squeezed very hard indeed in order to wring from them the interpretation Black adopts. Jonathan Elliot, *Debates on . . . the Federal Constitution . . .* (Washington, 1861), II, 50; III, 366–367; IV, 71.

[2] We have Wilson's own authority for doing so. In one of his law lectures he said: "Of the happiness of heaven, a part of the unerring description is—that it is 'full of glory.' " JHL *Works*, p. 594.

[3] JHL *Works*, p. 405.   [4] JHL *Works*, p. 71.

vation, the innovation itself would not have surprised him at all. This is only the latest in a long train of Wilsonian principles which have been embodied in the American polity in the years since his death. It is not too much to say that the ideas of James Wilson more nearly fore-shadowed the national future than those of any of his well-remembered contemporaries. No one of them — not Hamilton, or Jefferson, or Madison, or Adams, or Marshall — came so close to representing in his views what the United States was to become.

One who writes about Wilson must consciously restrain himself lest the reader suspect him of overstatement and discount his evaluations accordingly. Enthusiasts are prone to disinter comparatively minor figures — Pelatiah Webster,[5] Charles Pinckney[6] — and promote them to a new and doubtful eminence among the architects of the nation. Biographers can be infected by a vicarious egocentrism that inflates their subject and helps justify the time and labor invested in him. But Wilson is a special case, and if the past is any guide, the danger is not overstatement but understatement, not that he will be falsely magnified but that he will remain, in spite of the historical reality, little honored and almost forgotten.

The truth is that posterity's neglect of Wilson is nothing short of astonishing when it is measured against his claims to be remembered. A mere recitation of the roles he performed is sufficiently arresting. He was one of six men who signed both the Declaration of Independence and the Constitution; and his contribution to the deliberations of the Federal Convention was second only to Madison's. He was the principal figure in the struggle to secure ratification of the Constitution in Pennsylvania, the approval of that state being indispensable to the success of the whole constitutional movement. The important Pennsylvania state constitution of 1790 was very largely his work. He was one of the original justices of the Supreme Court of the United States and was commonly accepted in a nation already much dominated by lawyers as the most learned and profound legal scholar of his generation.

But this is very far from the whole story. Such a bare catalogue does not suggest the special attitudes that he brought to these activities or the striking parallels between those attitudes and the future lines of American constitutional and political development. The point is not that Wilson was especially "influential" in determining that future. No doubt he affected it some, but as an historical influence he does not remotely com-

---

[5] Charles Warren, *The Making of the Constitution* (Cambridge, Mass., 1947), pp. 48–49. Edward S. Corwin, "The Pelatiah Webster Myth" in *The Doctrine of Judicial Review* (Princeton, 1914), pp. 111–129.

[6] Charles C. Nott, *The Mystery of The Pinckney Draught* (New York, 1908). S. Sidney Ulmer, "Charles Pinckney, Father of the Constitution," *South Carolina Law Quarterly*, 10 (1958), 225–247.

pare with such peers as Hamilton and Jefferson and Marshall. Nor is it precisely right to say that he was more "prescient" than his fellows, if the word means that he consciously expected the Republic to evolve as it has evolved. He may have had such prophetic intimations, but he left small record of them. Perhaps the right word is "anticipate" in the sense of "to observe or practice in advance of the due date" rather than to foresee. Wilson's outlook was an anachronism, a prototype of the American system that has gradually emerged in the course of history.

This precursory quality of his mind is illustrated repeatedy in his intellectual biography. He seems to have been the first to conceive clearly — or at any rate to commit to paper — the view of the relationship between Crown and colonies that was an American dogma in the 1770's and became in the nineteenth century "the working compromise" [7] that preserved the British Empire, namely that Parliament has *no* authority over the colonies, which are bound to the Empire only by their obedience and loyalty to the British King. Wilson composed his *Considerations*[8] in 1768 (though it was not published until 1774, six months before John Adams made a similar argument in his *Novanglus*) and, as Page Smith says, Wilson "may thus be credited with formulating the idea of dominion status six years ahead of [Adams] and some seventy years ahead of the British Foreign Office." [9] In 1785, in the course of a defense of the Bank of North America, he advanced the doctrine that a corporate charter is an inviolable contract between the state and the company, and the doctrine that the national congress (even under the Articles of Confederation) enjoys, in addition to the powers specifically delegated, "general powers . . . resulting from the union of the whole." [10] The first of these ideas prefigures the holdings of Marshall in *Fletcher v. Peck*[11] and the *Dartmouth College* case;[12] the second certainly anticipates the "implied powers" conception of *McCulloch v. Maryland*,[13] and will further suggest to students of constitutional history the "inherent powers" doctrine of such relatively modern decisions as *Missouri v. Holland*[14] and *United States v. Curtiss-Wright*.[15] In the same tract he set forth what has been called the doctrine of "dual sovereignty":[16] that while the states are sovereign within their sphere, the nation is sovereign with respect to national affairs — that sovereignty is divisible. This all-important idea, which Wilson himself developed further in the Federal Convention and in *Chisholm v. Georgia*,[17] foreshadows Marshall's words

[7] Charles H. McIlwain, *The American Revolution: A Constitutional Interpretation* (New York, 1923), p. 116.
[8] *Considerations on the Nature and Extent of the Legislative Authority of the British Parliament*, JHL *Works*, p. 721.
[9] Charles Page Smith, *James Wilson* . . . (Chapel Hill, 1956), p. 58.
[10] JHL *Works*, p. 829.   [11] 6 Cranch 87 (1810).   [12] 4 Wheaton 518 (1819).
[13] 4 Wheaton 316 (1819).   [14] 252 U.S. 416 (1920).   [15] 299 U.S. 304 (1936).
[16] Smith, *Wilson*, pp. 152, 236.   [17] 2 Dallas 419 (1793).

in *Cohens v. Virginia:* "[the states] are members of one great empire —for some purposes sovereign, for some purposes subordinate." [18] His view of the nature of law rejected the Blackstonian idea of law based on the command of a superior and found the source of legal obligation rather in "the consent of those whose obedience the law requires," [19] such consent deriving, thought Wilson, from the gradual accumulation of custom. Accordingly he envisioned a judicial system very like that of subsequent American history, enjoying its authority by virtue not of superior power but of general acceptance, and extending that authority step by step as the growth of need and custom permitted. Of course the judiciary as he saw it would exercise the function of judicial review;[20] Wilson is one of those whose views on this matter were unmistakable.

Few if any of these insights were entirely unique. Most of them can be attributed to one or more of the other founding fathers, though it is worth re-emphasis that Wilson often achieved these positions somewhat sooner than his contemporaries and stated them with greater clarity. However, with respect to one immensely important prevision Wilson stands alone, if not in the general tendency of his conviction, at least in the degree and consistency of his commitment to it. His fellows were, almost without exception, prevented from accurate foreknowledge of the nation they were building by the confusions that were to be exemplified in the struggle between the Hamiltonian and the Jeffersonian persuasions. Hamilton wanted a strong national government and a firm union, but he hoped to base the government of that union on a merchant-manufacturer oligarchy because he dreaded the disorder and threats to property that majority rule might entail. Jefferson—or at any rate "Jeffersonians"—tended to accept majority rule but to distrust national union and national power. The result of these discordancies of opinion was the ambivalent constitutional arrangement of 1789 with its complex hedging on the questions of popular rule and national power; and the political struggles of the time continued to reflect the curious illusion that localism is inevitably linked to democracy, that a potent central government is the instrument of minority control and the enemy of liberty. The eventual historical solution of course was to reject these twin misconceptions and to recognize that democracy and national union were natural partners. This solution—which may be said to be still working itself out—began to appear soon after ratification and has been signalized in our history by such statements as Marshall's opinion in

---

[18] 6 Wheaton 264, 414 (1821).   [19] JHL *Works,* p. 121.
[20] John B. McMaster and Frederick D. Stone (eds.), *Pennsylvania and the Federal Constitution, 1787–1788* (Lancaster, Pa., 1888), p. 354. Max Farrand, *The Records of the Federal Convention of 1787* (New Haven, 1911), II, 73, 391. Elliot *Debates,* II, 445. Wilson, JHL *Works,* pp. 300, 329–331.

McCulloch v. Maryland, Webster's reply to Hayne, Jackson's reaction
to the nullification crisis, and the Gettysburg Address; and by such
developments as the *de facto* popular election of the President, the consequent emergence of the President as a puissant tribune of the national
will, the Seventeenth Amendment, and — only yesterday — the reapportionment decisions. Wilson could justifiably regard each of these as a
vindication of his own instincts.

Wilson saw, as Hamilton did not, that the union government could
only be based on the will of the whole people, and he had no fear that
such a popularly based government would plunder the rich and degrade
the nation.[21] Yet he also saw, as Jefferson did not, that excessive localism
was potentially incompatible with national well-being as well as with
democracy. He saw this even at the time of the Federal Convention
more clearly than anyone else, and he was more consistent than anyone
else, including Madison, in advocating political democracy. He favored
direct popular election of both Senate and House, as did most of the
other delegates from the large states, and he joined with Madison in
urging that the proposed Constitution be submitted to popularly elected
conventions in each state, a policy that has been called "the most au-
dacious and altogether unqualified appeal to the notion of popular sovereignty and majority rule that had ever been made, even in America." [22]
But when Madison supported a freehold qualification for voting, Wilson
opposed it,[23] and Wilson was practically alone in arguing that the president too should be elected directly by the people, the general opinion
being that it "would be as unnatural to refer the choice of a proper
character for chief Magistrate to the people as it would be to refer a
trial of colours to a blind man." [24] Add to all this the fact that his personal handiwork, the Pennsylvania constitution of 1790, provided only an
almost negligible tax qualification for voting,[25] and that Wilson led a
successful fight for direct election of the state senate,[26] and Wilson stands
forth as one of the most consistent democrats of his era. Add the further

[21] Charles Beard said: "Wilson shared the apprehensions of his colleagues as to
the dangers of democratic legislatures . . . ," *An Economic Interpretation of the
Constitution of the United States* (New York, 1949), p. 216; which leaves the impression that Wilson was, like many of the others, suspicious of democracy itself.
But this is to misunderstand him. He certainly opposed the tendency to exalt the
legislature as the all-powerful organ of the popular will, but that was because he
thought a political community would *function* most effectively as a democracy if
the other two branches of government — also deriving from the people — were not
overridden by the legislature. See JHL *Works,* p. 293.
[22] Corwin, "Webster Myth," p. 106.   [23] Farrand, *Records,* II, 201.
[24] George Mason of Virginia, quoted in Max Farrand, *The Framing of the Constitution of the United States* (New Haven, 1925), p. 116.
[25] Louis Hartz, *Economic Policy and Democratic Thought: Pennsylvania, 1776–
1860* (Cambridge, Mass., 1948), p. 23.
[26] JHL *Works,* pp. 781–793.

fact that he steadily supported a strong government (and particuarly a strong executive) as well as a democratic one, and he stands virtually alone among his contemporaries. "To render government efficient," he said, "powers must be given liberally: to render it free as well as efficient, those powers must be drawn from the people as directly and as immediately as possible." [27] This proposition cuts across the prejudices and suspicions that bedeviled the Federalists and anti-Federalists, the Hamiltonians, and the Jeffersonians;[28] it foreshadows what has appeared with increasing clarity in the course of the years as the essential feature of the American national experiment.

This then is a partial account of Wilson's claims to be remembered and celebrated among the founders of the Republic. Yet his actual repute has been greatly less than the claims would seem to warrant. To be sure, the Wilson-fancier can collect a few sentences of tribute from historians of high authority. Lord Bryce admired him and A. F. Pollard called him "possibly the profoundest theorist of the Revolution." [29] Andrew C. McLaughlin placed him "above all but one or two men of the convention" [30] and Max Farrand rated Wilson "second to Madison and almost on a par with him." [31] Morris R. Cohen included Wilson — along with Coke, Blackstone, Marshall, Kent, and Story — among the group "who may be said to have laid the foundation of the American common law." [32] In 1930 Randolph G. Adams edited a volume of Wilson's political essays,[33] and in an earlier book he devoted a chapter to Wilson's contributions to legal theory.[34] In 1956 Charles Page Smith produced a valuable biography, the first and only one so far published. But the noteworthy thing is that these gleanings are so comparatively sparse, that most of the references to Wilson are so perfunctory even when they acknowledge his great importance, that those few who have paid special attention to him, such as McLaughlin, Adams, and Smith, are all successively astonished by posterity's neglect. Adams felt that Wilson's fame had been steadily gaining ground and that he would soon in the natural course of events get his deserts from the nation he had served. Smith's biography was a step in that direction even though it came twenty-seven years after Adams' sanguine prediction. But it seems fair to say that even today Wilson is well-known only to a few consti-

[27] JHL *Works*, p. 791.
[28] Jackson T. Main, *The Antifederalists* (Chapel Hill, 1961), p. xiv.
[29] Randolph G. Adams, *Selected Political Essays of James Wilson* (New York, 1930), p. 19 and Editorial Foreword.
[30] "James Wilson in the Philadelphia Convention," *Political Science Quarterly*, 12 (1897), 1.
[31] *The Framing of The Constitution*, p. 197.
[32] *Law and the Social Order* (New York, 1933), p. 333.
[33] *Selected Political Essays of James Wilson*.
[34] *Political Ideas of the American Revolution* (Durham, N.C.), 1922.

tutional historians, that he is not much more than a name to most other American historians, and that to educated Americans in general he is not even a name. The discrepancy between Wilson's historic importance and his posthumous reputation is one of the intriguing paradoxes of our national hagiography.

However, this is only the first of the paradoxes that present themselves to one who examines Wilson's story. There are at least two others, equally striking, equally tantalizing; and a knowledge of these others is necessary to an understanding of the first. One is the enigma of his contemporary reputation. In spite of the remarkable and seemingly unquestionable devotion to popular democracy which has been described above, he was widely regarded by contemporaries as a conservative of deepest dye and was stigmatized repeatedly as one who "has always been tainted with the spirit of high aristocracy" and who "despises what he calls the inferior order of the people." [35] The final paradox is in the career and character of the man himself. Although he deeply wished to be esteemed as one of the chief statesmen-heroes of the American pantheon, although he gave much of his heart and mind to the public service, he also wanted with equal passion to be rich, to create a personal financial empire side by side with the republican dominion he was helping to secure. And he pursued this material aim so obsessively and ruthlessly that in a peculiarly American tragedy he lost, not only the fame he had wanted and earned, but the wealth for which the fame had been traded.

Each of these three apparent contradictions in Wilson's life and repute is linked to the others. Each of them calls for explanation, and the quest for those explanations requires us to look more fully into Wilson's personal biography, into the nature of politics and ideas in his time, and into the evolving character of America in the years that followed.

II

Although many of the external facts of Wilson's life are of course known, a deeper understanding of the man is hard to come by. He left few of those personal vestiges that are so vital to the biographer — the private journal or memoir, the revealing, confidential letter. Nor is there much that is very illuminating about him in the writings of his contemporaries; even his death was unmarked — for reasons that will appear — by the reminiscent funeral elegies that usually follow the passing of a great man and that may provide some clues to his character. Wilson's own writings were substantial enough, and some hints of the man behind them shine through. But the fact remains that our impressions of his inner life must rest very largely on guess and inference.

He was born in Fifeshire, Scotland, in 1742, the first son of William

---

[35] Quoted in Smith, *Wilson*, p. 266.

Wilson, who seems to have been the typical diligent small farmer of that time and place. Both his father and mother were pious to a degree that may have been special even in the land of John Knox; and James Wilson, as the oldest son, was promised at birth to the ministry. After his father's death, when he himself was about twenty years old, Wilson decided against a career in the Kirk, but by then his whole youth had been colored by the pledge his parents had made for him in babyhood. It is difficult to be sure how much of the character he displayed later in life can be traced back to the rigorous, Calvinistic devoutness of his home and to the assumption that the boy was destined to do God's work. One would particularly like to know what ordeal of conscience he may have suffered when he determined to repudiate his dead father's wish, whether his impulse toward public service in later years was a kind of surrogate for the holy task he had abandoned, whether the lifelong conflict between statesmanship and self-enrichment was not prefigured in this youthful crisis. He was evidently an immensely ambitious and energetic young man: that much can be confidently inferred from the boundless vigor, the endless projects, of his mature life; and from the fact that he was unwilling to settle for the lot that faced him in Scotland. It was not a very bad lot as Old World prospects went; his life at home would not have been opulent, but it would probably have been quite bearable. Wilson was not one of those emigrants who were driven to the New World by intolerable poverty or persecution; he was rather one of those whose inner needs impelled them to exchange a safe, cramped future for a prospect less certain but perhaps far more spacious. Such men are more than ordinarily ambitious; they are a special restless breed. If they are unencumbered by ethical misgivings, their aspirations need create no problems for them: they can steer a single, ruthless course. But if by temperament and upbringing they are burdened with a sense of high moral duty, they may agonize over the conflicts between avidity and altruism, behave erratically as one impulse or the other is ascendant, or persuade themselves, when it is possible, that they serve a higher purpose by serving themselves.

Whatever may have been the ultimate effect on Wilson's soul of this early religious commitment, one of its effects on his future career is perfectly tangible and beyond conjecture. In preparation for the ministry, he received an education that not many of his station and means could have expected, and this training was to prove invaluable when he took it with him to the burgeoning society of the New World. After an elementary education in a nearby grammar school, Wilson went at the age of fifteen to the University of St. Andrews, where he studied for five years. Scotland was undergoing at that time the eruption of energy and ideas that has been called the Scottish Renaissance. St. Andrews was not Edinburgh, but it was a respectable university, and had recently been revitalized by the advent of new faculty members primed with the new learning. Wilson's education there was not far from the best that the Old World could provide. In America, where perhaps no more than one in a thousand colonists had attended college,[36] where men with European education were even rarer, this burden of learning that his father's pledge had imposed on him turned out to be precious beyond price. Wilson was certainly one of the best-educated men in America when he arrived there in 1765. His training and natural bookishness were admirably suited for a society already much dominated by lawyers and men of learning, already dreaming that enlightenment could lift a whole nation to millennial heights, already preparing to think anew the ancient problem of political obligation.

If his education supplied Wilson with the formal credentials for advancement in the New World, it may also have contributed to a mental set that was to characterize his career in that world. Throughout his life one senses a quality of mind that is curiously abstractive and romantic, a confidence in ideas and an impulse to push them to the limits of their implications without great regard for practicalities, a taste for large intellectual constructs and grand schemes. He was in a way unworldly even when his objectives seemed most mundane. This bent made it possible sometimes for him to pierce through confusion to essences; it helps account for some of those precursory insights already mentioned. But it also sometimes carried him headlong down rocky paths that others would have trod more hesitantly and safely.

The quality is illustrated by that noteworthy pamphlet he composed in 1768, *Considerations on the Nature and Extent of the Legislative Authority of the British Parliament.* Wilson had disembarked in New York in 1765, had gone directly to Philadelphia, and had, by flourishing his rare educational credentials, found employment as a tutor at the College of Philadelphia. But though his taste for scholarship was always strong, it was never all-absorbing. He wanted a more spectacular success than the study alone could offer, and the law must have immediately seemed a calling nicely adapted to his talents and ambitions. It was both scholarly and worldly. Wilson's erudite background and propensities would serve him well in the law; and by happy chance the legal profession was at this very time developing the prestige and importance that were to elevate lawyers to such a vital place in the future history of America.[37] He made an arrangement to read law under one of the luminaries of the colonial bar, John Dickinson, who had himself studied at

[36] Evarts B. Greene, *The Revolutionary Generation, 1763–1790* (New York, 1943), p. 123.
[37] *Ibid.*, p. 280.

the London Inns of Court, and in 1767 Wilson began practice in the town of Reading. Meanwhile he had been caught up in the controversy over the worsening relationships between the English motherland and the colonies. His mentor, Dickinson, published in 1767–68 the *Farmer's Letters,* challenging Parliament's power to tax the colonies for the purpose of raising revenue but conceding the authority to regulate external trade and levy duties in order to control imperial commerce. Wilson says in the preface to his own paper — and there is no reason to doubt him — that he had sat down "with a view and expectation of being able to trace some constitutional line between those cases in which we ought, and those in which we ought not, to acknowledge the power of parliament over us," but became convinced somewhat to his own surprise that such power must be denied "in every instance." [38] Starting with the premise drawn from "the law of nature" that government must rest on consent, that a people must be enabled to express their consent by restraining those who govern them, and noting that the colonists had no means of choosing or influencing the Parliament, he was driven inexorably to the conclusion that Parliament should have no voice whatever in the affairs of the colonies. There is no basis for drawing distinctions that allow Parliament to pass general laws but not taxes, or to regulate external but not internal affairs. The tie that binds the colonies to the Empire is the "faith and obedience" which they owe the Crown, and only that.

It was indeed a tight and formidable argument once the premise was granted. Wilson buttressed his contention with legalistic citations purporting to show that the colonial status he described was the traditional one, and here there was of course room for considerable argument. But "the law of nature" was quite enough to carry his point. Nor is the apparent concession of allegiance to the Crown as great as might seem. For, in the first place, Wilson was obviously assuming that the King's prerogative in America could be checked by colonial assemblies, just as it could be checked in England by the House of Commons. If the consent of the House of Commons, or a colonial legislature, is necessary to pass a law, and if the populace is represented in those bodies, then the principle of consent is protected and popular liberties can be ensured. [39] And, in the second place, Wilson was careful to say that the "faith and obedience" to the King were founded on the "protection" which the King reciprocally owed his subjects, [40] and it followed (though Wilson stopped

---

[38] JHL *Works,* p. 721.   [39] JHL *Works,* p. 724.

[40] *Ibid.,* p. 743. See also the speech delivered in the Provincial Convention in January 1775: " 'it [the British constitution] binds the king as much as the meanest subject.' The measures of his power, and the limits, beyond which he cannot extend it, are circumscribed and regulated by the same authority, and with the same precision, as the measures of the subject's obedience, and the limits, beyond

short of saying so) that the allegiance could be withdrawn if the protection was denied. Some question might be raised, and a friend did raise it, whether the nation was in 1768 or even 1774 quite ready for a set of views so in advance of their times, or whether "the wisest system that the Colonies can adopt at present" might be "to temporize a little."[41] But when Wilson saw an idea and a pen, his natural inclination was to proceed as far as they would carry him.

III

Yet this is not to say that he was an extremist in politics, much less a "radical" in the popular meaning of that term; nor that he was intransigent in holding out for his own views. On the contrary, he could usually be found among the "moderates" in factional disputes, and his political career was marked by frequent compromises. As a delegate to the Continental Congress in 1775 and 1776, he resisted until nearly the last moment the drift toward a Declaration of Independence. He temporized so long in fact that the radicals attacked him bitterly, and the charge of having opposed independence pursued him all his life; even in 1829, long after his death, Goodrich in the *Lives of the Signers* felt obliged to refute the "slander."[42] And in 1787, in the course of the ratification controversy, Wilson said: "I will confess, indeed, that I am not a blind admirer of this plan of government, and that there are some parts of it, which if my wish had prevailed, would certainly have been altered. But, when I reflect how widely men differ in their opinions, and that every man . . . has an equal pretension to assert his own, I am satisfied that anything nearer to perfection could not have been accomplished."[43]

Both of these examples are perfectly characteristic of Wilson's statesmanship, and may seem incompatible with the doctrinaire, rationalistic tendency attributed to him in this essay. We expect that axiomatic thinkers will be prepared, as Wilson's fellow émigré and rationalist Tom Paine was, to upset existing social and political arrangements. We expect them to be impatient and obstinate when other men "differ in their opinions" and claim "an equal pretension to assert their own." But in Wilson's case the commitment to ideas was often combined with and moderated by a quality that might be described — without disparagement — as the will to succeed, to "get along." It is evident that he wanted acceptance, position, respectability; that he was drawn to the solid folk

which he is under no obligation to practise it, are fixed and ascertained. . . . The duties of the king and those of the subject are plainly reciprocal: they can be violated on neither side, unless they be performed on the other." *Ibid.*, pp. 753–754.
[41] Smith, *Wilson*, p. 58.
[42] Charles A. Goodrich, *The Lives of the Signers of the Declaration of Independence* (New York, 1829), p. 303.
[43] McMaster and Stone, *Constitution*, p. 149.

of Reading (where he met his first wife, Rachel Bird, daughter of one of the leading citizens), and of Carlisle and Philadelphia, where he successively made his home. His ambition was to share the power and prestige of these substantial citizens, not to disrupt the order of their world, and he had every reason to expect that his ambition would be realized, for by the time of his marriage in 1771 he was already clearly on his way to success at the bar. To Tom Paine the established order made no appeal. It had done nothing for him in England except to provoke in him the spirit of revolt, and so he was already disposed when he came to America to drive in a straight line from his premises to dogmatic revolutionary conclusions. Wilson, with a different life experience and different prospects, took a different course. Like Paine, he was inclined to follow where his reason led him, but — again like Paine — he was led by his reason to conclusions that were congenial to his own aspirations and tastes. Wilson's proposal of dominion status with the King's prerogative checked by colonial legislatures was no less logical than Paine's proposal of outright separation — until it became apparent that the King would not tolerate such derogation of either Parliament's power or his own; and it was a proposal less calculated to disörganize the order that, to Wilson, meant so much. Wilson may have been rather slow to recognize that the King's intractability had become apparent, and even after he came to realize that separation was inevitable, he hung back from supporting the resolution for independence on the plea that the Pennsylvania delegation was still formally bound by the Assembly's instructions against such a policy. But when the vote came he voted for the policy and signed the Declaration, which had now become in the light of circumstances the unequivocal outcome of his cherished principle of popular consent.

However, while Wilson often managed, as in this instance, to maintain considerable accord between his liking for logic and his liking for comfort and order, it must be conceded that they were not always compatible, and that he was then quite capable of accepting a compromise that would, to an extent, dilute the principle. This is evident from his ratification speech quoted above, and one even has a feeling that his reluctance about independence, though arguably consistent enough with his premises, was also explainable partly as a reluctance to break ties with such friends as Dickinson and Robert Morris who continued to oppose separation after Wilson had given in. This willingness to make do with something less than the perfect symmetry of rationalism, to modify one's own ends in order to accommodate to the opinions of others, is usually associated with the pragmatic temper; and of course it would be idle to deny that Wilson had, like most men, a strain of the pragmatist in his makeup. He had sense enough to know that a half a loaf can be better than none, and that in order to get along it is sometimes necessary to go along. Not many men who are not saints are entirely lacking in this sense. But since most men are a mixture of the conceptualist and the pragmatist, the meaningful question is how and in what proportion these impulses are conjoined. Men like Henry Clay or Franklin Roosevelt, for example, seem to have been instinctively pragmatic, which is not to say that they were devoid of principled conviction but that their natural impulse was to think first and most often in terms of concrete problems and practical arrangements. Wilson's inclinations ran the other way, which is, again, not to say that he was incapable of compromise or even opportunism, but that his first and powerful impulse was to conceptualize, that abstractions always attracted him greatly, and that he was often tempted to pursue them unless unmistakable reality held him down to earth.

This impulse, this quality of mind, may explain much about the attitude toward popular democracy which he professed so ardently before, during, and after the Federal Convention; and which is, as I have said, so remarkable in a declared Federalist partisan. There is of course nothing particularly noteworthy in the fact that he espoused the doctrine of popular consent in some form: by 1776 only Tories dared to repudiate it. But for most of the founding fathers the will of the people was the necessary but not sufficient condition for an acceptable political order. Government must indeed *derive* its just powers from the consent of the governed, and the majority must enjoy a continuing *share* in the governmental process. But at this point most of Wilson's fellows became ambivalent about the "democratical principle" and began to hedge their bets, fearing like Hamilton the "imprudence" of unchecked democracy,[44] and hoping, like John Adams, to restrain it by giving a measure of power to branches of government not popularly based.[45] Wilson did not share these misgivings. Just as he had been unable, once the premise was granted, to find a line distinguishing the legitimate from the illegitimate powers of Parliament, so he was unable to recognize a logical stopping point for the principle of popular rule. His view of the matter is summarized in a metaphor which he offered the Federal Convention and which he often recurred to in later years: that government was a "pyramid" and that, since he proposed to raise it to a considerable altitude, it ought to have "as broad a basis as possible." [46] In short, all branches of government should rest on the popular will, not only because the people have a right to a full voice in controlling their destinies, but because they alone can provide the support the government will need for the great

[44] Farrand, *Records*, I, 299.
[45] *The Life and Works of John Adams* (Boston, 1850–1856), IV, 228.
[46] Farrand, *Records*, I, 49.

task of unifying and controlling the nation. The simplest way of ensuring that support was direct election based on manhood suffrage, and Wilson opposed devices for refining the popular will, such as the choice of senators by state legislatures or of the President by the Congress. Yet he evidently felt that the measures ultimately agreed on approximated his design, for he always insisted that all departments of the American government did in fact rest on the popular will [47] and derived their sinews from that source. And he was confident that a government so chosen and controlled would be wise and restrained as well as potent. "Conceiving that all men, wherever placed have equal rights and are equally entitled to confidence, he viewed without apprehension the period when a few states should contain the superior number of people. The majority of people, wherever found ought in all questions to govern the minority";[48] and all will be well, for the right of suffrage has "a powerful tendency to open, to enlighten, to enlarge, and to exalt the mind." [49]

Whence did Wilson derive this unwavering commitment to popular rule and, even more, this serene conviction that the people would rule soberly and well? Democracy was, after all, a novel experiment in the modern world; it is not surprising that most of the solid citizens at the Philadelphia Convention entertained some uncertainties about it. And as for societies of the past, John Adams' exhaustive journey through history had led him to the precept, proved by "the experience of all ages," that "tumults arise in all governments; but they are certainly most remediless and certainly most fatal in a simple democracy." [50] Wilson was a solid citizen himself; he had much to lose if the "excesses of democracy" [51] turned out to be as malignant as his fellows feared; and the history of ancient societies was as familiar to him as it was to Adams. Why was he so single-minded about it, and so confident?

Perhaps a part of the answer can be found in the social structure of his native Fifeshire, where, as Smith says, property was very evenly

---

[47] JHL *Works*, p. 293. It is evident from the discussion in this chapter that Wilson found no difficulty in reconciling either separation of powers or judicial review with his belief in popular sovereignty. All three branches of government derive their authority from the Constitution, which is the product of the popular will. And, it is worth noting, Wilson insisted that the sovereign power to alter the Constitution is continuous, that in the people's hands "it is as clay in the hands of the potter" (*ibid.*, p. 304), that there must be "a proper regard to the original and inherent and continued power of the society to change its constitution." (*Ibid.*, p. 305.) For his belief that all branches of government derived from the people, and his enthusiasm for that arrangement, see also his speech to the ratifying convention. (*Ibid.*, p. 759.)

[48] Quoted in McLaughlin, "Wilson in the Philadelphia Convention," p. 16.

[49] JHL *Works*, p. 403.   [50] John Adams, *Life and Works*, VI, 152.

[51] Elbridge Gerry, quoted in Farrand, *Records*, I, 48.

divided and the lairds were sometimes no richer than their tenants. Wilson's idea of democratic man may well have been shaped in the image of the comparatively poor but self-reliant and property-respecting Scottish farmer of his boyhood. Perhaps too his hopefulness about democracy can be traced to a certain natural optimism in his character. Though he seemed outwardly dour in the traditional manner of the Scot, there is much evidence of a sanguine temper beneath: throughout his life he built air castles and looked trustfully forward to a gloriously expanding future for himself and America.[52] Yet many of his fellow Federalists had also grown up in an egalitarian environment, had reason to respect the self-sufficiency and steadiness of the American yeoman and pioneers; and even in the eighteenth century optimism was already a pervasive American trait. Wilson's social origins and his inherent hopefulness may have helped to make him a democrat, but they are not alone enough to account for his outlook.

The root explanation really seems to lie in a fortuitous meeting of man and idea, in the fact that Wilson, with his peculiarly conceptualist quality of mind, encountered in his formative years the Scottish "common sense" philosophy with its peculiar emphasis on the intuitive perception of reality and the benevolence of human nature. This school of thought, whose leading exemplar was Thomas Reid, was taking form during Wilson's university years. It represented a reaction against Hume's radical empiricism, which held that direct knowledge of the real world was impossible, denied the reality of moral insights, natural law, and "self-evident truths," and based human motivation on naked self-interest. Reid insisted to the contrary that existence was in fact perceptible to man, that common sense and customary belief were good and reliable ways of "knowing," and that moral convictions such as those represented by customary beliefs and the natural law tradition were not fictions of the mind but unmistakable reality.[53] Wilson seems to have embraced these conceptions with youthful zeal, and he adhered to them throughout his life with the enthusiastic commitment of a born lover of ideas. His law lectures in 1790–91 are strewn with references to Reid and heavily de-

[52] "It is the glorious destiny of man to be always progressive. . . . In the order of Providence, as has been observed on another occasion, the progress of societies towards perfection resembles that of an individual. This progress has hitherto been but slow: by many unpropitious events, it has often been interrupted: but may we not indulge the pleasing expectation, that, in future, it will be accelerated; and will meet with fewer and less considerable interruptions. . . . Many circumstances seem — at least to a mind anxious to see it, and apt to believe what it is anxious to see — many circumstances seem to indicate the opening of such a glorious prospect." JHL *Works*, p. 146.
[53] Arnaud B. Leavelle, "James Wilson and the Relation of the Scottish Metaphysics to American Political Thought," *Political Science Quarterly*, 57 (1942), 394–410.

voted to Wilson's own deeply-thought-out restatement of the common-sense philosophy. "Morality, like mathematics, has its intuitive truths";[54] "the law of nature is universal";[55] "I feel, but I cannot prove; I can find no previous truth more certain or more luminous, from which this can derive either evidence or illustration." [56] And since he thus assumed that intuitive perception was reliable, Wilson could argue that the capacity to make sound judgments is very widespread (since intuition is not a monopoly of philosophers or natural aristocrats); that men are naturally social, veracious, and benevolent creatures (which is confirmed by our own common-sense observation of their propensities); and that men's intuitive senses can be improved with practice so as to carry society "above any limits which we can now assign." [57]

It is easy to see how such a view of the cognitive process and of human nature might lead its exponent to an intellectual acceptance of majoritarian democracy and to popular, "Jacksonian" nationalism. If intuitive insight is both dependable and evenly distributed among mankind, and if human motivations are largely social and benevolent, it follows that the "right" judgment will be the one most people approve. And it further follows that there is no basis for Jeffersonians to exalt the agrarian man's special political virtue, nor for the Federalists to place special trust in "the wise, the rich, and the good." Indeed, such an outlook as Wilson's cuts across all the class and sectional divisions that were the stuff of contemporary American politics and looks forward to a view of democratic national community that suggests the "New Nationalism" of Theodore Roosevelt and, even more, Herbert Croly.

It is thus not difficult to see how the logic of the "Scottish common sense" premises would bring a man to such conclusions in the armchair. What is remarkable, what distinguishes Wilson, is that he was prepared, without flinching, to convert his intellectual construct into operative political institutions. His philosophic commitments were strong enough not merely to transcend the unreasonable fears and jealousies of his America, but also to obscure for him the evidence — as his contemporaries saw it — of very real conflict of interest and very human propensities toward selfishness and evil. His fellows were not unfamiliar with comparable ideas about the benevolence and perfectibility of human nature: a version of these ideas had played a part in the thinking of many of them since the heyday of the doctrine of popular consent in the prerevolutionary controversy. But almost all of them drew back from a full acceptance of its implications in the face of what they regarded as the brute realities of human conduct and the plain facts of economic and sectional strife. Even Jefferson in his less sanguine moments would concede that any given group was likely to include more rogues

[54] JHL *Works,* p. 133.   [55] *Ibid.,* p. 145.   [56] *Ibid.,* p. 205.   [57] *Ibid.,* p. 236.

than virtuous citizens, and the qualms of most Federalists were pro-
founder and more consistently expressed. Only Wilson was armored
against such allegedly practical doubts; only he had the temperament
to build a complete faith on a single-minded philosophic conviction. No
doubt his optimistic disposition helped him to this steadiness of vision:
it was characteristic and convenient for Wilson to believe that the unfettered popular will would maintain in its wisdom the orderly, rule-of-
law, property-respecting society of his own preference. But there is
also no doubt that the philosophy itself was a decisive factor in his credo,
that Wilson was one of those comparatively rare men who are genuinely
devoted to ideas in their own right.

IV

All these temperamental qualities — the curious capacity to regard
abstractions and dreams as the veriest reality; the incurably optimistic
and romantic belief in what a twentieth-century novelist was to call
"the green light, the orgiastic future"; the driving ambition to succeed,
to attain status in material terms as well as the good opinion of others —
are plausibly reflected in what is known of Wilson's personal and professional life in the years following independence. And it begins to be
apparent how the intertwining of his private and his public careers
affected his image in the popular mind and helped to deny him his due
as a champion of democracy. Even before the Revolution, in Carlisle, he
had launched modest land speculations to augment the income from his
growing legal practice, and had established personal and business relationships with the local commercial princelings. But in 1777, when a shift
in Pennsylvania political alignments deprived him of his seat in the
Congress, he returned to Carlisle equipped with opportunities and visions
well beyond his pre-war horizons. His congressional experience had
brought him into contact with affluent and ambitious men throughout
the colonies — men like Silas Deane, Charles Carroll, William Duer, and
above all Robert Morris — and he, like so many of his contemporaries,
had been half-intoxicated by the vast commercial prospects that he saw
unfolding with the birth of the nation. The war was already generating
a novel spirit of national economic unity; "men of business abilities and
propensities" tended to congregate, as they had not before, in the commercial centers such as Philadelphia and New York;[58] and the basis
seemed to be laid for America to become the Promised Land where both
political and economic felicities would be limitless. As the adventurous,
dreaming entrepreneurs saw it, America could look forward to winning
"such a stake as defied mathematics": "Not only were artificial barriers

[58] Joseph S. Davis, *Essays in the Earlier History of American Corporations* (Cambridge, Mass., 1917), p. 179.

carefully removed, but every influence that could appeal to ordinary ambition was applied. No brain or appetite active enough to be conscious of stimulants could fail to answer to the intense incentive." [59]

Moreover, though Europeans might be repelled by the grossness of this commercial spirit, "the hard, practical, money-getting American democrat" could be seen from another point of view as "living in a world of dream, and acting a drama more instinct with poetry than all the avatars of the East, walking in gardens of emerald and rubies, in ambition already ruling the world and guiding Nature with a kinder and wiser hand than had ever yet been felt in human history." [60] This brave, new, half-imaginary world in which high hopes seemed accomplished realities, in which personal enrichment and public welfare and romance were linked, was Wilson's natural element. His ambition rose far above the ordinary; his brain and appetite were tirelessly active even without stimulants. His instinctive tendency to push an idea to its limits and beyond could be fully indulged, for in the New World, by hypothesis, there were no limits, only "the orgiastic future." Speculation, chiefly in land, but also in various entrepreneurial ventures, obsessed him continually for the remainder of his life, robbed him of time and energy he might have devoted to statesmanship, clouded his repute beyond remedy, and finally helped quite literally to drive him to the grave.

Evidently a man of such imperial aspirations required an ampler universe than Carlisle, and in 1778 Wilson moved to Philadelphia, then the financial, political, and literary capital of the nascent United States. There as a lawyer he could quickly build up what was to become "one of the largest and most successful practices in America";[61] there he could enlarge and consolidate his associations with men of property and prospects; there he could copiously slake his thirst for speculation. In the courtroom he defended Quaker Tories against the hasty rage of the professional patriots, writing thereby the beginning of a significant chapter in the history of American treason law, but also earning the hot suspicion of the patriotic radicals — together of course with the gratitude and regard of his clients and their affluent friends. He developed a special reputation in arguing admiralty cases, which often involved large sums and correspondingly large fees. He represented "Aaron Lopez, one of the richest merchants in America, his friend [Robert] Morris, the Penns, a score of Tories, and the Commonwealth of Pennsylvania." [62] And as the fees poured in, he poured them back into an endless train of extravagant and daring business schemes.

The details of these ventures are too numerous and complicated to be

[59] Henry Adams, *History of the United States of America During the First Administration of Thomas Jefferson* (New York, 1889), I, 159.
[60] *Ibid.*, p. 172.   [61] Smith, *Wilson*, p. 128.   [62] *Ibid.*, p. 128.

recited here, but it is important to understand their nature and dimensions in order to understand Wilson. His interests at one time or another touched on a wide variety of enterprises, including banking, ironworks, and a grandiose plan for selling ship masts to European powers. But land was his passion, and he plunged in his land speculations with the rashness, optimism, and growing desperation of a compulsive gambler. His methods from the first invited disaster — unless of course the dice should behave in that miraculous way they sometimes do and turn up nothing but sevens. He would buy, for a fraction of the ultimate purchase price, a "warrant" which authorized him to survey a tract of land and to buy the tract outright when the survey was done. Before the first transaction was completed, another tract would tempt him, and he would make a similar arrangement, perhaps borrowing the money for the warrants and hoping no doubt that proceeds from the first tract would pay the full cost of the second when the bill came due. However, unless the first transaction proceeded swiftly and very successfully, his investment in both was endangered, and he seems to have compounded these obvious risks by continually plunging into still more such marginal ventures and by engaging himself for amounts of land far beyond his even putative capacity to pay. The amounts ran very high: 8,334 acres in Pennsylvania; 56,000 acres in one Virginia purchase, 321,000 acres in another. In some of these enterprises Wilson of course had partners to share the burdens and rewards, but his own "holdings" were immense: in the Illinois-Wabash Company, of which he was president, his share exceeded 1,000,000 acres. Once on the accelerating treadmill of borrowings and postponed payments and more borrowings it was increasingly hard to keep pace with it, much less get off: his measures to survive became more and more desperate and less and less scrupulous. Moreover, it is doubtful whether, even in his most critical straits, he ever really wanted to get off; for his optimism was indelible, the green light always allured him.

V

Meanwhile the obligations and prizes of statesmanship also continued to allure him, although his political career was always encumbered by the reputation he had earned in his financial affairs. In the light of his business associates, his wealth, and his methods, the populace tended to view him as merely another purse-conscious conservative, at one with the would-be oligarchs who feared the rule of the people above all political ills. The evaluation had been confirmed to the satisfaction of many when he had joined with men like Morris, Benjamin Rush, Dickinson, and George Ross to oppose the Pennsylvania constitution of 1776. That document, blessed by Benjamin Franklin and Tom Paine, was regarded as the very symbol of democracy and, with its test oath to disfranchise rich Quakers and crypto-Tories, as "a mighty stumbling block in the way of our gentry." [63] In the view of populists like George Bryan and William Findley, to oppose the constitution was to favor oligarchy and to despise the people.

But in truth the 1776 constitution was in many ways a poorly conceived instrument of government, and even its vaunted democracy was open to question. With a unicameral legislature, an executive weak to the point of helplessness, and a judiciary appointed for a term rather than during good behavior, the arrangement flouted the separation of powers principle, which was already an article of faith for Wilson and for practically all other Americans who had reflected about the process of government in a free society. [64] It is worth emphasis that devotion to this principle was not a conservative, Federalist peculiarity: on the contrary, as the struggle over the national Constitution was to show, the more popular elements looked upon alleged departures from it with profound suspicion. [65] Moreover, the Pennsylvania constitution of 1776 had never been submitted to popular ratification, but had been simply proclaimed by the Radicals who then controlled the state machinery of government. Still further, its test oath requirements were nicely calculated to prevent the formation of an anti-Radical majority; although all Pennsylvanians were equal, some were more equal than others. [66] In short, Wilson could find plenty to object to in the constitution of 1776, without in the least compromising his belief in political democracy. As usual, his interests and associations may have helped to buttress his principled disapproval; no doubt he thought that the Radical leaders might subvert property rights as well as republican procedures. But their sins on the latter count were quite enough to warrant his censure. Nevertheless the "honest well-meaning Country men" [67] of Pennsylvania suspected, probably with some justice, that many of Wilson's colleagues in the sixteen-year campaign against the constitution were concerned more for their fortunes and their privileges than for principle; and Wilson, the rich speculator, was tarred by the same brush. It made no

[63] Robert L. Brunhouse, *The Counter-Revolution in Pennsylvania, 1776–1790* (Philadelphia, 1942), p. 20.

[64] Benjamin F. Wright, "The Federalist on the Nature of Man," *Ethics*, 59 (1949), 8.

[65] Cecilia M. Kenyon, "Men of Little Faith: Anti-Federalists on the Nature of Representative Government," *William and Mary Quarterly*, 12 (1955), 23.

[66] The spirit of the test oath defenders is suggested by the rhetorical salvo of a radical reported by Smith: "The non-jurors it was said instead of 'acknowledging their past misconduct, expressing their sorrow and penitence, promising . . . to be faithful citizens in the future, and . . . humbly praying forgiveness' for their sins, have the arrogance to speak of their rights. Such men are, indeed, but 'mean, skulking cowards.' " *Wilson*, p. 149.

[67] Brunhouse, *Counter-Revolution*, p. 13.

difference that his constitution of 1790 — the final victory in the campaign — retained the virtual manhood suffrage of the former regime, while omitting the test oath; or that he joined in a coalition of Radicals and moderates to prevent ultraconservatives from providing for indirect election of state senators. The popular imagination could not believe that a man who defended Tories and hobnobbed with rich Quakers and who disparaged the 1776 constitution could himself be a sincere democrat.

Nor were these popular suspicions in any way assuaged by Wilson's other postrevolutionary political activities, including those that culminated in the composition and ratification of the federal Constitution. He consistently lined up, in factional disputes, with the conservative mercantile elite of Philadelphia and America, and his political opponents naturally lumped him together with his allies. In 1779, a mob of disgruntled militia joined by other "patriotic" odds and ends of humanity had determined to expel from Philadelphia "all disaffected persons and those who supported them."[68] They besieged Wilson and a band of his fellow substantial citizens in Wilson's own house; shots were fired, and men on both sides were killed. Wilson himself was forced to flee the city and to hide in the attic of Robert Morris' country house until the passion of the mob died down. By 1782, however, the Pennsylvania conservatives began to recapture the political favor they had lost to the radicals during the Revolution: Wilson was again elected to Congress, and he served in it thereafter off and on throughout the Articles of Confederation period. The spectacle of a purportedly national legislature rendered nearly impotent by localist jealousies reconfirmed his already powerful nationalist leanings. He argued for congressional rather than state control of western lands; he joined with Hamilton and other advocates of more vigorous central government to urge that Congress be given power to collect and maintain general funds and to control commerce. As a commissioner in a land controversy between Pennsylvania and Connecticut, he became convinced of the need for a national judiciary to resolve such conflicts; and his participation in the struggle to preserve the Bank of North America against local hostility led him, as has been said above, to an expansive view of national power. In the light of subsequent American history these positions may seem to represent the obvious common sense of the matter, but in the 1780's they further certified Wilson's identification with a supposedly antidemocratic American elite.

The affair of the Bank of North America is an almost perfect example of the way in which Wilson's personal interests and political convictions intertwined, to the detriment of his reputation as a selfless, democratic

[68] Smith, *Wilson*, p. 133.

statesman; and his essay "Considerations on the Bank of North America" also illustrates his willingness to make daring departures, his capacity for "brilliant conceits." [69] The Bank had been chartered in 1781 by both the Continental Congress and the state of Pennsylvania. Robert Morris had helped to found it, partly for the patriotic purpose of aiding the nation in its fiscal affairs, and partly, no doubt, for less altruistic reasons. At any rate it quickly became the center of a political controversy very like the one that swirled about the Bank of the United States some years later. Wilson was a member of its first board of directors, its attorney, and its champion against detractors. He also soon established himself, characteristically, as "its most persistent debtor." [70] When the radical foes of the Bank proposed in 1785 that the Pennsylvania Assembly revoke its charter, the management called on Wilson to help repel the onslaught, and he obliged by composing "a very ingenious Pamphlet" aimed at both Congress and the Assembly. The "Considerations" there set forth certainly reflected Wilson's sincere convictions about public policy, but he would have been in no position to argue differently even if he had wished; for he then owed the Bank about $30,000. [71]

His objectives in composing the pamphlet were two: to persuade his readers that the congressional charter was alone enough to preserve the Bank's lawful existence; and to persuade them that in any event the Assembly ought not revoke the state charter. As to the first point, the difficulty was that the Articles of Confederation seemed to grant no power to incorporate the Bank in the first place, and that Article II reserved to the states all powers not expressly delegated to the Congress. But Wilson was undaunted. To be sure, he said, Congress is forbidden to exercise, without express delegation, powers that once belonged to the states. But no individual state ever had the power to legislate on a national scale for national objects; hence Article II does not apply to such powers (the state cannot "retain" what it never possessed). In fact, the Congress can, under the Articles, act to accomplish any general, national objects that the individual states are incompetent to effect. That is the meaning of Article V, which provides that delegates shall be annually appointed to Congress "for the more convenient management of the *general interests* of the United States." [72] If this argument is pressed to its logical conclusion, it suggests, as Corwin has remarked, that the

---

[69] The phrase is that of a contemporary, cited in McMaster and Stone, *Constitution*, p. 759.

[70] Smith, *Wilson*, p. 146.

[71] Janet Wilson, "The Bank of North America and Pennsylvania Politics," *Pennsylvania Magazine of History and Biography* 66 (1942), 11.

[72] JHL *Works*, p. 829. The italics are, of course, Wilson's. In fact, this clause was a frail reed to support such a weighty interpretation. Article V was simply concerned with the selection and organization of Congress, not with its powers.

supposedly feeble Confederation Congress enjoyed a greater structure of derived powers than did the Congress of the United States as late as 1925![73]

As for the second matter — the Assembly's threat to repeal the state charter — not even Wilson was quite bold enough to argue unambiguously that such a revoking act would be legally invalid. His precise question was whether it would be "wise or politick" for the legislature to do this. But his discussion of the question nicely intermingles issues of morality and policy with issues of power (in a manner, as I have said above, suggestive of Marshall in *Fletcher v. Peck*); and the reader is left with at least a strong hint that the repealing act would be a nullity, partly because the corporation would continue to exist under its congressional charter, and partly because the act would violate "the rules and maxims, by which compacts are governed."[74]

It was a powerful effort; but it failed, as did all the other appeals and stratagems that Wilson and others devised to stay the Assembly's hand. The state charter was repealed, to the resounding applause of the Radicals; Wilson's role had only strengthened the popular impression that he was not a disinterested patriot but a self-seeker "who can bewilder the truth in all the mazes of sophistry"[75] for the benefit of the aristocracy he aspired to and served. One is reminded of Macaulay's essays on the two Pitts, in which he attributes their popularity to what he calls in the father "ostentatious purity" and in the son "pecuniary disinterestedness." "About treaties, wars, expeditions, tariffs, budgets, there will always be room for dispute. The policy which is applauded by half the nation may be condemned by the other half. But pecuniary disinterestedness everybody comprehends. It is a great thing for a man who has only three hundred a year to be able to show that he considers three thousand a year as mere dirt beneath his feet, when compared with the public interest and the public esteem."[76] Far from thus spurning material gains, Wilson notoriously coveted them; and the populace judged him accordingly.

It must be said that these misgivings about Wilson were always to some degree mitigated by the widespread respect for his intellect and his erudition — although it must also be said that these very gifts probably excited some further suspicions, classically expressed by Amos Singletary

[73] Edward S. Corwin, "The Progress of Constitutional Theory Between the Declaration of Independence and the Meeting of the Philadelphia Convention," *American Historical Review*, 30 (1925), 529.

[74] JHL *Works*, p. 834.

[75] McMaster and Stone, *Constitution*, p. 642. The words were written by "Centinel" (either George or Samuel Bryan) during the ratification controversy.

[76] Thomas B. Macaulay, *Critical, Historical, and Miscellaneous Essays and Poems* . . . (Boston, 1880), III, 334.

in the Massachusetts ratifying convention, that "these lawyers, and men of learning, and moneyed men that talk so finely and gloss over matters so smoothly . . . will swallow up all us little folks, like the great leviathan, Mr. President; yes, just as the whale swallowed up Jonah." [77] But Wilson was recognized as one of the most learned men in the young nation; he did know more about history and government than almost anyone else. It would have been absurd for Pennsylvania to deny him a place in its delegation to the Federal Convention, where such talents would be needed as never before. Nevertheless, although Wilson was chosen by the Assembly, he received fewer votes than any other delegate except Gouverneur Morris, who had very recently moved to Pennsylvania; and it seems unlikely that Wilson would have been chosen at all if it were not that the conservative "Republicans" had won a majority in the state elections of 1786.

The "assembly of demigods" would have felt his absence; the nation would be poorer if a shift in the Pennsylvania political breezes had kept Wilson out of the Convention. No one, except perhaps Madison, worked harder at the business of statesmanship during that hot Philadelphia summer of 1787; no one, again except Madison, played a larger part in shaping the Convention's deliberations. Plainly both Wilson and Madison were in their element in a small conclave of generally sober and earnest men, where under the protection of privacy they could speak to the point rather than to galleries, where their scholarly readiness to do their homework would be appreciated, where their aptitude for mediation could serve so well.

Wilson had already progressed by 1787 to a set of views that were in themselves a kind of synthesis of the Convention's divided mind. The delegates' problem was to reconcile the need for a more perfect union with the stubborn fact of localism, the concern for property rights and commercial stability with the rise of democracy. Wilson had already achieved such a reconciliation on his own account, and what is more he had already thought deeply about the institutional implications of his position. He had, as has been said, fully accepted the doctrine of popular democracy and had enlarged it into the notion of "the people of the United States." [78] His confidence in the good judgment of a free electorate insulated him against the fears of popular rapacity, and the idea that this electorate transcended state lines provided him with a basis for a vigorous national government. All of its branches should rest on the people, since their "authority, interests, and affections . . . are the only

[77] Samuel B. Harding, *The Contest Over the Ratification of the Federal Constitution in the State of Massachusetts* (New York, 1896), p. 77.

[78] JHL *Works*, p. 402. See also Farrand, *Records*, I, 52, 69; and Elliot, *Debates*, II, 443–444, 457.

foundation on which a superstructure, supposed to be at once durable and magnificent, can be rationally erected." [79] This combination of ideas led him to endorse a single, strong executive as an instrument and symbol of national unity, for he saw that it was delusory to fear "monarchy" and to regard the legislature alone as the people's branch, when the people also chose the executive.[80] It helped him see at once the need for a national judiciary including inferior courts as well as a Supreme Court, so that the national government could enforce its will without local interference.[81] It caused him, in short, to take the lead in supporting every measure that strengthened the union or strengthened popular government, for he was convinced in advance that by strengthening either he would strengthen both. This solid and in general preconceived set of beliefs gave him an advantage over all but a very few of his fellows, and helped ensure that he would play a major role in the making of the Constitution.

That role was, as I have emphasized, to steer the Convention on all points toward a democratic nationalism. Yet though his critics found no difficulty in believing that he advocated centralism, they continued skeptical about his devotion to popular government. Daniel Redick of Pennsylvania was voicing this common opinion when he said during the Convention: "I acknowledge I have still my fears whilst such as Guvero [Gouverneur Morris] and Turner the caledonian [Wilson] are in the council, not that I think they lack knowledge: but that they are artfull, plausable men of influence, and I fear they may not be lovers of mankind." [82] On the last point he was perfectly right with respect to the haughty Morris, but it is hard to see how anyone reading the debates could bracket Wilson with him. Of course Redick had not read the debates, which were to remain unpublished for many years to come, and whatever may have been the other merits of preserving the rule of secrecy after the Convention was over,[83] the policy was costly to Wilson's contemporary reputation. It helped anti-Federalists to cling to the presupposition that he was merely another of the band of aristocrats who in the "secret conclave" of the Convention had forged "gilded chains" to fetter "the liberties of a free people." [84]

Perhaps, however, it would have made no difference if the debates had been exposed to public view, for the preconceived image was ob-

[79] JHL *Works*, p. 403.
[80] Farrand, *Records*, I, 65, 80; Elliot, *Debates*, II, 510–511.
[81] Farrand, *Records*, I, 125.
[82] Jackson T. Main, *The Antifederalists: Critics of the Constitution, 1781–1788* (Chapel Hill, 1961), p. 118.
[83] On the reasons for secrecy, Warren, *Constitution*, pp. 134–139; on the effects of secrecy, *ibid.*, pp. 761–762.
[84] Albert J. Beveridge, *The Life of John Marshall* (New York, 1916), I, 333, 336.

stinately entrenched. The proceedings of the ratifying convention in Pennsylvania were *not* secret, and Wilson bore in that conclave not only the responsibility of leader and strategist, but the task of chief spokesman as well. His speeches were closely listened to and widely reported, and they were full of apostrophes to "the people" and of protestations that the Constitution he espoused would establish a "democracy" [85] (there is some significance in Wilson's willingness to use that word: it was not in high favor at the time, especially among Federalists). Nevertheless he continued to be one of the main targets of anti-Federalist artillery, and in the popular mind he remained a high aristocrat devoted to the patrician interest and despising the people. He had played a vital part in framing the proposed Constitution; now he was the leading figure in securing the indispensable assent of Pennsylvania; he believed with perfect sincerity that in both efforts he had labored to create not only a nation but a democracy. His reward was not the "well founded and distinguishing applause" [86] of the people in whose behalf he had toiled, but a reputation as a subtle foe of the democratic ideal.

As has already been suggested, Wilson's own behavior had contributed to this popular misunderstanding of his principles. His far-flung financial machinations did not easily suggest to the mind the image of a selfless democratic statesman. His natural tendency was to form connections with men of affluence and influence, and these men were often skeptical about democracy: it was natural for observers to suppose that Wilson was a bird of the same feather. In the Pennsylvania ratification controversy itself, he and his costrategists were open to the charge of steamrolling through to a decision before there was time for adequate popular debate. Moreover Wilson's manner was always a handicap. He lacked the easy, hail-fellow-well-met qualities that are so useful for a popular leader. His bearing seemed to many cold and aloof and proud. As McLaughlin said: "he must have been a curious and angular being, given to repellent learning and possessed of prolix and voluble wisdom." [87] Such personal qualities stamped him in the public mind as "aristocratick," and there was little that Wilson could do about either his stiff bearing or the impression it made. When the Society of the Cincinnati, that curious flower of New World aristocratic yearnings, invited him to become an honorary member in 1789 (there is no evidence that he actually joined) it was reflecting the common and unsurprising view of Wilson's tastes in political principles and associations.

But there is another and deeper explanation of the general contemporary failure to credit Wilson with the democratic values he indisputably held, and it has to do with that antecedent, precursory quality of

[85] Elliot, *Debates*, II, 434. [86] JHL *Works*, p. 405.
[87] McLaughlin, "Wilson in the Philadelphia Convention," p. 20.

his outlook, which was emphasized earlier. In the climate of the 1780's and 1790's, it was most difficult to conceive that a man could be a financial tycoon and a democrat; and the difficulty was greatly compounded if he was also an ardent nationalist and a declared Federalist. We know that the anti-Federalists were by no means all zealous democrats.[88] Nevertheless in their campaign against the Constitution they heavily emphasized the twin themes that the proposed national government would be controlled by the rich and wellborn and that it would destroy the autonomous states, which were the only security for popular rights. On the other hand, although Federalists like young John Marshall replied that the Constitution would in fact ensure "a well regulated democracy," [89] most of them, including Marshall,[90] had recorded, privately or publicly, misgivings about democratic excesses, and their opponents suspected — not entirely without justice — that they cared more about establishing a "well regulated" national union than about making sure it would be democratic. This tendency to connect democracy with states' rights and elitism with nationalism was already strong before the ratification struggle. In the course of that controversy it hardened into a dogma, most firmly anchored perhaps in the minds of the anti-Federalists, but more or less shared — with more or less frankness — by many Federalists as well. Wilson was, as we have seen, entirely and almost eccentrically innocent of these Federalist doubts about the virtues of popular rule; his faith in union was exactly what he said it was: a faith in democratic nationalism. But by the time the ratification controversy had run its bitter course, the stereotypes had become so fixed that neither side could quite believe in such a hybrid. Wilson was irremediably "James the Caledonian, Leut. Gen. of the Myrmidons of power." [91] When the Radicals of Carlisle burned him in effigy after the Pennsylvania ratification vote, they were testifying to the obstinacy of the stereotypes; and Wilson was paying the price for being as usual in advance of his generation.

VI

The composition and ratification of the Constitution marked the high point of Wilson's life-service to his country. America had made one of those great leaps forward that occur so rarely in history, and Wilson had played a central part in that momentous development. When he further managed, in 1790, to remold the Pennsylvania constitution to his tastes, one might expect that his cup would run over. Conceding that the agrarian, populist faction would never, for reasons just described, properly value him, he could nevertheless legitimately hope to be revered by the

---

[88] Kenyon, "Men of Little Faith," p. 3.   [89] Beveridge, *Marshall*, I, 410.
[90] *Ibid.*, p. 302.   [91] McMaster and Stone, *Constitution*, p. 631.

nation in general as one of the chief begetters of American constitution-alism. This hope might have been reinforced by the glow of public approval that was soon shed over the fruits of his constitutional labors. The 1790 Pennsylvania constitution won almost unanimous acceptance,[92] in spite of the bitterness of the political struggles that had gone before. As for the federal Constitution, it was transmuted soon after adoption into an object of remarkable public devotion. In the words of Woodrow Wilson: ". . . hostile criticism of its provisions . . . not only ceased, but gave place to an undiscriminating and almost blind worship of its principles. . . . The divine right of kings never ran a more prosperous course than did the unquestioned prerogative of the Constitution to receive universal homage." [93] James Wilson had a solid claim to bask in this glory, to be canonized by a grateful nation.

To a degree in fact his just expectations were fulfilled, his claim was honored. Except in certain partisan circles, he was respected as one of the statesmen of the rising sun; and his reputation as a legal scholar already meant much in a land where law was becoming a quasi religion. But his ambitions outran such comparatively moderate recognitions of his status. He desired fame and position commensurate with his service and abilities, and these rewards were forever denied him. He had the judgment to see that his best chance for acknowledged greatness lay in the field of jurisprudence, where he could exploit his known gifts. He must have realized that he lacked the talent for achieving high elective office; on the other hand his characteristic foresight must have given him an inkling of the part that law would play in the folklore of America. A man who was received as the nation's chief lawgiver could take his place in that folklore with the topmost leaders of battle and politics. Wilson foresaw, as it were, the stature that a John Marshall would attain, and he coveted that eminence.

He proposed himself to Washington as chief justice of the new Supreme Court,[94] explaining that delicacy had heretofore restrained him but that he now spoke so that the President would be spared the embarrassment of offering the post to one who would scorn it. When the honor was tendered instead to John Jay, Wilson consoled himself for the time with an associate justiceship and sought to augment his juristic repute in other ways. The College of Philadelphia appointed him to its first law professorship, and Wilson patently hoped that his course of lectures there would lay the foundation for an American system of law based on Wilsonian principles. They represented the major written work

---

[92] Brunhouse, *Counter-Revolution*, p. 227.

[93] *Congressional Government* (New York, 1956), p. 27.

[94] Charles Warren, *The Supreme Court in United States History* (Boston, 1937) I, 33–34.

of his life, his pretension to challenge the renown of the *Federalist Papers* but extending to a far wider terrain. Wilson planned them to be so extensive, in fact — embracing, *inter alia*, epistemology, political theory, natural law, the law of nations, and the common law, as well as commentaries on the constitutions of the United States and Pennsylvania — that he was unable to complete their delivery in the winter of 1790–91. He broke off in order to attend to his circuit duties as a Supreme Court justice and to his endless business affairs. But a few months later he had not only taken them up again, but had absorbed himself in another vast scheme, or rather two of them: to produce by his own hand complete digests of the laws of Pennsylvania and of the United States. He importuned the legislature of Pennsylvania and President Washington to commission him for these stupendous tasks which would, when completed, establish him as the American Lycurgus and ensure his state and country a jurisprudence befitting its glorious republican future.

One is caught between awe and sympathy. Such energy and vaulting ambition are admirable in both senses of that word, but they tempt fortune to provide disappointments in equal measure. And disappointed Wilson was, partly perhaps because he was asking too much for any man; but partly because of the contradictions within his own character; and because — his perennial tragedy — the moment for his kind of greatness was not quite ripe: he was born too soon and his time was limited. Washington bypassed him for the chief justiceship not only at the time of Jay's appointment, but again in 1795 and 1796 when John Rutledge and Oliver Ellsworth were chosen. None of the three really matched Wilson in legal learning and in intellect, but Jay and Ellsworth were powerful political figures, and Rutledge enjoyed the personal esteem of Washington. Moreover Wilson suffered from the handicap that seems to have increasingly clouded his name: the reputation for reckless and potentially disastrous financial adventuring. This may not have been greatly important in explaining the preference of Jay over him;[95] indeed, there is no hard evidence that it was decisive in the disappointments of 1795 and 1796, although by this time the tangle of Wilson's affairs had become more notorious than ever. But it is highly plausible that the vision of impending scandal helped Washington to pass over the foremost legal scholar of the time. Iredell, Wilson's closest associate on the bench, thought his friend would resign in chagrin after Ellsworth's appointment.

Nevertheless, although the chief justiceship eluded him, he was an associate justice of the tribunal that was to be more powerful than any

[95] In 1789 Jay's "prestige as a lawyer and statesman" was very great. Charles Warren, "The First Decade of the Supreme Court," *University of Chicago Law Review,* 7 (1940), 633.

other court, anywhere, has ever been. In that position he was an equal among equals; his weight in shaping judgments and doctrines was no less than the chief's. It might be thought that this opportunity was ample enough for his aspirations. The most illustrious molders of American constitutional law have not all been chief justices.

But here the trouble was that the Court of the 1790's was not yet ready for the great work of its future, nor was the country prepared to accept the judicial leadership of later years. The status of the fledgling Court in the fledgling Republic was ambiguous and, for the moment, comparatively minor. The paramount governmental tasks were legislative and executive. The great pyramid of subordinate courts and causes leading up to the Supreme Court was still in the process of formation, and as Wilson himself said in another connection the apex of a pyramid depends on the breadth of its base. The constitutional issues left unresolved by the framers in 1789 were numerous and imposing, and Wilson was primed with answers to most of them. But before a Supreme Court justice could play a major part in resolving those issues both the Court and the nation needed time to mature.

Within this limited range of judicial possibilities Wilson labored manfully to stamp his impress on the American governmental structure, but the range must have seemed constricting to a man of his aspirations, and the occasions were distressingly few. The total of his written opinions on the Supreme Court sums up to little more than twenty pages in the *Reports*, some ten pages less than Marshall's single opinion in *Marbury v. Madison*. Even when we supplement this arithmetic by including the cases in which he cast a vote without an opinion and by reflecting that he was concurrently judging circuit cases, the record is slim. Those years from February 1, 1790, when he first took his seat, and August 21, 1798, when he died, were simply not years of great opportunity for a justice of the Supreme Court, even one with Wilson's intellect and drive.

With one exception therefore his Supreme Court opinions provide little inkling of his stature and potentiality. The "famous" cases of the 1790's are a mere handful and, though Wilson participated in most of them, his performances were seldom greatly memorable. To be sure, his role in the "First Hayburn Case" has a certain historical interest. Congress had in the Invalid Pension Act of 1792 directed circuit courts to act as pension commissioners. In the New York circuit, three judges, headed by Chief Justice Jay, had expressed grave doubts about this assignment on the ground that its functions were not "properly judicial," but had avoided a direct statement that the law was unconstitutional. However, in the Pennsylvania circuit, Wilson and two of his brethren, confronted by a pension claim from one William Hayburn, met the issue squarely and addressed a letter to the President:

Before you . . . we think it our duty to lay the sentiments which, on a late painful occasion, governed us with regard to an act passed by the Legislature of the Union. . . . Upon due consideration, we have been unanimously of the opinion, that under this act, the Circuit Court . . . could not proceed. . . . Be assured that though it became necessary, it was far from pleasant. To be obliged to act contrary, either to the obvious direction of Congress, or to a constitutional principle in our judgment equally obvious, excited feelings in us, which we hope never to experience again.[96]

There is no question, as Max Farrand says,[97] that Wilson was the dominant member of this judicial trio; it is probable that he composed the letter; and it is beyond reasonable doubt that the "painful occasion" referred to was the first holding by a federal court that a congressional act was unconstitutional. Wilson of course had made it plain — in the Federal Convention,[98] in the Pennsylvania ratifying convention,[99] and in his law lectures[100] — that he envisioned the power of judicial review. In the Hayburn case he was acting on that basis, and in *Hylton v. United States*[101] he seconded the rest of the Court in confirming it once again by implication and at the same time upholding a broad interpretation of national powers. This case, involving a national tax that was important to Hamilton's fiscal program, had come before Wilson in circuit court, where he had upheld it against constitutional attack. He refrained therefore from actually joining in the Supreme Court's similar judgment, merely remarking that his "sentiments in favor of the constitutionality of the tax . . . have not been changed." Of course by considering the question of constitutionality at all, even to decide it affirmatively, both courts were assuming that they had the authority to disallow an act of Congress.

Wilson's short opinion in *Ware v. Hylton* (1796)[102] is also moderately interesting. The case raised the salient question whether a 1777 Virginia law confiscating and sequestrating debts due British citizens was valid against the 1783 treaty of peace with Great Britain — that is, whether the national treaty power overrode state law. The treaty power granted in the proposed Constitution had troubled the opponents of ratification in Pennsylvania[103] and elsewhere,[104] and Wilson himself in the Federal Convention had objected that the role assigned to the Senate in treaty-making had "a dangerous tendency to aristocracy," diminishing the

[96] 2 Dallas 410 (1792).
[97] "The First Hayburn Case, 1792," *American Historical Review*, 13 (1908), 284.
[98] Farrand, *Records*, II, 73, 391.   [99] Elliot, *Debates*, II, 445, 478, 489.
[100] JHL *Works*, pp. 455–456.   [101] 3 Dallas 171 (1796).
[102] 3 Dallas 199 (1796).
[103] McMaster and Stone, *Constitution*, pp. 463, 476.
[104] Charles H. Butler, *The Treaty-Making Power of the United States* (New York, 1902), vol. I, ch. vii.

chance that the president would be "the man of the people, as he ought to be." [105] But these were reservations based on his solid belief in democracy and in separation of powers with a strong executive. They did not impair his equally solid belief in national supremacy over the states,[106] which he joined the Court in now affirming. Indeed, he went beyond his fellow justices, for they had either conceded, or chosen not to question, Virginia's power to confiscate before the signing of the treaty; and Wilson came very close to declaring the Virginia law invalid as a violation of "the law of nations in its modern state of purity and refinement." [107] "But even if Virginia had the power to confiscate," he continued, "the treaty annuls the confiscation." The other justices, especially Chase and Iredell (the only dissenter), had gone on at considerable length in their opinions out of deference to the "uncommon magnitude of the subject" and the "awful situation" [108] of the judges who must decide it; but for Wilson the matter depended on "a few plain principles" and he disposed of it in less than a page. Concise and lucid though that page is, revealing Wilson's justified self-confidence as a constitutional lawyer, it is, like most of his other performances on the supreme bench, not the stuff of which judicial immortality is made.

VII

The single exception to this relatively unimpressive record of Wilson's Supreme Court service is his opinion in *Chisholm v. Georgia* (1793).[109] The case presented what was probably the most heated constitutional question of the Federalist period: whether a state was amenable in the federal courts to suit by a citizen of another state. Fears had been voiced in the ratification controversy that the clause extending judicial power to "controversies between a state and citizens of another state" would permit a private citizen to hale a state before the bar of federal justice. Defenders of the Constitution had assured opponents that no such incongruous thing was intended.[110] Yet as soon as the new government was established the fears were revived, and with good reason. Creditors at once began suits against New York, Virginia, and Maryland; and all the

[105] Farrand, *Records*, II, 522–523.

[106] The issue of national supremacy also had been raised earlier in connection with this very question of British debts and treaty rights. See Wilson's views during the ratification controversy in Elliot, *Debates*, II, 490.

[107] 3 Dallas at 281.   [108] Iredell's phrases. *Ibid*. at 256.

[109] 2 Dallas 419 (1793).

[110] See, e.g., Hamilton in *The Federalist* . . . (Cambridge, Mass., 1961), pp. 511–512; and Madison and Marshall in the Virginia Convention, Elliot, *Debates*, III, 533, 555. Wilson himself had alluded to the clause in the Pennsylvania ratification debates and had defended it only with the generality that when "a citizen has a controversy with another state, there ought to be a tribunal where both parties may stand on a just and equal footing." *Ibid.*, II, 491. It is not clear whether this meant that he thought a citizen could sue a state. Perhaps he was purposefully avoiding the issue.

states were threatened. *Chisholm* involved a suit by two South Carolina citizens against Georgia.

Underlying the issue of the state's amenability to suit was of course a broader and far greater one: whether the Constitution had created a nation or a league of sovereign states. The ratification of the Constitution had not settled that issue, fervently as the Philadelphia delegates — and most especially Wilson — had hoped that it would. The clauses that bore on the matter of nation-state relationships, like the one in question here, were certainly susceptible of nationalistic interpretations. But the spirit of state sovereignty was still running strong; its proponents, defeated by a narrow margin in the ratification struggle, were still prepared to resist such interpretations with all their might. They continued to argue that the national government was a creature of the states and that it could not therefore claim supremacy over them. Nor was it by any means clear in 1793 that their cause would fail; indeed it was not to become fully clear until the matter was brought to its final test on the battlefields of the Civil War. In *Chisholm v. Georgia*, then, the Court was being asked not merely whether a state could be sued; it was being asked to define the nature of the American Union.

Wilson had already thought deeply about the question whether states should be exempt from suit on the ground that they were "sovereign." In his law lectures he had contended, in accordance with his democratic principles, that sovereignty resides not in states but in the people, in "the free and independent man";[111] and that if a man can submit himself without loss of dignity to the courts, the state, "which is compounded of the dignity of its members," should do likewise. Now in the *Chisholm* case these anti-Blackstone precepts of jurisprudence were reinforced by his belief in the need for a potent national judicial power to cement national union. He joined in a four-to-one holding that the suit could be entertained and wrote in defense of the decision his only really substantial Supreme Court opinion.

Wilson was no doubt mindful that the case provided him with his first chance to cast his views about American constitutionalism in the form of memorable judicial statement, though he could not know that this first chance was also to be the last. He poured into the opinion a distillation of the ideas that had been ripening since his days at St. Andrews. He began, appropriately, with a quotation from Thomas Reid to the effect that those who would think anew must give old terms new meanings; and then plunged into the task of examining the case by the light of "the principles of general jurisprudence," "the laws and practices of particular states and kingdoms," and the Constitution of the United States. The jurisprudence he explicated was of course his own version of a

[111] JHL *Works*, p. 497. See also Elliot, *Debates*, II, 443.

jurisprudence for America, and it called for a redefinition of the terms "state" and "sovereign." A state, though an excellent human contrivance, is not an independent and superior entity but merely a "body of free persons united together for their common benefit." It derives its existence from the people and is obviously subordinate to them. As for "sovereignty," that quality is found, not in the state, or in the agencies of government where Blackstone would place it, but — again — in the people. In theory the people might surrender this sovereignty to the state or its government, but in fact the citizens of Georgia have not done so: they have chosen a republican form of government, which means by definition that they have reserved the supreme, sovereign power in their own hands. It was that reserved sovereign power which the people were exercising when they created a national government for certain national purposes, and "as to the purposes of the Union, therefore, Georgia is not a sovereign state." In short, though the people always retain sovereignty, they have given the stamp of their sovereign will to the functions of the national government, and the state, being inferior to the people, cannot claim immunity from their mandates.

After this all that remained was to inquire whether the suing of one state by a citizen of another was one of these "purposes of the Union" which the sovereign people ordained. But Wilson was too much the historian and too proud of his historical learning to go directly to that question. He must try to demonstrate by an excursion through "the laws and practices of different states and kingdoms" that history recognizes the right of subjects to sue their sovereigns and *a fortiori* supports the present suit where no subject-superior relationship exists. This show of erudition was typical of Wilson and may have impressed contemporaries, but to a modern it dilutes the argument with dubious analogies to the practices of Spanish law at the time of Columbus, the Spartan *ephori*, and — a favorite idea of Wilson's — the fabled egalitarianism of Saxon England. Having made this bow to the past, he was now ready, one might think, to ask whether the American Constitution does authorize the suit. But still that question was postponed while he returned for a reprise and amplification of his first theme. *Could* the Constitution of the United States vest federal courts with jurisdiction over the state of Georgia? Again we are told that states are inferior to the "majesty of the people" who create them, that the people of the United States, including the people of Georgia, have the sovereign power to subordinate the state of Georgia to the national authority which they ordain. These pages include another slap at Wilson's villain Blackstone and at Louis XIV, as well as encomiums on Athens and "the most magnificent object which a nation could present": "the people of the United States"; but they do not advance the argument beyond the stage it had previously reached.

Now at length, however, the final query can be posed: did the people mean to exercise their undoubted power to subject states to federal authority? Did they prescribe this as one of "the purposes of the Union"? Both deduction and the constitutional text suggest that they did. Certainly they granted Congress power to revise and control state laws in certain instances.[112] Since that power would be nugatory without executive enforcement and judicial interpretation, it follows that all three branches of the national government were empowered by the people to act directly to control the states. The people intended to form themselves into a nation for national purposes, and it would be incongruous to assume that, having this intent, they meant to exempt either states or natural persons from national jurisdiction. Moreover, their contrary design, if it should need more verification, they expressed in so many words: extending "the judicial power of the United States" to "controversies between a State and citizens of another State." No more strict and appropriate language could be devised to describe the cause of Mr. Chisholm. "The combined inference is, that the action lies." The people, exercising their indefeasible sovereignty, did subject Georgia to the judicial power.

Jay said that he had been forced to write his own opinion in *Chisholm* hastily "between the intervals of the daily adjournments and while my mind was occupied and wearied by the business of the day." [113] If Wilson endured comparable handicaps (and they must have been at least as great, for he was chronically overburdened with distractions) his opinion was a notable performance, despite its superfluities and repetitions. His essential argument is not easy to refute on logical grounds, and his analysis of the nature of "state" and "sovereignty" was hard to challenge without repudiating the dogma of popular supremacy on which it rested. Indeed, his argument in *Chisholm* is worth comparing with Marshall's in *McCulloch v. Maryland* (1819) and in *Cohens v. Virginia* (1821), for it anticipates "the great Chief Justice's" main contention that the will of the people of the United States had made the national government in its sphere superior to the states and that as to the purposes of the Union the states were not sovereign. To be sure, Wilson's fellow justices in *Chisholm* made this point as well, for it was a common idea in their generation[114] among men of their political views. But Wilson had thought the point through more fundamentally and his opinion carries it further than the others. It deserves a significant place among American state papers.

Yet the mention of John Marshall suggests the reason why that place

[112] Wilson's specific instance is Art. I, #10, providing that state duties on imports or exports are "subject to the Revision and Control of the Congress."

[113] 2 Dallas at 478.

[114] See Edward S. Corwin, *The Doctrine of Judicial Review . . . and other Essays* (Princeton, 1914), p. 99.

is not more exalted and why Wilson could not, in his years on the bench, establish title as the premier lawgiver of the American constitutional tradition. To begin with, he lacked Marshall's personal gifts. Though far more erudite and a deeper thinker than Marshall, he was unable to match the lucidity, simplicity, and persuasiveness of Marshall's prose style. When we lay a page of his *Chisholm* opinion beside a page from *McCulloch* or *Cohens* the contrast is arresting. Wilson's argumentative talent was by no means slight. But he could seldom resist adorning the essential point of his contention with scholarly references and grandiloquent asides, and his sentences sometimes develop a labyrinthine complexity. At its worst his prose seems the result of a cross-fertilization between a pedant and a Fourth of July orator, and the intervening passages of clear and even memorable English cannot quite save it. "Marshall's maxim," William Wirt said, was to "aim exclusively at strength," and Wirt went on to advise his correspondent: *"let argument strongly predominate. . . . Avoid as you would the gates of death, the reputation for floridity. . . . imitate . . . Marshall's simple process of reasoning."* [115] Such counsel might have been useful to Wilson. Add to all this the fact that Wilson was singularly deficient in the man-to-man charm that Marshall possessed in such abundance, and his relative disadvantage becomes further apparent. Perhaps no one could have dominated Wilson's Court as Marshall did the Court of later times; at any rate such easy ascendancy was beyond likelihood for Wilson.

But more important than these differences in personal attributes is the fact that the times were right for Marshall in 1821 as they were not for Wilson in 1793: the most decisive contrast between *Chisholm* and *Cohens* is in their dates. The aftermath of the *Chisholm* case is a gauge of the constricted potential of Wilson's Court and of Wilson's opportunity for judicial renown. Throughout the nation all but the extreme Federalists were taken aback by a decision so contrary to the assurances given in the ratification debates and so irreverent toward state sovereignty. Within little more than a year the Congress had resoundingly passed a resolution to reverse the decision by altering the Constitution, and this measure, ratified in 1798, became the Eleventh Amendment. On the other hand, Marshall dared, some three decades later, to emasculate that amendment itself, [116] and although the outraged furor was substantial, the interpretations stuck: they became the law of the land. The Supreme Court's capacity to act as a bellwether for the nation depends at any given time on two factors, the alignment of political interests and the prestige of the Court. In Wilson's time neither of these factors was auspicious. He was

---

[115] Beveridge, *Marshall*, II, 192–193.

[116] *Cohens v. Virginia*, 6 Wheaton 264 (1821); *Osborn v. Bank*, 9 Wheaton 738 (1824).

ready with a doctrine of constitutional nationalism that would anticipate the Marshallian canon. But America and its judiciary had not reached the canonical age; the nation as usual was not ready for him.

VIII

Wilson's other apparent opportunity for magisterial achievement during the post-ratification period came with his appointment to the Philadelphia law professorship in 1790. He was not quite America's first professor of law, but he was, as his biographer says, the first to be appointed after the establishment of the Federal Republic;[117] Philadelphia was the seat of government and the greatest city of America; Wilson was a founding father and a Supreme Court Justice, and was widely acknowledged as the preeminent legal scholar of his generation. In such a place and time such a preceptor could expect to be heard and heeded. He might be able to implant his ideas in the seedbed of American law at a uniquely opportune moment and thus be recognized as the founder of an American jurisprudence.

The inaugural lecture was accompanied by ceremonial flourishes that must have further kindled these expectations. President Washington, Vice-President Adams, and a galaxy of other republican worthies turned out, some with their ladies at their sides, to honor the speaker and to be enlightened.

Wilson had in mind nothing less than the presentation of a complete political theory, grounded on theology and psychology, and leading to a philosophy of American law. This grand design was, as has been intimated earlier, never wholly carried out. No more than half of the lectures composed were actually delivered; even the complete written text (unpublished until after the author's death) leaves serious gaps in the analytic structure, and some of the chapters deteriorate into turgid generality or into the dreary recitation of hornbook facts, as if the professor lacked time to do his homework properly. But even when the omissions are allowed for and the superfluous is discounted, the residue is impressive. In a scattered and imperfect way the lectures touch on most of the great issues of political philosophy and jurisprudence, and they are the most nearly full treatment we have of those matters by an eminent American of Wilson's generation.

Yet they are not "typical" of that generation, any more than their author was. To be sure, many of the ideas must have sounded familiar and even axiomatic to the listeners. Wilson was concerned, as he said at the outset, to treat with the chief "glory of America": its "love of liberty and the love of law." [118] His audience might well have nodded, both in weariness and in agreement. But the unique thing is that Wilson really

[117] Smith, *Wilson*, p. 309.   [118] JHL *Works*, p. 72.

was seeking to bring together and synthesize those two propensities of the American spirit. Most of his contemporaries did cherish "the love of liberty" (by which he meant chiefly popular rule) and the rule of law; but they varied — from time to time and from person to person — in the degree of their attachment to one or the other of these values. It is probably fair to say that most of the Federalists in the 1790's were more anxious to preserve the rule of law than they were to assert the rights of popular sovereignty, and that their political opponents tended toward an opposite emphasis. Wilson shared neither of these preferences. For him liberty and law were not polarities to be compromised: they were intertwined and complementary. If, as Edward Corwin has said, the great theoretical problem of the time was to reconcile the venerable Western idea of a binding higher law with the relatively new idea of the will of the people,[119] Wilson felt prepared to supply a comprehensive solution.

His analysis rests on two premises: a concept of natural law and a concept of human nature. The law of nature is prescribed by the will of God; it is universal and immutable; and it is the basis of legal obligation. As directed to individuals it is properly called the "law of nature"; as directed to states, it is called the "law of nations." Among the several things that might be emphasized about this Wilsonian concept of natural law, perhaps the most important are its explicitly deistic origin and its normative quality. This is not the secularized natural law of some eighteenth century rationalists nor is it merely a morally indifferent rule of necessity like the "laws" of motion. It is God's ordainment, and it imposes ethical duties on men and on states.

It might seem to this point that the doctrine presented, far from providing foundations for a new American jurisprudence, has turned back to a remote past in which neither America nor its precious ideas of popular sovereignty had been heard of. God's will had often been invoked to vindicate archaic and tyrannical legal systems, as Wilson well knew. But when the concept of human nature is joined to the theologically oriented natural law concept, the possibility of a modern, American outlook begins to take shape. For God, having willed such a rule to guide men's conduct, has not been so inconsiderate as to withhold from men the means of apprehending it, or the inclination to obey it. God's truth, like all truth, is discoverable to man because He has given men conscience or intuition, which enables them to perceive His first principles; reason, which is secondary, but which may clarify and refine the perceptions of conscience; and scriptural revelation, which may corroborate and make explicit the precepts discerned by conscience and reason. Not only are men endowed with these divine benefactions. By virtue of these benefac-

[119] Edward S. Corwin, *The Higher Law Background of American Constitutional Law* (Ithaca, 1955), p. 89.

tions, their propensity is toward "social affection" rather than mere self-interest. Society based on moral notions like contract and mutual trust, on the recognition of freedom and of equality in rights and obligations, is the natural state of man. All this is not to say that men are automatically perfect in perceiving God's design and in conforming their lives and their governments to it. Both the moral sense and reason need to be improved by exercise; and revelation supplies only some answers, not all. But it is to say that man's perception of the good through these means is the best guide we currently have and that it *can* be improved almost indefinitely as humanity presses on toward its progressively more glorious destiny.

From these premises Wilson sought to draw out a theory of law and of good government. His *bête noire* was Blackstone and especially Blackstone's definition of law as a "rule of action prescribed by some superior, and which the inferior is bound to obey." [120] The definition must be incorrect, says Wilson, for one man cannot be naturally superior to another, nor is there any means by which a human agency can bestow superiority on other humans. God might indeed do so, but He has provided no clues for recognizing these distinctions, and we can presume that he intended them not to exist. The actual basis of law is not then superiority but "the consent of those whose obedience the law requires." For, given the premise of an innately moral and essentially social human nature, it follows that popular consent will tend to reflect God's natural law.

God's will, then, as interpreted by popular consent, is the source of legal obligation. Sovereignty resides not in states or in governments, but in "the free and independent man." [121] In practice, this freeman's consent to the law may be expressed in compacts, in majority votes, or, most importantly of all, in custom. The great virtue of the common law is that it is a customary law, representing the consent of those it affects, and adapting itself by innumerable adjustments and alterations to the needs and desires of the people. It is a mistake to argue as Blackstone does that the legislature is supreme or as some Americans do that it is peculiarly the representative of the people's will. At least in America where the "revolution principle" of popular consent is acknowledged, all branches of government represent the people: the pronouncements of the judiciary, no less than the enactments of the legislature, speak with the sovereign authority of that "free and independent man" who has consented to be bound by them. Because quick popular judgment, though generally good, may be imperfect, it is desirable that it be refined and perhaps retarded by such devices as separation of powers, bicameralism, and judicial review. And because that judgment can be made more nearly perfect by

[120] JHL *Works*, p. 103.　　[121] JHL *Works*, p. 81.

exercise, the suffrage should be granted to every independent man so as to cultivate in him the wisdom and high-mindedness social decision requires; and he should develop a knowledge of the law which depends on him as both its sovereign and its object. Needless to say, this knowledge should be of American law, which rests on the American-discovered principle of popular consent, and which is simple enough in its main outlines for general apprehension.

Wilson's attitude toward the common law seems at first glance contradictory: he appears both to eulogize it and to reject it. But the explanation is simple. He greatly admired the English common law because it was based on custom and because he conceived that custom is based "on nothing else but free and voluntary *consent*." [122] The common law anticipates, then, unlike the enactments of parliament or the fiat of kings, the American principle of law derived wholly from the consent of the governed. For that reason the method of the common law is peculiarly appropriate to America, but precisely because that law must be based on custom-consent, English common law precedents must be rejected or adapted very cautiously; we must have in this country an *American* common law drawing its doctrines from American wants and needs.

The United States faces the first great historical opportunity to show how such a democratically based legal system will maintain order, keep faith, and improve the future. "Where liberty prevails, the arts and sciences lift up their heads and flourish. Where the arts and sciences flourish, political and moral improvements will likewise be made. All will receive from each; and each will receive from all, mutual support and assistance: mutually supported and assisted, all may be carried to a degree of perfection hitherto unknown; perhaps, hitherto not believed." [123] America is even offering the world an example that may demonstrate how to prevent war among nations; for the Supreme Court is, so to speak, the prototype of an international tribunal, resolving in accordance with the law of nations the questions between states which were formerly decided by force.

IX

This brief account of Wilson's law lectures, while by no means complete, may be sufficient to indicate the scope and character of the political and legal theory he hoped to fasten on America. It is obviously a curious amalgam of ideas drawn from both the recent and the remote past and filtered through the special predilections of its author. Locke and

[122] JHL *Works*, p. 184. Wilson was sometimes inspired to poetic flights by his enthusiasm for this point: "In the countenance of that law, every lovely feature beams consent." *Ibid.*, p. 182.
[123] JHL *Works*, p. 146.

the "spirit of '76" are there; but Wilson is more emphatic than Locke in deriving the force of natural law from divine mandate; and he lays much less emphasis on natural rights, particularly the right of property. Richard Hooker and the medieval tradition on which he drew are a more important source, but Wilson, unlike Hooker, recognized the right of revolution, and recognized, as he had to, that consent must often be expressed in actual votes, not merely in the assumed, tacit agreement of the community with its governors. Perhaps the most noteworthy thing about the theory is its synthetic quality: the refusal to dispense with either the old or the new, the tendency to claim the best of both worlds — or of any of the several worlds that Wilson cherished. The virtue of this quality is that it reflects the eclectic, ambivalent disposition of the American mind itself. America was attached to both the ancient idea of an immutable moral law and the new idea of popular sovereignty, to the concept of order and the concept of liberty, to the need for continuity and the need for progressive change. Wilson's theory embraced all these New World prepossessions and asserted, in spite of logical difficulties, their compatibility.

One of the defects of this assertive method is of course that the logical problems are not so tractable; the accommodations between the various elements of the system of values are not made easily. If the "free and independent individual" is really sovereign, then it must be explained how the law can compel him to do what he prefers not to do, as it plainly sometimes does. If the answer is that he has consented to be bound by the law, then it must be explained how and when this consent was given. If God's moral law expresses itself in custom, then how can customs change? how are we to choose between a customary observance and a contradictory demand of the electorate which by hypothesis is also divinely guided? If the answer to all these queries is that human consent does not yet infallibly discover natural law, but that it will progressively improve in its capacity to do so (and thereby in its willingness to submit to law), we are provided with an assurance for the future, but no guide for the present; and the problem of political obligation, of sovereignty, of social and political judgment, cannot be conveniently postponed.

The truth is that the pattern of Wilson's law lectures is strikingly analogous to the pattern of Wilson's own character and career. Like his theory, he was a conglomerate of values and impulses drawn from widely variant worlds, of incompatibilities brought together only by his own attachment to them, and reconciled only by his own incurable optimism that they *could* be reconciled in some apocalyptic day that never quite arrived. He wanted to be a scholar, a lawgiver, a statesman, and a Napoleon of finance; a political theorist and a political manager; a respected crony of high-toned Federalists and a man of the people, enjoying their "well-founded and distinguishing applause." [124] He seems not to have re-flected that these goals might be contradictory, that one must choose among them or at the very least assign them relative priorities. It was as if the very fact that he wanted them so much would be itself enough to resolve the conflicts and to achieve them all. And so it was with the law lectures. They bring together in a cluster the political and legal values Wilson himself happened to cherish, as if the act of assembling and asserting those values was itself enough to establish their validity. If he had had the time, Wilson might have been able to reconcile some of their dissonances, to answer some of the questions they left unan-swered, and to construct a rounded and comprehensive political philoso-phy for America. No one was better qualified in native intellect or in erudition to do that job. But, as always, he was beset by other cares and drawn to other preoccupations — his judicial tasks, his grandiose codifica-tion plans, most of all his business affairs, which were now becoming ominously chaotic. So the aim of the lectures, which might well have absorbed a man for a lifetime, could be allotted only a portion of two winter seasons; and the chance was lost that he might be known and remembered as the John Locke of America's Glorious Revolution.

Yet, although the logical structure of the lectures was imperfect and although they were cast in an ungainly form, there was in their basic viewpoint a rightness that rose above logical inconsistencies and omis-sions. As so often with Wilson, his instinctive trenchancy had enabled him to strike closer to the real American grain than any of his peers. The most thoughtful of them, like John Adams and James Madison, were cur-rently much concerned with the menace of majority tyranny which they feared might arise from the bitter factional warfare of democratic so-ciety. Earlier thinkers such as Locke and Hooker had avoided this prob-lem by simply assuming the traditional, narrow electoral system, so that the consent of the governed was more metaphorical than real.[125] For Wil-son of course it was completely real — popular institutions created and controlled by manhood suffrage — and to his contemporaries this pros-pect of genuine rather than figurative popular influence created the dan-ger that the majority could oppress minorities and despoil property-holders. To talk otherwise, as John Adams said, is "either to babble like a new-born infant, or to deceive like an unprincipled imposter." [126] Yet Wilson did talk otherwise. He did not undertake the task that seemed inescapable to most of his contemporaries — of constructing a theory in

[124] JHL *Works*, p. 405.

[125] J. W. Gough, *John Locke's Political Philosophy* (Oxford, 1950), p. 64. Caroline Robbins, *The Eighteenth-Century Commonwealthman* (Cambridge, Mass., 1959), p. 16.

[126] John Adams, *Life and Works*, VI, 62.

which these popular propensities were somehow mitigated and balanced. In his view separation of powers and judicial review were not obstructions to the popular will, but means of improving and expressing it. He assumed that the alleged propensities were, if not entirely chimerical, at least greatly exaggerated, that the American majority would, by and large, behave justly and with self-restraint. Optimism like this seemed fatuously unrealistic to his hardheaded fellows, and even in retrospect their qualms are understandable. But in the final event Wilson was more nearly right about America than they were. American society and politics have not been characterized by the factional struggles-to-the-death which they dreaded; the majority has in general been restrained, law-respecting, and tame. Whatever the faults of the law lectures in organization and logic, history, which is sometimes cavalier about these auctorial virtues, has ratified the basic point. Just as Wilson contended, popular government and the rule of law have been more complementary than antithetical in the American historical experience.

But the law lectures, pragmatically right though they may have been in their fundamental point of view, failed to produce the impact that their author probably hoped for. Neither his own current repute nor contemporary legal philosophy was likely to be much altered by a series of classroom addresses hurriedly composed and loosely organized, broken off before completion, and unpublished until after the speaker's death. A teacher may transform the thought of his generation, but he needs decades to accomplish this, and Wilson had only months to spare. The outcome of the law lectures, like the record of his achievement on the Supreme Court, must have disappointed this greatly ambitious, optimistic, and energetic man.

X

By now in fact the clouds were gathering fast, and further, graver disappointments were in the making. The business affairs that continually entrenched on his time as a scholar and judge, that probably helped to rob him of the chief justiceship, were becoming more than a handicap and an embarrassment. They were beginning to take on the proportions of the kind of disaster that ruins a life.

As always, the enterprises were numerous, varied, and extravagant. As always they were propped up mainly by a scaffolding of loans and optimism. He had bought on mortgage the Birdsboro Ironworks that once belonged to his wife's father. As late as 1794 he conceived and began to develop an extensive industrial complex at Wilsonville on Lake Wallenpaupack, including sawmills, cloth mills, and dye works. The lure of land and more land — in Pennsylvania, in Carolina, in Virginia, in the west — continued to entice him. The house of cards rose higher and higher, and he was repeatedly forced to turn away from his judicial duties and his scholarly pursuits in order to deal with a procession of crises. Yet each time he managed somehow to forestall collapse, emerging from each trial with unimpaired ambition and energy, not only for fresh financial sallies, but for life's other gambles as well. In 1793, Wilson, now a widower in his fifties, married Hannah Gray of Boston, who was not more than nineteen; and in 1796, a terrible and desperate year for her husband, she bore him a son to add to the six children he had already fathered by his first wife. Wilson was never one to hesitate about giving hostages to fortune, but this offering seems exorbitant even for him.

By 1796 the often-postponed calamity was unmistakably at hand. European money, which Wilson and many others had counted on to vindicate their speculations, was flowing not to America but into Europe's own wars. The emigrants who had been expected to people the mortgaged acres did not appear: they were fighting and dying on the battlefields of the Old World. Credit could no longer be had on any terms, and credit was essential to Wilson's survival. He was caught in the maelstrom that was currently engulfing his old friend Robert Morris, William Duer (who had suffered one spectacular downfall in 1792 and was now again in trouble), James Greenleaf, and many others heretofore "of reputed fortunes and prudence." [127]

His remaining years were a tragic ordeal of penury, harassment, imprisonment, and failing health. He who had lately been regarded as one of America's nabobs lacked now the money to clothe and feed his family adequately. Even while he rode circuit as a justice of the Supreme Court aggrieved business associates and creditors besieged him, threatening denunciation and debtors' prison. After his circuit duties in the spring of 1797, he hid from them in Bethlehem: to return to Philadelphia would have meant jail. Nevertheless they caught up with him and had him imprisoned in Burlington, New Jersey. When his son managed to squeeze from stones enough money to provide bail, Wilson fled southward to a squalid temporary sanctuary in Edenton, North Carolina. But he owed Pierce Butler $197,000, and Butler's agents sought him out and jailed him once more. He was, as he said, being "hunted like a wild beast," and his formerly robust health began to deteriorate alarmingly. In July 1798, still in Edenton, he caught malaria; a few weeks later he suffered a stroke; and on August 21, with only his young wife at his side in the Hornblow Tavern, he died.

For Wilson, who had always expected so much from life, those final days when his visions of fame and riches lay in shambles about him must have been a very special hell. Although he held fast until the very end

---

[127] Edward Channing, *A History of the United States* (New York, 1917), IV, 111.

to hopes of retrieving his fortunes, even he surely realized at last that those hopes were implausible, more the figments of lifetime habit than of conviction. He was ruined in estate and health and reputation, and he must have known it.

Yet it is charitable to hope that he never understood while he lived the extent of the ruination, the full measure of the disappointment of his dreams. As Smith says, he had become by 1798 an object of derision to his enemies and an embarrassment to his friends; and the death of one of the chief founding fathers therefore passed by almost unobserved. His surviving contemporaries seldom mentioned him, and within a very little time he was as obscure in the nation's memory as he has been ever since. In the inaugural law lectures, during one of those florid digressions he loved so well, Wilson had deplored posterity's neglect of Lord Baltimore:

. . . why should an ungracious silence be observed, with regard to the name and character of Calvert? . . . He was truly the father of his country. . . . Similar to that of Calvert, has been the fate of many other valuable characters in America. They have been too little known. . . . Will America refuse a temple to her patriots and her heroes? No; she will not. The glorious dome already rises. . . . In its front a number of niches are formed. In some of them statues are placed.[128]

He felt, and rightly, that he had earned a niche in the forefront of that hall of fame. But the fate of Calvert, as Wilson described it, was to be his own.

XI

That fate, considered in contrast to both the achievements of his lifetime and the shape of American government since his death, is — as was said at the outset of this essay — the first great paradox in the strange case of James Wilson. Why should America have neglected so shamefully the author of *Considerations on the . . . Authority of the British Parliament*, a signer of the Declaration, one of the primary figures in the Constitutional Convention, the leader of the ratification movement in Pennsylvania, the architect of the Pennsylvania constitution of 1790, one of the six original justices of the Supreme Court, the new Republic's first law professor, and the only founding father to essay a general theory of government and law? Why should it not only have neglected him but persistently failed to rediscover him in the light of the fact that his views more nearly foreshadowed the actual political future of America than those of any of his celebrated contemporaries? The answers to this riddle have already, I believe, been in large part suggested in the foregoing ac-

[128] JHL *Works*, pp. 71–72.

count of Wilson's career. The time has now come to draw the strands together in summary and conclusion.

The answers are numerous and complex; and they depend to a considerable extent on an understanding of Wilson and the climate of opinion in his own times. He was, as we have seen, himself a paradox: a man whose driving ambition to be revered as a philosopher-statesman was equalled only by his equally compulsive drive to forge a personal financial empire, whose mind was capable of the most acute perceptions but also of wishful thinking on a remarkable scale. Perhaps he had achieved a personally satisfying inner harmony between his desire to serve America and his desire to serve himself, between his love of honor and his love of gain. American capitalists have often been attracted by the simple but grand idea that the opening up and development of the continent is no less God's work because it is personally profitable. Wilson, who was peculiarly given to such acts of faith, probably had little difficulty in reconciling, in moral terms, the public good and his private welfare, just as he was able to reconcile his belief in popular sovereignty, national union, and the rule of law by positing a national democracy whose people would faithfully adhere to the laws of nature and of nature's God.

But however easy these accommodations were in Wilson's mind, they were not so readily obvious either in the public mind or in the world of fact. The populace found difficulty in believing that doing well and doing good were identical. Nor could most contemporary Americans rise enough above the factional dogmatisms of their time to understand that a Federalist, nationalist, legalist capitalist could be a sincere devotee of popular rule, much less to realize that he was fundamentally right in asserting the congruence of those seemingly disparate values. Moreover both the workings of the economic order and the boundaries of individual capacity were unaffected by Wilson's optimistic disbelief in their existence. When loans were called in, faith was no substitute for cash. No amount of self-confidence could stretch a day beyond twenty-four hours or prevent arteries from hardening. Wilson's failure in life to build the monuments he yearned for is explained by the circumstance that he was born too variously ambitious and was born and died too soon. If he had coveted fewer of life's rewards, he might have gained more. If he had lived twenty years later or twenty years longer, the financial shoals might have been navigated, the books and judicial opinions might have been written, America might have been readier to believe in and be taught by a champion of democratic nationalism. 1742–1798 was the wrong span for a man of Wilson's propensities and views to achieve enduring fame.

Yet if Wilson's own era was not right for him, if he was the familiar prophet without honor in his own time and country, one might expect that the future would redress the balance of the past, that as America came to practice what he preached it would canonize him posthumously. The man who anticipated the alliance of democracy and union, who recognized the law-regarding temper of American political society and who would have shaped our political institutions in accordance with those insights, might expect to be rescued from the back room of history when the nation so shaped those institutions, sometimes tacitly, sometimes by explicit constitutional amendment or judicial decision. That those expectations have been groundless is explained by several factors having to do with the sociology of fame and with Wilson's own special qualities. To begin with, continuity alone probably has much bearing on historic repute. Romantic myth to be contrary, the great whom the present recognizes tend to be those who were thought of as great in their time. Tomorrow may enhance or diminish yesterday's reputation; it does not often create a wholly new one. Wilson's name had been so thoroughly clouded at his death — by his own errors of omission and commission, by the handicaps which the times had imposed on his range of opportunity — that resurrection was unlikely. As Smith says, the pietistic biographers of the nineteenth century drew back from a man who had, whatever his statesmanly virtues, played fast and loose with his own and other people's money and died in bankrupt disgrace. And Wilson had not really completed the comprehensive work on American philosophy and law which the plan of the law lectures envisioned; he had not molded the working machine of government like Hamilton, nor held great positions of political leadership like Jefferson and Madison. He lacked both Marshall's title and Marshall's gifts of personality and persuasiveness. When the nation came to accept some of Wilson's precepts, it preferred to hear them stated by the living Marshall and Webster and Lincoln, rather than by a dead and largely forgotten Scot.

These considerations all play a part in explaining Wilson's historical obscurity. But they need to be supplemented by a further point which might alone have been decisive: that Wilson has been encumbered in death as in life by the precursive quality of mind that was his most extraordinary attribute. He was underrated while he lived partly because his thinking was too far in advance of the nation's development; he has been neglected in afterlife because America has even yet never quite managed to catch up with him. To be sure, the practice of American government has tended progressively to follow his guidelines: majority rule and nationalism have grown concurrently and have mutually supported each other; the majority has been sober and law-abiding; the legal system has grown and the authority of the Supreme Court has developed by the slow accretion of general consent, not by Blackstonian commands. This *de facto* political system closely corresponds to Wilson's vision. But while American political actuality has been increasingly Wilsonian, American political myth has remained in large degree wedded to the illusions of the past, to the ideological cleavages spawned by Jefferson and Hamilton. Local autonomy is still often confused with liberty. Though strong, purposeful national government exists, we acknowledge it only halfheartedly, because we have never stopped to decide whether we want it to exist. We pretend that the majority is prevented from having its way by constitutional barriers and by procedural devices like the filibuster when as a matter of fact it is prevented only by its own sense of self-restraint. Our courts continue to announce decisions in the rhetoric of eternal mandates, when in truth those decisions rest on the evolution of custom, the accumulation of consent. Perhaps these fictions, or some of them, merit preservation; perhaps it is desirable for a nation to act one way and think another. But for James Wilson this national propensity has meant permanent exclusion from America's Olympus. If a man wants to be remembered he should not forecast the realities of a society; he should nourish its myths.

A NOTE ON THE TEXT

As indicated in the Introduction, the version of the *Works* here reprinted was first published in three volumes in Philadelphia in 1804 under the editorship of Bird Wilson, the statesman's son. In 1896 James DeWitt Andrews edited a two-volume version (Callaghan and Company, Chicago) which omitted some of the papers Bird Wilson had included and rearranged some of the remainder but was otherwise substantially identical. Both editions have long been out of print.

Few changes have been made in the text. I have corrected the *errata* listed in the final volume of the original edition and a small number of other patent errors of typography or spelling. Otherwise spelling, capitalization, and punctuation have been left unchanged. James Wilson's footnotes have been left largely intact, as have those of Bird Wilson. It did seem desirable to translate for the modern reader the Latin quotations Wilson used so copiously, and the translations have been incorporated in the footnotes. Footnotes with alphabetic indicators are those of James Wilson himself; "Ed." indicates Bird Wilson; and notes enclosed in square brackets indicate the present editor. All the notes appear together at the foot of the page.

Another change perhaps worth noting is in the table of contents. In the 1804 edition there was no general table of contents, only a separate one for each volume. Moreover, the miscellaneous papers beginning at page 711 were in the 1804 edition grouped together without chapter numbers at the end of the last volume, so that the casual reader might mistake them for a continuation of the "Lectures on Law." It has seemed best to provide them with chapter numbers, and to construct a page of contents for the *Works* as a whole.

The original title page of Volume I (see below, page 53) has been reproduced from the 1804 edition.

Wilson was obviously proud of his reputation as a scholar, and he had reason to be. His writings are adorned with a wealth of reference that is all the more remarkable when we consider that public, professional, and personal affairs were always competing for his time. The books he cited in the works here reprinted are drawn together in the glossary (pp. 849–856), and his range of allusion is further suggested by the index. His footnotes include references to something over two hundred separate sources, ancient and modern. To be sure, a certain number of these were partly decorative, for Wilson like other of his contemporaries could seldom forbear reminding his readers that he was learned beyond the ordinary. But the bulk of them were actually germane to the argument he was pursuing, and in any event his copious use of them demonstrates that he was, as has been suggested, a profoundly bookish man.

Unfortunately he employed for his citations an abbreviation system that is often initially baffling. Most of the footnotes occur in the law lectures, and these were of course in manuscript until his son edited them after his death. I suppose that Wilson might have translated the shorthand if he himself had been spared to revise and edit the lectures. Some of the abbreviations, especially the legal ones, would have been comprehensible enough to the sophisticated. But what could he have expected a reader to make of "Stu.V. cites Com.Per.," especially since the context suggests a work on the American Indians? or of "Bac.on Gov.," which is *not* a reference to Francis Bacon, who is however cited in his own right (usually as "Ld.Bac." but sometimes as "Bac.") over forty times? At any rate I have tried to identify them all in the glossary, because I thought it would be interesting to see at a glance a full list of the sources he drew on; and the performance of this modest task has suggested a few further observations about Wilson's scholarly qualities and methods.

It is of some interest, for example, to note whom Wilson cites and how frequently. He refers to most of the standard British legal authorities of the time, to a large number of historians, and to a fair number of philosophers. The *Works* do not suggest a man greatly devoted to belles-lettres. His few literary quotations — from Pope, Shakespeare, and Milton, for example — are obvious and sometimes rather gratuitous. Among legal writers the name of Blackstone leads all the rest, which is perhaps not surprising considering the grip of the author of the *Commentaries* on the contemporary Anglo-American legal mind. But Wilson of course often mentions Blackstone not to invoke his authority but to challenge it. "My Lord Coke" is an easy second, and "My Lord Bacon" seems to be third. As might be expected, Scottish authors appear frequently. John Millar, the Whiggish law professor at Glasgow, and Thomas Reid are among the most common. Among the writers of the European Enlightenment, Pufendorf, Vattel, Beccaria, and Montesquieu are most often referred to. It is of some interest that Locke's *Two Treatises of Government* is cited only twice. As for Hume, his *Treatise on Human Nature* is referred to in order to refute it, but his *History* is not mentioned at all. Among classical authors, Cicero is quoted by far the most frequently and Tacitus the next. Others are cited much less often, but there are enough of them to suggest that Wilson was indeed a competent Latinist. He sometimes misquotes, but Richard Gummere suggests that when he does it is because he is depending on memory. Surely he read

Latin easily. His knowledge of Greek is, on the other hand, much more doubtful. Most of his references to Greek writers turn out to be drawn from secondary sources like Gillies or Pufendorf; and it is hard to believe that he would not have cited the writers directly if he had read them firsthand. As for French authors, his references are usually to translations, and I at first suspected that he did not know the language. But he does occasionally cite the original (Bouchaud and Brissot, for example), and my guess is that, being an able Latinist, he knew French well enough to read it when he had to.

At this point the reader should perhaps be warned that, as has already been intimated, a citation does not necessarily mean that Wilson actually used the book cited. He sometimes drew his reference from a secondary source, and while he usually acknowledges this in his footnote, he does not always do so. For example, he may have actually examined the "Gentoo Code," but it seems more likely that he culled the reference from Gilbert Stuart, whose own voluminous footnotes make much of it. Yet if he did this kind of thing my impression is that he did it seldom enough so that the citations (as distinguished from the mere name references in the text) can be taken as a fairly reliable list of books he genuinely consulted.

A second caveat can be offered with more assurance. The reader is cautioned against appraising Wilson's prose style on the basis of passages from the law lectures. No doubt most of the language is indeed his own. But he sometimes paraphrases a source quite closely and even neglects to use quotation marks when he has in fact transcribed a whole passage verbatim. For example, page 351 encloses in quotes one passage from Whitaker's *History of Manchester* (slightly misquoted) but then does not indicate that the sentences that follow are also direct quotations. The passage about the provability of the existence of ideas on page 220, including the sardonic tone, is drawn directly from Kames's *Elements of Criticism* (which is cited only as "Elem. Crit.") with no indication of the authorship.

These points are not brought up in order to disparage Wilson's scholarship. The lectures *were* lectures, after all. They were not seen into print by the author himself. Even modern classroom lecturers have been known to lean rather heavily on their sources or to borrow a citation from them. In fact the net result of a journey through Wilson's references is a feeling of solid respect for his erudition and industry. Their number and range are impressive, and it is worth emphasizing that they are for the most part woven through the analysis, not merely tossed in to certify the author's membership in the company of learned men. It is easy enough to cite Bacon or Reeves or Goguet once or twice for window dressing: a single trip to the shelves will do the trick. But Wilson's references to these and many others are not only frequent; they are distributed throughout the lectures in a way that suggests he really had read them and was using them constantly, returning to them again and again as his shifting subject matter required. It is interesting to speculate what a mark he might have left on American scholarship if distractions and early death had not cut his time so short.

Dr. Morton Horowitz provided valuable aid in the preparation of the Introduction, and Mr. Sanford Levinson has been extremely helpful throughout, particularly in the identification of Wilson's references. Mr. Leslie Threatte translated most of the Latin passages. A number of Wilson's more obscure references would have remained obscure but for the erudition and kindness of Professor Mason Hammond. Professors Samuel H. Beer and Don K. Price read the Introduction and offered helpful counsel. The editor's thanks are extended to all of them, though the final responsibility for any errors or inadequacies is of course his own.

THE

WORKS

OF

THE HONOURABLE

JAMES WILSON, L. L. D.

LATE ONE OF THE ASSOCIATE JUSTICES OF THE SUPREME
COURT OF THE UNITED STATES, AND PROFESSOR OF LAW
IN THE COLLEGE OF PHILADELPHIA.

PUBLISHED UNDER THE DIRECTION

OF

BIRD WILSON, ESQUIRE.

LEX FUNDAMENTUM EST LIBERTATIS, QUA FRUIMUR. LEGUM
OMNES SERVI SUMUS, UT LIBERI ESSE POSSIMUS.

CIC.

VOL. I.

PHILADELPHIA:

AT THE LORENZO PRESS, PRINTED FOR BRONSON AND CHAUNCEY

1804.

CONTENTS

Preface by Bird Wilson   59

LECTURES ON LAW
PART ONE

I.	Of the study of the law in the United States.	69
II.	Of the general principles of law and obligation.	97
III.	Of the law of nature.	126
IV.	Of the law of nations.	148
V.	Of municipal law.	168
VI.	Of man, as an individual.	197
VII.	Of man, as a member of society.	227
VIII.	Of man, as a member of a confederation.	247
IX.	Of man, as a member of the great commonwealth of nations.	270
X.	Of government.	284
XI.	Comparison of the constitution of the United States, with that of Great Britain.	309
XII.	Of the common law.	334
XIII.	Of the nature and philosophy of evidence.	369

PART TWO

I.	Of the constitutions of the United States and of Pennsylvania — Of the legislative department.	399
II.	— Of the executive department.	436

[VOLUME TWO]

II.	— Of the executive department, *continued*.	441
III.	— Of the judicial department.	446
IV.	Of the nature of courts.	494
V.	Of the constituent parts of courts — Of the judges.	500

VI. The subject continued — Of juries. 503

VII. The subject continued — Of sheriffs and coroners. 550

VIII. The subject continued — Of counsellors and attornies. 556

IX. The subject continued — Of constables. 568

X. Of corporations. 570

XI. Of citizens and aliens. 573

XII. Of the natural rights of individuals. 585

PART THREE

I. Of the nature of crimes; and the necessity and proportion of punishments. 611

II. Of crimes against the right of individuals to their property. 637

III. Of crimes against the right of individuals to liberty, and to reputation. 647

IV. Of crimes against the right of individuals to personal safety. 653

V. Of crimes immediately against the community. 663

VI. Of crimes affecting several of the natural rights of individuals. 670

VII. Of crimes against the rights of individuals acquired under civil government. 672

VIII. Of the persons capable of committing crimes; and of the different degrees of guilt incurred in the commission of the same crime. 677

IX. Of the direct means used by the law to prevent offences. 680

X. Of the different steps prescribed by the law, for apprehending, detaining, trying, and punishing offenders. 684

MISCELLANEOUS PAPERS

[I] On the history of property. 711

[II] Considerations on the nature and extent of the legislative authority of the British Parliament. Published in the year 1774. 721

[III] Speech delivered in the convention for the province of Pennsylvania, held at Philadelphia, in January, 1775. 747

[IV] Speech delivered on 26th November, 1787, in the convention of Pennsylvania, assembled to take into consideration
the constitution framed, by the federal convention, for the
United States. 759

[V] Oration delivered on 4th July, 1788, at the procession
formed at Philadelphia to celebrate the adoption of the
constitution of the United States. 773

[VI] Speech on choosing the members of the senate by electors;
delivered, on 31st December, 1789, in the convention of
Pennsylvania, assembled for the purpose of reviewing, altering, and amending the constitution of the state. 781

[VII] Speech delivered, on 19th January, 1790, in the convention
of Pennsylvania, assembled for the purpose of reviewing,
altering, and amending the constitution of the state; on a
motion that "no member of congress from this state, nor
any person holding or exercising any office of trust or
profit under the United States, shall at the same time, hold
and exercise any office whatever in this state." 794

[VIII] A charge delivered to the grand jury in the circuit court
of the United States for the district of Virginia, in May,
1791. 803

[IX] Considerations on the Bank of North America. Published in
the year 1785. 824

Appendix to the Preceding Considerations. 841

BIBLIOGRAPHICAL GLOSSARY 849

INDEX 857

PREFACE

THE incomplete state of the lectures on law, notwithstanding the lapse of several years between the time at which those now published were delivered and the death of the Author, is a circumstance of which the publick will naturally inquire the cause. The circumstance itself is certainly much to be lamented; but its cause presents a subject of still deeper regret.

The law professorship, in the college of Philadelphia, was established in the year 1790; and the Author was appointed the first professor. The extent of his plan of lectures rendered it impossible for him to go through his whole subject in one season: three courses were necessary for the purpose. The first course, which was delivered in the winter of 1790–91, consisted of those lectures contained in what the Editor has entitled the *first part*. The second course, which was, in a great measure, delivered in the following winter, would have consisted of the remaining two parts now published. In April, 1792, the college of Philadelphia and the university of Pennsylvania were, by an act of assembly, united into one seminary, under the latter title. A law professorship was erected in the new seminary, and the Author again appointed to fill the chair; but no lectures were delivered after the union. The preceding course had been interrupted and was not completed. The causes of these circumstances are not within the Editor's knowledge. He knows, however, that, though the delivery of the lectures was discontinued, the Author designed to complete his plan for publication. From this design his attention was drawn by another object of more importance, in which he was engaged.

In March, 1791, the house of representatives in the general assembly of Pennsylvania, resolved to appoint a person to revise and digest the laws of the commonwealth; to ascertain and determine how far any British statutes extended to it; and to prepare bills, containing such alterations, additions, and improvements as the code of laws, and the principles and forms of the constitution then lately adopted might require. The Author was unanimously appointed for that purpose. The nature of the plan which he formed in consequence of this resolution, will appear from the following letter on the subject, delivered to the speaker of the house of representatives on 24th August, 1791.

Sir,

While I am employed in executing the trust committed to me by the house of representatives, it is, I conceive, my duty, from time to time, to inform them, through you, of the steps which I have taken, and of those which I mean to take, in order to accomplish the great end which is in contemplation.

From the records deposited in the rolls office, I have taken an account of all the laws made in Pennsylvania from its first settlement till the beginning of the last session of the legislature. They are in number one thousand seven hundred and two. Their titles I have entered into a book, in the order, usually chronological, in which they are recorded. On some of them, especially those of an early date, I have made and minuted remarks: and have left ample room for more, in the course of my further investigations. I have also reduced their several subjects into an alphabetical order, by entering them regularly in a common place book. This process required time, and care, and a degree of minute drudgery; but it was absolutely requisite to the correct execution of the design. How can I make a digest of the laws, without having all the laws upon each head in my view? This view can in the first instance be obtained only by ranging them in an exact common place.

But something more must still be done. To rank, in a correct edition, the several laws according to their seniority or to the order of the alphabet would, by no means, be correspondent to the enlarged plan signified by the resolutions of the house. It is obvious, and it was certainly expected, that, under each head, the different regulations, however dispersed, at present, among numerous laws, should, in the digest, be collected in a natural series, and reduced to a just form. This I deem an indispensable part of my business.

But the performance of this indispensable part gives rise to a new question. In what order should the methodised collections be arranged?

A chronological order would, from the nature of those collections, be impracticable: an alphabetical order would be unnatural and unsatisfactory. The order of legitimate system is the only one, which remains. This order, therefore, is necessarily brought into my contemplation. My contemplation of it has been attended with the just degree of diffidence and solicitude. To form the mass of our laws into a body compacted and well proportioned, is a task of no common magnitude. Arduous as it is, the enlarged views of the house of representatives stimulate me to attempt it. In such an attempt it will not be dishonourable — even to fail.

Of this system, I have begun to sketch the rough outlines. In finishing them, and in filling them up, I mean to avail myself of all the assistance, which can possibly be derived from every example set before me. But, at the same time, I mean to pay implicit deference to none.

The acts of the legislature of Pennsylvania, though very numerous, compose but a small proportion of her laws. The common law is a part, and, by far, the most important part of her system of jurisprudence. Statute regulations are intended only for those cases, comparatively few, in which the common law is defective, or to which it is inapplicable: to that law, those regulations are properly to be considered as a supplement. A knowledge of that law should, for this reason, precede, or, at least, accompany the study of those regulations.

"To know what the common law was before the making of any statute," says my Lord Coke, in his familiar but expressive manner, "is the very lock and key to set open the windows of the statute." [a] To lay the statute laws before one who knows nothing of the common law, amounts, frequently, to much the same thing as laying every third or fourth line of a deed before one who has never seen the residue of it. It would, therefore, be highly eligible, that, under each head of the statute law, the common law, relating to it, should be introduced and explained. This would be a useful commentary on the text of the statute law, and would, at the same time, form a body of the common law reduced into a just and regular system.

With such a commentary, the digest which I shall have the honour of reporting to the house will be accompanied. The constitution of the United States and that of Pennsylvania, compose the supreme law of the land: they contain and they suggest many of the fundamental principles of jurisprudence, and must have a governing and an extensive influence over almost every other part of our legal system. They should, therefore, be explained and understood in the clearest and most distinct manner, and they should be pursued through their numerous and important, though remote and widely ramified effects. Hence it is proper, that they also should be attended with a commentary. These commentaries will not, however, form a part of my report: they must stand or fall by their own merit or insignificance.

Another question, of very considerable importance, has occurred to me: the result of my reflections upon it, I beg leave to lay before the house.

In what manner should the digest of the laws of Pennsylvania be composed? Should it imitate the style of the British acts of parliament and those statutes, which have been framed upon their model—or should it be written in the usual forms of composition?

To professional gentlemen it is well known, that, in England, all bills were anciently drawn in the form of petitions; that these petitions, with the king's answer, were entered upon the parliament rolls; and that, at the end of each parliament, they were reduced into statutes by the judges. Hence the form, "may it please your majesty, that it may be enacted" and "be it enacted, &c." This form, like many others, has been

[a] 3. Ins. 308.

continued in England long after the reason of it has ceased. This form, like many others, has been introduced into the colonies, and, among the rest, into Pennsylvania, where the reason of it never existed. Thus almost every sentence in our acts of assembly begins with a "be it enacted."

This form, though without foundation in Pennsylvania, is not, however, without its inconveniences. To introduce every sentence under the government of a verb, gives a stiffness — to introduce every sentence under the government of the same verb, gives a monotony as well as stiffness, to the composition. To avoid the frequent reiteration of those blemishes, the sentences are lengthened. By being lengthened, they are crowded with multifarious, sometimes with heterogeneous and disjointed, circumstances and materials. Hence the obscure, and confused, and embarrassed periods of a mile, with which the statute books are loaded and disgraced.

But simplicity and plainness and precision should mark the texture of a law. It claims the *obedience*—it should be level to the *understanding* of all.

By the first assembly of Pennsylvania an act was made "for teaching the laws in the schools." [b] This noble regulation is countenanced by the authority and example of the most enlightened nations and men. Cicero[c] informs us, that when he was a boy, the laws of the twelve tables were learned "ut necessarium carmen," as a piece of composition at once necessary and entertaining. The celebrated legislator of the Cretans used all the precautions, which human prudence could suggest, to inspire the youth with the greatest respect and attachment to the maxims and customs of the state. This was what Plato found most admirable in the laws of Minos.

If youth should be educated in the knowledge and love of the laws: it follows, that the laws should be proper objects of their attachment, and proper subjects of their study. Can this be said concerning a statute book drawn up in the usual style and form? Would any one select such a composition to form the taste of his son, or to inspire him with a relish for literary accomplishments? It has been remarked, with truth as well as wit, that one of the most irksome penalties, which could be inflicted by an act of parliament, would be, to compel the culprit to read the statutes at large from the beginning to the end.

But the knowledge of the laws, useful to youth, is incumbent on those of riper years.

From the manner, in which other law books, as well as statute laws, are usually written, it may be supposed that law is, in its nature, unsusceptible of the same simplicity and clearness as the other sciences. It is high time that law should be rescued from this injurious imputation.

[b] R. O. book. A. p. 22.   [c] De leg. l. 2. c. 23.

Like the other sciences, it should now enjoy the advantages of light, which have resulted from the resurrection of letters; for, like the other sciences, it has suffered extremely from the thick veil of mystery spread over it in the dark and scholastick ages.

Both the divinity and law of those times, says Sir William Blackstone,[d] were frittered into logical distinctions, and drawn out into metaphysical subtilties, with a skill most amazingly artificial. Law in particular, which (being intended for universal reception) ought to be a plain rule of action, became a science of the greatest intricacy; especially when blended with the new and oppressive refinements ingrafted upon feodal property: which refinements were, from time to time, gradually introduced by the Norman practitioners, with a view to supersede (as they did in a great measure) the more homely, but the more free and intelligible, maxims of distributive justice among the Saxons.

As were the divinity and the law, such likewise was the philosophy of the schools during many ages of darkness and barbarism. It was fruitful of words, but barren of works, and admirably contrived for drawing a veil over human ignorance, and putting a stop to the progress of knowledge.[e] But at last the light began to dawn. It has dawned, however, much slower upon the law, than upon religion and philosophy. "The laws," says the celebrated Beccaria,[f] "are always several ages behind the actual improvement of the nation which they govern." If this observation is true, and I believe it to be true, with regard to law in general; it is peculiarly true, and its truth is of peculiar importance, with regard to criminal law in particular. It is the observation of Sir William Blackstone, that, in every country of Europe, the criminal is more rude and imperfect than the civil law. Unfortunate it is that this should be the case. For on the excellence of the criminal law the liberty and happiness of the citizens chiefly depend.

We are told by Montesquieu, that the knowledge, with regard to the surest rules, observed in criminal judgments, is more interesting to mankind than any other thing in the universe. We are told by him further, that liberty can be founded only on the practice of this knowledge. But how can this knowledge be acquired — how can it become the foundation of practice, if the laws, and particularly the criminal laws, are written in a manner in which they cannot be clearly known or understood?

Deeply penetrated with the truth and the force of these remarks, which are supported by the most respectable authorities, I shall not justly incur the censure of innovation, if I express my opinion, that the law should be written in the same manner, which we use when we write on other subjects, or other sciences. This manner has been already adopted, with

[d] 4. Bl. Com. 410. 2. Id. 58.   [e] Reid. Ess. Int. 127.   [f] C. 29.

success, in the Constitution of the United States, and in that of Pennsylvania.

As, however, the observations, which I have made and quoted, bear particularly upon the criminal code; I propose to make, in that code, the first experiment of their justness and efficacy.

The criminal law, though the most important, is by far the least voluminous part of the system; and it can be easily formed into a separate report. This I mean to do. By doing so, I shall have a fair opportunity of exhibiting a specimen of the manner and the merits both of my plan and of its execution.

To the Speaker of the House of Representatives.

In the execution of this plan, the Author made very considerable progress. It had been undertaken, however, under the authority of only one of the houses of the assembly, without the sanction of the other; and, in the course of its execution, it was found, that the want of legislative sanction, and of a provision for making pecuniary compensation to persons necessarily employed as assistants in a work of so much labour and importance, joined with the difficulty of obtaining many useful and necessary books connected with the subject of the work, had retarded its progress, and thrown considerable impediments in the way of its completion. An attempt was made to remove these obstacles; and a bill was passed for that purpose by the house of representatives; but it was unfortunately negatived by the senate. The design of framing a digest under the authority of the legislature was, of course, relinquished. But the Author still contemplated the execution of a similar design, as a private work; supported only by his own name; and it occupied, for a long time, his assiduous attention. He had, in a great degree, prepared the materials; but did not live to arrange them, and compose the contemplated digest.

From these causes, the lectures continued in the state, in which they now appear. The Editor has not thought himself at liberty to make any alterations in the language of the Author: the lecturing style is, therefore, retained. He has, however, been obliged to adopt a division not, perhaps, strictly in unison with that style, but the only one which was in his power — that into parts and chapters, according to the subjects. They were never divided by the Author into distinct lectures; as, according to his mode of delivering them, they were frequently attended with recapitulations, and often embraced parts of his observations on different subjects.

Of the other parts of the contents of these volumes, the tracts on the legislative authority of parliament over the colonies, and on the Bank of

North America, were before published; as were also the speech in convention on 26th November, 1787, and the oration on 4th July, 1788.
These, with the other speeches now published, appear to have been
selected for publication by the Author himself. His charges to grand
juries in the federal courts, the Editor has not thought it proper to insert;
because, as they related generally to the history, powers, and duties of
juries, the contents of them are to be found in the lectures. One, however, he has selected and inserted, because it contains a concise and hand-
some view of the criminal law of the United States, nearly as it stands
at present, and many important observations not to be found in the
other works.

Of the value and merit of these volumes, the Editor will say nothing.
He leaves that subject to the judgment of those who can estimate them
with greater impartiality. In some parts, perhaps, they want that degree
of polish, which the farther attention and corrections of the Author
might have bestowed on them; and repetitions, which sometimes occur,
and which, in lectures delivered, are not only excusable but proper,
would probably not have been met with, had they been corrected by
himself for the press. On the whole, however, the Editor trusts, that
they will not be thought unworthy, either in style or sentiment, of the
reputation of their Author.

[Bird Wilson]

LECTURES ON LAW

DELIVERED IN THE

COLLEGE OF PHILADELPHIA

IN THE YEARS ONE THOUSAND SEVEN HUNDRED AND NINETY,
AND ONE THOUSAND SEVEN HUNDRED AND NINETY ONE

PART ONE

I

OF THE STUDY OF THE LAW IN THE UNITED STATES

L ADIES and gentlemen, though I am not unaccustomed to speak in publick, yet, on this occasion, I rise with much diffidence to address you. The character, in which I appear, is both important and new. Anxiety and selfdistrust are natural on my first appearance. These feelings are greatly heightened by another consideration, which operates with peculiar force. I never before had the honour of addressing a *fair* audience. Anxiety and selfdistrust, in an uncommon degree, are natural, when, for the first time, I address a fair audience so brilliant as this is. There is one encouraging reflection, however, which greatly supports me. The whole of my very respectable audience is as much distinguished by its politeness, as a part of it is distinguished by its brilliancy. From that politeness, I shall receive — what I feel I need — an uncommon degree of generous indulgence.

It is the remark of an admired historian, that the high character, which the Grecian commonwealths long possessed among nations, should not be ascribed solely to their excellence in science and in government. With regard to these, other nations, he thinks, and particularly that of which he was writing the history, were entitled to a reputation, not less exalted and illustrious. But the opinion, he says, of the superiour endowments and achievements of the Grecians has arisen, in a considerable degree, from their peculiar felicity in having their virtues transmitted to posterity by writers, who excelled those of every other country in abilities and elegance.

Alexander, when master of the world, envied the good fortune of Achilles, who had a Homer to celebrate his deeds.

The observation, which was applied to Rome by Sallust, and the force of which appears so strongly from the feelings of Alexander, permit me to apply, for I can apply it with equal propriety, to the States of America.

They have not, it is true, been long or much known upon the great theatre of nations: their immature age has not hitherto furnished them with many occasions of extending their renown to the distant quarters of the globe. But, in real worth and excellence, I boldly venture to compare them with the most illustrious commonwealths, which adorn the records of fame. When some future Xenophon or Thucydides shall arise to do justice to their virtues and their actions; the glory of America will rival — it will outshine the glory of Greece.

Were I called upon for my reasons why I deem so highly of the American character, I would assign them in a very few words — That character has been eminently distinguished by the love of liberty, and the love of law.

I rejoice in my appointment to this chair, because it gives me the best opportunities to discover, to study, to develop, and to communicate many striking instances, hitherto little known, on which this distinguished character is founded.

In free countries — in free countries, especially, that boast the blessing of a common law, springing warm and spontaneous from the manners of the people — Law should be studied and taught as a historical science.

The eloquent Rousseau complains, that the origin of nations is much concealed by the darkness or the distance of antiquity.

In many parts of the world, the fact may be as he represents it; and yet his complaint may be without foundation: for, in many parts of the world, the origin of nations ought to be buried in oblivion. To succeeding ages, the knowledge of it would convey neither pleasure nor instruction.

With regard to the States of America, I am happy in saying, that a complaint concerning the uncertainty of their first settlements cannot be made with propriety or truth; though I must add, that, if it could be made with propriety or truth, it would be a subject of the deepest regret.

If the just and genuine principles of society can diffuse a lustre round the establishment of nations; that of the States of America is indeed illustrious. Fierce oppression, rattling, in her left hand, the chains of tyranny; and brandishing, in her right hand, the torch of persecution, drove our predecessors from the coasts of Europe: liberty, benevolent and serene, pointing to a cornucopia on one side, and to a branch of olive on the other, invited and conducted them to the American shores.

In discharging the duties of this office, I shall have the pleasure of presenting to my hearers what, as to the nations in the Transatlantick world, must be searched for in vain — an original compact of a society, on its first arrival in this section of the globe. How the lawyers, and statesmen, and antiquarians, and philosophers of Europe would exult, on discovering a similar monument of the Athenian commonwealth! and yet, perhaps, the historical monuments of the states of America are not, intrinsically, less important, or less worthy of attention, than the historical monuments of the states of Greece. The latter, indeed, are gilded with the gay decorations of fable and mythology; but the former are clothed in the neater and more simple garb of freedom and truth.

The doctrine of toleration in matters of religion, reasonable though it certainly is, has not been long known or acknowledged. For its reception and establishment, where it has been received and established, the world has been thought to owe much to the inestimable writings of the celebrated Locke. To the inestimable writings of that justly celebrated man, let the tribute of applause be plenteously paid: but while immortal honours are bestowed on the name and character of Locke; why should an ungracious silence be observed, with regard to the name and character of Calvert?

Let it be known, that, before the doctrine of toleration was published in Europe, the practice of it was established in America. A law in favour of religious freedom was passed in Maryland, as early as the year one thousand six hundred and forty nine.

When my Lord Baltimore was afterwards urged — not by the spirit of freedom — to consent that this law should be repealed; with the enlightened principles of a man and a christian, he had the fortitude to declare, that he never would assent to the repeal of a law, which protected the natural rights of men, by ensuring to every one freedom of action and thought.

Indeed, the character of this excellent man has been too little known. He was truly the father of his country. To the legislature of Maryland he often recommended a maxim, which deserves to be written in letters of gold: "By concord a small colony may grow into a great and renowned nation; but, by dissensions, mighty and glorious kingdoms have declined and fallen[a] into nothing."

Similar to that of Calvert, has been the fate of many other valuable characters in America. They have been too little known. To those around them, their modest merits have been too familiar, perhaps too uniform, to attract particular and distinguished attention: by those at a distance, the mild and peaceful voice of their virtue has not been heard. But to their memories, justice should be done, as far as it can be done, by a just and grateful country.

In the European temple of fame, William Penn is placed by the side of Lycurgus. Will America refuse a temple to her patriots and her heroes?

[a] Chal. 363.

No; she will not. The glorious dome already rises. Its architecture is of the neatest and chastest order: its dimensions are spacious: its proportions are elegant and correct. In its front a number of niches are formed. In some of them statues are placed. On the left hand of the portal, are the names and figures of Warren, Montgomery, Mercer. On the right hand, are the names and figures of Calvert, Penn, Franklin. In the middle, is a niche of larger size, and decorated with peculiar ornaments. On the left side of it, are sculptured the trophies of war: on the right, the more precious emblems of peace. Above it, is represented the rising glory of the United States. It is without a statue and without a name. Beneath it, in letters very legible, are these words — "FOR THE MOST WORTHY." By the enraptured voice of grateful America — with the consenting plaudits of an admiring world, the designation is unanimously made. Late — very late — may the niche be filled.[b]

But while we perform the pleasing duties of gratitude, let not other duties be disregarded. Illustrious examples are displayed to our view, that we may imitate as well as admire. Before we can be distinguished by the same honours, we must be distinguished by the same virtues.

What are those virtues? They are chiefly the same virtues, which we have already seen to be descriptive of the American character — the love of liberty, and the love of law. But law and liberty cannot rationally become the objects of our love, unless they first become the objects of our knowledge. The same course of study, properly directed, will lead us to the knowledge of both. Indeed, neither of them can be known, because neither of them can exist, without the other. Without liberty, law loses its nature and its name, and becomes oppression. Without law, liberty also loses its nature and its name, and becomes licentiousness. In denominating, therefore, that science, by which the knowledge of both is acquired, it is unnecessary to preserve, in terms, the distinction between them. That science may be named, as it has been named, the science of law.

The science of law should, in some measure, and in some degree, be the study of every free citizen, and of every free man. Every free citizen and every free man has duties to perform and rights to claim. Unless, in some measure, and in some degree, he knows those duties and those rights, he can never act a just and an independent part.

Happily, the general and most important principles of law are not removed to a very great distance from common apprehension. It has been said of religion, that though the elephant may swim, yet the lamb may wade in it. Concerning law, the same observation may be made.

[b] General Washington, then President of the United States, was present when this lecture was delivered. *Ed.*

The home navigation, carried on along the shores, is more necessary, and more useful too, than that, which is pursued through the deep and expanded ocean. A man may be a most excellent coaster, though he possess not the nautical accomplishments and experience of a Cook.

As a science, the law is far from being so disagreeable or so perplexed a study, as it is frequently supposed to be. Some, indeed, involve themselves in a thick mist of terms of art; and use a language unknown to all, but those of the profession. By such, the knowledge of the law, like the mysteries of some ancient divinity, is confined to its initiated votaries; as if all others were in duty bound, blindly and implicitly to obey. But this ought not to be the case. The knowledge of those rational principles on which the law is founded, ought, especially in a free government, to be diffused over the whole community.

In a free country, every citizen forms a part of the sovereign power: he possesses a vote, or takes a still more active part in the business of the commonwealth. The right and the duty of giving that vote, the right and the duty of taking that share, are necessarily attended with the duty of making that business the object of his study and inquiry.

In the United States, every citizen is frequently called upon to act in this great publick character. He elects the legislative, and he takes a personal share in the executive and judicial departments of the nation. It is true, that a man, who wishes to be right, will, with the official assistance afforded him, be seldom under the necessity of being wrong: but it is equally true, and it ought not to be concealed, that the publick duties and the publick rights of every citizen of the United States loudly demand from him all the time, which he can prudently spare, and all the means which he can prudently employ, in order to learn that part, which it is incumbent on him to act.

On the publick mind, one great truth can never be too deeply impressed — that the weight of the government of the United States, and of each state composing the union, rests on the shoulders of the people.

I express not this sentiment now, as I have never expressed it heretofore, with a view to flatter: I express it now, as I have always expressed it heretofore, with a far other and higher aim — with an aim to excite the people to acquire, by vigorous and manly exercise, a degree of strength sufficient to support the weighty burthen, which is laid upon them — with an aim to convince them, that their duties rise in strict proportion to their rights; and that few are able to trace or to estimate the great danger, in a free government, when the rights of the people are unexercised, and the still greater danger, when the rights of the people are ill exercised.

At a general election, too few attend to the important consequences of voting or not voting; and to the consequences, still more important, of voting right or voting wrong.

The rights and the duties of jurors, in the United States, are great and extensive. No punishment can be inflicted without the intervention of one — in much the greater number of cases, without the intervention of more than one jury. Is it not of immense consequence to the publick, that those, who have committed crimes, should not escape with impunity? Is it not of immense consequence to individuals, that all, except those who have committed crimes, should be secure from the punishment denounced against their commission? Is it not, then, of immense consequence to both, that jurors should possess the spirit of just discernment, to discriminate between the innocent and the guilty? This spirit of just discernment requires knowledge of, at least, the general principles of the law, as well as knowledge of the minute particulars concerning the facts.

It is true, that, in matters of law, the jurors are entitled to the assistance of the judges; but it is also true, that, after they receive it, they have the right of judging for themselves: and is there not to this right the great corresponding duty of judging *properly?*

Surely, therefore, those who discharge the important and, let me add, the dignified functions of jurors, should acquire, as far as they possibly can acquire, a knowledge of the laws of their country; for, let me add further, the dignity, though not the importance of their functions, will greatly depend on the abilities, with which they discharge them.

But in the administration of justice — that part of government, which comes home most intimately to the business and the bosoms of men — there are judges as well as jurors; those, whose peculiar province it is to answer questions of law, as well as those, whose peculiar province it is to answer questions of fact.

In many courts — in many respectable courts within the United States, the judges are not, and, for a long time, cannot be gentlemen of professional acquirements. They may, however, fill their offices usefully and honourably, the want of professional acquirements notwithstanding. But can they do this, without a reasonable degree of acquaintance with the law?

We have already seen, that, in questions of law, the jurors are entitled to the assistance of the judges: but can the judges give assistance, without knowing what answers to make to the questions which the jury may propose? can those direct others, who themselves know not the road?

Unquestionably, then, those who fill, and those who expect to fill the offices of judges in courts, not, indeed, supreme, but rising in importance and in dignity above the appellation of inferiour, ought to make the strongest efforts in order to obtain a respectable degree of knowledge in the law.

Let me ascend to a station more elevated still. In the United States, the doors of publick honours and publick offices are, on the broad principles of equal liberty, thrown open to all. A laudable emulation, an emulation that ought to be encouraged in a free government, may prompt a man to legislate as well as to decide for his fellow citizens — to legislate, not merely for a single State, but for the most august Union that has yet been formed on the face of the globe.

Should not he, who is to supply the deficiencies of the existing law, know when the existing law is defective? Should not he, who is to introduce alterations into the existing law, know in what instances the existing law ought to be altered?

The first and governing maxim in the interpretation of a statute is, to discover the meaning of those, who made it. The first rule, subservient to the principle of the governing maxim, is, to discover what the law was, before the statute was made. The inference, necessarily resulting from the joint operation of the maxim and the rule, is this, that in explaining a statute, the judges ought to take it for granted, that those, who made it, knew the antecedent law. This certainly implies, that a competent knowledge of, at least, the general principles of law, is of indispensable necessity to those, who undertake the transcendent office of legislation.

I say, a knowledge of the general principles of law for though an accurate, a minute, and an extensive knowledge of its practice and particular rules be highly useful; yet I cannot conceive it to be absolutely requisite to the able discharge of a legislative trust.

Upon this distinction — and it is an important one — I cannot, perhaps, explain myself better, than by delivering the sentiments, which were entertained, some centuries ago, by a very learned and able judge — I mean the Lord Chancellor Fortescue.

In his excellent book, which he wrote in praise of the laws of England, he uses a number of arguments with his pupil, the prince of Wales, to excite him to the study of the law. Of these arguments the prince feels and acknowledges the full force. "But," says he, "there is one thing, which agitates my mind in such a manner, that, like a vessel tossed in the tumultuous ocean, I know not how to direct my course: it is, that when I recollect the number of years, which the students of the law employ, before they acquire a sufficient degree of knowledge, I am apprehensive lest, in studies of this nature, I should consume the whole of my youth."

To relieve his pupil from this anxiety, the chancellor cites a passage from the writings of Aristotle, to the following purpose: "We are then supposed to know a thing, when we apprehend its causes and its principles, as high as its original elements."

This maxim the chancellor illustrates, by a reference to several of the sciences; and then draws this general conclusion. "Whoever knows the principles and elements of any science, knows the science itself — generally, at least, though not completely." This conclusion he then applies to the science of law. "In the same manner, when you shall become acquainted with the principles and the elements of law, you may be denominated a lawyer. It will not be necessary for *you*, at a great expense of your time, to scrutinize curious and intricate points of discussion. I know the quickness of your apprehension, and the strength of your genius. Though the legal knowledge accumulated in a series of twenty years is not more than sufficient to qualify one for being a judge; yet, in one year, you will be able to acquire a degree of it sufficient for you; without, even in that year, neglecting your other studies and improvements." [e]

That a law education is necessary for gentlemen intended for the profession of the law, it would be as ridiculous to prove as to deny. In all other countries, publick institutions bear a standing testimony to this truth. Ought this to be the only country without them? Justinian, who did so much for the Roman law, was, as might have been expected, uncommonly attentive to form and establish a proper plan for studying it. All the modern nations of Europe have admitted the profession of their municipal jurisprudence, into their universities and other seminaries of liberal education.

In England, numerous and ample provisions have been made for this purpose. For young gentlemen, there are eight houses of chancery, where they learn the first elements of law. For those more advanced in their studies, there are four inns of court. "All these together," says my Lord Coke,[d] with conscious professional pride, "compose the most illustrious university in the world, for the profession of law." Here lectures have been read, exercises have been performed, and degrees in the common law have been conferred, in the same manner as degrees in the civil and canon law, in other universities.

Besides all these, the Vinerian professorship of law has, not many years ago, been established in the university of Oxford. Of this professorship, the celebrated Sir William Blackstone was the first, who filled the chair.

A question deeply interesting to the American States now presents itself. Should the elements of a law education, particularly as it respects

[e] Fort. de Laud. c. 7. 8.   [d] 3 Rep. Pref. 20.

publick law, be drawn entirely from another country — or should they be drawn, in part, at least, from the constitutions and governments and laws of the United States, and of the several States composing the Union?

The subject, to one standing where I stand, is not without its delicacy: let me, however, treat it with the decent but firm freedom, which befits an independent citizen, and a professor in independent states.

Surely I am justified in saying, that the principles of the constitutions and governments and laws of the United States, and the republicks, of which they are formed, are materially different from the principles of the constitution and government and laws of England; for that is the only country, from the principles of whose constitution and government and laws, it will be contended, that the elements of a law education ought to be drawn. I presume to go further: the principles of our constitutions and governments and laws are materially *better* than the principles of the constitution and government and laws of England.

Permit me to mention one great principle, the *vital* principle I may well call it, which diffuses animation and vigour through all the others. The principle I mean is this, that the supreme or sovereign power of the society resides in the citizens at large; and that, therefore, they always retain the right of abolishing, altering, or amending their constitution, at whatever time, and in whatever manner, they shall deem it expedient.

By Sir William Blackstone, from whose Commentaries, a performance in many respects highly valuable, the elements of a foreign law education would probably be borrowed — by Sir William Blackstone, this great and fundamental principle is treated as a political chimera, existing only in the minds of some theorists; but, in practice, inconsistent with the dispensation of any government upon earth. Let us hear his own words.

"It must be owned that Mr. Locke and other theoretical writers have held, that "there remains still inherent in the people, a supreme power to alter the legislative, when they find the legislative act contrary to the trust reposed in them; for when such trust is abused, it is thereby forfeited, and devolves to those, who gave it." "But, however just this conclusion may be in theory, we cannot admit it, nor argue from it, under any dispensation of government, at present actually existing. For this devolution of power to the people at large, includes a dissolution of the whole form of government established by that people; reduces all the members to their original state of equality; and, by annihilating the sovereign power, repeals all positive laws whatsoever before enacted. No human laws will therefore suppose a case, which at once must destroy all law, and compel men to build afresh upon a new foundation, nor will they make provision for so desperate an event, as must render all legal provisions ineffectual." [e]

[e] 1 Bl. Com. 161. 162.

And yet, even in England, there have been revolutions of government: there has been one within very little more than a century ago. The learned Author of the Commentaries admits the fact; but denies it to be a ground on which any constitutional principle can be established.

If the same precise "conjunction of circumstances" should happen a second time; the revolution of one thousand six hundred and eighty eight would form a precedent: but were only one or two of the circumstances, forming that conjunction, to happen again; "the precedent would fail us." [t]

The three circumstances, which formed that conjunction, were these: 1. An endeavour to subvert the constitution, by breaking the original contract between the king and people. 2. Violation of the fundamental laws. 3. Withdrawing out of the kingdom.

Now, on this state of things, let us make a supposition — not a very foreign one — and see the consequences, which would unquestionably follow from the principles of Sir William Blackstone. Let us suppose, that, on some occasion, a prince should form a conjunction of only two of the circumstances; for instance, that he should only violate the fundamental laws, and endeavour to subvert the constitution: let us suppose, that, instead of completing the conjunction, by withdrawing out of his government, he should only employ some forty or fifty thousand troops to give full efficacy to the two first circumstances: let us suppose all this — and it is surely not unnatural to suppose, that a prince, who shall form the two first parts of the conjunction, will not, like James the second, run away from the execution of them — let us, I say, suppose all this; and what, on the principles of Sir William Blackstone, would be the undeniable consequence? In the language of the Commentaries, "our precedent would fail us."

But we have thought, and we have acted upon revolution principles, without offering them up as sacrifices at the shrine of revolution precedents.

Why should we not teach our children those principles, upon which we ourselves have thought and acted? Ought we to instil into their tender minds a theory, especially if unfounded, which is contradictory to our own practice, built on the most solid foundation? Why should we reduce them to the cruel dilemma of condemning, either those principles which they have been taught to believe, or those persons whom they have been taught to revere?

It is true, that the learned Author of the Commentaries concludes this very passage, by telling us, that "there are inherent, though latent powers of society, which no climate, no time, no constitution, no contract can ever destroy or diminish." But what does this prove? not that revolution

[t] 1 Bl. Com. 245.

principles are, in his opinion, recognized by the English constitution; but that the English constitution, whether considered as a law, or as a contract, cannot destroy or diminish those principles.

It is the opinion of many, that the revolution of one thousand six hundred and eighty eight did more than set a mere precedent, even in England. But be that as it may: a revolution principle certainly is, and certainly should be taught as a principle of the constitution of the United States, and of every State in the Union.

This revolution principle — that, the sovereign power residing in the people, they may change their constitution and government whenever they please — is not a principle of discord, rancour, or war: it is a principle of melioration, contentment, and peace. It is a principle not recommended merely by a flattering theory: it is a principle recommended by happy experience. To the testimony of Pennsylvania — to the testimony of the United States I appeal for the truth of what I say.

In the course of these lectures, my duty will oblige me to notice some other important principles, very particularly his definition and explanation of law itself, in which my sentiments differ from those of the respectable Author of the Commentaries. It already appears, that, with regard to the very first principles of government, we set out from different points of departure.

As I have mentioned Sir William Blackstone, let me speak of him explicitly as it becomes me. I cannot consider him as a zealous friend of republicanism. One of his survivors or successours in office has characterized him by the appellation of an antirepublican lawyer. On the subject of government, I think I can plainly discover his jealousies and his attachments.

For his jealousies, an easy and natural account may be given. In England, only one specimen of a commonwealth has been exhibited to publick examination; and that specimen was, indeed, an unfavourable one. On trial, it was found to be unsound and unsatisfactory. It is not very surprising that an English lawyer, with an example so inauspicious before his eyes, should feel a degree of aversion, latent, yet strong, to a republican government.

An account, perhaps equally natural and easy, may be given for his attachments. With all reigning families, I believe, it is a settled maxim, that every revolution in government is unjustifiable, except the single one, which conducted them to the throne. The maxims of the court have always their diffusive influence. That influence, in favour of one species of government, might steal imperceptibly upon a mind, already jealous of another species, viewed as its rival, and as its enemy.

But, with all his prejudices concerning government, I have the pleasure of beholding him, in one conspicuous aspect, as a friend to the rights of men. To those rights, the author of the beautiful and animated dissertations concerning juries could not be cold or insensible.

As author of the Commentaries, he possessed uncommon merit. His manner is clear and methodical; his sentiments — I speak of them generally — are judicious and solid; his language is elegant and pure. In publick law, however, he should be consulted with a cautious prudence. But, even in publick law, his principles, when they are not proper objects of imitation, will furnish excellent materials of contrast. On every account, therefore, he should be read and studied. He deserves to be much admired; but he ought not to be implicitly followed.

This last admonitory remark should not be confined to Sir William Blackstone: it ought to be extended to all political writers — must I say? — almost without exception. This seems a severe sentence: but, if it is just, it must be pronounced. The cause of liberty, the rights of men require, that, in a subject essential to that cause and to those rights, errour should be exposed, in order to be avoided.

The foundations of political truth have been laid but lately: the genuine science of government, to no human science inferiour in importance, is, indeed, but in its infancy: and the reason of this can be easily assigned. In the whole annals of the Transatlantick world, it will be difficult to point out a single instance of its legitimate institution: I will go further, and say, that, among all the political writers of the Transatlantick world, it will be difficult to point out a single model of its unbiassed theory.

The celebrated Grotius introduces what he says concerning the interesting doctrine of sovereignty, with the following information. "Learned men of our age, each of them handling the argument, rather according to the present interest of the affairs of his country, than according to truth, have greatly perplexed that, which, of itself, was not very clear." [g] In this, the learned men of every other age have resembled those of the age of Grotius.

Indeed, it is astonishing, in what intricate mazes politicians and philosophers have bewildered themselves upon this subject. Systems have been formed upon systems, all fleeting, because all unfounded. Sovereignty has sometimes been viewed as a star, which eluded our investigation by its immeasurable height: sometimes it has been considered as a sun, which could not be distinctly seen by reason of its insufferable splendour.

In Egypt, the Nile is an object truly striking and grand. Its waters, rising to a certain height, and spreading to a certain distance, are the cause of fertility and plenty: swelling higher, and extending further, they produce devastation and famine. This stupendous stream, at some times

[g] Gro. b. i. c. 3. s. 5.

so beneficial, at other times so destructive, has, at all times, formed a subject of anxious inquiry. To trace its source has been the unceasing aim of the mighty and the learned. Kings, attended with all the instruments of strength; sages, furnished with all the apparatus of philosophy, have engaged, with ardour, in the curious search; but their most patient and their most powerful enterprises have been equally vain.

The source of the Nile continued still unknown; and because it continued still unknown, the poets fondly fabled that it was to be found only in a superiour orb; and, of course, it was worshipped as a divinity.

We are told, however, that, at last, the source of the Nile has been discovered; and that it consists of — what might have been supposed before the discovery — a collection of springs small, indeed, but pure.

The fate of sovereignty has been similar to that of the Nile. Always magnificent, always interesting to mankind, it has become alternately their blessing and their curse. Its origin has often been attempted to be traced. The great and the wise have embarked in the undertaking; though seldom, it must be owned, with the spirit of just inquiry; or in the direction, which leads to important discovery. The source of sovereignty was still concealed beyond some impenetrable mystery; and, because it was concealed, philosophers and politicians, in this instance, gravely taught what, in the other, the poets had fondly fabled, that it must be something more than human: it was impiously asserted to be divine.

Lately, the inquiry has been recommenced with a different spirit, and in a new direction; and although the discovery of nothing very astonishing, yet the discovery of something very useful and true, has been the result. The dread and redoubtable sovereign, when traced to his ultimate and genuine source, has been found, as he ought to have been found, in the free and independent man.

This truth, so simple and natural, and yet so neglected or despised, may be appreciated as the first and fundamental principle in the science of government.

Besides the reasons, which I have already offered; others may be suggested, why the elements of a law education ought to be drawn from our own constitutions and governments and laws.

In every government, which is not altogether despotical, the institution of youth is of some publick consequence. In a republican government, it is of the greatest. Of no class of citizens can the education be of more publick consequence, than that of those, who are destined to take an active part in publick affairs. Those who have had the advantage of a law education, are very frequently destined to take this active part. This deduction clearly shows, that, in a free government, the principles of a law education are matters of the greatest publick consequence.

Ought not those principles to be congenial with the principles of government? By the revolution in the United States, a very great alteration — a very great improvement — as we have already seen, has taken place in our system of government: ought not a proportioned alteration — ought not a proportioned improvement to be introduced into our system of law education?

We have passed the Red Sea in safety: we have survived a tedious and dangerous journey through the wilderness: we are now in full and peaceable possession of the promised land: must we, after all, return to the flesh pots of Egypt? Is there not danger, that when one nation teaches, it may, in some instances, give the law to another?

A foundation of human happiness, broader and deeper than any that has heretofore been laid, is now laid in the United States: on that broad and deep foundation, let it be our pride, as it is our duty, to build a superstructure of adequate extent and magnificence.

But further; many parts of the laws of England can, in their own nature, have neither force nor application here. Such are all those parts, which are connected with ecclesiastical jurisdiction and an ecclesiastical establishment. Such are all those parts, too, which relate to the monarchical and aristocratick branches of the English constitution. Every one, who has perused the ponderous volumes of the law, knows how great a proportion of them is filled with the numerous and extensive titles relating to those different subjects. Surely they need not enter into the elements of a law education in the United States.

I mean not, however, to exclude them from the subsequent investigation of those, who shall aspire at the character of accomplished lawyers. I only mean, that they ought not to be put into the hands of students, as deserving the same time and the same attention with other parts, which are to have a practical influence upon their future conduct in their profession.

The numerous regulations, in England, respecting the poor, and the more artificial refinements and distinctions concerning real estates, must be known, but known as much in order to be avoided as to be practised. The study of them, therefore, need not be so minute here as in England.

Concerning many other titles of the English law, similar observations might be made. The force and the extent of each will increase day after day, and year after year.

All combine in showing, that the *foundation*, at least, of a separate, an unbiassed, and an independent law education should be laid in the United States.

Deeply impressed with the importance of this truth, I have undertaken the difficult, the laborious, and the delicate task of contributing to lay that foundation. I feel most sensibly the weight of the duty, which I have engaged to perform. I will not promise to perform it successfully — as well as it might be performed: but I will promise to perform it faithfully — as well as I can perform it. I feel its full importance.

It may be asked — I am told it has been asked — is it proper that a judge of the supreme court of the United States should deliver lectures on law? It will not surely be suspected, that I deem too lightly of the very dignified and independent office, which I have the honour to hold, in consequence of the favourable sentiments entertained concerning me by those, whose favourable sentiments are indeed an honour. Had I thought that the dignity of that seat could be disparaged by an alliance with this chair, I would have spurned it from me. But I thought, and I still think in a very different manner. By my acceptance of this chair, I think I shall certainly increase my usefulness, without diminishing my dignity, as a judge; and I think, that, with equal certainty, I shall, as a judge, increase my usefulness, I will not say my dignity, in this chair. He, who is well qualified to teach, is well qualified to judge; and he, who is well qualified to judge, is well qualified to teach. Every acquisition of knowledge — and it is my duty to acquire much — can, with equal facility, and with equal propriety, be applied to either office: for let it be remembered, that both offices view the same science as their common object.

Any interference as to the times of discharging the two offices — the only one that strikes me as possible — will be carefully avoided.

But it may be further asked — ought a judge to commit himself by delivering his sentiments in a lecture? To this question I shall give a very explicit answer: and in that answer I shall include the determination, which I have taken both as a professor and as a judge. When I deliver my sentiments from this chair, they shall be my honest sentiments: when I deliver them from the bench, they shall be nothing more. In both places I shall make — because I mean to support — the claim to integrity: in neither shall I make — because, in neither, can I support — the claim to infallibility.

My house of knowledge is, at present, too small. I feel it my duty, on many accounts, to enlarge it. But in this, as in every other kind of architecture, I believe it will be found, that he, who adds much, must alter some.

When the greatest judges, who ever adorned or illuminated a court of justice, have candidly and cheerfully acknowledged their mistakes; shall *I* be afraid of committing myself?

The learned and indefatigable Spelman, after all the immense researches, which enabled him to prepare and publish his Glossary, published it with this remarkable precaution: "under the protestation of adding, retracting, correcting, and polishing, as, upon more mature consideration, shall seem expedient." [h]

I hope I have now shown, that my acceptance of this chair, instead of diminishing, is calculated to increase my usefulness, as a judge. Does it derogate from my dignity? By no means, in my opinion.

Let things be considered as they really are. As a judge, I can decide whether property in dispute belongs to the man on my right hand, or to the man on my left hand. As a judge, I can pass sentence on a felon or a cheat. By doing both, a judge may be eminently useful in preserving peace, and in securing property.

Property, highly deserving security, is, however, not an end, but a means. How miserable, and how contemptible is that man, who inverts the order of nature, and makes his property, not a means, but an end!

Society ought to be preserved in peace; most unquestionably. But is this all? Ought it not to be improved as well as protected? Look at individuals: observe them from infancy to youth, from youth to manhood. Such is the order of Providence with regard to society. It is in a progressive state, moving on towards perfection. How is this progressive state to be assisted and accelerated? Principally by teaching the young "ideas how to shoot," and the young affections how to move.

What intrinsically can be more dignified, than to assist in preparing tender and ingenuous minds for all the great purposes, for which they are intended! What, I repeat it, can intrinsically be more dignified, than to assist in forming a future Cicero, or a future Bacon, without the vanity of one, and without the meanness of the other!

Let us see how things have been considered in other ages and in other countries.

Philip of Macedon, a prince highly distinguished by his talents, though not by his virtues, was fully sensible of the value of science. An heir was born to his kingdom and his throne. Could any thing be more interesting to a father and a king? There was, it seems, a circumstance, which, in his opinion, enhanced the importance even of this event. His heir was born at a time, when he could receive a most excellent education.

Philip wrote to Aristotle the following letter: "You are to know that a son hath been born to us. We thank the gods, not so much for having bestowed him on us, as for bestowing him, at a time when Aristotle lives. We assure ourselves, that you will form him a prince worthy to be our successour, and a king worthy of Macedon." [i]

On Aristotle, accordingly, was devolved the charge of superintending

[h] Sub protestatione de addendo, retrahendo, corrigendo, poliendo, prout opus fuerit et consultius videbitur. Sir. H. Spelman.
[i] 1 Lel. L. Phil. 98.

the education of the young prince, "that he may be taught," said Philip, "to avoid those errours, which I have committed, and of which I now repent."

What price Alexander the Great set upon his education, before his mind was fatally poisoned by the madness of ambition, will appear by a letter from him to Aristotle, in which we find this sentiment: "I am not so anxious to appear superiour to the rest of mankind in power, as in the knowledge of excellent things." [j] We see here the impetus of strong ambition; but it had not then taken its pernicious direction.

In the most shining periods of the Roman republick, men of the first distinction made the science of law their publick profession, and taught it openly in their houses as in so many schools. The first of these publick professors was Tiberius Coruncanius, who was raised to the office of chief pontiff — the highest in the whole scale of Roman honours. His example was followed by many distinguished characters, among whom we find the celebrated names of the two Scevolæ, of Cato, of Brutus, and of others well known to such as are conversant with the writers of the classical ages. Even Cicero himself, after he had been consul of Rome, after he had had kings for his clients, projected this very employment, as his future "honour and ornament." [k]

Whether, therefore, we consider the intrinsick or the external dignity of this chair; we shall find that it is, by no means, beneath an alliance with the highest offices and the highest characters.

If any example, set by me, can be supposed to have the least publick influence; I hope it will be in raising the care of education to that high degree of respectability, to which, every where, but especially in countries that are free, it has the most unimpeachable title.

I have been zealous — I hope I have not been altogether unsuccessful — in contributing the best of my endeavours towards forming a system of government; I shall rise in importance, if I can be equally successful — I will not be less zealous — in contributing the best of my endeavours towards forming a system of education likewise, in the United States. I shall rise in importance, because I shall rise in usefulness.

What are laws without manners? How can manners be formed, but by a proper education? [l]

Methinks I hear one of the female part of my audience exclaim — What is all this to us? We have heard much of societies, of states, of governments, of laws, and of a law education. Is every thing made for your sex? Why should not we have a share? Is our sex less honest, or less virtuous, or less wise than yours?

[j] 2 Lel. L. Phil. 126.   [k] Decus et ornamentum. De orat. l. i. c. 45.
[l] The ancient wisdom of the best times did always make a just complaint, that states were too busy with their laws; and too negligent in point of education. 2. Ld. Bacon 423.

Will any of my brethren be kind enough to furnish me with answers to these questions? — I must answer them, it seems, myself? and I mean to answer them most sincerely.

Your sex is neither less honest, nor less virtuous, nor less wise than ours. With regard to the two first of these qualities, a superiority, on our part, will not be pretended: with regard to the last, a pretension of superiority cannot be supported.

I will name three women; and I will then challenge any of my brethren to name three men superiour to them in vigour and extent of abilities. My female champions are, Semiramis of Nineveh; Zenobia, the queen of the East; and Elizabeth of England. I believe it will readily be owned, that three men of superiour active talents cannot be named.

You will please, however, to take notice, that the issue, upon which I put the characters of these three ladies, is not that they were *accomplished;* it is, that they were *able* women.

This distinction immediately reminds you, that a woman may be an able, without being an accomplished female character.

In this latter view, I did not produce the three female characters I have mentioned. I produced them as women, merely of distinguished abilities — of abilities equal to those displayed by the most able of our sex.

But would you wish to be tried by the qualities of our sex? I will refer you to a more proper standard — that of your own.

All the three able characters, I have mentioned, had, I think, too much of the masculine in them. Perhaps I can conjecture the reason. Might it not be owing, in a great measure — might it not be owing altogether to the masculine employments, to which they devoted themselves?

Two of them were able warriors: all of them were able queens; but in all of them, we feel and we regret the loss of the lovely and accomplished woman: and let me assure you, that, in the estimation of our sex, the loss of the lovely and accomplished woman is irreparable, even when she is lost in the queen.

For these reasons, I doubt much, whether it would be proper that you should undertake the management of publick affairs. You have, indeed, heard much of publick government and publick law: but these things were not made for themselves: they were made for something better; and of that something better, you form the better part — I mean society — I mean particularly domestick society: there the lovely and accomplished woman shines with superiour lustre.

By some politicians, society has been considered as only the scaffolding of government; very improperly, in my judgment. In the just order of things, government is the scaffolding of society: and if society could be built and kept entire without government, the scaffolding might be thrown down, without the least inconvenience or cause of regret.

Government is, indeed, highly necessary; but it is highly necessary to a fallen state. Had man continued innocent, society, without the aids of government, would have shed its benign influence even over the bowers of Paradise.

For those bowers, how finely was your sex adapted! But let it be observed, that every thing else was finished, before Heaven's "last best gift" was introduced: let it be also observed, that, in the pure and perfect commencement of society, there was a striking difference between the only two persons, who composed it. His "large fair front and eye sublime" declared that, "for contemplation and for valour he was formed."

> "For softness, she, and sweet attractive grace.
> Grace was in all her steps, Heav'n in her eye;
> In every gesture, dignity and love.
> A thousand decencies unceasing flow'd
> From all her words and actions, mixt with—
> ———mild compliance." *

Her accomplishments indicated her destination. Female beauty is the expression of female virtue. The purest complexion, the finest features, the most elegant shape are uninteresting and insipid, unless we can discover, by them, the emotions of the mind. How beautiful and engaging, on the other hand, are the features, the looks, and the gestures, while they disclose modesty, sensibility, and every sweet and tender affection! When these appear, there is a "Soul upon the countenance."

These observations enhance the value of beauty; and show, that to possess and to admire it, is to possess and to admire the exhibition of the finest qualities, intellectual and moral. These observations do more: they show how beauty may be acquired, and improved, and preserved. When the beauties of the mind are cultivated, the countenance becomes beautifully eloquent in expressing them.

I know very well, that mere complexion and shape enter into the composition of beauty: but they form beauty only of a lower order. Separate them from animation — separate them from sensibility — separate them from virtue: what are they? The ingredients that compose a beautiful picture or a beautiful statue. I say too much; for the painters and the statuaries know, that expression is the soul of mimick as well as of real life.

As complexion and shape will not supply the place of the higher orders of beauty; so those higher orders have an independent existence, after the inferiour influence of complexion and shape are gone. Though the bloom of youth be faded; though the impressions of time be distinctly marked; yet, while the countenance continues to be enlivened by the beaming

* [The quotation, which is somewhat inaccurate, is drawn from *Paradise Lost,* Book VIII.]

emanations of the mind, it will produce, in every beholder possessed of sensibility and taste, an effect far more pleasing, and far more lasting, than can be produced by the prettiest piece of uninformed nature, however florid, however regular, and however young.

How many purposes may be served at once, if things are done in the proper way! I have been giving a recipe for the improvement and preservation of female beauty; but I find that I have, at the same time, been delivering instructions for the culture and refinement of female virtue; and have been pointing at the important purposes, which female virtue is fitted and intended to accomplish.

If nature evinces her designs by her works; you were destined to embellish, to refine, and to exalt the pleasures and virtues of social life.

To protect and to improve social life, is, as we have seen, the end of government and law. If, therefore, you have no share in the formation, you have a most intimate connexion with the effects, of a good system of law and government.

That plan of education, which will produce, or promote, or preserve such a system, is, consequently, an object to you peculiarly important.

But if you would see such a plan carried into complete effect, you must, my amiable hearers, give it your powerful assistance. The pleasing task of forming your daughters is almost solely yours. In my plan of education for your sons, I must solicit you to cooperate. Their virtues, in a certain proportion — the refinement of their virtues, in a much greater proportion, must be moulded on your example.

In your sex, too, there is a natural, an easy, and, often, a pure flow of diction, which lays the best foundation for that eloquence, which, in a free country, is so important to ours.

The style of some of the finest orators of antiquity was originally formed on that of their mothers, or of other ladies, to whose acquaintance they had the honour of being introduced.

I have already mentioned the two Scevolæ among the illustrious Roman characters. One of them was married to Lælia, a lady, whose virtues and accomplishments rendered her one of the principal ornaments of Rome. She possessed the elegance of language in so eminent a degree, that the first speakers of the age were ambitious of her company. The graces of her unstudied elocution were the purest model, by which they could refine their own.

Cicero was in the number of those, who improved by the privilege of her conversation. In his writings, he speaks in terms of the warmest praise concerning her singular talents. He mentions also the conversation of her daughters and grand daughters, as deserving particular notice.

The province of early education by the female sex, was deemed, in Rome, an employment of so much dignity, that ladies of the first rank did not disdain it. We find the names of Aurelia and Attia, the mothers of Julius Cæsar and of Augustus, enumerated in the list of these honourable patronesses of education.

The example of the highly accomplished Cornelia, the daughter of the great Africanus, and the mother of the Gracchi, deserves uncommon attention. She shone, with singular lustre, in all those endowments and virtues that can dignify the female character.

She was, one day, visited by a lady of Campania, who was extremely fond of dress and ornament. This lady, after having displayed some very rich jewels of her own, expressed a wish to be favoured with the view of those which Cornelia had; expecting to see some very superb ones, in the toilet of a lady of such distinguished birth and character. Cornelia diverted the conversation, till her sons came into the room: "These are my jewels," said she, presenting them to the Campanian lady.

Cicero had seen her letters: his expressions concerning them are very remarkable. "I have read," says he, "the letters of Cornelia, the mother of the Gracchi; and it appears, that her sons were not so much nourished by the milk, as formed by the style of their mother." [m]

You see now, my fair and amiable hearers, how deeply and nearly interested you are in a proper plan of law education. By some of you, whom I know to be well qualified for taking in it the share, which I have described, that share will be taken. By the younger part of you, the good effects of such a plan will, I hope, be participated: for those of my pupils, who themselves shall become most estimable, will treat you with the highest degree of estimation.

PLAN

Gentlemen, permit me, at this time, to address, in a very few words, the younger and more inexperienced part of those who attend my lectures — I say the younger and more inexperienced part; because my lectures are honoured with the presence of some, whose learning, talents, and experience fit them for communicating instead of receiving instruction here. For the honour of their presence, I must consider myself indebted to the importance of my subject; and to a desire, generous and enlightened, of countenancing and encouraging every attempt, however feeble, to diffuse knowledge on a subject so important.

You have seen, my young friends, in what a high point of view I consider your education. Is this on your own account? Partly it is — that you may be great and good men. But solely it is not; for more extended

[m] Legimus epistolas Corneliæ, matris Gracchorum: apparet filios non tam in gremio educatos, quam in sermone matris. Cic. de clar. orat. c. 58.

hopes are entertained concerning you: you are designated by your education, and by your country, to be great and good citizens.

In no other part of the world, and in no former period, even in this part of it, have youth ever beheld so glorious and so sublime a prospect before them. Your country is already respectable for its numbers; it is free; it is enlightened; it is flourishing; it is happy: in numbers; in liberty; in knowledge; in prosperity; in happiness it is receiving great and rapid accessions. Its honours are already beginning to bud: in a few years, they will "blossom thick" upon you. You ought certainly, by proper culture, to qualify yourselves in such a manner, that when the blossoms fade and fall, the fruit may begin to appear. Remember that, in a free government, every honour implies a trust; that every trust implies a duty; and that every duty ought to be performed.

I mean not, that such of you as are designed for the practice of the law, should be inattentive to the emoluments of your profession; but I mean that you should consider it as something higher than a mere instrument of private gain. By being fitted for higher purposes, it will not be less fit, it will be more fit for accomplishing this.

It is peculiarly necessary, that you should, as soon as possible, form proper conceptions of what ought to be your objects in your course of study. Let them not be fixed too low: the higher your aims, the higher your attainments will be. To assist you in fixing those aims, let me lay before you the sentiments of a writer, who wrote on some subjects most excellently, and on others most contemptibly — I mean Lord Bolingbroke. When he wrote on politicks or business, he wrote well; because he wrote on what he knew: when he wrote concerning religion, he wrote ill; because he wrote concerning that, of which he was ignorant. The passage I am about to quote to you is vouched by the respectable authority of Lord Kaims, who considered it, and justly, as a master piece of expression and thought.

"I might instance," says he, "in other professions, the obligations men lie under of applying themselves to certain parts of history; and I can hardly forbear doing it in that of the law, in its nature, the noblest and most beneficial to mankind, in its abuse and debasement, the most sordid and the most pernicious. A lawyer now is nothing more, I speak of ninety nine in a hundred at least" (the proportion in this country, I believe, is much smaller) "to use some of Tully's words, "nisi liguleius quidam cautus, et acutus præco actionum, cantor formularum, aucepts syllabarum:" but there have been lawyers that were orators, philosophers, historians: there have been Bacons and Clarendons. There will be none such any more, till, in some better age" (I hope that better age has found you, my young friends) "true ambition or the love of fame prevail over avarice; and till men find leisure and encouragement for the exercise of this profession, by climbing up to the vantage ground, so my Lord Bacon calls it, of science,[n] instead of groveling all their lives below, in a mean but gainful application to all the little arts of chicane. Till this happen, the profession of law will scarce deserve to be ranked among the learned professions: and whenever it happens, one of the vantage grounds, to which men must climb, is metaphysical, and the other, historical knowledge." By metaphysical knowledge, his lordship evidently means the philosophy of the human mind; for he goes on in this manner. "They must pry into the secret recesses of the human heart, and become well acquainted with the whole moral world, that they may discover the abstract reason of all laws: and they must trace the laws of particular states, especially of their own, from the first rough sketches to the more perfect draughts; from the first causes or occasions that produced them, through all the effects, good and bad, that they produced." [o]

Such, my young friends, are the great prospects before you; and such is the general outline of those studies, by which you will be prepared to realize them. Suffer me to recommend most earnestly this outline to the utmost degree of your attention. It comes to you supported with all the countenance and authority of Bacon, Bolingbroke, Kaims — two of them consummate in the practice, as well as in the knowledge of the law — all of them eminent judges of men, of business, and of literature; and all distinguished by the accomplishments of an active, as well as those of a contemplative life. The propriety, the force, and the application of their sentiments will be gradually unfolded, fully explained, and warmly urged to you in the course of my lectures.

It is by no means an easy matter to form, to digest, and to arrange a plan of lectures, on a subject so various and so extensive as that of law. With great deference to some of you, with anxious zeal for the information of others, I lay before you the following analysis: reserving, however, to myself, the full right and force of the protestation, which I have already borrowed from Sir Henry Spelman, of adding, retracting, correcting, and polishing, as, on more mature consideration, shall appear to me to be expedient.[p]

I begin with the general principles of law and obligation. These I shall investigate fully and minutely; because they are the basis of every legal system; and because they have been much misrepresented, or much misunderstood.

[n] It is not possible to discover the more remote, and deeper parts of any science, if you stand but upon the level of the same science, and ascend not to a higher science. 2. Ld. Bac. 432.

[o] Boling. of the Study of History. let. 5. p. 149.

[p] Some alterations, as the reader will observe, were afterwards made in the plan; but they are neither numerous nor important and need not be here particularized. *Ed.*

Next, I shall proceed to give you a concise and very general view of the law of nature, of the law of nations, and of municipal law.

I shall then consider man, who is the subject of all, and is the author as well as the subject of the last, and part of the second of these species of law. This great title of my plan, dignified and interesting as it is, must be treated in a very cursory manner in this course. I will, however, select some of the great truths which seem best adapted to a system of law. I will view man as an individual, as a member of society, as a member of a confederation, and as a part of the great commonwealth of nations.

His situation, under the third relation, is, in a great measure, new; and, to an American, peculiarly important: It will, therefore, merit and obtain peculiar attention.

The proper discussion of this title will draw on a discussion of the law of nations, under an aspect, almost wholly new. How far, on the principles of the confederation, does the law of nations become the municipal law of the United States? The greatness of this question is self-evident: it would be very unwise, at present, even to hint at an answer.

After having examined these important preparatory topicks, I shall trace the causes, the origin, the progress, the history, the kinds, the parts, and the properties of government.

Under this title, I shall have occasion to treat concerning legislative, executive, and judicial power; and to investigate and compare the simple and the mixt species of governments and constitutions — one, particularly, that is simple in its principle, though diversified in its form and operations.

This will lead me to a particular examination of the constitution and government of the United States, of Pennsylvania, and of her sister commonwealths.

By this time, we shall be qualified to enter, with proper advantage, upon the illustration of the different parts of our municipal law. The common law is the first great object, which will here present itself. I shall think it my duty to investigate very carefully its principles, its nature, and its history; particularly the great event of its transmigration from Europe to America; and the subsequent juridical history of the American States.

Our municipal law, I shall consider under two great divisions. Under the first, I shall treat of the law, as it relates to persons: under the second, I shall treat of it, as it relates to things.

The division of the United States into circuits, districts, states, counties, and townships will, probably, be introduced here, with some remarks concerning the causes, the operation, and the consequences of those divisions.

In considering the law as it relates to persons, the legislative department of the United States will occupy the first place; the executive department, the second; and the judicial department, the third.

Under the first, the institution and powers of congress will come into view. The principles on which the senate and house of representatives are separately established, will be carefully discriminated; and the necessary remarks will be made on the great doctrine of representation. The importance and the manner of legislation will also claim a portion of our regard.

In considering the executive authority of the United States, the appointment, the powers, and the duties of the president, will first attract our notice. We will then proceed to consider the number and the nature of the subordinate executive departments. We shall here have an opportunity of taking a very general view of the civil, commercial, fiscal, maritime, and military establishments of the United States.

When we come to the judicial department, our attention will be first drawn to the supreme court of the United States. Its establishment and its jurisdiction will be particularly considered; as also the establishment and jurisdiction of the circuit and district courts.

Here the nature, the history, and the jurisdiction of courts in general; and the powers and duties of judges, juries, sheriffs, coroners, counsellors, and attornies will be naturally introduced.

Perhaps this may be the proper place, likewise, for some general observations on the nature and philosophy of evidence; a proper system of which is the greatest desideratum in the law.

The investigation of the different parts of the constitution and government of the United States, will lay the foundation of a very interesting parallel between them and the pride of Europe — the British constitution.

If the consideration of the legislative, executive, and judicial departments of the sister states can, without intricacy or confusion, be severally arranged under the three corresponding articles in the constitution of the United States; the parts of my plan will be considerably reduced in their number. I hope, but I am not confident, that this can be done. Upon this, as upon every other part of my plan, I shall be thankful for advice.

Bodies politick and inferiour societies will be described and distinguished.

The relations of private and of domestick life will pass in review before us; and after these, the rights and duties of citizens will come under consideration.

Here the important principles of election will receive the merited attention.

The rights, privileges, and disabilities of aliens will then be examined.

Happy would it be, if the great division of the law, which relates to persons, could be closed here. But it cannot be done. We are under the

sad necessity of viewing law as sometimes violated, and man as sometimes guilty. Hence the ungracious doctrine of punishment and crimes.

I will introduce this disagreeable part of my system with general observations concerning the nature of crimes, and the necessity and the
proportion of punishments: next, I will descend into a particular enumeration and description of each: and I will afterwards point out the different steps prescribed by the law for apprehending, detaining, trying, and
punishing offenders.

Here warrants, arrests, attachments, bail, commitments, imprisonment,
appeals, informations, indictments, presentments, process, arraignments,
pleas, trials, verdicts, judgments, attainders, pardons, forfeitures, corruption of blood, and executions will be considered.

With regard to criminal law, this observation may be made even in a
summary: it greatly needs reformation. In the United States, the seeds of
reformation are sown.

As to the second great division of our municipal law, which relates to
things; it may be all comprehended under one word — property. Claims,
it is true, may arise from a variety of sources, almost infinite: but the
declaration of every claim concludes by alleging a damage or a demand;
and the decision of every successful claim concludes by awarding a satisfaction or a restitution in property.

I shall trace the history of property from its lowest rude beginnings to
its highest artificial refinements; and, by that means, shall have an opportunity of pointing out the defects of the first, and the excesses of the last.

Property is of two kinds; publick and private. Under publick property,
common highways, common bridges, common rivers, common ports are
included. In the United States, and in the states composing the Union,
there is much land belonging to the publick.

Private property is divided into two kinds; personal and real: things
moveable are comprehended under the first division: things immoveable,
under the second.

Estates in real property are measured by their duration. An estate of
the greatest duration, is that which is in fee, or "to a man and his heirs,"
in the language of the common law. Real property of shorter duration
is known by the names of estates tail, estates in tail after possibility of
issue extinct, estates by the curtesy of England, estates in dower, estates
for life, estates for years, estates by sufferance, and estates at will.

Estates may be either absolute or conditional. Under the title of conditional estates, the excellent law of Pennsylvania with regard to mort-
gages will deserve particular consideration.

Estates may be in possession or in expectancy. Under the last head,
reversions, remainders, vested and contingent, and executory devises will
be treated.

Property may be joint or cotemporary, as well as separate and successive. Here we will treat concerning coparceners, partners, joint tenants, and tenants in common.

Property may be acquired by occupancy, conveyance, descent, succession, will, custom, forfeiture, judgment in a court of justice. In much the greatest number of instances, the acquisition of property by one is accompanied with the transfer of it by another.

Conveyances are by matter of record; as a fine, a common recovery, a deed enrolled: or by matter in pais; as livery, deed: here the nature and different kinds of deeds, at common law, and by virtue of statutes, will be particularly considered.

Property may consist of things in possession, or of things in action.

Land, money, cattle, are instances of the first kind; debts, rights of damages, and rights of action are instances of the second kind.

These are prosecuted by suit.

You have heard much concerning the forms of process, and proceedings, and pleadings. Much has been written in praise, and much has been written in ridicule, of this part of law learning. It has certainly been abused: in some hands, it has become, and daily does become ridiculous. And what is there that has been exempted from a similar fate! religion herself, elegant and simple as she is, yet, when dressed in the tawdry or tattered robes put upon her by the false taste of her injudicious friends, assumes an awkward and ridiculous appearance.

Law has experienced the same treatment with her elder sister. But though the learning with regard to pleas and pleading has been abused, it may certainly be employed for the most excellent purposes.

When properly directed and properly used, the science of well pleading is, indeed, in the language of Littleton, "one of the most honourable, laudable, and profitable things in our law." [q] Let me also adduce, in its favour, the weighty testimony of Earl Mansfield.[r] "The substantial rules of pleading," says this very able judge, "are founded in strong sense, and in the soundest and closest logick; and so appear when well understood and explained: though, by being misunderstood and misapplied, they are too often made use of as the instruments of chicane."

Permit me to add, that some of the forms of writs and pleas, particularly those that are most ancient, are models of correct composition, as well as of just sentiment.

The history of a suit at law, from its commencement, through all the different steps of its progress, to its conclusion, presents an object very interesting to a mind sensible to the beauty of strict and accurate arrangement. The dispositions of the drama are not made with more exactness

---

[q] Litt. s. 534.   [r] 1. Burr. 319.

and art. Every thing is done by the proper persons, at the proper time, in the proper place, in the proper order, and in the proper form.

This history may be comprised under the following titles — original writ, process, return, appearance — in person, by guardian, by next friend, by attorney — bail, declaration, profert, oyer, imparlance, continuance, pleas — in abatement and bar — replication, rejoinder, issue, demurrer, trial, demurrer to evidence, bill of exceptions, verdict, new trial, judgment, appeal, writ of error, execution.

II

OF THE GENERAL PRINCIPLES
OF LAW AND OBLIGATION

ORDER, proportion, and fitness pervade the universe. Around us, we see; within us, we feel; above us, we admire a rule, from which a deviation cannot, or should not, or will not be made.

On the inanimate part of the creation, are impressed the continued energies of motion and of attraction, and other energies, varied and yet uniform, all designated and ascertained. Animated nature is under a government suited to every genus, to every species, and to every individual, of which it consists. Man, the *nexus utriusque mundi*,* composed of a body and a soul, possessed of faculties intellectual and moral, finds or makes a system of regulations, by which his various and important nature, in every period of his existence, and in every situation, in which he can be placed, may be preserved, improved, and perfected. The celestial as well as the terrestrial world knows its exalted but prescribed course. This angels and the spirits of the just, made perfect, do "clearly behold, and without any swerving observe." Let humble reverence attend us as we proceed. The great and incomprehensible Author, and Preserver, and Ruler of all things — he himself works not without an eternal decree.

Such — and so universal is law. "Her seat," to use the sublime language of the excellent Hooker,[s] "is the bosom of God; her voice, the harmony of the world; all things in heaven and earth do her homage; the very least as feeling her care, and the greatest as not exempted from her power. Angels and men, creatures of every condition, though each in different sort and manner, yet all with uniform consent, admiring her as the mother of their peace and joy."

Before we descend to the consideration of the several kinds and parts of this science, so dignified and so diversified, it will be proper, and it will be useful; to contemplate it in one general and comprehensive view; and to select some of its leading and luminous properties, which will serve to guide and enlighten us in that long and arduous journey, which we now undertake.

It may, perhaps, be expected, that I should begin with a regular defini-

* [Binding together of both worlds.]   [s] Hooker 34.

tion of law. I am not insensible of the use, but, at the same time, I am not insensible of the abuse of definitions. In their very nature, they are not calculated to extend the acquisition of knowledge, though they may be well fitted to ascertain and guard the limits of that knowledge, which is already acquired. By definitions, if made with accuracy — and consummate accuracy ought to be their indispensable characteristick — ambiguities in expression, and different meanings of the same term, the most plentiful sources of errour and of fallacy in the reasoning art, may be prevented; or, if that cannot be done, may be detected. But, on the other hand, they may be carried too far, and, unless restrained by the severest discipline, they may produce much confusion and mischief in the very stations, which they are placed to defend.

You have heard much of the celebrated distribution of things into genera and species. On that distribution, Aristotle undertook the arduous task of resolving all reasoning into its primary elements; and he erected, or thought he erected, on a single axiom, a larger system of abstract truths, than were before invented or perfected by any other philosopher. The axiom, from which he sets out, and in which the whole terminates, is, that whatever is predicated of a genus, may be predicated of every species contained under that genus, and of every individual contained under every such species.[t] On that distribution likewise, the very essence of scientifick definition depends: for a definition, strictly and logically regular, "must express the genus of the thing defined, and the specifick difference, by which that thing is distinguished from every other species belonging to that genus." [u]

From this definition of a definition — if I may be pardoned for the apparent play upon the word — it evidently appears that nothing can be defined, which does not denote a species; because that only, which denotes a species, can have a specifick difference.

But further: a specifick difference may, in fact, exist; and yet language may furnish us with no words to express it. Blue is a species of colour; but how shall we express the specifick difference, by which blue is distinguished from green?

Again: expressions, which signify things simple, and void of all composition, are, from the very force of the terms, unsusceptible of definition. It was one of the capital defects of Aristotle's philosophy, that he attempted and pretended to define the simplest things.

Here it may be worth while to note a difference between our own abstract notions, and objects of nature. The former are the productions of our own minds; we can therefore define and divide them, and distinctly designate their limits. But the latter run so much into one another, and their essences, which discriminate them, are so subtile and latent, that

[t] 1. Gill. (4to.) 690.   [u] Reid's Ess. Int. 10. 11.

it is always difficult, often impossible, to define or divide them with the necessary precision. We are in danger of circumscribing nature within the bounds of our own notions, formed, frequently, on a partial or defective view of the object before us. Fettered thus at our outset, we are restrained in our progress, and govern the course of our inquiries, not by the extent or variety of our subject, but by our own preconceived apprehensions concerning it.

This distinction between the objects of nature and our own abstract notions suggests a practical inference. Definitions and divisions in municipal law, the creature of man, may be more useful, because more adequate and more correct, than in natural objects.

By some philosophers, definition and division are considered as the two great nerves of science. But unless they are marked by the purest precision, the fullest comprehension, and the most chastised justness of thought, they will perplex, instead of unfolding — they will darken, instead of illustrating, what is meant to be divided or defined. A defect or inaccuracy, much more an impropriety, in a definition or division, more especially of a first principle, will spread confusion, distraction, and contradictions over the remotest parts of the most extended system.

Errours in science, as well as in life, proceed more frequently from wrong principles, than from ill drawn consequences. *Prava regula prima** may be the parent of the most fatal enormities.

The higher an edifice is raised, the more compactly it is built, the more precisely it is carried up in a just direction — in proportion to all these excellencies, a rent in the foundation will increase and become dangerous.

The case is the same with a radical errour at the foundation of a system. The more accurately and the more ingeniously men reason, and the farther they pursue their reasonings, from false principles, the more numerous and the more inveterate will their inconsistencies, nay, their absurdities be. One advantage, however, will result — those absurdities and those inconsistencies will be more easily traced to their proper source. When the string of a musical instrument has a fault only in one place, you know immediately how and where to find and correct it.

Influenced by these admonitory truths, I hesitate, at present, to give a definition of law. My hesitation is increased by the fate of the far greatest number of those, who have hitherto attempted it. Many, as it is natural to suppose, and laboured have been the efforts to infold law within this scientifick circle; but little satisfaction — little instruction has been the result. Almost every writer, sensible of the defects, the inaccuracies, or

* ["The ruler awry at first." The words are drawn from a passage in Lucretius, *de Rerum Natura* IV 513-516, the point of which is that, if initial measurements are faulty, the whole building will be askew; if the premises of reasoning are incorrect, the conclusions will be erroneous.]

the improprieties of the definitions that have gone before him, has endeavoured to supply their place with something, in his own opinion, more proper, more accurate, and more complete. He has been treated by his successours, as his predecessors have been treated by him: and his definition has had only the effect of adding one more to the lengthy languid list. This I know, because I have taken the trouble to read them in great numbers; but because I have taken the trouble to read them, I will spare you the trouble of hearing them — at least, the greatest part of them.

Some of them, indeed, have a claim to attention: one, in particular, will demand it, for reasons striking and powerful — I mean that given by the Commentator on the laws of England.

Let us proceed carefully, patiently, and minutely to examine it. If I am not deceived, the examination will richly compensate all the time, and trouble, and investigation, that will be allotted to it; for it will be uncommonly fruitful in the principles, and in the consequences of the great truths and important disquisitions, which it will lead in review before us.

"Law," says he, "in its most general and comprehensive sense, signifies a rule of action." [v] In its proper signification, a rule is an instrument, by which a right line — the shortest and truest of all — may be drawn from one point to another. In its moral or figurative sense, it denotes a principle or power, that directs a man surely and concisely to attain the end, which he proposes.

Law is called a rule, in order to distinguish it from a [w] sudden, a transient, or a particular order: uniformity, permanency, stability, characterize a law.

Again; law is called a rule, to denote that it carries along with it a power and principle of obligation. Concerning the nature and the cause of obligation, much ingenious disputation has been held by philosophers and writers on jurisprudence. Indeed the sentiments entertained concerning it have been so various, that an account of them would, in the estimation of my Lord Kaims, be a "delicate historical morsel."

This interesting subject will claim and obtain our attention, next after what we have to say concerning law in general.

When we speak of a rule with regard to human conduct, we imply two things. 1. That we are susceptible of direction. 2. That, in our conduct, we propose an end. The brute creation act not from design. They eat, they drink, they retreat from the inclemencies of the weather, without considering what their actions will ultimately produce. But we have faculties, which enable us to trace the connexion between actions and their effects; and our actions are nothing else but the steps which we take,

[v] 1. Bl. Com. 38.   [w] 1. Bl. Com. 44.

or the means which we employ, to carry into execution the effects which we intend.

Hooker, I think, conveys a fuller and stronger conception of law, when he tells us, that "it assigns unto each thing the kind, that it moderates the force and power, that it appoints the form and measure of working." [x] Not the direction merely, but the kind also, the energy, and the proportion of actions is suggested in this description.

Some are of opinion, that law should be defined [y] "a rule of acting or not acting;" because actions may be forbidden as well as commanded. But the same excellent writer, whom I have just now cited, gives a very proper answer to this opinion, and shows the addition to be unnecessary, by finely pursuing the metaphor, which we have already mentioned. "We must not suppose that there needeth one rule to know the good, and another to know the evil by. For he that knoweth what is straight, doth even thereby discern what is crooked. Goodness in actions is like unto straightness; wherefore that which is well done, we term right." [z]

After this dry description of the literal and metaphorical meaning of a rule, permit me to relax your strained attention by a critical remark. In the philosophy of the human mind, it is impossible altogether to avoid metaphorical expressions. Our first and most familiar notions are suggested by material objects; and we cannot speak intelligibly of those that are immaterial, without continual allusions to matter and the qualities of matter.

Besides, in teaching moral science, the use of metaphors is not only necessary, but, if prudent, and honest, and guarded, it is highly advantageous. Nature has endowed us with the faculty of imagination, that we may be enabled to throw warming as well as enlightening rays upon truth — to embellish, to recommend, and to enforce it. Truth may, indeed, by reasoning, be rendered evident to the understanding; but it cannot reach the heart, unless by means of the imagination. To the imagination metaphors are addressed.

From this short excursion into the field of criticism, let us return to our legal tract. Law is a rule "prescribed." A simple resolution, confined within the bosom of the legislator, without being notified, in some fit manner, to those for whose conduct it is to form a rule, can never, with propriety, be termed a law.

There are many ways by which laws may be made sufficiently known. They may be printed and published. Written copies of them may be deposited in publick libraries, or other places, where every one interested may have an opportunity of perusing them. They may be proclaimed in general meetings of the people. The knowledge of them may be dissemi-

---

[x] Hooker 2.   [y] Daws. Orig. Laws, 4. 14.   [z] Hooker 11.

nated by long and universal practice. "Confirmed custom," says a writer on Roman jurisprudence, "is deservedly considered as a law. For since written laws bind us for no other reason than because they are received by the judgment of the people; those laws, which the people have approved, without writing, are also justly obligatory on all. For where is the difference, whether the people declare their will by their suffrage, or by their conduct? This kind of law is said to be established by[a] manners." [b]

Of all yet suggested, the mode for the promulgation of human laws by custom seems the most significant, and the most effectual. It involves in it internal evidence, of the strongest kind, that the law has been introduced by common *consent;* and that this consent rests upon the most solid basis — experience as well as opinion. This mode of promulgation points to the strongest characteristick of liberty, as well as of law. For a consent thus practically given, must have been given in the freest and most unbiassed manner.

With pleasure you anticipate the prospect of a species of law, to which these remarks have already directed your attention. If it were asked — and it would be no improper question — who of all the makers and teachers of law have formed and drawn after them the most, the best, and the most willing disciples; it might be not untruly answered — custom.

Laws may be promulgated by reason and conscience, the divine monitors within us. They are thus known as effectually, as by words or by writing: indeed they are thus known in a manner more noble and exalted. For, in this manner, they may be said to be engraven by God on the hearts of men: in this manner, he is the promulgator as well as the author of natural law.

If a simple resolution cannot have the force of a law before it be promulgated; we may certainly hazard the position — that it cannot have the force of a law, before it be made: in other words, that *ex post facto* instruments, claiming the title and character of laws, are impostors.

Peculiarly striking, upon this subject, are the sentiments of the criminal and unfortunate Strafford. I call him criminal, because he acted; I call him unfortunate, because he suffered, against the laws of his country. His sentiments must make a deep impression upon others; because, when he spoke them, he must have been deeply impressed with them himself. When he spoke them, he stood under a bill of attainder, suspended only by the slender thread of political justice, and ready, like the sword of Damocles, to fall on his devoted head. "Do we not live by laws? And must we be punished by laws before they are made? Far better were it to

[a] D. l. 1. t. 3. 32. p. 1.
[b] The first written laws in Greece were given only six centuries before the christian era.—1. Gill. 7. (4to.)

live by no laws at all, than to put this necessity of divination upon a man, and to accuse him of the breach of a law, before it be a law at all." [e]

In criminal jurisprudence, a Janus statute, with one face looking backward, and another looking forward, is a monster indeed.

The definition of law in the Commentaries proceeds in this manner. "Law is that rule of action, which is prescribed by some superiour, and which the inferiour is bound to obey." A superiour! Let us make a solemn pause — Can there be *no* law without a superiour? Is it *essential* to law, that inferiority should be involved in the obligation to obey it? Are these distinctions at the root of *all* legislation?

There is a law, indeed, which flows from the Supreme of being — a law, more distinguished by the goodness, than by the power of its allgracious Author. But there are laws also that are human; and does it follow, that, in these, a character of superiority is inseparably attached to him, who makes them; and that a character of inferiority is, in the same manner, inseparably attached to him, for whom they are made? What is this superiority? Who is this superiour? By whom is he constituted? Whence is his superiority derived? Does it flow from a source that is human? Or does it flow from a source that is divine?

From a human source it cannot flow; for no stream issuing from thence can rise higher than the fountain.

If the prince, who makes laws for a people, is superiour, in the terms of the definition, to the people, who are to obey; how comes he to be vested with the superiority over them?

If I mistake not, this notion of superiority, which is introduced as an *essential* part in the definition of a law — for we are told that a law *always*[d] supposes some superiour, who is to make it — this notion of superiority contains the germ of the divine right — a prerogative impiously attempted to be established — of princes, arbitrarily to rule; and of the corresponding obligation — a servitude tyrannically attempted to be imposed — on the people, implicitly to obey.

Despotism, by an artful use of "superiority" in politicks; and scepticism, by an artful use of "ideas" in metaphysicks, have endeavoured — and their endeavours have frequently been attended with too much success — to destroy all true liberty and sound philosophy. By their baneful effects, the science of man and the science of government have been poisoned to their very fountains. But those destroyers of others have met, or must meet, with their own destruction.

We now see, how necessary it is to lay the foundations of knowledge deep and solid. If we wish to build upon the foundations laid by another, we see how necessary it is cautiously and minutely to examine them.

[e] Whitlocke 230.   [d] 1. Bl. Com. 43.

If they are unsound, we see how necessary it is to remove them, however venerable they may have become by reputation; whatever regard may have been diffused over them by those who laid them, by those who built on them, and by those who have supported them.

But was Sir William Blackstone a votary of despotick power? I am far from asserting that he was. I am equally far from believing that Mr. Locke was a friend to infidelity. But yet it is unquestionable, that the writings of Mr. Locke have facilitated the progress, and have given strength to the effects of scepticism.

The high reputation, which he deservedly acquired for his enlightened attachment to the mild and tolerating doctrines of christianity, secured to him the esteem and confidence of those, who were its friends. The same high and deserved reputation inspired others of very different views and characters, with a design to avail themselves of its splendour, and, by that means, to diffuse a fascinating kind of lustre over their own tenets of a dark and sable hue. The consequence has been, that the writings of Mr. Locke, one of the most able, most sincere, and most amiable assertors of christianity and true philosophy, have been perverted to purposes, which he would have deprecated and prevented, had he discovered or foreseen them.

Berkeley, the celebrated bishop of Cloyne, wrote his Principles of human Knowledge — a book intended to disprove the existence of matter — with the express view of banishing scepticism both from science and from religion. He was even sanguine in his expectations of success. But the event has proved that he was egregiously mistaken; for it is evident, from the use to which later authors have applied it, that his system leads directly to universal scepticism.

Similar, though in an inferiour degree, have been, and may be, the fate and the influence of the writings and character of Sir William Blackstone, even admitting that he was as much a friend to liberty, as Locke and Berkeley were friends to religion.

But in prosecuting the study of law on liberal principles and with generous views, our business is much less with the character of the Commentaries or of their author, than with the doctrines which they contain. If the doctrines, insinuated in the definition of law, can be supported on the principles of reason and science; the defence of other principles, which I have thought to be those of liberty and just government, becomes — I am sorry to say it — a fruitless attempt.

Sir William Blackstone, however, was not the first, nor has he been the last, who has defined law upon the same principles, or upon principles similar and equally dangerous.

This subject is of such radical importance, that it will be well worth while to trace it as far as our materials can carry us; for errour as well as truth should be examined historically, and pursued back to its original springs.

By comparing what is said in the Commentaries on this subject, with what is mentioned concerning it in the system of morality, jurisprudence, and politicks written by Baron Puffendorff, we shall be satisfied that, from the sentiments and opinions delivered in the last mentioned performance, those in the first mentioned one have been taken and adopted. "A law," says Puffendorff, "is the command of a superiour." [e] "A law," says Sir William Blackstone, "always supposes some superiour, who is to make it." [f]

The introduction of superiority, as a necessary part of the definition of law, is traced from Sir William Blackstone to Puffendorff. This definition of Puffendorff is substantially the same with that of Hobbes. "A law is the command of him or them, that have the sovereign power, given to those that be his or their subjects." [g] It is substantially the same also with that of Bishop Saunderson. "Law is a rule of action, imposed on a subject, by one who has power over him." [h]

Let us now inquire what is meant by superiority, that we may be able to ascertain and recognise those qualities, inherent or derivative, which entitle the superiour or sovereign to the transcendent power of imposing laws.

We can distinguish two kinds of superiority. 1. A superiority merely of power. 2. A superiority of power, accompanied with a right to exercise that power. Is the first sufficient to entitle its possessor to the character and office of a legislator? If we subscribe to the doctrines of Mr. Hobbes, we shall say, that it is. "To those," says he, "whose power is irresistible, the dominion of all men adhereth naturally, by their excellence of power." [i]

This position, strange as it is, has had its advocates in ancient as well as in modern times. Even the accomplished Athenians, who excluded it from their municipal code, seem to have considered it as part of the received law of nations. "We follow," says their ambassadour in the name of his commonwealth, "the common nature and genius of mankind, which appoints those to be masters, who are superiour in strength. We have not made this law; nor are we the first, who have appealed to it. We received it from antiquity: we are determined to transmit it to the most distant futurity: and we claim and use it in our own case." [j]

Brennus, at the head of his victorious and ferocious Gauls, with more

[e] Puff. B. 1. c. 2. s. 6. p. 16. B. 1. c. 6. s. 1. 2. p. 56. 57.   [f] 1. Bl. Com. 43.
[g] 3. Dagge 95. 96.   [h] Daws. Orig. L. 3. cites Saund. Præl. 5. s. 3.
[i] De Cive 187. (Puff. 64.)   [j] Puff. 65. (Thucyd. l. 5. c. 105) 1. Anac. 351.

conciseness, and with a less striking inconsistency of character, tells the vanquished Romans "omnia fortium esse." [k] Every thing belongs to the bold and the strong.

The prudent Plutarch thinks it "the first and principal law of nature, that he whose circumstances require protection and deliverance, should admit him for his ruler, who is able to protect and deliver him." [l]

For us, it is sufficient, as men, as citizens, and as states, to say, that power is nothing more than the right of the strongest, and may be opposed by the same right, by the same means, and by the same principles, which are employed to establish it. Bare force, far from producing an obligation to obey, produces an obligation to resist.

Others, unwilling to rest the office of legislation and the right of sovereignty simply on superiority of power, have to this quality super-added preeminence or superiour excellence of nature.

Let it be remembered all along, that I am examining the doctrine of superiority, as applied to human laws, the proper and immediate object of investigation in these lectures. Of the law that is divine, we shall have occasion, at another time, to speak, with the reverence and gratitude which become us.

"It is a law of nature," says Dionysius of Halicarnassus, "common to all men, and which no time shall disannul or destroy, that those, who have more strength and *excellence*, shall bear rule over those, who have less." [m] The favourers of this opinion are unfortunate, both in the illustrations, by which they attempt to evince it; and in the inferences, to which they contend it gives rise.

Because Cicero, by a beautiful metaphor, describes the government of the other powers of the mind as assigned, by nature, to the understanding; does it follow that, in strict propriety of reasoning, the right of legislation is annexed, without any assignment, to superiour excellence?

Aristotle, it seems, has said, that if a man *could* be found, excelling in *all* virtues, such an one would have a *fair title* to be king. These words may well be understood as conveying, and probably were intended to convey, only this unquestionable truth — that excellence in every virtue furnished the strongest recommendation, in favour of its happy possessor, *to be elected* for the exercise of authority. If so, the opinion of Aristotle is urged without a foundation properly laid in the fact.

But let us suppose the contrary: let us suppose it to be the judgment of Aristotle, that the person, whom he characterizes, derived his right to the exercise of power, not from the donation made to him by a voluntary election, but solely from his superiour talents and excellence; shall the judgment of Aristotle supersede inquiry into its reasonableness?

[k] Puff. 65. (Livy.)   [l] Puff. 65. (Plut. in Pelop.)
[m] Puff. 65. (Dion. Hal. b. 1. c. 5.)

Shall the judgment of Aristotle, if found, on inquiry, to be unreasonable, silence all reprehension or confutation? Decent respect for authority is favourable to science. Implicit confidence is its bane. Let us adopt — for it is necessary, in the cause of truth and freedom, that we should adopt — the manly expostulation, which the ardent pursuit of knowledge drew from the great Bacon — "Why should a few received authors stand up like Hercules's columns, beyond which there should be no sailing or discovery?"

To Aristotle, more than to any other writer, either ancient or modern, this expostulation is strictly applicable. Hear what the learned Grotius says on this subject. "Among philosophers, Aristotle deservedly holds the chief place, whether you consider his method of treating subjects, or the acuteness of his distinctions, or the weight of his reasons. I could only wish that the authority of this great man had not, for some ages past, degenerated into tyranny; so that truth, for the discovery of which Aristotle took so great pains, is now oppressed by nothing more than by the very name of Aristotle." [n]

Guided and supported by the sentiments and by the conduct of Grotius and Bacon, let us proceed, with freedom and candour combined, to examine the judgment — though I am very doubtful whether it was the judgment — of Aristotle, that the right of sovereignty is founded on superiour excellence.

To that superiority, which attaches the right to command, there must be a corresponding inferiority, which imposes the obligation to obey. Does this right and this obligation result from every kind and every degree of superiority in one, and from every kind and every degree of inferiority in another? How is excellence to be rated or ascertained?

Let us suppose three persons in three different grades of excellence. Is he in the lowest to receive the law immediately from him in the highest? Is he in the highest to give the law immediately to him in the lowest grade? Or is there to be a gradation of law as well as of excellence? Is the command of the first to the third to be conveyed through the medium of the second? Is the obedience of the third to be paid, through the same medium, to the first? Augment the number of grades, and you multiply the confusion of their intricate and endless consequences.

Is this a foundation sufficient for supporting the solid and durable superstructure of law? Shall this foundation, insufficient as it is, be laid in the contingency — allowed to be improbable, not asserted to be even possible — "if a man can be found, excelling in *all* virtues?"

Had it been the intention of Providence, that some men should govern the rest, without their consent, we should have seen as indisputable marks distinguishing these superiours from those placed under them, as those

[n] Gro. Prel. 28.

which distinguish men from the brutes. The remark of Rumbald, in the nonresistance time of Charles the second, evinced propriety as well as wit. He could not conceive that the Almighty intended, that the greatest part of mankind should come into the world with saddles on their backs and bridles in their mouths, and that a few should come ready booted and spurred to ride the rest to death.[o] Still more apposite to our purpose is the saying of him, who declared that he would never subscribe the doctrine of the divine right of princes, till he beheld subjects born with bunches on their backs, like camels, and kings with combs on their heads, like cocks; from which striking marks it might indeed be collected, that the former were designed to labour and to suffer, and the latter, to strut and to crow.[p]

These pretensions to superiority, when viewed from the proper point of sight, appear, indeed, absurd and ridiculous. But these pretensions, absurd and ridiculous as they are, when rounded and gilded by flattery, and swallowed by pride, have become, in the breasts of princes, a deadly poison to their own virtues, and to the happiness of their unfortunate subjects. Those, who have been bred to be kings, have generally, by the prostituted views of their courtiers and instructors, been taught to esteem themselves a distinct and superiour species among men, in the same manner as men are a distinct and superiour species among animals.

Lewis the fourteenth was a strong instance of the effect of that inverted manner of teaching and thinking, which forms kings to be tyrants, without knowing or even suspecting that they are so. That oppression, under which he held his subjects, during the whole course of his long reign, proceeded chiefly from the principles and habits of his erroneous education. By this, he had been accustomed to consider his kingdom as his patrimony, and his power over his subjects as his rightful and undelegated inheritance. These sentiments were so deeply and strongly imprinted on his mind, that when one of his ministers represented to him the miserable condition to which those subjects were reduced, and, in the course of his representation, frequently used the word "l'etat," the state; the king, though he felt the truth, and approved the substance of all that was said, yet was shocked at the frequent repetition of the word "l'etat," and complained of it as an indecency offered to his person and character.

And, indeed, that kings should imagine themselves the final causes, for which men were made, and societies were formed, and governments were instituted, will cease to be a matter of wonder or surprise, when we find that lawyers, and statesmen, and philosophers have taught or favoured principles, which necessarily lead to the same conclusions.

[o] 1. Burgh. Pol. Dis. 3.   [p] Boling. Rem. 209.

Barbeyrac, whose commentaries enrich the performances of the most distinguished philosophers, at one time, taught and favoured principles, which necessarily led to the conclusions, so degrading and so destructive to the human race. On this subject, it will be worth while to pursue his train of thought.

In the formation of societies and civil governments, three different conventions or agreements are supposed, by Puffendorff and many other writers, to have taken place. The first convention is an engagement, by those who compose the society or state, to associate together in one body, and to regulate, with one common consent, whatever regards their preservation, their security, their improvement, and their happiness. The second convention is, to specify the form of government, that shall be established among them. The third convention is an engagement between the following parties; that is to say, the person or persons, on whom the sovereignty, or superiority, or majesty — for it is called by all these names — is conferred, on one hand; and, on the other hand, those who have conferred this sovereignty, this superiority, this majesty; and are now, by that step, as it seems, become subjects. By this third convention, the sovereign engages to consult the common security and advantage of the subjects; and the subjects engage to observe fidelity and allegiance to the sovereign. From this last convention, the state is supposed to receive its final completion and perfection.

This account of the origin of society and government will be fully considered afterwards. I introduce it now, in order to show the force and import of Barbeyrac's observation concerning it. "The first convention," says he, "is only, with regard to the second, what scaffolding is with regard to the building, for whose construction it was erected." [q]

And is it so? Is society nothing more than a scaffolding, by the means of which government may be erected; and which, consequently, may be prostrated, as soon as the edifice of civil government is built? If this is so, it must have required but a small portion of courtly ingenuity to persuade Lewis the fourteenth, that, in a monarchy, government was nothing but a scaffolding for the king.

For the honour of Barbeyrac, however, let not this account be concluded, till it be told, that this did not continue to be always his sentiment; that, on consideration and reflection, this sentiment was changed; and that, when it was changed, he, as every other great and good man will do on similar occasions, freely and nobly retracted it. But although it has been retracted by Barbeyrac, it has neither been retracted nor abandoned by some others.

To evince that I speak not without foundation, and to show, what will

[q] Puff. 641. note to b. 7, c. 2. s. 8.

not be suspected till they are shown, the extravagant notions which have been entertained on this head, I will adduce a number of sentences and quotations, which Grotius[r] has collected together, in order to combat the sentiments of those, who hold that the supreme power is, always and without exception, in the people.

Historians and philosophers, poets and princes, bishops and fathers, are all summoned to oppose the dangerous doctrine.

When Tacitus says, "that, as we must bear with storms, barrenness, and the inconveniences of nature, so we must bear with the luxury or avarice of princes;" Grotius tells us, "'tis admirably said." Marcus Antoninus, the philosopher, is produced as an authority, "that magistrates are to judge of private persons, princes of magistrates, but God alone of princes." King Vitigis declares, that "what regards the royal power is to be judged by the powers above; because it is derived from heaven, and is accountable to heaven alone." Ireneus, we are informed, says excellently, "by whose orders men are born, by his command kings are ordained." The same doctrine is contained in the constitutions of Clement. "You shall fear the king, knowing that he is chosen of God."

In a tragedy of Æschylus, the suppliants use this language to the king. "Sir, you are the city and the publick; you are an independent judge. Seated upon your throne as upon an altar, you alone govern all by your absolute commands."

Here we have the very archetype of the idea of Lewis the fourteenth, sanctioned by the name of Grotius. If the king was the city and the publick; to mention "l'etat" in his presence, as something separate and distinct, was certainly an indecency; because it contained an implied though distant limitation of his power.

The reverend bishop of Tours addresses the king of France in this very remarkable manner: "If any of us, O king! should transgress the bounds of justice, he may be punished by you: but if you yourself should offend, who shall call you to account? When we make representations to you, if you please, you hear us: but if you will not, who shall condemn you? There is none but he, who has declared himself to be justice itself."

Let me also mention what Heineccius says, in much more recent times, in his System of Universal Law. "The doctrine,[s] which makes the people superiour to the king or prince, and places in the former the real, and in the latter only personal majesty, is a most petulant one. It is the doctrine of Hottoman, Sidney, Milton, and others. Since a people, when they unite into a republick, renounce their own will, and subject themselves to the will of another, with what front can they call themselves superiour to their sovereign?"

[r] Grotius 68 — 71.   [s] 2. Hein. 120, 121.

And yet Heineccius himself allows, that "Grotius (i. 3. 8.) is thought by not a few, to have given some handle to the doctrine of passive obedience and nonresistance."

Indeed, the lawyers of almost all the states of Europe represent kings as legislators: and we know, that, in the dictionaries of many, legislative and unlimited power are synonimous terms. To unlimited power, the correlative is passive obedience.

Even Baron de Wolfius, the late celebrated philosopher of Hall, lays down propositions concerning patrimonial kingdoms, without re-jecting or contradicting a distinction, so injurious to the freedom and the rights of men.

Domat, in his book on the civil law, derives the power of governours from *divine* authority. "It is always he (God) who places them in the seat of authority: it is from him alone that they derive all the power and authority that they have; and it is the ministry of his justice that is committed to them. And seeing it is God himself whom they represent, in the rank which raises them above others; he will have them to be considered as holding his place in their functions. And it is for this reason, that he himself gives the name of gods to those, to whom he communicates the right of governing and judging men." [t]

To diminish the force of the foregoing citations, it may be said, that, in all probability, Lewis the fourteenth — and the same may be said of other princes equally ignorant — never read the tragedies of Æschylus, nor the history of Gregory of Tours. It is highly probable that he never did: but it is equally probable, that their sentiments were known in his court, and found the way, through the channels of flattery, to the royal ear. But the writings of Grotius must have been well known in France, and probably to Lewis the fourteenth himself. This very book of the Rights of War and Peace was dedicated to his father, Lewis the thir-teenth; and its author, we are told, had credit with some of the ministers of that prince.

Every plausible notion in favour of arbitrary power, appearing in a respectable dress, and introduced by an influential patron, is received with eagerness, protected with vigilance, and diffused with solicitude, by an arbitrary government. The consequence is, that, in such a government, political prejudices are last of all, if ever, overcome or eradicated.

But these doctrines, it may be replied, are not now believed, even in France. But they have been believed — they have been believed, even in France, to the slavery and misery of millions. And if, happily, they are not still believed there; unfortunately, they are still believed in other countries.

But I ask — why should they be believed at all? I ask further: if they

[t] 1. Domat XXII.

are not, and ought not to be believed; why is their principle suffered to lie latent and lurking at the root of the science of law? Why is that principle continued a part of the very definition of law?

The pestilent seed may seem, at present, to have lost its vegetating power: but an unfriendly season and a rank soil may still revive it. It ought to be finally extirpated. It has, even within our own remembrance, done much real mischief. The position, that law is inseparably attached to superiour power, was the political weapon used, with the greatest force and the greatest skill, in favour of the despotick claims of Great Britain over the American colonies. Of this, the most striking proofs will appear hereafter. Let me, at present, adopt the sentiments expressed, on a similar subject, by Vattel. "If the base flatterers of despotick power rise up against my principles; I shall have, on my side, the friend of laws, the true citizen, and the virtuous man." [u]

Let us conclude our observations upon this hypothesis concerning the origin of sovereignty, by suggesting, that were it as solid as it is unsound in speculation, it would be wholly visionary and useless in practice. Where would minions and courtly flatterers find the objects, to which they could, even with courtly decency, ascribe superiour talents, superiour virtue, or a superiour nature, so as to entitle them, even on their own principles, to legislation and government?

We have now examined the inherent qualities, which have been alleged as sufficient to entitle, to the right and office of legislation, the superiour, whose interposition is considered as essential to a law. We have weighed them in the balance, and we have found them wanting.

If this superiour cannot rest a title on any inherent qualities; the qualities, which constitute his title, if any title he has, must be such as are derivative. If derivative; they must be derived either from a source that is human, or from a source that is divine. "Over a whole grand multitude," says the judicious[v] Hooker, "consisting of many families, impossible it is, that any should have complete lawful power, but by consent of men, or by immediate appointment of God." We will consider those sources separately.

How is this superiour constituted by *human* authority? How far does his superiority extend? Over whom is it exercised? Can any person or power, appointed by human authority, be superiour to those by whom he is appointed, and so form a necessary and essential part in the definition of a law?

On these questions, a profound, I will not say a suspicious silence is observed. By the Author of the Commentaries, this superiour is announced in a very questionable shape. We can neither tell who he is, nor whence he comes. "When society is once formed, government results of

[u] Vattel Pref. 14.   [v] Hooker. b. 1. s. 10. p. 18.

course" — I use the words[w] of the Commentary — "as necessary to preserve and to keep that society in order. Unless some superiour be constituted, whose commands and decisions all the members are bound to obey, they would still remain as in a state of nature, without any judge upon earth to define their several rights, and redress their several wrongs. But as all the members of the society are naturally equal, it may be asked" — what question may be asked? The most natural question, that occurs to me, is — how is this superiour, without whom there can be no law, without whom there can be no judge upon earth — how is this superiour to be constituted? This is the question, which, on this occasion, I would expect to see proposed: this is the question, to which I would expect to hear an answer. But how suddenly is the scene shifted! Instead of the awful insignia of superiority, to which our view was just now directed, the mild emblems of confidence make their appearance. The person announced was a dread superiour: but the person introduced is a humble trustee. For, to proceed, "it may be asked, in whose hands are the reins of government to be *intrusted?*"

I very well know how "a society once formed" constitute a trustee: but I am yet to learn, and the Commentator has not yet informed me, how this society can constitute their superiour. Locke somewhere says that "no one can confer more power on another, than he possesses himself." [x]

If the information, how a superiour is appointed, be given in any other part of the valuable Commentaries; it has escaped my notice, or my memory. Indeed it has been remarked by his successour in the chair of law, that Sir William Blackstone "declines speaking of the origin of government." [y]

The question recurs — how is this superiour constituted by human authority? Is he constituted by a law? If he is, that law, at least, must be made without a superiour; for by that law the superiour is constituted. If there can be no law without a superiour, then the institution of a superiour, by human authority, must be made in some other manner than by a law. In what other manner can human authority be exerted? Shall we say, that it may be exerted in a covenant or an engagement? Let us say, for we may say justly, that it may. Let us suppose the authority to be exerted, and the covenant or engagement to be made. Still the question recurs — can this authority so exerted, can this covenant or engagement so made, produce a superiour?

If he is now entitled to that appellation, he must be so by virtue of some thing, which he has received. But has he received more than was given? Could more be given than those, who gave it, possessed?

We can form clear conceptions of authority, original and derived,

[w] 1. Bl. Com. 48.   [x] Lock Gov. p. 2. s. 6.   [y] El. Jur. 23.

entire and divided into parts; but we have no clear conceptions how the parts can become greater than the whole; nor how authority, that is derived, can become superiour to that authority, from which the derivation is made.

If these observations are well founded; it will be difficult — perhaps we may say, impossible — to account for the institution of a superiour by human *authority*.

Is there any other human source, from which superiority can spring? 'Tis thought there is: 'tis thought that human *submission* can effectuate a purpose, for the accomplishment of which human authority has been found to be unavailing.

And is it come to this! Must submission to an equal be the yoke, under which we must pass, before we can diffuse the mild power, or participate in the benign influence of law? If such is indeed, our fate, let resignation be our aim: but before we resign ourselves, let us examine whether our fate be so hard.

That I may be able to convey a just and full representation of opinions, which have been entertained on this subject, I shall give an abstract of the manner, in which Puffendorff has reasoned concerning it, in his chapter on the generation of civil sovereignty.

His object is, "to examine whence that sovereignty or supreme command, which appears in every state, and which, as a kind of soul, informs, enlivens, and moves the publick body, is immediately produced."

In this inquiry, he supposes that civil authority requires natural strength and a title. "Both these requisites," says he, "immediately flow from those pacts, by which the state is united and subsists." With regard to the former — natural strength — he observes, "that since all the members of the state, in submitting their wills to the will of a single director, did, at the same time, thereby oblige themselves to nonresistance, or to obey him in all his desires and endeavours of applying their strength and wealth to the good of the publick; it appears that he, who holds the sovereign rule, is possessed of sufficient force to compel the discharge of the injunctions, which he lays."

"So, likewise," adds he, "the same covenant affords a full and easy title, by which the sovereignty appears to be established, not upon violence, but in a lawful manner, upon the voluntary consent and *subjection* of the respective members."

"This, then," continues he, "is the nearest and immediate cause, from which sovereign authority, as a moral quality, doth result. For if we suppose *submission* in one party, and, in another, the *acceptance* of that submission; there accrues, presently, to the latter, a right of imposing commands on the former; which is what we term sovereignty or rule. And as, by private contract, the right of any thing which we possess, so, by *submission*, the right to dispose of our strength and our liberty of acting, may be conveyed to another."

He illustrates this immediate cause of sovereign authority, by the following instance. "If any person should voluntarily and upon covenant deliver himself to me in servitude, he thereby really confers on me the power of a master." "Against which way of arguing, to object the vulgar maxim, *quod quis non habet, non potest in alterum transferre,*[z] is but a piece of trifling ignorance." [a]

Shall we, for a moment, suppose all this to be done? What is left to the people? Nothing. What are they? Slaves. What will be their portion? That of the beasts — instinct, compliance, and punishment. So true it is, that in the attempt to make one person more than man, millions must be made less.

We now see the price, at which law must be purchased; for we see the terms, on which a superiour, of such absolute necessity to a law, is constituted, according to the hypothesis, of which I have given an account. We see the covenants which must be entered into, the consent which must be given, the submission which must be made, the subjection which must be undergone, the state, analogous to servitude, which must be supposed, before this system of superiority can be completed. Has this been always done — must this be always done, in every state, where law is known or felt?

Without examining its incongruity with reason, with freedom, and with fact; without insisting on the incoherence of the parts, and the unsoundness of the whole, I shall again, for a moment, take it all for granted: and, on that supposition, I shall put the question — Is even all this sufficient to constitute a superiour? Is it in the power of the meanest to prostitute, any more than it is in the power of the greatest to delegate, what he does not possess? [b] The arguments, therefore, which we used

---

[z] Puff. b. 7. c. 3. s. 1. p. 654. 655. [What a man does not have he cannot hand over to another.]

[a] All this, it is true, has been done, in fact. This act of legal suicide has been often perpetrated; and, in the history of some periods, we find the prescribed form, by which liberty was extinguished — a form truly congenial with the transaction — a form expressed in terms the most disgraceful to the dignity of man. "Licentiam habeatis, mihi qualemcunque volueritis disciplinam ponere, vel venumdare, aut quod vobis placuerit de me facere." [Take every liberty, place whatever restriction you wish upon me, or sell me as a slave, or do whatever you please with me.] (6. Gibbon 361. cites Marculf. Formul.) But these periods were the periods which introduced and established the feudal law. "The majesty of the Roman law protected the liberty of the citizen against his own distress or despair." 6. Gibbon. 360.

[b] Let individuals, in any number whatever, become severally and successively subject to one man, they are all, in that case, nothing more than master and slaves; they are not a people governed by their chief; they are an aggregate, if you will; but they do not form an association; there subsists among them neither commonwealth nor body politick. Such a superiour, though he should become master of half the

with regard to the appointment of a superiour by human authority, will equally apply to his appointment by human submission. The manner may be different: the result will be the same.

Indeed, the author of this system betrays a secret consciousness, that it is too weak and too disjointed to stand without an extrinsick support. "Yet still," says he, "to procure to the supreme command an especial efficacy, and a sacred respect, there is need of another additional principle, besides the submission of the subjects. And therefore he who affirms sovereignty to result immediately from compact, doth not, in the least, detract from the *sacred* character of civil government; or maintain that princes bear rule, by human right *only*, and not by divine." [c]

It deserves remark, that, in this passage, Puffendorff assumes the divine right of princes to bear rule, as an admitted principle; and seems only solicitous to show, that the account, which he has given, of the origin of sovereignty, is not inconsistent with their sacred character.

After some further observations with regard to the source of government and the cause of sovereignty, the author acknowledges, that there is very little difference between his sentiments on the subject, and those of Bœcler. What Bœcler's sentiments were, we learn from the account given of them by our author. "The supreme authority," [d] says Bœcler, "is not to be derived from the bare act of man, but from the command of God, and from the law of nature; or from such an act of men, by which the law of nature was followed and obeyed."

So far Puffendorff seems willing to go. He adopts a kind of compromising principle. He founds the right of the sovereign immediately upon the submission of the subjects; but, to complete the efficacy of supreme command, he calls in the aid of an additional principle, the sacred character of civil government, and the divine right of princes to bear rule. Further he was unwilling to proceed.

It has been often the fate of a compromise between two parties, that it has given entire satisfaction to neither. Such has been the fate of that adopted by Puffendorff. Some will certainly think, that he has given too much countenance to the claim, which princes have boldly made, of a divine right to rule. Others have thought, that, into his composition of a sovereign, he has infused too great a proportion of human authority. They pursue the source of sovereignty further than he is willing to accompany them, and maintain, that it is the Supreme Being, who confers immediately the supreme power on princes, without the intervention or concurrence of man.

---

world, would be still a private person, and his interest, separate and distinct from that of his people, would be still no more than a private interest. Rousseau's **Orig. Comp.** 17. 18.

    [c] Puff. 655. b. 7. c. 3. s. 1. — 2. Burl. 39.   [d] Puff. 655. b. 7. c. 3. s. 1.

This doctrine, in some countries, and at some periods, has been carried, and is still carried, to a very extravagant height, and has been supported and propagated, and still is supported and propagated, with uncommon zeal. It has been, and still is, a favourite at courts; and has been, and still is, treated with every appearance of profound respect by courtiers, and, in too many instances, by philosophers and by statesmen, who have imitated, and still imitate courtiers in their practice of the slavish art. In the reign of James the second, "the immediate emanation of divine authority" was introduced on every occasion, and ingrafted, often with the strangest impropriety, on every subject. Even in the present century, a book has been burnt by the hangman, because its author maintained, "that God is not the immediate cause of sovereignty." [e]

It cannot escape observation, that, in one particular, those who carry this doctrine the furthest, seem to challenge, with some success, the palm of consistency from those, who refuse to accompany them. Both entertain the same sentiments — and they are certainly overcharged ones — concerning sovereignty and superiority. Thus far they march together. But here, one division halt. The other proceed, and, looking back on those behind them, demand, why, having gone so far, they refuse to accomplish the journey. They insist, that all human causes are inadequate to the production of that superiority or sovereignty, about the august and sacred character of which they are both agreed. They say, that neither particular men, nor a multitude of men, are themselves possessed of this sovereignty or superiority; and that, therefore, they cannot confer it on the prince. The consequence is, that, as this superiority is admitted to exist, and as it cannot be conferred by men, it must derive its origin from a higher source.

It is in this manner that Domat reasons concerning the origin of sovereignty and government. "As there is none but God alone who is the natural sovereign of man; so it is likewise from him that they who govern derive all their power and authority. It is one of the ceremonies in the coronation of the kings of France, for them to take the sword from the altar; thereby to denote, that it is immediately from the hand of God that they derive the sovereign power, of which the sword is the principal emblem." [f]

In the same train of sentiment, Bishop Taylor[g] observes, "that the legislative or supreme power is not the servant of the people, but the minister, the trustee, and the representative of God: that all just human power is given from above, not from beneath; from God, not from the people."

Indeed, on the principle of superiority, Caligula's reasoning was con-

[e] Puff. 656. note to b. 7. c. 3. s. 3.   [f] 2. Domat 298, 299.
[g] Rule of Conscience 429.

cise and conclusive. "If I am only a man, my subjects are something less: if they are men, I am something more." [h]

The answer to the foregoing reasoning appears to me to be more ingenious than solid, and to be productive of amusement, rather than of conviction. I shall deliver it from Burlamaqui, who, on this subject, has followed the opinions of Puffendorff. "This argument," says he, "proves nothing. It is true, that neither each member of the society, nor the whole multitude collected, are formally invested with the supreme authority; but it is sufficient that they possess it virtually; that is, that they have within themselves all that is necessary to enable them, by the concurrence of their free will and consent, to produce it in the sovereign. Since every individual has a natural right of disposing of his own natural freedom, according as he thinks proper; why should he not have a power of transferring to another, that right which he has of directing himself? Now is it not manifest, that, if all the members of the society agree to transfer this right to one of their fellow members, this cession will be the nearest and immediate cause of sovereignty? It is, therefore, evident, that there are, in each individual, the seeds, as it were, of the supreme power. The case is here very near the same, as in that of several voices collected together, which, by their union, produce a harmony, that was not to be found separately in each." [i]

The metaphors from vegetation and musick may illustrate and please; but they cannot prove nor convince. The notion of virtual sovereignty is as unsatisfactory to me, on this occasion, as that of virtual representation has been, on many others. Indeed, I see but little difference between a claim to derive from another that, which he is willing to give, but of which he is not possessed, and a claim to derive from him that, which he possesses, but which he has not given, and will not give.

Besides; let me repeat the questions, which I formerly put. — Have these degrading steps been always taken? must they be always taken, in every state, where law is known or felt? For let it not be forgotten, that superiority is introduced as a *necessary* part of the definition of law.

I will not attempt to paint the hideous consequences that have been drawn, nor the still more hideous practices that have claimed impunity, indulgence, and even sanction, from the pretended principle of the divine right of princes. Absolute, unlimited, and indefeasible power, nonresistance, passive obedience, tyranny, slavery, and misery walk in its train.

On this subject — its importance cannot be overrated — let us receive instruction from a well informed and a well experienced master — from one, who, probably, in some periods of his life, had felt what he so

[h] Rous. Or. Com. 6.   [i] 2. Burl. 41, 42.

feelingly describes — from one, who had been bred to the trade of a prince, and who had been perfectly initiated in all the mysteries of the profession — from the late Frederick of Prussia.

"If my reflections," says he, "shall be fortunate enough to reach the ears of some princes, they will find among them certain truths, which they never would have heard from the lips of their courtiers and flatterers. Perhaps they will be struck with astonishment, to see such truths placed, by their side, on the throne. But it is time, that, at last, they should learn, that their false principles are the most empoisoned source — *la source la plus empoisonée* — of the calamities of Europe.

"Here is the errour of the greatest part of princes. They believe that God has expressly, and from a particular attention to their grandeur, their happiness, and their pride, formed their subjects for no other purpose, than to be the ministers and instruments of their unbridled passions. As the principle, from which they set out, is false; the consequences cannot be otherwise than infinitely pernicious. Hence the unregulated passion for false glory — hence the inflamed desire of conquest — hence the oppressions laid upon the people — hence the indolence and dissipation of princes — hence their ambition, their injustice, their inhumanity, their tyranny — hence, in short, all those vices, which degrade the nature of man.

"If they would disrobe themselves of these erroneous opinions; if they would ascend to the true origin of their appointment; they would see, that their elevation and rank, of which they are so jealous, are, indeed, nothing else than the work of the people; they would see, that the myriads of men, placed under their care, have not made themselves the slaves of one single man, with a view to render him more powerful and more formidable; have not submitted themselves to a fellow citizen, in order to become the sport of his fancies, and the martyrs of his caprice; but have chosen, from among themselves, the man, whom they believed to be the most just, that he might govern them; the best, that he might supply the place of a father; the most humane, that he might compassionate and relieve their misfortunes; the most valiant, that he might defend them against their enemies; the most wise, that he might not engage them inconsiderately in ruinous and destructive wars; in one word, the man the most proper to represent the body of the state, and in whom the sovereign power might become a bulwark to justice and to the laws, and not an engine, by the force of which tyranny might be exercised, and crimes might be committed with impunity.

"This principle being once established, princes would avoid the two rocks, which, in all ages, have produced the ruin of empires, and distraction in the political world — ungoverned ambition, and a listless inattention to affairs." [j] "They would often reflect that they are men, as well as the least of their subjects — that if they are the first judges, the first generals, the first financiers, the first ministers of society; they are so, for the purpose of fulfilling the duties, which those names import. They will reflect, that they are only the first servants of the state, bound to act with the same integrity, the same caution, and the same entire disinterestedness, as if, at every moment, they were to render an account of their administration to the citizens." [k]

I will not charge to the authors, whose opinions I have examined, all the consequences that have been drawn, practically as well as theoretically, from their principles. From their principles, however, admitted by themselves without due caution and scrutiny, those consequences have been drawn by others, and drawn too accurately and too successfully for the peace, liberty, and happiness of men.

After all, I am much inclined, for the honour of human nature, to believe, that all this doctrine concerning the divine right of kings was, at first, encouraged and cherished by many, from motives, mistaken certainly, but pardonable, and even laudable; and that it was intended not so much to introduce the tyranny of princes, as to form a barrier against the tyranny of priests.

One of them, at the head of a numerous, a formidable, and a well disciplined phalanx, claimed to be the Almighty's vicegerent upon earth; claimed the power of deposing kings, disposing crowns, releasing subjects from their allegiance, and overruling the whole transactions of the christian world. Superstition and ignorance dreaded, but could not oppose, the presumptuous claim. The Pope had obtained, what Archimedes wanted, *another* world, on which he placed his ecclesiastical machinery; and it was no wonder that he moved *this* according to his will and pleasure. Princes and potentates, states and kingdoms were prostrate before him. Every thing human was obliged to bend under the incumbent pressure of divine control.

It is not improbable, that, in this disagreeable predicament, the divine right of kings was considered as the only principle, which could be opposed to the claims of the papal throne; and as the only means, which could preserve the civil, from being swallowed by the ecclesiastical powers.

This conjecture receives a degree of probability from a fact, which is mentioned in the history of France.

In a general assembly of the states of the kingdom, it was proposed to canonize this position — "that kings derive their authority immediately from God." That such a proposition was made in an assembly of the

[j] K. Prus. works. v. 6. p. 48. 50.   [k] Id. p. 83. 84.

states, the most popular body known in the kingdom, will, no doubt, occasion surprise. This surprise will be increased, when it is mentioned, that the proposition was patronized by the most popular part of that assembly: it was the third estate, which wished to pass it into a law. But every thing is naturally and easily accounted for, when it is mentioned further, that the principal object, which the third estate had in view by this measure, was to secure the sovereign authority from the detestable maxims of those, who made it depend upon the pope, by giving him a power of absolving subjects from their oath of allegiance, and authorizing those who assassinated their princes as hereticks.[1]

The proposal did not pass into a law; because, among other reasons, the question was thought proper for the determination of the schools. But this much may safely be inferred, that what was thought proper by the third estate to be passed into a law, would be generally received through the kingdom, as popular and wholesome doctrine.

I confess myself pleased with indulging the conjecture I have mentioned.

When I entered upon the disquisition of the doctrine of a superiour as necessary to the very definition of law; I said, that, if I was not mistaken, this notion of superiority contained the germ of the divine right of princes to rule, and of the corresponding obligation on the people implicitly to obey. It may now be seen whether or not I have been mistaken; and, if I have not been mistaken, it appears, how important it is, carefully and patiently to examine a first principle; to trace it, with attention, to its highest origin; and to pursue it, with perseverance, to its most remote consequences. I have observed this conduct with regard to the principle in question. The result, I think, has been, that, as to human laws, the notion of a superiour is a notion unnecessary, unfounded, and dangerous; a notion inconsistent with the genuine system of human authority.

Now that the will of a superiour is discarded, as an improper principle of obligation in human laws, it is natural to ask — What principle shall be introduced in its place? In its place I introduce — the consent of those whose obedience the law requires. This I conceive to be the true origin of the obligation of human laws. This principle I shall view on all its sides; I shall examine it historically and legally; I shall consider it as a question of theory, and as a question of fact.

Let us ascend to the first ages of societies. Customs, for a long time, were the only laws known among them. The Lycians[m] had no written laws; they were governed entirely by customs. Among the ancient Britons also, no written laws were known: they were ruled by the tra-

[1] Puff. 656. n.   [m] 1. Gog. Or. Laws. 8.

ditionary — and if traditionary, probably, the customary — laws of the Druids.

Now custom is, of itself, intrinsick evidence of consent. How was a custom introduced? By voluntary adoption. How did it become general? By the instances of voluntary adoption being increased. How did it become lasting? By voluntary and satisfactory experience, which ratified and confirmed what voluntary adoption had introduced. In the introduction, in the extension, in the continuance of customary law, we find the operations of consent universally predominant.

"Customs," in the striking and picturesque language of my Lord Bacon, "are laws written in living tables." [n] In regulations of justice and of government, they have been more effectual than the best written laws. The Romans, in their happy periods of liberty, paid great regard to customary law. Let me mention, in one word, every thing that can enforce my sentiments: the common law of England is a customary law.

Among the earliest, among the freest, among the most improved nations of the world, we find a species of law prevailing, which carried, in its bosom, internal evidence of consent. History, therefore, bears a strong and a uniform testimony in favour of this species of law.

Let us consult the sentiments[o] as well as the history of the ancients. I find a charge against them on this subject — "that they were not accurate enough in their expressions; because they frequently applied to laws the name of *common agreements*." [p] This, it is acknowledged, they do almost every where in their writings. He, however, who accuses the ancient writers of inaccuracy in expression, ought himself to be consummately accurate. "Let those teach others, who themselves excel." Whether the Baron Puffendorff was entitled to be a teacher in this particular, we stay not to examine. It is of more consequence to attend to the ground of his accusation.

One reason, why he urges their expressions to be inaccurate, is, that "neither the divine positive laws, nor the laws of nature had their rise from the agreement of men." All this is, at once, admitted; but the present disquisition relates only to laws that are human. What is said with regard to them? With regard to them it is said, that "the Grecians,

[n] 4. Ld. Bac. 5.
[o] Mens, et animus, et consilium, et sententia civitatis posita est in legibus. Ut corpora nostra sine mente; sic civitas sine lege, suis partibus, ut nervis, ac sanguine, et membris, uti non potest. Legum ministri, magistratus; legum interpretes, judices: legum denique idcirco omnes servi sumus, ut liberi esse possimus. [The mind, the soul, the wisdom, and the judgment of the state rests in the laws. Just as we cannot use our bodies without the mind, so that state, without the law, cannot use its own parts, as though they were nerves, blood, and limbs. The laws' administrators are the magistrates; their interpreters the judges; we are all the laws' slaves, so that we may be free.] Cicero pro Cluen. c. 53.
[p] Puff. 59. b. 1. c. 6. s. 7.

as in their other politick speeches, so in this too, had an eye to their own democratical governments; in which, because the laws were made upon the proposal of the magistrate, with the knowledge, and by the command, of the people, and so, as it were, in the way of bargain and stipulation; they gave them the name of covenants and agreements."

I am now unsolicitous to repel the accusation: it seems, it was conceived to arise from a reference, by the ancients, to their democratical governments. Let them be called covenants, or agreements, or bargains, or stipulations, or any thing similar to any of those, still I am satisfied; for still every thing mentioned, and every thing similar to every thing mentioned, imports consent. Here history and law combine their evidence in support of consent.

Law has been denominated "a general convention of the citizens:" such is the definition of it in the Digest: for the Roman law was not, in every age of Rome, the law of slavery. A similar mode of expression has been long used in England. Magna Charta was made "by the common assent of all the realm." [q]

Let us listen to the judicious and excellent Hooker: what he says always conveys instruction. "The lawful power of making laws to command whole politick societies of men, belongeth so properly unto the same entire societies, that for any prince or potentate of what kind soever upon earth, to exercise the same of himself, and not either by express commission immediately and personally received from God, or else by authority derived, at the first, from their consent, upon whose persons they impose laws, it is no better than mere tyranny. Laws they are not, therefore, which publick approbation hath not made so." [r] "Laws human, of what kind soever, are available by consent." [s]

My Lord Shaftesbury, who formed his taste and judgment upon ancient writers and ancient opinions, delivers it as his sentiment, "That no people in a civil state can possibly be free, when they are otherwise governed, than by such laws as they themselves have constituted, or to which they have freely given consent." [t]

This subject will receive peculiar illustration and importance, when we come to consider the description and characters of municipal law. I will not anticipate here what will be introduced there with much greater propriety and force.

Of law there are different kinds. All, however, may be arranged in two different classes. 1. Divine. 2. Human laws. The descriptive epithets employed denote, that the former have God, the latter, man, for their author.

The laws of God may be divided into the following species.

I. That law, the book of which we are neither able nor worthy to

[q] Sulliv. Pref. 18.   [r] Hooker. b. 1. s. 10. p. 19.   [s] Id. p. 20.
[t] 3. Shaf. 312.

open. Of this law, the author and observer is God. He is a law to himself, as well as to all created things. This law we may name the "law eternal."

II. That law, which is made for angels and the spirits of the just made perfect. This may be called the "law celestial." This law, and the glorious state for which it is adapted, we see, at present, but darkly and as through a glass: but hereafter we shall see even as we are seen; and shall know even as we are known. From the wisdom and the goodness of the adorable Author and Preserver of the universe, we are justified in concluding, that the celestial and perfect state is governed, as all other things are, by his established laws. What those laws are, it is not yet given us to know; but on one truth we may rely with sure and certain confidence — those laws are wise and good. For another truth we have infallible authority — those laws are strictly obeyed: "In heaven his will is done."

III. That law, by which the irrational and inanimate parts of the creation are governed. The great Creator of all things has established general and fixed rules, according to which all the phenomena of the material universe are produced and regulated. These rules are usually denominated laws of nature. The science, which has those laws for its object, is distinguished by the name of natural philosophy. It is sometimes called, the philosophy of body. Of this science, there are numerous branches.

IV. That law, which God has made for man in his present state; that law, which is communicated to us by reason and conscience, the divine monitors within us, and by the sacred oracles, the divine monitors without us. This law has undergone several subdivisions, and has been known by distinct appellations, according to the different ways in which it has been promulgated, and the different objects which it respects.

As promulgated by reason and the moral sense, it has been called natural; as promulgated by the holy scriptures, it has been called revealed law.

As addressed to men, it has been denominated the law of nature; as addressed to political societies, it has been denominated the law of nations.

But it should always be remembered, that this law, natural or revealed, made for men or for nations, flows from the same divine source: it is the law of God.

Nature, or, to speak more properly, the Author of nature, has done much for us; but it is his gracious appointment and will, that we should also do much for ourselves. What we do, indeed, must be founded on what he has done; and the deficiencies of our laws must be supplied by the perfections of his. Human law must rest its authority, ultimately, upon the authority of that law, which is divine.

Of that law, the following are maxims — that no injury should be done — that a lawful engagement, voluntarily made, should be faithfully fulfilled. We now see the deep and the solid foundations of human law.

It is of two species. 1. That which a political society makes for itself. This is municipal law. 2. That which two or more political societies make for themselves. This is the voluntary law of nations.

In all these species of law — the law eternal — the law celestial — the law natural — the divine law, as it respects men and nations—the human law, as it also respects men and nations — man is deeply and intimately concerned. Of all these species of law, therefore, the knowledge must be most important to man.

Those parts of natural philosophy, which more immediately relate to the human body, are appropriated to the profession of physick.

The law eternal, the law celestial, and the law divine, as they are disclosed by that revelation, which has brought life and immortality to light, are the more peculiar objects of the profession of divinity.

The law of nature, the law of nations, and the municipal law form the objects of the profession of law.

From this short, but plain and, I hope, just statement of things, we perceive a principle of connexion between all the learned professions; but especially between the two last mentioned. Far from being rivals or enemies, religion and law are twin sisters, friends, and mutual assistants. Indeed, these two sciences run into each other. The divine law, as discovered by reason and the moral sense, forms an essential part of both.

From this statement of things, we also perceive how important and dignified the profession of the law is, when traced to its sources, and viewed in its just extent.

The immediate objects of our attention are, the law of nature, the law of nations, and the municipal law of the United States, and of the several states which compose the Union. It will not be forgotten, that the constitutions of the United States, and of the individual states, form a capital part of their municipal law. On the two first of these three great heads, I shall be very general. On the last, especially on those parts of it, which comprehend the constitutions and publick law, I shall be more particular and minute.

III

OF THE LAW OF NATURE

IN every period of our existence, in every situation, in which we can be placed, much is to be known, much is to be done, much is to be enjoyed. But all that is to be known, all that is to be done, all that is to be enjoyed, depends upon the proper exertion and direction of our numerous powers. In this immense ocean of intelligence and action, are we left without a compass and without a chart? Is there no pole star, by which we may regulate our course? Has the all-gracious and all-wise Author of our existence formed us for such great and such good ends; and has he left us without a conductor to lead us in the way, by which those ends may be attained? Has he made us capable of observing a rule, and has he furnished us with no rule, which we ought to observe? Let us examine these questions — for they are important ones — with patience and with attention. Our labours will, in all probability, be amply repaid. We shall probably find that, to direct the more important parts of our conduct, the bountiful Governour of the universe has been graciously pleased to provide us with a law; and that, to direct the less important parts of it, he has made us capable of providing a law for ourselves.

That our Creator has a supreme right to prescribe a law for our conduct, and that we are under the most perfect obligation to obey that law, are truths established on the clearest and most solid principles.

In the course of our remarks on that part of Sir William Blackstone's definition of law, which includes the idea of a superiour as essential to it, we remarked, with particular care, that it was only with regard to human laws that we controverted the justness or propriety of that idea. It was incumbent on us to mark this distinction particularly; for with regard to laws which are divine, they truly come from a superiour — from Him who is supreme.

Between beings, who, in their nature, powers, and situation, are so perfectly equal, that nothing can be ascribed to one, which is not applicable to the other, there can be neither superiority nor dependence. With regard to such beings, no reason can be assigned, why any one should assume authority over others, which may not, with equal propriety, be assigned, why each of those others should assume authority over that one.

To constitute superiority and dependence, there must be an essential difference of qualities, on which those relations may be founded.[a]

Some allege, that the sole superiority of strength, or, as they express it, an irresistible power, is the true foundation of the right of prescribing laws. "This superiority of power gives," say they, "a right of reigning, by the impossibility, in which it places others, of resisting him, who has so great an advantage over them." [b]

Others derive the right of prescribing laws and imposing obligations from superiour excellence of nature. "This," say they, "not only renders a being independent of those, who are of a nature inferiour to it; but leads us to believe, that the latter were made for the sake of the former." For a proof of this, they appeal to the constitution of man. "Here," they tell us, "the soul governs, as being the noblest part." "On the same foundation," they add, "the empire of man over the brute creation is built." [c]

Others, again, say, that "properly speaking, there is only one general source of superiority and obligation. God is our creator: in him we live, and move, and have our being: from him we have received our intellectual and our moral powers: he, as master of his own work, can prescribe to it whatever rules to him shall seem meet. Hence our dependence on our Creator: hence his absolute power over us. This is the true source of all authority." [d]

With regard to the first hypothesis, it is totally insufficient; nay, it is absolutely false. Because I cannot resist, am I obliged to obey? Because another is possessed of superiour force, am I bound to acknowledge his will as the rule of my conduct? Every obligation supposes motives that influence the conscience and determine the will, so that we should think it wrong not to obey, even if resistance was in our power. But a person, who alleges only the law of the strongest, proposes no motive to influence the conscience, or to determine the will. Superiour force may reside with predominant malevolence. Has force, exerted for the purposes of malevolence, a right to command? Can it impose an obligation to obey? No. Resistance to such force is a right; and, if resistance can prove effectual, it is a duty also. On some occasions, all our efforts may, indeed, be useless; and an attempt to resist would frustrate its own aim: but, on such occasions, the exercise of resistance only is suspended; the right of resistance is not extinguished: we may continue, for a time, under a constraint; but we come not under an obligation: we may suffer all the external effects of superiour force; but we feel not the internal influence of superiour authority.[e]

The second hypothesis has in it something plausible; but, on examination, it will not be found to be accurate. Wherever a being of superiour

[a] 1. Burl. 82.   [b] 1. Burl. 83.   [c] Id. 83.   [d] Id. 83. 87.
[e] 1. Burl. 85. 86.

excellence is found, his excellence, as well as every other truth, ought, on proper occasions, to be acknowledged; we will go farther; it ought, as every thing excellent ought, to be esteemed. But must we go farther still? Is obedience the necessary consequence of honest acknowledgment and just esteem? Here we must make a pause: we must make some inquiries before we go forward. In what manner is this being of superiour excellence connected with us? What are his dispositions with regard to us? By what effects, if by any, will his superiour excellence be displayed? Will it be exerted for our happiness; or, as to us, will it not be exerted at all? We acknowledge — we esteem excellence; but till these questions are answered, we feel not ourselves under an obligation to obey it.[f] If the opinion of Epicurus concerning his divinities — that they were absolutely indifferent to the happiness and interests of men — was admitted for a moment;[g] the inference would unquestionably be — that they were not entitled to human obedience.

The third hypothesis contains a solemn truth, which ought to be examined with reverence and awe. It resolves the supreme right of prescribing laws for our conduct, and our indispensable duty of obeying those laws, into the omnipotence of the Divinity. This omnipotence let us humbly adore. Were we to suppose — but the supposition cannot be made — that infinite goodness could be disjoined from almighty power — but we cannot — must not proceed to the inference. No, it never can be drawn; for from almighty power infinite goodness can never be disjoined.

Let us join, in our weak conceptions, what are inseparable in their incomprehensible Archetype — infinite power — infinite wisdom — infinite goodness; and then we shall see, in its resplendent glory, the supreme right to rule: we shall feel the conscious sense of the perfect obligation to obey.

His infinite power enforces his laws, and carries them into full and effectual execution. His infinite wisdom knows and chooses the fittest means for accomplishing the ends which he proposes. His infinite goodness proposes such ends only as promote our felicity. By his power, he is able to remove whatever may possibly injure us, and to provide whatever is conducive to our happiness. By his wisdom, he knows our nature, our faculties, and our interests: he cannot be mistaken in the designs, which he proposes, nor in the means, which he employs to accomplish

[f] 1. Burl. 86. 87.

[g] Epicurus re tollit, oratione relinquit deos. Deinde, si maxime talis est deus, ut nulla gratia, nulla hominum caritate teneatur: valeat. Quid enim dicam, propitius sit? [Epicurus in fact takes away the gods, though he professes to leave them. In fine, if god is precisely such as is held by no sense of gratitude, by no love of mankind, then goodbye to him! for why should I say "may he be gracious toward me?"] Cic. de Nat. Deo. l. 1. c. 44.

them. By his goodness, he proposes our happiness: and to that end directs the operations of his power and wisdom. Indeed, to his goodness alone we may trace the principle of his laws. Being infinitely and eternally happy in himself, his goodness alone could move him to create us, and give us the means of happiness. The same principle, that moved his creating, moves his governing power. The rule of his government we shall find to be reduced to this one paternal command — Let man pursue his own perfection and happiness.

What an enrapturing view of the moral government of the universe! Over all, goodness infinite reigns, guided by unerring wisdom, and supported by almighty power. What an instructive lesson to those who think, and are encouraged by their flatterers to think, that a portion of divine right is communicated to their rule. If this really was the case; their power ought to be subservient to their goodness, and their goodness should be employed in promoting the happiness of those, who are intrusted to their care. But princes, and the flatterers of princes, are guilty, in two respects, of the grossest errour and presumption. They claim to govern by divine institution and right. The principles of their government are repugnant to the principles of that government, which is divine. The principle of the divine government is goodness: they plume themselves with the gaudy insignia of power.

Well might nature's poet say —

> ———————— Could great men thunder,
> As Jove himself does, Jove would ne'er be quiet;
> For every pelting, petty officer
> Would use his heaven for thunder;
> Nothing but thunder. Merciful heaven!
> Thou rather with thy sharp and sulphurous bolt
> Split'st the unwedgeable and gnarled oak,
> Than the soft myrtle: O, but man, proud man,
> Dressed in a little brief authority,
> Most ignorant of what he's most assured,
> His glassy substance; like an angry ape,
> Plays such fantastick tricks before high heaven,
> As make the angels weep.
>
> *Shak. Meas. for Meas. Act II.*

Where a supreme right to give laws exists, on one side, and a perfect obligation to obey them exists, on the other side; this relation, of itself, suggests the probability that laws will be made.

When we view the inanimate and irrational creation around and above us, and contemplate the beautiful order observed in all its motions and appearances; is not the supposition unnatural and improbable — that the rational and moral world should be abandoned to the frolicks of chance, or to the ravage of disorder? What would be the fate of man and of society, was every one at full liberty to do as he listed, without any fixed rule or principle of conduct, without a helm to steer him — a sport of the fierce gusts of passion, and the fluctuating billows of caprice?

To be without law is not agreeable to our nature; because, if we were without law, we should find many of our talents and powers hanging upon us like useless incumbrances. Why should we be illuminated by reason, were we only made to obey the impulse of irrational instinct? Why should we have the power of deliberating, and of balancing our determinations, if we were made to yield implicitly and unavoidably to the influence of the first impressions? Of what service to us would reflection be, if, after reflection, we were to be carried away irresistibly by the force of blind and impetuous appetites?

Without laws, what would be the state of society? The more ingenious and artful the twolegged animal, man, is, the more dangerous he would become to his equals: his ingenuity would degenerate into cunning; and his art would be employed for the purposes of malice. He would be deprived of all the benefits and pleasures of peaceful and social life: he would become a prey to all the distractions of licentiousness and war.

Is it probable — we repeat the question — is it probable that the Creator, infinitely wise and good, would leave his moral world in this chaos and disorder?

If we enter into ourselves, and view with attention what passes in our own breasts, we shall find, that what, at first, appeared probable, is proved, on closer examination, to be certain; we shall find, that God has not left himself without a witness, nor us without a guide.

We have already observed, that, concerning the nature and cause of obligation, many different opinions have been entertained, and much ingenious disputation has been held, by philosophers and writers on jurisprudence. It will not be improper to take a summary view of those opinions.

Some philosophers maintain, that all obligation arises from the relations of things[h]; from a certain proportion or disproportion, a certain fitness or unfitness, between objects and actions, which give a beauty to some, and a deformity to others. They say, that the rules of morality are founded on the nature of things; and are agreeable to the order necessary for the beauty of the universe.[i]

Others allege, that every rule whatever of human actions carries with it a moral necessity of conforming to it; and consequently produces a sort of obligation. Every rule, say they, implies a design, and the will of attaining a certain end. He, therefore, who proposes a particular end,

[h] 1. Ruth. 9.   [i] Gro. 10.

and knows the rule by which alone he can accomplish it, finds himself under a moral necessity of observing that rule. If he did not observe it, he would act a contradictory part; he would propose the end, and neglect the only means, by which he could obtain it. There is a reasonable necessity, therefore, to prefer one manner of acting before another; and every reasonable man finds himself engaged to this, and prevented from acting in a contrary manner. In other words, he is obliged: for obligation is nothing more than a restriction of liberty produced by reason. Reason, then, independent of law, is sufficient to impose *some* obligation on man, and to establish a system of morality and duty.[j]

But, according to others, the idea of obligation necessarily implies a being, who obliges, and must be distinct from him, who is obliged. If the person, on whom the obligation is imposed, is the same as he who imposes it; he can disengage himself from it whenever he pleases: or, rather, there is no obligation. Obligation and duty depend on the intervention of a superiour, whose will is manifested by law. If we abstract from all law, and consequently from a legislator; we shall have no such thing as right, obligation, duty, or morality.[k]

Others, again, think it necessary to join the last two principles together, in order to render the obligation perfect.[l] Reason, say they, is the first rule of man, the first principle of morality, and the immediate cause of all primitive obligation. But man being necessarily dependent on his Creator, who has formed him with wisdom and design, and who, in creating him, has proposed some particular ends; the will of God is another rule of human actions, another principle of morality, obligation, and duty. On this distinction, the kinds of obligation, external and internal, are founded. These two principles must be united, in order to form a complete system of morality, really founded on the nature and state of man. As a rational being, he is subject to reason: as a creature of God, to his supreme will. Thus, reason and the divine will are perfectly reconciled, are naturally connected, and are strengthened by their junction.[m]

The cause of obligation is laid, by some philosophers, in utility.[n] Actions, they tell us, are to be estimated by their tendency to promote happiness. Whatever is expedient, is right. It is the utility, alone, of any moral rule, which constitutes its obligation.

Congenial with this principle, is another, which has received the sanction of some writers — that sociability, or the care of maintaining society properly, is the fountain of obligation and right: for to every right, there must be a corresponding obligation. From this principle the inference is

[j] Hein. 63. 1. Burl. 207. 210. 212. Puff. 17. b. 1. c. 2. s. 6.
[k] 1. Burl. 210. 212. 202. Hein. 10.   [l] 1. Ruth. 9.   [m] 1. Burl. 214. 216. 219. 220.
[n] 1. Paley 82. Hein. 51.

drawn, that every one is born, not for himself alone, but for the whole human kind.[o]

Further — many philosophers derive our obligation to observe the law of nature from instinctive affections, or an innate moral sense.[p] This is the sense, they tell us, by which we perceive the qualities of right and wrong, and the other moral qualities in actions.

With regard, then, both to the meaning and the cause of obligation, much diversity of sentiment, much ambiguity, and much obscurity have, it appears, prevailed. It is a subject of inquiry, however, that well deserves to be investigated, explained, illustrated, and placed in its native splendour and dignity. In order to do this, it will be proper to ascertain the precise state of the question before us. It is this — what is the efficient cause of moral obligation — of the eminent distinction between right and wrong? This has been often and injudiciously blended with another question, connected indeed with it, but from which it ought to be preserved separate and distinct. That other question is — how shall we, in particular instances, learn the dictates of our duty, and make, with accuracy, the eminent distinction, which we have just now mentioned? The first question points to the *principle* of obligation: the second points to the *means* by which our obligation to perform a specified action, or a series of specified actions, may be deduced. The first has been called by philosophers — principium essendi — the principle of existence; the principle which *constitutes* obligation. The second has been called by them — principium cognoscendi — the principle of knowing it; the principle by which it may be *proved* or *perceived*. In a commonwealth, the distinction between these two questions is familiar and easy. If the question is put — what is the efficient cause of the obligation upon the citizens to obey the laws of the state? — the answer is ready — the will of those, by whose authority the laws are made. If the other question is put — how shall we, in a particular instance, or in a series of particular instances, ascertain the laws, which the citizens ought to obey? — reference is immediately made to the code of laws.

Having thus stated the question — what is the efficient cause of moral obligation? — I give it this answer — the will of God. This is the supreme law.[q] His just and full right of imposing laws, and our duty in obeying them, are the sources of our moral obligations. If I am asked — why do you obey the will of God? I answer — because it is my duty so to do. If I am asked again — how do you know this to be your duty? I answer again — because I am told so by my moral sense or conscience. If I am

---

[o] Hein. 50. Gro. Prel. 17. Puff. 139. b. 2. c. 3. s. 15.   [p] 1. Ruth. 9.

[q] Principem legem illam et ultimam, mentem esse dicebant, omnia ratione aut cogentis, aut vetantis dei. [That first and final law, they used to say, is the mind of God, who forces or prohibits everything by reason.] Cic. de leg. l. 2. c. 4.

asked a third time — how do you know that you ought to do that, of which your conscience enjoins the performance? I can only say, I *feel* that such is my duty. Here investigation must stop; reasoning can go no farther. The science of morals, as well as other sciences, is founded on truths, that cannot be discovered or proved by reasoning. Reason is confined to the investigation of unknown truths by the means of such as are known. We cannot, therefore, begin to reason, till we are furnished, otherwise than by reason, with some truths, on which we can found our arguments. Even in mathematicks, we must be provided with axioms perceived intuitively to be true, before our demonstrations can commence. Morality, like mathematicks, has its intuitive truths, without which we cannot make a single step in our reasonings upon the subject.[r] Such an intuitive truth is that, with which we just now closed our investigation. If a person was not possessed of the feeling before mentioned; it would not be in the power of arguments, to give him any conception of the distinction between right and wrong. These terms would be to him equally unintelligible, as the term *colour* to one who was born and has continued blind. But that there is, in human nature, such a moral principle, has been felt and acknowledged in all ages and nations.

Now that we have stated and answered the first question; let us proceed to the consideration of the second — how shall we, in particular instances, learn the dictates of our duty, and make, with accuracy, the proper distinction between right and wrong; in other words, how shall we, in particular cases, discover the will of God? We discover it by our conscience, by our reason, and by the Holy Scriptures. The law of nature and the law of revelation are both divine: they flow, though in different channels, from the same adorable source. It is, indeed, preposterous to separate them from each other. The object of both is — to discover the will of God — and both are necessary for the accomplishment of that end.

I. The power of moral perception is, indeed, a most important part of our constitution. It is an original power — a power of its own kind; and totally distinct from the ideas of utility and agreeableness. By that power, we have conceptions of merit and demerit, of duty and moral obligation. By that power, we perceive some things in human conduct to be right, and others to be wrong. We have the same reason to rely on the dictates of this faculty, as upon the determinations of our senses, or of our other

[r] Quæ est gens, aut quod genus hominum, quod non habeat sine doctrina anticipationem quandam, id est, anticeptam animo rei quandam informationem, sine qua nec intelligi quidquam, nec quæri, nec disputari potest. [What nation, what species if man is there which does not have, without teaching, some sort of foreknowledge, that is, a certain image of the thing conceived beforehand by the mind, without which nothing can be understood, investigated or discussed?] Cic. de nat. Deor. l. 1. c. 16.

natural powers. When an action is represented to us, flowing from love, humanity, gratitude, an ultimate desire of the good of others; though it happened in a country far distant, or in an age long past, we admire the lovely exhibition, and praise its author. The contrary conduct, when represented to us, raises our abhorrence and aversion. But whence this secret chain betwixt each person and mankind? If there is no moral sense, which makes benevolence appear beautiful; if all approbation be from the interest of the approver; "What's Hecuba to us, or we to Hecuba?" [s]

The mind, which reflects on itself, and is a spectator of other minds, sees and feels the soft and the harsh, the agreeable and the disagreeable, the foul and the fair, the harmonious and the dissonant, as really and truly in the affections and actions, as in any musical numbers, or the outward forms or representations of sensible things. It cannot withhold its approbation or aversion in what relates to the former, any more than in what relates to the latter, of those subjects. To deny the sense of a sublime and beautiful and of their contraries in actions and things, will appear an affectation merely to one who duly considers and traces the subject. Even he who indulges this affectation cannot avoid the discovery of those very sentiments, which he pretends not to feel. A Lucretius or a Hobbes cannot discard the sentiments of praise and admiration respecting some moral forms, nor the sentiments of censure and detestation concerning others. Has a man gratitude, or resentment, or pride, or shame? If he has and avows it; he must have and acknowledge a sense of something benevolent, of something unjust, of something worthy, and of something mean. Thus, so long as we find men pleased or angry, proud or ashamed; we may appeal to the reality of the moral sense. A right and a wrong, an honourable and a dishonourable is plainly conceived. About these there may be mistakes; but this destroys not the inference, that the things are, and are universally acknowledged — that they are of nature's impression, and by no art can be obliterated.

This sense or apprehension of right and wrong appears early, and exists in different degrees. The qualities of love, gratitude, sympathy unfold themselves, in the first stages of life, and the approbation of those qualities accompanies the first dawn of reflection. Young people, who think the least about the distant influences of actions, are, more than others, moved with moral forms. Hence that strong inclination in children to hear such stories as paint the characters and fortunes of men. Hence that joy in the prosperity of the kind and faithful, and that sorrow upon the success of the treacherous and cruel, with which we often see infant minds strongly agitated.

There is a natural beauty in figures; and is there not a beauty as natural in actions? When the eye opens upon forms, and the ear to sounds; the

[s] Hamlet.

beautiful is seen, and harmony is heard and acknowledged. When actions are viewed and affections are discerned, the inward eye distinguishes the beautiful, the amiable, the admirable, from the despicable, the odious, and the deformed. How is it possible not to own, that as these distinctions have their foundation in nature, so this power of discerning them is natural also?

The universality of an opinion or sentiment may be evinced by the structure of languages. Languages were not invented by philosophers, to countenance or support any artificial system. They were contrived by men in general, to express common sentiments and perceptions. The inference is satisfactory, that where all languages make a distinction, there must be a similar distinction in universal opinion or sentiment. For language is the picture of human thoughts; and, from this faithful picture, we may draw certain conclusions concerning the original. Now, a universal effect must have a universal cause. No universal cause can, with propriety, be assigned for this universal opinion, except that intuitive perception of things, which is distinguished by the name of common sense.

All languages speak of a beautiful and a deformed, a right and a wrong, an agreeable and disagreeable, a good and ill, in actions, affections, and characters. All languages, therefore, suppose a moral sense, by which those qualities are perceived and distinguished.

The whole circle of the arts of imitation proves the reality of the moral sense. They suppose, in human conduct, a sublimity, a beauty, a greatness, an excellence, independent of advantage or disadvantage, profit or loss. On him, whose heart is indelicate or hard; on him, who has no admiration of what is truly noble; on him, who has no sympathetick sense of what is melting and tender, the highest beauty of the mimick arts must make indeed, but a very faint and transient impression. If we were void of a relish for moral excellence, how frigid and uninteresting would the finest descriptions of life and manners appear! How indifferent are the finest strains of harmony, to him who has not a musical ear!

The force of the moral sense is diffused through every part of life. The luxury of the table derives its principal charms from some mixture of moral enjoyments, from communicating pleasures, and from sentiments honourable and just as well as elegant — "The feast of reason, and the flow of soul."

The chief pleasures of history, and poetry, and eloquence, and musick, and sculpture, and painting are derived from the same source. Beside the pleasures they afford by imitation, they receive a stronger charm from something moral insinuated into the performances. The principal beauties of behaviour, and even of countenance, arise from the indication of affections or qualities morally estimable.

Never was there any of the human species above the condition of an idiot, to whom all actions appeared indifferent. All feel that a certain temper, certain affections, and certain actions produce a sentiment of approbation; and that a sentiment of disapprobation is produced by the contrary temper, affections, and actions.

This power is capable of culture and improvement by habit, and by frequent and extensive exercise. A high sense of moral excellence is approved above all other intellectual talents. This high sense of excellence is accompanied with a strong desire after it, and a keen relish for it. This desire and this relish are approved as the most amiable affections, and the highest virtues.

This moral sense, from its very nature, is intended to regulate and control all our other powers. It governs our passions as well as our actions. Other principles may solicit and allure; but the conscience assumes authority, it must be obeyed. Of this dignity and commanding nature we are immediately conscious, as we are of the power itself. It estimates what it enjoins, not merely as superiour in degree, but as superiour likewise in kind, to what is recommended by our other perceptive powers. Without this controlling faculty, endowed as we are with such a variety of senses and interfering desires, we should appear a fabrick destitute of order: but possessed of it, all our powers may be harmonious and consistent; they may all combine in one uniform and regular direction.

In short; if we had not the faculty of perceiving certain things in conduct to be right, and others to be wrong; and of perceiving our obligation to do what is right, and not to do what is wrong; we should not be moral and accountable beings.

If we be, as, I hope, I have shown we are, endowed with this faculty; there must be some things, which are immediately discerned by it to be right, and others to be wrong. There must, consequently, be in morals, as in other sciences, first principles, which derive not their evidence from any antecedent principles, but which may be said to be intuitively discerned.

Moral truths may be divided into two classes; such as are selfevident, and such as, from the selfevident ones, are deduced by reasoning. If the first be not discerned without reasoning, reasoning can never discern the last. The cases that require reasoning are few, compared with those that require none; and a man may be very honest and virtuous, who cannot reason, and who knows not what demonstration means.

If the rules of virtue were left to be discovered by reasoning, even by demonstrative reasoning, unhappy would be the condition of the far greater part of men, who have not the means of cultivating the power of reasoning to any high degree. As virtue is the business of all men, the first principles of it are written on their hearts, in characters so legible,

that no man can pretend ignorance of them, or of his obligation to practise them. Reason, even with experience, is too often overpowered by passion; to restrain whose impetuosity, nothing less is requisite than the
vigorous and commanding principle of duty.

II. The first principles of morals, into which all moral argumentation
may be resolved, are discovered in a manner more analogous to the perceptions of sense than to the conclusions of reasoning. In morality, however, as well as in other sciences, reason is usefully introduced, and performs many important services. In many instances she regulates our
belief; and in many instances she regulates our conduct. She determines
the proper means to any end; and she decides the preference of one
end over another. She may exhibit an object to the mind, though the
perception which the mind has, when once the object is exhibited, may
properly belong to a sense. She may be necessary to ascertain the circumstances and determine the motives to an action; though it be the
moral sense that perceives the action to be either virtuous or vicious,
after its motive and its circumstances have been discovered. She discerns
the tendencies of the several senses, affections, and actions, and the comparative value of objects and gratifications. She judges concerning subordinate ends; but concerning ultimate ends she is not employed. These
we prosecute by some immediate determination of the mind, which, in
the order of action, is prior to all reasoning; for no opinion or judgment
can move to action, where there is not a previous desire of some end. —
This power of comparing the several enjoyments, of which our nature
is susceptible, in order to discover which are most important to our happiness, is of the highest consequence and necessity to corroborate our
moral faculty, and to preserve our affections in just rank and regular
order.

A magistrate knows that it is his duty to promote the good of the
commonwealth, which has intrusted him with authority. But whether one
particular plan or another particular plan of conduct in office, may best
promote the good of the commonwealth, may, in many cases, be doubtful. His conscience or moral sense determines the end, which he ought
to pursue; and he has intuitive evidence that his end is good: but the
means of attaining this end must be determined by reason. To select and
ascertain those means, is often a matter of very considerable difficulty.
Doubts may arise; opposite interests may occur; and a preference must be
given to one side from a small over-balance, and from very nice views.
This is particularly the case in questions with regard to justice. If
every single instance of justice, like every single instance of benevolence,
were pleasing and useful to society, the case would be more simple, and
would be seldom liable to great controversy. But as single instances of
justice are often pernicious in their first and immediate tendency; and as

the advantage to society results only from the observance of the general rule, and from the concurrence and combination of several persons in the same equitable conduct; the case here becomes more intricate and involved. The various circumstances of society, the various consequences of any practice, the various interests which may be proposed, are all, on many occasions, doubtful, and subject to much discussion and inquiry. The design of municipal law (for let us still, from every direction, open a view to our principal object) the design of municipal law is to fix all the questions which regard justice. A very accurate reason or judgment is often requisite, to give the true determination amidst intricate doubts, arising from obscure or opposite utilities.

Thus, though good and ill, right and wrong are ultimately perceived by the moral sense, yet reason assists its operations, and, in many instances, strengthens and extends its influence. We may argue concerning propriety of conduct: just reasonings on the subject will establish principles for judging of what deserves praise: but, at the same time, these reasonings must always, in the last resort, appeal to the moral sense.

Farther; reason serves to illustrate, to prove, to extend, to apply what our moral sense has already suggested to us, concerning just and unjust, proper and improper, right and wrong. A father feels that paternal tenderness is refined and confirmed, by reflecting how consonant that feeling is to the relation between a parent and his child; how conducive it is to the happiness, not only of a single family, but, in its extension, to that of all mankind. We feel the beauty and excellence of virtue; but this sense is strengthened and improved by the lessons, which reason gives us concerning the foundations, the motives, the relations, the particular and the universal advantages flowing from this virtue, which, at first sight, appeared so beautiful.

Taste is a faculty, common, in some degree, to all men. But study, attention, comparison operate most powerfully towards its refinement. In the same manner, reason contributes to ascertain the exactness, and to discover and correct the mistakes, of the moral sense. A prejudice of education may be misapprehended for a determination of morality. 'Tis reason's province to compare and discriminate.

Reason performs an excellent service to the moral sense in another respect. It considers the relations of actions, and traces them to the remotest consequences. We often see men, with the most honest hearts and most pure intentions, embarrassed and puzzled, when a case, delicate and complicated, comes before them. They feel what is right; they are unshaken in their general principles; but they are unaccustomed to pursue them through their different ramifications, to make the necessary distinctions and exceptions, or to modify them according to the circumstances of time and place. 'Tis the business of reason to discharge this

duty; and it will discharge it the better in proportion to the care which
has been employed in exercising and improving it.

The existence of the moral sense has been denied by some philosophers
of high fame: its authority has been attacked by others: the certainty
and uniformity of its decisions have been arraigned by a third class.[t] We
are told, that, without education, we should have been in a state of perfect indifference as to virtue and vice; that an education, opposite to that
which we have received, would have taught us to regard as virtue that
which we now dislike as vice, and to despise as vice that which we now
esteem as virtue. In support of these observations, it is farther said, that
moral sentiment is different in different countries, in different ages, and
under different forms of government and religion; in a word, that it is
as much the effect of custom, fashion, and artifice, as our taste in dress,
furniture, and the modes of conversation. Facts and narratives have been
assembled and accumulated, to evince the great diversity and even contrariety that subsists concerning moral opinions. And it has been gravely
asked, whether the wild boy, who was caught in the woods of Hanover,
would feel a sentiment of disapprobation upon being told of the conduct
of a parricide. An investigation of those facts and narratives cannot find
a place in these lectures; though the time bestowed on it might be well
employed. It may, however, be proper to observe, that it is but candid to
consider human nature in her improved, and not in her most rude or
depraved forms. "The good experienced man," says Aristotle, "is the last
measure of all things." [u] To ascertain moral principles, we appeal not to
the common sense of savages, but of men in their most perfect state.

Epicurus, as well as some modern advocates of the same philosophy,
seem to have taken their estimates of human nature from its meanest and
most degrading exhibitions; but the noblest and most respectable philosophers of antiquity have chosen, for a much wiser and better purpose,
to view it on the brightest and most advantageous side. "It is impossible,"
says the incomparable Addison,[v] "to read a passage in Plato or Tully,
and a thousand other ancient moralists, without being a greater and a
better man for it. On the contrary, I could never read some modish modern authors, without being, for some time, out of humour with myself,
and at every thing about me. Their business is to depreciate human nature, and consider it under its worst appearances. They give mean interpretation and base motives to the worthiest actions — in short, they endeavour to make no distinction between man and man, or between the
species of men and that of brutes." True it is, that some men and some
nations are savage and brutish; but is that a reason why their manners
and their practices should be generally and reproachfully charged to the

[t] 1. Paley 12 — 24. Kaims Pr. Eq. 8.   [u] 1. Hutch. 237. 121.
[v] Tatler No. 103.

account of human nature? It may, perhaps, be somewhat to our purpose to observe, that in many of these representations, the picture, if compared with the original, will be found to be overcharged. For, in truth, between mankind, considered even in their rudest state, and the *mutum et turpe pecus,* a very wide difference will be easily discovered. In the most uninformed savages, we find the *communes notitiae,* the common notions and practical principles of virtue, though the application of them is often extremely unnatural and absurd. These same savages have in them the seeds of the logician, the man of taste, the orator, the statesman, the man of virtue, and the saint. These seeds are planted in their minds by nature, though, for want of culture and exercise, they lie unnoticed, and are hardly perceived by themselves or by others. Besides, some nations that have been supposed stupid and barbarous by nature, have, upon fuller acquaintance with their history, been found to have been rendered barbarous and depraved by institution. When, by the power of some leading members, erroneous laws are once established, and it has become the interest of subordinate tyrants to support a corrupt system, errour and iniquity become sacred. Under such a system, the multitude are fettered by the prejudices of education, and awed by the dread of power, from the free exercise of their reason. These principles will account for the many absurd and execrable tenets and practices with regard to government, morals, and religion, which have been invented and established in opposition to the unbiassed sentiments, and in derogation of the natural rights of mankind. But, after making all the exceptions and abatements, of which these facts and narratives, if admitted in their fullest extent, would justify the claim, still it cannot be denied, but is even acknowledged, that some sorts of actions command and receive the esteem of mankind more than others; and that the approbation of them is general, though not universal. It will certainly be sufficient for our purpose to observe, that the dictates of reason are neither more general, nor more uniform, nor more certain, nor more commanding, than the dictates of the moral sense. Nay, farther; perhaps, upon inquiry, we shall find, that those obliquities, extravagancies, and inconsistencies of conduct, that are produced as proofs of the nonexistence or inutility of the moral sense, are, in fact, chargeable to that faculty, which is meant to be substituted in its place. We shall find that men always approve upon an opinion — true or false, but still an opinion — that the actions approved have the qualities and tendencies, which are the proper objects of approbation. They suppose that such actions will promote their own interest; or will be conducive to the publick good; or are required by the Deity; when, in truth, they have all the contrary properties — may be forbidden by the Deity, and may be detrimental both to publick and to private good. But when all this happens, to what cause is it to be traced? Does it prove the nonexistence of a moral sense, or does it prove, in such instances, the weakness or perversion of reason? The just solution is, that, in such instances, it is our reason, which presents false appearances to our moral sense.

It is with much reluctance, that the power of our instinctive or intuitive faculties is acknowledged by some philosophers. That the brutes are governed by instinct, but that man is governed by reason, is their favourite position. But fortunately for man, this position is not founded on truth. Our instincts, as well as our rational powers, are far superiour, both in number and in dignity, to those, which the brutes enjoy; and it were well for us, on many occasions, if we laid our reasoning systems aside, and were more attentive in observing the genuine impulses of nature. In this enlarged and elevated meaning, the sentiment of Pope[w] receives a double portion of force and sublimity.

> And reason raise o'er instinct as you can,
> In this, 'tis God directs, in that, 'tis man.

This sentiment is not dictated merely in the fervid glow of enraptured poetry; it is affirmed by the deliberate judgment of calm, sedate philosophy. Our instincts are no other than the oracles of eternal wisdom; our conscience, in particular, is the voice of God within us: it teaches, it commands, it punishes, it rewards. The testimony of a good conscience is the purest and the noblest of human enjoyments.

It will be proper to examine a little more minutely the opinions of those, who allege reason to be the sole directress of human conduct. Reason may, indeed, instruct us in the pernicious or useful tendency of qualities and actions: but reason alone is not sufficient to produce any moral approbation or blame. Utility is only a tendency to a certain end; and if the end be totally indifferent to us, we shall feel the same indifference towards the means. It is requisite that *sentiment* should intervene, in order to give a preference to the useful above the pernicious tendencies.

Reason judges either of relations or of matters of fact. Let us consider some particular virtue or vice under both views. Let us take the instance of *ingratitude*. This has place, when good will is expressed and good offices are performed on one side, and ill will or indifference is shown on the other. The first question is — what is that matter of fact, which is here called a vice? Indifference or ill will. But ill will is not always, nor in all circumstances a crime: and indifference may, on some occasions, be the result of the most philosophick fortitude. The vice of ingratitude, then, consists not in matter of fact.

Let us next inquire into the relations, which reason can discover, among the materials, of which ingratitude is composed. She discovers good will

[w] Ess. on Man. Ep. 3. v. 99.

and good offices on one side, and ill will or indifference on the other. This is the relation of *contrariety*. Does ingratitude consist in this? To which side of the contrary relation is it to be placed? For this relation of contrariety is formed as much by good will and good offices, as by ill will or indifference. And yet the former deserves praise as much as the latter deserves blame.

If it shall be said, that the morality of an action does not consist in the relation of its different parts to one another, but in the relation of the whole actions to the rule; and that actions are denominated good or ill, as they agree or disagree with that rule; another question occurs — What is this rule of right? by what is it discovered or determined? By reason, it is said. How does reason discover or determine this rule? It must be by examining facts or the relations of things. But by the analysis which has been given of the particular instance under our consideration, it has appeared that the vice of ingratitude consists neither in the matter of fact, nor in the relation of the parts, of which the fact is composed. Objects in the animal world, nay inanimate objects, may have to each other all the same relations, which we observe in moral agents; but such objects are never supposed to be susceptible of merit or demerit, of virtue or vice.

The *ultimate* ends of human actions, can never, in any case, be accounted for by reason. They recommend themselves entirely to the sentiments and affections of men, without dependence on the intellectual faculties. Why do you take exercise? Because you desire health. Why do you desire health? Because sickness is painful. Why do you hate pain? No answer is heard. Can one be given? No. This is an ultimate end, and is not referred to any farther object.

To the second question, you may, perhaps, answer, that you desire health, because it is necessary for your improvement in your profession. Why are you anxious to make this improvement? You may, perhaps, answer again, because you wish to get money by it. Why do you wish to get money? Because, among other reasons, it is the instrument of pleasure. But why do you love pleasure? Can a reason be given for loving pleasure, any more than for hating pain? They are both ultimate objects. 'Tis impossible there can be a progress *in infinitum*; and that one thing can always be a reason, why another is hated or desired. Something must be hateful or desirable on its own account, and because of its immediate agreement or disagreement with human sentiment and affection.

Virtue and vice are ends; and are hateful or desirable on their own account. It is requisite, therefore, that there should be some sentiment, which they touch — some internal taste or sense, which distinguishes moral good and evil, and which embraces one, and rejects the other. Thus are the offices of reason and of the moral sense at last ascertained.

The former conveys the knowledge of truth and falsehood: the latter, the sentiment of beauty and deformity, of vice and virtue. The standard of one, founded on the nature of things, is eternal and inflexible. The standard of the other is ultimately derived from that supreme will, which bestowed on us our peculiar nature, and arranged the several classes and orders of existence. In this manner, we return to the great principle, from which we set out. It is necessary that reason should be fortified by the moral sense: without the moral sense, a man may be prudent, but he cannot be virtuous.

Philosophers have degraded our senses below their real importance. They represent them as powers, by which we have sensations and ideas only. But this is not the whole of their office; they judge as well as inform. Not confined to the mere office of conveying impressions, they are exalted to the function of judging of the nature and evidence of the impressions they convey. If this be admitted, our moral faculty may, without impropriety, be called the *moral sense*. Its testimony, like that of the external senses, is the immediate testimony of nature, and on it we have the same reason to rely. In its dignity, it is, without doubt, far superiour to every other power of the mind.

The moral sense, like all our other powers, comes to maturity by insensible degrees. It is peculiar to human nature. It is both intellectual and active. It is evidently intended, by nature, to be the immediate guide and director of our conduct, after we arrive at the years of understanding.

III. Reason and conscience can do much; but still they stand in need of support and assistance. They are useful and excellent monitors; but, at some times, their admonitions are not sufficiently clear; at other times, they are not sufficiently powerful; at all times, their influence is not sufficiently extensive. Great and sublime truths, indeed, would appear to a few; but the world, at large, would be dark and ignorant. The mass of mankind would resemble a chaos, in which a few sparks, that would diffuse a glimmering light, would serve only to show, in a more striking manner, the thick darkness with which they are surrounded. Their weakness is strengthened, their darkness is illuminated, their influence is enlarged by that heaven-descended science, which has brought life and immortality to light. In compassion to the imperfection of our internal powers, our all-gracious Creator, Preserver, and Ruler has been pleased to discover and enforce his laws, by a revelation given to us immediately and directly from himself. This revelation is contained in the holy scriptures. The moral precepts delivered in the sacred oracles form a part of the law of nature, are of the same origin, and of the same obligation, operating universally and perpetually.

On some important subjects, those in particular, which relate to the

Deity, to Providence, and to a future state, our natural knowledge is greatly improved, refined, and exalted by that which is revealed. On these subjects, one who has had the advantage of a common education in a christian country, knows more, and with more certainty, than was known by the wisest of the ancient philosophers.

One superiour advantage the precepts delivered in the sacred oracles clearly possess. They are, of all, the most explicit and the most certain. A publick minister, judging from what he knows of the interests, views, and designs of the state, which he represents, may take his resolutions and measures, in many cases, with confidence and safety, and may presume, with great probability, how the state itself would act. But if, besides this general knowledge, and these presumptions highly probable, he was furnished also with particular instructions for the regulation of his conduct; would he not naturally observe and govern himself by both rules? In cases, where his instructions are clear and positive, there would be an end of all farther deliberation. In other cases, where his instructions are silent, he would supply them by his general knowledge, and by the information, which he could collect from other quarters, concerning the counsels and systems of the commonwealth. Thus it is with regard to reason, conscience, and the holy scriptures. Where the latter give instructions, those instructions are supereminently authentick. But whoever expects to find, in them, particular directions for every moral doubt which arises, expects more than he will find. They generally presuppose a knowledge of the principles of morality; and are employed not so much in teaching new rules on this subject, as in enforcing the practice of those already known, by a greater certainty, and by new sanctions. They present the warmest recommendations and the strongest inducements in favour of virtue: they exhibit the most powerful dissuasives from vice. But the origin, the nature, and the extent of the several rights and duties they do not explain; nor do they specify in what instances one right or duty is entitled to preference over another. They are addressed to rational and moral agents, capable of previously knowing the rights of men, and the tendencies of actions; of approving what is good, and of disapproving what is evil.

These considerations show, that the scriptures support, confirm, and corroborate, but do not supercede the operations of reason and the moral sense. The information with regard to our duties and obligations, drawn from these different sources, ought not to run in unconnected and diminished channels: it should flow in one united stream, which, by its combined force and just direction, will impel us uniformly and effectually towards our greatest good.

We have traced, with some minuteness, the efficient principle of obligation, and the several means, by which our duty may be known. It will be proper to turn our attention back to the opinions that have been held, in philosophy and jurisprudence, concerning this subject. On a review of them, we shall now find that, in general, they are defective rather than erroneous; that they have fallen short of the mark, rather than deviated from the proper course.

The fitness of things denotes their fitness to produce our happiness: their nature means that actual constitution of the world, by which some things produce happiness, and others misery. Reason is one of the means, by which we discern between those things, which produce the former, and those things, which produce the latter. The moral sense feels and operates to promote the same essential discriminations. Whatever promotes the greatest happiness of the whole, is congenial to the principles of utility and sociability: and whatever unites in it all the foregoing properties, must be agreeable to the will of God: for, as has been said once, and as ought to be said again, his will is graciously comprised in this one paternal precept — Let man pursue his happiness and perfection.

The law of nature is immutable, not by the effect of an arbitrary disposition, but because it has its foundation in the nature, constitution, and mutual relations of men and things. While these continue to be the same, it must continue to be the same also. This immutability of nature's laws has nothing in it repugnant to the supreme power of an all-perfect Being. Since he himself is the author of our constitution; he cannot but command or forbid such things as are necessarily agreeable or disagreeable to this very constitution, He is under the glorious necessity of not contradicting himself. This necessity, far from limiting or diminishing his perfections, adds to their external character, and points out their excellency.

The law of nature is universal. For it is true, not only that all men are equally subject to the command of their Maker; but it is true also, that the law of nature, having its foundation in the constitution and state of man, has an essential fitness for all mankind, and binds them without distinction.

This law, or right reason, as Cicero[x] calls it, is thus beautifully described by that eloquent philosopher. "It is, indeed," says he, "a true law, conformable to nature, diffused among all men, unchangeable, eternal. By its commands, it calls men to their duty: by its prohibitions, it deters them from vice. To diminish, to alter, much more to abolish this law, is a vain attempt. Neither by the senate, nor by the people, can its powerful obligation be dissolved. It requires no interpreter or commentator. It is not one law at Rome, another at Athens; one law now, another hereafter: it is the same eternal and immutable law, given at all

[x] De Rep. l. 3.

times and to all nations: for God, who is its author and promulgator, is always the sole master and sovereign of mankind."

"Man never *is*," says the poet, in a seeming tone of complaint, "but always *to be* blest." The sentiment would certainly be more consolatory, and, I think, it would be likewise more just, if we were to say — man ever *is; for* always to be blest. That we should have more and better things before us, than all that we have yet acquired or enjoyed, is unquestionably a most desirable state. The reflection on this circumstance, far from diminishing our sense or the importance of our present attainments and advantages, produces the contrary effects. The present is gilded by the prospect of the future.

When Alexander had conquered a world, and had nothing left to conquer; what did he do? He sat down and wept. A well directed ambition that has conquered worlds, is exempted from the fate of that of Alexander the Great: it still sees before it more and better worlds as the objects of conquest.

It is the glorious destiny of man to be always progressive. Forgetting those things that are behind, it is his duty, and it is his happiness, to press on towards those that are before. In the order of Providence, as has been observed on another occasion, the progress of societies towards perfection resembles that of an individual. This progress has hitherto been but slow: by many unpropitious events, it has often been interrupted: but may we not indulge the pleasing expectation, that, in future, it will be accelerated; and will meet with fewer and less considerable interruptions?

Many circumstances seem — at least to a mind anxious to see it, and apt to believe what it is anxious to see — many circumstances seem to indicate the opening of such a glorious prospect. The principles and the practice of liberty are gaining ground, in more than one section of the world. Where liberty prevails, the arts and sciences lift up their heads and flourish. Where the arts and sciences flourish, political and moral improvements will likewise be made. All will receive from each, and each will receive from all, mutual support and assistance: mutually supported and assisted, all may be carried to a degree of perfection hitherto unknown; perhaps, hitherto not believed.

"Men," says the sagacious Hooker, "if we view them in their spring, are, at the first, without understanding or knowledge at all. Nevertheless, from this utter vacuity, they grow by degrees, till they become at length to be even as the angels themselves are. That which agreeth to the one now, the other shall attain to in the end: they are not so far disjoined and severed, but that they come at length to meet." [y]

[y] Hooker, b. 1. s. 6. p. 8.

Our progress in virtue should certainly bear a just proportion to our progress in knowledge. Morals are undoubtedly capable of being carried to a much higher degree of excellence than the sciences, excellent as they are. Hence we may infer, that the law of nature, though immutable in its principles, will be progressive in its operations and effects. Indeed, the same immutable principles will direct this progression. In every period of his existence, the law, which the divine wisdom has approved for man, will not only be fitted, to the cotemporary degree, but will be calculated to produce, in future, a still higher degree of perfection.

A delineation of the laws of nature, has been often attempted. Books, under the appellations of institutes and systems of that law, have been often published. From what has been said concerning it, the most finished performances executed by human hands cannot be perfect. But most of them have been rude and imperfect to a very unnecessary, some, to a shameful degree.

A more perfect work than has yet appeared upon this great subject, would be a most valuable present to mankind. Even the most general outlines of it cannot, at least in these lectures, be expected from me.

IV

OF THE LAW OF NATIONS

THE law of nature, when applied to states or political societies, receives a new name, that of the law of nations. This law, important in all states, is of peculiar importance in free ones. The States of America are certainly entitled to this dignified appellation. A weighty part of the publick business is transacted by the citizens at large. They appoint the legislature, and, either mediately or immediately, the executive servants of the publick. As the conduct of a state, both with regard to itself and others, must greatly depend upon the character, the talents, and the principles of those, to whom the direction of that conduct is intrusted; it is highly necessary that those who are to protect the rights, and to perform the duties of the commonwealth, should be men of proper principles, talents, and characters: if so, it is highly necessary that those who appoint them should be able, in some degree at least, to distinguish and select those men, whose principles, talents, and characters are proper. In order to do this, it is greatly useful that they have, at least, some just and general knowledge of those rights that are to be protected, and of those duties that are to be performed. Without this, they will be unable to form a rational conjecture, concerning the future conduct of those whom they are to elect. Nay, what is more; without some such general and just knowledge, they will be unable to form a rational judgment, concerning the past and present conduct of those whom they have already elected; and, consequently, will be unable to form a rational determination whether, at the next election, they should reappoint them, or substitute others in their place. As the practice of the law of nations, therefore, must, in a free government, depend very considerably on the acts of the citizens, it is of high import that, among those citizens, its knowledge be generally diffused.

But, if the knowledge of the law of nations is greatly useful to those who appoint, it must surely be highly necessary to those who are appointed, the publick servants and stewards of the commonwealth. Can its interests be properly managed, can its character be properly supported, can its happiness be properly consulted, by those who know not what it owes to others, what it owes to itself, what it has a right to claim from others, and what it has a right to provide for itself? In a free commonwealth, the path to publick service and to publick honour is open to all. Should not all, therefore, sedulously endeavour to become masters of such qualifications, as will enable them to tread this path with credit to themselves, and with advantage to their country?

In the United States, a system of republicks, the law of nations acquires an importance still more peculiar and distinguished. In the United States, the law of nations operates upon peculiar relations, and upon those relations with peculiar energy. Well am I justified, on every account, in announcing the dignity and greatness of the subject, upon which I am now to enter.

On all occasions, let us beware of being misled by names. Though the law, which I am now to consider, receives a new appellation; it retains, unimpaired, its qualities and its power. The law of nations, as well as the law of nature, is of obligation indispensable: the law of nations, as well as the law of nature, is of origin divine.

The opinions of many concerning the law of nations have been very vague and unsatisfactory; and if such have been the opinions, we have little reason to be surprised, that the conduct of nations has too often been diametrically opposite to the law, by which it ought to have been regulated. In the judgment of some writers, it would seem, for instance, that neither the state which commences an unjust war, nor the chief who conducts it, derogates from the general sanctity of their respective characters. An ardent love of their country they seem to have thought a passion too heroick, to be restrained within the narrow limits of systematick morality; and those have been too often considered as the greatest patriots, who have contributed most to gratify the publick passion for conquest and power. States, as well as monarchs, have too frequently been blinded by ambition. Of this there is scarcely a page in ancient or in modern history, relating to national contentions, but will furnish the most glaring proofs. The melancholy truth is, that the law of nations, though founded on the most solid principles of natural obligation, has been but imperfectly viewed in theory, and has been too much disregarded in practice.

The profound and penetrating Bacon was not inattentive to the imperfect state, in which he found the science of the law of nations. As, in another science, that enlightened philosophical guide pointed to the discoveries of a Newton; so in this, in all probability, he laid a foundation for the researches of a Grotius. For we have reason to believe, as we are told by Barbeyrac,[a] that it was the study of the works of Lord Bacon, that first inspired Grotius with the design of writing a system

---

[a] Pref. to Puff. s. 29. p. 79.

concerning the law of nations. In this science Grotius did much; for he was well qualified to do much. Extensive knowledge, prodigious reading, indefatigable application to study, all these were certainly his. Yet with all these, he was far from being as successful in law, as Sir Isaac Newton was in philosophy. He was unfortunate in not setting out on right and solid principles. His celebrated book of the Rights of War and Peace is indeed useful; but it ought not to be read without a due degree of caution: nor ought all his doctrines to be received, without the necessary grains of allowance. At this we ought not to wonder, when we consider the extent, the variety, and the importance of his subject, and that, before his time, it was little known, and much neglected. His opinion concerning the source and the obligation of the law of nations is very defective. He separates that law from the law of nature, and assigns to it a different origin. "When many men," says he, "at different times and places, unanimously affirm the same thing for truth; this should be ascribed to a general cause. In the subjects treated of by us, this cause can be no other than either a just inference drawn from the principles of nature, or a universal consent. The first discovers to us the law of nature, the second the law of nations." [b] The law of nations, we see, he traces from the principle of universal consent. The consequence of this is, that the law of nations would be obligatory only upon those by whom the consent was given, and only by reason of that consent. The farther consequence would be, that the law of nations would lose a part, and the greatest part, of its obligatory force, and would also be restrained as to the sphere of its operations. That it would lose the greatest part of its obligatory force, sufficiently appears from what we have said at large concerning the origin and obligation of natural law, evincing it to be the will of God. That it would be restrained as to the sphere of its operations, appears from what Grotius himself says, when he explains his meaning in another place. He qualifies the universality of his expression by adding these words, "at least the most civilized nations;" and he afterwards says that this addition is made "with reason." [c] On the *least* civilized nations, therefore, the law of nations would not, according to his account of it, be obligatory.

I admit that there are laws of nations — perhaps it is to be wished that they were designated by an appropriate name; for names, after all, will have their influence on operations — I freely admit that there are laws of nations, which are founded altogether upon consent. National treaties are laws of nations, obligatory solely by consent. The customs of nations become laws solely by consent. Both kinds are certainly voluntary. But the municipal laws of a state are not more different from the

[b] Gro. Prel. s. 41.   [c] Gro. 14.

law of nature, than those voluntary laws of nations are, in their source and power, different from the law of nations, properly so called. Indeed, those voluntary laws of nations are as much under the control of the law of nations, properly so called, as municipal laws are under the control of the law of nature. The law of nations, properly so called, is the law of nature applied to states and sovereigns. The law of nations, properly so called, is the law of states and sovereigns, obligatory upon them in the same manner, and for the same reasons, as the law of nature is obligatory upon individuals. Universal, indispensable, and unchangeable is the obligation of both.

But it will naturally be asked, if the law of nations bears, as from this account it bears, the same relation to states, which the law of nature bears to individuals; if the law of nature and the law of nations are accompanied with the same obligatory power, and are derived from the same common source; why should the law of nations have a distinct name? Why should it be considered as a separate science? Some have thought that the difference was only in name; and if only in name, there could surely be no solid reason for establishing even that difference. Of those, who thought so, Puffendorff was one. "Many," says he,[a] "assert the law of nature and of nations to be the very same thing, differing no otherwise than in external denomination. Thus Mr. Hobbes divides natural law, into the natural law of men, and the natural law of states, commonly called the law of nations. He observes, that the precepts of both are the same; but that as states, when once instituted, assume the personal properties of men, what we call the law of nature, when we speak of particular men, we denominate the law of nations, when we apply it to whole states, nations, or people. This opinion," continues Puffendorff, "we, for our part, readily subscribe to; nor do we conceive, that there is any other voluntary or positive law of nations, properly vested with a true and legal force, and obliging as the ordinance of a superiour power." By the way, we may here observe, that, with regard to the law of nations, Grotius and Puffendorff seem to have run into contrary extremes. The former was of opinion, that the whole law of nations took its origin and authority from consent. The latter was of opinion, that every part of the law of nations was the same with the law of nature, that no part of it could receive its obligatory force from consent; because, according to his favourite notion of law, no such thing could exist without the intervention of a superiour power. The truth seems to lie between the two great philosophers. The law of nations, properly so called, or, as it may be termed, the natural law of nations, is a part, and an important part, of the law of nature. The voluntary

[a] Puff. p. 149. b. 2. c. 3. s. 23.

law of nations falls under the class of laws that are positive. If a particular name had been appropriated to this last species of law, it is probable that much confusion and ambiguity, on this subject, would have been
avoided; and the distinction between the different parts of that law,
comprehended, at present, under the name of the law of nations, would
have been as clearly marked, as uniformly preserved, and as familiarly
taken, as the well known and well founded distinction between natural
and municipal law. But to return.

As Puffendorff thought that the law of nature and the law of nations
were precisely the same, he has not, in his book on these subjects, treated
of the law of nations separately; but has every where joined it with the
law of nature, properly so called. His example has been followed by the
greatest part of succeeding writers. But the imitation of it has produced
a confusion of two objects, which ought to have been viewed and studied
distinctly and apart. Though the law of nations, properly so called, be a
part of the law of nature; though it spring from the same source, and
though it is attended with the same obligatory power; yet it must be
remembered that its application is made to very different objects. The law
of nature is applied to individuals: the law of nations is applied to states.
The important difference between the objects, will occasion a proportioned difference in the application of the law.[e] This difference in the
application renders it fit that the law of nature, when applied to states,
should receive an appropriate name, and should be taught and studied as
a separate science.

Though states or nations are considered as moral persons; yet the
nature and essence of these moral persons differ necessarily, in many
respects, from the nature and essence of the individuals, of whom they
are composed. The application of a law must be made in a manner
suitable to its object. The application, therefore, of the law of nature
to nations must be made in a manner suitable to nations: its application
to individuals must be made in a manner suitable to individuals. But as
nations differ from individuals; the application of the law suitable to
the former, must be different from its application suitable to the latter.
To nations this different application cannot be made with accuracy, with
justness, and with perspicuity, without the aid of new and discriminating
rules. These rules will evince, that, on the principles themselves of the
law of nature, that law, when applied to nations, will prescribe decisions
different from those which it would prescribe, when applied to individuals. To investigate those rules; to deduce, from the same great and leading
principles, applications differing in proportion to the difference of the
persons to which they are applied, is the object of the law of nations,

  [e] Vat. Pref. 1.

considered as a science distinct and separate from that of the law of
nature.

Having given you this general idea and description of the law of
nations; need I expatiate on its dignity and importance? The law of
nations is the law of sovereigns. In free states, such as ours, the sovereign
or supreme power resides in the people. In free states, therefore, such as
ours, the law of nations is the law of the people. Let us again beware of
being misled by an ambiguity, sometimes, such is the structure of
language, unavoidable. When I say that, in free states, the law of nations
is the law of the people; I mean not that it is a law made by the people,
or by virtue of their delegated authority; as, in free states, all municipal
laws are. But when I say that, in free states, the law of nations is the
law of the people; I mean that, as the law of nature, in other words, as
the will of nature's God, it is indispensably binding upon the people, in
whom the sovereign power resides; and who are, consequently, under
the most sacred obligations to exercise that power, or to delegate it to
such as will exercise it, in a manner agreeable to those rules and maxims,
which the law of nature prescribes to every state, for the happiness of
each, and for the happiness of all. How vast — how important — how
interesting are these truths! They announce to a free people how exalted
their rights; but, at the same time, they announce to a free people how
solemn their duties are. If a practical knowledge and a just sense of these
rights and these duties were diffused among the citizens, and properly
impressed upon their hearts and minds; how great, how beneficial, how
lasting would be their fruits! But, unfortunately, as there have been and
there are, in arbitrary governments, flatterers of princes; so there have
been and there are, in free governments, flatterers of the people. One
distinction, indeed, is to be taken between them. The latter herd of flatterers persuade the people to make an improper use of the power, which
of right they have: the former herd persuade princes to make an improper use of power, which of right they have not. In other respects,
both herds are equally pernicious. Both flatter to promote their private
interests: both betray the interests of those whom they flatter.

It is of the highest, and, in free states, it is of the most general importance, that the sacred obligation of the law of nations should be
accurately known and deeply felt. Of all subjects, it is agreeable and
useful to form just and adequate conceptions; but of those especially,
which have an influence on the practice and morality of states. For it is
a serious truth, however much it has been unattended to in practice, that
the laws of morality are equally strict with regard to societies, as to the
individuals of whom the societies are composed. It must be owing either
to ignorance, or to a very unjustifiable disregard to this great truth,

that some transactions of publick bodies have often escaped censure, nay, sometimes have received applause, though those transactions have been such, as none of the individuals composing those bodies would have dared to introduce into the management of his private affairs; because the person introducing them would have been branded with the most reproachful of names and characters. It has been long admitted, by those who have been the best judges of private life and manners, that integrity and sound policy go hand in hand. It is high time that this maxim should find an establishment in the councils of states, and in the cabinets of princes. Its establishment there would diffuse far and wide the most salutary and benign effects.

Opinions concerning the extent of the law of nations have not been less defective and inadequate, than those concerning its origin and obligatory force. Some seem to have thought, that this law respects and regulates the conduct of nations only in their intercourse with each other. A very important branch of this law — that containing the duties which a nation owes itself — seems to have escaped their attention. "The general principle," says Burlamaqui,[f] "of the law of nations, is nothing more than the general law of sociability, which obliges nations to the same duties as are prescribed to individuals. Thus the law of natural equality, which prohibits injury and commands the reparation of damage done; the law of beneficence, and of fidelity to our engagements, are laws respecting nations, and imposing, both on the people and on their respective sovereigns, the same duties as are prescribed to individuals." Several other writers concerning the law of nations appear to have formed the same imperfect conceptions with regard to its extent. Let us recur to what the law of nature dictates to an individual. Are there not duties which he owes to himself? Is he not obliged to consult and promote his preservation, his freedom, his reputation, his improvement, his perfection, his happiness? Now that we have seen the law of nature as it respects the duties of individuals, let us see the law of nations as it respects the duties of states, to themselves: for we must recollect that the law of nations is only the law of nature judiciously applied to the conduct of states. From the duties of states, as well as of individuals, to themselves, a number of corresponding rights will be found to arise.

A state ought to attend to the preservation of its own existence. In what does the existence of a state consist? It consists in the association of the individuals, of which it is composed. In what consists the preservation of this existence? It consists in the duration of that association. When this association is dissolved, the state ceases to exist; though all the members, of whom it was composed, may still remain. It is the duty of a state, therefore, to preserve this association undissolved and unimpaired.

[f] 2. Burl. 3. 4. 1. Burl. 196.

But in this, as in many other instances, a difference between the nature of states and the nature of individuals will occasion, for the reasons already mentioned, a proportioned difference in the application of the law of nature. Nations, as well as men, are taught by the law of nature, gracious in its precepts, to consider their happiness as the great end of their existence. But without existence there can be no happiness: the means, therefore, must be secured, in order to secure the end. But yet, between the duty of self-preservation required from a state, and the duty of self-preservation required from a man, there is a most material difference; and this difference is founded on the law of nature itself. A nation has a right to assign to its existence a voluntary termination: a man has not. What can be the reasons of this difference? Several may be given. By the voluntary act of the individuals forming the nation, the nation was called into existence: they who bind, can also untie: by the voluntary act, therefore, of the individuals forming the nation, the nation may be reduced to its original nothing. But it was not by his own voluntary act that the man made his appearance upon the theatre of life; he cannot, therefore, plead the right of the nation, by his own voluntary act to make his exit. He did not make; therefore, he has no right to destroy himself. He alone, whose gift this state of existence is, has the right to say when and how it shall receive its termination.

Again; though nations are considered as moral persons, and, in that character, as entitled, in many respects, to claim the rights, and as obliged, in many respects, to perform the duties of natural persons; yet we must always remember that of natural persons those moral persons are composed; that for the sake of natural persons those moral persons were formed; and that while we suppose those moral persons to live, and think, and act, we know that they are natural persons alone, who really exist or feel, who really deliberate, resolve, and execute. Now none of these observations resulting from the nature and essence of the nation, can be applied, with any degree of propriety, to the nature and essence of the man: and, therefore, the inferences drawn from these observations, with regard to the case of the nation, are wholly inapplicable to the case of the man.

One of these inferences is, that as it was for the happiness of the members that the moral existence of the nation was produced; so the happiness of the members may require this moral existence to be annihilated. Can this inference be applied to the man?

Further; there may be a moral certainty, that, of the voluntary dissolution of the nation, the necessary consequence will be an increase of happiness. Can such a consequence be predicted, with moral certainty, concerning the voluntary death of the man?

This instance shows, in a striking manner, how, on some occasions, the law of nature, when applied to a nation, may dictate or authorize a measure of conduct very different from that, which it would authorize and dictate with regard to a man.

As it is, in general, the duty of a state to preserve itself; so it is, in general, its duty to preserve its members. This is a duty which it owes to them, and to itself. It owes it to them, because their advantage was the final cause of their joining in the association, and engaging to support it; and they ought not to be deprived of this advantage, while they fulfil the conditions, on which it was stipulated. This duty the nation owes to itself, because the loss of its members is a proportionable loss of its strength; and the loss of its strength is proportionably injurious both to its security, and to its preservation. The result of these principles is, that the body of a nation should not abandon a country, a city, or even an individual, who has not forfeited his rights in the society.

The right and duty of a state to preserve its members are subject to the same limitations and conditions, as its right and duty to preserve itself. As, for some reasons, the society may be dissolved; so, for others, it may be dismembered. A part may be separated from the other parts; and that part may either become a new state, or may associate with another state already formed. An illustration of this doctrine may be drawn from a recent instance, which has happened in the commonwealth of Virginia. The district of Kentucky has, by an amicable agreement, been disjoined from the rest of the commonwealth, and has been formed into a separate state. It is a pleasure, perhaps I may add it is a laudable pride, to be able to furnish, to the world, the first examples of carrying into practice the most sublime parts of the most sublime theories of government and law.

When a nation has a right, and is under an obligation to preserve itself and its members; it has, by a necessary consequence, a right to do everything, which, without injuring others, it can do, in order to accomplish and secure those objects. The law of nature prescribes not impossibilities: it imposes not an obligation, without giving a right to the necessary means of fulfilling it. The same principles, which evince the right of a nation to do every thing, which it lawfully may, for the preservation of itself and of its members, evince its right, also, to avoid and prevent, as much as it lawfully may, every thing which would load it with injuries, or threaten it with danger.

It is the right, and generally it is the duty, of a state, to form a constitution, to institute civil government, and to establish laws. If the constitution formed, or the government instituted, or the laws established shall, on experience, be found weak, or inconvenient, or pernicious; it is the right, and it is the duty of the state to strengthen, or alter, or abolish them. These subjects will be fully treated in another place.

A nation ought to know itself. It ought to form a just estimate of its own situation, both with regard to itself and to its neighbours. It ought to learn the excellencies, and the blemishes likewise of its own constitution. It ought to review the instances in which it has already attained, and it ought to ascertain those in which it falls short of, a practicable degree of perfection. It ought to find out what improvements are peculiarly necessary to be promoted, and what faults it is peculiarly necessary to avoid. Without a discriminating sagacity of this kind, the principle of imitation, intended for the wisest purposes in states as well as in individuals, would be always an uncertain, sometimes a dangerous guide. A measure extremely salutary to one state, might be extremely injurious to another. What, in one situation, would be productive of peace and happiness, might, in another, be the unfortunate cause of infelicity and war. Above all things, the genius and manners of the people ought to be carefully consulted. The government ought to be administered agreeably to this genius and these manners; but how can this be done, if this genius and these manners are unknown? This duty of self-knowledge is of vast extent and of vast importance, in nations as well as in men.

To love and to deserve honest fame, is another duty of a people, as well as of an individual. The reputation of a state is not only a pleasant, it is also a valuable possession. It attracts the esteem, it represses the unfriendly inclinations of its neighbours. This reputation is acquired by virtue, and by the conduct which virtue inspires. It is founded on the publick transactions of the state, and on the private behaviour of its members.

A state should avoid ostentation, but it should support its dignity. This should never be suffered to be degraded among other nations. In transactions between states, an attention to this object is of much greater importance than is generally imagined. Even the marks and titles of respect, to which a nation, and those who represent a nation, are entitled, ought not to be considered as trivial: they should be claimed with firmness: they should be given with alacrity. The dignity, the equality, the mutual independence, and the frequent intercourse of nations render such a tenour of conduct altogether indispensable.

It is the duty of a nation to intrust the management of its affairs only to its wisest and best citizens. The immense importance of this duty is easily seen; but it is not sufficiently regarded. The meanest menial of a family will not be received without examination and cautious inquiry. The most important servants of the publick will be voted in without consideration and without care. In electioneering, as it is called, we frequently find warm recommendations and active intrigues in favour of candidates for the highest offices, to whom the recommenders and intriguers would not, if put to the test, intrust the management of the smallest part of their own private interest. An election ground, the great theatre of original sovereignty, on which nothing but inviolable integrity and independent virtue should be exhibited, is often and lamentably transformed into a scene of the vilest and lowest debauchery and deception. An election maneuvre, an election story, are names appropriated to a conduct, which, in other and inferiour transactions, would be branded, and justly branded, with the most opprobrious appellations. Even those, who may be safely trusted every where else, will play false at elections. The remarks, which I have made concerning general elections, may be too often made, with equal truth, concerning other appointments to offices. But these things ought not to be. When the obligation and the importance of the great national duty required at elections — a duty prescribed by him who made us free — a duty prescribed that we may continue free — when all this shall be sufficiently diffused, and known, and felt; these things will not be. The people will then elect conscientiously; and will require conscientious conduct from those whom they elect.

A nation ought to encourage true patriotism in its members. The first step towards this encouragement is to distinguish between its real and its pretended friends. The discrimination, it is true, is often difficult, sometimes impracticable: but it is equally true, that it may frequently be made. Let the same care be employed, let the same pains be taken, to ascertain the marks of deceit and the marks of sincerity in publick life, and in intriguing for publick office, which are usually taken and employed in private life, and in solicitations for acts of private friendship. The care and pains will sometimes, indeed, be fruitless; but they will sometimes, too, be successful; at all times, they will be faithful witnesses, that those, who have employed them, have discharged their duty.

If a nation establish itself, or extend its establishment in a country already inhabited by others; it ought to observe strict justice, in both instances, with the former inhabitants. This is a part of the law of nations, that very nearly concerns the United States. It ought, therefore, to be well understood. The whole earth is allotted for the nourishment of its inhabitants, but it is not sufficient for this purpose, unless they aid it by labour and culture. The cultivation of the earth, therefore, is a duty incumbent on man by the order of nature. Those nations that live by hunting, and have more land than is necessary even for the purposes of hunting, should transfer it to those who will make a more advantageous use of it: those who will make this use of it ought to pay, for they can afford to pay, a reasonable equivalent. Even when the lands are no more than sufficient for the purposes of hunting, it is the duty of the new inhabitants, if advanced in society, to teach, and it is the duty of the original inhabitants, if less advanced in society, to learn, the arts and uses of agriculture. This will enable the latter gradually to contract, and the former gradually to extend their settlements, till the science of agriculture is equally improved in both. By these means, the intentions of nature will be fulfilled; the old and the new inhabitants will be reciprocally useful; peace will be preserved, and justice will be done.

It is the duty of a nation to augment its numbers. The performance of this duty will naturally result from the discharge of its other duties: by discharging them, the number of persons born in the society will be increased; and strangers will be incited to wish a participation in its blessings. Among other means of increasing the number of citizens, there are three of peculiar efficacy. The first is, easily to receive all strangers of good character, and to communicate to them the advantages of liberty. The state will be thus filled with citizens, who will bring with them commerce and the arts, and a rich variety of manners and characters. Another means conducive to the same end is, to encourage marriages. These are the pledges of the state. A third means for augmenting the number of inhabitants is, to preserve the rights of conscience inviolate. The right of private judgment is one of the greatest advantages of mankind; and is always considered as such. To be deprived of it is insufferable. To enjoy it lays a foundation for that peace of mind, which the laws cannot give, and for the loss of which the laws can offer no compensation.

A nation should aim at its perfection. The advantage and improvement of the citizens are the ends proposed by the social union. Whatever will render that union more perfect will promote these ends. The same principles, therefore, which show that a man ought to pursue the perfection of his nature, will show, likewise, that the citizens ought to contribute every thing in their power towards the perfection of the state. This right involves the right of preventing and avoiding every thing, which would interrupt or retard the progress of the state towards its perfection. It also involves the right of acquiring every thing, without which its perfection cannot be promoted or obtained.

Happiness is the centre, to which men and nations are attracted: it is, therefore, the duty of a nation to consult its happiness. In order to do this, it is necessary that the nation be instructed to search for happiness where happiness is to be found. The impressions that are made first, sink deepest; they frequently continue through life. That seed, which is sown in the tender minds of youth, will produce abundance of good, or abundance of evil. The education of youth, therefore, is of prime importance to the happiness of the state. The arts, the sciences, philosophy, virtue, and religion, all contribute to the happiness, all, therefore, ought to receive the encouragement, of the nation. In this manner, publick and private felicity will go hand in hand, and mutually assist each other in their progress.

When men have formed themselves into a state or nation, they may reciprocally enter into particular engagements, and, in this manner, contract new obligations in favour of the members of the community; but they cannot, by this union, discharge themselves from any duties which they previously owed to those, who form no part of the union. They continue under all the obligations required by the universal society of the human race — the great society of nations. The law of that great and universal society requires, that each nation should contribute to the perfection and happiness of the others. It is, therefore, a duty which every nation owes to itself, to acquire those qualifications, which will fit and enable it to discharge those duties which it owes to others. What those duties are, we shall now very concisely and summarily inquire.

The first and most necessary duty of nations, as well as of men, is to do no wrong or injury. Justice is a sacred law of nations. If the law of the great society of nations requires, as we have seen it to require, that each should contribute to the perfection and happiness of others; the first degree of this duty surely is, that each should abstain from every thing, which would positively impair that perfection and happiness. This great principle prohibits one nation from exciting disturbances in another, from seducing its citizens, from depriving it of its natural advantages, from calumniating its reputation, from debauching the attachment of its allies, from fomenting or encouraging the hatred of its enemies. If, however, a nation, in the necessary prosecution of its own duties and rights, does what is disagreeable or even inconvenient to another, this is not to be considered as an injury; it ought to be viewed as the unavoidable result, and not as the governing principle of its conduct. If, at such conduct, offence is taken, it is the fault of that nation, which takes, not of that nation, which occasions it.

But nations are not only forbidden to do evil; they are also commanded to do good to one another. The duties of humanity are incumbent upon nations as well as upon individuals. An individual cannot subsist, at least he cannot subsist comfortably, by himself. What is true concerning one, is true concerning all. Without mutual good offices and assistance, therefore, happiness could not be procured, perhaps existence could not be preserved. Hence the necessity of the duties of humanity among individuals. Every one is obliged, in the first place, to do what he can for himself; in the next, to do what he can for others; beginning with those with whom he is most intimately connected. The consequence is, that each man is obliged to give to others every assistance, for which they have a real occasion, and which he can give without being wanting to himself. What each is obliged to perform for others, from others he is entitled to receive. Hence the advantage as well as the duty of humanity. These principles receive an application to states as well as to men. Each nation owes to every other the duties of humanity. It is true, there may be some difference in the application, in this as well as in other instances: but the principles of the application are the same. A nation can subsist by itself more securely and more comfortably than an individual can; therefore the duty of mutual assistance will not, at all periods, be equally indispensable, or return with equal frequency. But when it becomes, as it may become, equally indispensable; and when it returns, as it may return, with equal frequency; it ought, in either case, to be equally performed. One individual may attack another daily: a longer time is necessary for the aggression of one nation upon another. The assistance, therefore, which ought to be given to the individual daily, will be necessary for the nation only at more distant intervals of time. But between nations, what the duties of humanity lose in point of frequency, they gain in point of importance, in proportion, perhaps, to the difference between a single individual, and all those individuals of whom the nation is composed.

One nation ought to give to another, not only the assistance necessary to its preservation, but that also which is necessary to its perfection, whenever it is wanted, and whenever, consistently with other superiour duties, it can be given. The cases in which assistance ought to be demanded, and those in which it ought to be given, must be decided respectively by that nation which demands, and by that of which the demand is made. It is incumbent on each to decide properly; not to demand, and not to refuse, without strong and reasonable cause.

It may, perhaps, be uncommon, but it is certainly just, to say that nations ought to love one another. The offices of humanity ought to flow from this pure source. When this happily is the case, then the principles of affection and of friendship prevail among states as among individuals: then nations will mutually support and assist each other with zeal and ardour; lasting peace will be the result of unshaken confidence; and kind and generous principles, of a nature far opposite to mean jealousy, crooked policy, or cold prudence, will govern and prosper the affairs of men. And why should not this be the case? When a number of individuals, by the social union, become fellow citizens, can they, by that union, devest themselves of that relation, which subsists between them and the other — the far greater — part of the human species? With regard to those, can they cease to be men?

The love of mankind is an important duty and an exalted virtue. Much has been written, much has been said concerning the power of *intellectual* abstraction, which man possesses, and which distinguishes him so eminently from the inferiour orders of animals. But little has been said, and little has been written, concerning another power of the human mind, still more dignified, and, beyond all comparison, more amiable — I may call it the power of *moral* abstraction.

All things in nature are individuals. But when a number of individuals have a near and striking resemblance, we, in our minds, class them together, and refer them to a species, to which we assign a name. Again; when a number of species have a resemblance, though not so near and striking, we, in the same manner, class them also together, and refer them to a genus, to which we likewise assign a name. Different genera may have a resemblance, though still less close and striking; we refer them to a higher genus, till we arrive at *being*, the highest genus of all. This is the progress of intellectual abstraction.

We are possessed of a moral power, similar in its nature and in its progress — a principle of good will as well as of knowledge. This principle of benevolence is indeed primarily and chiefly directed towards individuals, those especially, with whom we are or wish to be most intimately connected. But this principle, as well as the other, is capable of abstraction, and of embracing general objects. The culture, the improvement, and the extension of this principle ought to have made, in the estimation of philosophers, as important a figure among the moral, as the other has made among the intellectual powers and operations of the mind; for it is susceptible of equal culture, of equal improvement, and of equal extension.

"After having," says the illustrious Neckar, in his book concerning the importance of religious opinions,[g] "proved myself a citizen of France, by my administration, as well as my writings, I wish to unite myself to a fraternity still more extended, that of the whole human race. Thus, without dispersing our sentiments, we may be able to communicate ourselves a great way off, and enlarge, in some measure, the limits of our circle. Glory be to our thinking faculties for it! to that spiritual portion of ourselves, which can take in the past, dart into futurity, and intimately associate itself with the destiny of men of all countries and of all ages!"

To the same purpose is the sentiment of Cicero, in his beautiful treatise on the nature and offices of friendship.[h] "In tracing the social laws of nature," says he, "it seems evident, that man, by the frame of his moral constitution, is supposed to consider himself as standing in some degree of social relation to the whole species in general; and that this principle acts with more or less vigour, according to the distance at which he is placed with respect to any particular community or individual of his kind."

This principle of benevolence and sociability, which is not confined

[g] Pref. 19.   [h] c. 5.

to one sect or to one state, but ranges excursive through the whole
expanded theatre of men and nations, instead of being always acknowledged and always recommended, as it ought to have been, has been altogether omitted by some philosophers: by some, its existence seems to
have been doubted or denied.

"Some sort of union," says Rutherforth, in his institutes of natural
law,[1] "there is between all nations: they are all included in the collective
idea of mankind, and are frequently spoken of under this general name.
But this is not a social union: the several parts of the collective idea,
whether we consider the great body of mankind as made up of individuals or of nations, are not connected, as the several parts of a civil
society are, by compact among themselves: the connexion is merely
notional, and is only made by the mind, for its own convenience."

The very enlarged active power, concerning which I speak, is, to this
day, so far as I know, without an appropriated name. The term *philan-
thropy* approaches near, but does not reach it. We sometimes call it
patriotism, by a figurative extension of that term, which, in its proper
meaning, denotes a circle of benevolence limited by the state, of which
one is a member. When we speak of the most exalted of all characters,
of the man who possesses this virtue, we generally describe him, by a
metaphor, a "citizen of the world." A "man of the world," which would
be the more natural expression, though it is in common use, is used to
convey a very different idea.

If the general observations, which I have before made concerning the
nature, the structure, and the evidence of language, be well founded, the
particular remarks I have now made will appear to be striking and just.

This power of moral abstraction should be exercised and cultivated
with the highest degree of attention and zeal. It is as necessary to the
progress of exalted virtue, as the power of intellectual abstraction is to the
progress of extensive knowledge. The progress of the former will be
accompanied with a degree of pleasure, of utility, and of excellence,
far superiour to any degree of those qualities, which can accompany
the latter. The purest pleasures of mathematical learning spring from
the source of accurate and extended intellectual abstraction. But those
pleasures, pure as they are, must yield the palm to those, which arise from
abstraction of the moral kind.

By this power, exerted in different proportions, the commonwealth
of Pennsylvania, the empire of the United States, the civilized and commercial part of the world, the inhabitants of the whole earth, become
objects of a benevolence the warmest, and of a spirit the most patriotick;
for custom, the arbitress of language, has not yet authorized a more

[1] Vol. 2. 463. 464.

appropriate epithet. By this power, a number of individuals, who, considered separately, may be so minute, so unknown, or so distant, as to elude the operations of our benevolence, yet, comprehended under one important and distinguished aspect, may become a general and complex object, which will warm and dilate the soul. By this power the capacity of our nature is enlarged; men, otherwise invisible, are rendered conspicuous; and become known to the heart as well as to the understanding.

This enlarged and elevated virtue ought to be cultivated by nations with peculiar assiduity and ardour. The sphere of exertion, to which an individual is confined, is frequently narrow, however enlarged his disposition may be. But the sphere, to the extent of which a state may exert herself, is often comparatively boundless. By exhibiting a glorious example in her constitution, in her laws, in the administration of her constitution and laws, she may diffuse reformation, she may diffuse instruction, she may diffuse happiness over this whole terrestrial globe.

How often and how fatally are expressions and sentiments perverted! How often and how fatally is perverted conduct the unavoidable and inveterate effect of perverted sentiment and expression! What immense treasures have been exhausted, what oceans of human blood have been shed, in France and England, by force of the expression "natural enemy!" 'Tis an unnatural expression. The antithesis is truly in the thought: for natural enmity forms no title in the genuine law of nations, part of the law of nature. It is adopted from a spurious code.

The foregoing rules and maxims of national law, though they are the sacred, the inviolable, and the exalted precepts of nature, and of nature's Author, have been long unknown and unacknowledged among nations. Even where they have been known and acknowledged, their calm still voice has been drowned by the solicitations of interest, the clamours of ambition, and the thunder of war. Many of the ancient nations conceived themselves to be under no obligations whatever to other states or the citizens of other states, unless they could produce in their favour a connexion formed and cemented by a treaty of amity.

At last, however, the voice of nature, intelligible and persuasive, has been heard by nations that are civilized: at last it is acknowledged that mankind are all brothers: the happy time is, we hope, approaching, when the acknowledgment will be substantiated by a uniform corresponding conduct.

How beautiful and energetick are the sentiments of Cicero on this subject. "It is more consonant to nature," that is, as he said a little before, to the law of nations, "to undertake the greatest labours, and to undergo the severest trouble, for the preservation and advantage of all nations, if such a thing could be accomplished, than to live in solitary repose, not only without pain, but surrounded with all the allurements of pleasure and wealth. Every one of a good and great mind, would prefer the first greatly before the second situation in life." "It is highly absurd to say, as some have said, that no one ought to injure a parent or a brother, for the sake of his own advantage; but that another rule may be observed concerning the rest of the citizens: such persons determine that there is no law, no bonds of society among the citizens, for the common benefit of the commonwealth. This sentiment tends to dissolve the union of the state. Others, again, admit that a social regard is to be paid to the citizens, but deny that this regard ought to be extended in favour of foreigners: such persons would destroy the common society of the human race; and if this common society were destroyed, the destruction would involve, in it, the fate also of beneficence, liberality, goodness, justice. Which last virtue is the mistress and the queen of all the other virtues." [j] By justice here, Cicero clearly means that universal justice, which is the complete accomplishment of the law of nature.

It has been already observed, that there is one part of the law of nations, called their voluntary law, which is founded on the principle of consent: of this part, publick compacts and customs received and observed by civilized states form the most considerable articles.

Publick compacts are divided into two kinds — treaties and sponsions. Treaties are made by those who are empowered, by the constitution of a state, to represent it in its transactions with other nations. Sponsions are made by an inferiour magistrate or officer, on behalf of the state, but without authority from it. Such compacts, therefore, do not bind the state, unless it confirms them after they are made. These take place chiefly in negotiations and transactions between commanding officers, during a war.

Though the power of making treaties is usually, it is not necessarily annexed to sovereign power. Some of the princes and free cities of Germany, though they hold of the emperour and the empire, have nevertheless the right of making treaties with foreign nations: this right, as well as several other rights of sovereignty, the constitution of the empire has secured to them.

With a policy, wiser and more profound, because it shuts the door against foreign intrigues with the members of the union, no state comprehended within our national government, can enter into any treaty, alliance, or confederation. [k]

It is in the constitution or fundamental laws of every nation, that we must search, in order to discover what power it is, which has sufficient authority to contract, with validity, in the name of the state.

A treaty is valid, if there has been no essential defect in the manner, in which it has been made; and, in order to guard against essential defects,

[j] Cic. de off. 1. 3. c. 5. 6.   [k] Cons. U.S. art. 1. s. 10.

it is only necessary that there be sufficient power in the contracting parties, that their mutual consent be given, and that that consent be properly declared.

It is a truth certain in the law of nature, that he who has made a promise to another, has given to that other a perfect right to demand the performance of the promise. Nations and the representatives of nations, therefore, ought to preserve inviolably their treaties and engagements: by not preserving them, they subject themselves to all the consequences of violating the perfect right of those, to whom they were made. This great truth is generally acknowledged; but too frequently an irreligious disregard is shown to it in the conduct of princes and states. But such a disregard is weak as well as wicked. In publick as in private life, among sovereigns as among individuals, honesty is the best policy, as well as the soundest morality. Among merchants, credit is wealth; among states and princes, good faith is both respectability and power.

A state, which violates the sacred faith of treaties, violates not only the voluntary, but also the natural and necessary law of nations; for we have seen that, by the law of nature, the fulfilment of promises is a duty as much incumbent upon states as upon men. Indeed it is more incumbent on the former than on the latter; for the consequences both of performing and of violating the engagements of the former, are generally more important and more lasting, than any which can flow from engagements performed or violated by individuals. Hence the strict propriety, as well as the uncommon beauty of the sentiment — that if good faith were banished from every other place, she should find an inviolable sanctuary at least in the bosoms of princes.

Every treaty should be illuminated by perspicuity and candour. A tricking minister is, in real infamy, degraded as much below a vulgar cheat, as the dignity of states is raised above that of private persons. Ability and address in negotiation may be used to avoid, never to accomplish a surprise.

Fraud in the subsequent interpretation, is equally base and dishonourable as fraud in the original structure of treaties. In the scale of turpitude, it weighs equally with the most flagrant and notorious perfidy.

Treaties and alliances are either personal or real. The first relate only to the contracting parties, and expire with those who contract. The second relate to the state, in whose name and by whose authority the contract was made, and are permanent as the state itself, unless they determine, at another period, by their own limitation.

Every treaty or alliance made with a commonwealth is, in its own nature, real; for it has reference solely to the body of the state. When a free people make an engagement, it is the nation which contracts. Its stipulations depend not on the lives of those, who have been the instruments in forming the treaty: nor even on the lives of those citizens, who were alive when the treaty was formed. They change; but the commonwealth continues the same.

Hence the stability and the security of treaties made with commonwealths. By the faithful observance of their treaties, the Cantons of Switzerland have rendered themselves respectable and respected over all Europe. Let it be mentioned to the honour of the parliament of Great Britain, that it has frequently thanked its king for his zeal and attachment to the treaties, in which he has engaged the nation.

The corruption of the best things and institutions, however, always degenerates into the worst. The citizens of Carthage prostituted the character of their republick to such a degree, that, if we may believe the testimony of an enemy, *Punica fides* became proverbial, over the ancient world, to denote the extreme of perfidy.

As the United States have surpassed others, even other commonwealths, in the excellence of their constitution and government; it is reasonably to be hoped, that they will surpass them, likewise, in the stability of their laws, and in their fidelity to their engagements.

In the great chart of the globe of credit, we hope to see American placed as the very antipode of Carthaginian faith.

V

OF MUNICIPAL LAW

I NOW proceed to the consideration of municipal law — that rule, by which a state or nation is governed. It is thus defined by the learned Author of the Commentaries on the Laws of England. "A rule of civil conduct, prescribed by the *supreme power* of the state, commanding what is right and prohibiting what is wrong." [a] In my observations upon Sir William Blackstone's definition of law in general, I did him the justice to mention, that he was not the first, and that he has not been the last, who has defined law upon the same principles, or upon principles similar, and equally dangerous. Here it is my duty to mention, and, in one respect, I am happy in mentioning, that he was the first, though, I must add, he has not been the last, who has defined municipal law, as applied to the law of England, upon principles, to which I must beg leave to assign the epithets, dangerous and unsound. It is of high import to the liberties of the United States, that the seeds of despotism be not permitted to lurk at the roots of our municipal law. If they shall be suffered to remain there, they will, at some period or another, spring up and produce abundance of pestiferous fruit. Let us, therefore, examine, fully and minutely, the extent, the grounds, the derivation, and the consequences of the abovementioned definition.

"Legislature," we are told, "is the greatest act of superiority, that can be exercised by one being over another. Wherefore it is requisite to the very essence of a law, that it be made by the supreme power. Sovereignty and legislature are, indeed, convertible terms; one cannot subsist without the other." [b] "There must be in every government, however it began, or by whatsoever right it subsists, a supreme, irresistible, absolute, uncontrolled authority, in which the *jura summi imperii*, or the rights of sovereignty reside." "By sovereign power is meant the making of laws; for wherever that power resides, all others must conform to and be directed by it, whatever appearance the outward form and administration of the government may put on. For it is at any time in the option of the legislature to alter that form and administration, by a new edict or rule, and to put the execution of the laws into whatever hands it pleases: and all the

[a] 1. Bl. Com. 44.   [b] 1. Bl. Com. 46.

other powers of the state must obey the legislative power in the execution of their several functions, or else the constitution is at an end." ᶜ "In the British parliament, is lodged the sovereignty of the British constitution." ᵈ "The power of making laws constitutes the supreme authority." ᵉ "In the British parliament," therefore, which is the legislative power, "the supreme and absolute authority of the state is vested." ᶠ "This is the place, where that absolute despotick power, which must, in all governments, reside somewhere, is intrusted by the constitution of these kingdoms." "Its power and jurisdiction is so transcendent and absolute, that it cannot be confined, either for causes or persons, within any bounds." ᵍ "It can change and create afresh even the constitution of the kingdom and of parliaments themselves. It can, in short, do every thing that is not naturally impossible." "What the parliament doth, no authority upon earth can undo." ʰ "So long as the English constitution lasts, we may venture to affirm, that the power of parliament is absolute and without control." ⁱ "Hence the known apothegm of the great Lord Treasurer Burleigh, that England could never be ruined but by a parliament." ʲ

It is obvious, that though this definition of municipal law, and this account of legislative authority be applied particularly to the law of England and the legislature of Great Britain; yet they are, in their terms and in their meaning, extended to every other state or nation whatever — "to every government, however it began, or by whatever right it subsists." Indeed, the opinion of Mr. Locke and other writers, "that there remains still inherent in the people a supreme power to remove and alter the legislature," is considered to be so merely theoretical, that "we cannot adopt it, nor argue from it, under any dispensation of government at present actually existing." ᵏ

The doctrines contained in the foregoing quotations from the Commentaries on the laws of England, may be comprised under the two general propositions, which follow. 1. That in every state, there is and must be a supreme, irresistible, absolute, uncontrolled authority, in which the rights of sovereignty reside. 2. That this authority, and these rights of sovereignty must reside in the legislature; because "sovereignty and legislature are convertible terms," and because "it is requisite to the very essence of a law, that it be made by the supreme power." In the first general proposition, I have the pleasure of agreeing entirely with Sir William Blackstone. Its truth rests on this broad and fundamental principle — that, by the constitutions of nature, men and nations are equal and free. In the second general proposition, I am under the necessity of differing altogether from the learned Author of the Commentaries. I differ from him, not only in the opinion, that the foregoing chain of reasoning must be

ᶜ Id. 48. 49.   ᵈ Id. 51.   ᵉ Id. 52.   ᶠ 1. Bl. Com. 147.   ᵍ Id. 160.
ʰ Id. 161.   ⁱ Id. 162.   ʲ Id. 161.   ᵏ Id. 161.

applicable to every government and to every system of municipal law;
I differ from him likewise in the opinion, that the foregoing chain of reasoning can be justly applied even to the government of Great Britain
and to the municipal law of England. I think I can safely pledge myself
to show, that, in both, I differ from him on the most solid and satisfactory
grounds.

It deserves to be remarked, that, for his definition of municipal law,
he cites the authority of no English court, nor of any English preceding
writer, lawyer, or judge. Indeed, so far as I know, he could cite no such
authority. So far as I have examined the English law books and authorities, upon this important subject — and I have examined them, as it has
been my duty to do, with no small degree of attention — this definition
stands entirely unsupported in point of authority. I may, however, be
mistaken — I pretend not to have read, far less to remember, every thing
in the law. If I am mistaken, I will thank the friendly monitor, that will
advise me of the mistake. As at present advised, I can say, that, so far as
I know, this definition is unsupported by authority in the English law. I
shall hereafter have occasion to show that, concerning acts of parliament,
to which the definition is particularly applied, our law authorities hold,
and even parliament itself holds, a very different language.

The introduction of the principle of superiority into the definition of
law in general, we traced, when we examined that subject, from Sir
William Blackstone to Baron Puffendorff. The introduction of the same
principle into the definition of municipal law, can be traced to the same
source. "Human laws," says he, "are nothing else, but the decrees of the
supreme power, concerning matters to be observed by the subjects." [1]
The celebrated Heineccius, in his system of Universal Law, gives a definition much to the same purpose — "Civil laws," says he, "are the commands of the supreme power in a state." [m] Why was this principle transplanted into the law of England?

It deserves to be further remarked, that, for all the strong sentiments
and expressions concerning the necessary connexion, and indeed the convertibility of the sovereign and the legislative powers, no authority is
produced from the English law; and — I speak under the guard as before
— so far as I know, none could be produced, except in one instance, of
which I shall soon take notice. The observation, which I have already
made with regard to the definition of municipal law, may, therefore, be
applied, with equal propriety, to the necessary connexion between the
sovereign and the legislative powers. This connexion is not attempted to
be supported by authority in the English law. I excepted one instance. It
is this — "The power and jurisdiction of parliament is so transcendent

---

[1] Puff. 688. b. 7. c. 6. s. 3.   [m] 2. Hein. s. 150. p. 152.

and absolute, that it cannot be confined, either for causes or persons, within any bounds." [n] For this, the authority of my Lord Coke in his fourth Institute is quoted. I have examined the passage. It stands thus. "Of the power and jurisdiction of the parliament, *for making of laws in proceeding by bill*, it is so transcendent and absolute, as it cannot be confined, either for causes or persons, within any bounds." [o] From this authority, I think it may be fairly and justly inferred — that, by the British constitution, the legislative authority of that nation is, without any exception of causes or persons, vested in the British parliament. In the same manner, by the constitution of Pennsylvania, the legislative power of this commonwealth is vested in a general assembly. But can it be inferred from this authority, that the sovereign power of Great Britain is vested in her parliament? Can it be inferred from the constitution of Pennsylvania, that her sovereign power is vested in her general assembly? I think, therefore, I may now venture to say, that both in his definition of municipal law, and in his opinion concerning the convertibility of the legislative and the sovereign authority, Sir William Blackstone stands unsupported by authority. Is he supported by reason and by principle? By neither, in my humble opinion.

The discussion of this question necessarily leads me to consider the establishment of government, and the division of its powers. That this subject may be fully understood, — for, in the United States, it ought to be understood fully — I shall examine the sentiments, which have been generally entertained and received concerning it, and then compare those sentiments with what I consider as the true state of things. No sooner is government mentioned, than the fine flattering images of power, dominion, and sovereignty dance in the fancy, as the beautiful and magnificent effects of its establishment. But the truth is, that sovereignty, dominion, and power are the parents, not the offspring of government. Let us, however, see what has been thought, and what ought to be thought, concerning those splendid objects.

The theory of the establishment of government has been generally such as I am about to explain.

It has been supposed, that, if a multitude of people, who had formerly lived independent of each other, wished to unite in a political society, and to establish a government, they would find it necessary to take the following steps. 1. Each individual would engage with all the others to join in one body, and to manage, with their joint powers and wills, whatever should regard their common preservation, security, and happiness. In consideration of this engagement, made by each individual with all the others, all those others would engage with each individual to protect and

[n] 1. Bl. Com. 160.   [o] 4. Ins. 36.

defend him from injury, and to secure him in the prosecution of every just and laudable pursuit. These reciprocal engagements from each individual to all the others, and from all the others to each individual form the political association. Those who do not enter into them are not considered as a part of the society.

The society being formed, some measures must be taken in order to regulate its operations; otherwise it could never adopt or pursue a system of measures for promoting, jointly and effectually, the publick security and happiness. These measures involve the formation of government.

A third step, we are told, must also be taken, before government can be completed. In addition to the engagement of political association, another engagement must be made: to that engagement, there must be a new party. What he is — whence he comes — from what source his equal and independent powers of contracting originate, have never, to this moment, been explained. Such an account of him as I have received, I will give: if it is not satisfactory, you must not blame me. "This party is one or more persons, on whom the supreme authority is conferred," says one.[p] By another, we are told, that this party is one or more persons, on whom "the sovereignty is conferred." [q] The sovereignty or supreme authority! How has it started up all of a sudden? Why does it make its first appearance in a derivative state? Where do we find it originally? — for it must exist originally before it can be conferred. To these questions we receive no explicit answer. We are told at one time, that "there are, in each individual, the seeds, as it were, of the supreme power." [r] We are told, more cautiously, at another time, that the voluntary consent and subjection of the respective members of the society, is the "nearest and immediate cause, from which sovereign authority, as a moral quality, results." [s] But, to make the most of these different pieces of information, let us suppose that this cause will produce its proper effects; that these seeds will yield, in due time, their natural fruits; and that this conferred sovereignty existed originally in those who conferred it. What is this sovereignty? Is it divisible or indivisible? Was the whole or only a part of it conferred? Was it conferred unconditionally, or upon certain conditions? Was it conferred gratuitously, or for a valuable consideration? Why hear we nothing concerning these important steps, which, upon the opinion generally received, must have been taken previously to the complete formation of a government? This, I confess, is far from being satisfactory: let us, however, take it as it is; and proceed to the remaining step, which, we are told, is taken for the complete establishment of government. This is an engagement by those, who are to be the future governours, that they will consult most carefully and act most honestly for

---

[p] 2. Burl. 28.   [q] Puff. 640. b. 7. c. 2. s. 8.   [r] 2. Burl. 42.
[s] Puff. 654. b. 7. c. 3. s. 1.

the common security and happiness; and a reciprocal engagement by those, who are, in future, to be governed, that they will observe fidelity and allegiance to those invested with the sovereign authority.

It is admitted not to be probable, that, in the formation of the several governments, these three steps have been actually and regularly taken; yet, we are told, in every just institution of power, there must have been such transactions as implicitly contain the full force and import of all of them.[t]

That the two first steps have been sometimes taken, and must be always supposed, in the regular structure of a government, I readily agree; because it is not easy to discover how a government could be formed without them. But with regard to the third, I see no necessity for it: I see no propriety in it: it is derogatory, in my humble judgment, from the genuine principles of legitimate sovereignty, and inconsistent with the best theory, and the best exercise too, of supreme power. But the full illustration of these dignified subjects is reserved for another place.

With regard, however, to the British constitution, we must allow the supposition, that a contract took place at its establishment. For this we have high political authority. A full assembly of the lords and commons, met in convention in the year 1688, declared that James the second had broke the original contract between the king and people.[u] What the terms of that contract were, at what time it was made, and what duties it enjoined, have been subjects of dark and doubtful disputation. For this reason, as we are told by Sir William Blackstone, it was, after the revolution, judged proper to declare these duties expressly, and to reduce that contract to a plain certainty. So that, whatever doubts might be formerly raised, by weak and scrupulous minds, about the existence of such an original contract, they must now entirely cease; especially with regard to every prince, who has reigned since that revolution.[v]

But, after all, what will this prove with regard to the supreme power of parliament? Do we hear, in the British constitution, of any contract between *them* and the people? How came *they* to be invested with such immense authority? The usual theories of government support no hypothesis of this kind, even in favour of the British legislature; far less, in favour of the legislature of every other government, "however formed, or by whatever right subsisting."

Let us trace this matter a little farther: let us endeavour to form some just conceptions concerning this supreme and sovereign power, concerning which so much has been said, and concerning which so little has been said justly. Let us turn our eyes, for a while, from books and systems: let us fix them upon men and things. While those, who were about to form a society, continued separate and independent men, they possessed

[t] 2. Hutch. 227.   [u] 1. Bl. Com. 211, 212.   [v] Id. 233.

separate and independent powers and rights. When the society was formed, it possessed jointly all the previously separate and independent powers and rights of the individuals who formed it, and all the other powers and rights, which result from the social union. The aggregate of these powers and these rights composes the sovereignty of the society or nation. In the society or nation this sovereignty originally exists. For whose benefit does it exist? For the benefit of the society or nation. Is it necessary for the benefit of the society or nation, that, the moment it exists, it should be transferred? — This question ought, undoubtedly, to be seriously considered, and, on the most solid grounds, to be resolved in the affirmative, before the transfer is made. Has this ever been done? Has it ever been evinced, by unanswerable arguments, that it is necessary to the benefit of a society to transfer all those rights and powers, and the results of all those rights and powers, which the members once possessed separately, but which the society now possess jointly? I think such a position has never been evinced to be true. Those powers and rights were, I think, collected to be exercised and enjoyed, not to be alienated and lost. All these powers and rights, indeed, cannot, in a numerous and extended society, be exercised personally; but they may be exercised by representation. One of those powers and rights is to make laws for the government of the nation. This power and right may be delegated for a certain period, on certain conditions, under certain limitations, and to a certain number of persons. I ask — Is it necessary that, along with this power and this right, all the other powers and rights of the nation should be delegated to the same persons? I ask farther — is it necessary, that all those other powers and rights should be delegated without any right of resumption? — Another of those powers and rights is that of carrying the laws into execution. May not the society delegate this right for another period, on other conditions, with other limitations, and to other persons? A third right and power of the society is that of administering justice under the laws. May not this right be delegated for still another period, on still other conditions, under still other limitations, and to still other persons? Or may not this power and right be partly delegated and partly retained in personal exercise? For, in the most extended communities, an important part of the administration of justice may be discharged by the people themselves. All this certainly may be done. All this certainly has been done, as I shall have the pleasure of showing, when I come to examine the American governments, and to point out, by an enumeration and comparison of particulars, how beautifully, how regularly, and how usefully we have established, by our practice in this country, principles concerning the reservation, the distribution, the arrangement, the direction, and the uses of publick authority, of which even the just theory is still unknown in other nations,

Let us now pause and reflect. After what we see can be done, after what we see has been done, in the delegation and distribution of the rights and powers of society; can we subscribe to the doctrine of the Commentaries — that the authority, which is legislative must be *supreme?* Can we consent, that this doctrine should form a first principle in our system of municipal law? Certainly not. This definition is not calculated for the meridian of the United States.

I go farther — It is not calculated for the meridian of Great Britain. In order to show this, as it ought to be shown, it will be necessary to enter into a disquisition concerning the component parts and powers of the British parliament, and the origin, kinds, and properties of the English municipal law; the greatest and best proportion of which was never made by a parliament at all.

The British parliament consists of three distinct branches; the king, the house of lords, and the house of commons. To that species of English law, which is called a statute, the assent of all the three branches is necessary. When it has received the assent of all the three, it becomes a law and is obligatory upon the nation; but it is obligatory upon different parts of it for different reasons. "An act of parliament," says my Lord Hale, "is made, as it were, a tripartite indenture, between the king, the lords, and commons; for without the concurrent consent of all those three parts of the legislature, no such law is or can be made." [w] What is an indenture? The Commentaries will tell us, that it is a species of deed, to which there are more parties than one.[x] What is the first requisite of a deed? The Commentaries will also tell us, "that there be persons able to contract, and be contracted with." [y] If a deed is a contract or agreement; if an indenture is a species of deed, to which there are more parties than one; if an act of parliament may be called an indenture tripartite, because there are three parties to it — the king, the lords, and the commons; we find, that an act, which, considered indistinctly and dignified by the name of law, requires the whole supreme power of the nation to give it birth, is, when viewed more closely and analyzed into the component parts of its authority, properly arranged under the class of contracts. It is a contract, to which there are three parties; those, who constitute one of the three parties, not acting even in publick characters. A peer represents no one; he votes for himself; and when he is absent, he may transfer his right of voting to another. This may be thought a very free way of treating what is represented as necessarily an emanation of sovereign authority; but it is treating it truly; and give me leave to add, it is treating it accurately. Besides; I shall not be ashamed of treading in a path, though even a foot path, to which I am directed by the finger of the enlightened Lord Hale. That path, to which he points, will lead to instruction. Let us pursue it —

[w] Hale's Hist. 2.   [x] 2. Bl. Com. 295.   [y] Id. 296.

To this indenture there are three parties: to an indenture the power of contracting in each of the parties is necessary. What is the power of contracting in the different parts? The king contracts for himself, and as representing the executive authority of the nation. The peers engage in their private and personal rights. The members of the house of commons bind themselves and those whom they represent. They represent, or are supposed — how justly is immaterial to our present argument — to represent "all the commons of the whole realm." [z] We all know, that one may execute an instrument, either in person, or by an attorney: we all know that an instrument may be executed by a person in his own right and as attorney also. Perhaps it would not be improper if, on some occasions at least, the forms, as well as the principles, of private, were copied into publick, transactions. Permit me to mention an instance, in which this was lately done. In the ratification of the constitution of the United States by the convention of Pennsylvania, the distinct characters, in which the members of that convention acted, are distinctly marked. "We the delegates of the people of the commonwealth of Pennsylvania, in general convention assembled, do, in the name and by the authority of the same people, and for ourselves, assent to and ratify the foregoing constitution for the United States of America."

The foregoing, though a very familiar, must, I think, be admitted to be a very intelligible and satisfactory illustration and analysis of the manner, in which acts of parliament are made and become obligatory. For my own part, I cannot conceive how the truth, or the real dignity of a subject, can suffer by being closely inspected. When the exclamation — procul este — is made, I am led to suspect, that a secret conscious want of dignity or integrity is the cause. The plain and simple analysis, which I have given, of the nature and obligation of acts of parliament is evidently countenanced by the expressive legal language of my Lord Hale — It is supported and confirmed by the very respectable authority of my Lord Hardwicke. "The binding force — " I use his very words, as they are reported — "the binding force of these acts of parliament arises from that prerogative, which is in the king, as our sovereign liege lord; from that personal right, which is inherent in the peers and lords of parliament to bind themselves and their heirs and successours in their honours and dignities; and from the delegated power vested in the commons, as the representatives of the people; and, therefore, Lord Coke says, 4. Inst. 1. these represent the whole commons of the realm, and are trusted for them. By reason of this representation, every man is said to be a party to, and the consent of every subject is involved in, an act of parliament." [a] "Every man in England," says the Author of the Commentaries himself,

[z] 4. Ins. 1.   [a] 2. Atk. 654.

"is, in judgment of law, party to the making of an act of parliament, being present thereat by his representatives." [b] What is there in all this, that necessarily implies the irresistible energy of power, which is sovereign and supreme, without limits and without control?

We have already seen all the parties to an act of parliament. Let us, again, take a deliberate and distinct view of them: where shall we find the sovereign and supreme power? In the king? It is true, that he is called by my Lord Hardwicke "sovereign liege lord," and that his prerogative, as such, is assigned, and with much propriety, as one of the sources, from which "the binding force of acts of parliament arises." The legal and constitutional import of the expressions, sovereign liege lord, is well known. They present the king to his subjects as the object of their allegiance: they present him to foreigners as exercising the whole authority of the nation in foreign transactions. To foreign transactions, the British parliament is no party: to foreign nations, the British parliament is totally unknown. Alliances, treaties of peace, even declarations of war, are made in the name, and by the constitutional authority, of the king alone. But, it has never been pretended, that the prerogative of the king, as sovereign liege lord, extended so far as to bind his subjects by his laws. Even Henry the eighth, tyrant as he was, knew that an act of parliament was necessary, if even that could be sufficient, to endow his proclamations with legal obligatory force. But the king, by assenting to an act of parliament, can bind himself; and he can bind all that portion of the sovereign power of the nation, which is intrusted to his management and care. And it is certainly proper, that, as he represents the executive and the foreign powers of the nation, he should be consulted in the making of the national laws. From this short and clear deduction, we evidently see, that the absolute, uncontrolled power, mentioned by Sir William Blackstone as inseparable from legislative authority, is not to be found in the king. Is it to be found in the house of lords? That will not be pretended. Their votes bind not a single person in the nation, except themselves and the heirs and successours of their honours and dignities. Let us go to the house of commons: is this supreme power, which elsewhere we have searched for in vain, to be found among the members of this house? In what character? In their own right? This will not be alleged. As representatives? As representatives, they act, not by their own power, but by the power of those whom they represent. This power, therefore, whatever it is, cannot be found among the members of the house of commons, it must be looked for among their constituents. There, indeed, we shall find it: and the moment we find it, we shall discover its nature and extent. The king and the commons assembled in parliament are invested by the whole nation,

[b] 1. Bl. Com. 185.

except the house of lords, who act in their own right, not with "transcendent and absolute power and jurisdiction" *generally,* as one would naturally conclude from the unqualified expressions of Sir William Blackstone; but with this "transcendent and absolute power and jurisdiction
for the *making of laws,*" as we find in the determinate language of my
Lord Coke. To the making of laws, this power and jurisdiction of the
British parliament is strictly and rigidly confined. A single law the British
parliament cannot execute: in a single cause, the British parliament cannot
administer justice. Why then should "absolute despotick power," to use
the language of the Commentaries, be ascribed to the British parliament?
Has this doctrine a solid foundation? I presume it has not. But though
it has not a solid foundation, it has produced, as I shall hereafter show, the
most pernicious effects. I will acknowledge freely, that the bounds, which
circumscribe the authority of the British parliament, are not sufficiently
accurate: I will acknowledge farther, that they are not sufficiently strong.
But can this suggest a reason or a motive for denying their existence? It
strongly suggests, indeed, reasons and motives of a very different kind.
It suggests the strongest reasons and motives for circumscribing the authority of the British parliament by limits more accurate, for fortifying
those limits with an additional degree of strength, and for rendering the
practice more conformable than it now is, to the theory of its institution
— for rendering the house of commons in fact, what it is presumed to be
in law, "a representation of all the commons of the whole realm." If any
thing coming from this chair could be supposed, by possibility, to produce the smallest effect in that nation, I would warmly recommend to
it the accomplishment of those great objects, as consummations most
devoutly to be wished. The maxim of the great Lord Burleigh has prevailed long enough: let it make way for a better. Instead of saying, that
"England can never be ruined but by a parliament;" let it be said, and
truly said, that "England can never be ruined but by herself."

The learned Author of the Commentaries distinguishes between a
law and a counsel; and also between a law and an agreement. I will examine the principle of these distinctions, in order that its strength or
weakness may appear. It will be necessary to mention what is said in
the Commentaries upon this subject. "Municipal law is called a *rule,* to
distinguish it from *advice* or *counsel,* which we are at liberty to follow or
not, as we see proper, and to judge of the reasonableness or unreasonable-
ness of the thing advised: whereas our obedience to the law depends not
upon our approbation, but upon the maker's will. Counsel is only matter
of persuasion; law is matter of injunction: counsel acts only upon the
willing; law upon the unwilling also.

"It is also called a *rule,* to distinguish it from a *compact* or *agreement:*
for a compact is a promise proceeding *from* us; law is a command di-

rected *to* us. The language of a compact is, 'I will, or will not, do this;' that of a law is, 'thou shalt, or shalt not, do this.' It is true, that there is an obligation, which a compact carries with it, equal, in point of conscience, to that of a law; but then the original of the obligation is different. In compacts, we ourselves determine and promise what shall be done, before we are obliged to do it; in laws, we are obliged to act, without ourselves determining or promising any thing at all." [e]

The examination of the principle, which lies at the root of these distinctions, is an interesting subject indeed. If these distinctions can be supported, we may bid a last adieu to the maxim which I have always deemed of prime importance in the science of government and human laws — a free people are governed by laws, of which they approve. Before we part from this darling position, let us, at least, cast behind us, a "longing, lingering look."

Upon these passages in the Commentaries, I make remarks similar to those, which I made upon the passages examined some time ago. No authority in the English law is adduced — none, so far as I know, could be adduced to support them. These sentiments concerning law, as well as the definitions of municipal law, and law in general, may be traced to the performance of Baron Puffendorff. Let us see what this performance says. "*Law* differs from *counsel* in this, that by the latter a man" — "has no proper power, so as to lay any direct obligation on another; but must leave it to his pleasure and choice whether he will follow the counsel or not." "But law, though it ought not to want its reasons, yet these reasons are not the cause why obedience is paid to it, but the power of the exacter, who, when he has signified his pleasure, lays an obligation on the subject to act in conformity to his decree." "We obey laws, not principally on account of the matter of them, but upon account of the legislator's will. And thus law is the injunction of him, who has a power over those, to whom he prescribes; but counsel comes from him, who has no such power." "Counsel is only given to those, who are willing to have it; but law reaches the unwilling." [d]

"Neither are those ancients accurate enough in their expressions, who frequently apply to laws the name of *common agreements*." "The points of distinction between a compact or covenant and a law, are obvious. For a *compact* is a *promise*, but a *law* is a *command*. In *compacts*, the form of speaking is, I will do so and so; but in *laws*, the form runs, do thou so, after an imperative manner. In *compacts*, since they depend, as to their original, on our will, we first determine what is to be done, before we are obliged to do it; but in *laws*, which suppose the power of others over us, we are, in the first place, obliged to act, and afterwards the manner of acting is determined. And, therefore, he is not bound by a *compact*

[e] 1. Bl. Com. 44. 45.   [d] Puff. 58. 59. b. 1. c. 6. s. 1.

who did not freely tie himself by giving his consent: but we are, for this reason, obliged by a *law;* because we owed an antecedent obedience to its author." [e]

You now see, that these distinctions between a law and an agreement, a law and a compact are adopted from Baron Puffendorff: whence he derived them, it is immaterial to inquire. But it is material to show, as I think I can do unanswerably, that these distinctions, if they could be supported, would overturn the beautiful temple of liberty from its very foundations. It is material also to show, as I think I can do unanswerably, that the fair temple of liberty stands unshaken and undefaced; and that the sole legitimate principle of obedience to human laws is human consent. This consent may be authenticated in different ways: in its different stages of existence, it may assume different names — approbation — ratification — experience: but in all its different shapes — under all its different appellations, it may easily be resolved into this proposition, simple, natural, and just — All human laws should be founded on the consent of those, who obey them. This great principle I shall, in the course of these lectures, have occasion to follow in a thousand agreeable directions. My present business, while I examine the principles of municipal law as delivered in the Commentaries, is to apply them and the examination of them to the law of England. In that law, we shall find the stream of authority running, from the most early periods, uniform and strong in the direction of the principle of consent — consent, given originally — consent, given in the form of ratification — and, what is most satisfactory of all, consent given after long, approved, and uninterrupted experience. This last, I think, is the principle of the common law. It is the most salutary principle of obedience to human laws, that ever was diffused among men. With such a Byzantium before him, is it not astonishing, indeed, that the attention — must I say the attachment? — of Sir William Blackstone should have been attracted towards a Chalcedon? [f]

The ancient coronation oath of the kings of England obliged them, to the utmost of their power, to cause those laws to be observed, "which the men of the people have made and chosen." [g]

Let us next pay the respect, which is due to the celebrated sentiment of the English Justinian, Edward the first. "Lex justissima, ut quod omnes tangit, ab omnibus approbetur." It is a most just law, that what affects all should be approved by all. This golden rule is, with great propriety, inserted in his summons to his parliament. The Lord Chancellor Fortescue, in his most excellent tractate concerning the English laws, informs his royal pupil, that the statutes of England are framed, not by the will of the prince, but by that and by the assent of the whole kingdom. "Angliæ, sta-

---

[e] Puff. 59. b. 1. c. 6. s. 2.   [f] 3. Gibbon. 6. 7. Tac. Ann. XII. 62.
[g] 1. Bl. Com. 236, note. "que lez gentez du people avont faitez et esliez."

tuta, nedum principis voluntate, sed et totius regni assensu, ipsa conduntur." And if a statute, though passed with the greatest caution and solemnity, should be found, on experience, not to reach those purposes, which were intended by its framers, it can soon be reformed; but not without the same assent of the peers and commonalty of the kingdom, from which it originally flowed. "Et si statuta hæc, tanta solennitate et prudentia edita, efficaciæ tantæ, quantæ conditorum cupiebat intentio, non esse contingant, correcto reformari ipsa possunt; et nonsine communitatis et procerum regni illius assensu, quali ipsa primitus emanarunt." [h] "To an act of law, statute or common, every man," says Lord Chief Justice Vaughan, "is as much consenting, and more solemnly, than he is to his own private deed." [i] Authorities to the same purpose might, without end, be heaped upon authorities from the law books. I forbear to trouble you with any more of them. Let us have recourse to what I may properly call a perpetually standing authority upon this very important subject — the writ for choosing members of parliament. It commands the sheriff of each county to cause two knights, the most fit and discreet of the county, and two citizens from every city, and two burgesses from every borough within the county, to be chosen according to law — "So that the said knights have full and sufficient power for themselves,[j] and the commonalty of the said county, and the said citizens and burgesses for themselves and the commonalty[k] of the said cities and boroughs, severally from them, to do and consent to those things, which, by the favour of God, shall happen to be ordained by the common council of the kingdom: so that for default of such power, or through improvident election of the said knights, citizens, or burgesses, the said affairs remain not undone." [l] Can language be more explicit to show the principle, upon which acts of parliament must be made, and consequently the principle, upon which alone they ought to be obeyed? It is directed, that the members have full and sufficient powers *for themselves*, and for their constituents *from their constituents*. This is precisely according to the analysis, which we have already given of the power of parliament. Why are those powers

[h] Fortes. c. 18.   [i] Vaugh. 392.

[j] It is the wisdom of the English law, that acts of parliament are equally binding to the makers of them as to the rest of the people. The makers are empowered for themselves, as well as for their constituents; and themselves, as well as their constituents must taste the sweet or bitter fruits of their own works. This suggests a powerful motive for caution and justice in their determinations (2. Whitlocks 87.) But this doctrine ill agrees with the new and foreign theory, introduced into the Commentaries — "A law always supposes some superiour, who is to make it." 1. Bl. Com. 43.

[k] It is a great trust reposed in members of parliament, to have the power of the whole commonalty of a county, or city, or borough conferred on them. The acts of the members are the acts of the commonalty, from whom they have their power, and who are bound by them. 2. Whitlocke 89.

[l] 1. Whitlocke 2. 3.

necessary? To do and *consent* to those things, which shall be ordained by parliament. Those powers are absolutely necessary; for, without them, the business of the nation would remain undone. Is it possible, that any one, who has ever seen this venerable and authentick legal instrument, could suppose, that the sovereign power of the nation was vested in the parliament of Great Britain? Is it possible, that one who has seen this writ could forget the rock, from which the members were hewn, and the hole of the pit from which they were dug? The humble servants, who must come furnished with "full and sufficient power from" their masters "the commonalty of the county, and the burgesses and the citizens separately — " "*Divisim*," one by one — have those humble servants, when assembled together, the uncontrolled powers of the nation in their hands? When they are intrusted with the legislative, may they, therefore, assume also the executive and the judicial powers of their country?

We now see, in a very striking point of view, the strong and expressive import of the language of my Lord Hale, when he says, that an act of parliament is, as it were, a tripartite indenture, between the king, the lords, and the commons. They form three parties: each party has power to contract. The king contracts in his own right — for the king is also a man — and in consequence of the powers devolved on him by that original contract, long supposed, but, at the revolution of 1688, expressly recognized to have been made between him and the people. The lords of parliament contract solely in their own right. The members of the house of commons contract in their own right, for themselves, and in right of their constituents, for the commonalty of the whole realm. Thus we find every party and every power to form a contract, a compact, or an agreement — for these terms are synonimous — in the strictest and most proper sense of the words. The vital principle of every contract is the consent of the mind. My Lord Hale did not draw the obligatory principle of an act of parliament from a foreign fountain: he drew it, pure and clear, from its native springs.

Sir William Blackstone tells us, that the original of the obligation, which a compact carries with it, is different from that of a law. The original of the obligation of a compact we know to be consent: the original of the obligation of an act of parliament we have traced minutely to the very same source.

But acts of parliament are not the only — let us add, they are not the principal — species of law, known and obligatory in England. That kingdom boasts in the common law. In the countenance of that law, every lovely feature beams consent. This law is of vast importance. By it, the proceedings and decisions of courts of justice are regulated and directed. It guides the course of descents and successions to real estates, and limits their extent and qualifications: it appoints the forms and solemnities of acquiring, of securing, and of transferring property: it prescribes the manner and the obligation of contracts: it establishes the rules, by which contracts, wills, deeds, and even acts of parliament are interpreted.[m] This law is founded on long and general custom. A custom, that has been long and generally observed, necessarily carries with it intrinsick evidence of consent. Caution and prudence are universally recommended in the introduction of new laws: can caution and prudence be so strongly exemplified — can their fruits be so certainly reaped in any other laws, as in those that are established by custom? The prospect of convenience invites to the first experiment: a first experiment, successful, encourages to make a second. The successful experiments of one man or one body of men induce another man or another body of men to venture upon similar trials. The instances are multiplied and extended, till, at length, the custom becomes universal and established. Can a law be made in a manner more eligible? Experience, the faithful guide of life and business, attends it in its every step. Other laws demand to be taken upon trust: a good countenance is their only recommendation. Those, who introduce them, can only say, in their favour, that they look well. A customary law, with a modesty appropriate to conscious merit, asks for admittance only upon trial, and claims not to be considered as a part of the political family, till she can establish a character, founded on a long and intimate acquaintance. The same means, by which the character of one law is known and approved, are employed to try and discriminate the character of every other. In favour of every one that is recommended, it can be said, not only, that it has lived unexceptionably by itself, but also that it has lived in peace and harmony with all the others. In this manner, a system of approved and concording laws is gradually, though slowly, collected and formed. By a process of this kind, the immortal Newton collected, arranged, and formed his just and beautiful system of experimental philosophy. By the same kind of process, our predecessors and ancestors have collected, arranged, and formed a system of experimental law, equally just, equally beautiful, and, important as Newton's system is, far more important still. This system has stood the test of numerous ages: to every age it has disclosed new beauties and new truths. In improvement, it is yet progressive; and what has been said poetically on another occasion, may be said in the strictest form of asseveration on this, — it acquires strength in its progress. From this system, we derive our dearest birthright and richest inheritance. The rise, the progress, the history, and the component parts of this invaluable system; its extension to America, and the principles of its establishment in the several states and in the national government, it will be my duty and my pleasure to trace and to exhibit in the course of these lectures. My present business is, to ascertain the ori-

[m] Hale's Hist. 24.

gin of its obligatory force. Surely, this may be done with ease. The common law is founded on long and general custom. On what can long and general custom be founded? Unquestionably, on nothing else, but free and voluntary *consent*. The regions of custom afford a most secure asylum from the operations of absolute, despotick power. To the cautious, circumspect, gradual, and tedious probation, which a law, originating from custom, must undergo, a law darted from compulsion will never submit.

"Sic volo, sic jubeo, stet pro ratione voluntas," * is the motto of edicts, proclaimed, in thunder, by the voice of a human superiour. Far dissimilar are the sentiments expressed in calm and placid accents by a customary law. I never intruded upon you: I was invited upon trial: this trial has been had: you have long known me: you have long approved me: shall I now obtain an establishment in your family? A customary law carries with it the most unquestionable proofs of freedom in the country, which is happy enough to be the place of its abode.

Some truths are too plain to be proved. That a law, which has been established by long and general custom, must have received its origin and introduction from free and voluntary consent, is a position that must be evident to every one, who understands the force and meaning of the terms, in which it is expressed. My object is to imprint, as well as to prove, this great political doctrine. Perhaps this cannot be done better, than by laying before you the sentiments, which an English parliament held upon this subject, above two hundred years ago. You will see how strongly they support the principle — that the obligation of human laws arises from consent. The sentiments were expressed on an occasion similar to one, which will still suggest matter of very interesting recollection to many minds — They were expressed when an attempt was made to establish, in England, a foreign jurisdiction. With becoming indignation against it, the parliament declare — "This realm is free from subjection to any man's laws, but only to such as have been devised, made, and obtained within this realm, for the wealth of the same, or to such as, by sufferance of your grace and your progenitors, the people of this your realm have taken at their free liberty, with their *own consent* to be used amongst them, and have *bound themselves* by *long use and custom* to the observance of the same, not as to the observance of laws of any foreign prince, potentate, or prelate, but as to the customed and ancient laws of this realm, originally established as laws of the same, by the said sufferance, consents, and customs, and none otherwise." [n]

Some writers, when they describe that usage, which is the foundation of common law, characterize it by the epithet *immemorial*. The parlia-

* [Thus I will, thus I command, let my will stand as the reason.]
[n] St. 25. H. 8. c. 21. s. 1.

mentary description is not so strong. "Long use and custom" is assigned as the criterion of law, "taken by the people at their free liberty, and by their own consent." And this criterion is surely sufficient to satisfy the principle: for consent is certainly proved by long, though it be not immemorial usage.

That consent is the probable principle of the common law, is admitted by the Author of the Commentaries himself. "It is one of the characteristick marks of English liberty," says he,[o] "that our common law depends upon custom, which carries this internal evidence of freedom along with it, that it probably was introduced by the voluntary consent of the people." I search not for contradictions: I wish to reconcile what is seemingly contradictory. But, if the common law could be introduced, as it is admitted it probably was, by the voluntary consent of the people; I confess I can not reconcile with this — certainly a solid — principle, the principle that "A law always supposes some superiour, who is to make it," nor another principle, that "sovereignty and legislature are indeed convertible terms."

A power, far beneath the sovereign power, may be invested with legislative authority; and its laws may be as obligatory as any other human laws. Of this, instances occur even in the government of Great-Britain.

It is necessarily and inseparably incident to all corporations, to make by-laws, or private statutes, for their government. These laws are binding upon themselves, unless contrary to the laws of the land, and then they are void.[p] From these positions, we clearly infer, that laws, obligatory upon those for whom they are made, may be enacted by a power, so far from being absolute and supreme, that its laws are void, when contrary to those enacted by a superiour power: so far do sovereignty and legislature, in this instance at least, appear to be from convertible terms: so far is it from being requisite to the very essence of a law, that it be made by the supreme power. Sir William Blackstone tells us, that in the provincial establishments in America, the assemblies had the power of making local ordinances; that subordinate powers of legislation subsisted in the proprietary governments; and that, in the charter governments, the assemblies made laws, suited to their own emergencies:[q] and yet, in these instances, he certainly did not admit, that "by sovereign power is meant the making of laws."

I hope I have now shown, that the definition of municipal law in the Commentaries is not calculated even for the meridian of Great-Britain: it is still less calculated for that of many other governments: for, in many other governments, the distinction is still more strongly marked between the sovereign and legislative powers.

[o] 1. Bl. Com. 74.   [p] 1. Bl. Com. 475.   [q] 1. Bl. Com. 108.

In the original constitution of Rome, the sovereign power, the *dominium eminens*, as it is called by the civilians, always resided in the collective body of the people. But the laws of Rome were not always made by that collective body. To the senate was indulged a privilege of legislation; partial and subordinate, it is true; but still a privilege of legislation. An act of the senate was not considered as a permanent law; but it was allowed to continue in force for one year; not longer, unless it was ratified by the people. To the plebeians, exclusive of the senators and patricians, a privilege of legislation was also indulged; but their laws bound only themselves. While we are taking notice of the different bodies, that possessed the power of legislation in Rome, it is proper to mention one very great defect, which existed in the constitution of that celebrated republick. A power, inferiour to that which made a law, could dispense with it. The senate, by its own decree, could dispense with a law, made by the whole collective body of the people. This power, dangerous in every free government, was often exercised, in Rome, to accomplish the most pernicious purposes.[r]

In the United States, and in each of the commonwealths, of which the union is composed, the legislative is very different from the supreme power. Instead of being uncontrollable, the legislative authority is placed, as it ought to be, under just and strict control. The effects of its extravagancies may be prevented, sometimes by the executive, sometimes by the judicial authority of the governments; sometimes even by a private citizen, and, at all times, by the superintending power of the people at large. These different points will afterwards receive a particular explication. At present, perhaps, this general position may be hazarded — That whoever would be obliged to obey a constitutional law, is justified in refusing to obey an unconstitutional act of the legislature — and that, when a question, even of this delicate nature, occurs, every one who is called to act, has a right to judge: he must, it is true, abide by the consequences of a wrong judgment.

Puffendorff, from whom the idea of a superiour, as forming a necessary ingredient in the idea of law, seems to have been transplanted into the Commentaries, insists much upon what he calls a maxim — *that a person cannot oblige himself*; "and this maxim," he tells us, "is not confined to single men, but extends to whole bodies and societies:"[s] "for a person to oblige himself under the notion of a lawgiver, or of a superiour, is an impossibility."[t] Hence the inference seems to be drawn, that "obligations are laid on human minds by a superiour." To different

[r] In the government of Media, an opposite extreme prevailed. When an edict was once published, it was not in the power of the legislator to alter or repeal it. The same power, which is sufficient to make, should be sufficient to abrogate a law. 3. Gog. Or. Laws. 11.
[s] Puff. 63. b. 1. c. 6. s. 7.   [t] Id. 688. b. 7. c. 6. s. 2.

minds, the same things, sometimes, appear in a very different manner. If I was to make a maxim upon this subject, it would be precisely the reverse of the maxim of Baron Puffendorff. Instead of saying, that a man cannot oblige himself; I would say, that no other person upon earth can oblige him, but that he certainly can oblige himself. Consent is the sole principle, on which any claim, in consequence of human authority, can be made upon one man by another. I say, in consequence of human authority; for, in consequence of the divine authority, numerous are the claims that we are reciprocally entitled to make, numerous are the duties, that we are reciprocally obliged to perform. But none of these can enter into the present question. We speak of authority merely human. Exclusively of the duties required by the law of nature, I can conceive of no claim, that one man can make upon another, but in consequence of his own consent. Let us, upon this occasion, as we have done upon some others, simplify the object by a plain and distinct analysis. Let us take for the subject of our analysis the very question we are upon — Whether a man can be bound by any human authority, except his own consent? Let us suppose, that one demands obedience from me to a certain in-junction, which he calls a law, by performing some service pointed out to me: I ask him, why am I obliged to obey it? He says it is just I should do it. Justice, I tell him, is a part of the law of nature; give me a reason drawn from human authority. He tells me, he had promised it. Very well, perform your promise. Suppose he rises in his tone, and tells me, he orders it. Equal and free, I see no reason for obeying the order of one, who is only equal and free. Repelled from this attack upon my inde-pendence, he assails me on a very different quarter; and, softening his accents, represents how generous, nay how humane, it would be, to do as he desires. Humanity is a duty; generosity is a virtue; but neither is to be referred to human authority. Let invention be put upon the rack, and the severest torture will not draw from it a discovery of any external human authority, by which I am obliged to obey the supposed law, or to perform the supposed service. He tells me, next, that I promised to do it. Now, indeed, I discover a human source of obligation. If I promised to do it, I am bound to do it; unless the promise is either un-lawful, or discharged; dissolved by an equal, or prohibited by a superiour authority. But this promise originated from consent; for if it was the abortion of compulsion — the effect sometimes of exterior and superiour human *power*, but never of human *authority* — I am not bound to con-sider it as my act and deed.

Let us now vary the supposition a little. Suppose this demand to be made upon me by one, of whose superiour judgment and unimpeached veracity I had the strongest and best founded belief: suppose me at that period of life — for there is such a period of life — when I should

believe implicitly whatever was taught me by one, whom I knew I could
so well trust: suppose this person, respected for his knowledge and integrity, should tell me, that he really thought it my duty to comply with
the demand. I think I should probably feel a sense of obligation arise
within me. But why? because this respectable person says it? No. But
for a reason, which may be easily mistaken for this: because I believe,
that what this respected person says must be true. Here, indeed, is a
species of external human authority, exerted and obeyed for the wisest
purposes: But this is very different from that external human authority,
which is assigned by some as the source of obligation in human laws.
This species of authority is said to have been carried to a very great
height by Pythagoras, the celebrated philosopher. He delivered it as a
maxim, and it was received as such in his school, that whatever he said
must be true. *Ipse dixit* was an undisputed authority. But if folly and
falsehood had been as inseparably associated with the character of
Pythagoras, as veracity and wisdom were, in the minds of his followers,
I ask — would his *ipse dixit* have been received as an undisputed authority? I presume not. To recur, then, to the supposition, which I last
made; I should feel the sense of obligation arise in me, not because I
should think it his will, that I should comply with the demand; but
because I should believe in his opinion, that it was my duty to do so. This
refers to a very different source. For let me suppose a little farther, that,
after feeling this sense of obligation arise within me, I should come to
learn, either from my own observation, or from authority still superiour
to that of the person in whom I placed confidence, that this confidence
was misplaced; that what he told me proceeded either from mistake, or
from something worse than mistake; his will might continue the same,
and my opinion concerning it might continue the same, but my sense of
obligation would be greatly altered. These remarks, I hope, will be
sufficient to show, that no exterior human authority can bind a free and
independent man.

    The next question is — can a man bind himself? Baron Puffendorff
lays it down as a maxim, that he cannot: and on this maxim, applied to
publick bodies as well as private individuals, he builds a very interesting
series of argumentation — just, indeed, and unanswerable, if the basis, on
which it rests, be solid and sound.

    We have, at last, reached the bottom of the business. We are now
come to the important question, the resolution of which must, in my
opinion, decide the fate of all human laws. I say, in my opinion; for I
have already given my reasons for thinking, that if a man cannot bind
himself, no human authority can bind him. For one man, equal and free,
cannot be bound by another, who is no more. The consequence necessarily is, that if a man can be bound by any human authority, it must be

by himself. A farther consequence necessarily is, that if he cannot bind himself, there is an end of all human authority, and of all human laws. How differently, sometimes, things turn out, from what was expected from them! The idea of superiority, it was probably thought, would strengthen the obligation of human laws. When traced minutely and accurately, we find, that it would destroy their very existence. If no human law can be made without a superiour; no human law can ever be made.

First principles ought to be admitted with caution indeed. When you first read, in the Commentaries, this principle — "a law always supposes some superiour, who is to make it;" you did not suspect, I presume, that this principle is subversive of all human laws. You now perceive, that, if a man can be bound by human authority, it must be by his own. But is he his own superiour? The creative imagination of a Theobald himself could not suggest the fancy. He could only go so far as to say

> None but himself can be his *parallel.*

Even the master of a show, who boasted, that his elephant was "the greatest elephant in the world," thought it necessary, for preventing mistakes, to add — except himself.

But to resume seriously the important question — can a man bind himself? Simple facts have sometimes led to the greatest discoveries. The sublime theory of gravitation was first suggested to Newton by an apple falling from a tree.

At the end of the second volume of the Commentaries are precedents of some useful instruments, known to the law of England. Among others, there is a precedent of a common bond. In that bond, there are these words written — *I bind myself.* This form of a bond has been known and used and approved in England from time immemorial. If a man cannot bind himself, then all the bonds, which have been executed in England, have been mere nullities. The substantial parts of that bond are parts of the common law of England. The part, which I have mentioned, is certainly a most substantial one. All parts of the precedent are not substantial: many of them may be omitted or altered without vitiating the force of the bond. The law does not require any particular form of words: but one thing it strictly requires — such words as declare the intention of the party, and denote his being bound: such words will be sufficient: such words will be carried into effect by the judgment of the law.

Let us examine the obligatory principle of a bond by legal tests, by triers at the common law. Suppose one applies to a court of justice to enforce the obligation of a bond, and proposes it as the foundation of his demand. In what manner is he directed by the law to express the legal import of the instrument? He is directed to declare, that, by this instrument, the party who executed it, "acknowledged himself to be bound," [u] or "bound himself." [v] The precedents are in both forms. When the action is properly instituted, the party, against whom it is instituted, is next called upon, with all legal solemnity, to make his defence — for against no man ought a decision to be pronounced till he has an opportunity of being heard. He appears: the instrument is produced. What can he say, why a decision should not be pronounced against him? The common law furnishes him with forms to suit almost every case, certainly every case that has been brought before a court of justice. If the case of the present defendant is so very peculiar, that nothing similar to it ever happened before; the common law will protect him in forming a defence, suited to his very peculiar case. Among all the different kinds of pleas, fitted for every case that has happened, for almost every case that can happen, are there any furnished, which bear towards this principle — that the defendant could not oblige himself? There are. But they are furnished only for those, who, by reason of their infancy, or any other cause, appear to want a common degree of understanding. For without understanding it, no obligation can be legitimately formed. There are others too, that respect another situation, which it will be proper to examine particularly; because it is probable, that it will throw much light upon the principle of obligation to human laws. The understanding, though necessary, is not, of itself, sufficient to form a legitimate obligation: in a legitimate obligation, the *will* must concur; compulsion will not be received as a substitute for consent. The common law is a law of liberty. The defendant may plead, that he was compelled to execute the instrument. He cannot, indeed, deny the execution of it; but he can state, in his plea, the circumstances of compulsion attending its execution;[w] and these circumstances, if sufficient in law, and established in fact, will procure a decision in his favour, that, in such circumstances, he did not bind himself. If he never executed the instrument at all; he can state the fact; and unless the execution of it be proved against him, he will, upon this plea likewise, obtain a decision, that he did not bind himself. But if he can do none of these things — if he executed the instrument; if he executed it voluntarily; if he executed it knowingly; the law will pronounce, that he bound himself. This has been the regular course of the law during time immemorial — a course, uninterrupted and unrepealed. In the municipal law of England, therefore, the doctrine is established — that a man can bind himself. This doctrine is established by strict legal inference from the principles and the practice of the common law. The consequence is, that, on the principles of the municipal law of England, a superiour is not necessary to the existence of obligation. A man can

[u] Boh. Ins. Leg. 102.   [v] 2. Mod. Ent. 178.   [w] 5. Rep. 119.

bind himself. But is his bond a law? Yes, it is a law binding upon himself. Farther it ought not to bind. But shall a private contract be viewed
in the venerable light of a law? Why not, if it has all its essential properties? Suppose this contract to have been made by millions, contracting
on each side: it would have been dignified by the name of a treaty: as
such, had the United States been the contractors on one side, it would
have become a law of the land: as such, it would have become an important part of the law of nations. Is the act of millions more binding upon
those millions, than the act of one is binding upon that one? Light will
break in upon us by degrees.

By the law of England, a man can bind himself. The law of England
speaks not a language contrary to that of the law of nature. By this law
also, a man can bind himself. "If among men," says Barbeyrac,[x] "the
immediate reason why one ought to be subject to the command of another is ordinarily this, that he has voluntarily consented to it" — and
we have shown, that this is not only *ordinarily*, but *always* the reason —
"then," continues he, "this consent, and all other engagements whatever
are only obligatory through that maxim of natural law, which tells us,
that every one ought to observe what he has engaged himself to." This
maxim is, indeed, a part of the law of a superiour; but this maxim is
founded upon the previous truth — that a man can engage himself: I
need not surely prove, that an engagement must be made before it can be
observed. "That we should be faithful to our engagements," says the
very learned President Goguet,[y] "is one of those maxims, which derive
their origin from those sentiments of equity and justice, which God has
engraven on the hearts of all men: they are taught us by that internal
light, which enables us to distinguish between right and wrong." The
same important lesson is delivered to nations, as well as to men.[z]

We see now, that, both by the law of England, and by the superiour
law of nature, men and nations can bind themselves. Can they be bound
without their consent? Is it necessary to dig for another foundation, on
which the obligatory force of human laws can be laid? Can any other
solid foundation be found?

That this foundation is sufficient to support the whole beautiful
structure of human law, will abundantly appear.

"The union of families," says the same respectable author, whom I
quoted just now, "could not have taken place but by an agreement of
wills. When we view society as the effect of unanimous concord, it necessarily supposes certain covenants. These covenants imply conditions.
These conditions are to be considered as the first laws."[a] We have already

[x] Puff. 67. n. 2. to b. 1. c. 6. s. 12.   [y] 1. Gog. Or. Laws. 7. 8.
[z] Vat. Pref. 12.   [a] 1. Gog. Or. Laws. 7.

seen the sentiments of the excellent Hooker — that "human edicts, derived from any other human source, than the consent of those, upon whom they are imposed, are nothing better than mere tyranny. Laws they are not, because they have not the publick approbation."[b] "The mother of civil law," says Grotius,[c] "is that very obligation, which arises from consent." "So that the civil law," says his commentator, Barbeyrac,[d] "is, at the bottom, no more than a consequence of that inviolable law of nature — every man is obliged to a religious observance of his promise." "The legislative power of a civil society," says Dr. Rutherforth, in his Institutes of Natural Law,[e] "is acquired by the immediate and direct consent of the several individuals, who make themselves members of such society. And the legislative body acquires it, as by the immediate and direct consent of the collective body of the society, so by the remote and indirect consent of the several members."

I hope I have now performed my engagement: I hope I have evinced, from authority and from reason, from precedent and from principle, that *consent* is the sole obligatory principle of human government and human laws. To trace the varying but powerful energy of this animating principle through the formation and administration of every part of our beautiful system of government and law, will be a pleasing task in the course of these lectures. Can any task be more delightful than to pursue the circulation of liberty through every limb and member of the political body? This kind of anatomy has a peculiar advantage — it traces, without destroying, the principle of life.

Before I conclude, it will be proper to take a concise view of the consequences, necessarily resulting from the doctrine, that the legislative power must be "absolute, uncontrolled, irresistible, and supreme." 1. The power, which makes the laws, cannot be accountable for its conduct; it cannot be submitted either to human judgment, or to human punishment. For both these, says Puffendorff,[f] suppose a superiour; but a superiour to the supreme, in the same order of men, and the same notion of government, is a contradiction. 2. If to every human law, a superiour is necessary: and if the power, which makes a human law, must be supreme; the consequence unquestionably is, that that power cannot be bound by the laws, which it makes: for where shall we find a superiour to what is supreme? "When a civil power," says Puffendorff,[g] "is constituted supreme, it must, on this very score, be supposed exempt from human laws; or, to speak more properly, above them. Human laws are nothing else but the decrees of the supreme power, concerning matters to be observed, by the subjects, for the publick good of the state. That no such edicts can directly oblige the sovereign is manifest; because his very

[b] Hooker. b. 1. s. 10. p. 19. 20.   [c] Pref. 20. s. 16.   [d] Id. note to s. 16.
[e] Vol. 2. 222.   [f] B. 7. c. 6. s. 2. p. 687.   [g] B. 7. c. 6. s. 3. p. 688.

name and title supposeth, that no bond or engagement can be laid on him by any other mortal hand: and for a person to oblige himself, under the notion of a lawgiver, or of a superiour, is an impossibility." 3. If the legislative power be absolute, uncontrolled, and supreme; all opposition to its acts must be unlawful. This, indeed, is not so much a consequence, as a part of the doctrine. In the language of the Commentaries, this power is "irresistible," [h] Many recollect the numerous and the extravagant inferences, which, at a former period, were drawn from the supposed absolute, irresistible, uncontrolled, and supreme power of the British parliament. They will fall under our notice, when we come to examine the principles, the rise, and the progress of the American constitutions and governments.

I have already mentioned, that though Sir William Blackstone was the first, he has not been the last, who defined municipal law, as applied to the law of England, upon unsound and dangerous principles. This doctrine has been adopted by his successour in the Vinerian chair, though with some degree of apparent hesitation. "Every state," says he, "must, like individuals, be subject to certain rules." "The necessity of rules infers the necessity of political superiours." [i] "The giving of laws to a people, forms the most exalted degree of human sovereignty; and is, perhaps, in effect, or in strict propriety of speech, the only truly supreme power of the state." [j] The sensible and decided Mr. Paley, in his principles of moral and political philosophy, has propagated the same doctrine without limitation and without reserve. "As a series of appeals," says he, "must be finite, there necessarily exists, in every government, a power, from which the constitution has provided no appeal; and which power, for that reason, may be termed absolute, omnipotent, uncontrollable, arbitrary, despotick; and is alike so, in all countries. The person, or assembly, in whom this power resides, is called the sovereign or the supreme power of the state. Since to the same power universally appertains the office of establishing publick laws, it is also called the legislature of the state." [k] It is not improbable, that the doctrine is disseminated wherever the Commentaries are generally received as authority.

I have already intimated, that there is a period in our lives, when we receive implicitly whatever we are taught, especially by those, in whom, we think, we can confide. "It is the intention of nature," says the ingenious Dr. Reid,[l] "that we should be carried in arms before we are able to walk upon our legs; and it is likewise the intention of nature, that our belief should be guided by the authority and reason of others, before it can be guided by our own reason." At this very period of life, the Commentaries, as a book of authority, are put into the hands of young gentle-

[h] 1. Bl. Com. 49.   [i] El. Jur. (4to) 26. 27.   [j] El. Jur. (4to) 43.
[k] 2. Paley 185.   [l] Inq. 433.

men, to form the basis of their law education. Is it surprising, that the
reception of its doctrines should be indiscriminate, as well as implicit?
Indeed the former is the unavoidable consequence of the latter. But
doctrines received implicitly, at this period of life, are not so easily dismissed in its subsequent stages. "For," says the same experienced judge
of human nature,[m] "the novelty of an opinion, to those who are too fond
of novelties; the gravity and solemnity, with which it is introduced; the
opinion we have entertained of the author; and, above all, its being fixed
in our minds at that time of life, when we receive implicitly what we
are taught; may cover its absurdity, and fascinate the understanding for a
time" — I will add — for a long time. These observations explain, and,
while they explain, they justify my conduct in examining, so fully and so
minutely, the definitions of law in general and of municipal law given in
the Commentaries on the laws of England. This full and minute examination has, at the same time, given me a fit opportunity of discovering,
of illustrating, and, I hope, of establishing very different principles, as
the foundation of the science of law. In this, as in every other science, it
is all important, that the foundation be properly and surely laid.

Permit me to close this subject with the sentiments, which a very
learned and ingenious judge expressed, on an occasion somewhat similar
to this, and in a situation somewhat similar to mine. The principles of
the revolution in England have been dear to whigs: they have been opposed inveterately and pertinaciously by tories. Some passages in the law
performances of the great and good Lord Chief Justice Hale were conceived, on both sides, and justly, to militate against the principles of that
revolution. These passages were cited with uncommon exultation, and
were, no doubt, disseminated by the votaries of the abdicated family with
extraordinary zeal. Seventy years after the revolution, and sixteen years
after the last rebellion, which was raised in order to overturn its happy
establishment, Mr. Justice Foster thought it his duty to publish some
observations on those passages, with a view to detect and expose their
mistakes, which were great, and to defend the principles, on which the
revolution and the subsequent establishment were founded. Concerning
these observations, and their publication, he thus speaks, "The cause of
the Pretender seems now to be absolutely given up. I hope in God it is
so. But whether the root of bitterness, the principles which gave birth,
and growth, and strength to it, and have been, twice within our memory,
made a pretence for rebellion, at seasons very critical, whether those
principles be totally eradicated, I know not. These I encounter, by showing that certain historical facts, which the learned Judge hath appealed
to in support of them, either have no foundation in truth, or, were they
true, do not warrant the conclusions drawn from them.

[m] Reid. Ess. In. 568.

"The passages I animadvert upon have been cited with an uncommon degree of triumph by those, who, to say no worse of them, from the dictates of a misguided conscience, have treated the revolution and present establishment as founded in usurpation and rebellion; and they are in every student's hand. Why, therefore, may not a good subject, be it in season or out of season, caution the younger part of the profession against the prejudices, which the name of Lord Chief Justice Hale, a name ever honoured and esteemed, may otherwise beget in them? I, for my part, make no apology for the freedom I have taken with the sentiments of an author whose memory I can love and honour, without adopting any of his mistakes on the subject of government.

"It cannot be denied, and I see no reason for making a secret of it, that the learned Judge hath, in his writings, paid no regard to the principles, upon which the revolution and present happy establishment are founded. The prevailing opinion of the times, in which he received his first impressions, might mislead him. And it is not to be wondered at, if the detestable use the parliamentary army made of its success in the civil war did contribute to fix him in the prejudices of his early days. For, in the competition of parties, extremes, on one side, almost universally produce their contraries on the other. And even honest minds are not always secured against the contagion of party prejudice.

"But, it matters not with us, whether his opinion was the effect of prejudices early entertained, or the result of cool reflection; since the opinion of no man, how great or good soever, is or ought to be the sole standard of truth." [n]

The next great title in my course of lectures is MAN, the subject of all, and the author, as well as the subject of part of those kinds of law, of which I have now given a general and summary view. Man I shall consider as an individual, as a member of society, as a member of a confederation, and as a part of the great commonwealth of nations.

On a slight glance of this subject, it may seem, perhaps, not to be very intimately connected with a system of lectures on law. And, indeed, it must be owned, that as law, or what is called law, is sometimes taught, and sometimes practised, there is but a slender and very remote alliance between law and man. But, in the real nature of things, the case is very different.

You have not, I am sure, forgotten, that, in an early address, which I made to you, I recommended, most earnestly, to the utmost degree of your attention, an outline of study, supported with all the countenance and authority of three distinguished and experienced characters — Bacon, Bolingbroke, Kaims: it will not, I am sure, be forgotten, that metaphysical knowledge, or the philosophy of the human mind, formed a very conspic-

[n] Fost. Pref. 6. 7.

uous part of that outline; one of those "vantage grounds," which every one must climb, who aims to be really a master in the science of law.

"Natura juris a natura hominis repetenda est," * is the judgment of Cicero. It is a judgment, not more respectable on account of the high authority, which pronounces it, than on account of its intrinsick solidity and importance.

You have heard me mention, that a proper system of evidence is the greatest *desideratum* in the law. From a distinct and accurate knowledge of the human mind, and of its powers and operations, the principles and materials of such a system must be drawn and collected.

Whatever produces belief may be comprehended under the name of evidence. Belief is a simple and undefinable operation of the mind; but, by the constitution of our nature, it is intimately and inseparably associated with many other powers and operations. This association should be minutely traced: all its properties and consequences should be distinctly marked. Belief attends on the perceptions of our external senses, on the operations of our internal consciousness, on those of memory, on those of intuition, on those of reason: it is attendant, likewise, on the veracity, the fidelity, and the judgment of others. Hence the evidence of sense, the evidence of recollection, the evidence of consciousness, the evidence of intuition, the evidence of demonstration, probable evidence, the evidence of testimony, the evidence of engagements, the evidence of opinion, and many other kinds of evidence; for this is, by no means, a complete enumeration of them.

It is difficult, perhaps it is impossible, to discover any common principle, to which all these different kinds of evidence can be reduced. They seem to agree only in this, that, by the constitution of our nature, they are fitted to produce belief.

It is superfluous to add, that the social operations of the mind should be well known and studied by him, who wishes to reach the genuine principles of legal knowledge.

* [The nature of the law is to be sought from the nature of man himself.]

VI

OF MAN, AS AN INDIVIDUAL

"KNOW thou thyself," is an inscription peculiarly proper for the porch of the temple of science. The knowledge of human nature is of all human knowledge the most curious and the most important. To it all the other sciences have a relation; and though from it they may seem to diverge and ramify very widely, yet by one passage or another they still return.

In every art and in every disquisition, the powers of the mind are the instruments, which we employ; the more fully we understand their nature and their use, the more skilfully and the more successfully we shall apply them. In the sublimest arts, the mind is not only the instrument, but the subject also of our operations and inquiries. The poet, the orator, the philosopher work upon man in different ways and for different purposes. The statesman and the judge, in pursuit of the noblest ends, have the same dignified object before them. An accurate and distinct knowledge of his nature and powers, will undoubtedly diffuse much light and splendour over the science of law. In truth, law can never attain either the extent or the elevation of science, unless it be raised upon the science of man.

The knowledge of human nature is not more distinguished by its importance, than it is by its difficulty. Though the mind — the noblest work of God, which reason discovers — is of all objects the nearest to us, and seems the most within our view; yet it is no easy matter to attend to its operations and faculties, in such a manner as to obtain clear, full, and distinct conceptions concerning them. The consequence has been, that in no branch of knowledge have greater errours, and even absurdities, insinuated themselves, than in the philosophy of the human mind. Instead of proceeding slowly and cautiously by observation and experience, those who have written on this subject have adopted the more easy, but the less certain mode of process by hypothesis and analogy. The event has been such as might have been expected: those who have cultivated other sciences, have made progress, because they have set out in the right road, and have consulted the proper guides: those who have speculated on human nature have, too many of them, been involved in a dark and inextricable labyrinth, because they commenced their journey in an improper direction, and have listened to the information of those, whose information was the result of conjecture and not of experience. But this darkness will not last for ever. Some future sun of science will arise, and illuminate this benighted part of the intellectual globe. When the powers of the human mind shall be delineated truly and according to nature, those, whose vision is not distorted by prejudice, will recognise their own features in the picture. They will be surprised that things, in themselves so clear, could be so long involved in absurdity; and, when the truth is to be found in their own breasts, that they have been led so far from it by false systems and theories.

The only instrument, by which we can have any distinct notion of the faculties of our own and of others' minds, is reflection. By this power, the mind makes its own operations the object of its attention, and views and examines them on every side. This power of reflection or self-examination, so absolutely indispensable in the investigation of what is so near and so important to us, is neither soon nor easily acquired or exerted. The mind, like the eye, contemplates, with facility, every object around it; but is with difficulty turned inward upon its own operations. Whoever has attempted to experiment on the philosophy of the mind — the only legitimate way in which a knowledge of it can be acquired — must have found how utterly impossible it is to make any clear and distinct observations on our faculties of thought, unless the passions, as well as the imagination, be silent and still. The materials on which we reflect are so minute, so mixed, and so volatile, that the strongest minds alone can, in any degree, arrange them, even in their quietest state. The least breath of passion moves and agitates them, so as to render every thing distorted and deformed.

Reflection, like all our other powers, is greatly improved by exercise: it thus becomes habitual; the difficulty attending it daily diminishes; and the advantages resulting from it are many and great. One who is accustomed habitually to reflection, can think and speak with accuracy on every subject; and can judge and discriminate for himself in many cases, in which others must trust to notions borrowed, confused, and indistinct.

Assisting and subservient to accurate reflection, is the structure of language, which is of much use in developing the operations of the mind. The language of mankind is expressive of their thoughts. The various operations of the understanding, will, and passions have various forms of speech corresponding to them, in all languages; a due attention to the signs, throws light on the things signified by them. There are, in all languages, modes of speech, by which men signify their judgment, or give their testimony, or accept, or refuse, or command, or threaten, or supplicate, or ask information or advice, or plight their faith in promises or contracts. If such operations were not common to mankind, we should not find, in all languages, forms of speech by which they are expressed.

A system of human nature is not expected from this chair. The undertaking, indeed, is too vast for me; it is too vast for any one man, however great his genius or abilities may be. But it comes directly within our plan, to consider it so far as to have just conceptions of man in two most important characters, as an author, and as a subject of law; as accountable for his own conduct, as capable of directing the conduct both of himself and of others. The laws, which God has given to us, are strictly agreeable to our nature; they are adjusted with infallible correctness to our perfection and happiness. On those, which we make for ourselves, the same characters, as deeply and as permanently as possible, ought to be impressed. But how, unless we study and know our nature, shall we make laws fit for it, and calculated to improve it?

I mean not — for it would be uninstructive — to give you an account of the divisions and subdivisions, into which metaphysicians have attempted to class and arrange our mental powers and principles. No division has been more common, and, perhaps, less exceptionable, than that of the powers of the mind into those of the understanding and those of the will. And yet even this division, I am afraid, has led into a mistake. The mistake I believe to be this; it has been supposed, that in the operations ascribed to the will, there was no employment of the understanding; and that in those ascribed to the understanding, there was no exertion of the will. But this is not the case. It is probable, that there is no operation of the understanding, in which the mind is not in some degree active; in other words, in which the will has not some share. On the other hand, there can be no energy of the will, which is not accompanied with some act of the understanding. In the operations of the mind, both faculties generally, if not always, concur; and the distinction between them can be of no farther use, than to arrange each operation under that faculty, which has the largest share in it. Thus by the perceptive powers, we are supposed to acquire knowledge, and by the powers of volition, we are said to exert ourselves in action.

If even this division, long and generally received as it has been, has given occasion to a mistake; we have no great reason to indulge a partiality for others. The truth is, that they have been generally superficial and inaccurate; they have depended more on fancy than on nature; and have proceeded more from presumptuous attempts to accommodate the mind to a system, than from respectful endeavours to accommodate a system to the mind. Abhorrent from the first, restrained by propriety from aiming at the second; let my humble task be to select and make such observations concerning our powers, our dispositions, our principles, and our habits, as will illustrate the intimate connexion and reciprocal influence of religion, morality, and law.

Simplicity is the favourite object of system. In the material world, attachment to this simplicity misled the penetrating Des Cartes. Even the great Newton, patient, faithful, and attentive as he was in tracing Nature's footsteps, was, on one occasion, almost seduced, by the same attachment, to follow hypothesis, the ape of Nature. A body of morality, pretending to be complete, has sometimes been built on a single pillar of the inward frame: the entire conduct of life has been accounted for, at least the attempt has been made to account for it, from a single quality or power. Many systems of this kind have appeared, calculated merely to flatter the mind. According to some writers, man is entirely selfish; according to others, universal benevolence is the highest aim of his nature. One founds morality upon sympathy solely: another exclusively upon utility. But the variety of human nature is not so easily comprehended or reached. It is a complicated machine; and is unavoidably so, in order to answer the various and important purposes, for which it is formed and designed.

How wretched are oftentimes the representations and the imitations of Nature's works! A puppet may make a few motions and gesticulations; but how unlike it is to that, which it represents! How contemptible, when compared to the body of a man, whose structure the more we know, the more we discover its wonders, and the more sensible we are of our ignorance! Is the mechanism of the mind so easily comprehended, when that of the body is so difficult? Yet, by some systems, which are offered to us, with pretensions the most lofty and magnificent, a few laws of association, joined to a few original feelings, explain the whole mechanism of sense, imagination, memory, belief, and of all the actions and passions of the mind. Is this the man that Nature made? It is a puppet surely, contrived to mimick her work. The more we know of other parts of nature, the more we approve and admire them. But when we look within, and consider the mind itself, which makes us capable of all our prospects and enjoyments; if it is indeed what some late systems of high pretensions make it, we find we have only been in an enchanted castle, imposed upon by spectres and apparitions. We blush to think how we have been deluded; we are ashamed of our frame; and can hardly forbear expostulating with our destiny. Is this thy pastime, O Nature, to put such tricks upon a silly creature, and then take off the mask, and show him how he has been befooled? If this is the philosophy of human nature; my soul! enter thou not into her secrets. It is surely the forbidden tree of knowledge: I no sooner taste of it, than I perceive myself naked. — Such, in substance, has been the well founded expostulation[a] against some of the

[a] Reid's Inq. 26. 28.

late and famed theories concerning the human mind. The theory, which we adopt, because we think it grounded in truth and reality, will open very different — the most enrapturing prospects.

The mind itself, indeed, is *one* internal principle: but its operations many, various, connected, and complicated: its perceptions are mixed, compounded, and decompounded, by habits, associations, and abstractions: its powers both of action and perception, on account either of a diversity in their objects, or in their manner of operating, are considered as separate and distinct faculties. This I take to be a just state of things with regard to the mind, and its perceptions, operations, and powers. But I think it is highly probable, that, in opposition to this account, the mind has been too often considered as distributed into different divisions and departments: and that the operations, in each department, have been considered as simple and unmixed. Each one of you, by recalling to remembrance your manner of thinking upon these subjects, will be able to say whether this has not been the case.

Again; the mind is an *active* principle. It has been the opinion of some modern philosophers, that, in thinking and sensation, the mind is merely passive. In all ages, and in all languages, the various modes of thinking have been expressed by words of active signification; such as seeing, hearing, reasoning, willing. It seems, therefore, to be the natural judgment of mankind, that the mind is active in its various ways of thinking; and for this reason, they are called its operations, and are expressed by active verbs. Sensation, imagination, memory, and judgment have, in all ages, been considered, by the vulgar, as *acts* of the mind. This is shown by the manner, in which they are expressed in all languages. When the mind is much employed in them, we say it is very active; whereas, if they were impressions only, as the *ideal* philosophy would lead us to conceive, we ought, in such a case, rather to say, that the mind is very passive. The paper which I hold in my hand was not active, when it received the characters written on it.

Man is composed of a body and a soul intimately connected; but at what time and in what manner connected, we do not know. In consequence of this connexion, the body lives and performs the functions necessary to life for a certain time; increases for a certain time in stature and in strength; is nourished with food, and is refreshed by sleep. In consequence of the same connexion, the body moves; the hands fulfil their various and active offices; the tongue expressive speaks; and the eyes sometimes still more expressive look. The body, and the things of the body, are far from being beneath our regard. In its present state, it is a mansion well fitted for the temporary residence of its noble inhabitant: in its renewed state, it will be endowed with the power of retaining that fitness for ever.

The fabrick of the human mind, however, is more astonishing still. The faculties of this are, with no less wisdom, adapted to their several ends, than the organs of the other. Nay, as the mind is of an order higher than that of the body, even more of the wisdom and skill of the divine Architect is displayed in its structure. In all respects, fearfully and wonderfully are we made.

From experience we find, that when external things are within the sphere of our perceptive powers, they affect our organs of sensation, and are perceived by the mind. That they are perceived we are conscious; but the manner in which they are perceived, we cannot explain; for we cannot trace the connexion between our minds and the impressions made on our organs of sense; because we cannot trace the connexion which subsists between the soul and the body. Frequent and laborious have been the attempts of philosophers to investigate the manner, in which things external are perceived by the mind. Let us imitate them, neither in their fruitless searches to discover what cannot be known; nor in framing hypotheses which will not bear the test of reason, or of intuition; nor in rejecting selfevident truths, which, though they cannot be proved by reasoning, are known by a species of evidence superiour to any that reasoning can produce.

Many philosophers allege that our mind does not perceive external objects themselves; that it perceives only *ideas* of them; and that those ideas are actually in the mind. When it has been intimated to them, that, if this be the case; if we perceive not external objects themselves, but only ideas; the necessary consequence must be, that we cannot be certain that any thing, except those ideas, exists; the consequence has been admitted in its fullest force. Nay, it has been made the foundation of another theory, in which it has been asserted, that men and other animals, the sun, moon, and stars, every thing which we think we see, and hear, and feel around us, have no real existence; that what we dignify with such appellations, and what we suppose to be so permanent and substantial, are nothing more than "the baseless fabrick of a vision" — are nothing more than ideas perceived in the mind. The theory has been carried to a degree still more extravagant than this; and the existence of mind has been denied, as well as the existence of body. We shall have occasion to examine these castles, which have not even air to support them. Suffice it, at present, to observe, that the existence of the objects of our external senses, in the way and manner in which we perceive that existence, is a branch of intuitive knowledge, and a matter of absolute certainty; that the constitution of our nature determines us to believe in our senses; and that a contrary determination would finally lead to the total subversion of all human knowledge. For this belief we cannot, we pretend not to assign an argument; it is a simple and original, and therefore an inexplicable act of the mind. It can neither be described nor defined. But one thing we shall engage to do, though, at present, we are not prepared for it. When those philosophers prove by argument, that we ought to receive the testimony of reason; we then will prove, by argument, that we ought to receive the testimony of sense. Till that time, let us receive the testimony of both, as of faculties, with which we have been endowed, for wise and benevolent purposes, by him who is all-true. The senses were intended by him to give us all that information of external objects, which he saw to be proper for us in our present state. This information they convey without reasoning, without art, without investigation on our part. They are five in number. Tastes are referred to the sense of tasting: odours, to that of smelling: sounds, to that of hearing: light and colours, to that of seeing: all other bodily sensations, to that of touch.

Our external senses are not indeed the most exalted of our powers; but they are powers of real use and importance; and, to powers of a more dignified nature, they are most serviceable and necessary instruments. It has been the endeavour of some philosophers to degrade them below that rank, in which they ought to be placed. They have been represented as powers, by which we receive sensations only of external objects. Even this part of their service is far from being unimportant. The perception of external objects is a principal link of that mysterious chain, which connects the material with the intellectual world. But this, as I before mentioned,[b] is not the whole of the functions discharged by the senses: they judge, as well as inform: they are not confined to the task of conveying impressions; they are exalted to the office of deciding concerning the nature and the evidence of the impressions, which they convey.

The senses are the vehicles of pleasures, less elevated indeed than those which are intellectual, still less elevated than those which are moral, but pleasures not beneath the regard of a rational and a moral mind. The pleasures of sense, it is true, ought, like every thing else that is subordinate, to be prevented from transgressing their natural and proper bounds: but that is no reason why they should be either neglected or despised. To be without the senses even of tasting and smelling, would be a real misfortune, because it would be a real inconvenience, and would be attended with the loss of sensations innocent and agreeable. The organ of smelling is often the speediest and the surest instrument to prevent or to recover a person from a fainting fit. The senses are susceptible of improvement; and they ought to be improved; for they are the sources both of pleasures and of advantage. Some of the senses are the sources of pleasures of a very elegant kind. The ear is the welcome messenger of melody and harmony, as well as of sound: the eye, of beauty, as well as of light and colours: and the man who feels not agreeable emotions from the contem-

[b] Ante. p. 143.

plation of beauty, and is not moved with concord of sweet sounds — I will not finish the fine poetical description — I will only say, that he has no reason to exult in the absence of those enjoyments. Both the eyes and the ear are capable of being refined to a very great height. For this I need only appeal to judges of musick, of painting, of statuary, of architecture. In many mechanick arts, a good eye, as it is called, is of excellent service. Gentlemen of the military profession — a profession which has something singular in it; a profession which should be learned, that it may never be used — know the importance of a military eye.

It is not without design that I have said thus much concerning the utility and importance of our senses. It has been the custom of certain philosophers, and, I must here add, of certain divines, to represent human nature as in a state of hostility endless and uninterrupted, internal as well as external. According to these philosophers, and according to these divines, he is at war with all the world, as well as with himself. The senses have been considered as incorrigible rebels, who aspired to be tyrants: the inference has been, that they ought to be treated as the vilest slaves. The monk, who built a dead wall before his window, that he might not be seduced by the beauties of creation, introduced no new doctrine; he only carried to an unusual height a doctrine already received. This doctrine embraces the two vicious extremes, and excludes the golden mean. Whence this sombre system derives its origin, I care and inquire not. Of one thing I am certain; it is not that wisdom which cometh from above: for the ways of that wisdom are the ways of pleasantness, and all her paths are peace. Our senses ought to be deemed, as they really are, and as they are intended to be, the useful and pleasing ministers of our higher powers. Let it be remembered, however, that, of the pleasures of sense, temperance and prudence are the necessary and inseparable guides and guardians; detached from whom, those pleasures lose themselves in another nature and in other names: they become vices and pains.

As the external senses convey to us information of what passes without us; we have an internal sense, which gives us information of what passes within us. To this we appropriate the name of consciousness. It is an immediate conception of the operations of our own minds, joined with the belief of the existence of those operations. In exerting consciousness, the mind, so far as we know, makes no use of any bodily organ. This operation seems to be purely intellectual. Consciousness takes knowledge of every thing that passes within the mind. What we perceive, what we remember, what we imagine, what we reason, what we judge, what we believe, what we approve, what we hope, all our other operations, while they are present, are objects of this.

This, like many other operations of the mind, is simple, peculiar, inaccessible equally to definition and analysis. For its existence every one must make his appeal to himself. Are you conscious that you remember, or that you think? We have already seen, that the existence of the objects of sense is one great branch of intuitive knowledge: of the same kind of knowledge, the existence of the objects of consciousness is another branch, more extensive and important still. When a man feels pain, he is certain of the existence of pain; when he is conscious that he thinks, he is certain of the existence of thought. If I am asked to prove that consciousness is a faithful and not a fallacious sense; all the answer which I can give is — I feel, but I cannot prove; I can find no previous truth more certain or more luminous, from which this can derive either evidence or illustration. But some such antecedent truth is necessarily the first link in a chain of proof. For proof is nothing else than the deduction of truths less known or less believed, from others that are more known or better believed. "What can we reason, but from what we know?" [c] The immediate and irresistible conviction, which I have of the real existence of those things, of whose existence I am conscious, is a conviction produced by intuition, not by reason. He who doubted, or pretended to doubt, concerning every other information, deemed himself justified in taking for granted the veracity of that information, which was given to him by his consciousness. He was conscious that he thought; and therefore he was satisfied that he really thought. — "Cogito" was a first principle, which he who pronounced it dangerous and unphilosophical to assume any thing else, judged it safe and wise to assume. And when he had once assumed that he thought, he gravely set to work to prove, that because he thought he existed. His existence was true, but he could not prove it; and all his attempts to prove it have been shown, by a succeeding philosopher, to be inconsistent with the rules of sound and accurate logick. But even this succeeding philosopher, who showed that Des Cartes had not proved his existence, and who, from the principles of his own philosophy could not assume this existence without proof — even this philosopher has assumed the truth of the information given by consciousness. "Mr. Hume, after annihilating body and mind, time and space, action and causation, and even his own mind, acknowledges the reality of the thoughts, sensations, and passions, of which he is conscious." [d] He has left them — how philosophically I will not pretend to say — to "stand upon their own bottom, stript of a subject, rather than call in question the reality of their existence." [e] Let us felicitate ourselves, that there is, at least, one principle of common sense, which has never been called in question. It is a first principle, which we are required and determined, by the very constitution of our nature and faculties, to believe. Perhaps we shall find other first principles, which, by the same constitution of our nature and facul-

[c] Pope's Ess. on Man. Ep. i. v. 18.   [d] Reid's Ess. Int. 579.
[e] Reid's Inq. 39. 139.

ties, we are equally required and determined to believe. Such principles are parts of our constitution, no less than the power of thinking: reason can neither make nor destroy them: like a telescope, it may assist, it may extend, but it cannot supply natural vision.

Possessed of the senses and of consciousness; and believing, as we must believe, the truth of the information, which they give, we cannot complain that our knowledge is a *baseless* fabrick; but if we were possessed only of those powers, we might well complain, that our knowledge was a *fleeting* fabrick. The moment that an external object is removed from the operation of our senses, that moment our perception of it is lost: the moment our attention is withdrawn from the consideration of any of the powers of the mind, that moment our immediate conception of it is gone. The external object may, indeed, return; but it will return as a stranger: the internal power may become again the object of our consciousness; but it will appear as an object hitherto unknown. As to the purpose of accumulating knowledge, every succeeding moment would be as the first moment of our existence. We should perceive what is present; but we should have no power of connecting what is present, with what is past. Without this connecting power, we should have no means of forming any conjecture concerning what is to come. But the divine hand that made us, leaves not its workmanship unfinished. We are endowed with a power, by which we have an immediate knowledge of things past. We are provided with a storehouse, fitted to preserve things new and old. And of this storehouse it is the extraordinary property, that the more it is filled with treasure, the more capacious and retentive it becomes. You know I speak of the memory. Much might be usefully said concerning this necessary and important power; but my plan, which comprehends such a variety of parts, forbids me to enlarge upon each of them.

Of the immediate cause of remembrance we know nothing: and all attempts to trace and discover that cause have, to say the least of them, proved vain and illusory: it is one of those things, of which we must be contented to remain ignorant. But while of some things we ought to acquiesce in our ignorance; of others, we should be satisfied with our knowledge: though we cannot assign a cause *why* we remember, we know the fact that we *do* remember; and we know likewise another fact, that our remembrance is true. What we distinctly remember, we believe as strongly as what we distinctly perceive. To give a reason why we believe the information of our perceptions, I have already declared myself incapable: the same declaration I now make, concerning the information of our memory. By the constitution of our nature, it is always accompanied with belief.

I had occasion to rescue the senses from the unjust disparagement, which they have sometimes suffered: let me now perform the same just office to the memory. You know it to be the fashion of some to exclaim, with a degree of affectation, how wretched their memories are. The design is not declared; but it is obvious. At the expense of their memory, they insinuate a compliment to their judgment: for it has somehow been received as an opinion, that a strong memory and a strong judgment have seldom been united in the same mind. Perhaps the beautiful lines of Mr. Pope may have contributed to give a currency to this sentiment: but the sentiment is ill founded. I will, indeed, admit, on one hand, that a great memory is often found without a great genius: but I will not admit, on the other, that a great genius is often found without a great memory. The contrary I believe to be generally, I will not say always, the case. Men of the most extensive abilities have been men also of the most extensive memories: witness Themistocles, Cicero, Cæsar, Bolingbroke. If these remarks be true, the compliment to judgment at the cost of memory is but a left-handed one. Instead of being rivals, judgment and memory are mutual assistants. Memory furnishes the materials which judgment selects, adjusts, and arranges. Those materials selected, adjusted, and arranged are more at the call of memory than before: for it is a well known fact, that those things, which are disposed most methodically and connected most naturally, are the most distinct, as well as the most lasting objects of remembrance: hence, in discourse, the utility as well as beauty of order. Strength, as well as clearness in our perceptions greatly aids the memory: hence, in discourse, the utility as well as beauty of vivacity. Agreeable emotions, attending our perceptions, contribute to render them both clear and strong: hence, in discourse, the utility as well as beauty of every chaste and elegant ornament. That which is conveyed through the channel of two senses makes a stronger and more lasting impression, than that which is conveyed through the channel of one: hence, in discourse, the utility as well as beauty of just and expressive action. To associate the pleasing with the useful, is Nature's example as well as precept.

I have already intimated that memory is greatly susceptible of improvement: it is so to a surprising degree. This improvement is acquired by vigorous but prudent exercise; and by habitual but lively attention. I assign limitations both to exercise and attention, because both are liable to run into excess. A memory overloaded will make but little useful progress either in literature or business. An attention overstrained is apt to degenerate into what is, with singular propriety, termed absence of thought. To counterfeit this absent kind of thoughtfulness, has been the affectation of those, who wish to be deemed deep thinkers, without the trouble of thinking. To feel it is frequently the lot of those, who think too much. But it is a failing, not an excellence: it is to be avoided, not to be courted. When it begins to steal upon a studious person, he should relieve his attention by changing its object.

In all the ways, in which the objects of our thoughts have hitherto presented themselves to us, they have been necessarily attended with the act or operation of belief. But they may be presented to us in another way, unaccompanied with that act or operation. Let me exemplify this by a set of very familiar instances: for things may be exemplified, that cannot be defined. You see this handkerchief. You are necessarily determined to believe that you see it. You remember that, but a moment ago, I showed you a handkerchief. You are now necessarily determined to believe that you saw it. In the first instance, the handkerchief was seen: that was necessarily accompanied with the belief of its then present existence. In the second instance, the handkerchief was remembered: that was necessarily accompanied with the belief of its past existence. You may hereafter think of a handkerchief, certainly without seeing, probably without recollecting, the handkerchief, which I just now showed you. In the first instance, the perception was accompanied with the belief of present existence: in the second instance, the remembrance was accompanied with the belief of past existence: in the third and last instance, the conception is not accompanied with any belief at all. Conception is an operation of the mind, by which we apprehend a thing, without any belief or judgment concerning it, without referring it to present or past existence. Every one is conscious that he can conceive a thousand things, of whose present or past existence he has not the least belief. You have seen a mountain: you have seen gold: you can conceive a golden mountain: but can you believe its existence?

Conception enters into every operation of the mind. Our sense and our consciousness cannot convey to us information concerning any object, without, at the same time, giving some conception of that object. If we remember any thing, we must have some conception of that, which we remember. In conception there is neither truth nor falsehood; for conception neither affirms nor denies. But though all the other operations of the mind include conception; conception itself may exist, detached from all the others, excepting consciousness. By logicians, conception is frequently called *simple apprehension*.

The powers of sensation, of consciousness, and of memory are exerted upon objects which exist, or have existed. Conception is often exerted upon objects, which have neither past, nor present, nor even future existence. The creative powers of conception and description possessed by Shakespeare were, by no means, confined to actual existence, past, present, or to come.

Judgment is an important operation of the mind, and is employed upon the materials of perception and knowledge. It is generally described to be, that act of the mind, by which one thing is affirmed or denied of another. But this description is, in one respect, too limited; in another, it is too extensive. It is too limited in this respect, that though our judgments, when expressed, are indeed expressed by affirmation or denial, yet it is not necessary to a judgment that it be expressed at all. Men may judge without affirming or denying any thing; nay, they may judge contrary to what they affirm or deny. The description is too extensive in this respect, that it includes testimony as well as judgment. When a judge pronounces his decree, he delivers it in the affirmative or negative: when a witness delivers his testimony, he uses the affirmative or negative likewise. Judgment and testimony are, however, operations very different from one another: wrong judgment is only an errour: false testimony is something more.

In persons arrived at the years of discretion, their perceptions, their consciousness, their memory are objects of their judgment. Evidence is the ground of judgment; and where evidence is, it is impossible not to judge.

To every determination of the mind concerning what is true or what is false, the name of judgment may be assigned. Some consider knowledge[f] as a separate faculty, conversant about truth and falsehood: perhaps it is more accurate to consider it as a species of judgment; for without judgment, how can there be any knowledge? Judgments are intuitive, as well as discursive, founded on truths that are selfevident, as well as on those that are deduced from demonstration, or from reasoning of a less certain kind. The former, or intuitive judgments, may, in the strictest sense, be called the judgments of nature.

Sense and judgment are sometimes used, especially by some modern philosophers, in contradistinction to each other — very improperly. In common language, and in the writings of the best authors, sense always implies judgment: a man of sense is a man of judgment: common sense is that degree of judgment, which is to be expected in men of common education and common understanding.

With the power of judging, the power of reasoning is very nearly connected. Both powers are frequently included under the general appellation of reason. But reasoning is strictly the process, by which we pass from one judgment to another, which is the consequence of it. In all reasoning, there must be one proposition, which is inferred, and another, at least, from which the inference is made.

Reason, as well as judgment, has truth and falsehood for its objects: both proceed from evidence; both are accompanied with belief.

The power of reasoning is frequently selected as the characteristick quality, which distinguishes the human race from the inferiour part of the creation. From nature the capacity of reasoning is unquestionably derived; but it may be wonderfully strengthened, improved, and ex-

[f] Locke on Hum. Und. b. 4. c. 14.

tended by art. Imitation and exercise are the two great instruments of improvement.

In a chain of reasoning, the evidence must proceed regularly and without interruption from link to link: the evidence of the last conclusion can be no greater than that of the weakest link in the chain; because if even the weakest link fails, the whole chain is broken.

In reasoning, the most useful and the most splendid talent is the invention of intermediate proofs. In all productions of the understanding, invention is entitled to the highest praise. It implies a luminous view of the object proposed, and sagacity and quickness in discerning, selecting, and employing, to the utmost advantage, the means that are best fitted for accomplishing that object. In the assemblage of those qualities consists that superiority of understanding, which is denominated genius.

Reasoning is distinguished into two kinds; that, which is demonstrative; and that, which is only probable. In demonstrative reasoning there are no degrees; the inference, in every step of the series, is necessary; and it is impossible but that, from the premises, the conclusion must flow. Hence demonstrative reasoning can be applied only to such truths as are necessary; not to such as are contingent.

With regard to reasoning, which is only probable, the connexion between the premises and the conclusion is not a necessary connexion. Probability is susceptible of numerous and widely differing degrees of strength and weakness. The degrees of evidence are measured by their effect upon a clear, a sound, and an unprejudiced understanding. Every degree of evidence produces a proportioned degree of knowledge and belief.

Probable evidence may be distributed into a number of different kinds. One, and a very important one, is that of human testimony. On this a great part of human knowledge depends. History and law resort to it for the materials of decision and faith. To examine, to compare, and to appreciate this kind of evidence is the business of the judge, the juryman, the counsel, and the party. Without some competent discernment concerning it, no man can act with common prudence or safety in the ordinary occurrences of life.

Another kind of probable evidence is, the opinion of those, who are professional judges of the point in question. In England, a reference is sometimes made to the judges for their opinions in a matter of law. On a trial, recourse is frequently had to the professional sentiments of a physician. A shoemaker could point out to Apelles himself a defect in the picture of a shoe. A tyrant, nutured and practised in the tyrant's art, could, at the first glance, discover a mistake in the representation of a decollated head.

A third kind of probable evidence is that, by which we recognise the identity of the same thing, and the diversity of different things. This kind of evidence is of the greatest consequence in the affairs of life. By it, the identity of persons and things is determined in courts of justice. In acquiring, retaining, and applying this kind of evidence, there is a wonderful diversity of talents in different men. Some will recollect and distinguish almost all the faces they have ever seen: others are much more slow, and much less retentive in this species of recollection and discrimination.

There are many other kinds of probable evidence, that well deserve the study of the lawyer, the philosopher, and the man. But this is not the proper occasion to attempt an enumeration of them.

Every free action has two causes, which cooperate in its production. One is moral; the other is physical: the former is the will, which determines the action; the latter is the power, which carries it into execution. A paralytick may will to run: a person able to run, may be unwilling: from the want of will in one, and the want of power in the other, each remains in his place.

Our actions and the determinations of our will are generally accompanied with liberty. The name of liberty we give to that power of the mind, by which it modifies, regulates, suspends, continues, or alters its deliberations and actions. By this faculty, we have some degree of command over ourselves: by this faculty we become capable of conforming to a rule: possessed of this faculty, we are accountable for our conduct.

But the existence of this faculty has been boldly called in question. It has been asserted, that we have no sense of moral liberty; and that, if we have such a sense, it is fallacious.

With regard to the first question, let every one ask it of himself. Have I a sense of moral liberty? Have I a conviction that I am free? If you have; this sense — this conviction is a matter of fact, or an object of intuition; and vain it is to reason against its truth or existence.

If it exists; why is it to be deemed fallacious? Are there peculiar marks of deception discoverable in it? Can any reason be assigned why we should suspect it, and not every other sense or power of our nature? He that made one, made all. If we are to suspect all; we ought to believe nothing.

But by what one especial power are we told that we ought to suspect all others? On which is this exclusive character of veracity impressed? If Nature is fallacious; how do we learn to detect the cheat? If she is a juggler by trade; is it for us to attempt to penetrate the mysteries of her art, and take upon us to decide when it is that she presents a true, and when it is that she presents a false appearance? If she is false in every other instance, how can we believe her, when she says she is a liar?

But she does not say so. She is, and she claims to be honest; and the law of our constitution determines us to believe her. When we feel, or when we perceive by intuition, that we are free; we may assume the doctrine of moral liberty, as a first and selfevident, though an undemonstrable principle.

I have frequently mentioned *first principles*. The evidence, on which they ought to be received, well deserves discussion and attention. This is a subject which has been greatly misunderstood, and, perhaps, misrepresented. It is a subject, in which inferences, destructive of all knowledge and virtue, have been drawn, with all the pomp and parade of metaphysical sagacity. It is a subject, concerning which proper conceptions are essentially necessary to the progress of all science, that is truly valuable. They are peculiarly necessary in the study of law, in which evidence bears such an active and distinguished part. To believe our senses — to give credit to human testimony, has been considered as unphilosophical, and, consequently, irrational, if not absurd. The connexion, on this subject, between the principles of law, of philosophy, and of human nature has never, so far as I know, been sufficiently traced or explained.

Of some philosophers of no small fame, and of no small influence in propagating a certain fashionable — creed, I was going to say; but that would be peculiarly improper — system I will call it, by a particular indulgence — Of such philosophers it has been the favourite doctrine, that reason is the supreme arbitress of human knowledge; that by her solely we ought to be governed; that in her solely we ought to place confidence; that she can establish first principles; that she can ascertain and correct the mistakes of common sense.

Reason is a noble faculty, and when kept within its proper sphere, and applied to its proper uses, exalts human creatures almost to the rank of superiour beings. But she has been much perverted, sometimes to vile, sometimes to insignificant purposes. By some, she has been chained like a slave or a malefactor; by others, she has been launched into depths, unknown or forbidden.

Are the dictates of our reason more plain, than the dictates of our common sense? Is there allotted to the former a portion of infallibility, which has been denied to the latter? If reason may mistake; how shall the mistake be rectified? shall it be done by a second process of reasoning, as likely to be mistaken as the first? Are we thus involved, by the constitution of our nature, in a labyrinth, intricate and endless, in which there is no clue to guide, no ray to enlighten us? Is this true philosophy? is this the daughter of light? is this the parent of wisdom and knowledge? No. This is not she. This is a fallen kind, whose rays are merely sufficient to shed a "darkness visible" upon the human powers; and to disturb the security and ease enjoyed by those, who have not become apostates to the pride of science. Such degenerate philosophy let us abandon: let us renounce its instruction: let us embrace the philosophy which dwells with common sense.

This philosophy will teach us, that first principles are in themselves apparent; that to make nothing selfevident, is to take away all possibility of knowing any thing; that without first principles, there can be neither reason nor reasoning; that discursive knowledge requires intuitive maxims as its basis; that if every truth would admit of proof, proof would extend to infinity; that, consequently, all sound reasoning must rest ultimately on the principles of common sense — principles supported by original and intuitive evidence.

In the investigation of this subject, we shall have the pleasure to find, that those philosophers, who have attempted to fan the flames of war between common sense and reason, have acted the part of incendiaries in the commonwealth of science; that the interests of both are the same; that, between them, there never can be ground for real opposition: that, as they are commonly joined together in speech and in writing, they are inseparable also, in their nature.

We assign to reason two offices, or two degrees. The first is, to judge of things selfevident. The second is, from selfevident principles, to draw conclusions, which are not selfevident. The first of these is the province, and the sole province, of common sense, and, therefore, in its whole extent, it coincides with reason; and is only another name for one branch or one degree of reason. Why then, it may be said, should it have a particular name assigned to it, since it is acknowledged to be only a degree of reason? To this it may be answered, why would you abolish a name, which has found a place in all civilized languages, and has acquired a right by prescription? But this degree of reason ought to be distinguished by a particular name, on two accounts. 1. In the greatest part of mankind, no other degree of reason is to be found. It is this degree of reason, and this only, which makes a man capable of managing his own affairs, and answerable for his conduct towards others. 2. This degree of reason is purely the gift of heaven; and where heaven has not given it, no education can supply it; though, where it is given, it may, in a certain degree, be improved. But the second degree of reason is learned by practice and rules, where the first is wanting.

From the age of Plato down to the present century, it has been the opinion of philosophers, that nothing is perceived but what is in the mind which perceives it: that the mind takes no direct cognizance of external things; but that it perceives them through the medium of certain shadows or images of them: those images were called by the ancients *species, forms, phantasms;* by the moderns they are called *ideas.*

On this foundation the systems of Des Cartes and Locke have been built. The doctrines of Mr. Locke have been received, not only in England, but in many other parts of Europe, with unbounded applause; and to his theory of the human understanding the same kind of respect and deference has been paid, as to the discoveries of Sir Isaac Newton in the natural world.

The school of Mr. Locke has given rise to two sects: at the head of one are Berkely and Hume: at the head of the other are Hartley and Priestley.

In the extension of Mr. Locke's principles, the Bishop of Cloyne conceived that he saw reason to deny the reality of matter; and to resolve all existence into mind. In his own sublime language, he thought he discovered, "that all the choir of heaven and furniture of the earth; all those bodies that compose the frame of the universe, are merely ideas, and exist only in the mind."

Mr. Hume, proceeding on the same principles of reasoning, advances boldly a step farther: he thinks he sees reason for denying the existence of mind as well as of matter; he annihilates spirit as well as body; and reduces mankind — I use his own words — to "a bundle or collection of different perceptions, which succeed each other with an inconceivable rapidity, and are in a perpetual flux and movement." "There is properly no simplicity in the mind at one time; nor identity in it at different times; whatever natural propensity" — tis indeed natural — "we may have to imagine that simplicity and identity: they are successive perceptions only, that constitute the mind." [g]

On the other hand, Dr. Hartley, assuming the existence of an immaterial principle, and of an external world, has endeavoured to trace the connexion between them. By a chain of hypotheses, he has attempted to illustrate the nature of the impressions, which the senses receive from external objects; the laws, by which those impressions influence our ideas; and the rules of association, by which these ideas are connected in our mind. He has thus formed a system, which, in the opinion of some enlightened men, explains, in a satisfactory manner, most of the operations of the thinking faculty.

Dr. Priestley has embraced these doctrines with his usual warmth; and has propagated them with his well known zeal. He is of opinion, however, that they ought to be further simplified. A principle, separate from body, he contends is an incumbrance on Dr. Hartley's system. On the principles of deduction, satisfactory to him, he asserts, that to matter, we should ascribe the capacity of intelligence, as well as the property of gravitation. Thought he believes to arise necessarily from a certain organization of the brain; and, resting on this, he denies the existence of an immaterial principle.

Different — exceedingly different indeed — nay, totally irreconcilable are these illustrious men in the conclusions, which they draw. But how-

[g] Tr. on hum. nat. 439. 440.

ever widely they differ, however impracticable it may be to reconcile them with regard to their conclusions; they all agree concerning their fundamental principles. They all agree in *assuming* the *existence* of *ideas*. This is the fundamental principle of Mr. Locke's philosophy.

Strange has been the fate of this principle! Strange have been the vicissitudes, with which it has been attended! Strange have been the revolutions, which it has been thought capable of producing! What a powerful engine it has been! In skilful and experienced hands, how tremendous have been its operations! Wielded by one philosopher, it attaches itself solely to matter, and destroys mind. Wielded by another, it attaches itself solely to mind, and destroys matter. Wielded by a third, it becomes equally fatal to matter and mind: by a single fiat of uncreating omnipotence, it strikes body and spirit, time and space into annihilation; and leaves nothing remaining but impressions and ideas!

We have hitherto been apt, perhaps, with unphilosophick credulity, to imagine, that thought supposed a thinker; and that treason implied a traitor. But correct philosophy, it seems, discovers, that all this is a mistake; for that there may be treason without a traitor, laws without a legislator, punishment without a sufferer. If, in these cases, the *ideas* are the traitor, the legislator, the sufferer; the author of this discovery ought to inform us, whether ideas can converse together; whether they can possess rights, or be under obligations; whether they can make promises, enter into covenants, fulfil, or break them; whether, if they break them, damages can be recovered for the breach. If one set of ideas make a covenant; if another successive set — for be it remembered they are all in succession — break the covenant; and if a third successive set are punished for breaking it; how can we discover justice to form any part of this system? These professional questions naturally suggest themselves.

Will these philosophers forgive me, if, from this dreary prospect — if a view of nothing can be called a prospect — I turn my eyes, and direct them to another scene, not indeed so solemn or awful, but such as, in one particular, bears to it a certain strong, though, perhaps, a ridiculous analogy. I would wish to pay all becoming deference to a system, venerable by its high antiquity, and fortified by the authority of philosophers without number. The images, and species, and phantasms of the ancients, and the ideas of the moderns, I wish to contemplate and treat with all imaginable respect. But there is an unlucky object of comparison, which constantly presents itself to my view. I cannot think of this doctrine of ideas, so versatile in its nature and application, without thinking, at the same time, of another doctrine, which has likewise been uncommonly powerful in its operations and effects. Shall I be forgiven? — I repeat the question — if, upon this occasion, I introduce — my Lord Peter's brown loaf. His lordship presented it once: it was excellent mutton. He presented it a second time: it was delicious beef. He presented it a third time: it was exquisite plumb pudding.

Shall I be permitted to ask one question — I think, a very natural one — did the brown loaf ever exist? If it never existed at all; my Lord Peter was equally infallible, when he called it mutton, as when he called it plumb pudding; and when he called it plumb pudding, as when he called it mutton or beef.

Shall I be permitted to ask another question — equally natural as the former? These images, and species, and phantasms of the ancients; these ideas of the moderns — did they ever exist? You will unquestionably be surprised when I tell you, that though, from the time of Plato and Aristotle to the time of Berkely and Hume, ideas and species have been supposed to lie at the foundation of the philosophy of the human mind, and, consequently, of all philosophy and knowledge; yet that foundation has never, till lately, been examined; but that the existence of ideas and species has always been assumed as a doctrine taken for granted. You will, perhaps, be further surprised, on being told, that, when lately the rubbish, which, during the long course of two thousand years, had covered and concealed the foundations of philosophy, was removed; and when those foundations were examined by an architect of uncommon discernment and skill; no such things as the ideas of the moderns, or the species of the ancients were to be discovered there.

"I acknowledge," says the enlightened and candid Dr. Reid,[h] "that I never thought of calling in question the principles commonly received with regard to the human understanding, until the Treatise of Human Nature was published." This is the performance of Mr. Hume, from which I cited a passage a little while ago. It appeared in the year 1739. "The ingenious author," continues Dr. Reid, "of that treatise, upon the principles of Locke, who was no sceptick, hath built a system of scepticism, which leaves no ground to believe any one thing rather than its contrary. His reasoning appeared to me to be just: there was, therefore, a necessity to call in question the principles, upon which it was founded; or admit the conclusion.

"But can any ingenious mind admit this sceptical system without reluctance? I truly could not: for I am persuaded that absolute scepticism is not more destructive of the faith of a christian, than of the science of a philosopher, and of the prudence of a man of common understanding." — I may add — or the sound principles of a lawyer or statesman. "I am persuaded," continues the Doctor, "that the unjust live by faith, as well as the just; and that, if all belief could be laid aside, piety, patriotism, friend-

[h] Inq. Ded. 4 — 8.

ship, parental affection, and private virtue would appear as ridiculous as knight errantry; and that the pursuits of pleasure, of ambition, and of avarice must be grounded upon belief, as well as those that are honourable and virtuous.

"For my own satisfaction, I entered into a serious examination of the principles, upon which this sceptical system is built; and was not a little surprised to find, that it leans with its whole weight upon a hypothesis, which is ancient indeed and hath been very generally received by philosophers; but of which I could find no solid proof. The hypothesis I mean is, that nothing is perceived but what is in the mind, which perceives it; that we do not really perceive things that are external, but only certain images and pictures of them imprinted upon the mind, which are called *impressions* and *ideas*.

"If this be true; supposing certain impressions and ideas to exist in my mind, I cannot, from their existence, infer the existence of any thing else; my impressions and ideas are the only existences, of which I can have any knowledge or conception, and they are such fleeting and transitory beings, that they can have no existence at all, any longer than I am conscious of them. So that, upon this hypothesis, the whole universe about me, bodies and spirits, sun, moon, stars and earth, friends and relations, all things without exception, which I imagined to have a permanent existence, whether I thought of them or not, vanish at once,

> And like the baseless fabrick of a vision,
> Leave not a track behind.

"I thought it unreasonable, upon the authority of philosophers, to admit a hypothesis, which, in my opinion, overturns all philosophy, all religion and virtue, and all common sense, and finding that all the systems concerning the human understanding, which I was acquainted with, were built upon this hypothesis, I resolved to inquire into this subject anew, without regard to any hypothesis."

The fruits of his inquiries have been published; and richly deserve your perusal and attention. Others have sown and cultivated the same seeds of knowledge, with the most encouraging success; and there is reason to hope, that the philosophy of human nature will not much longer continue the reproach of the human understanding.

Monopoly and exclusive privilege are the bane of every thing — of science as well as of commerce. The sceptical philosophers claim and exercise the privilege of assuming, without proof, the very first principles of their philosophy; and yet they require, from others, a proof of every thing by reasoning. They are unreasonable in both points. Some things, which ought to be believed, ought to be believed without proof. The first principle of their philosophy — the existence of ideas — is none of those things. If it be true; it is a discursive, not an intuitive truth; and, therefore, it can be proved. For this reason, unless it be proved, it should not be believed.

After having mentioned the sceptical philosophers, it is with a degree of reluctance that I so soon introduce the respected name of Mr. Locke. I introduce him not as one of those philosophers, but as one, who has unfortunately given a sanction to principles, the consequences of which he certainly did not foresee. But from his principles, those consequences have been ably and unanswerably drawn by others. His principles, therefore, ought to be minutely examined, that we may see whether, on a strict examination, they will stand the test.

I shall examine his leading principle by the very test, which he himself proposes for its trial. Cautious and candid as he was, it is very remarkable, that, while he recommends it to others to be careful in the admission of principles, he admits his own leading principle without sufficient examination and care. "I take leave to say" — I use his own words[i] — "I take leave to say, that every one ought very carefully to beware what he admits for a principle, to examine it strictly, and see whether he certainly knows it to be true of itself by its own evidence; or whether he does only, with assurance, believe it to be so upon the authority of others." And yet he begins his observations on ideas and their original, by assuming their existence, as his leading principle. "Every man being conscious to himself that he thinks; and that which his mind is applied about, whilst thinking, being the *ideas* that are *there*, tis past doubt, that men have in their minds several ideas." "It is, in the *first* place, then, to be inquired *how* he comes by them." [j]

With all deference for the character and talents of Mr. Locke — and I have, indeed, a high respect for them — I think that a previous inquiry ought to have been made — *Does* he come by them? To assume, without proving, that the things, which the mind is applied about, whilst thinking, are the ideas that are *there;* is certainly to assume too much.

In another place,[k] he expresses a hope, that it will be received as an intuitive truth — as one of that species of intuitive truths, which arise from consciousness. "I presume," says he, "it will be easily granted me, that there are such ideas in men's minds." Why so easily granted? Why should the leading principle of a philosophy, which, if true, necessarily draws us to such consequences as have been represented — why should such a leading principle be taken on trust? "Because," continues Mr. Locke,[l] "every one is conscious of them in himself."

Here is a fair and candid appeal: for if every one is conscious of ideas

[i] On Hum. Und. b. 4. c. 20. s. 8.   [j] Id. b. 2. c. 1. s. 1.   [k] Id. Introd.
[l] On Hum. Und. b. 1. c. 1. s. 8.

in his own mind, he must believe that such ideas are *there:* for consciousness is unquestionably a first principle of evidence. In this appeal I have
the pleasure of joining with Mr. Locke. In one thing we certainly agree
— the object of both is to discover the truth. Of this truth, you shall be
the judges, or rather the triers between us; for consciousness is a matter of
fact.

But before we enter upon the trial of this appeal, let us be sure that the
point to be tried is clearly ascertained and understood: let us not be misled by verbal ambiguity, nor drawn into the field of verbal disputation.
Many errours, and some of no inconsiderable importance, have arisen
from the vague, the doubtful, or the inaccurate application of the term
idea.

By ideas are sometimes meant the acts or operations of our minds in
perceiving, remembering, or imagining objects. In this sense, the existence
of ideas is far from being called in question. We are conscious of them
every day and every hour of our lives.

Sometimes *idea* is used to denote *opinion* — Thus, when we speak of
the ideas of Cicero; we mean his opinions or doctrines.

But there is a third sense, in which the term *idea* has been used. It has
been used to denote those images and pictures of things, which, and not
the things themselves, are the immediate objects perceived by the mind.
Those, who speak the most intelligibly, explain their doctrine in this
manner. Suppose me to look at a mirrour; and, while I am looking at it,
suppose a person to come behind me; I see, in the mirrour, not the person
himself, but his image. In the same manner, when, without a mirrour, I
am supposed to see a house or a tree; I see only an image of those objects
in my mind. This image is the immediate object of my perception.

It is in this last sense, now explained, that an appeal is made to your
consciousness for the truth of the existence of ideas.

You look at me: now I call for your conscious verdict. Are you conscious, that you really see me: or are you conscious, that you see, not me,
but only a certain image or picture of me, imprinted upon your own
minds? If the latter; your consciousness decides in favour of Mr. Locke:
if the former; it decides in favour of me. In whose favour does your
verdict decide? Before you finally declare it, it may, perhaps, be urged,
that you perceive me by means of intervening resemblances of me, distinctly painted on the retinæ of your eyes.

This shows, that I am willing to give the cause an impartial trial, nay,
an advantageous one, on the side of my admired antagonist. From those
parts only of our knowledge, which are disclosed by the sense of seeing,
could this objection be urged.

I admit, that the resemblances mentioned are distinctly painted on the
retinæ of your eyes. But suffer me to ask you — do you *perceive* those

resemblances, *so* painted? I presume you do not: for the existence of those resemblances was never, so far as I know or have heard, perceived by any of the innumerable race of men: it was not so much as suspected, till in the last century. Then the discovery was made by Kepler: but even to Kepler the discovery was not disclosed by consciousness: it was the result of deep and accurate researches into the philosophy of vision.

But I have not yet done with my answer to this objection. That you do not perceive me by the intervention of any perception of the resemblances painted on the retinæ of the eyes, is evident from two circumstances. In the first place, the resemblances of me are painted on the retinæ of both eyes: therefore, if you saw me through the intervention of those resemblances, you would see me double. In the second place, the resemblances of me on the retinæ are inverted: therefore, if you saw me through the intervention of those resemblances, you would see me turned upside down.

Are you now ready finally to declare your verdict? Do you perceive me? or do you only perceive, in your own minds, an image or picture of me?

I presume I may say, that the existence of ideas is not the dictate of consciousness. Is the existence of ideas entitled, in any other manner, or from any other source, to be considered as an intuitive truth? I have not heard it suggested. If it is a truth, and not an intuitive one; it is a truth capable of being proved: if it is capable of being proved; it ought to be proved, as we have already said, before it be believed.

A proof has been attempted: let us examine it. "No being, it is said, can act or be acted upon, but where it is; and, consequently, our mind cannot act upon, or be acted upon by any subject at a distance." [m]

This argument possesses one eminent advantage: its obscurity, like that of an oracle, is apt to impose on the hearer, who is willing to consider it as demonstration, because he does not, at first, discover its fallacy. Let it undergo a fair examination; let it be drawn out of its obscurity: let it be stated and analyzed in a clear point of view. Then it will appear as follows.

"No subject can be perceived, unless it acts upon the mind, or is acted upon by the mind: but no distant object can act upon the mind, or be acted upon by the mind; for no being can act but where it is: therefore the immediate object of perception must be something in the mind, so as to be able to act upon, or to be acted upon by the mind."

Now you see, fairly stated in all its parts, the argument, which is supposed to prove the necessity of phantasms or ideas in the mind, as the only objects of perception. It is singularly unfortunate for this argument, that

[m] Reid's Ess. Int. 203. 2 Elem. Crit. 513. n.

it concludes directly against the very hypothesis, of which it is the only foundation: for how can phantasms or ideas be raised in the mind by things at a distance, if things at a distance cannot act upon, or be acted upon by the mind.

Again; the argument assumes a proposition as true, without evidence — that no distant subject can act upon, or be acted upon by the mind. This proposition requires evidence; for it is not intuitively certain. Till this proposition, therefore, be proved, every man may rationally rely upon the conviction of his senses, that he sees and hears objects at a distance.

But further; to render the foregoing argument conclusive, it ought to be proved, that when we perceive objects, either they act upon us, or we act upon them. This is not selfevident; nor is it proved. Indeed reasons may be well offered against its admission.

When we say, that one being acts upon another, we mean that some power is exerted by the agent, which produces, or tends to produce a change in the thing acted upon. Now, there appears no reason for asserting, that, in perception, either the object acts upon the mind, or the mind upon the object. An object, in being perceived, does not act at all. I perceive the desk before me; but it is perfectly inactive; and, therefore, cannot act upon my mind. Neither does the mind, in perception, act upon the object. To perceive an object is one thing: to act upon it is another thing. To say, that I act upon the paper before me, when I look at it, is an abuse of language. We have, therefore, no evidence, that, in perception, the mind acts upon the object, or the object upon the mind; but strong evidence to the contrary. The consequence is, that the very foundation of the only argument brought to prove the existence of ideas is sandy and unsound.

Thus the first principle of the ideal philosophy is supported neither by intuition nor by proof. On what pretension, then, can it lay any just claim to our regard?

And yet this principle, unsupported, absurd, and unphilosophical as it is, will, I believe, be found to be the sole foundation laid, so far as any is laid, in our law books, for the philosophy of the law of evidence. My Lord Chief Baron Gilbert, the most approved, and deservedly the most approved writer on this part of the law, grounds his general observations on the doctrine of Mr. Locke, that knowledge is nothing but the perception of the agreement or disagreement of our *ideas*.[n]

In one of my early lectures,[o] I made the following observations. "Despotism, by an artful use of 'superiority' in politicks; and scepticism, by an artful use of 'ideas' in metaphysicks, have endeavoured — and their endeavours have frequently been attended with too much success — to

[n] Gilb. Ev. 1 — 3.   [o] Ante. p. 103.

destroy all true liberty and sound philosophy. By their baneful effects, the science of man and the science of government have been poisoned to their very fountains. But those destroyers of others have met, or must meet with their own destruction." I have put you in possession of materials to judge for yourselves whether these observations are or are not well founded.

At first sight, it would seem strange that the principles of law, as they are laid down in a book, which is very generally received for authority, should be destructive of liberty; and that the principles of the philosophy of the human mind, as they likewise are generally received and taught, should be subversive of all truth and knowledge. But after what we have seen; is it not as true as strange?

This investigation has cost me some trouble: to you I hope it will be attended with some advantage. I thought it my duty to make and to communicate it; because, without it, any superstructure of system, which I could build, would not satisfy me as resting on a solid foundation. Could I have been justified in palming upon you a system leaning on such principles as do not satisfy myself?

I know very well, that in the business of life, the dictates of common sense will always, and that in the business of government, the spirit of liberty will sometimes prevail over false theories of politicks and philosophy. But is this a reason why those false theories should be received, or encouraged, or propagated? Ought not our conduct as men and as citizens to receive benefit instead of detriment from the systems of our education? One, whose practice is in diametrical opposition to his principles, stands always in an awkward, often in a painful, sometimes in a dangerous situation.

I have said, that the spirit of liberty will sometimes prevail over false theories of politicks. Unhappily I could not say more: I could not say, generally: far less could I say, always. Let us look around us and behold the sons of men, who inhabit this globe. What an immense proportion of them are the wretched slaves of perverted opinion, of perverted system, of perverted education, and of perverted example in matters relating to the principles of society, and the rights of the human kind!

I hope I have now shown, that the philosophers before mentioned unreasonably claimed the exclusive privilege of assuming the first principle of their philosophy, without proof: I now proceed to show, that they are equally unreasonable in requiring, from others, a proof of every thing by reasoning.

The defects and blemishes of the received philosophy, which have most exposed it to ridicule and contempt, have been chiefly owing to a prejudice of the votaries of this philosophy in favour of reason. They have endeavoured to extend her jurisdiction beyond its just limits; and to

call before her bar the dictates of common sense. But these will not submit to this jurisdiction: they plead to its authority; and disdain its trial;
they claim not its aid; they dread not its attacks.

In this unequal contest between reason and common sense, the former
will always be obliged to retreat both with loss and with dishonour; nor
can she ever flourish, till this rivalship is dropt, till these encroachments
are given up, and till a cordial friendship is restored. For, in truth, reason
has no other root than the principles of common sense: it grows out of
them: and from them it draws its nourishment.

There are some common principles, which are the foundation of all
science, and of all reasoning. Before men can argue together, they must
agree in such principles; for it is impossible for two to reason, but from
principles held by them in common. Such common principles seldom admit of direct proof; they need none; they are such as men of common
understanding will acknowledge as soon as they are proposed and understood.

Such principles, when we have occasion to use them in science, are
called *axioms*. Upon such, the finest, the most elaborate, and the most
sublime reasonings in mathematicks are founded.

In every other science, as well as in mathematicks, there are some
common principles, upon which all the reasonings in that science are
grounded, and into which they may be resolved. If these were pointed out
and considered, we should be better able to judge concerning the strength
and certainty of the conclusions in that science.

It is not impossible, that what is only a vulgar prejudice may be mistaken for a first principle. Nor is it impossible, that what is really a first
principle, may, by the enchantment of words, have such a mist thrown
about it, as to hide its evidence, and make a man of candour doubt concerning it.

The peripatetick philosophy, instead of being deficient, was redundant
in first principles; instead of rejecting those, which are truly such, it
adopted, as such, many vulgar prejudices and rash judgments. This seems,
in general, to have been the spirit of ancient philosophy.

How naturally one extreme produces its opposite! Des Cartes, at the
head of modern reformers in philosophy, anxious to avoid the snare, in
which Aristotle and the peripateticks had been caught — that of admitting things too rashly as first principles — resolved to doubt of every
thing, till it was clearly proved. He would not assume, as a first principle,
even his own existence. In what manner he supposed nonexistence could
institute, or desire to institute a series of proof to prove existence or any
thing else, we are not informed.

He thought he could prove his existence by his famous enthymem —
Cogito, ergo sum. I think, therefore, I exist. Though he would not assume

the existence of *himself* as a first principle, he was obliged to assume the existence of his *thoughts* as a first principle. But is this entitled to any degree of preference? Can one, who doubts whether he exists, be certain that he thinks? And may not one, who, without proof, takes it for granted that he thinks — may not such an one, without the imputation of unphilosophick credulity, take it for granted, likewise without proof, that he exists?

In every just proof, a proposition less evident is inferred from one, which is more evident. How is it more evident that we think, than that we exist? Both are equally evident: one, therefore, ought not to be first assumed, and then used as a proof of the other.

But further; if we attend to the strict rules of proof; the existence of Des Cartes was not legitimately inferred from the existence of his thoughts. If the inference is legitimate; it must become legitimate by establishing this proposition — that thought cannot exist without a thinking being. But did Des Cartes, or has any of his followers proved this proposition? They have not proved it: they cannot prove it. Mr. Hume has denied it; and has triumphantly challenged the world to establish it by proof. The basis of his philosophy is, as we have already seen — "that a train of successive perceptions constitute the mind."

Let me not here be misunderstood. When I say, that the existence of a thinking principle, called the mind, has not been and cannot be proved; I am far from saying, that it is not true, that such a thinking principle exists. I know — I feel — it to be true; but I know it not from proof: I know it from what is greatly superiour to proof: I *see* it by the shining light of intuition.

Why will philosophers, by a preposterous pride, wish and endeavour to be indebted, for the discovery of every thing, to the feeble and glimmering rays of their own tapers, when they have only to throw the window open, and they will behold every thing illuminated by the splendour of the meridian sun?

Let me, upon this subject, further observe, that strongly as Des Cartes was seized with this phobia of first principles, he was obliged, in one instance at least, to suffer the detested liquid to touch his lips. Cogito, says he: I think. You think! How do you prove that? You, who will not believe your own existence without proof — can you consistently dispense with the proof of the existence of your thoughts? He is obliged to submit to the inconsistency. He assumes the existence of his thoughts, as a first principle. Why did he not pursue the same course with regard to other intuitive truths?

As the last observation on this subject, I beg leave to take notice, that, in this remarkable enthymem, Des Cartes assumed the very thing to be proved. Cogito, *I* think. Who *are you?* Existence is implied in the very proposition, that *one* thinks.

To the distinction between first principles and those principles, which may be ascribed to the power of reasoning, it is not a just objection, that there may be some judgments, concerning which we may be doubtful, to which class they should be referred. In painting and in nature, two colours, very different, may so run into one another, as to render it difficult to perceive where one ends and the other begins.

Let us then conclude — for we may safely conclude — that all knowledge, obtained by reasoning, must be built on first principles. When we examine, by analysis, the evidence of any proposition; we find, either that it is selfevident; or that it rests upon one or more propositions, which support it. The same thing may be said of the propositions, which support it; and of those again, which support them. But we cannot go back, in this tract, to infinity. Where, then, must the analysis stop? When we come to propositions, which support all that are built upon them, but are themselves supported by none: in other words, when we come to selfevident propositions.

All first principles must be the immediate dictates of our natural faculties; nor is it possible that we should have any other evidence of their truth. In different sciences, the faculties, which dictate these first principles, are very different: the eye, in astronomy and opticks: the ear, in musick: the moral sense, in morals.

Some first principles yield conclusions, which are certain; others yield such only as are probable. In just reasoning, the strength or weakness of the conclusion will always correspond to the strength or weakness of the principles, on which it is grounded. But the lowest degree of probability, as well as absolute certainty, must be grounded ultimately on first principles.

After hearing so much concerning first principles, the question will naturally suggest itself — are they ascertained and pointed out? That they were so, is most ardently to be desired. In mathematicks, they have been so, as far back as the annals of literature can carry us. And the consequence has been, that, in mathematicks, we find no sects, or contrary systems. This science, founded upon first principles, as upon a rock, has been increased from age to age, till it has become the loftiest and most solid fabrick, which human reason can boast.

Till within these two hundred years, natural philosophy was in the same fluctuating state with the other sciences. Every new system pulled up the old one by the roots. The great Lord Bacon first marked out the only foundation, on which natural philosophy could be built. His celebrated successour, Sir Isaac Newton, gave the first and noblest examples of that chaste induction, of which his guide in the principles of science could only delineate the theory. He reduced the principles of Lord Bacon into a few axioms, which he calls "regulæ philosophandi," — rules of philosophising. From these, together with the phenomena observed by the senses, which he likewise assumes as first principles, he deduces, by strict reasoning, the propositions of his philosophy; and, in this manner, has erected an edifice, which stands immovable upon the basis of first and selfevident principles. This edifice has been enlarged by the accession of new discoveries, made since his time; but it has not been subjected to alterations in the plan.

The other sciences have not, as yet, been so fortunate as those of mathematicks and natural philosophy. Indeed the other sciences, compared with these, have this disadvantage, that it is more difficult to form distinct and determinate conceptions of the objects, about which they are employed. But this difficulty, though great, is not insurmountable: it may afford a reason why the other sciences have had a longer infancy; but it can afford none, why they may not, at last, arrive at maturity by the same steps as those of a quicker growth.

If the same unanimity concerning first principles could be introduced into the other sciences, as in those of mathematicks and natural philosophy; this might be considered as a new era in the progress of human reason.[p]

Some first principles I have already had occasion to notice: in the course of my system, others will come forward into view; and will receive particular attention; especially in the important law of evidence, upon which the practical use of the whole municipal law entirely rests. For the facts must be ascertained by evidence, before they are susceptible of an application of the law. "Ex facto oritur jus." How can facts be satisfactorily established, unless the genuine philosophy of evidence be known?

Investigation will, perhaps, disclose to us, that this part of philosophy has been best known, where the knowledge of it has been least expected.

[p] Reid's Inq. 483.

VII

OF MAN, AS A MEMBER OF SOCIETY

"IT is not fit that man should be alone," said the all-wise and all-gracious Author of our frame, who knew it, because he made it; and who looked with compassion on the first solitary state of the work of his hands. Society is the powerful magnet, which, by its unceasing though silent operation, attracts and influences our dispositions, our desires, our passions, and our enjoyments. That we should be anxious to share, and, by sharing, to divide our afflictions, may, to some, appear by no means strange, because a certain turn of thinking will lead them to ascribe this propensity to the selfish rather than to the social part of our nature. But will this interested solution account for another propensity, equally uniform and equally strong? We are no less impatient to communicate our pleasures than our woes. Does self-interest predominate here? No. Our social affection acts here unmixed and uncontrolled.

> There's not a blessing individuals find,
> But some way leans and hearkens to the kind.
> No bandit fierce, no tyrant mad with pride,
> No caverned hermit rests self-satisfied.
> Who most to shun or hate mankind pretend
> Seek an admirer, or would fix a friend.
> Abstract what others feel, what others think,
> All pleasures sicken, and all glories sink.[a]

In all our pictures of happiness, which, at certain gay and disengaged moments, appear, in soft and alluring colours, to our fancy, does not a partner of our bliss always occupy a conspicuous place? When, on the other hand, phantoms of misery haunt our disturbed imaginations, do not solitary wanderings frequently form a principal part of the gloomy scenes? It is not an uncommon opinion, and, in this instance, our opinions must be vouched by our feelings, that the most exquisite punishment, which human nature could suffer, would be, in total solitude, to languish out a lengthened life.

"These deep solitudes" is the circumstance that first bursts from the

[a] Pope's Ess. Man. Ep. 4. v. 39.

labouring bosom of the cloistered Eloisa, when she describes the "awful cells," where "ever musing melancholy reigns."

How various and how unwearied are the workings of the social aim! Deprived of one support, it lays hold on another: deprived of that other, it lays hold on another still. While an intelligent, or even an animate being can be found, it will find an object for its unremitted pursuit and attachment.

We may extract sweet lessons of liberty and sociability from the prison of barbarous and despotick power. A French nobleman was long immused in a dreary and solitary apartment. When he had uttered many an unavailing sigh after society, he, at last, was fortunate enough to discover a spider, who had taken up his abode in the same room. Delighted with the acquisition, he immediately formed a social intercourse with the joint inhabitant of his sequestered mansion. He enjoyed, without molestation, this society for a considerable time. But the correspondence was, at last, discovered by his keeper, long tutored and accustomed to all the ingenious inventions and refinements of barbarity. By an effort, which evinced him a consummate master of his art, he killed the spider, and reduced his prisoner again to absolute solitude. The nobleman, after his release, used frequently to declare, that he had seldom experienced more poignant distress, than what he had suffered from the loss of his companion in confinement.

Some philosophers, however, have alleged, that society is not natural, but is only adventitious to us; that it is the mere consequence of direful necessity; that, by nature, men are wolves to men; not wolves to wolves; for between them union and society have a place; but as wolves to sheep, destroyers and devourers. Men, say they, are made for rapine; they are destined to prey upon one another: each is to fight for victory, and to subdue and enslave as many of his fellow creatures, as he possibly can, by treachery or by force. According to these philosophers, the only natural principles of man are selfishness, and an insatiable desire of tyranny and dominion. Their conclusion is, that a state of nature, instead of being a state of kindness, society, and peace, is a state of selfishness, discord, and war. By a strange perversion of things, they would so explain all the social passions and natural affections, as to denominate them of the selfish species. Humanity and hospitality towards strangers or those in distress are represented as selfishness, only of a more deliberate kind. An honest heart is only a cunning one; and good nature is a well regulated self-love. The love of posterity, of kindred, of country, and of mankind — all these are only so many different modifications of this universal self-love.

But if we attend to our nature and our state; if we listen to the operations of our own minds, to our dispositions, our sensations, and our propensities; we shall be fully and agreeably convinced, that the narrow and hideous representation of these philosophers is not founded on the truth of things; but, on the contrary, is totally repugnant to all human sentiment, and all human experience. Indeed, an appeal to themselves will evince, that their philosophy is not consistent even with the instinctive principles of their own hearts — principles, of which the native lustre will, at some times, beam forth, notwithstanding all the care employed to cover or extinguish it. The celebrated Sage of Malmesbury, savage and unsociable as he would make himself and all mankind appear, took the utmost pains that, during his life, and even after his death, others might be kindly rescued from the unhappy delusions, by which they were prevented from discovering the truth.[b] He told us "that both in religion and in morals, we were imposed on by our governours; that there is nothing, which, by nature, inclines us either way; and that nothing naturally draws us to the love of what is without or beyond ourselves." And yet he was the most laborious of all men in composing and publishing systems of this kind — *for our use.*

To such philosophers, animated with this preposterous zeal, this answer, in the spirit of their own doctrines, is plain and easy. If there is nothing to carry you without yourselves; what are we to you? From what motives do you give yourselves all this concern about us? What can induce you to trim your midnight lamp, and waste your spirits in laborious vigils, for our instruction? You disclaim all social connexion with your species; what, then, we say again, are we to you?

But a subject, in itself so material to the sciences of philosophy and of law, merits a serious, a full, and a patient discussion. For it is of high practical importance, that the principles of society should be properly explained and well understood. It has been one of the happy characteristicks of the present age, both on this and on the other side of the Atlantick, that the spirit of philosophy has been wisely directed to the just investigation of those principles; and that the spirit of patriotism has been vigorously exerted in their support.

In a very early part of these lectures,[e] it was observed, concerning definitions and divisions, that by them we are in danger of circumscribing nature within the limits of our own notions, formed frequently on partial and defective views. A very remarkable instance of this occurs in the subject, on the examination of which we now enter.

The intellectual powers of the mind have been commonly divided into simple apprehension, judgment, and reasoning. This division has received the sanction of high antiquity, and of a very extensive adoption; yet it

[b] 1. Shaft. Char. 90.   [e] Ante. p. 99.

is far from being complete. From it many of the operations of the understanding are excluded, such as consciousness, moral perception, taste, memory, and our perception of objects by means of our external senses. But, besides all these, there is a whole class, and a very important one too, of our intellectual operations, which, because they were not fortunate enough to be included within the foregoing division, have been overlooked by philosophers, and have not even yet been distinguished by a name. Some operations of the mind may take place in a solitary state: others, from their very nature, are social; and necessarily suppose a communication with some other intelligent being. In a state of absolute solitude, one may apprehend, and judge, and reason. But when he bears or hears testimony; when he gives or receives a command; when he enters into an engagement by a promise or a contract; these acts imply necessarily something more than apprehension, judgment, and reasoning; they imply necessarily a society with other beings, social as well as intelligent.

Simple apprehension is unaccompanied with any judgment or belief, concerning the object apprehended. Judgment is formed, as these philosophers say, by comparing ideas, and by perceiving their agreements and disagreements. Reasoning is an operation, by which, from two or more judgments, we deduce a conclusion. Now, from this account of these three operations of the mind, it appears unquestionably, that testimony is neither apprehension, nor judgment, nor reasoning. The same observation will apply, with the same propriety, to a promise, to an agreement, to a contract. Testimony, agreements, contracts, promises form very distinguished titles in that law, which it is the object of these lectures to delineate: perhaps it has already been evinced to your satisfaction, that some of them form its very basis.

That system of human nature must, indeed, appear extremely inadequate and defective, by which articles of such vast importance, both in theory and in the business of life, are left without a place, and without a name.

The attempts of some philosophers to reduce the social operations under the common philosophical divisions, resemble very much the attempts of others, to reduce all our social affections to certain modifications of self love. The Author of our existence intended us to be social beings; and has, for that end, given us social intellectual powers. They are original parts of our constitution; and their exertions are no less natural than the exertions of those powers, which are solitary and selfish.

Our social intellectual operations appear early in life, and before we are capable of reasoning; yet they suppose a conviction of the existence of other intelligent and social beings. A child asks a question of his nurse, and waits for her answer: this implies a conviction that she is intelligent and social; that she can receive and return a communication of thoughts and sentiments.

All languages are fitted to express the social as well as the solitary operations of the mind. To express the former is indeed the primary and the direct intention of language. A man, who had no interchange of sentiments with other social and intelligent beings, would be as mute as the irrational animals that surround him. By language, we communicate to others that, which we know: by language, we learn from others that, of which we are ignorant: by language, we advise, persuade, console, encourage, soothe, restrain: in consequence of language, we are united by political societies, government, and laws: by means of language, we are raised from a situation, in which we should be as rude and as savage as the beasts of the woods.

In the more imperfect societies of mankind, such as those composed of colonies scarcely settled in their new seats, it might pass for sufficient good fortune, if the people proved only so far masters of language, as to be able to understand one another, to confer about their wants, and to provide for their common necessities. Their exposed and indigent state would not afford them either that leisure or that easy disposition, which is requisite for the cultivation of the fine arts. They, who were neither safe from violence, nor secure from want, would not be likely to engage in unnecessary pursuits. It could not be expected that they would turn their attention towards the numbers of their language, or to its best and most perfect application and arrangement. But when, in process of time, the affairs of the society were settled on an easy and secure foundation; when debates and discourses, on the subjects of common interest and of publick good, were become familiar; when the speeches of distinguished characters were considered and compared; then there would be observed, between one speaker and another, a difference, not only with regard to a more agreeable measure of sound, but to a happier and more easy arrangement of sentiment.

The attention paid to language is one distinguishing mark of the progress of society towards its most refined period: as society improves, influence is acquired by the means of reasoning and discourse: in proportion as that influence is felt to increase, in proportion will be the care bestowed upon the methods of expressing conceptions with propriety and elegance. In every polished community, this study has been considered as highly important, and has possessed a place in every plan of liberal education.

In all languages, a question, a promise, a contract, which are social acts, can be expressed as easily and as properly, as a judgment, which is a solitary act. The expression of a judgment has been dignified with a par ticular appellation; it has been denominated a *proposition*. It has been analyzed, with great logical parade, into its several parts: its elements of subject, predicate, and copula have been exhibited in ostentatious arrangement: their various modifications have been traced and examined in laborious and voluminous tracts. The expression of a question, of a covenant, or of a promise is as susceptible of analysis as the expression of a judgment: but this has not been attempted; these operations of the mind have not been honoured even with a distinct and appropriate name. Why has so much pains been taken, why has so much labour been bestowed in analyzing, and assigning appropriate names to the solitary operations, and the expression of the solitary operations of the understanding; while so little attention has been allotted to such of its operations as are social? Perhaps it will be difficult to assign any other reason than this: in the divisions, which have been made of the operations of the mind, the social ones have been omitted; and, consequently, have not been introduced to notice or regard.

Our moral perceptions, as well as the other powers of our understanding, indicate, in the strongest manner, our designation for society. Veracity, and its corresponding quality, confidence, show this, in a very striking point of view. If we were intended for solitude, those qualities could have neither operation nor use. On the other hand, without those qualities, society could not be supported. Without the latter, the former would be useless: without the former, the latter would be dangerous. Without confidence in promises, for instance, we must, in the greatest part of our conduct, proceed entirely upon the calculations of chance: but there could be no confidence in promises, if there was no principle, from which their performance might be reasonably expected.

Some may imagine, that though this principle did not exist, yet human affairs might, perhaps, be carried on as well; for that general caution and mutual distrust would be the necessary result; and where no confidence would be reposed, no breach of it could happen. But, not to mention the uneasiness and anxiety which would unavoidably attend such a situation, it is not considered how much, in every hour of our lives, we trust to others; and how difficult, if not entirely impracticable, it would be to perform the most common as well as the most important business of human life, without such trust. The conclusion is, that the performance of promises is essential to society.

Deeply laid in human nature, we now behold the basis of one of the principal pillars of private municipal law; that, which enforces the obligation of promises, agreements, and covenants.

Again; the moral sense restrains us from harming the innocent: it teaches us, that the innocent have a right to be secure from harm. These are two great principles, which prepare us for society; and, with regard to them, the moral sense discovers peculiar inflexibility: it dictates, that we should submit to any distress or danger, rather than procure our safety and relief by violence upon an innocent person.

Similar to the restraint, respecting personal safety and security, is the restraint, which the moral sense imposes on us, with regard to property. Robbery and theft are indulged by no society: from a society even of robbers, they are strictly excluded.

The necessity of the social law, with regard to personal security, is so evident, as to require no explanation. Its necessity, with regard to property, will be explained and made evident by the following remarks.

Man has a natural propensity to store up the means of his subsistence: this propensity is essential, in order to incite us to provide comfortably for ourselves, and for those who depend on us. But this propensity would be rendered ineffectual, if we were not secured in the possession of those stores which we collect; for no one would toil to accumulate what he could not possess in security. This security is afforded by the moral sense, which dictates to all men, that goods collected by the labour and industry of individuals are their property; and that property ought to be inviolable.

We beheld, a little while ago, one of the principal pillars of *civil* law founded deeply in our nature: we now perceive the great principles of *criminal* law laid equally deep in the human frame. Violations of property and of personal security are, as we shall afterwards show particularly, the objects of that law. To punish, and, by punishing, to prevent them, is or ought to be the great end of that law, as shall also be particularly shown.

That we are fitted and intended for society, and that society is fitted and intended for us, will become evident by considering our passions and affections, as well as by considering our moral perceptions, and the other operations of our understandings. We have all the emotions, which are necessary in order that society may be formed and maintained: we have tenderness for the fair sex: we have affection for our children, for our parents, and for our other relations: we have attachment to our friends: we have a regard for reputation and esteem: we possess gratitude and compassion: we enjoy pleasure in the happiness of others, especially when we have been instrumental in procuring it: we entertain for our country an animated and vigorous zeal: we feel delight in the agreeable conception of the improvement and happiness of mankind.

> The centre mov'd, a circle straight succeeds,
> Another still, and still another spreads.
> Friend, parent, neighbour first it will embrace,
> His country next, and next all human race;
> Wide and more wide, th' o'erflowings of the mind

Take ev'ry creature in, of ev'ry kind;
Earth smiles around, with boundless bounty blest,
And heav'n beholds its image in his breast.[a]

How naturally, and sometimes how strongly, are our passions communicated from one to another, without even the least knowledge of the cause, by which they were originally produced! They are conveyed by aspect: the very countenance is infectious: the emotion flies from face to face: it is no sooner seen than experienced: like the electrick shock, it is felt instantaneously by a whole multitude; though, perhaps, only one of them knows from whence it proceeds. Such is the force of society in the passions.

This sympathy is an important quality of many of our passions: in particular, it invites and produces a communication of joys and sorrows, hopes and fears. Spirits, the most generous and the most susceptible of strong impressions, are the most social and combining. They delight most to move in concert; and feel, in the strongest manner, the force of the confederating charm.

The social powers and dispositions of our minds discover themselves in the earliest periods of life. So soon as a child can speak, he can ask, and he can answer a question: before he can speak, he shows signs of love, of resentment, and of other affections necessarily pointed to society. He is capable of social intercourse long before he is capable of reasoning. We behold this charming intercourse between his mother and him, before he is a year old. He can, by signs, ask and refuse, threaten and supplicate. In danger, he clings to his mother — for I will not, on this occasion, distinguish between the mother and the nurse — he enters into her joy and grief, is happy in her caresses, and is unhappy in her displeasure.

As sociability attends us in our infancy; she continues to be our companion through all the variegated scenes of our riper years. By an irresistible charm, she insinuates herself into the hearts of every rank and class of men, and mixes in all the various modes and arrangements of human life. Let us suppose a man of so morose and acrimonious a disposition, as to shun, like Timon of Athens, all communication with his species; even such a misanthropist would wish for at least one associate, into whose bosom he might discharge the rancour and virulence of his own heart.

Society is necessary as well as natural to us. To support life, to satisfy our natural appetites, to obtain those agreeable enjoyments of which our nature is susceptible, many external things are indispensable. In order to live with any degree of comfort, we must have food, clothing, habitations, furniture, and utensils of some sort. These cannot be procured

[a] Pope's Ess. on Man. Ep. 4. v. 365.

without much art and labour; nor without the friendly assistance of our fellows in society.

Let us suppose a man of full strength, and well instructed in all our arts of life, to be reduced suddenly to solitude, even in one of the best of soils and climates: could he procure the grateful conveniences of life? It will not be pretended. Could he procure even its simple necessaries? In an ingenious and excellent romance, we are told this has been done. But it will be remembered, that the foundation of Robinson Crusoe's future subsistence, and of all the comforts which he afterwards provided and collected, was laid in the useful instruments and machines, which he saved from his shipwreck. These were the productions of society.

Could one, uninstructed in our arts of life, and unfurnished with the productions of society, subsist in solitude, though he were of full age, and possessed of health and strength? the probabilities would run strong against him.

Could one subsist in solitude during the weak, uninformed, and in-experienced period of his infancy? This he could not do, unless, like an-other Romulus and Remus, he owed his subsistence to the social aid of the wolves.

But let us, for a moment, suppose, that food, raiment, and shelter were supplied even by a miracle; a solitary life must be continually harassed by dangers and fears. Suppose those dangers and fears to be removed; could he find employment for the most excellent powers and instincts of his mind? Could he indulge affection or social joy? could he communicate, or could he receive social pleasure or social regard? Dispositions very different indeed — sour discontentment, sullen melancholy, listless languor — must prey upon his soul.

The reciprocal assistance of those, who compose a single family, may procure many of the necessaries of life; and may diminish its dangers. In this state some room will be afforded for social enjoyments, and for the finer operations of the mind. Still greater pleasures and advantages would be obtained by the union of a few families in the same neighbourhood. They would undertake and execute laborious works for the common good of all; and social emotions would operate in a less contracted circuit. Associations, still larger, will enlarge the sphere of pleasure and enjoy-ment; and will furnish more diversified and delightful exercise to our powers of every kind. Knowledge is increased: inventions are discov-ered: experience improves them: and the inventions, with their improve-ments, are spread over the whole community. Designs of durable and extensive advantage are boldly formed, and vigorously carried into effect. The social and benevolent affections range in an ample sphere; and attain an eminent degree of strength and refinement.

On what does our security — on what do our enjoyments depend?

On our mutual services and sympathetick pleasures. Other animals have strength or speed sufficient for their preservation and defence. Man is, in all states, encompassed with weakness and dangers: but the strength and safety, which he wants by himself, he finds, when he is united with his equals. Nature has endowed him with a principle, which gives him force and superiority, where otherwise he would be helpless and in-feriour. By sociability, they, who separately could make no effectual re-sistance, conquer and tame the various kinds of the brute creation. Society is the cause, that, not satisfied with the element on which he was born, man extends his dominion over the sea. Society supplies him with remedies in his diseases, with comfort in his afflictions, and with assistance in his old age. Take away society, and you destroy the basis, on which the preservation and happiness of human life are laid.

"There is nothing more certain," says Cicero,[e] "than the excellent maxim of Plato — that we are not intended solely for ourselves; but that our friends and our country claim a portion of our birth. Since, according to the doctrine of the stoicks, the productions of the earth are designed for men, and men are designed for the mutual aid of one another; we should certainly pursue the design of Nature, and promote her benign intention, by contributing our proportion to the general interest, by mutually performing and receiving good offices, and by employing our care, our industry, and even our fortune, in order to strengthen the love and friendship, which should always predominate in human society."

In point of dignity, the social operations and emotions of the mind rise to a most respectable height. The excellency of man is chiefly dis-cerned in the great improvements, of which he is susceptible in society: these, by perseverance and vigour, may be carried on progressively to degrees higher and higher, above any limits which we can now assign.

Our social affections and operations acquire still greater importance, in another point of view: they promote and are necessary to our happiness. "If we could suppose ourselves," says Cicero,[f] who knew so well how to illustrate law by philosophy — "if we could suppose ourselves transported by some divinity into a solitude, replete with all the delicacies which the heart of man could desire, but excluded, at the same time, from every possible intercourse with our kind, there is not a person in the world of so unsocial and savage a temper, as to be capable, in these forlorn cir-cumstances, of relishing any enjoyment." "Nothing," continues he, "is more true, than what the philosopher Archytas is reported to have said: If a man were to be carried up into heaven, and see the beauties of universal nature displayed before him, he would receive but little pleasure from the wonderful scenes, unless there was some person, to whom he could relate the glories, which he had viewed. Human nature is so con-

[e] De off. l. 1. c. 7.   [f] De Amic. 23.

stituted, as to be incapable of solitary satisfaction. Man, like those plants which are formed to embrace others, is led, by an instinctive impulse, to recline on those of his own kind."

> Man, like the gen'rous vine, supported lives;
> The strength he gains is from th' embrace he gives.[g]

The observations, which we make in common life, vouch the justness of these sentiments. We see those persons possess the greatest share of happiness, who have about them many objects of love and endearment. To the want of these objects, may be ascribed the moroseness of monks, and of those who, without entering into any religious order, lead the lives of monks.

Of the same nature with the indulgence of domestick affections, and equally refreshing to the spirit, is the pleasure, which flows from acts of beneficence, either in bestowing pecuniary favours, or in imparting, to those who want it, the benefit of our advice, or the assistance of our professional skill. The last consideration is urged, with peculiar propriety, by the professor of law. Innumerable instances occur, in which gentlemen of the bar, who possess abilities and character, can bestow what may be called favours, even on those, who are both able and willing to pay well for their services. When a client has an important business depending, entire confidence in the integrity and talents of his counsel diffuses over his mind a degree of composure and serenity, against which a fee, weighed in the balance, would be found wanting. This is particularly the case, when the life or the reputation of the client is at stake.

The foregoing observations may also be applied to publick services done for the state, by assisting her in her councils, or by defending or prosecuting her interests. Even if no suitable return, as it sometimes happens, should be received from the state for such services; yet a mind, nurtured to the refined and enlarged exercise of the social passion, will find no trivial pleasure in the reflection that it has performed them, and that those, for whom they were performed, enjoy the advantages resulting from them. Virtue, in such an instance, will prove herself her own reward. A man, whose soul vibrates in unison with the benevolent affections, will always find within him an encouragement, and a compensation too, for discharging his duty — an encouragement and a compensation, of which ingratitude itself cannot deprive him.

I will not appeal to vanity, and ask, if any thing can be more flattering, than to *obtain* the praises and acclamations of others. But I will appeal to conscious rectitude, and ask, whether any thing can be more satisfactory, than to *deserve* their regard and esteem.

The possession of science is always attended with pleasure: but science,

[g] Pope's Ess. on Man. Ep. 3. v. 311.

believe me, acquires an increased relish, when we have an opportunity of pouring it into the bosoms of others. We receive a redoubled satisfaction from the agreeable, though, perhaps, the flattering opinion, that we communicate entertainment and instruction; and from the opinion, better founded, that even weak attempts to communicate entertainment and instruction are received with reflected social emotions.

What can be more productive of happiness than even those wants, which are the foundations of so many blessings — love and friendship, generosity and reliance, kindness and gratitude? The gratifications even of sense lose their relish, if not heightened by the "spes mutui credula animi" — corresponding social emotions.

Our esteem of others, too, arising from the approbation of their conduct, is a most pleasing affection. The contemplation of a great and good character warms the heart, and invigorates the whole frame.

The wisest and most benign constitution of a rational and moral system is that, in which the degree of private affection, most useful to the individual, is, at the same time, consistent with the greatest interest of the system; and in which the degree of social affection, most useful to the system, is, at the same time, productive of the greatest happiness to the individual. Thus it is in the system of society. In that system, he who acts on such principles, and is governed by such affections, as sever him from the common good and publick interest, works, in reality, towards his own misery: while he, on the other hand, who operates for the good of the whole, as is by nature and by nature's God appointed him, pursues, in truth, and at the same time, his own felicity.

Regulated by this standard, extensive, unerring, and sublime, self-love and social are the same.

To a state of society, then, we are invited from every quarter. It is natural; it is necessary; it is pleasing; it is profitable to us. The result of all is, that for a state of society we are designated by Him, who is all-wise and all-good.

Society may be distinguished into two kinds, natural and civil. This distinction has not been marked with the accuracy, which it well merits. Indeed some writers have given little or no attention to the latter kind; others have expressly denied it, and said, that there can be no civil society without civil government. But this is certainly not the case. A state of civil society must have existed, and such a state, in all our reasonings on this subject, must be supposed, before civil government could be regularly formed and established. Nay, 'tis for the security and improvement of such a state, that the adventitious one of civil government has been instituted. To civil society, indeed, without including in its description the idea of civil government, the name of *state* may be assigned, by way of excellence. It is in this sense that Cicero seems to use it, in the following beautiful passage. "Nothing, which is exhibited on our globe, is more acceptable to that divinity, which governs the whole universe, than those communities and assemblages of men, which, lawfully associated, — jure sociati — are denominated states." [h]

How often has the end been sacrificed to the means? Government was instituted for the happiness of society: how often has the happiness of society been offered as a victim to the idol of government! But this is not agreeable to the true order of things: it is not consistent with the orthodox political creed. Let government — let even the constitution be, as they ought to be, the handmaids; let them not be, for they ought not to be, the mistresses of the state.

A state may be described — a complete body of free persons, united together for their common benefit, to enjoy peaceably what is their own, and to do justice to others. It is an artificial person: it has an understanding and will peculiar to itself: it has its affairs and its interests: it deliberates and resolves: it has its rules; it has its obligations; and it has its rights. It may acquire property, distinct from that of its members: it may incur debts, to be discharged out of the publick stock, not out of the private fortunes of individuals: it may be bound by contracts, and for damages arising *quasi ex contractu*.

In order to constitute a state, it is indispensably necessary, that the wills and the power of all the members be united in such a manner, that they shall never act nor desire but one and the same thing, in whatever relates to the end, for which the society is established. It is from this union of wills and of strength, that the state or body politick results. The only rational and natural method, therefore, of constituting a civil society, is by the convention or consent of the members, who compose it. For by a civil society we properly understand, the voluntary union of persons in the same end, and in the same means requisite to obtain that end. This union is a benefit, not a sacrifice: civil is an addition to natural order.

This union may rationally be supposed to be formed in the following manner: if a number of people, who had hitherto lived independent of each other, wished to form a civil society, it would be necessary to enter into an engagement to associate together in one body, and to regulate, with one common consent, whatever regards their preservation, their security, their improvement, their happiness.

In the social compact, each individual engages with the whole collectively, and the whole collectively engage with each individual. These engagements are obligatory, because they are mutual. The individuals who are not parties to them, are not members of the society.

Smaller societies may be formed within a state by a part of its members. These societies also are deemed to be moral persons; but not in a

[h] Somn. Scip. c. 3.

state of natural liberty: their actions are cognizable by the superiour power of the state, and are regulated by its laws. To these societies the name of corporations is generally appropriated, though somewhat improperly; for the term is strictly applicable to supreme as well as to inferiour bodies politick.

The foregoing account of the formation of civil society, which refers it to original engagements; and consequently resolves the duty of submission to the laws of the society, into the universal obligation of fidelity in the performance of promises, is warmly attacked by a sensible and ingenious writer.[1] He represents it, as founded on a supposition, false in fact; as insufficient, if it was true, for the purposes, for which it is produced; and as leading to dangerous consequences. He acknowledges, however, that, in the United States, transactions have happened, which bear the nearest resemblance to this political idea, of any, of which history has preserved the account or the memory. This subject has already received some; it will afterwards receive more attention and examination. At present, it is sufficient, and it is proper, to intimate to you the point of discussion; for it is a very important one in the science of government.

In civil society, previously to the institution of civil government, all men are equal. Of one blood all nations are made; from one source the whole human race has sprung.

When we say, that all men are equal; we mean not to apply this equality to their virtues, their talents, their dispositions, or their acquirements. In all these respects, there is, and it is fit for the great purposes of society that there should be, great inequality among men. In the moral and political as well as in the natural world, diversity forms an important part of beauty; and as of beauty, so of utility likewise. That social happiness, which arises from the friendly intercourse of good offices, could not be enjoyed, unless men were so framed and so disposed, as mutually to afford and to stand in need of service and assistance. Hence the necessity not only of great variety, but even of great inequality in the talents of men, bodily as well as mental. Society supposes mutual dependence: mutual dependence supposes mutual wants: all the social exercises and enjoyments may be reduced to two heads — that of giving, and that of receiving: but these imply different aptitudes to give and to receive.

Many are the degrees, many are the varieties of human genius, human dispositions, and human characters. One man has a turn for mechanicks; another, for architecture; one paints; a second makes poems; this excels in the arts of a military; the other, in those of civil life. To account for these varieties of taste and character, is not easy; is, perhaps, impossible.

[1] 2. Paley 140.

But though their efficient cause it may be difficult to explain; their final cause, that is, the intention of Providence in appointing them, we can see and admire. These varieties of taste and character induce different persons to choose different professions and employments in life: these varieties render mankind mutually beneficial to each other, and prevent too violent oppositions of interest in the same pursuit. Hence we enjoy a variety of conveniences; hence the numerous arts and sciences have been invented and improved; hence the sources of commerce and friendly intercourse between different nations have been opened; hence the circulation of truth has been quickened and promoted; hence the operations of social virtue have been multiplied and enlarged.

> Heaven, forming each on other to depend,
> Bids each on other for assistance call,
> 'Till one man's weakness grows the strength of all.
> Wants, frailties, passions closer still ally
> The common interest, or endear the tie:
> To these we owe true friendship, love sincere,
> Each home-felt joy, that life inherits here.[j]

How insipidly uniform would human life and manners be, without the beautiful variety of colours, reflected upon them by different tastes, different tempers, and different characters!

But however great the variety and inequality of men may be with regard to virtue, talents, taste, and acquirements; there is still one aspect, in which all men in society, previous to civil government, are equal. With regard to all, there is an equality in rights and in obligations; there is that "jus æquum," that equal law, in which the Romans placed true freedom. The natural rights and duties of man belong equally to all. Each forms a part of that great system, whose greatest interest and happiness are intended by all the laws of God and nature. These laws prohibit the wisest and the most powerful from inflicting misery on the meanest and most ignorant; and from depriving them of their rights or just acquisitions. By these laws, rights, natural or acquired, are confirmed, in the same manner, to all; to the weak and artless, their small acquisitions, as well as to the strong and artful, their large ones. If much labour employed entitles the active to great possessions, the indolent have a right, equally sacred, to the little possessions, which they occupy and improve.

As in civil society, previous to civil government, all men are equal; so, in the same state, all men are free. In such a state, no one can claim, in preference to another, superiour right: in the same state, no one can claim over another superiour authority.

Nature has implanted in man the desire of his own happiness; she has

[j] Pope. Ess. Man. Ep. 2. v. 249.

inspired him with many tender affections towards others, especially in the near relations of life; she has endowed him with intellectual and with active powers; she has furnished him with a natural impulse to exercise his powers for his own happiness, and the happiness of those, for whom he entertains such tender affections. If all this be true, the undeniable consequence is, that he has a right to exert those powers for the accomplishment of those purposes, in such a manner, and upon such objects, as his inclination and judgment shall direct; provided he does no injury to others; and provided more publick interests do not demand his labours. This right is natural liberty. Every man has a sense of this right. Every man has a sense of the impropriety of restraining or interrupting it. Those who judge wisely, will use this liberty virtuously and honourably: those, who are less wise, will employ it in meaner pursuits: others, again, may, perhaps, indulge it in what may be justly censured as vicious and dishonourable. Yet, with regard even to these last, while they are not injurious to others; and while no human institution has placed them under the control of magistrates or laws, the sense of liberty is so strong, and its loss is so deeply resented, that, upon the whole, more unhappiness would result from depriving them of their liberty on account of their imprudence, than could be reasonably apprehended from the imprudent use of their liberty.

The right of natural liberty is suggested to us not only by the selfish parts of our constitution, but by our generous affections; and especially by our moral sense, which intimates to us, that in our voluntary actions consist our dignity and perfection.

The laws of nature are the measure and the rule; they ascertain the limits and the extent of natural liberty.

In society, when the sentiments of the members are not unanimous, the voice of the majority must be deemed the will of the whole. That the majority, by any vote, should bind not only themselves, but those also who dissent from that vote, seems, at first, to be inconsistent with the well known rules — that all men are naturally equal; and that all men are naturally free. From these rules, it may be alleged, that no one can be bound by the act of another, without his own consent. But it is to be remembered, that society is constituted for a certain purpose; and that each member of it consents that this purpose shall be carried on; and, consequently, that every thing necessary for carrying it on shall be done. Now a number of persons can jointly do business only in three ways — by the decision of the whole, by the decision of the majority, or by the decision of the minority. The first case is not here supposed, nor is there occasion to make a question concerning it. The only remaining question, then, which can be proposed, is, which is most reasonable and equitable — that the minority should bind the majority — or that the majority should bind the minority? The latter, certainly. It is most reasonable; because it is not so probable, that a greater number, as that a smaller number concurring in judgment, should be mistaken. It is most equitable; because the greater number are presumed to have an interest in the society proportioned to that number. Besides; though, in the case supposed, the minority are bound without their *immediate* consent; they are bound by their consent originally given to the establishment of the society, for the purposes which it was intended to accomplish. For it has been already observed, that those, who enter not into the original engagements forming the society, are not to be considered as members: all the members, therefore, must have originally given their consent.

The rule, which we have mentioned, may be altered and modified by positive institution. In some cases, the consent of a number larger than a mere majority: in others, even unanimity may be required.

This is the proper place for considering a question of very considerable importance in civil society, and concerning which there has been much diversity in the sentiments of writers, and in the laws and practice of states: has a state a right to prohibit the emigration of its members? may a citizen dissolve the connexion between him and his country?

On the principles of the compact of association, which I have already stated, there seems to be but little doubt that one article of it may be, that each individual binds himself indissolubly to the society, while the society performs, on its part, the stipulated conditions. This engagement each individual may make for himself:[k] but can he make it for his children and his posterity? must they be and continue bound by the act of their father and ancestor?

The notion of natural, perpetual, and unalienable allegiance from the citizen to the society, or to the head of the society, of which he was born a member, has, by some writers and in some countries, been carried very far indeed: and their practice has been equally rigorous with their principles. The well known maxim, which the writers upon the law of England have adopted and applied to this case is,[1] "Nemo potest exuere patriam." It is not, therefore, as is holden by that law, in the power of any private subject to shake off his allegiance, and to transfer it to a foreign prince. Nor is it in the power of any foreign prince, by naturalizing or employing a subject of Great Britain, to dissolve the bond of

---

[k] Connecticut was originally settled by emigrants from the neighbourhood of Boston. They applied to the general court of Massachusetts for permission to go in quest of new adventures: and could not be satisfied, until they had obtained the leave of the court. For it was the general sense, as we are assured, that the inhabitants were all mutually bound to one another by the oath of a freeman, as well as the original compact; so as not to be at liberty to separate without the consent of the whole. Chal. 286.

[1] Fost. 184. [No man can renounce his own country.]

allegiance between that subject and the crown. Hence it has been adjudged, that a cartel for the exchange or ransom of prisoners of war cannot extend to the case of a subject born, though clothed with a commission from the party to the cartel. The reason assigned is, that by the laws of all nations, subjects taken in arms against their lawful prince are not considered as prisoners of war, but as rebels; and are liable to the punishments ordinarily inflicted on rebels.[m] This doctrine was, so late as the year one thousand seven hundred and forty seven, applied to the case of a native of Great Britain, who had received his education in France from his early infancy; and who had spent his riper years in a profitable employment in that kingdom, where all his hopes were centred.[n]

The reasons in favour of the position, that a citizen cannot dissolve the political connexion between him and his country, may be stated in the following manner. Every citizen, as soon as he is born, is under the protection of the state, and is entitled to all the advantages arising from that protection: he, therefore, owes obedience to that power, from which the protection, which he enjoys, is derived. But while he continues in infancy and nonage, he cannot perform the duties of obedience. The performance of them must be respited, till he arrive at the years of discretion and maturity. When he arrives at those years, he owes obedience, not only for the protection, which he then enjoys, but also for that, which, from his birth, he has enjoyed. Obedience now becomes a duty founded upon principles of gratitude, as well as upon principles of interest: it becomes a debt, which nothing but the performance of the duties of citizenship, during a whole life, will discharge.[o]

But, notwithstanding this train of thought and reasoning, there are certainly cases, in which a citizen has an unquestionable right to renounce his country, and go in quest of a settlement in some other part of the world. One of these cases is, when, in his own country, he cannot procure a subsistence. Another is, when the society neglects to fulfil its obligations to the citizen. A third is, when the society would establish laws, on things, to which the original social compact cannot oblige the citizen to submit.[p]

In answer to the inferences drawn from principles of gratitude, it may be observed, that every man being born free, a native citizen, when he arrives at the age of discretion, may examine whether it be convenient for him to join in the society, for which he was destined by his birth. If, on examination, he finds, that it will be more advantageous to him to remove into another country, he has a right to go, making to that which he leaves a proper return for what it has done in his favour, and preserving for it, as far as it shall be consistent with the engagements, which

[m] Id. 60.   [n] Fost. 59.   [o] 2. P. Wms. 123. 124.
[p] Vat. 96. b. 1. s. 223 — 225.

his new situation and connexions may require, the sentiments of respect and attachment.

The sentiments of Mr. Locke on this subject go much further. " 'Tis plain," says he,[q] "by the law of right reason, that a child is born a subject of no country or government. He is under his father's tuition and authority, till he comes to the age of discretion; and then he is a freeman, at liberty what government he will put himself under; what body politick he will unite himself to."

"O glorious regulations!" says Cicero,[r] "originally established for us by our ancestors of Roman name; that no one of us should be obliged to belong to more than one society, since a dissimilitude of societies must produce a proportioned variety of laws; that no one, contrary to his inclination, should be deprived of his right of citizenship; and that no one, contrary to his inclinations, should be obliged to continue in that relation. The power of retaining and of renouncing our rights of citizenship, is the most stable foundation of our liberties."

In the digest of the Roman laws,[s] it is laid down as a rule, that every one is at liberty to choose the state, of which he wishes to be a member.

Indeed, excepting in some very particular cases, every one ought to be at liberty to leave the state. This general liberty is not only just, but may be productive of much generous emulation among states, and of extensive advantages to their citizens. Those states, which manage their affairs best, will offer the strongest inducements to their own citizens to remain, and to others to incorporate among them. On the other hand, it is both inhuman and unjust to convert the state into a prison for its citizens, by preventing them from leaving it on a prospect of advantage to themselves. True it is, that they ought to make compensation for any advantages, which they have derived from the state at its expense: but equally true it is, that this compensation is generally made, by their having contributed annually, during their past residence, towards the publick revenue, by paying taxes on property, as all men, even minors, do; and by consuming goods, on which imposts or duties have been levied.

Emigration may arise from various causes. It may be occasioned by the population of a country. In this case, great numbers may be constantly leaving the state, and yet the state may be increasing in population. It has been suggested by some writers, that the right of exposing children has been one cause of the populousness of China. Surely the prospect that they will be comfortably provided for, if not in their own, yet in another country, must be a much more powerful, as well as more humane incentive to marriages.

Insecurity, hardships, oppression may be the causes of emigration. A nation whose inhabitants are in a predicament so disagreeable, may be in

<hr>

[q] On Civ. Gov. s. 118.   [r] Pro. Balb. c. 13.   [s] Dig. l. 49. t. 15.

declining circumstances; but those circumstances, indicating a decline, are not the effects of emigration; they are the effects of the evils and calamities which occasion it. Two things, which are commonly considered as cause and effect, are often no more than two collateral effects of the same cause.

Independently, therefore, of the question of right, there can be but few cases, in which emigration could be prohibited on the sound principles of policy. Emigration, it is true, may be a symptom of languor and decay; but it may also be an evidence and a consequence of the overflowing vigour and prosperity of the state.

Permit me to suggest a still further reason — to me it appears a strong one — in favour of unrestrained emigration. In a free state, the consent of every citizen to its institution and government ought to be evinced either by express declarations, or by the strongest and justest presumptions. When a state is formed, the residence of a citizen is presumed a sufficient evidence of his assent and acquiescence in its institutions: to reside in any country is universally deemed a submission to its authority. But that these presumptions may be fairly drawn, we must be understood as speaking of a state, from which the citizens have liberty to depart with their effects at pleasure. Where this liberty is not enjoyed, the considerations of family, of property, and many other considerations that are without a name, may detain a man, much against his inclination, in a country, in which he finds himself trammelled. In such case, his residence is no reasonable evidence of his consent to the formation, the constitution, the government, or the laws of the state.

Upon the whole it appears, that the right of emigration is a *right*, advantageous to the citizen, and generally useful even to the state. It may, however, in the fundamental laws, be reduced to a certainty. The citizens of Neufchatel in Switzerland may quit the country, and carry off their effects, in whatever manner they please, without paying any duties.[t] By the constitution of Pennsylvania,[u] it is declared "that emigration from the state shall not be prohibited."

These remarks on the rights and principles of emigration, prepare the way for remarks, more important, on the principles and rights of colonization, which will form the subject of inquiry in a future part of our lectures.

[t] Vat. 96. b. 1. s. 225.   [u] Art. 9. s. 25.

VIII

OF MAN, AS A MEMBER OF A CONFEDERATION

A NUMBER of states or societies may associate or confederate together for their mutual security and advantage. In some respects, such
confederacies are to be considered as forming only one nation: in other
respects, they are to be considered as still retaining their separate political
capacities, characters, rights, and powers. Associations of this kind have
made their appearance but seldom on the great theatre of human affairs;
and when they have appeared, the part they have acted has generally been
but a short one; and even that short part has, in most instances, been
defaced, or mutilated, or rendered obscure by the effect of all-corroding
time. The appearance, however, of personages, so peculiarly interesting
to the United States, well deserves to be marked, to be traced, to be
distinguished, with the most sedulous precision and exactness.

The first association of this kind, of which we have any information
from history, is that of the Amphyctionick Council, so called from
Amphyction, by whom it was instituted. In the time of this wise and
patriotick prince, the condition of Greece demanded his most serious
and deep reflection. That country was divided into a great number of
small independent sovereignties. That division was likely to occasion controversies, and produce ruinous intestine wars. Weakness and confusion,
the inseparable concomitants of such wars, might invite the attacks of the
barbarous nations, by whom Greece was surrounded. Her destruction,
total and irretrievable, might prove the necessary consequence.

To prevent calamities, so probable and so great, Amphyction meditated and formed the plan of uniting all the different states of Greece in
one common bond, as well as in one common interest; that, availing themselves of the advantages and strength acquired by this union, they might
labour together in maintaining their internal peace and security, and in
rendering themselves respectable, and, if necessary, formidable to the
neighbouring nations. With this view, and on these principles, he formed
a league among twelve Grecian cities, whose deputies were to meet twice
a year at Thermopylæ, where Amphyction reigned.[a] Difference of times
and circumstances produced many successive alterations in this assembly;

[a] 2. Gog. Or. Laws. 26.

but the general intention and invariable object of all its modellers and directers was, to form a complete representation of all Greece.[b]

Each city sent two deputies; and had, of consequence, two votes in their deliberations, without distinction or preeminence.

We should consider the Council of the Amphyctions as the Congress of the United States of Greece. The delegates, who composed that august assembly, represented the body of the nation; and were invested with full power to deliberate and resolve upon whatever appeared to them to be most conducive to the publick prosperity.[c] Besides those laws, by which each particular city was governed, others were enacted by the Council of Amphyctions, of general force and obligation on all. Those were called Amphyctionick laws. All contests between the Grecian states and cities came under the particular cognizance of the Amphyctions. To their tribunal, an appeal also lay in all private controversies.[d] To the same tribunal, individuals were amenable for their publick crimes.[e] Their authority extended to the raising of forces, and to compel the obstinate to submit to the execution of their decrees. The three religious wars, undertaken by the order of the Amphyctions, are striking instances of the extent of their power.[f]

Among the Grecians, it was esteemed a high honour to have a right to send delegates to this kind of states-general. The least mark of infidelity to their country was sufficient to prevent their admission, or to procure their expulsion. The Lacedemonians, however important, and the Phocians were, for some time, excluded; and could not obtain a readmission, till, by unequivocal proofs of service and attachment to the publick, they had made reparation for the fault, which they had committed.

The effects, produced by the Council of the Amphyctions, fully answered the most sanguine expectations of the prince, by whom it was instituted. From the moment of its establishment, the interests of their country became the common concern of all the people of Greece. The different states, of which the union was composed, formed only one and the same republick: and this union it was, which made the Greeks so formidable afterwards to the barbarians.[g] To the Amphyctions we may ascribe the salvation of Greece from the invasion of Xerxes. It was by means of this association, that she performed such wonderful actions, and supported, for so long a time, the character of the pride of nations.

Amphyction ought to be esteemed one of the greatest men, that Greece ever produced; and the establishment of the Council of the Amphyctions should be admired, as a great master-piece in human politicks.

While the generous principles, on which the Council of the Amphyc-

[b] Lel. L. P. Prel. 43.   [c] 2. Gog. Or. Laws. 27.   [d] Lel. L. P. Prel. 39. 53.
[e] Lel. Dem. Int. to oration de corona.   [f] 2. Gog. Or. Laws. 27.
[g] 2. Gog. Or. Laws. 28.

tions was formed, continued to preserve their due vigour, that illustrious body was respectable, august, and powerful. But when Greece herself began to degenerate, her representative body was contaminated with the general corruption. The decline of this council we may date particularly from the time, when Philip of Macedon, artful and intriguing, practised on its venal members by bribes, and succeeded in having his kingdom annexed to the Hellenick Body. It continued, however, for ages after the destruction of Grecian liberty, to assemble, and to exercise some remains of its authority.[h]

The next confederacy, which claims our attention, is that of the Lycians. In this republick, the just rights of suffrage were observed with great accuracy. It was an association of twenty three towns. These were arranged into three classes, in proportion to their strength. In the first class, six states were included. The numbers of which the second and third classes were composed, are uncertain. Every city had its own magistrates and government, and managed its own internal affairs. But all, uniting together, formed only one common republick, and had one common council. In that council, they deliberated and resolved concerning war, concerning peace, concerning alliances; in a word, concerning the general interests and welfare of the Lycians. The towns of the first class had three votes; the towns of the second class had two votes; and the towns of the third class had one vote, in the common council. In the same proportion, they contributed to the publick expenses, and appointed the publick magistrates of the union.

This republick was celebrated for its moderation and justice. Respected and unimpaired, it continued till the Romans, by their extending conquests, overpowered every thing in Asia.

Concerning the Lycians, one observation is made, which merits our particular notice. They observed customs more than written laws.[i]

"Was I to give," says the celebrated Montesquieu,[j] "the model of an excellent confederate republick, I would select that of Lycia." The happy experience, however, of the United States, has evinced, that, even upon that model, immense improvements have been made.

The Achæan League comes now in review before us. The cities composing it retained, like those of Lycia, the government of their interiour police, and appointed their own magistrates and publick officers. The senate, in which they were represented, had the sole and exclusive right of declaring war and making peace; of receiving and sending ambassadours; of entering into treaties, and forming alliances. It appointed a chief magistrate, called a pretor, who commanded their armies, and who, assisted by a council of ten of the senators, not only administered the gov-

[h] Lel. L. P. Prel. 56. 57.   [i] 2. Ub. Em. 320. 323.   [j] Sp. Laws. b. 9. c. 3.

ernment during the recess of the senate; but, when the senate was assembled, had also a large share in its deliberations. At first, there were two pretors; but experience taught them to prefer one.

In Achaia, all the cities had the same money, the same weights and measures, the same customs and laws. The popular government, we are told, was not so tempestuous in the cities of Achaia, as in some of the other cities of Greece; because, in Achaia, it was tempered by the authority and laws of the confederacy. Indeed it is unquestionable, that, in this confederacy, there was much more moderation and justice, than was to be found in any of the cities exercising singly all the prerogatives of sovereignty.

When Lacedæmon was admitted into the Achæan League; she was obliged to abolish the institutions of Lycurgus, and to adopt the laws of the Achæans. But Lacedæmon had been long a member of the Amphyctionick Council; and, during all the time, she had been left in the full possession of her own government and laws. This circumstance discloses a very important difference between those two confederate systems.[k]

The Ætolian League was similar to that of the Achæans; and therefore it is unnecessary to make particular observations concerning it.[l]

The Germanick Body has been generally considered as a confederate state. From the feudal system, which has itself many of the important features of a confederacy, the federal system, which constitutes the empire of Germany, has grown. Its powers are vested in a diet, representing the component members of the confederacy; in the emperour, who is the executive magistrate, with a negative on the decrees of the diet; and in the imperial chamber and aulick council, two tribunals possessed of supreme jurisdiction in controversies, which concern the empire, or happen among its members.

The diet possesses the power of legislation for the empire, of making peace and war, contracting alliances, assessing quotas of troops and money, constructing fortresses, regulating coin, admitting new members, and subjecting disobedient members to the ban of the empire; by which the party is degraded from his sovereign rights, and his possessions are forfeited. The members of the confederacy are expressly restricted from entering into compacts prejudicial to the empire; from imposing tolls and duties on their mutual intercourse, without the consent of the emperour and diet; from altering the value of money; from doing injustice to one another; and from affording assistance or retreat to the disturbers of the publick peace. The ban is denounced against such as shall violate any of these restrictions.

The members of the diet, as such, are subject, in all cases, to be judged

[k] 1. Pub. 114. 2. Ub. Em. 240. 243.   [l] 2. Ub. Em. 257.

by the emperour and diet; and, in their private capacities, by the aulick council and imperial chamber.

The prerogatives of the emperour are numerous. The most important of them are — his exclusive right to make propositions to the diet, to negative its resolutions, to name ambassadours, to confer dignities and titles, to fill vacant electorates, to found universities, to grant privileges not injurious to the states of the empire, to receive and apply the publick revenues, and generally to watch over the publick safety. In certain cases, the electors form a council to him. In the character of emperour, he possesses no territory within the empire; and receives no revenue for his support.

The fundamental principle, on which this confederacy rests, is — that the empire is a community of sovereigns — that the diet is a representation of sovereigns — and that the laws are addressed to sovereigns.[m] The princes and free states of Germany may treat with foreign powers.[n]

The Swiss Cantons are frequently mentioned as forming a confederacy; but they are improperly mentioned in that character. They are no more than states connected together by a close and perpetual alliance. They have no common treasury; they have no national troops, even in war; they have no common coin; they have no common tribunal; they have no common characteristick of sovereignty.

When a dispute happens among the cantons, there is a provision, that the parties to that dispute shall each choose four judges out of the neutral cantons, who, in case of disagreement, choose an umpire. This tribunal, under an oath of impartiality, pronounces definitive sentence. This sentence all the cantons are bound to enforce.[o]

The United Netherlands are generally represented as a confederacy. If the term can, with propriety, be applied to them; they are a confederacy of republicks, or rather of aristocracies, of a very remarkable texture.

The union is composed of seven coequal and sovereign states or provinces;[p] and each state or province is a composition of equal and independent cities. In all important cases, not only the states, but the cities, must be unanimous.

The sovereignty of the union is represented by the states-general, consisting of deputies appointed by the provinces. Some hold their seats for life; some, for six years; some, for three years; some, for one year; some, during pleasure.

The states-general have authority to enter into treaties and alliances; to make war and peace; to raise armies and equip fleets; to ascertain

---

[m] 1. Pub. 119. 120.   [n] Vat. 171.   [o] 1. Pub. 123.

[p] We may exceed the United Provinces by having, not many sovereignties *in* one commonwealth, but many commonwealths under one sovereignty. Milt. 370.

quotas, and demand contributions. In all these cases, however, unanimity and the sanction of their constituents are requisite. They have authority to appoint and receive ambassadours; to execute treaties and alliances already formed; to provide for the collection of duties on imports and exports; to regulate the mint, with a saving to the provincial rights; to govern, as sovereigns, the dependent territories.

The particular states or provinces are restrained, unless with the general consent, from entering into foreign treaties; from establishing imposts injurious to others; and from charging higher duties upon their neighbours than upon their own citizens.

A council of state; a chamber of accounts; and five colleges of admiralty, aid and fortify the federal administration.

The executive magistrate of the union is the stadtholder, who is now an hereditary prince. As stadtholder, he is invested with very considerable prerogatives. In his civil capacity, he has power to settle disputes between the provinces; to assist at the deliberations of the states-general; to give audiences to foreign ambassadours; and to keep agents, for his particular affairs, at foreign courts. In his military capacity, he commands the federal troops; provides for garrisons; regulates military affairs; disposes of military appointments, and of the government of fortified towns. In his marine capacity, he is admiral, and superintends every thing relative to naval affairs; presides in the admiralties in person or by proxy; appoints naval officers; and establishes councils of war, whose sentences are not executed till he approve them. He is stadtholder in the several provinces, as well as in the union; and, in this provincial character, he has the appointment of town magistrates; executes provincial decrees; and presides, when he pleases, in the provincial tribunals. Throughout all, he has the power of pardon.[q]

After the independence of the United Netherlands was recognised by Spain, the individual states began to pay very little regard to the decrees of the states-general: even particular towns and lordships seemed desirous of maintaining entire independence on the states of the provinces, within which they were situated. The Dutch government, which had greatly relaxed, and was even threatened with dissolution, recovered its tone through the dangers, to which the United Provinces were exposed by the war of thirty years, which was terminated by the peace of Westphalia. Since that time, dissensions among the Dutch have prevailed, or have been composed, according as they have dreaded or trusted their ambitious neighbours.[r]

In the Saxon Heptarchy, a confederacy certainly existed; though, perhaps, a confederacy weak, defective, and interrupted; and from all the

[q] 1. Pub. 125. 126.   [r] 2. Anal. Rev. 337.

confederated states a wittenagemote was frequently called.[s] This general
superintending body was sometimes called a *pananglicum*.

Among the ancient Germans, the genius of confederacy pervaded the
whole structure of society. They sojourned in huts, which served them
as strong holds, to which they carried their property in time of danger.
These strong holds or *pagi*, as the Greeks and Romans called them, were
the natural resort of the tribes in their neighbourhood, and seem to have
been the embryos of the little states, with which ancient Europe so much
abounded. A point of union being thus formed among a few tribes, it was
natural that the warriors should frequently assemble at that point. In
those assemblies, a king, or common leader in war, and an executive
magistrate in peace, was chosen.[t] "Eliguntur," says Tacitus,[u] "in iisdem
consiliis principes, qui jura per pagos vicosque reddunt."

Though, in general, each pagus acknowledged no superiour, yet particular circumstances of society induced numbers of them to confederate;
and, when wars happened, a common leader of the confederacy was
chosen of course. When a confederacy of neighbouring pagi had subsisted for a considerable time, a sentiment of national union and of national character began, at last, to appear and operate. The common leader,
occasionally chosen for a war, was so often elected, that he became a
king, like the chief of a pagus; that he was a *princeps regionis*, with several *principes pagorum* in such a subordination under him, as the chiefs
of *vici*, or of primary tribes, were originally held under the chiefs of the
pagi.

These combined associates became, again, the members of a greater and
less consolidated confederacy. According to Tacitus, the Suevi, one of
the greatest communities of Germany, were not comprehended in a
single people, but were divided into several nations, all bearing distinct
names, though they were all included under the common appellation of
Suevi. The Semnones, a single nation, though, indeed, the most noble and
the most ancient nation, comprehended under this great confederacy,
inhabited no fewer than a hundred pagi. Over the largest portion of Germany the confederacy of the Suevi extended.[v] Thus the Semnones,
though but a single member of the great confederacy of the Suevi, were
themselves, considered with regard to the pagi which they inhabited, a
very considerable national confederacy.

Of a confederacy, whether supreme or subordinate, every member
possessed, within itself, legislative, executive, and judicial powers, similar, but inferiour to those exercised by the confederacy itself. In this

[s] Mil. 52.   [t] 3. Edin. Phil. Trans. 18.
[u] De mor. Germ. c. 12. [At the same assemblies are chosen leaders, who administer law through the cantons and villages.]
[v] Tac. de mor. Germ. c. 38. 39.

way the form of society was nearly indestructible.[w] The bonds of association were in just, though inverse, number and proportion to the extent and greatness of the parts associated.

Let us conclude this general view of confederacies with an account of one, which was established, where we should little expect to find it, in Iceland. That obscure and sequestered region — but what place or what people are there, from whence instruction may not be drawn — was peopled by a series of colonies from Norway. These colonists relinquished their country, when it was conquered by Harold with the beautiful hair, in the year eight hundred and seventy eight. In their new settlements, they formed small communities with elective chiefs. These, by degrees, combined together, and held assemblies, under a common leader, in each of the four great provinces, into which the ridges of Mount Hecla divide the island. At last, these four provinces likewise confederated, and formed, in the year nine hundred and twenty eight, a republick, under one chief magistrate.

The whole country was arranged into regular divisions, called provinces, hundreds, and reeps. The magistrates held their offices for life. Diets were held for the districts; and an alting, or great annual assembly, was held for the nation. In that assembly, besides the arrangement of political matters, appeals were received from the provincial courts, and rejudged, in its presence, and under its inspection, by the former judges. The duty of the lagman, or chief of the nation, was to carry into execution what the alting ordered and decreed. There was a succession of thirty eight lagmans, which continued till the year one thousand two hundred and sixty two, when the republick was destroyed by the Danes.

This account is taken from the Icelandick historian, Arngrimus Jonas, a native of the island, and a person, who appears to have had abundance of materials for his work.[x]

On a subject of such magnitude, not only that which has been done, but also that which has been proposed to be done, well deserves attention and examination. I allude to the grand plan of a general confederacy in Europe, formed by the immense genius of Henry the Fourth of France; in which he received most essential assistance from the genius, no less penetrating and active, of Elizabeth of England.

It is very remarkable, that, by several writers, and even by some very profound ones, this very enlarged plan of government is considered as nothing better than a mere visionary project; and doubts are proposed whether it could ever engage the serious contemplation of Henry the Great. To me, I confess, the matter appears in a very different light; and I feel myself justified and supported in directing your close and earnest

[w] 3. Edin. Phil. Trans. 22.   [x] 3. Edin. Phil. Trans. 23.

attention to it, when I consider the fact as authenticated by the testimony of Sully, Henry's faithful and confidential minister, and the plan itself as occupying, for a series of years, the unremitted application of Henry and Elizabeth; who were distinguished by their wisdom, as well as by their enterprise; and who knew, if ever princes knew, how to draw the important line between what is extravagant and what is great.

An investigation of this sublime system, from its commencement through the various and successive stages of its progress and preparation, must be instructive to all: to Americans, it must be interesting as well as instructive.

Sully enters upon his account of it with expressing some sagacious apprehensions, that — as, in fact, has since been the case — it would be considered as one of those darling chimeras, or idle political speculations, in which a mind susceptible of singular and uncommon conceptions, is sometimes easily engaged. He confesses, that at the first time the king suggested to him the idea of a political system, by which all Europe might be managed and governed as a single family, he received the suggestion, supposing that Henry meant by it nothing more than to amuse himself with an agreeable speculation, or, at most, to show, that his contemplations on political subjects were more profound and more extensive than those of others.

How modest is conscious merit! Henry often afterwards owned to his confidential friend, that he had long concealed even from him what he meditated upon this great subject, from a principle of shame, lest he should disclose designs, which might appear ridiculous or impracticable.

Inattentive to this great design, when it was first suggested, the cold and cautious Sully was averse to it when the suggestion was renewed. An endless series of difficulties and obstructions presented itself to his circumspect mind. The extent of a design, which supposed a union of all the states in Europe; the concatenation of events, almost infinite, that would be necessary for its accomplishment; the immense expenses, which, if it could be accomplished, would thereby be rolled upon France at a crisis, when she was scarcely able to supply her own necessities — all these considerations induced him to consider the scheme as a vain one, and even to suspect, that, in it, there was something illusory. The disposition of the princes of Europe to become jealous of France, when she should have assisted them to dissipate their fears from the overgrown power of the house of Austria, appeared, of itself, an insurmountable obstacle. His own sentiments he endeavoured to infuse into the mind of the king, with an honest desire to undeceive him, as he thought. Henry begged him to consider the plan in its several parts, and not to pass an indiscriminate sentence of condemnation upon the whole. This solicitation, so reasonable and so unassuming, it was impossible to refuse. The result of Sully's consideration was what Henry expected it would be — the conversion of the minister to the opinions of the prince. After having seen all the parts of the fabrick from their proper points of view, after having made the necessary examinations and the necessary calculations, he found himself engaged and confirmed in the sentiment, that the plan was just in its intention, and that it would be practicable in the execution, and glorious in its consequences.

Great minds frequently unite, without intercommunication, upon the same great object. This exalted system presented itself to the penetration and magnanimity of Elizabeth, before it had occurred to the expansive comprehension of Henry. Indeed it appears doubtful, whether he was not indebted to her for the first hint of the design. But between two such minds, there was no mean jealousy about the right or the merit of the prior discovery. The family of Sully is still possessed of a letter written by Henry, evidently to Elizabeth, though her name does not appear either in the superscription or in the letter itself. It is addressed to "her who merits immortal praise." In it, Henry speaks of a certain object, which he calls "the most excellent and rare enterprise that the human mind ever conceived" — "a thought rather divine than human." He mentions, with rapture, "a discourse so well connected and demonstrative of what would be necessary for the government of empires and kingdoms," and those "conceptions and resolutions," from which nothing less could be hoped, than "most remarkable issues both of honour and glory." These expressions can point to no other person than Elizabeth — to no other object than that, in the investigation of which we are now engaged.

It is well known that Henry and Elizabeth were anxious to have a personal interview; and that, in the year 1601, the latter came to Dover and the former to Calais for this purpose. The ceremonials, established among princes, prevented the satisfaction of a conference; but those communications, which Henry could not make in person, he transmitted by the faithful Sully. This minister found that she was deeply engaged in the means, by which the great design might be happily executed; and that, notwithstanding the difficulties, which, in some points, she apprehended, she did not appear at all to doubt of success. This she chiefly expected for a reason, of the solidity and justness of which, Sully declares that he was afterwards well convinced. It was, that as the plan was, in truth, contrary only to the designs of some princes, whose ambitious views were sufficiently known to all Europe, the obstacles interposed by those princes, instead of retarding, would promote the design; since they would place its necessity in a more striking point of view.

"A very great number, says Sully, of the articles, conditions, and different dispositions is due to this queen; and sufficiently evince, that, in respect of wisdom, penetration, and all the other perfections of the mind, she was not inferiour to any king, the most truly deserving of that title."

The death of this great princess gave such a violent shock to the whole plan, that Henry and his minister were almost induced to abandon their fondest hopes. The successour to the throne was the successour neither to the virtues nor to the talents of Elizabeth; and Henry had too much penetration to expect that assistance, which James had too much pusil-lanimity to give. After some time, however, favourable circumstances oc-curred again, which induced him to reassume the plan, and to prepare, with renewed vigour, for its execution. Of its execution, he was on the very eve, when the fatal poignard of Ravaillac interrupted it.

The leading object in the great design was to reduce, within reasonable bounds, the formidable power of the house of Austria. With this view, it was proposed to devest that house of its possessions in Germany, Italy, and the Low Countries; and to confine it to the kingdom of Spain, bounded by the ocean, the Mediterranean, and the Pyrenean mountains. That it might, however, be equally powerful with the other sovereigns in Europe, it was intended to allot to it Sardinia, Majorca, Minorca, the Canaries, the Azores, and its possessions in Asia, Africa, and America.

"If there be any where," says Vattel,[y] "a state restless and mischievous, always ready to injure others, to traverse their designs, and to foment domestick troubles within them, it is not to be doubted, that all have a right to join in order to repress it, and deprive it of the power to molest them in future. The conduct of Philip the second of Spain was adapted to unite all Europe against him; and it was from just reasons that Henry the Great formed the design of humbling a power, formidable by its forces, and pernicious by its maxims."

Between Henry and Elizabeth, it was a settled point, that neither of them should, by the different dismemberments proposed to be made, re-ceive any thing, except the glory of distributing them with equity and impartiality. Henry even sometimes said, with equal moderation and good sense, that were the meditated dispositions once firmly established, he would have consented that the extent of France should have been determined by a majority of suffrages. With regard to England, the conduct of Elizabeth was probably influenced by an observation, which she made, that the Britannick isles, in all the different states, through which they passed, and among all the variations of their laws and policy, had never experienced great misfortunes, but when their sovereigns had interfered in matters beyond the sphere of their little continent. It seems, indeed, as if they were concentred in it, even by nature; and their happi-

[y] B. 2. s. 53.

ness appears to depend entirely on themselves, provided they aim only to maintain peace in the three nations subject to them, by governing each according to its own laws and customs.

The ultimate design of the great plan was, to divide Europe equally among a certain number of powers, in such a manner, that no one might have reason for either envy or fear, from the power or possessions of the others. The number of states were reduced to fifteen. They were of three different kinds; hereditary monarchies; elective monarchies; republicks. The hereditary monarchies were six — France, Spain, Britain, Denmark, Sweden, Lombardy. The elective monarchies were five — the Empire, the Papacy, Poland, Hungary, Bohemia. The republicks were four — the Venetian, the Italian, the Helvetick, the Belgick.

There was to have been a general council, representing all the states of Europe. The establishment of this would have been the happiest invention that could have been conceived for preventing those innovations, and for applying a remedy to those inconveniences or defects, which time often introduces or discovers in the wisest and the most useful institutions. The model of this general council of Europe was formed on that of the ancient Amphyctions of Greece (a delineation of which I have already laid before you) with such alterations only as rendered it suitable to the alterations of customs, climate, and policy. It was to consist of a certain number of delegates from all the governments of the Christian Republick, who were to be constantly assembled as a senate. This body was to discuss the different interests, decide the controversies, and determine all the civil, political, and religious affairs of Europe, whether within itself or with its neighbours. The senate was to consist of four delegates from each of the following powers — the Emperour, the Pope, the kings of France, Spain, England, Denmark, Sweden, Lombardy, Poland, and the republick of Venice; and of two only from the other republicks and inferiour powers. All together would have composed a senate of about sixty six persons. They were to be chosen every three years. With regard to the place of meeting, it was undetermined whether it would be better for the council to be fixed or ambulatory; united in one, or divided into three. If it were divided into three, each containing twenty two magistrates, then each of them must have been fixed in such a centre as should appear to be most commodious. If it were judged more expedient not to divide the assembly, whether fixed or ambulatory, it must have been nearly in the centre of Europe.

Besides this general council, it would have been proper to have constituted subordinate councils: but whatever the number or form of those subordinate councils had been, it would have been absolutely necessary that an appeal should have lain from them to the general council, whose decisions, when considered as proceeding from the united authority of all the sovereigns, pronounced in a manner equally free and absolute; must have been regarded as so many final and irrevocable decrees.

A particular account is given by Sully of the measures taken to secure the success of this great and glorious design.

Henry was indefatigable in his negotiations in the different courts of Europe, particularly in the United Provinces, and in the circles of Germany. The council of the states-general were very soon unanimous in their determinations. The states-general were, in a short time, followed by the landgrave of Hesse, and the prince of Anhalt, to whom, as well as to the prince of Orange, the confederacy was obliged for being increased by the duke of Savoy; by all of the reformed religion in Hungary, Bohemia, and lower Austria; by many princes and towns in Germany; and by a great proportion of the Swiss Cantons. But a discovery either of the true motives, or of the full extent of the design, was cautiously avoided. It was, at first, concealed from all, without exception; and it was afterwards revealed, only to a few persons of approved discretion; and even of those, only to such as were absolutely to engage others to join the confederacy.

The king, on his side, had actually set on foot two good and well furnished armies; one of which he was to have commanded in person. It was to have consisted of twenty thousand foot, all native French, eight thousand Swiss, four thousand Lansquenets or Walloons, five thousand horse, and twenty cannons. The second was to have been commanded by Lesdiguires, consisting of ten thousand foot, one thousand horse, and ten cannons; besides a flying camp of four thousand foot, six hundred horse, and ten cannons; and a reserve of two thousand foot to garrison places, where they might be necessary. Magazines were collected and deposited in proper places, for facilitating the execution of the enterprise: and, with the same view, manifestoes were composed with the greatest care. In them, a spirit of justice, of good policy, of honesty, of disinterestedness, and of inviolable faith was universally apparent.

It is impossible to dismiss a design, so interesting to humanity, without indulging a few observations concerning its nature, and its probable effects. That it was bold and magnificent, it will be unanimously agreed: but was it nothing more? was it not presumptuous and extravagant? We have seen that, as such, it was, at first, considered by Sully. As such, even the least difficult and most unimportant parts of it were considered by the other counsellors of France: for it was only on the least difficult and most unimportant parts, that he could venture to consult them. "Could it be imagined," says Sully, "that Henry, in his whole council, could not find one person, besides myself, to whom he could, without danger, disclose the whole of his designs; and that the respect due to him could scarce restrain those, who appeared most devoted to his service, from treating what, with the greatest circumspection, he had intrusted to them, as wild and extravagant chimeras." So true is sometimes the poet's exclamation —

> Truths would you teach, or save a sinking land?
> All fear, none aid you, and few understand.*

But nothing discouraged that great prince, who was an abler politician and a better judge than all his council, and than all his kingdom. When he perceived that affairs, both at home and abroad, began to wear a favourable aspect, he then considered his success as infallible.

At this distance of time, and with our present imperfect knowledge of particular circumstances, it would be unwise to attempt a judgment, or even a conjecture, upon a detail of facts, existing at that age, and in the different states of Europe. But from general principles, and from our knowledge of some eminent characters, inferences, plausible and even satisfactory, may be drawn.

One inference may be drawn from the nature of the design, which Henry had formed. It was not a design inspired by mean and despicable ambition: it was not a design, guided by base and partial interests: it was a design, in the first place, to render France happy, and permanently happy: but as he well knew that France could not enjoy permanent felicity, unless in conjunction with the other parts of Europe; and as he was well pleased that the other parts of Europe should participate in the felicity of France; it was the happiness of Europe in general which he laboured to procure; and to procure in a manner so solid and so durable, that nothing should afterwards be able to shake its foundations. May we not conclude, that, every thing else being equal, the probability is in favour of a great and good design? The fury and ravage of conquests have extended farther and wider, than the benevolent system of Henry the Great was meant or proposed to extend. Why should evil be more powerful or more enlarged in its operations than good? In private life, success is most frequently, though not universally, on the side of virtue: is it natural to expect a contrary rule in the administration of states and kingdoms? Is there not reason to hope that publick virtue will, on the whole, be triumphant; and that publick flagitiousness must, and should, and, at a proper time, will be degraded to the deepest abyss of humiliation?

These observations suggest general reasons in favour of the great design: other reasons may be drawn from the character, and talents, and virtues of the great man, who undertook its execution. It could not have been formed by one more eminently qualified to accomplish it. He possessed a courage capable of surmounting the greatest obstacles: he possessed a presence of mind, which saw and seized every opportunity of

* [Pope, *Essay on Man,* Ep. IV, 1. 265.]

advantage: he possessed a prudence, which would not precipitate, but would calmly and patiently wait for the fit season of action: he possessed consummate experience, the result jointly of talents and of time. With all those great qualities as a soldier, as a statesman, and as a patriot, what was there, fair, or honest, or honourable, to which he could not form just pretension? Had this enterprise failed in his hands, it would probably have failed for no other reason than this — that he was too great and too enlightened for the age in which he lived.

Had he been successful, the consequences of his success would, indeed, have been beneficial, lasting, and extensive. Those consequences would have reached not only his own subjects, not only the christian nations of Europe, but the whole world in general: of those consequences, the generation, at that time alive, the generations that have since succeeded, and those generations that are still to succeed, would have participated, down to the latest periods of time: those consequences would have been the source of all the sweets, which naturally flow from an uninterrupted and universal tranquillity.

Let me add another remark, which has been made in Europe, and which, with pride and joy, may be transferred to America. "Henry the Great has always had the honour of being considered as the author of the most important invention for the benefit of mankind, that has yet appeared in the world; the execution of which may, perhaps, be reserved by Providence, for the greatest and most capable of his successours." This rich succession has been reaped in America. Here the sublime system of Henry the Great has been effectually realized, and completely carried into execution.

When the political bonds, by which the American States had been connected with Great Britain, were dissolved; when they assumed, among the powers of the earth, the seperate and equal station, to which the laws of nature and of nature's God entitled them, the form of government, which each should institute for herself, and that form, if any, which all should institute for all, became objects of the most serious and interesting deliberation. With regard to this last, which is the object of our present discussion, four different systems lay before them; any one of which they might have adopted. They might have consolidated themselves into one government, in which the separate existence of the states would have been entirely absorbed. They might have rejected any plan of union or association, and have acted as distinct and unconnected states. They might have formed two or more confederacies. They might have united in one federal republick.

To support, with vigour, a single government over the whole extent of the United States, would, I apprehend, demand a system of the most unqualified and the most unremitted despotism: even despotism herself, extended so far and so wide, would totter under the weight of her own unwieldiness.

Separate states, numerous as those of America are, still more numerous as they must become, contiguous in situation, unconnected and disunited in government, would, at one time, be the prey of foreign force, foreign influence, and foreign intrigue; at another, the victims of mutual rage, rancour, and revenge.

Would it have been proper to have divided the United States into two or more confederacies? It will not be unadvisable to examine this object with accuracy and attention. Some aspects, under which it may be viewed, are far from being, at first sight, uninviting. Two or more confederacies would be each more compact and more manageable, than a single one extending over the same territory. By dividing the United States into two or more confederacies, the great collision of interests, apparently or really different or contrary, in the whole extent of their dominion, would be broken, and, in a great measure, disappear in the several parts. But these advantages, which are discovered from certain points of view, are greatly overbalanced by inconveniences, which will appear on a closer inspection. Animosities and, perhaps wars would arise from assigning the extent, the limits, and the rights of the different confederacies. The expenses of governing would be multiplied by the number of federal governments. The danger, resulting from foreign influence and mutual dissensions, would not, perhaps, be less great and alarming in the instance of different confederacies, than in the instance of different, though more numerous, unassociated states. These observations, and many others which might be made on the subject, will be sufficient to evince, that a division of the United States into a number of separate confederacies would probably be an unsatisfactory and an unsuccessful experiment.

The only remaining system, that is to be considered, is the union of the American States into one confederate republick. It will not be necessary to employ many arguments to show, that this is the most eligible system, which could have been proposed. By adopting it, the vigour and decision of a wide spreading monarchy may be associated with the freedom and beneficence of a compacted commonwealth. On one hand, the extent of territory; the diversity of climate and soil; the number, and greatness, and connexion of lakes and rivers, with which the United States are intersected and almost surrounded, all indicate an enlarged government to be fit and advantageous for them. On the other hand, the principles and dispositions of their citizens indicate, that, in this enlarged government, liberty shall reign triumphant.

Agreeably to these principles, the United States have been formed into one confederate republick; first, under the articles of confederation;

afterwards, under our present national government. The weakness and inefficiency of the former; the excellencies, the advantages, and the imperfections of the latter — for it has its imperfections, though neither many nor dangerous — we shall hereafter have an opportunity of showing. Our present purpose will be best answered by taking a general view of those principles, characters, and properties, which distinguish or ought to distinguish a confederate republick and its members.

"An overgrown republick," says the Marquis of Beccaria, in the exquisite performance, with which he has enriched the treasures of legislation — "an overgrown republick can be saved from despotism, only by subdividing it into a number of confederate republicks. But how is this practicable? By a despotick dictator, who, with the courage of Sylla, has as much genius for building up, as that Roman had for pulling down. If he be an ambitious man; his reward will be immortal glory: if a philosopher; the blessings of his fellow citizens will sufficiently console him for the loss of authority, though he should not be insensible to their ingratitude." [z] In the United States, there is no occasion for the assumption of dictatorial power, in order to be enabled to perform supereminent services for the publick. Powers amply sufficient for the performance of the greatest services, the enlightened citizens of the United States know how to give. As they know how to give those powers, so they know how to confine them within the proper and reasonable limits.

If a commonwealth is small, it may be destroyed by a foreign power; if it is extensive, it carries within it the internal causes of its destruction. This double disadvantage affects equally democracies and aristocracies, whether they are well, or whether they are ill constituted. The former disadvantage is selfevident; and, therefore, requires no illustration. The latter may be evinced from the following considerations. In a very extended commonwealth, it is difficult, if not impracticable, to provide, at the same time, the three following requisites — a number of representatives, which will not be too large; opportunities of minute and local information, which will be sufficiently frequent and convenient; and a connexion between the constituent and representative, which will be sufficiently intimate and binding. The experience of ages evinces, that, where a certain excess in numbers prevails, regularity, decency, and the convenient despatch of business are expected in vain. On the other hand, when, to avoid an excessive number of representatives, one representative is allotted to too great a number of constituents; it is improbable, that the former should possess a sufficient degree of accurate and circumstantial knowledge, or of an interest, common, and, at the same time, peculiar, with the latter, to qualify him for the zealous and well informed discharge of his confidential trust. Add to these considerations, that, in a

[z] Bec. c. 26.

commonwealth, the proceedings and deliberations are too complicated and too slow for the emergencies of an extended government; to whose affairs and interests, simplicity and secrecy in council, and vigour and despatch in execution are of indispensable necessity. For these reasons, it is not unlikely, that mankind would, at last, have been obliged to submit always to the government of a single person, if they had not invented the form of a constitution, which is recommended by all the internal advantages of a republican government, and, at the same time, by all the force and energy of a government, which is monarchical. This form is a federal republick.

This form of government is a convention, by which several states consent to become citizens of a larger state, which they wish to form.[a] It is a society formed of other societies, which make a new one. This new one may be enlarged and aggrandized by the union of associates still new.

This kind of republick, fitted for resistance against exteriour attacks, is equally fitted to maintain its greatness without interiour corruption. It is formed for avoiding the inconveniences of that government, which is bad; and for securing the benefits of that, which is good.

In this kind of republick, the rights of internal legislation may be reserved to all the states, of which it is composed; while the adjustment of their several claims, the power of peace and war, the regulation of commerce, the right of entering into treaties, the authority of taxation, and the direction and government of the common force of the confederacy may be vested in the national government.

A confederate republick should consist of states, whose government is of the same nature; and it is proper that their government should be of the republican kind. Small monarchies are unfriendly to the genius of confederation. The spirit of monarchy is too often dominion and war; that of a commonwealth is more frequently moderation and peace. It is not likely, therefore, that these two kinds of government should subsist, on amicable terms, in the same confederated republick. Thus Germany, which consists of free cities and arbitrary monarchies, forms a confederacy, jarring and disjointed. Thus Greece was ruined, when the kings of Macedon obtained a seat among the Amphyctions. Hence we may see the propriety and wise policy of that article in the constitution of the United States,[b] which provides, that they shall guaranty to every state in the union a republican form of government.

When we say, that the government of those states, which unite in the same confederacy, ought to be of the same nature; it is not to be understood, that there should be a precise and exact uniformity in all their particular establishments and laws. It is sufficient that the fundamental

---

[a] Mont. Sp. Laws. b. 9. c. 1.   [b] Art. 4. s. 4.

principles of their laws and constitutions be consistent and congenial; and that some general rights and privileges should be diffused indiscriminately among them. Among these, the rights and privileges of naturalization hold an important place. Of such consequence was the intercommunication of these rights and privileges in the opinion of my Lord Bacon, that he considered them as the strongest of all bonds to cement and to preserve the union of states. "Let us take a view," says he, "and we shall find, that wheresoever kingdoms and states have been united, and that union incorporated by a bond of mutual naturalization, you shall never observe them afterwards, upon any occasion of trouble or otherwise, to break and sever again." [c] Machiavel, when he inquiries concerning the causes, to which Rome was indebted for her splendour and greatness, assigns none of stronger or more extensive operation that this — she easily compounded and incorporated with strangers.[d] This important subject has received a proportioned degree of attention in forming the constitution of the United States. "The citizens of each state shall be entitled to all privileges and immunities of citizens in the several states." [e] In addition to this, the congress have power to "establish a uniform rule of naturalization throughout the United States." [f]

Though a union of laws is, by no means, necessary to a union of states; yet a similarity in their code of *publick*[g] laws is a most desirable object. The publick law is the great sinew of government. The sinews of the different governments, composing the union, should, as far as it can be effected, be equally strong. "In this point," says my Lord Bacon, "the rule holdeth, which was pronounced by an ancient father, touching the diversiy of rites in the church; for finding the vesture of the queen in the psalm (who prefigured the church) was of divers colours; and finding again that Christ's coat was without a seam, concludeth well, in veste varietas sit, scissura non sit." [h]

Non omnibus facies una; sed qualis decet esse sororum.[*]

OVID.

In a confederated republick, consisting of states of unequal numbers, extent, and power, the influence of each ought to bear a corresponding proportion. The Lycian republick was an association of twenty three towns. The large ones had three votes in the common council, the middling ones two, the small ones one. They contributed to the national expenses according to the proportion of suffrages. "Were I to give a

---

[c] 4. Ld. Bac. 243.   [d] Id. 214.   [e] Art. 4. s. 2.   [f] Art. 1. s. 8.
[g] 4. Ld. Bac. 224. 225.
[h] 4. Ld. Bac. 215. [In clothing let there be variety, but no seam.]
[*] [They have not all the same appearance; but such as it befits sisters to have.]

model," says the celebrated Montesquieu,[1] "of an excellent confederate republick, I would pitch upon that of Lycia."

No one state, comprehended within a confederated republick, should be permitted to conclude an alliance with a foreign nation. This salutary regulation subsists not in the constitution of the Germanick Body. Hence the frequent dissensions and calamities, to which that great confederacy is constantly exposed, and with which it is frequently visited, through the rashness or the ambition of a single member.

With regard to foreign transactions, and with regard to those matters, which affect the general interests of the whole union, a confederated republick should be considered and should act as a single government or nation.

A union of hearts and affections, as well as a union of counsels and interests, is the very life and soul of a confederated republick. This is a subject, on which it is almost impossible to say too much, or to speak with too much zeal. We have, in former lectures,[j] seen how strong, how active, and how persevering are the operations and aims of our social powers. They are capable of being raised to the greatest height. They are capable of being enlarged to the greatest extent. But they partake of human imperfection: in their most useful and amiable forms, they sometimes degenerate into irregularity, abuse, and what I may call an excess of concentricity: by this I mean, overstrained exertions within a narrow and contracted sphere. Faction itself is frequently nothing else than a warm but inconsiderate ebullition of our social propensities.

How easily is the esprit du corps generated! How powerfully is it felt! How universally does it operate! How early does it appear! How ardent we see it in boys of different schools; and of different classes in the same school! With what emulation do they strive to outshine one another in their several tasks or sports! With what eagerness do the young men of neighbouring and rival towns — rival because they are neighbouring — contend for victory in their rural and manly exercises! Let the distinction be once formed — it is immaterial on what occasion, or from what cause — and its effects will be both strong and lasting. They will be beneficial or pernicious, according to the direction, which it first receives, and the objects to which it ultimately tends. How frivolous; how fierce; how obstinate; and how bloody were the contests of the Blues and Greens in the Hippodrome of Constantinople! The empire was sometimes shaken to its centre; and those, who produced the strong convulsions, could tell neither what they wished, nor why they were agitated. On the other hand; how often has the reputation of a regiment been preserved or heightened — how often, in battle, has vic-

[1] Sp. Laws. b. 9. c. 3.   [j] Ante ch. 7.

tory been obtained or retrieved, by the wise encouragement and skilful application of the esprit du corps! This spirit should not be extinguished: but in all governments, it is of vast moment — in confederated governments, it is of indispensable necessity — that it should be regulated, guided, and controlled.

"The associating genius of man," says my Lord Shaftesbury, "is never better proved, than in those very societies, which are formed in opposition to the general one of mankind, and to the real interest of the state." [k] Extensive governments are particularly exposed to this inconvenience: to this inconvenience a national government, such as ours, composed of a great number of states, powerful, extensive, and separated, to a great distance, by situation, and, sometimes too, by an opinion of interest, not only from one another, but from the superintending power, by which they are connected — to this inconvenience, I say, such a national government is, of all, the most exposed — by this inconvenience, I add, such a national government is, of all, the most endangered. To embrace the whole, requires an expansion of mind, of talents, and of temper. To the trouble, though the generous trouble, of expanding their mind, their talents, and their temper, some will be averse from indolence, or what the indolent call moderation; others will be averse from interest, or what the interested call prudence. The former will encourage a narrow spirit by their example; the latter will encourage it by their exertions also. These last will introduce and recommend the government of their state, as a rival, for social and benevolent affection, to the government of the United States. The simplicity of some, the inexperience of others, the unsuspecting confidence, again, of others will be won by plausible and seducing representations; and, in this manner, and by these arts, the patriotick emanations of the soul, which would otherwise be diffused over the whole Union, will be refracted and converged to a very narrow and inconsiderable part of it.

Against this ungenerous application of one of the noblest propensities of our nature, the system of our education and of our law ought to be directed with the most vigorous and unremitted ardour. This application of that noble propensity is not merely ungenerous: it is no less unwise. It is unwise, as to the person, who makes it; it is unwise, as to the state, to the advantage of which it is supposed to be made. Apply and extend, in favour of the Union, the same train of reflection and argument which is used in favour of the state. With regard to the latter, will it not be allowed — will it not be urged — will it not be properly urged, that the interest of the whole should never be sacrificed to that of a part, nor the interest of a greater part to that of a part, which is smaller? Will it not

[k] I. Shaft. 114.

be allowed — will it not be urged, that to think or act in a contrary manner, would be improper and unwise? Why should not the same reasoning and the same conduct be allowed — why should they not be urged — for they may be urged with equal propriety — in favour of the interests of the Union, or of the greater part of the Union, compared with those of a single member, of which that Union is composed?

But it will be seldom, if ever, necessary that the interest of a single state should be sacrificed to that of the United States. The laws, and government, and policy of the union operate universally and not partially; for the accomplishment of general and not of local purposes. On the other hand, the laws, and government, and policy of a particular state, compared with the Union, operate partially and not universally; for the accomplishment of purposes, which are local, and not general. If, then, on any subject, a difference should take place between the sentiments, and designs, and plans of the national government and those of the government of a single state; on whose side are justice and general utility likely to be found? It is to be presumed that they will be found on the side of the national government. That government is animated and directed by a representation of the whole Union: the government of a single state is animated and directed by a representation of only a part, inconsiderable when compared with the whole. Is it not more reasonable, as well as more patriotick, that the interests of every part should be governed, since they will be embraced, by the counsels of the whole, than that the interests of the whole should be governed, since they will not be embraced, by the counsels of a part?

Expanded patriotism is a cardinal virtue in the United States. This cardinal virtue — this "passion for the commonweal," superiour to contracted motives or views, will preserve inviolate the connexion of interest between the whole and all its parts, and the connexion of affection as well as interest between all the several parts.

Let us, then, cherish; let us encourage; let us admire; let us teach; let us practise this "devotion to the publick," so meritorious, and so necessary to the peace, and greatness, and happiness of the United States.

> "The central parent-publick calls
> Its utmost effort forth, awakes each sense,
> The comely, grand, and tender. Without this,
> This awful pant, shook from sublimer powers
> Than those of self, this heaven-infused delight,
> This moral gravitation, rushing prone
> To press the publick good, *our* system soon,
> Traverse, to several *selfish* centres drawn,
> Will reel to ruin."

2. *Thom. Works.* 158.

          " — To avoid this fate,
Let worth and virtue —
Exerted full, from every quarter shine,
Commix'd in heightened blaze. Light flash'd to light,
Moral or intellectual, more intense
By giving glows. As on pure winter's eve,
Gradual, the stars effulge; fainter, at first,
They, straggling, rise: but when the radiant host,
In thick profusion poured, shine out immense,
Each casting vivid influence on each,
From pole to pole a glittering deluge plays,
And worlds above rejoice, and men below."

                                    2. *Thom. Works.* 162.

IX

OF MAN, AS A MEMBER OF THE GREAT COMMONWEALTH OF NATIONS

EVERY civil society, under whatever form it appears, whether governed merely by the natural laws of such a society, or by them and civil institutions superadded — every such society, not subordinate to another, is a sovereign state.

Those, who unite in society, lived, before their union, in a state of nature: a state of nature is a state of equality and liberty. That liberty and that equality, belonging to the individuals, before the union, belong, after the union, to the society, which those individuals compose. The consequence is, that a society is subjected to no power or authority without it; that it may do what is necessary for its preservation; that it may exercise all its rights, and is obliged to give an account of its conduct to no one. But these things constitute what is called sovereignty. Every state, therefore, composed of individuals, free and equal, is a state sovereign and independent. The aggregate body possesses all the rights of the individuals, of whom it is formed.

Another consequence is, that the rights of any one state are naturally the same as those of every other. States are moral persons, who live together in a natural society, under the law of nations. To give a state a right to make an immediate figure in the great society of nations, it is sufficient, if it be really sovereign and independent; that is, it must govern itself by its own authority.[a] Thus, when the United Colonies found it necessary to dissolve the political bonds, which had connected them with Great Britain, and to assume among the powers of the earth the separate and equal station, to which the laws of nature and of nature's God entitled them; they had a right to publish and declare, as, in fact, they did publish and declare, that "they were free and independent states; and that, as free and independent states, they had full power to levy war, to conclude peace, contract alliances, establish commerce, and to do all other acts and things, which independent states may of right do;" though, at that time, no articles of confederation were agreed upon; nor was any form of civil government instituted by them.

[a] Vat. b. 1. s. 4.

A number of individuals, who have formed themselves into a society or state, are, with regard to the purposes of the society, bound to consider themselves as one moral person. But the rest of mankind, who are not parties to this social compact, are under no obligation to take notice of it; and may still consider the society as a large number of unconnected persons. This personality — I know no better expression for it — of a state must, as to other nations, be derived from their consent and agreement. But when a society have once associated, and considered and announced themselves to other nations as a moral person, this consent and agreement ought not to be refused, without solid and special reasons, which will justify the refusal. On this consent and agreement, the mutual and mutually beneficial intercourse of nations is founded: whatever, therefore, promotes this intercourse, should be zealously encouraged; whatever prevents or interrupts it, should be cautiously avoided.

Though one state has, by an unequal alliance, formed a connexion with another state more powerful; still the weaker state is to be reckoned in the class of sovereigns. To the weaker state, the unequal alliance may secure the most assistance; on the stronger, it may reflect the most honour; but it leaves both the same rank among the society of nations.

We may go further; if a state, in order to provide for its own safety, finds it necessary to place itself under the protection of another; and, in consideration of that protection, stipulates to perform equivalent offices, without devesting itself of the right of self-government; such a state ceases not to preserve its place among sovereigns. The payment even of tribute, though it may diminish the dignity of the society, by no means destroys or impairs its sovereignty or its rights.

Two sovereign states may employ the same executive magistrate, or bear allegiance to the same prince, without any dependence on each other; and each may retain all its national rights, free and undiminished. This last, under the house of Stuart, was the case of England and Scotland, before the nation of Great Britain was formed by their union. This last, also, as shall be hereafter shown at large, was the case of Great Britain and the American colonies, before the political connexion between them was declared to be dissolved.

But one people who have passed under the *dominion* of another, can no longer form a state: they can no longer retain a place in the great society of nations. Of that great society, equality is the basis and the rule. To this equality, the inferiority of subjection and the superiority of command are, alike, repugnant.

This equality of nations is the great and general foundation of national rights. In this matter, no regard is had to names. On the great theatre of the world, empires, kingdoms, commonwealths, principalities, dukedoms,

free towns, are all equally imperial. A society, which, without subordination to any other, exercises within itself all the essential powers of society, is sovereign, and has all the rights of a sovereign and independent
state; however narrow its territories; however small its numbers may be.

Every nation deserves consideration and respect; because it makes an
immediate figure in the grandest society of the human race; because it
is independent of all earthly power; and because it is an assemblage of a
number of men, who, doubtless, are more considerable than any individual.

With regard to precedency, or the first place among equals, power
and antiquity are grounds, upon which it is claimed or allowed. Into
this question, the forms of government do not enter.

The natural state of individuals we have already seen to be a state of
society and peace: such also is the natural state of nations. This state, it
is the duty of nations, as well as of individuals, to preserve and improve.
But among nations, as well as among individuals, differences and causes
of difference will, sometimes, unavoidably arise. Over independent
nations there is no coercive authority, to which recourse may be had for
a decision of their controversies. What, then, shall be done, in order to
terminate or adjust them? Much may be done; much ought to be done,
before the fatal appeal is made to the dernier resort of sovereigns.

In some peculiar situations, it is more prudent, as well as more honourable, to abandon than to claim a right; to disregard, than to resent an
injury: but, by nations, even this laudable and generous conduct should
be observed with great prudence and circumspection, and in such a
manner as, instead of cowardice, to discover magnanimity. When this
conduct can be so observed, what a glorious example does it exhibit to
the world! "A king of France ought not to revenge the wrongs of a
duke of Orleans," was nobly said by a monarch of an elevated mind.
Might it not also be said, that it is not every petty offence, which ought
to provoke the dignified energy of sovereign power? Suppose a picture,
disrespectful to Lewis the fourteenth, had been exhibited in Holland; was
this a sufficient occasion for drawing forth the great monarch at the
head of the armies of France? Was it a sufficient occasion for drawing
him forth at the head of those armies against a power, comparatively
inconsiderable, and trembling to its centre from a conscious sense of its
own inferiority?

Nec deus intersit, nisi nodus vindice dignus.*

On some occasions, it may be proper to claim a right, or take notice
of an injury, merely with a determined and heroick purpose of ceding

* [Nor would God intervene, unless the predicament be worthy of a helper to
untangle it. Horace, *Ars Poetica*, 191.]

the former, and of forgiving the latter. This mode of proceeding, adopted at a proper time, in a proper manner, and by a proper person, has a great and a useful effect. It displays the good sense and superiour judgment of him, who observes it; and secures the esteem, perhaps the friendship of him, towards whom it is observed.

Controversies often happen, when neither of the parties to them is intentionally wrong: they arise from misapprehensions or mistakes. In such cases, nothing more is necessary for an amicable accommodation, than candid conference and mutual explanation. "There are two kinds of disputation," says Cicero,[b] "one, by argument and reason; the other, by violence and force. To determine controversies by the former belongs to man; by the latter, to the brutes. To the latter we ought never to have recourse, but when all hopes of success by the former are proved to be unavailing." If in every minute particular, an entire coincidence of sentiment and interest cannot take place; concessions, in the course of a negotiation, may be made on both sides; and, in this manner, a satisfactory adjustment of every difference may be effectuated.

If the parties themselves, notwithstanding their peaceful and proper inclinations, cannot finally agree upon the terms, according to which the difference should be adjusted; those terms may, in many instances, be arranged and settled by the kind and benevolent mediation of a common friend. Delicate, indeed, but highly useful is the office of a mediator. Address, prudence, a winning smoothness, but, above all, a most strict impartiality are the rare qualifications, which he ought to possess. Possessing these, he will favour what is due to justice and right; but remembering, at the same time, that his office is to conciliate, and not to judge, his leading effort will be to preserve or to procure peace, and to prevail on him, who has even justice on his side, to relax something, if such a relaxation shall be necessary for accomplishing a purpose so desirable and so humane. In the Alcoran, it is delivered as an indispensable injunction, that if two nations of the faithful will go to war, the others shall interpose and force the aggressor to make satisfaction, and afterwards lay both under an obligation to live, for the future, in peace and friendship.[c]

If, unfortunately, neither negotiation nor friendly interposition of disinterested and benevolent powers shall prove effectual, for determining a controversy between two nations; there is another method remaining, by which mutual irritation and, much more, dreadful extremities may be prevented between those, who have no common judge upon earth, to whom they can appeal. This method is, to refer the matter in dispute to the award of arbitrators.

[b] De off. l. 1. c. 11.   [c] Puff. 556. b. 5. c. 13. s. 7.

This mode of decision has been embraced by nations, the most powerful and the most wise. When the Athenians and the citizens of Megara had a dispute concerning the property of the island of Salamis, five Lacedemonian umpires were chosen to settle their contested claims. Some of the Italian states, in the early ages of Rome, submitted their controversies to the determination of the Romans. The Romans themselves, haughty and domineering as they were, and proud of the character *debellare superbos,* proposed to the Samnites, that the subject of their contention should be referred to the arbitration of their common friends and allies.[d] The Druids, those revered ministers of a mysterious superstition, were the umpires between nations at war, and frequently brought matters to an accommodation, when the belligerent powers were on the very instant of an engagement. "It is cruel and detestable," says Thucydides, "to treat him as an enemy, who is willing to submit his case to an arbitration." [e]

In all their alliances with one another, and even in those, which they have formed with the neighbouring powers, the Swiss have used the wise precaution to ascertain, beforehand, the manner, in which their differences should be left to the award of arbitrators, in case it should prove impracticable to adjust them upon amicable terms. This prudent and judicious policy has contributed, in no small degree, to maintain the Helvetian republick in that flourishing state, which has secured its liberty, and rendered it respectable over all Europe.[f]

When the sentence of the arbitrators is given, it ought to be obeyed; unless it be flagrantly partial, manifestly unjust, or clearly beyond the powers given by the submission. If the award is upon the very point disputed, it can never be manifestly unjust, since it has been rendered doubtful by the dissension of the parties.

It has been the opinion of some very respectable and well informed writers, that it would be highly convenient, and even somewhat necessary, that congresses of a number of states should be held, in which the differences of contending parties might be determined by those altogether disinterested in them; and in which, likewise, some effectual means might be devised and carried into execution, for compelling nations at war to conclude a peace upon fair and equitable conditions. In the course of the present century, two general congresses have been held in Europe — one at Cambray; the other at Soissons: but they were nothing more than pompous farces, acted, with great parade, by those, who wished to appear solicitous for an accommodation, but who, in fact, were little solicitous to promote it.[g]

If justice cannot be obtained in any of the peaceful modes above-

[d] Liv. l. 8. c. 23.   [e] Gro. 486. 487.   [f] Vat. b. 2. s. 329.
[g] Vat. b. 2. s. 330.

mentioned; a nation has then a right to do itself justice. But even this ought to be done, when it can possibly be done, without proceeding to the last direful necessity of commencing a war. Reprisals may be made. If one nation has got into its possession what belongs to another, and will not restore it; if it refuses to pay a just debt, or to make reparation for an injury; that other nation may seize property belonging to the first, may apply it for its own benefit, in discharge of what is due, together with interest and damages; or it may hold the property in pledge, until satisfaction be made.

The subject of reprisals is so delicate and interesting that the nature and the extent of the right to make them deserve a careful and accurate investigation.

We have already seen,[h] that a nation is to be considered as a moral person, having an understanding and will peculiar to itself: as such it is considered by the law of nations. The consequence necessarily is, that every act of this moral or collective person must, in the view of that law, be the concurrent act of its several members.

From the same principles, the property of each of the members must, with regard to other states, be deemed the property of the whole nation. In some degree, this is, in truth, the case; because the nation has power over the riches of the citizens; and because those riches form a part of the national wealth. All those, who compose a nation, making, in the consideration of foreign states, one whole, or one single person; all their property must be considered as the property of that single person. It is in the power of a nation to establish, among its citizens, a community of goods; but whether this is done, or is not done, the separate property of those citizens can neither be known nor discriminated by other states. The unavoidable result is, that, if one nation has a right to any part of the goods of another, it has a right to the goods of its citizens, till the right be satisfied or discharged. The unavoidable result, again, is, that when it is justifiable to make reprisals, they may be made on the property of any of the citizens, as well as on that of the nation. From this rule, one exception has been made, and deserves to be established. This exception is made in favour of a deposit trusted to the faith of the nation, which has a right to make reprisals. This deposit has been made only in consequence of the reliance, which the owner had on this faith: this faith ought to be respected, even in the case of an open and declared war. For this reason, in France, in England, and in some other countries of Europe, the money, which hostile foreigners have placed in the publick funds, has been considered as sacred from the rights of reprisals, and even of war.

He who, for the injustice done by a nation, makes reprisals upon the

[h] Ante. p. 239.

property of its citizens indiscriminately, cannot be accused of seizing the property of one person in order to satisfy the debt of another. It is a demand against the state, to the discharge of which every citizen is bound to contribute his just proportion. It is the duty and business of the nation to provide, that those citizens, upon whom the reprisals fall immediately, should be indemnified for every thing beyond that share, which, on a fair assessment, they ought to pay. The nation ought to go farther; if the reprisals have been occasioned originally by the injustice or violence of some of its members; those members should be compelled to make satisfaction for every loss, which has arisen from their conduct.

Though the property of the private citizens, from the nature and the necessity of the case, must, in many, perhaps, in most instances, be considered by foreign states as liable for their demands against the nation; yet where publick property can be known and certainly distinguished, it is unquestionably proper, that such property should, in the first place, be the selected object of reprisals, if to reprisals it be easily or conveniently accessible. The principles of humanity and the dictates of magnanimity suggest, with equal force, the reasonableness and propriety of this discrimination, whenever it can be made.

As the property of a nation, or of the citizens of a nation, may be seized by reprisals, in order to compel it to do justice; so, on some occasions, the citizens themselves may be seized, in consequence of the same principles, and may be detained until full satisfaction has been received. This mode of proceeding was known among the Grecians by a name, which may be literally translated *mancatching;* 'Ανδροληψια. At Athens, the law permitted the relations of him, who had been assassinated in a foreign country, to apprehend three persons of that country, and detain them, till the assassin was punished or delivered up.

In making reprisals, three precautions should be inviolably observed. 1. They ought not to be made without the authority of the nation. Though reprisals are not war; and though their proper use is to prevent war; yet they approach to a war, and are often followed by one. They are, therefore, proceedings of too much publick moment, to be carried on under the direction and at the discretion of individuals; probably, of individuals immediately and particularly interested in them. In all civilized countries, therefore, it is the unvaried practice, that when a citizen considers himself as injured by a foreign state, he applies to the sovereign power of his nation for permission to make reprisals. 2. Reprisals ought to be made only for a demand, which is both just and certain. If it be doubtful or unliquidated, the first application should be for such steps as may be necessary to ascertain its reasonableness and its extent. 3. The reprisals should be in a due proportion to the demand. General reprisals, the grand pensionary De Wit used to say, were scarcely to be distinguished from an open war.

We have now seen that the citizens, in their persons and in their fortunes, may be accountable for the conduct of the nation: so, on the other hand, the nation may sometimes be accountable for the conduct of its private citizens.

The state should protect the citizen, should defend him from injury, and should procure reparation for injuries which he has sustained. So, likewise, the nation should not suffer its citizens to commit injuries against the citizens of other states, it ought to disclaim the conduct of such as offer injuries; and ought to compel or to give satisfaction for the injuries which have been offered.

It is impossible, however, that, even in the best regulated state, the government should be able to superintend the whole conduct of all the citizens, and to restrain them within the precise bounds of duty and obedience: it would be unjust, therefore, to impute to the nation, or to the government, all the faults or offences, which its members may commit. Hence it does not necessarily follow, that one has received an injury from a nation, merely because he has received an injury from a citizen belonging to that nation. To a whole state, the follies, the injuries, or the crimes of a particular person ought not to be immediately ascribed: in every state, wicked and disorderly citizens are unhappily to be found: let such be held responsible for the consequences of their crimes and disorders.

This doctrine is certainly reasonable and just; but if a nation wishes not to be involved in the punishment of her citizens, she should sedulously avoid the impropriety and the offence of becoming an accomplice in their injuries and crimes. In their injuries and crimes she becomes an accomplice, when she approves or ratifies them, and when she affords protection and security to those, who have committed them. In such cases, the nation may justly be considered as even the author, and the citizens as only the instruments, of the wrong or outrage which has been done.

When the offending citizen escapes into his own country, his nation should oblige him to repair the damage, if reparation can be made; should punish him according to the measure of his offence; or, when the nature and the circumstances of the case require it, deliver him up to the offended state to meet his doom there. This is frequently done with regard to atrocious crimes, such as are equally contrary to the laws and the safety of all nations.

In states, which are most strictly connected by friendship and good neighbourhood, they go farther still. Even with regard to common in-

juries, which are prosecuted civilly, whether for reparation of damage, or
for a slight civil punishment, the citizens of two neighbouring states are
reciprocally compelled to appear before the magistrate of the country,
in which they are accused of having offended. On a requisition of this
magistrate, which is called a letter rogatory, they are cited judicially,
and compelled by their own proper magistrates to appear. "An admirable institution!" exclaims Vattel,[i] in a tone of admiration, "by which
many neighbouring states live together in peace and harmony, and seem
to form but one and the same commonwealth." This institution is in
force through all Switzerland.

If we could restrain, would it be proper to restrain the pleasing and
animating reflection, that even the most admired institutions of Europe
are improved, while they are adopted by the United States? For the trial
and punishment of every kind of offence, prosecuted criminally, and,
therefore, on common law principles, locally, the following provision is
made in our national constitution.[j] "A person charged, in any state,
with treason, felony, or other crime, who shall flee from justice, and be
found in another state, shall, on demand of the executive authority of
the state from which he fled, be delivered up, to be removed to the
state, having jurisdiction of the crime." In civil causes of a transitory
nature, no such provision is necessary; but a much better one is made.
In Switzerland, controversies depending between citizens of different
states must be decided by the magistrates of a state, of which one party,
but not the other, is a citizen. But, in the United States, for controversies
depending between citizens of two different states, a tribunal is formed
and established, impartial, and equally independent of both.

The foregoing remarks exhibit, in a very striking point of view, the
numerous, the near, and the important relations, by which states and the
members of states may be connected together. We here discover the
much famed institutions of Alfred the Great, extended on a national
scale. In the great society of nations, we see each citizen bound for the
good behaviour of all, and all bound for the good behaviour of each.
As the principles of society, humanity, benevolence, and liberality shall
become more and more regarded and cultivated, the rights and duties
of different nations, and of the citizens of different nations, will become
more and more studied, and will be better and better practised and
observed. In this study, the present century has witnessed great and
manifest improvements. In this study all men are interested: it is rich in
delight: it is inestimable in importance: its maxims should be known by
every citizen of every free state.

The relations existing between different states and the citizens of

[i] B. 2. s. 76.   [j] Art. 4. s. 2.

different states, and the rights and duties arising from those relations, form a constituent part of the common law. In that country, from which the common law has been brought, the law of nations has always been most respectfully and attentively adopted and regarded by the municipal tribunals, in all matters, concerning which it is proper to have recourse to that rule of decision. The law of nations, in its full extent, is a part of the law of England.[k] The infractions of that law form a portion of her code of criminal jurisprudence. In civil transactions between the citizens of different states, that law has, in England, been received in its most ample latitude.

One branch of that law, which, since the extension of commerce, and the frequent and liberal intercourse between different nations, has become of peculiar importance, is called the law of merchants. This system of law has been admitted to decide controversies concerning bills of exchange, policies of insurance, and other mercantile transactions, both where citizens of different states, and where citizens of the same state only, have been interested in the event.[l] This system has, of late years, been greatly elucidated, and reduced to rational and solid principles, by a series of adjudications, for which the commercial world is much indebted to a celebrated judge, long famed for his comprehensive talents and luminous learning in general jurisprudence.

Another branch of the law of nations, which has also become peculiarly important by the extension of commerce, is the law maritime. In a cause depending in the court of king's bench in England, and tried at one of the assizes, my Lord Mansfield, the great judge to whom allusion has been just now made, was desirous to have a case made of it for solemn adjudication; not because he himself entertained great doubts concerning it; but in order to settle the point, on which it turned, more deliberately, solemnly, and notoriously; as it was of an extensive nature; and especially as the maritime law is not the law of a particular country, but the general law of nations: non erit alia lex Romæ, alia Athenis; alia nunc, alia posthac; sed et apud omnes gentes et omni tempore, una eademque lex obtinebit.[m]

In the plan of my lectures, I proposed a question, the greatness of which is selfevident — How far, on the principles of the confederation, does the law of nations become the municipal law of the United States? I mentioned, that it would be unwise, at that time, to hint at an answer.

[k] 3. Burr. 1481.
[l] In commercial cases, all nations ought to have their laws conformable to each other. Fides servanda est; simplicitas juris gentium prævaleat. [Faith must be kept; the simplicity of the law of nations must prevail.] 3. Burr. 1672.
[m] 2. Burr. 887. [There will not be one law in Rome, another in Athens; one now, another later; but both among all peoples and at every time one and the same law will prevail.]

An answer I mean not to give even now: but I deem it highly proper now to state the nature, the extent, and the importance of the question. It points to a course new and unexplored.

We have seen the divine origin; we have seen the amazing extent; we have seen the uncommon magnitude of the law of nations: we have, in part, seen, likewise, how ineffective the execution of that law, under human authority, has hitherto been.

Amicable agreement between parties in controversy has been recommended, and recommended with great propriety, where the recommendation can take effect: but controversy, which has arisen, and which, from the very supposition of the case, subsists between the parties, is certainly not the most natural guide to lead to an amicable accommodation. The mediation of a disinterested and benevolent power has been recommended likewise: but this mediation, though it enhances the merit and displays the beauty of the candid, the peaceful, and the disinterested virtues, affords no reasonable security, that the exertion of those virtues will be accompanied with the wished for effect. To arbitration recourse has been advised: but to the institution of arbitrators, the previous consent of the parties in controversy is requisite: and how, against the unwilling, is the award of the arbitrators to be enforced?

What is next to be done? The same disposition or the same mistake, which, on one of the sides, must have given birth to the controversy, will probably communicate to it vigour and perseverance. Nay, that disagreement of mind between the parties, which must have taken place when the controversy commenced, is likely to be increased, instead of being diminished, by the frequent, numerous, and mutual irritations, which will unavoidably happen in the prosecution of it. All the modes of adjustment, which have been hitherto mentioned, presuppose the reconciliation of irritated minds. But must the peaceful adjustment of controversies between states — an adjustment so salutary and so necessary to the human race — depend on events so very precarious, so very improbable? Must the alternatives in disputes and differences between the dignified assemblages of men, known by the name of nations, be the same, which are the prerogatives of savages in the rudest and most deformed state of society — voluntary accommodation, or open war, or violent reprisals, inferiour, in odium, only to war? Individuals unite in civil society, and institute judges with authority to decide, and with authority also to carry their decisions into full and adequate execution, that justice may be done and war may be prevented. Are states too wise or too proud to receive a lesson from individuals? Is the idea of a common judge between nations less admissible than that of a common judge between men? If admissible in idea, would it not be desirable to have an opportunity of trying whether the idea may not be reduced to practice? To return to the original question — has or has not our national constitution given us an opportunity of making this great and interesting trial?

Let us turn our most scrutinizing attention to the situation, in which, on the principles of that system, the states and the people, composing the American Union, stand with regard to one another; the situation, in which they stand with regard to foreign nations; and the situation, in which they stand with regard to the government of the United States.

With regard to one another, they have, by ordaining and establishing the national constitution, engaged to "form a more perfect union," "to ensure domestick tranquillity," "to establish justice:" [n] they have engaged "that the citizens of each state shall be entitled to all privileges and immunities of citizens in the several states:" [o] they have engaged that no state shall enter into "any treaty, alliance, or confederation;" [p] "nor, without the consent of congress, into any agreement or compact with another state." [q]

With regard to foreign nations, the states, composing the American Union, have made an engagement precisely in the terms of the last mentioned engagement, which they have made with regard to one another — absolutely to enter into no treaty, alliance, or confederation with foreign nations; and to enter into no agreement or compact with them, unless with the consent of congress. [r]

With regard to the government of the United States, they have engaged that the judicial power of the United States shall extend "to controversies between two or more states; between a state and the citizens of another state; between citizens of different states; between citizens of the same state claiming lands under grants of different states; and between a state, or the citizens thereof, and foreign states, citizens, or subjects." [s]

The law of nations respecting treaties, alliances, and confederations must be thrown entirely out of the question: these are absolutely interdicted.

The law of nations respecting agreements and compacts between two or more states; between a state and the citizens of another state; between citizens of different states; between citizens of the same state claiming lands under grants of different states; and between a state, or the citizens thereof, and foreign states, citizens, or subjects, will still be applicable, as before the national constitution was established, to controversies arising in all those different enumerated cases.

In all those different enumerated cases, the tribunals of the United

[n] Preamb.   [o] Art. 4. s. 2.   [p] Art. 1. s. 10.   [q] Ibid.   [r] Ibid.
[s] Art. 3. s. 2.

States have judicial authority to decide. By what law shall their decisions be governed? Before the establishment of the national government, controversies happening in those enumerated cases, if determined at all, must have been determined by the principles and rules of the law of nations. But before that establishment, there was no power to determine them judicially by any law.

We have already seen that, in England, the courts of common law, in cases, to which the law of nations, and particularly in cases, to which one great branch of it, the law of merchants is applicable, have made approved application of that law, and have received it, in its fullest extent, as a part of the law of England. Should a similar conduct be observed by the tribunals of the United States, in the numerous and very important cases, to which the national constitution extends their judicial authority?

If a similar conduct ought to be observed by those tribunals; what an immense improvement has taken place in the application and administration of the law of nations! Hitherto that great law has been applied and administered by the force or by the pleasure of the parties in controversy: in the United States, it can now be applied and administered by impartial, independent, and efficient, though peaceful authority.

This deduction, if properly founded, places the government of the United States in an aspect, new, indeed, but very conspicuous. It is vested with the exalted power of administering judicially the law of nations, which we have formerly seen to be the law of sovereigns.

It has been already observed, that the maxims of this law ought to be known by every citizen of every free state. Reasons, and very sufficient ones, were suggested, why this should be the case. A new reason, striking and illustrious, now appears, why the maxims of this law ought to be particularly known and studied by every citizen of the United States. To every citizen of the United States, this law is not only a rule of conduct, but may be a rule of decision. As judges and as jurors, the administration of this law is, in many important instances, committed to their care.

What a beautiful and magnificent prospect of government is now opened before you! The sluices of discord, devastation, and war are shut: those of harmony, improvement, and happiness are opened! On earth there is peace and good will towards men! On contemplating such a prospect, though only by the eye of a sublime imagination, well might the ardent and elevated Henry address the congenial ardour and elevation of Elizabeth — O most excellent and rare enterprise — Thought rather divine than human!

To us this prospect is realized by happy experience: how thankful ought we to be in enjoying it! how zealous should we be to secure it to ourselves and to our latest posterity! how anxious should we be to extend its example, its influence, and its advantages to the remotest regions of the habitable globe!

X

OF GOVERNMENT

W E have already seen, that society may exist without civil government: indeed, if we would think and reason with accuracy on the subject, we shall necessarily be led to consider, in our contemplation, the formation of society as preexistent to the formation of those regulations, by which the society mean, that their conduct should be influenced and directed.

It is necessary that this distinction be plainly made, and clearly understood. It has been controverted by some: an inattention to it has produced, in the minds of others, practical inferences, which are both ill founded and dangerous. A change of government has been viewed as a desperate event, as an object of the most terrifick aspect; because it has been thought, that government could not be changed, without tearing up the very foundations of the social establishment. It has been supposed, that, in a transition from one government to another, the body making it must be dissolved; that every thing must be reduced to a state of nature; and that the rights and obligations of the society must be lost and discharged.

In many parts of the world, indeed, the idea of revolutions in government is, by a mournful and indissoluble association, connected with the idea of wars, and of all the calamities attendant on wars.[a] But joyful experience teaches us, in the United States, to view them in a very different and much more agreeable light — to consider them only as progressive steps in improving the knowledge of government, and increasing the happiness of society and mankind.

It is true, that institutions, which depend on the form or structure of the preceding government, must fall, when that form or structure is taken away. But establishments, whose foundations rest on the society itself, cannot be overturned by any alteration of the government, which the society can make. The acts and compacts which form the political association, are very different from those by which the associated body, when formed, may choose to maintain and regulate itself.

[a] Changes in course of government are looked at as uncouth motions of the celestial bodies, portending judgments or dissolution. Bac. on Gov. 7.

But though, without government, society may exist; yet it must be admitted, that, without government, society, in the present state of things, cannot flourish; far less, can it reach perfection. In a state of nature, it is true, any one individual may act uncontrolled by others; but it is equally true, that, in such a state, every other individual may act uncontrolled by him. Amidst this universal independence, the dissensions and animosities between the interfering members of the society, would be numerous and ungovernable. The consequence would be, that each member, in such a natural state, would enjoy less liberty, and suffer more interruption and inconvenience, than he would under a civil government.

Again; it is true, that, by the fundamental laws of society, obedience is stipulated on the part of the members, and protection is stipulated on the part of the body. But the modes, and extent, and particular objects of this obedience, and the modes, and extent, and particular instruments of this protection, are all equally unascertained. Precision and certainty in these points, so important to the peace and order of society, can be obtained only by a system of government. In addition, therefore, to the rules, which necessarily enter into the formation of society, other rules — those, which compose government — have been gradually introduced into every community, which has attained any considerable degree of improvement.[b]

How the different governments, which have successively appeared in the different parts of the world, began; on what principles they were originally formed; what share in their formation should be ascribed to stratagem, what to force, what to necessity, what to conveniency, what to wisdom, what to patriotism — all these are questions, which would employ, and the answers to which would gratify curiosity: some of them would convey much pleasure and instruction: but, with regard to many of them, complete information cannot be obtained; and if it could, it would not be accompanied with a proportioned degree of satisfaction. The origin of many governments is obliterated or obscured by the impressions of all-corroding time. Some exceptions, however, there are; and of those exceptions, some deserve to be considered with careful and patient attention: they contain matter of wise example, or of prudent caution.

From ancient history I select one instance, the particulars of which are transmitted to us with a considerable degree of accuracy and minuteness. The Medes originally were included in the great empire of Assyria: from this empire they separated themselves by a successful revolt. After

[b] Sine imperio, nec domus ulla, nec civitas, nec gens, nec hominum universum genus stare, nec rerum natura omnis, nec ipse mundus potest. [Without authority neither any house, nor state, nor nation, nor the whole human race can stand, nor physical nature, nor the very universe itself.] Cic. de leg. l. 3. c. 1.

their separation, they continued, for some time, without any established form of government — in a state of self command, as the expression used by Herodotus denotes. Of this state, they soon began to experience the infelicities: injuries were committed; controversies arose; dissensions took place: there was no settled or acknowledged authority to repress animosities, to determine disputes, or to order reparation for injustice that had been done.

One man there was, whose integrity and wisdom taught his countrymen to revere him, and to apply to him as the judge and arbiter of their differences. This was the famed Dejoces. His decisions were equitable; but the execution of them depended on the pleasure of the parties, against whom they were made. Influence, however, and reputation supplied, in some tolerable degree, the place of regular and established authority; and the Medes confided and acquiesced in the prudence and justice of Dejoces.

Stimulated by latent principles of ambition, or directed by the admonitions of sagacity, Dejoces became dissatisfied with the situation, in which he stood. Perhaps he wisely foresaw, that unless he possessed authority at the same time that he deserved confidence, he could not be long safe in his own person, or useful to his fellow citizens. Another supposition there is likewise reason to make. Perhaps his ambition suggested to him, that the influence, which he already enjoyed, might, by an easy and a certain transition, be converted into power; that the voluntary acquiescence under his awards might be improved into implicit submission to his edicts; and that the respected judge might become the splendid monarch of Media. Whatever his motives were, we know what was their result. He would not exercise any longer the confidential office of administering justice among the Medes; but had recourse to a retired life, under the pretence, that he could no longer support the excessive fatigue of the business of others; and that it was now become absolutely necessary for him to devote his attention to the management of his own affairs.

The consequence, which was naturally expected, naturally followed. The disorders, which the character and influence of Dejoces had repressed, returned, upon his retirement, with redoubled violence; and increased to such a degree, that the Medes were obliged to convene a general council of the nation, in order to deliberate upon the proper methods of finding and applying a remedy to the publick miseries and dissensions. The expedient adopted by the general council was, that a king should be elected, who should have power to restrain the rage of violence, and to make laws for the government of the nation. When it was determined to elect a king; there was no hesitation concerning the person, on whom the election should fall. With common consent, De-joces was elected king of Media.[e]

With regard to the first establishment of civil government, it is prob-able, that the maintenance of publick peace and the promotion of pub-lick happiness were the ends originally proposed by the people, in many instances. It is certain, that, in every instance, they were the ends, which by all ought to have been proposed and prosecuted too. One thing is unquestionable, and this, indeed, is all that is necessary to be known upon the subject; that every man must have had his own advantage and happi-ness in view; and must have endeavoured, as much as possible, to preserve his natural liberty. This is founded on the constitution of mankind; and this invincible principle would operate with greater force on the first formation of government, than after it was fully established; for under es-tablished governments, the natural love of liberty is frequently counter-acted by education, by prejudice, by interest, by ambition. Of this mel-ancholy, but undeniable truth, the history of man and of government produces too many striking examples. The degeneracy of government, and the consequent degeneracy of the citizens, have been fruitful topicks of contemplation and complaint, in almost every age and country.

It is a question rather of curiosity than of utility — what kind of government is the most ancient? The different kinds have different ad-vocates in favour of their antiquity; and their different hypotheses are supported with much ingenuity and zeal. The ardour of polemical dis-quisition, however, upon this subject, might have been greatly softened by the obvious reflection, that it by no means follows, that the kind of government which is oldest, is the kind which is also best. That form which was most simple, and not that form which was most perfect, would, in all probability, attract the attention, and determine the choice, of a rude and inexperienced society. In many parts of the world, the science of government is even yet in a state of nonage: shall its first be deemed its most finished movements?

The most simple form of government is that of monarchy: reasonable conjecture, therefore, would lead us to presume, that this form is the most ancient. This presumption of reason is confirmed by the information of history, both sacred and profane. The most ancient nations mentioned by the inspired historian and legislator of the Hebrews — for instance, the Egyptians, the Babylonians, the Assyrians — were all under the govern-ment of kings. Homer, the true original of his own Ulysses, who knew societies as well as men, seems scarcely to have seen, or heard, or even imagined any other species of government, than that which was monar-chical. The most famous states of antiquity, Athens and Rome, were

[e] Rol. An. Hist. b. 3. c. 3.   3. Gog. Or. Laws. 8. 9.

monarchies at their first commencement. The history of China is said to reach a period of antiquity very remote; at the remotest period, monarchy was the form of government which prevailed in it.

But though monarchy is the most ancient form of government; monarchs were, at first, neither hereditary nor despotick. We have seen that Dejoces, the first monarch of Media, became a king by election. Crowns, in general, were originally elective. True, indeed, it is, that, from causes obvious and easy to be assigned, the office, which, at first, was elective, became afterwards hereditary.

The dominions of the first monarchs were far from being extensive. In the days of Abraham, there were five kings in the single Valley of Sodom. The kings defeated by Joshua in Palestine were thirty one in number. The different provinces, which, at present, compose the empire of China, formed anciently so many separate monarchies. "The ancient Britons," says Bacon in his Discourses on Government,[d] "had many chiefs in a little room; whom the Romans called kings, for the greater renown of their empire." For many ages, Greece was divided into a vast number of small and inconsiderable kingdoms.

The authority of those ancient monarchs was not more extensive than their dominions. It appears from many monuments, that, by the constitutions of the first kingdoms, the people had a great share in the government. Affairs of importance were debated and determined in the general assemblies of the nations.[e] "De majoribus omnes consultant," says Tacitus[f] of the ancient Germans. The first kings were, indeed, properly no more than judges, who had no power to inflict punishments by their own authority, and without the consent of the people. Hence the poet Hesiod says, that the muses give kings the art of persuasion, that they may engage the people to submit to their decisions, for which end they were placed in that exalted station.[g] "Principes jura per pagos vicosque reddunt," says Tacitus in the treatise just now cited.[h]

"In my opinion," says Cicero,[i] "it was not among the Medes only, as Herodotus informs us; but it was among our own ancestors likewise, that kings of good character were chosen, in order that the administration of justice might be enjoyed. For when the poor were oppressed by the rich, they fled for relief to some one, preeminent in virtue, who would protect the weak from injustice, and would dispense equal law to the high and to the low. If they could obtain this from the mouth of one just and

[d] P. 1.   [e] 1. Gog. Or. Laws. 15.
[f] De mor. Germ. c. 11. [On larger matters all consult.]
[g] Gro. 70. n. 53.
[h] De mor. Germ. c. 12. [The leaders administer law through the cantons and villages.]
[i] De off. l. 2. c. 12.

good man, they were satisfied; but, as they were often disappointed in this reasonable demand, they had, afterwards, recourse to general law, which spoke one language to all."

The course of things in other nations, was similar to that, which took place in Media and in Rome. "At first," says the excellent Hooker, "when some kind of regiment was once approved; it may be, that nothing was, then, further thought upon for the manner of governing; but all permitted to their wisdom and discretion, which were to rule; till, by experience, they found this, for all parts, very inconvenient, so as the thing, which they had devised for a remedy, did but increase the sore, which it should have cured. They saw, that to live by one man's will, became the cause of all men's misery. This constrained them to come unto law, wherein all men might see their duties beforehand, and know the penalties of transgressing them." [j]

This progress of government and law, we find remarkably exemplified in the history of Greece. At first, all the Grecian cities were under the government of kings, not arbitrarily, but agreeably to the laws and customs of the country. He was esteemed the best king, who was the justest and strictest observer of the laws, and who never departed from the established customs of his kingdom. This explains the true meaning of Homer, (who painted to the life) when he denominated kings, "men, who distribute justice." These small monarchies, thus limited, subsisted for a long time, as, for instance, that of the Lacedemonians. But, afterwards, some kings began to abuse their power, and to govern according to their pleasure, rather than according to the laws. This the Greeks could not endure; and, therefore, abolished the monarchical form of government, and established other kinds of government in its place.

To find out the best kind of government has been long the celebrated problem in the political world. In order to furnish some imperfect materials for the solution of this very important inquiry, let us consider and investigate the qualities and principles, by which a good government ought to be characterized.

Men, frail and imperfect as they are, must be the instruments, by which government is administered. But, in order to guard against the consequences of their frailties and imperfections, one effort, in the contrivance of the political system, is, to provide, that, for the offices and the departments of the state, the wisest and the best of her citizens be elected. A second effort is, to communicate to the operations of government as great a share as possible of the good, and as small a share as possible of the bad propensities of our nature. A third effort is, to increase, encourage, and strengthen those good propensities, and to lessen, discourage,

[j] Hooker. b. i. p. 18.

and correct those bad ones. A fourth effort is, to introduce, into the very form of government, such particular checks and controls, as to make it advantageous even for bad men to act for the publick good. When these efforts are successful, and happily united; then is accomplished what we truly mean, when we speak of a government of laws, and not of men; then every man does homage to the laws; the very least as feeling their care; the greatest as not exempted from their power.

What are the qualities in government, necessary for producing laws, properly designed, properly framed, and properly enforced? Goodness should inspire and animate the intention: wisdom should direct and arrange the means: power should render the means efficacious, by carrying the laws vigorously into execution. The more all those qualities prevail in any government, the nearer does that government approach to its perfection. In some kinds of government, one of the qualities is eminent in undue proportion: in others another: but the best are those, in which all the qualities are happily blended in their operation, and diffuse, through the whole society, their mingled and tempered influence.

We have now taken a general view of government, and have traced the qualities, which should operate through the whole: let us descend to a more minute examination of its different parts: let us view the structure and properties of each, considered by itself; and also the mutual dependencies and controls, which each ought to possess, and to which each ought to be subject, when considered relatively to others.

The powers of government are usually, and with propriety, arranged under three great divisions; the legislative authority, the executive authority, and the judicial authority. Let us consider each, as its greatness deserves to be considered.

The first remark, which I shall make on the structure of the legislative power, is, that it ought to be *divided*. In support of this position, which is, indeed, one of the most important in both the theory and the practice of government, many arguments may be advanced. Let me introduce one, by the declaration of an admired judge, whose manly candour must charm every generous mind. "It is the glory and happiness of our excellent constitution, that, to prevent any injustice, no man is concluded by the first judgment; but that, if he apprehends himself to be aggrieved, he has another court, to which he may resort for relief. For my part, I can say, that it is a consideration of great comfort to me, that, if I do err, my judgment is not conclusive to the party; but my mistake may be rectified, and so no injustice be done." [k] Is less skill required — should less caution be observed — in making laws, than in explaining them? Are mistakes less likely to happen — are they less dangerous — is it less necessary to prevent or rectify them, in the former case, than in the latter?

[k] Str. 565.

Which is most necessary? to preserve the streams, or to preserve the fountain from becoming turbid?

But the danger arising from mistakes and inaccuracies is not the only nor the greatest one, to be apprehended from a single body possessed of legislative power. It is impossible to restrain it in its operations. No other power in government can arrest the proceedings of that which makes the laws. Let us suppose, that this single body, in a lucky moment, should pass a law to restrain itself: in the next moment, an unlucky one, it might repeal the restraining law. Any mounds, which it might raise to confine itself, would still be within the sphere of its own motion; and whatever force should impel it, would necessarily impel those mounds along with it. To stop and to check, as well as to produce motion in this political globe, we must possess — what Archimedes wanted — another globe to stand upon.

A single legislature is calculated to unite in it all the pernicious qualities of the different extremes of bad government. It produces general weakness, inactivity, and confusion; and these are intermixed with sudden and violent fits of despotism, injustice, and cruelty.

But I will take the subject a little deeper: it is of the utmost consequence that it be fully discussed. In private life, how often and how fatally are we seduced, by our passions and by our prejudices, from those paths, which would lead us to our true interests? But are passions and prejudices less frequently to be found in publick bodies, than in individuals? Are they less powerful? Do they not become inflamed by mutual imitation and example? Will they not, if unrestrained, produce the most mischievous effects? Ye, who are versed in the science of human nature — ye, who have viewed it in the faithful mirrour of history — tell us, for you know, what answer should be given to these questions. Cannot you point out instances, in which the people have become the miserable victims of passions, operating upon their government without restraint? Cannot you point out other instances, in which the violence of one part of the government has been happily controlled by the constitutional interposition of another part?

There is not in the whole science of politicks a more solid or a more important maxim than this — that of all governments, those are the best, which, by the natural effect of their constitutions, are frequently renewed or drawn back to their first principles. When a single legislature is determined to depart from the principles of the constitution — and its incontrollable power may prompt the determination — there is no constitutional authority to arrest its progress. It may proceed, by long and hasty strides, in violating the constitution, till nothing but a revolution can stop its career. Far different will the case be, when the legislature consists of two branches. If one of them should depart, or attempt to depart from the principles of the constitution; it will be drawn back by the other. The very apprehension of the event will prevent the departure or the attempt.

In all the most celebrated governments both of ancient and of modern times, we find the legislatures composed of distinct bodies. Such was that formed at Athens by Solon. Such was that instituted at Sparta by Lycurgus. Such was that, which so long flourished at Rome. In our sister states, their legislatures consist of distinct bodies of men. Similar, upon this subject, is the constitution of the United States. And we can now happily say, that Pennsylvania no longer exhibits an instance to the contrary — that she no longer holds out to view a beacon to be avoided, instead of an example deserving imitation.

Thus much I have thought it necessary to say concerning that power of government, which is intrusted with the making of the laws. Let us next consider those powers, which are intrusted with their execution, and with the administration of justice under their authority. Wise and good laws are indeed essential; but though they are essential, they are so only as means. If we stop here, all that we have done is nugatory and abortive. The end is still unattained; and that can be attained only when the laws are vigorously and steadily executed; and when the administration of justice under them is unbiassed and enlightened.

Indeed, if I mistake not, an inferiour proportion of attention, in this and in most of our sister states, has been employed about these important parts of the political system. Laws have abounded: their multiplicity has been often a grievance: but their weak and irregular execution, and the unwise and unstable administration of justice, have been subjects of general and well grounded complaint.

Habits contracted before the late revolution of the United States, operate, in the same manner, since that time, though very material alterations may have taken place in the objects of their operations.

Before that period, the executive and the judicial powers of government were placed neither in the people, nor in those, who professed to receive them under the authority of the people. They were derived from a different and a foreign source: they were regulated by foreign maxims: they were directed to foreign purposes. Need we be surprised, that they were objects of aversion and distrust? Need we be surprised, that every occasion was seized for lessening their influence, and weakening their energy? On the other hand, our assemblies were chosen by ourselves: they were the guardians of our rights, the objects of our confidence, and the anchor of our political hopes. Every power, which could be placed in them, was thought to be safely placed: every extension of that power was considered as an extension of our own security.

At the revolution, the same fond predilection, and the same jealous dislike, existed and prevailed. The executive and the judicial as well as the legislative authority was now the child of the people; but, to the two former, the people behaved like stepmothers. The legislature was still discriminated by excessive partiality; and into its lap, every good and precious gift was profusely thrown.

Even at this time, people can scarcely devest themselves of those opposite prepossessions: they still hold, when, perhaps, they perceive it not, the language, which expresses them. In observations on this subject, we hear the legislature mentioned as the *people's representatives*. The distinction, intimated by concealed implication, though probably, not avowed upon reflection, is, that the executive and judicial powers are not connected with the people by a relation so strong, or near, or dear.

But it is high time that we should chastise our prejudices; and that we should look upon the different parts of government with a just and impartial eye. The executive and judicial powers are now drawn from the same source, are now animated by the same principles, and are now directed to the same ends, with the legislative authority: they who execute, and they who administer the laws, are as much the servants, and therefore as much the friends of the people, as they who make them. The character, and interest, and glory of the two former are as intimately and as necessarily connected with the happiness and prosperity of the people, as the character, and interest, and glory of the latter are. Besides, the execution of the law, and the administration of justice under the law, bring it home to the fortunes, and farms, and houses, and business of the people. Ought the executive or the judicial magistrates, then, to be considered as foreigners? ought they to be treated with a chilling indifference?

Having shown, that, on the principles of our new system, jealousies and prejudices concerning the executive and judicial departments ought to be discarded; let us now consider, in what manner those departments should be formed and constituted. We begin with the executive department.

The executive as well as the legislative power ought to be restrained. But there is a remarkable contrast between the proper modes of restraining them. The legislature, in order to be restrained, must be *divided*. The executive power, in order to be restrained, should be *one*. Unity in this department is at once a proof and an ingredient of safety and of energy in the operations of government.

The restraints on the legislative authority must, from its nature, be chiefly internal; that is, they must proceed from some part or division of itself. But the restraints on the executive power are external. These restraints are applied with greatest certainty, and with greatest efficacy, when the object of restraint is clearly ascertained. This is best done, when one object only, distinguished and responsible, is conspicuously held up to the view and examination of the publick.

In planning, forming, and arranging laws, deliberation is always becoming, and always useful. But in the active scenes of government, there are emergencies, in which the man, as, in other cases, the woman, who deliberates, is lost. Secrecy may be equally necessary as despatch. But, can either secrecy or despatch be expected, when, to every enterprise, and to every step in the progress of every enterprise, mutual communication, mutual consultation, and mutual agreement among men, perhaps of discordant views, of discordant tempers, and of discordant interests, are indispensably necessary? How much time will be consumed! and when it is consumed; how little business will be done! When the time is elapsed; when the business is unfinished; when the state is in distress, perhaps, on the verge of destruction; on whom shall we fix the blame? whom shall we select as the object of punishment?

Ruinous dissensions are not the only inconveniences resulting from a numerous executive body: it is equally liable to pernicious and intriguing combinations. When the first take place, the publick business is not done at all: when the last take place, it is done for mean or malicious purposes.

The appointment to offices is an important part of the executive authority. Much of the ease, much of the reputation, much of the energy, and much of the safety of the nation depends on judicious and impartial appointments. But are impartiality and fine discernment likely to predominate in a numerous executive body? In proportion to their own number, will be the number of their friends, favourites, and dependents. An office is to be filled. A person nearly connected, by some of the foregoing ties, with one of those who are to vote in filling it, is named as a candidate. His patron is under no necessity to take any part, particularly responsible, in his appointment. He may appear even cold and indifferent on the occasion. But he possesses an advantage, the value of which is well understood in bodies of this kind. Every member, who gives, on his account, a vote for his friend, will expect the return of a similar favour on the first convenient opportunity. In this manner, a reciprocal intercourse of partiality, of interestedness, of favouritism, perhaps of venality, is established; and, in no particular instance, is there a practicability of tracing the poison to its source. Ignorant, vicious, and prostituted characters are introduced into office; and some of those, who voted, and procured others to vote for them, are the first and loudest in expressing their astonishment, that the door of admission was ever opened to men of their infamous description. The suffering people are thus wounded and buffeted, like Homer's Ajax, in the dark; and have not even the melancholy satisfaction of knowing by whom the blows are given. Those who possess talents and virtues, which would reflect honour on office, will be reluctant to appear as candidates for appointments. If they should be brought into view; what weight will virtue, merit, and talents for office have, in a balance held and poized by partiality, intrigue, and chicane?

The person who nominates or makes appointments to offices, should be known. His own office, his own character, his own fortune should be responsible. He should be alike unfettered and unsheltered by counsellors. No constitutional stalking horse should be provided for him to conceal his turnings and windings, when they are too dark and too crooked to be exposed to publick view. Instead of the dishonourable intercourse, which I have already mentioned, an intercourse of a very different kind should be established — an intercourse of integrity and discernment on the part of the magistrate who appoints, and of gratitude and confidence on the part of the people, who will receive the benefit from his appointments. Appointments made and sanctioned in this highly respectable manner, will, like a fragrant and beneficent atmosphere, diffuse sweetness and gladness around those, to whom they are given. Modest merit will be beckoned to, in order to encourage her to come forward. Bare-faced impudence and unprincipled intrigue will receive repulse and disappointment, deservedly their portion.

If a contrary conduct should unfortunately be observed — and, unfortunately, a contrary conduct will be sometimes observed — it will be known by the citizens, whose conduct it is: and, if they are not seized with the only distemper incurable in a free government — the distemper of being wanting to themselves — they will, at the next general election, take effectual care, that the person, who has once shamefully abused their generous and unsuspecting confidence, shall not have it in his power to insult and injure them a second time, by the repetition of such an ungrateful return.

The observations, which I have made on the appointments to offices, will apply, with little variation, to the other powers and duties of the executive department.

When more than one person are engaged in the same enterprise, a difference of opinion, concerning the object or the means, is no improbable contingency. When the difference takes place among those of equal authority, where is the umpire to decide? A prevailing and undecided difference in sentiment, is the inauspicious parent of bitter and determined opposition in conduct. In business, which is merely deliberative, these differences may be concluded by a resolution or a vote: for, when a vote is taken, the majority is ascertained, and the business is done. But, in publick enterprises, the case is far otherwise. To the success of the enterprise, the zealous cooperation of the dissenting minority is no less indispensable, than that of the consenting majority. Is such cooperation to be expected? Would it be safe to calculate the motions of government upon an expectation, indeed, so extremely improbable? If we build on such a sandy foundation, will not the superstructure tumble in pieces, and bury, under its ruins, the dearest interests of the state?

If, on the other hand, the executive power of government is placed in the hands of one person, who is to direct all the subordinate officers of that department; is there not reason to expect, in his plans and conduct, promptitude, activity, firmness, consistency, and energy? These mark the proceedings of one man; at least, of one man, fit to be intrusted with the management of important publick affairs. May we not indulge, at least in imagination, the pleasing prospect, that this one man — the choice of those who are deeply interested in a proper choice — will be a man distinguished by his abilities? Will not those abilities pervade every part of his administration? Will they not diffuse their animating influence over the most distant corners of the nation? — May we not further indulge the pleased imagination in the agreeable prospect — in one instance, at least, it is realized by experience — that the publick choice will fall upon a man, in whom distinguished abilities will be joined and sublimed by distinguished virtues — on a man, who, on the necessary foundation of a private character, decent, respected, and dignified, will build all the great, and honest, and candid qualities, from which an elevated station derives its most beautiful lustre, and publick life its most splendid embellishments?

If these pleasing prospects should unhappily be blasted by a preposterous choice, and by the preposterous conduct of the magistrate chosen; still, at the next election, an effectual remedy can be applied to the mischief: and this remedy will be applied effectually, unless, as has been already intimated, the citizens should be wanting to themselves. For a people wanting to themselves, there is indeed no remedy in the political dispensary. From their power there is no appeal: to their errour there is no superiour principle of correction.

The third great division of the powers of government is the judicial authority. It is sometimes considered as a branch of the executive power; but inaccurately. When the decisions of courts of justice are made, they must, it is true, be executed; but the power of executing them is ministerial, not judicial. The judicial authority consists in applying, according to the principles of right and justice, the constitution and laws to facts and transactions in cases, in which the manner or principles of this application are disputed by the parties interested in them.

The very existence of a dispute is presumptive evidence, that the application is not altogether without intricacy or difficulty. When intricacy or difficulty takes place in the application, it cannot be properly made without the possession of skill in the science of jurisprudence, and the most unbiassed behaviour in the exercise of that skill. Clear heads, therefore, and honest hearts are essential to good judges.

As all controversies in the community respecting life, liberty, reputation, and property, must be influenced by their judgments; and as their judgments ought to be calculated not only to do justice, but also to give general satisfaction, to inspire general confidence, and to take even from disappointed suiters — for in every cause disappointment must fall on one side — the slightest pretence of complaint;[1] they ought to be placed in such a situation, as not only to be, but likewise to appear superiour to every extrinsick circumstance, which can be supposed to have the smallest operation upon their understandings or their inclinations. In their salaries, and in their offices, they ought to be completely independent: in other words, they should be removed from the most distant apprehension of being affected, in their judicial character and capacity, by any thing, except their own behaviour and its consequences.

"We are," says a very sensible writer on political subjects, "to look upon all the vast apparatus of government as having ultimately no other object or purpose, but the distribution of justice. All men are sensible of the necessity of justice to maintain peace and order; and all men are sensible of the necessity of peace and order for the maintenance of society." [m] "The pure, and wise, and equal administration of the laws," says Mr. Paley,[n] "forms the first end and blessing of social union." But how can society be maintained — how can a state expect to enjoy peace and order, unless the administration of justice is able and impartial? Can such an administration be expected, unless the judges can maintain dignified and independent characters? Can dignity and independence be expected from judges, who are liable to be tossed about by every veering gale of politicks, and who can be secured from destruction, only by dexterously swimming along with every successive tide of party? Is there not reason to fear, that in such a situation, the decisions of courts would cease to be the voice of law and justice, and would become the echo of faction and violence?

This is a subject, which most intimately concerns every one, who sets the least value upon his own safety, or that of his posterity. Our fortunes, our lives, our reputations, and our liberties are all liable to be affected by the judgments of the courts. How distressing and melancholy must the reflection be, that, while judges hold their salaries only at pleasure,

---

[1] Etiam quos contra statuit, æquos placatosque demisit; says Cicero of Brutus. [Even those against whom he made decisions, he sent away unruffled and placated. Cicero, *Orator ad M. Brutum*, 10, 34.]

[m] 1. Hume's Ess. 35.   [n] 2. Paley. 285.

and their commissions only for the term of a few years, our liberties, our fortunes, our reputations, and our lives may be sacrificed to a party, though we have done nothing to forfeit them to the law.

Though the foregoing great powers — legislative, executive, and judicial — are all necessary to a good government; yet it is of the last importance, that each of them be preserved distinct, and unmingled, in the exercise of its separate powers, with either or with both of the others. Here every degree of confusion in the plan will produce a corresponding degree of interference, opposition, combination, or perplexity in its execution.

Let us suppose the legislative and executive powers united in the same person: can liberty or security be expected? No. In the character of executive magistrate, he receives all the power, which, in the character of legislator, he thinks proper to give. May he not, then — and, if he may, will he not then — such is the undefined and undefinable charm of power — enact tyrannical laws to furnish himself with an opportunity of executing them in a tyrannical manner? Liberty and security in government depend not on the limits, which the rulers may please to assign to the exercise of their own powers, but on the boundaries, within which their powers are circumscribed by the constitution. He who is continually exposed to the lash of oppression, as well as he who is immediately under it, cannot be denominated free.

Let us suppose the legislative and judicial powers united: what would be the consequence? The lives, liberties, and properties of the citizens would be committed to arbitrary judges, whose decisions would, in effect, be dictated by their own private opinions, and would not be governed by any fixed or known principles of law. For though, as judges, they might be bound to observe those principles; yet, Proteus-like, they might immediately assume the form of legislators; and, in that shape, they might escape from every fetter and obligation of law.

Let us suppose a union of the executive and judicial powers: this union might soon be an overbalance for the legislative authority; or, if that expression is too strong, it might certainly prevent or destroy the proper and legitimate influences of that authority. The laws might be eluded or perverted; and the execution of them might become, in the hands of the magistrate or his minions, an engine of tyranny and injustice. Where and how is redress to be obtained? From the legislature? They make new laws to correct the mischief: but these new laws are to be executed by the same persons, and will be executed in the same manner as the former. Will redress be found in the courts of justice? In those courts, the very persons who were guilty of the oppression in their administration, sit as judges, to give a sanction to that oppression by their decrees. Nothing is more to be dreaded than maxims of law and reasons of state blended together by judicial authority. Among all the terrible instruments of arbitrary power, decisions of courts, whetted and guided and impelled by considerations of policy, cut with the keenest edge, and inflict the deepest and most deadly wounds.

Let us suppose, in the last place, all the three powers of government to be united in the same man or body of men: miserable indeed would this case be! This extent of misery, however, at least in Europe, is seldom experienced; because the power of judging is generally exercised by a separate department. But in Turkey, where all the three powers are joined in the Sultan's person, his slaves are crushed under the insupportable burthen of oppression and tyranny. In some of the governments of Italy, these three powers are also united. In such there is less liberty than in the European monarchies: and their governments are obliged to have recourse to as violent measures to support themselves, as even that of the Turks. At Venice, where an aristocracy, jealous and tyrannical, absorbs every power, behold the state inquisitors, and the lion's mouth, at all times open for the secret accusations of spies and informers. In what a situation must the wretched subjects be under such a government, all the powers of which are leagued, in awful combination, against the peace and tranquillity of their minds!

But further; each of the great powers of government should be independent as well as distinct. When we say this; it is necessary — since the subject is of primary consequence in the science of government — that our meaning be fully understood, and accurately defined. For this position, like every other, has its limitations; and it is important to ascertain them.

The independency of each power consists in this, that its proceedings, and the motives, views, and principles, which produce those proceedings, should be free from the remotest influence, direct or indirect, of either of the other two powers. But further than this, the independency of each power ought not to extend. Its proceedings should be formed without restraint, but, when they are once formed, they should be subject to control.

We are now led to discover, that between these three great powers of government, there ought to be a mutual dependency, as well as a mutual independency. We have described their independency: let us now describe their dependency. It consists in this, that the proceedings of each, when they come forth into action and are ready to affect the whole, are liable to be examined and controlled by one or both of the others.

So far are these different qualities of mutual dependency and mutual independency from opposing or destroying each other, that, without one, the other could not exist. Whenever the independency of one, or more than one, is lost, the mutual dependency of the others is, that moment, lost likewise: it is changed into a constant dependency of that one part on two; or, as the case may be, of those two parts on one.

An example may illustrate the foregoing propositions. They cannot be explained too fully. The congress is intrusted with the legislative power of the United States. In preparing bills, in debating them, in passing them, in refusing to pass them, their resolutions and proceedings should be uncontrolled and uninfluenced. Here is the independency of the legislative power. But after the proceedings of the legislature are finished, so far as they depend on it, they are sent to be examined, and are subjected to a given degree of control by the head of the executive department. Here is the dependency of the legislative power. It is subject also to another given degree of control by the judiciary department, whenever the laws, though in fact passed, are found to be contradictory to the constitution.

The salutary consequence of the mutual dependency of the great powers of government is, that if one part should, at any time, usurp more power than the constitution gives, or make an improper use of its constitutional power, one or both of the other parts may correct the abuse, or may check the usurpation.

The total disjunction of these powers would, in the end, produce that very union, against which it seems to provide. The legislature would soon become tyrannical, and would assume to itself the rights of the executive and judicial powers.

The important conclusion to be drawn from the premises, which we have established, is, that, in government, the perfection of the whole depends on the balance of the parts, and the balance of the parts consists in the independent exercise of their separate powers, and, when their powers are separately exercised, then in their mutual influence and operation on one another. Each part acts and is acted upon, supports and is supported, regulates and is regulated by the rest.

It might be supposed, that these powers, thus mutually checked and controlled, would remain in a state of inaction. But there is a necessity for movement in human affairs; and these powers are forced to move, though still to move in concert. They move, indeed, in a line of direction somewhat different from that, which each, acting by itself, would have taken; but, at the same time, in a line partaking of the natural direction of each, and formed out of the natural directions of the whole — the true line of publick liberty and happiness.

The works of human invention are progressive; and frequently are not completed, till after a slow and lengthened series of gradual improvements, remotely distant from one another both in place and in time. To the theory and practice of government, this observation is applicable with peculiar justness and peculiar force. In this science, few opportunities have been given to the human mind of indulging itself in easy and un-restrained investigation: still fewer opportunities have offered of verify-ing and correcting investigation by experiment. An age — a succession of ages — elapses, before a system of jurisprudence rises from its first rude beginnings. When we have made a little progress, and look forward; a few eminences in prospect are fondly supposed to form the greatest elevation, which we shall be obliged to ascend. But these, once gained, disclose, behind them, new and superiour degrees of excellence, yet un-attained. In beginning and continuing the pursuit of the arduous paths, through which this science leads us, we may well adopt the language of the philosophick poet;

> So pleas'd, at first, the tow'ring Alps we try,
> Mount o'er the vales, and seem to tread the sky.
> Th' eternal snows appear already past,
> And the first clouds and mountains seem the last:
> But these attain'd, we tremble to survey
> The growing labours of the lengthen'd way;
> Th' increasing prospect tires our wand'ring eyes,
> Hills peep o'er hills, and Alps on Alps arise! *

If the discoveries in government are difficult and slow, how much more arduous must it be to obtain, in practice, the advantage of those discoveries, after they have been made! Of some governments, the foun-dation has been laid in necessity; of others, in fraud; of others, in force; of how few, in deliberate and discerning choice! If, in their commence-ments, they have been so unpropitious to the principles of freedom, and to the means of happiness; shall we wonder, that, in their progress, they have been equally unfavourable to advances in virtue and excellence?

Let us ransack the records of history: in all our researches, how few fair instances shall we be able to find, in which a government has been formed, whose end has been the happiness of those, for whom it was designed! how few fair instances shall we find, in which such a govern-ment has been administered with a steady direction towards that end!

To all these circumstances, we must add others, which show still fur-ther the numerous and the strong obstacles that lie in the way of im-provement in jurisprudence. Government, founded in improper prin-ciples, and directed to improper objects, has a natural and powerful bias, both upon those who rule, and upon those who are ruled. Its bias upon the first will occasion no surprise: its bias upon the second, however surprising, is not, perhaps, less efficacious. How often have the vassals of absolute monarchy conceived their own dignity and happiness to be

* [The philosophick poet is, of course, Pope. The lines are from *An Essay on Criticism*.]

involved in the glory of their monarch! How often have they, in pursuit of projects for the accomplishment of his capricious desires, discovered a degree of courage and enthusiasm, worthy of a nobler object and a better cause! If such is the effect produced upon their conduct; will an inferiour effect be produced on their sentiments? Hence the principles of despotism become the principles of a whole nation, blinded and degraded by its pernicious influence.

But let us suppose that the light of liberty, at last, breaks in upon them; how slow must its progress; how feeble, for a long time, must its energy be! Power, splendour, influence, prejudice, fashion, all stand arranged in opposition to its operations.

Let us enlarge the sphere of our conjecture further, and suppose, that, notwithstanding all the efforts of opposition, the principles and doctrines of freedom are successfully propagated and established; yet how many and how formidable are the barriers, that remain to be surmounted, before those principles and doctrines can be carried successfully into practice? The friends of freedom, we shall suppose, are unanimous in their sentiments; does the same unanimity prevail with regard to their measures? does it prevail still farther with regard to the time and manner of pursuing them? In all these particulars, is unanimity attended with discretion, on one hand, and with decision, on the other? A failure in one circumstance, is a failure in all. Have not centuries passed without a single auspicious juncture, in which all, conjoined and cooperating, could have succeeded?

When we revolve, when we compare, when we combine the remarks, which we have been now making; when we take a slight glance of others, which might be offered; we shall be at no loss to account for the slow and small progress, which, after a lapse of ages, has been made in the science and practice of government.

Among the ancient political writers, no more than three regular forms of government were known and allowed. The first is that, in which the supreme power is lodged in the hands of a single person. This they denominated a monarchy. The second is that, in which the supreme power is vested in a select assembly, the members of which either fill up by election the vacancies of their own body, or succeed to their places by inheritance, property, tenure of lands, or in respect of some personal right or qualification. To this they gave the appellation of aristocracy. The third is that, in which the supreme power remains with the people at large, and is exercised either collectively, or by representation. On this they bestowed the name of democracy.

To each of these simple forms, conveniences and inconveniences, good and bad qualities are attached. In a democracy, publick virtue and purity of intention are likely to be found; but its counsels are often improvident, and the execution of them as frequently weak. In an aristocracy, we expect wisdom formed by education and experience; but, on the other hand, we may expect jealousies and dissensions among the nobles, and oppression of the lower orders. In a monarchy, there are strength and vigour; but there is danger, that they will not be employed for the happiness and prosperity of the state. A democracy is best calculated to direct the end of the laws; an aristocracy, to direct the means of attaining that end; a monarchy, to carry those means into execution.

The ancients considered all other species of governments as either corruptions of these three simple forms, or as reducible to some one of them. They had no idea of combining all the three together, and of uniting the advantages resulting from each. Cicero,[o] indeed, seems to have indulged a fond speculative opinion, that a government formed of the three kinds, properly blended and tempered, would, of all, be the best constituted. But this opinion was treated as visionary by his countrymen; and by Tacitus,[p] one of the wisest of them.

The example of Great Britain, however, has evinced that the sentiments of Cicero merited a very different reception; and that, if they did not point to the highest degree of excellence, they pointed, at least, to substantial improvement.

The government of that nation is composed of monarchical, aristocratical, and democratical parts. It possesses — we freely and with pleasure acknowledge — it possesses advantages over all that have preceded it: in dignity and in duration, in the maintenance of liberty, both publick and private, it has stood preeminent. But has it reached the lofty summit of perfection? In the race of excellence, has it gained a goal, which cannot be surpassed? Is it entitled, as, in less enlightened times, the columns of Hercules were thought to be, to the proud inscription of "ne plus ultra?"

For the western world, new and rich discoveries in jurisprudence have been reserved. We have found that, in order to arrive, in this first of human sciences, at a point of perfection hitherto unattained, it is not necessary to intermix the different species of government. We have discovered, that one of them — the best and purest — that, in which the supreme power remains with the people at large, is capable of being formed, arranged, proportioned, and organized in such a manner, as to exclude the inconveniences, and to secure the advantages of all the three. On the basis of goodness, we erect the pillars of wisdom and strength.

The formation and establishment of constitutions are an immense practical improvement, introduced by the Americans into the science of government and jurisprudence. By the invigorating and overruling energy of a constitution, the force and direction of the government are preserved

[o] Frag. de rep. l. 2.   [p] Ann. l. 4.

and regulated; and its movements are rendered uniform, strong, and safe.

It is proper that the nature and distinguishing characteristicks of a constitution should be clearly stated and explained. The sentiments and expressions, even of celebrated writers upon this subject, are uncommonly inaccurate and obscure.

By the term constitution, I mean that supreme law, made or ratified by those in whom the sovereign power of the state resides, which prescribes the manner, according to which the state wills that the government should be instituted and administered. From this constitution the government derives its power: by this constitution the power of government must be directed and controlled: of this constitution no alteration can be made by the government; because such an alteration would destroy the foundation of its own authority.

As to the people, however, in whom the sovereign power resides, the case is widely different, and stands upon widely different principles. From their authority the constitution originates: for their safety and felicity it is established: in their hands it is as clay in the hands of the potter: they have the right to mould, to preserve, to improve, to refine, and to finish it as they please. If so; can it be doubted, that they have the right likewise to change it? A majority of the society is sufficient for this purpose; and if there be nothing in the change, which can be considered as contrary to the act of original association, or to the intention of those who united under it; all are bound to conform to the resolution of the majority. If the act of original association be infringed, or the intention of those who united under it be violated; the minority are still obliged to suffer the majority to do as they think proper; but are not obliged to submit to the new government. They have a right to retire, to sell their lands, and to carry off their effects.

It may, perhaps, be asked — why is so much pains taken to prove and illustrate a principle, which, when detached from adventitious circumstances, and exhibited in its undisguised appearance, is so obvious, that few will be found disposed, in direct terms, to refuse their assent to its truth? Has it been denied, that those, who have a right to make, have a right to alter what they have made?

In England it has been denied: the successour of Sir William Blackstone in the Vinerian chair expresses himself upon this subject in the following manner. "However the historical fact may be of a social contract, government ought to be, and is generally considered as founded on consent, tacit or express, on a real or *quasi* compact. This theory is a material basis of political rights; and, as a theoretical point, is not difficult to be maintained. For what gives any legislature a right to act, where no express consent can be shown? what, but immemorial usage? and what is the intrinsick force of immemorial usage, in establishing this fundamental or any other law, but that it is evidence of common acquiescence and consent? Not," adds he, "that such consent is subsequently revocable, at the will even of all the subjects of the state, for that would be making a part of the community equal in power to the whole originally, and superiour to the rulers thereof, after their establishment." q "I am far," says he, in another place, "from maintaining, that any consent, tacit or express, is essential to induce the duty of subjection from individuals born under an established government." r The evident consequence of these positions is, that though the great and animating principle of consent is considered as necessary to the first formation of government, yet it is by no means necessary in the successive periods of its establishment. The theory is admitted; but the continued right to practise according to that theory is denied. In other words, an established government is treated as superiour to those, or, at least, to others possessing all the rights of those, who originally formed its establishment.

In America, indeed, the doctrine, which I have taken some pains to prove and illustrate, has not been denied, in words; yet unwearied attempts have, on more occasions than one, been made to elude its operation, and to destroy its force.

Besides; it is of high import, that the great principles of society and government should not only be known and recognised, but also that they should be so maturely considered and estimated, as, at last, to make a practical impression, deep and habitual, upon the publick mind. A proper regard to the original and inherent and continued power of the society to change its constitution, will prevent mistakes and mischiefs of very different kinds. It will prevent giddy inconstancy: it will prevent unthinking rashness: it will prevent unmanly languor.

Some have appeared apprehensive, that the introduction of this principle into our political creed would open the door for the admission of levity and unsteadiness in all our political establishments. The very reverse will be its effect. Let the uninterrupted power to change be admitted and fully understood, and the exercise of it will not be lightly or wantonly assumed. There is a *vis inertiae* in publick bodies as well as in matter; and, if left to their natural propensities, they will not be moved without a proportioned propelling cause. If, indeed, the prevailing opinion should be, that the society had not the regular power of altering, on every proper opportunity, its political institutions; an occasion, favourable in appearance, but deceptive in reality, might be suddenly fixed on, as a season for action. It might be allowed not to be, in every respect, unexceptionable; but when, it would be urged, will another, less exceptionable, present itself? The consequence would be, that the juncture, however unpropitious, would be seized with premature and improvident

q El. Jur. (4to.) 22.　　r Id. 23.

zeal, in order to accomplish the meditated change. Disappointments, arising from the want of due preparations, would take place; disasters, very
prejudicial to the publick and to individuals, would be produced; and the
enterprise would prove abortive, merely because it was pursued at an
unfit time, and under unfit circumstances.

On the other hand, how often and how long has degrading despotism
reigned triumphant, because the enfeebled and desponding sufferers
under it have not known, or, having once known, have, at last, forgotten,
that they retain, during every moment of their slavery, the right of rescu-
ing themselves from the proud and bloated authors and instruments of
their oppression! Hesitation about the right will be attended with a corresponding hesitation about the expediency of redress. A revolution,
surrounded, in prospect, so thickly with doubts, uncertainties, and
apprehensions, will wear a gloomy and formidable appearance; and the
miserable patients of tyranny will languish out their lives in excruciat-
ing and accumulated distress, merely because they will not undergo one
short operation, which would not be more painful than their disease, and
which would forever deliver them from all its ills and consequences.

The importance of a good constitution will, on reflection and examination, be easily conceived, deeply felt, and readily acknowledged. On the
constitution will depend the beneficence, the wisdom, and the energy, or
the injustice, the folly, and the weakness of the government and laws.
On the good or bad qualities of the government and laws, will depend
the prosperity or the decline of the state. On the same good or bad qualities will depend, on one hand, the excellence and happiness, and, on the
other, the depravity and infelicity of the citizens.

A state well constituted, well proportioned, and well conducted feels
her own importance, her own power, and her own vigour. Her importance, her power, and her vigour are seen by others, as well as felt by
herself. What are the consequences? Internal firmness; external respect:
the confidence of her citizens; the esteem of foreigners. What, again, are
the consequences of these? Peace; and dignity and security in the enjoyment of peace.

Let us reverse the scene — let us view a state ill constructed, ill proportioned, and ill directed. She may exhaust every stratagem, and employ
every art, to cover her weakness and her defects: but can she destroy
her own knowledge of them? will her arts and stratagems be successful
in concealing them from others? The very pains taken to conceal, will
facilitate the discovery, and enhance its importance. Her imperfections,
half seen behind the veil drawn over them, will appear greater, than if
fully exposed. What will be the result of this situation, thus felt and thus
viewed? Fluctuation in her councils; irresolution in her measures; pusil-
lanimity in her attempts to execute them: the distrust and alarm of

her own citizens: the contempt, and the unfriendly designs produced by the contempt, of the nations around her: the evils attending war, or the evils, little inferiour, attending a nation, which is equally incapable of securing peace and of repelling hostilities.

The influence of a good or bad constitution is not less powerful on the citizens, considered as individuals, than on the community, considered as a body politick. It is only under a good constitution that liberty — the precious gift of heaven — can be enjoyed and be secure. This exalting quality comprehends, among other things, the manly and generous exercise of our powers; and includes, as its most delicious ingredient, the happy consciousness of being free. What energetick, what delightful sensations must this enlivening principle diffuse over the whole man! His mind is roused and elevated: his heart is rectified and enlarged: dignity appears in his countenance, and animation in his every gesture and word. He knows that if he is innocent and upright, the laws and constitution of his country will ensure him protection. He trusts, that, if to innocence and integrity he adds faithful and meritorious services, his country, in addition to protection, will confer upon him honourable testimonies of her esteem. Hence he derives a cheerful and habitual confidence, this pervades and invigorates his conduct, and spreads a noble air over every part of his character. Hence, too, he is inspired with ardent affection for the publick: this stimulates and refines his strongest patriotick exertions. His heart, his head, his hands, his tongue, his pen, his fortune; all he is, and all he has, are devoted to his country's cause, and to his country's call.

A person of a very different description appears in view — pale, trembling, emaciated, faltering in his steps, not daring to look upwards, but, with marked anxiety, rolling his eager eyes on every side. Who is he? He is the slave of a bad constitution and a tyrannical government. He is afraid to act, or speak, or look. He knows that his actions and his words, however guarded, may be construed to be criminal: he knows that even his looks and countenance may be considered as the signs and evidences of treacherous thoughts and treasonable conspiracies; and he knows that the suspicion of his masters, upon any of these points, may be fatal: for he knows, that he is at the mercy of those, who, upon the slightest suspicion, may seize or hang him — who may do whatever they please with him, and with all those who are dear to him. What effects must this man's situation produce upon his mind and temper? Can his views be great or exalted? No. Such views, instead of being encouraged, would give offence; and he is well aware what would follow. Can openness and candour beam from his soul? No. Such light would be hateful to his masters; it must be extinguished. Can he feel affection for his country, its constitution, or its government? No. His country is his prison; its constitution is his curse; and its government is a rod of oppression, held continually over his head. What must this man be? He must be abject, fawning, dastardly, selfish, disingenuous, deceitful, cunning, base — but why proceed in the disgusting detail? He must receive the stamp of servility fully impressed on his person, on his mind, and on his manners.

Such are the influences of a constitution, good or bad, upon the political body: such are its influences upon the members, of which that body is composed. Surely, then, the first consideration of a state, and its most important duty, is to form that constitution, which will be best in itself; and best adapted to the genius, and character, and manners of her citizens. Such a constitution will be the basis of her preservation, her happiness, and her perfection.

XI

COMPARISON OF THE CONSTITUTION OF THE UNITED STATES, WITH THAT OF GREAT BRITAIN

THE British constitution has been celebrated in the most sublime and in the most elaborate strains by poets, by orators, by lawyers, and by statesmen. "As for us Britons," says the elegant Shaftesbury, comparing them, in the spirit of a fond and a just preference, with many other nations, "as for us Britons, thank heaven, we have a better sense of government, delivered to us from our ancestors. We have a notion of a publick, and a constitution; how a legislative and how an executive is modelled. We understand weight and measure in this kind; and can reason justly on the balance of power and property. The maxims we draw from hence, are as evident as those in mathematicks. Our increasing knowledge shows us every day, more and more, what common sense is in politicks." [a]

My Lord Bolingbroke,[b] in his masterly and animated style, represents this constitution as "a noble fabrick, the pride of Britain, the envy of her neighbours, raised by the labour of so many centuries, repaired at the expense of so many millions, and cemented by such a profusion of blood —a fabrick, which has resisted the efforts of so many races of giants."

You will be surprised on being told, that, if the nature and characteristick qualities, which I have described, are the true nature and characteristick qualities of a constitution; no such thing as a constitution, properly so called, is known in Great Britain. What is known, in that kingdom, under that name, instead of being the controller and the guide, is the creature and the dependent of the legislative power. The supreme power of the people is a doctrine unknown and unacknowledged in the British system of government. The omnipotent authority of parliament is the dernier resort, to which recourse is had in times and in doctrines of uncommon difficulty and importance. The natural, the inherent, and the predominating rights of the citizens are considered as so dangerous and so desperate a resource, as to be inconsistent with the arrangements of any government, which does or can exist.

---

[a] 1. Shaft. 108.   [b] Diss. on Part. let. 10. p. 151. 152.

The order of things in Britain is exactly the reverse of the order of things in the United States. Here, the people are masters of the government: there, the government is master of the people.

That, on this very interesting subject of contrast, you may be enabled to judge for yourselves, I shall lay before you some passages from British writers of high reputation. From those passages, you can draw your own inferences.

"Most of those," says Mr. Paley, "who treat of the British constitution, consider it as a scheme of government formally planned and contrived by our ancestors, in some certain era of our national history; and as set up in pursuance of such regular plan and design. Something of this sort is secretly supposed, or referred to, in the expressions of those, who speak of the principles of the constitution, of bringing back the constitution to its first principles, of restoring it to its original purity, or primitive model. Now this appears to me an erroneous conception of the subject. No such plan was ever formed; consequently no such first principles, original model, or standard exist.

"The constitution is one principal division, head, section, or title of the code of publick laws, distinguished from the rest only by the particular nature, or superiour importance of the subject, of which it treats. Therefore the terms *constitutional* and *unconstitutional*, mean *legal* and *illegal*. The distinction and the ideas, which these terms denote, are founded in the same authority with the law of the land upon any other subject; and to be ascertained by the same inquiries. The system of English jurisprudence is made up of acts of parliament, of decisions of courts of law, and of immemorial usages; consequently, these are the principles of which the constitution itself consists; the sources, from which all our knowledge of its nature and limitations is to be deduced, and the authorities, to which all appeal ought to be made, and by which every constitutional doubt or question can alone be decided. This plain and intelligible definition is the more necessary to be preserved in our thoughts, as some writers upon the subject absurdly confound what is constitutional with what is expedient; pronouncing forthwith a measure to be unconstitutional, which they adjudge in any respect to be detrimental or dangerous; whilst others again ascribe a kind of transcendent authority, or mysterious sanctity to the constitution, as if it was founded in some higher original, than that, which gives force and obligation to the ordinary laws and statutes of the realm, or were inviolable on any other account than its intrinsick utility.

"An act of parliament, in England, can never be unconstitutional, in the strict and proper acceptation of the term: in a lower sense it may; viz. when it militates with the spirit, contradicts the analogy, or defeats the provision of other laws, made to regulate the form of government.

Even that flagitious abuse of their trust, by which a parliament of Henry the eighth conferred upon the king's proclamation the authority of law, was unconstitutional only in this latter sense." [c]

Sir William Blackstone uses the term, constitution, as commensurate with the law of England. "Of a constitution," says he, "so wisely contrived, so strongly raised, and so highly finished, it is hard to speak with that praise, which is justly and severely its due. It hath been the endeavour of these Commentaries, however the execution may have succeeded, to examine its solid foundations, to mark out its extensive plan, to explain the use and distribution of its parts, and from the harmonious concurrence of those several parts to demonstrate the elegant proportion of the whole." [d]

Mr. Paley uses the word in a more confined and, perhaps, a more proper sense, when applied to Great Britain; as meaning that part of the law, which relates to the designation and form of the legislature; the rights and functions of the several parts of the legislative body; the construction, office, and jurisdiction of the courts of justice.[e] In this sense I shall use the term, when I speak of the British constitution. And, in this sense, the superiority of our constitution to that of Great Britain will eminently appear from the comparison, which we now institute, between their principles, their construction, their proportion, and their properties.

The extension of the theory and practice of representation through all the different departments of the state is another very important acquisition made, by the Americans, in the science of jurisprudence and government. To the ancients, this theory and practice seem to have been altogether unknown. To this moment, the representation of the people is not the sole principle of any government in Europe. Great Britain boasts, and she may boast with justice, that, by the admission of representation, she has introduced a valuable improvement into the science of jurisprudence. The improvement is certainly valuable, so far as it extends; but it is by no means sufficiently extensive.

Is the principle of representation introduced into the executive department of the constitution of Great Britain? This has never been attempted. Before the revolution of one thousand six hundred and eighty eight, some of the kings claimed to hold their thrones by divine, others by hereditary right; and even at the important era of that revolution, nothing farther was endeavoured or obtained, than the recognition of certain parts of an original contract, supposed, at some former period, to have been made between the king and the people. A contract seems to exclude, rather than to imply delegated power. The judges of Great Britain are appointed by the crown. The judicial department, therefore, does not depend upon a representation of the people, even in its remotest degree. Is

[c] 2. Paley. 203. 205.   [d] 4. Bl. Com. 435. 436.   [e] 2. Paley. 203.

representation a principle operating in the legislative department of Great Britain? It is; but it is not a predominating principle; though it may serve as a very salutary check. The legislature consists of three branches, the king, the lords, and the commons. Of these, only the latter are supposed, by the constitution, to represent the authority of the people. We now see clearly, to what a narrow corner of the British government the principle of representation is confined. In no other government in Europe does it extend farther: in none, I believe, so far. The American States enjoy the glory and the happiness of diffusing this vital principle throughout all the different divisions and departments of the government. Representation is the chain of communication between the people and those, to whom they have committed the important charge of exercising the delegated powers necessary for the administration of publick affairs. This chain may consist of one link, or of more links than one; but it should always be sufficiently strong and discernible.

As, in England, the house of commons alone represents, or is supposed to represent, the people at large; so, in that house alone are we to look for the constitutional and authoritative expression of the people's will. But even in that house, this will is but very feebly and very imperfectly expressed; for the representation in that house is very unequal and inadequate; and it is protracted through a period of time much too long.

It is very unequal and inadequate. In England, we may, from information which seems to be unexceptionable, compute six hundred and thirty nine thousand taxable inhabitants. This number would assign one representative to twelve hundred constituents. But the fact is, that a number not exceeding six thousand are sufficient to return more than one half of the members of the house of commons. This is in the proportion of twenty three constituents for one representative. The consequence is, that a majority of the house of commons may be returned by less than a fiftieth part of the constituents, that ought to be requisite for returning that majority. What is the situation of the other forty nine parts? Need I repeat, this representation is very unequal and inadequate? As to the number of electors, it certainly is.

It may, perhaps, be expected, that this deficiency in their numbers is, in some measure at least, compensated by the worth, the respectability, the independence, and the enlarged influence of the individuals, who are empowered to vote. To this expectation, the fact is directly reverse. That small part are the most dependent and the least respectable part of the commons of England. They are emphatically styled the *rotten* part of the constitution. In dignity and respectability, therefore, as well as in numbers, the representation of the commons of England is extremely inadequate and unequal.

The softness of a whisper may sometimes communicate sound with a more distinct impression than the report of a cannon. Sir William Blackstone admits that "if any alteration might be wished or suggested in the present frame of parliament, it should be in favour of a more complete representation of the people." [f]

The inequality of the representation of the people of England is evinced, in the most striking manner, by another comparative view, in which it may be placed. Ninety two members represent the landed interest; about one hundred members represent the great cities and towns; above three hundred members represent small and inconsiderable boroughs.

But further; the representation of the commons is not renewed by them at periods sufficiently near one another. Parliaments were at first annual; they were afterwards triennial; now they are septennial. This last period is surely too long. The members will be apt to forget the source from which they have received their powers. Every government, in order to preserve its freedom, has frequent need of some new provisions in favour of that freedom. Such new provisions are most likely to spring from those, who have been recently animated by the inspiration of the people.

A representation, inadequate, unequal, and continued too long, is inconsistent with the principles of free government: for by such a representation, it is probable that the sense of the people will be misapprehended, or misrepresented, or despised. This probability has, in England, been converted into fact and experience. During many years past, the politicks of the house of commons have been moved by the direction of the court and ministers, and not by the sense of the nation. Numerous and striking instances of this might be produced. But I can only point to those paths of investigation; I cannot pursue them.

How immensely different is the state of representation in the house of commons, from that which is established in the United States. With us, every freeman who possesses an attachment to the community, and a common interest with his fellow citizens, and is in a situation not necessarily dependent, is entitled to a vote for members. With us, no preference is given to any party, any interest, any situation, any profession, or any description over another. With us, those votes, equally, freely, and universally diffused, will have their frequent and powerful operation and influence. With us, therefore, it may be expected, that the voice of the representatives will be the faithful echo of the voice of the people.

Having seen that the house of representatives of the United States will not suffer by being compared, in its proportion and in its duration, with

[f] 1. Bl. Com. 172.

the house of commons of Great Britain; let us proceed to a comparison of the senate with the house of lords.

That house is divided into two orders; the lords spiritual, and the lords temporal. The lords spiritual are composed of the archbishops and bishops. All these hold, or are supposed to hold, certain ancient baronies under the crown; and, in right of succession to those baronies, which were inalienable from their respective dignities, they obtained their seats in the house of lords. With the other lords they intermix in their votes; and the majority of such intermixture binds both estates. The lords temporal consist of all the peers of the realm, by whatever title of nobility they are distinguished. Of these, some sit by descent, as all ancient peers; others, by creation, as all new made ones; others, since the union with Scotland, by election of the nobility of that country. The number of peers is indefinite; and may be increased at the pleasure of the crown.

The writers on the British constitution view the distinctions of rank and honours as necessary in every well governed state, in order to reward such as are eminent for their services to the publick; exciting thus a laudable ardour in others; and diffusing, by such ardour, life and vigour through the whole community. A body of nobility, they say, creates and preserves that gradual scale of dignity, which proceeds from the peasant to the prince; rising, like a pyramid, from a broad foundation, and diminishing as it rises, till, at last, it terminates in a single point. It is this ascending and contracting proportion, they conclude, which adds stability to any government.

That eminent services ought to be rewarded, that devotion to the publick ought to receive the warmest encouragement, will not be denied here. But does this encouragement — do these rewards grow only in an aristocratick soil? Has republicanism no rewards or honours for her meritorious sons? She is accused, it is true, of ingratitude. But the facts, which have given rise to the accusation, have not, we hope, been owing peculiarly to her disposition or principles, but have sprung from a spirit of envy and malevolence, predominating, alas! too much in all communities, and discovering too often more activity and zeal in doing mischief, than the opposite qualities display in doing good. Besides; instances have not been unfrequent, in which publick gratitude has been expressed by commonwealths, most generously and most effectually, both in words and actions. It is true, that the publick testimonials of gratitude and esteem have no hereditary descent among republicans; because it is true, that no regular course of descent is established in the qualities and services which merit them.

The nobility, we are told, are necessary in the British constitution, to form a barrier against the mutual encroachments of the king and of the people. In the government of the United States, separate orders of men do not exist; no encroachments of this kind can take place; and there is no occasion to provide barriers against them. The pyramid of government may certainly be raised with all the graces of fair proportion, and also with the more substantial qualities of firmness and strength, although the materials, of which it is constructed, be not an assemblage of different and dissimilar kinds. These are more likely to recall to our minds the composition and the fate of a heterogeneous and disjointed piece of workmanship, so well described by the prophet Daniel. But to drop the idea of approving and disapproving by metaphor; we find that, in Britain, there being two orders, the king and the people, it was necessary that there should be a third, to hold the balance between them. But different orders, we apprehend, may well be dispensed with in a good and perfect government.

Wisdom, it is said, is found in an aristocracy. Why? Because its members are formed by education, and matured by experience, for the discharge of their duty. Education and experience, it will be readily allowed, are excellent for forming and finishing the habits and characters of statesmen. But on whom will the best education be probably bestowed? On whom will it be likely to produce the strongest and most beneficial influence? On him, whose parents know, and who himself will soon know, that, whether he receive it or not, or, receiving it, whether he improve it or not, still he must succeed to all the preeminences of aristocratick power? — or on him, whose parents foresee, and who himself will be soon sensible, that his prospects of success in publick life must depend on the qualities, acquired as well as natural, which he can bring into publick life along with him? Whom will experience best teach? Him, who sees that, as estimable acquirements have not been necessary for introducing him to the dignities of the state, they are as little necessary for continuing him in the enjoyment of them? or him, who is aware, that, as the good opinion of his fellow citizens concerning his talents and virtues procured him admission to the honours of his country, his continuance in the possession of those honours must depend on his justifying that good opinion, on his improving it into confidence, and on his showing, by a progressive display of services and accomplishments, that his conduct becomes daily more and more worthy of publick sanction and esteem? He is, it is true, in some measure, dependent: but his dependence is not of an irrational or illiberal kind. It is of a kind, which, instead of depressing, will rouse and elevate the temper and character.

We thus seize the strong outworks of aristocracy, and successfully turn on herself her most formidable batteries.

In drawing a contrast between the executive magistrates of the United States and Great Britain, I wave every degree of comparison with regard to some of the characters applied to the latter, in the description given of him by the British law and the British lawyers. They ascribe to him certain qualities as inherent in his royal capacity, distinct from and superiour to those of any other individual in the nation: they assign to him certain properties of a great and transcendent nature: by these means, it is thought, the people will consider him in the light of a superiour being; and will pay him that awful respect, which may enable him, with greater ease, to carry on the business of government. The law clothes him with the attributes of sovereignty, of ubiquity, and of absolute perfection: he can do no wrong: he can think no wrong: in him no folly — in him no weakness can be found: royal wisdom is ascribed to the infant of a span long, as much as to the experienced sire, who has seen three generations: the man dies; but the king satisfies the wish of eastern adulation: he lives for ever!

Prepossessions long entertained, habits long formed, and practices long established may, possibly, have interwoven those ideas into the system of the British constitution in such a manner, that it would be difficult now to disentangle them, without tearing or injuring some more useful parts of the fabrick. But in forming a new system, it is certainly neither necessary nor proper to introduce into it qualities and pretensions so disproportioned to the sober consideration and management of human affairs. Power may be conferred without mystery; and may be exercised, for every wise and benevolent purpose, without challenging attributes, to which our frail and imperfect state of humanity stands in daily and marked contradiction.

On what foundation is the monarchical part of the British constitution supported? Are the rights of the monarch supposed, by it, to flow from the authority of those, over whom he is placed? Is the majesty of the people recognised as the august parent of the prerogative of the prince? No. Such principles have never received the sanction of the British constitution. Concerning the origin of the powers and rights of their monarchs, very different opinions have, at different times, been entertained and propagated. The dark foundations of conquest have, in some reigns, been uncovered and exposed to view. Divine right has, in others, been impiously summoned to sanctify claims and pretensions, too exorbitant to have derived their source from human authority. At some periods, the title to the crown has been supposed to be founded on hereditary right, a right derived, by succession, from a long list of ancestors. But, in tracing this succession upwards, we necessarily come, at last, in fact, or in idea, to some one, who was the first possessor. How did he acquire his possession? The solution, now received, of this question, is, that it was in consequence of an original contract, made, at some former distant period, between the king and the people. The terms of this contract have, indeed, been the subject of frequent and doubtful disputation. At the revolution, however, some of them were reduced to a certainty: and the existence of the contract itself was explicitly recognised. But a contract does not imply the idea of *derivative* power; it seems rather to imply an equality between the parties contracting. Besides; the crown, on whomever it may be devolved by virtue of this contract, still retains its descendible quality, and becomes hereditary in the wearer. Even in this enlightened century, the most determined champions of liberty in Great Britain have not instituted the claim, that the power of every part of government, the monarchical not excepted, should be founded on the authority of the people. Hear in what a humiliating manner one of their boldest and most energetick writers has described their power on this interesting subject. "The British liberties are not the grants of princes. They are original rights, conditions of original contracts, coequal with the prerogative, and coeval with the government." [g]

How different is this language, and how different are these sentiments, from the language and sentiments, which, under our improved systems of government, we are entitled to hold and express! We have no occasion to enter a caveat against the supposition, that our liberties are the grants of princes. With us, the powers of magistrates, call them by whatever name you please, are the grants of the people. With us, no prerogative or government can be set up as coequal with the authority of the people. The supreme power is in them; and in them, even when a constitution is formed, and government is in operation, the supreme power still remains. A portion of their authority they, indeed, delegate; but they delegate that portion in whatever manner, in whatever measure, for whatever time, to whatever persons, and on whatever conditions they choose to fix.

Those, who have traced and examined the subject of the appointment of governours, find, or think they find, an irreconcilable opposition between the principles of what they admit to be sound theory, and the rules of what they contend to be exclusively the safe and eligible practice. That what appears right in theory may be wrong in practice, is, no doubt, a possible case: but I am apt to believe that, generally, this contrariety is more apparent than real: and proceeds either from inaccurate investigation, or from improper conduct.

It has been the sentiment of many writers, that to have elective governours is best in speculation; but that to have hereditary ones is best in fact. The sense of nations has often, on this subject, coincided with the sentiments of writers; and therefore, they have trusted to chance rather than to choice, the succession of those, who hold the reins of power over them. They admit, that the chance is even a bad one. They admit that one born to govern is, by education, generally disqualified, both in

[g] Bol. Rem. let. 4.

body and mind, rather than qualified for government. They admit, that he will probably be debased by ignorance, enervated by pleasure, intoxicated by flattery, and corrupted by pride. They admit, that this chance may give them a fool, a madman, a tyrant, or a monster: and yet they hold it safer to depend on all the caprices of this very chance, than to commit their fortune and their fate to the discernment of choice.

And whence this strong antipathy to choice? Popular clamours, popular disturbances, popular distractions, popular tumults, and popular insurrections are ever present to their view. The unfortunate and fluctuating example of Poland dances perpetually before their eyes. They reflect not on the cause of this example. Poland is composed only of slaves, headed and commanded by a few despots. Those despots have private purposes to serve; and they head their slaves as the instruments for executing those private purposes. In Poland, we search in vain for a people. Need we be surprised, that, at an election in Poland, where there are only tyrants and slaves, all the detestable and pernicious extremes of tyranny and slavery should unite?

But surely, in the United States, we have no occasion to be apprehensive of such an odious and destructive union. In the United States, we have freemen and fellow citizens. To freemen and fellow citizens, and to those selected, for this very purpose, by freemen and fellow citizens, we may trust the appointment of our first and most important magistrate. In this appointment, no one can participate, either immediately or indirectly, who does not possess a common interest with the community. We are justified, therefore, in abandoning chance, and confiding in choice: our practice corresponds with our theory; and our theory is admitted to be just. An election made by those, whom we have described, authorized by the constitution, directed by the laws, held on the same day and for the same purpose, but at different and at distant places — such an election may certainly be carried on with fairness and with regularity; and its event may be considered as the genuine production of design, and not as the casual result of a "lottery." [h]

In one important particular — the unity of the executive power — the constitution of the United States stands on an equal footing with that of Great Britain. In one respect, the provision is much more efficacious.

The British throne is surrounded by counsellors. With regard to their authority, a profound and mysterious silence is observed. One effect, we know, they produce; and we conceive it to be a very pernicious one. Between power and responsibility, they interpose an impenetrable barrier. Who possesses the executive power? The king. When its baneful emana-

[h] See Bol. Pat. King. 89.

tions fly over the land; who are responsible for the mischief? His ministers. Amidst their multitude, and the secrecy, with which business, especially that of a perilous kind, is transacted, it will be often difficult to select the culprits; still more so, to punish them. The criminality will be diffused and blended with so much variety and intricacy, that it will be almost impossible to ascertain to how many it extends, and what particular share should be assigned to each.

But let us trace this subject a little further. Though the power of the king's counsellors is not, as far as I can discover, defined or described in the British constitution; yet their seats are certainly provided for some purpose, and filled with some effect. What is wanting in authority may be supplied by intrigue; and, in the place of constitutional influence, may be substituted that subtle ascendency, which is acquired and preserved by deeply dissembled obsequiousness. To so many arts, secret, unceasing, and well directed, can we suppose that a prince, in whose disposition is found any thing weak, indolent, or accommodating, will not be frequently induced to yield? Hence spring the evils of a partial, an indecisive, and a disjointed administration.

In the United States, our first executive magistrate is not obnubilated behind the mysterious obscurity of counsellors. Power is communicated to him with liberality, though with ascertained limitations. To him the provident or improvident use of it is to be ascribed. For the first, he will have and deserve undivided applause. For the last, he will be subjected to censure; if necessary, to punishment. He is the dignified, but accountable magistrate of a free and great people. The tenure of his office, it is true, is not hereditary; nor is it for life: but still it is a tenure of the noblest kind: by being the man of the people, he is invested; by continuing to be the man of the people, his investiture will be voluntarily, and cheerfully, and honourably renewed.

The president of the United States has such powers as are strictly and properly executive; and, by his qualified negative on the legislature, is furnished with a guard to protect his powers against their encroachments. Such powers and such a guard he ought to possess: but a just distribution of the powers of government requires that he should possess no more. In this important aspect, the constitution of the United States has much more regular, more correct, and better proportioned features, than are those of the constitution of Great Britain. It will be well worth while to trace this observation through various instances: its truth and its interesting consequences will, by this means, clearly appear.

As the king is the sole fountain of honour; he has, without limitation, the constitutional prerogative of creating peers; and of exalting to higher dignities those already created. He has also the power of appointing and promoting the bishops and archbishops. Those lords spiritual and temporal form one branch of the legislature. The number, therefore, and the rank of the members composing that branch depend entirely on the pleasure of the crown. This is a reprehensible dependency of the legislative on the executive power. Indeed, experience has proved it to be so. A single century has not yet revolved, since twelve peers were created at one time, with the avowed purpose of securing, by their necessary votes, the success of a favourite court system. A conviction, that, on any great crown emergency, recourse can be had to a similar expedient, will naturally lead the house of lords to be cautious, in an undue degree, of giving pointed opposition to the crown, however just or well grounded such opposition might be.

Another instance of the dependency of the house of lords on the king deserves to be mentioned: the speaker of that house, whose office it is to preside there and manage the forms of their business, is the lord chancellor, whose appointment and commission are at the pleasure of the crown.

Indeed, this undue and dangerous dependency of the house of lords seems to be acknowledged and dreaded — for, in one instance, provision is made against its effects — by the British constitution itself. It is the indisputable right of the house of commons — a right, over which they have constantly watched with a jealous solicitude — that all grants of parliamentary aid begin in their house. Several reasons have been assigned for this exclusive privilege: but the true one, arising from the spirit of the constitution, is this. The lords, being created, at pleasure, by the king, are supposed more liable to be influenced by the crown; and, being a permanent hereditary body, are, when once influenced, supposed more likely to continue so, than the commons, who are a temporary body elected by the people. It would, therefore, be extremely dangerous to give the lords any power of framing new taxes for the subject: it suffices that they have the power of rejecting, if they think the commons too lavish or improvident in their grants.

By the constitution of the United States, money bills originate in the house of representatives: the reason is, that as that house are more numerous than the other, and its members are elected more frequently; the most local and recent information of the circumstances of the people may be found there. But, as the senate derive their authority ultimately from the same origin with the other house; they have a right to propose and concur in amendments in these as well as in other bills.

But further; the power of conferring nobility is a source of influence, which the crown possesses over the house of commons, as well as over the house of lords. A coronet, and all the proud preeminences and gilded glories which encircle a coronet, are objects of ambition, whose tempting charms, few — very few indeed — are capable of resisting. Even the great commoner wishes and sighs to be something more. Will not his views be directed to that power, by which alone his wishes can be gratified? Will not his conduct receive a bias from the longing, expecting turn of his mind? When his towering hopes of elevation are suspended on the crown; will he easily run the risk of seeing them dashed to the ground, by speaking, and voting, and acting in opposition to its views and measures?

We are now arrived, in our progress, at another fountain, from which, in Great Britain, the waters of bitterness have plentifully flowed — I mean the fountain of office. We reprehend not the nature of this power, nor the place, where, by the British constitution, it is deposited. In every government there must be such a power; and it is proper, that it should be lodged in the hands of him, who is placed at the head of the executive department. What we censure is, that this power is not circumscribed by the necessary limitations. It may be — it is exercised in favour of the members of both houses of parliament. Offices of trust and profit are scattered, with a lavish hand, among those, by whom a return, very dangerous to the liberties of the nation, may be made; and from whom such a return is but too often expected.

This is the box of Pandora, which has been opened on Britain. To its poisonous emanations have been owing the contaminated and contaminating scenes of venality, of prostitution, and corruption, which have crowded and disgraced her political theatre. To the same efficacy have been owing the indiscriminate profligacy and universal degeneracy, which have been diffused through every channel, into which the treasures of the publick have procured admission. In the house of lords, this stream of influence may flow without measure and without end. Some attempts have been made to confine it in the house of commons; but they have been feeble and unavailing. If any member of that house accepts an office under the crown, his seat, it is true, is vacated; but he may be immediately reelected. This provision, flimsy as it is, extends not to officers in the army or navy accepting new commissions. The ardent aspirations after military preferment are thus left to be exerted, with all their energetick vigour, in promoting the designs of the crown, or of the ministers of the crown.

But fears, as well as hopes, operate in favour of the influence, which we have been tracing in so many directions. For the members hold their offices and commissions, and, consequently, may be dismissed from them, at the pleasure of the crown.

Indeed, this influence has been so great and so uniform, that for more than a century past, it has been found, that reliance could be placed on it implicitly. Accordingly, during that whole period, the king has never once been under the disagreeable necessity of interposing his negative to prevent the passing of an obnoxious law. It has been discovered to be a less ungracious, though not a less efficacious method, to stop its progress in one of the two houses of parliament.

To the power of the crown to confer offices on members of parliament, we may also ascribe those numerous and violent dissensions, which, on so many occasions, and some of them very critical ones, have convulsed the national councils, and sacrificed the national interests. Ample though the means are, which the crown can employ in gaining and securing members, by the offices in its gift, they are insufficient to gratify all. To a sure majority, the object must be confined. But of a majority, gained by the interest of the court, the necessary consequence is, a minority in opposition to its measures.[i]

The above is a plain and simple account of the manner, in which the parties in parliament have been formed, and in which they have, without interruption, been continued; though, on both sides, a very different account has been uniformly attempted to be palmed upon the publick. Neither side has chosen to give a true history and character either of themselves or of their antagonists: each finds its interest in appearing, and in representing the other, under a borrowed dress. While the influence of the crown, produced by offices of trust and profit bestowed upon members of parliament, shall continue, this state of formed and irreconcilable parties will continue also.

The result is, that a provision, by which the members of the legislature will be precluded, while they remain such, from offices, finds, with great propriety, a place in the constitution of the United States. In this important particular, it has a decided superiority over the constitution of Great Britain.

Perhaps the qualified negative of the president of the United States on the proceedings of the senate and house of representatives in congress, possesses advantages over an absolute negative, such as that vested in the crown of Great Britain over the proceedings of the lords and commons. To this last, recourse would not be had, unless on occasions of the greatest emergency. A determination not to interpose it without the last necessity, would prevent the exercise of it in many instances, in which it would be proper and salutary. In this manner, it would remain, like a sword always in the scabbard, an instrument, sometimes of distant apprehension, but not of present or practical utility. The exercise of the qualified negative is not an experiment of either dangerous or doubtful issue. A small bias it turns without noise or difficulty. To the operation of a powerful bias, which cannot be safely checked or diverted, it decently and leisurely gives way.

[i] It was the saying of King William, that if he had places enough to give, the names of whig and tory would soon be lost.

The qualified negative will be highly advantageous in another point of view: it will form an index, by which, from time to time, the strength and height of the current of publick opinions and publick movements may, with considerable exactness, be ascertained. Whenever it is exercised, the votes of all the members of both the houses must be entered on their journals. The single point, that there is a majority, will not be the only one, which will appear: it will be evinced also, how great that majority is. If it consists of less than two thirds of both houses, it seems reasonable, that the dissent of the executive department should suspend a business, which is already so nearly in equilibrio. On the other hand, if, after all the discussion, investigation, and consideration, which must have been employed upon a bill in its different stages, before its presentment to the president of the United States, and after its return from him with his objections to it, two thirds of each house are still of sentiment, that it ought to be passed into a law; this would be an evidence, that the current of publick opinion in its favour is so strong, that it ought not to be opposed. The experiment, though doubtful, ought to be made, when it is called for so long and so loudly.

Besides; the objections of the president, even when unsuccessful, will not be without their use. If the law, notwithstanding all the unfavourable appearances, which accurate political disquisition discovered against it, proves, upon trial, to be beneficial in practice; it will add one to the many instances, in which feeling may be trusted more than argument. If, on the contrary, experience shows the law to be replete with all the inconveniences, which sagacious scrutiny foresaw in its operations, the disease will no sooner appear, than the remedy will be known and applied.

Another advantage, of very general and extensive import, will flow from the qualified negative possessed by the president of the United States. His observations upon the bills and acts of the legislature will, in a series of time, gradually furnish the most valuable and the best adapted materials for composing a practical system of legislation. In every successive period, experience and reasoning will go hand in hand; and will, jointly, produce a collection of accurate and satisfactory knowledge, which could be the separate result of neither.

By the British constitution, the power of judging in the last resort is placed in the house of lords. It is allowed, by an English writer on that constitution, that there is nothing in the formation of the house of lords; nor in the education, habits, character, or professions of the members who compose it; nor in the mode of their appointment, or the right, by which they succeed to their places in it, that suggests any intelligible fitness, in the nature of this regulation.[j] Ecclesiasticks, courtiers, naval

[j] 2. Paley. 282. 283.

and military officers, young men, just of age, born to their elevated station, in other words, placed there by chance, are, for the most part, the members, who compose this important and supreme tribunal. These are the men, authorized and assigned to revise and correct the decisions, pronounced by the sages of the law, who have been raised to the seat of justice on account of their professional eminence, and have employed their lives in the study and practice of the jurisprudence of their country. There is surely something, which, at least in theory, appears very incongruous in this establishment of things. The practical consequences of its impropriety are, in a considerable degree, avoided, by placing in the house of lords some of the greatest law characters in the kingdom; by calling to their assistance the opinions of the judges upon legal questions, which come before the house for its final determination; and by the great deference which those, who are uninformed, naturally pay to those, who are distinguished by their information. After all, however, there is a very improper mixture of legislative and judicial authority vested and blended in the same assembly. This is entirely avoided in the constitution of the United States.

It may, perhaps, be objected, that, by this constitution, one branch of the legislature is to present, and the other is to try impeachments. The answer is obvious. Impeachments, and offences and offenders impeachable, come not, in those descriptions, within the sphere of ordinary jurisprudence. They are founded on different principles; are governed by different maxims, and are directed to different objects: for this reason, the trial and punishment of an offence on an impeachment, is no bar to a trial and punishment of the same offence at common law.

In the judicial establishments of Great Britain, there is, we cheerfully confess, much to admire, and much to imitate. The judges are the grand depository of the fundamental laws of the kingdom; and have gained a known and stated jurisdiction, regulated by certain and established rules, which cannot be altered, but by act of parliament. By the statute 13. W. III. c. 2. "An act for the further limitation of the crown, and better securing the rights and liberties of the subject," provision is made, that after the said limitation shall take effect, the commissions of the judges shall be, not, as formerly, "durante bene placito," but "quamdiu bene se gesserint;" * that their salaries shall be ascertained and established; but that it may be lawful to remove them on the address of both houses of parliament.

Though, in virtue of this law, the judges received commissions to hold their offices during their good behaviour; it was supposed, that their seats were immediately vacated by the demise of the crown. When

* [Not during good pleasure, but as long as they conduct themselves well.]

their seats were vacated, their salaries terminated. A new commission, it is true, might be given, and, if given, must be given during good behaviour; but a new commission might also be refused, by the successour to the throne. Under the new commission, if given, a different salary might be assigned. In this state of dependence, not so degrading, indeed, as it had been, but still very precarious, and, as it respected the heir apparent of the throne, very embarrassing and humiliating, the judges of England continued till the first year of the reign of George the third.

That Prince, soon after his accession, declared, from the throne, to both houses of parliament, that he looked upon the independency and uprightness of judges as essential to the impartial administration of justice, as one of the best securities to the rights and liberties of the subjects, and as most conducive to the honour of his crown. He, therefore, recommended it to the consideration of parliament, to make further provision for continuing the judges in the enjoyment of their offices during their good behaviour, notwithstanding the demise of the crown; and for enabling him to secure their salaries during the continuance of their commissions. Provision was accordingly made, by parliament, for both those purposes. But the judges are still liable to be removed by the king, upon the address of both houses of parliament.

This establishment for the administration of justice appears, in the opinion of Mr. Paley, no undiscerning judge of the subject, to approach so near to perfection, as to justify him in declaring, that a politician, who should sit down to delineate a plan for the dispensation of publick justice, guarded against all access to influence and corruption, and bringing together the separate advantages of knowledge and impartiality, would find, when he had done, that he had been transcribing the judicial constitution of England.[k] "It may teach," continues he, "the most discontented among us to acquiesce in the government of his country, to reflect that the pure, wise, and equal administration of the laws forms the first end and blessing of social union; and that this blessing is enjoyed by him in a perfection, which he will seek in vain in any other nation of the world."

Notwithstanding this high encomium, pronounced from a motive of which I cannot but approve, I hesitate not to institute a comparison between the judicial establishment of England, and that which is introduced by the constitution of the United States. Nay, I am sanguine, that, on a just comparison, the latter will be found to contain many very useful and valuable improvements on the former.

The laws, in England, respecting the independency of the judges, have been construed as confined to those in the superiour courts.[l] In the

k 2. Paley. 284. 285.   l 1. Bl. Com. 267.

United States, this independency extends to judges in courts inferiour as well as supreme. This independency reaches equally their salaries and their commissions.

In England, the judges of the superiour courts do not now, as they did formerly, hold their commissions and their salaries at the pleasure of the crown; but they still hold them at the pleasure of the parliament: the judicial subsists, and may be blown to annihilation, by the breath of the legislative department. In the United States, the judges stand upon the sure basis of the constitution: the judicial department is independent of the department of legislature. No act of congress can shake their commissions or reduce their salaries. "The judges, both of the supreme and inferiour courts, shall hold their offices during good behaviour, and shall, at stated times, receive for their services a compensation, which shall not be diminished during their continuance in office." [m] It is not lawful for the president of the United States to remove them on the address of the two houses of congress. They may be removed, however, as they ought to be, on conviction of high crimes and misdemeanors.

The judges of the United States stand on a much more independent footing than that on which the judges of England stand, with regard to jurisdiction, as well as with regard to commissions and salaries. In many cases, the jurisdiction of the judges of the United States is ascertained and secured by the constitution: as to these, the power of the judicial is coordinate with that of the legislative department. As to the other cases, by the necessary result of the constitution, the authority of the former is paramount to the authority of the latter.

It will be proper to illustrate, at some length, the nature and consequences of these important doctrines concerning the judicial department of the United States; and, at the same time, to contrast them with the doctrines held concerning the same department in England. Much useful and practical information may be drawn from this comparative review.

It is entertaining, and it may be very instructive, to trace and examine the opinions of the English courts and lawyers concerning the decision, which may be given, in the judicial department, upon the validity or invalidity of acts of parliament.

In some books we are told plainly, and without any circumlocution or disguise — that an act of parliament against law and reason is, therefore, void [n] — that, in many cases, the common law will control acts of parliament; and sometimes adjudge them to be utterly void: for when an act of parliament is against common right and reason, or repugnant, or impossible to be performed; the common law will control it, and adjudge such act to be void. Some statutes are made against law and right, which

---

[m] Con. U.S. art. 3. s. 1.   [n] 4. Rep. 13.

those who made them perceiving, would not put them in execution[o] — that an act of parliament made against natural equity, as to make a man judge in his own cause, is void in itself; for *jura naturae immutabilia*, and they are *leges legum.*[p]

My Lord Chief Justice Holt expresses himself, upon this delicate and embarrassing subject, in his usual blunt and decided manner: "It is a very reasonable and true saying, that if an act of parliament should ordain, that the same person should be a party and a judge, or, which is the same thing, judge in his own cause; it would be a void act of parliament; for it is impossible that one should be judge and party; for the judge is to determine between party and party, or between the government and the party; and an act of parliament can do no wrong; though it may do several things, that look pretty odd." [q]

These doctrines and sayings, however reasonable and true they appear to be, have been, nevertheless, deemed too bold; for they are irreconcilable with the lately introduced positions concerning the supreme, absolute, and uncontrollable power of the British parliament. Accordingly, Sir William Blackstone, on the principles of his system, expresses himself in the following manner, remarkably guarded and circumspect, as to the extent of the parliamentary power. "If there arise *out* of acts of parliament, *collaterally*, any absurd consequences, *manifestly* contradictory to common reason; they are, with regard to *those collateral* consequences, void. I lay down the rule with these restrictions; though I know it is generally laid down more largely — that acts of parliament contrary to reason are void. But if the parliament will *positively* enact a thing to be done, which is unreasonable; I know of no power that can control it: and the examples usually alleged in support of this sense of the rule do none of them prove, that, where the *main object* of a statute is unreasonable, the judges are at liberty to reject it: for that were to set the judicial power above that of the legislature, which would be subversive of all government." "No court has power to defeat the intent of the legislature, when couched in such evident and express words, as to leave no doubt concerning its intention." [r]

The successour of Sir William Blackstone in the Vinerian chair walks in his footsteps. "It is certain," he admits, "no human authority can rightfully infringe or abrogate the smallest particle of natural or divine law; yet a British judge, of highly deserved estimation, seems in some measure unguarded in asserting from the bench, that an act of parliament made against natural equity, is void in itself. The principle is infallibly true; the application of it, and the conclusion, dangerous. We must distinguish

[o] 8. Rep. 118.
[p] Hob. 87. [The laws of nature are immutable, and they are the laws of laws.]
[q] 12. Mod. 687. 688.   [r] 1. Bl. Com. 91.

between right and power; between moral fitness and political authority. We cannot expect that all acts of legislators will be ethically perfect; but if their proceedings are to be decided upon by their subjects, government and subordination cease." [s]

It is very true — we ought to "distinguish between right and power:" but I always apprehended, that the true use of this distinction was, to show that power, in opposition to right, was devested of every title, not that it was clothed with the strongest title, to obedience. Is it really true, that if "the parliament will positively enact an unreasonable thing — a thing manifestly contradictory to common reason — there is no power that can control it?" Is it really true that such a power, vested in the judicial department, would set it above the legislature, and would be subversive of all government? If all this is true; what will the miserable, but unavoidable consequence be? Is it possible, in the nature of things, that all which is positively enacted by parliament can be decreed and enforced by the courts of justice? It will not be pretended. The words in two different laws may be clearly repugnant to one another. The law supposes that, sometimes, this is the case; and accordingly has provided, as we are told in the Commentaries, that, in this case, the later law takes place of the elder. "Leges posteriores, priores contrarias abrogant," we are told, and properly told, is a maxim of universal law, as well as of the English constitutions.[t] Suppose two such repugnant laws to be produced in the same cause, before the same court: what must it do? It must control one, or obey neither. In this last instance, the remedy would be worse than the disease: but there is not the least occasion to have recourse to this desperate remedy. The rule which we have cited from the Commentaries, shows the method that should be followed. In the case supposed, the first law is repealed by the second: the second, therefore, is the only existing law.

Two contradictory laws, we have seen, may flow from the same source: and we have also seen, what, in that case, is to be done. But two contradictory laws may flow likewise from different sources, one superiour to the other: what is to be done in this case?

We are informed, in another part of the Commentaries, that, "on the two foundations of the law of nature, and the law of revelation, all human laws depend; that is to say, no human laws should be suffered to contradict these" — that, if any human law should enjoin us to commit what is prohibited by these, we are bound to transgress that human law, or else we must offend both the natural and the divine.[u] What! are we bound to transgress it? — And are the courts of justice forbidden to reject it? Surely these positions are inconsistent and irreconcilable.

[s] El. Jur. (4to.) 48.   [t] 1. Bl. Com. 59.   [u] Id. 42. 43.

But to avoid the contradiction, shall it be said, that we are bound to suppose every thing, positively and plainly enacted by the legislature, to be, at least, not repugnant to natural or revealed law? This may lead us out of intricate mazes respecting the omnipotence; but, I am afraid, it will lead us into mazes equally intricate and more dangerous concerning the infallibility of parliament. This tenet in the political creed will be found as heterodox as the other.

"I know of no power," says Sir William Blackstone, "which can control the parliament." His meaning is obviously, that he knew no *human* power sufficient for this purpose. But the parliament may, unquestionably, be controlled by natural or revealed law, proceeding from *divine* authority. Is not this authority superiour to any thing that can be enacted by parliament? Is not this superiour authority binding upon the courts of justice? When repugnant commands are delivered by two different authorities, one inferiour and the other superiour; which must be obeyed? When the courts of justice obey the superiour authority, it cannot be said with propriety that they control the inferiour one; they only declare, as it is their duty to declare, that this inferiour one is controlled by the other, which is superiour. They do not repeal the act of parliament: they pronounce it void, because contrary to an overruling law. From that overruling law, they receive the authority to pronounce such a sentence. In this derivative view, their sentence is of obligation paramount to the act of the inferiour legislative power.

In the United States, the legislative authority is subjected to another control, beside that arising from natural and revealed law; it is subjected to the control arising from the constitution. From the constitution, the legislative department, as well as every other part of government, derives its power: by the constitution, the legislative, as well as every other department, must be directed; of the constitution, no alteration by the legislature can be made or authorized. In our system of jurisprudence, these positions appear to be incontrovertible. The constitution is the supreme law of the land: to that supreme law every other power must be inferiour and subordinate.

Now, let us suppose, that the legislature should pass an act, manifestly repugnant to some part of the constitution; and that the operation and validity of both should come regularly in question before a court, forming a portion of the judicial department. In that department, the "judicial power of the United States is vested" by the "people," who "ordained and established" the constitution. The business and the design of the judicial power is, to administer justice according to the law of the land. According to two contradictory rules, justice, in the nature of things, cannot possibly be administered. One of them must, of necessity, give place to the other. Both, according to our supposition, come regularly before the court, for its decision on their operation and validity. It is the right and it is the duty of the court to decide upon them: its decision must be made, for justice must be administered according to the law of the land. When the question occurs — What is the law of the land? it must also decide this question. In what manner is this question to be decided? The answer seems to be a very easy one. The supreme power of the United States has given one rule: a subordinate power in the United States has given a contradictory rule: the former is the law of the land: as a necessary consequence, the latter is void, and has no operation. In this manner it is the right and it is the duty of a court of justice, under the constitution of the United States, to decide.

This is the necessary result of the distribution of power, made, by the constitution, between the legislative and the judicial departments. The same constitution is the supreme law to both. If that constitution be infringed by one, it is no reason that the infringement should be abetted, though it is a strong reason that it should be discountenanced and declared void by the other.

The effects of this salutary regulation, necessarily resulting from the constitution, are great and illustrious. In consequence of it, the bounds of the legislative power — a power the most apt to overleap its bounds — are not only distinctly marked in the system itself; but effectual and permanent provision is made, that every transgression of those bounds shall be adjudged and rendered vain and fruitless. What a noble guard against legislative despotism!

This regulation is far from throwing any disparagement upon the legislative authority of the United States. It does not confer upon the judicial department a power superiour, in its general nature, to that of the legislature; but it confers upon it, in particular instances, and for particular purposes, the power of declaring and enforcing the superiour power of the constitution — the supreme law of the land.

This regulation, when considered properly, is viewed in a favourable light by the legislature itself. "It has been objected," said a learned member[v] of the house of representatives, in a late debate, "that, by adopting the bill before us, we expose the measure to be considered and defeated by the judiciary of the United States, who may adjudge it to be contrary to the constitution, and therefore void, and not lend their aid to carry it into execution. This gives me no uneasiness. I am so far from controverting this right in the judiciary, that it is my boast and my confidence. It leads me to greater decision on all subjects of a constitutional nature, when I reflect, that, if from inattention, want of precision, or any other

[v] Mr. Elias Boudinot.

defect, I should do wrong, there is a power in the government, which can constitutionally prevent the operation of a wrong measure from affecting my constituents. I am legislating for a nation, and for thousands yet unborn; and it is the glory of the constitution, that there is a remedy for the failures even of the legislature itself."

It has already appeared, that the laws, in England, respecting the independency of the judges, have been construed as confined to those in the superiour courts. In many courts, nay in almost all the courts, which have jurisdiction in criminal, even in capital cases, the judges are still appointed and commissioned occasionally, and at the pleasure of the crown. Those courts, though possessing only a local jurisdiction, and confined to particular districts, are yet of a general nature, and are universally diffused over the kingdom. Such are the courts of oyer and terminer and general gaol delivery. They are held twice in every year in every county of the kingdom, except the four northern ones, in which they are held only once, and London and Middlesex, in which they are held eight times. By their commissions, the judges of those courts have authority to hear and determine all treasons, felonies, and misdemeanors; and to try and deliver every prisoner who shall be in the gaol, when they arrive at the circuit town, whenever indicted, or for whatever crime committed. Sometimes also, upon particular emergencies, the king issues a special or extraordinary commission of oyer and terminer and gaol delivery, confined to those offences which stand in need of immediate inquiry and punishment. Those courts are held before the king's commissioners, among whom are usually — but not necessarily, as it would seem — two judges of the courts at Westminster.[w]

It is somewhat surprising, that, in a nation where the value of liberty and personal security has been so long and so well known, less care has been taken to provide for the independency of the judges in criminal than in civil jurisdiction. Is property of more consequence than life or personal liberty? Is it more likely to become the selected and devoted object of ministerial vengeance or resentment? If peculiar precaution was necessary or proper to ensure the independence of the judges on the crown, one would think it most reasonable to apply that precaution to the independence of those judges, who exercise criminal jurisdiction. Even treason may be tried before judges, named, for the occasion, and during pleasure, by him, who, in law, is supposed to be personally as well as politically offended.

To the constitution of the United States, and to those who enjoy the advantages of that constitution, no judges are known, but such as hold their offices during good behaviour.

[w] 4. Bl. Com. 266. 267.

With regard to the institution and establishment of juries, as well as those of judges, an advantage is possessed under the constitution of the United States, greater than what is possessed under the constitution of Great Britain. This subject deserves to be placed in the clearest and strongest point of view.

To be tried only by men of one's own condition, is one of the greatest blessings — to know that one can be tried only by such men, is one of the greatest securities — which can be enjoyed under any government.

If the trial of causes was committed entirely to one selected body of men, deprived, by their situation, of having many opportunities of knowing particularly the circumstances and characters of the parties, who come before them; it could not be expected, that the proper and practical adjustment of facts to persons would, in every instance, be made. The transactions of life will be best investigated by a competent number of sensible and unprejudiced jurymen, summoned and assembled for each particular cause. Such men will be triers not only of the facts; but also of the credibility of the witnesses. They will know whom and what to believe, as well as whom and what to hear. Truth will be estimated by the character, and not by the number, of those, who give their testimony. The testimony of one witness will not be rejected merely because it stands single; nor will the testimony of two witnesses be believed, if it be encountered by reason and probability. These advantages of a trial by jury are important in all causes: in criminal causes, they are of peculiar importance.

In criminal causes, the accusation charges not only the particular fact, which has been committed, but also the motive or design, to which it owed its origin, and from which it receives its complexion. This design is often so closely interwoven with the transaction, that the elucidation of both depends on a collected view of particulars, arising not merely from the testimony, but also from the conduct and character of the witnesses, and sometimes likewise from the character and conduct of the person accused. Of such conduct and character, men of the same condition with that person, and probably of the same condition with the witnesses too, are the best qualified to make the proper comparison and estimate; and consequently to determine, upon the whole, whether the conduct of the prisoner, comprehending both the fact and the motives, is, or is not, within the meaning of the law, upon which the accusation against him is founded.

This institution does honour to human policy: it is the most excellent method for the investigation and discovery of truth; and the best guardian of both publick and private liberty, which has been hitherto devised by the ingenuity of man. We are told by the celebrated Montesquieu, that Rome, that Sparta, that Carthage — states, once so free and so prosperous — have lost their liberties, and have perished. Their fate he holds up to the view of other states, as a memento of their own. But there is one consolatory distinction, which he did not take, and which we will apply in our favour. In Rome, in Sparta, in Carthage, the trial by jury did not exist, or was not preserved. Liberty can never be insecure in that country, in which "the trial of all crimes is by jury." [x]

Is it not, then, of the last consequence, that, in criminal causes, this most excellent mode of trial should be placed on the most solid and permanent foundation? Is it enough that its establishment be legal, — supported by the legislature? Is it not proper that it should be constitutional — supported by authority superiour to that of the legislature? Such an establishment it has not in Great Britain; but it has in the United States.

I have now finished the parallel between the pride of Europe — the British constitution — and the constitution of the United States. Let impartiality hold the balance between them: I am not solicitous about the event of the trial.

[x] Con. U.S. art. 3. s. 2.

XII

OF THE COMMON LAW

"SAPIENTISSIMA res tempus," says the profound Lord Bacon,[a] in one of his aphorisms concerning the augmentation of the sciences — Time is the wisest of things. If the qualities of the parent may, in any instance, be expected in the offspring; the common law, one of the noblest births of time, may be pronounced the wisest of laws.

This law has, at different times, and for different reasons, been denominated by different appellations. It is sometimes called, by way of eminence, the law of the land, "lex terræ." At other times, it is called the law of England. At other times again, it is called the law and custom of the kingdom. But its most general and best known appellation is, the common law. Various are the reasons, which have been assigned for this appellation: the best seems to be this — that it is the common municipal law or rule of justice;[b] the law which is described in the code of king Edward the elder, as expressing the same equal right, law, or justice, due to persons of all degrees.[c]

The term *common law* is not confined to the law of England: It is not, says Sir Henry Finch, a word new and strange, or barbarous, and proper to ourselves, and the law, which we profess, as some unlearnedly would have it: it is the proper term for other laws also. Euripides mentions the common laws of Greece; and Plato defines common law in this manner: that which, being taken up by the common consent of a country, is called law. In another place, he names it, the golden and sacred rule of reason, which we call common law.

This place, continues the same author, in his discourse of law,[d] is very notable: it opens the original and first beginning of the common law: it shows the antiquity of the name; it teaches common law to be nothing else but common reason — that refined reason, which is generally received by the consent of all.

The antiquity of the common law of England is unquestionably very high. It is worth while to listen to what may be deemed the prejudices

[a] 1. Ld. Bacon. 252. Aph. 32.   [b] Hale. Hist. 55.   [c] El. Jur. (4to.) 94.
[d] Finch. 74. 75.

— certainly the pardonable ones — of its fond admirers, upon a point so interesting to their partiality.

The realm of England, says Lord Chancellor Fortescue,[e] was first inhabited by the Britons; it was afterwards ruled and civilized under the government of the Romans: then the Britons prevailed again: next it was possessed by the Saxons: afterwards the Danes lorded it over us: the Saxons were successful a second time: at last, the Norman conquest took place. But, during all that time, England has been constantly governed by the same customs, by which it is governed at present. Neither the laws of the Romans, which are celebrated beyond all others for their antiquity; nor yet the laws of the Venetians; nor, in short, the laws of any other kingdom in the world are so venerable for their antiquity. So that there is no pretence to insinuate to the contrary, but that the laws and customs of England are not only good, but the very best. — Thus far from the predilection of the chancellor.

But, in truth, it is extremely difficult, if not altogether impracticable, to trace the common law of England to the era of its commencement, or to the several springs, from which it has originally flowed. For this difficulty or impossibility, several reasons may be assigned. One may be drawn from the very nature of a system of common law. As it is accommodated to the situation and circumstances of the people, by whom it is appointed; and as that situation and those circumstances insensibly change; so, especially in a long series of time, a proportioned variation of the laws insensibly takes place; and it is often impossible to ascertain the precise period, when the change began, or to mark the different steps of its progress. Another reason may be drawn from the great number of different nations, which, at different successive periods, and sometimes even at the same period, possessed the government, or the divided governments of England. These added, undoubtedly, to the richness and variety of the common law; but they added likewise to the difficulty of investigating the origin of its different parts.

If this investigation is difficult, there is one consolation, that it is not of essential importance. For at whatever time the laws of England were introduced, from whatever person or country they were derived; their obligatory force arises not from any consideration of that kind, but from their free and voluntary reception in the kingdom.

Several writers, some of them very ingenious and learned, think they can discover, in the common law, features, which strongly indicate, that it is of a Grecian extraction. Without adopting implicitly the authenticity of this high descent, it may be well worth our while to examine the particulars, on which the opinion is founded. If they lead us not to this con-

[e] De Laud. c. 17.

clusion, they may, perhaps, lead us to something else, which will be, at least, equally valuable and instructive.

The similarity between the idiom of our language and that of the Grecians has persuaded some very sensible men to believe, that the inhabitants of Great Britain were, in a very remote age, connected, in some manner, with the inhabitants of Greece. This similarity is, indeed, very striking. No one, I believe, who is acquainted with the Greek, the Latin, and the English languages, will hesitate to declare, that there is a closer affinity of idiom between the Greek and the English, than between the English and the Latin, or between the Latin and the Greek.

The very idea of a traditionary law, transmitted from generation to generation merely by custom and memory, may be considered as derived, in part at least, from the practice of the Druids, who considered it as unlawful to commit their religious instructions to writing. But we are informed by the penetrating and intelligent Cæsar, that, in other business, whether of a publick or of a private nature, they used the Grecian letters — "Graecis literis utuntur." [f]

Pliny conjectures that the name of *Druid* was derived from the Greek word δρυς, quercus, an oak, because they performed their solemn ceremonies in the deep recesses of groves formed by oaks; and because, in their sacrifices, they used the leaves of those trees.[g] The missletoe, it is well known, was of sacred import in their religious mysteries.

Nathaniel Bacon, a gentleman of Gray's inn, wrote a historical and political discourse of the laws and government of England, particularly during the early periods of its history. This discourse, we are informed, was collected from manuscript notes of Mr. Selden, so famed for his various and extensive erudition. To the notes of an antiquarian, so celebrated and so profound, attention will be expected in an investigation of the present kind.

In that discourse we are told, that, though it be both needless and fruitless to enter the lists concerning the original of the Saxons; yet, about the time of Tiberius, their government was, in general, so suitable to that of the Grecians, as if not by the remains of Alexander's army, which was supposed to emigrate into the north, nevertheless, by the neighbourhood of Greece, much of the Grecian wisdom was disseminated among them, before the Roman glory was mounted up to the full pitch; and because this wisdom could never be thus imported but in vessels of men's flesh, rigged according to the Grecian guise, it may well be supposed that there is some consanguinity between the Saxons and the Grecians, although the degrees be not known.[h]

Their country, continues he, they divided into countries or circuits, all

---

[f] De bel. Gal. l. 6. c. 13.   [g] 3. Rep. Pref. 9 b.   [h] Bac. on Gov. 9.

under the government of twelve lords, like the Athenian territory under
the archontes. These had the judicial power of distributive justice committed to them, together with one hundred of the commons out of each
division. The election of these princes with their commission was concluded *inter majora*, by the general assembly, and they executed their
commission in circuits, like unto the Athenian heliastick or subdial court,
which was rural, and for the most part kept in the open air. In brief, their
judicial proceedings were very suitable to the Athenian, but their military
more like the Lacedæmonian, whom, above all others, in their manners,
they most resembled.[i]

Austin is generally considered as the apostle of the Saxons, who converted them to christianity: but our author suggests, that he was an apostle of another kind — to reconcile them to the see of Rome. To prove
this, he adduces a remarkable fact, that the Saxons kept Easter "more
Asiatico;" and, against Austin's will, retained that custom fifty years after
Austin began his mission among them.[j]

In enumerating the different manners of trial among the Saxons, he
says, that the last and most usual one was by witnesses, before the jurors,
and their votes thereupon: this made the verdict, and it determined the
matter in fact. In former time, questionless, it was a confused manner of
trial, by votes of the whole multitude; which made the votes hard to be
discerned. But time taught them better advice, to bring the voters to a
certain number, according to the Grecian way, who determined controversies by the suffrages of four and thirty, or the major part of them." [k]

Speaking of a certain regulation concerning dower, which was derived
from the Latins, he says; "but the Germans learned from the Greeks
otherwise: for the laws both of Solon and Lycurgus forbade it, lest marriages should be made for reward, and not grounded on affection." [l]

After having described, in detail, a number of particulars relative to the
Saxon government and laws, he makes this general remark: "Nor did the
fundamentals alter, either by the diversity and mixture of people of several nations in the first entrance, nor from the Danes or Normans in their
survenue; not only because in their original they all breathed one air of
the laws and government of Greece; but also they were no other than the
common dictates of nature, refined by wise men, which challenge a kind
of awe, in the sense of the most barbarous." [m]

He concludes his observations concerning the Saxon commonwealth in
this expressive manner. "It was a beautiful composure; mutually dependent in every part from the crown to the clown; the magistrates being all
choice men; and the king the choicest of the chosen: election being the

[i] Id. 10.　　[j] Bac. on Gov. 12.　　[k] Id. 56.　　[l] Id. 64.
[m] Bac. on Gov. 68.

birth of esteem, and that of merit: this bred love and mutual trust; which made them as corner stones, pointed forward to break the wave of danger.

"Lastly, it was a regular frame in every part, squared and made even by laws, which, in the people, ruled as *lex loquens*, and, in the magistrate, as *lex intelligens;* all of them being grounded on the wisdom of the Greeks, and the judicials of Moses." [n]

The history, says an inquisitive writer, of the constitutions of the different European nations may be much elucidated by institutions, ascertained to have existed in their sister countries, during the corresponding periods of their progress. The rise of the constitutions of the Greek and Italian states will derive light from what is known of the Gaulick, German, and Scandinavian tribes.[o]

Dr. Pettingal, in his very learned inquiry concerning the use and practice of juries, differs from Mr. Bacon with regard to the channel, through which the Grecian customs flowed into the Saxon commonwealths: but he admits that those customs were originally derived from Greece. "The likeness," says he, "of the Greek and Saxon government, supposed to be owing to the neighbourhood of Greece and Saxony, proceeded from a different cause. For, as the Romans took their laws and institutions from Greece, and particularly in the instance of the heliastick court, which was a court of trial by jury, and on which the Romans formed their *judicium* or jury; so when they sent their colonies into Germany, they sent also their laws and usages along with them, and by these means the wisdom of Greece and the practice of the heliastick court got among the Saxons in the shape of the Roman *judicia;* and the plan of the Greek government, through the channel of the Roman jurisprudence, laid the foundation of many customs that had a resemblance to the Greek, but in fact were no other than an imitation of the Roman polity, which originally was derived from Athens: so that the jury among the Saxons and northern nations was derived from the Roman *judicia,* as the *causa proxima;* but both of them drew their origin from the court of δικασται, or jury, among the Greeks. This was the manner, in which the resemblance between the Saxons and Greeks, spoken of by Bacon, was produced." [p]

With regard to the institution of juries, he afterwards observes; "where shall we go, with so much propriety, to look for its origin, as among those, who, of all mankind, were the depositaries and patrons of equal law and liberty, and which they themselves had learned from the wisdom and good government established in Athens by Solon? For nothing can be so absurd as to imagine, that such a noble political structure, as had distinguished the only two civilized nations of Europe, and whose legal

[n] Id. 70.   [o] 3. Edin. Phil. Trans. 10.   [p] Pett. on Jur. 154. 155.

limitations of power and obedience had done honour even to human nature, should, in times future, be the fortuitous result of a tumultuous deliberation, and that of Scythians and barbarians, rather than an imitation of the wisdom of those customs, which had been introduced among them by their conquerors." [q]

The particular history of juries will find its proper place elsewhere. Suffice it to mention them now among the group of institutions said to be derived from the Grecians to the Saxons either immediately, or through the intermediate channel of the Romans.

The laws and institutions of Greece flowed into Italy, and were conveyed to the many different states there, through a vast variety of channels.

The first inhabitants of this "terra potens virorum" were composed of Grecian tribes, the overflowings of their native habitations, who migrated, in early days, into the southern parts of the Italian continent; from this circumstance, it was denominated Magna Græcia. These colonists brought with them their own laws and customs. [r] These laws and customs were incorporated into one general body, and made a part of the unwritten or customary law of Rome. "The law of the ancient Romans," says Dr. Burn, in the preface to his book on ecclesiastical law, [s] "had its foundation in the Grecian republicks."

It is well known, that the Roman system of jurisprudence was much indebted to the wise and peaceful institutions of Numa. There was one, which produced strong, and extensive, and lasting consequences in the Roman republick; and which seems to have furnished an example for later times — the establishment of *pagi* or villages. The conquered and vacant lands he distributed among the citizens. These he divided into districts, and placed over each a superintendant, in order to induce them to improve in the arts of agriculture. The consequence of this wise regulation was, that the functions of war and peace were frequently discharged by one and the same person. The farmer, the soldier, and the magistrate were often united in the same character; and reflected on each other reciprocal ornament. The respected citizen stepped from the plough to the consulship without being elated; and, without being mortified, returned from the consulship to the plough. Thus the Cincinnati were formed.

Towards the latter end of the third century of Rome, a solemn deputation, consisting of three commissioners, was despatched to Athens, with instructions to obtain a transcript of the celebrated laws of Solon, and to make themselves fully acquainted with the regulations, the manners, and the institutions of the other states of Greece. [t]

[q] Pett. on Jur. 159.   [r] Bever. 2.   [s] P. I.   [t] Livy. l. 3. c. 31.

The constitution of Athens had lately received great improvements under the administration of some of her most illustrious citizens, Aristides, Themistocles, and Cimon; and, at this very time, the splendid Pericles was at the head of her government.

After an absence of about two years, the commissioners returned, with copies of the Athenian laws. The decemvirs, of whom the commissioners were three, were then appointed, with full powers to form and propose a digest of laws for Rome. With much alacrity and zeal they entered upon the execution of the very important trust, with which they were invested by their confiding country. In the arduous business, they received the most valuable assistance from a wise Ephesian, who had been driven, by the hand of envy, from his native country; and who, during his exile, had opportunities of personally observing the principles and characters of men, and the establishments and forms of society. His accumulated treasures of observation and reflection were imparted liberally to the decemvirs. The name of Hermodorus was gratefully transmitted to posterity, by a statue erected to his honour in the forum.

The code, which the decemvirs composed, consisted partly of entire laws transcribed from the Grecian originals; partly of such as were altered and accommodated to the constitution and manners of the Romans; and partly of the former laws received and approved in Rome. It was engraved on ten tables, and fixed up in the most conspicuous part of the forum; that the whole people might have an opportunity of perusing and examining it at their conveniency and leisure. When sufficient time had been allowed for those purposes, an assembly of the people was convened. In that assembly, after invocations that what might be done should prove happy and auspicious to the commonwealth, the proposed laws were read. The decemvirs declared, that they had provided, as far as their abilities could provide, that the laws should be equal and impartial to the high and to the low; but that on the counsels and deliberations of the citizens at large, more reliance could be placed; for that the Roman people should have no laws, but such as were ratified as well as ordered by the consent of all.[u] The ten tables received the solemn ratification of the people. Two more were afterwards added in a second decemvirate. All these formed the celebrated code of the twelve tables; the fountain, as Livy honourably denominates them, of all publick and private law. They constituted the foundation of that immense fabrick of jurispudence, which has extended the influence and the glory of Rome, far beyond the limits and existence of the Roman power.

To the twelve tables, after some time, the *responsa prudentum* began to be superadded. These were the commentaries of lawyers, who accommodated them to the successive practice and proceedings of the courts of

[u] Livy. l. 3. c. 34.

justice. This part of the law was denominated, in contradistinction to the laws of the twelve tables, the *jus non scriptum*, or unwritten law; and having no other name, began then to be called the *civil* law. By Justinian, it is styled the *jurisprudentia media;* because it intervened between the laws of the twelve tables, and the imperial constitutions.[v]

In the free and happy periods of the Roman commonwealth, great regard was paid to customary law. We have already seen,[w] on another occasion, that it was thought immaterial whether a law received the sanction of the people by their formal suffrage, or by the uniform course of their conduct and manners. Thus did Romans speak and reason while they enjoyed the blessings of liberty. Nor did the spirit of their law change immediately with the spirit of their government. Long after the impure air of despotism tainted the latter, the vital principles of freedom continued the former in a tolerable state of internal health and soundness. Even under the emperours, the opinions of the Roman lawyers, and the decisions of the Roman courts, with regard to property, and to the rights of private persons, seem not to have been vitiated by the principles of their government. The rules of justice among individuals could not prejudice, in the most remote degree, the power or the interest of the emperour, placed above the reach of all private regards; their rights were, therefore, investigated and enforced with a balanced impartiality.[x]

I have observed, that, in the free and happy periods of the Roman commonwealth, great regard was paid to customary law. Even so late as the time of Justinian, the unwritten law constituted one of the two great divisions, into which the system of Roman jurisprudence was thrown. "Constat," [y] says the emperour, "autem jus nostrum, quo utimur, aut scripto, aut sine scripto; ut apud Græcos των νομων ὁι μεν εγγραφοι ὁι δε αγραφοι." "Our law, which we use, consists, like the law of Grecians, of what is written, and of what is unwritten." This passage, by the by, strongly intimates, in the Institutes, a principle of attachment and imitation operating in favour of the Grecian system. This principle appears, in the most explicit manner, from what we find in the next section of the Institutes. "Et non ineleganter in duas species jus civile distributum esse videtur; nam origo ejus ab institutis duarum civitatum, Athenarum scilicet et Lacedæmoniorum, fluxisse videtur. In his enim civitatibus ita agi solitum erat, ut Lacedæmonii quidem ea, quæ pro legibus observabant, memoriæ mandarent: Athenienses vero ea quæ in legibus scripta comprehendissent, custodirent." "The civil or municipal law is divided, with some degree of elegance, into two kinds. For its origin seems to be

---

[v] Burn's Ecc. Law. Pref. 1.   [w] Ante. p. 102.
[x] Consult Gibbon's Rom. Emp. c. 44. vol. 8. p. 19. and the authorities cited in his notes.
[y] Just. Ins. l. 1. t. 2. s. 3.

derived from the institutions of two states — that of the Athenians, and that of the Lacedæmonians. In those states, the manner of transacting their legislative business was such, that the Lacedæmonians trusted to memory for the preservation of their laws; whereas the laws of the Athenians were committed to writing."

Concerning unwritten or customary law, Justinian thus expresses himself. "Sine scripto jus venit, quod usus approbavit; nam *diuturni* mores, consensu utentium comprobati, legem imitantur." "The unwritten law supervenes upon the approbation of usage; for long customs, approved by the consent of those who use them, acquire the qualities of a law." By the way, it deserves to be remarked here, that the expression, which, on a former occasion,[y] I cited from an act of parliament as characteristick of the common law of England, is the literal translation of the expression used by Justinian to characterize the unwritten law of the Roman empire — diuturnus — long. The epithet *immemorial* is used by neither of those very high authorities.

If unwritten law possessed such a dignified rank in the system of Roman jurisprudence so late as even the reign of Justinian; we may be well justified in supposing that this species of law was entitled to a still greater proportion of regard, four or five centuries before that time. Four or five centuries before that time, it was extended to the island of Great Britain.

The jurisprudence, which had been grossly adapted to the wants of the first Romans, was polished and improved, towards the latter years of the commonwealth, by the infusion and operation of the Grecian philosophy. The Scævolas had been taught by precedents and experience. But Servius Sulpicius was the first civilian, who established his art on certain and general principles. For the discernment of truth and falsehood, he applied, as an infallible rule, the logick of Aristotle and the Stoicks, reduced particular cases to general principles, and diffused, over the dark and shapeless mass, the light of order, and the graces of eloquence.

The jurisprudence of Rome was adorned and enriched by the exquisite genius of Cicero, which, like the touch of Midas, converts every object into gold. In imitation of Plato, he composed a republick: and for the use of his republick, formed a system of laws. In this system, he expatiates on the wisdom and excellency of the Roman constitution.[z]

Julius Cæsar was the first Roman who visited the island of Great Britain; and, perhaps, he had no great reason to exult in the success of his visit. His own account of his retreat is unfurnished with a decent apology. The poet, whose republican spirit was unbroke to the pliant arts of flattery, says in explicit terms,

[y] Ante. p. 185.
[z] Consult Gib. Rom. Emp. c. 44. vol. 8. p. 26. 27. and the authorities cited.

Territa quæsitis ostendit terga Britannis.*

The first foundations of an effective conquest and a permanent settlement, which were laid in Britain under the auspices of Rome, were those,
which were begun in the reign of the emperour Claudius.

The character of his administration may be thus described. From the
general tenour of his conduct it is plain, that he contemplated the senate
as the sovereign power of the whole empire. He made many attempts
to introduce an improvement of the constitution, by reviving or reform-
ing antiquated laws, and by enacting salutary new ones: but these attempts he meditated and prosecuted by the advice and with the concurrence of the senate. So far, therefore, as the establishments in Britain
were carried on during the administration of Claudius, it is not likely
that they were marked by circumstances of uncommon rigour or oppression. Indeed, the acquisitions made in the island during that and some
succeeding reigns were both very limited and very precarious.

Julius Agricola, who governed it in the reign of Vespasian, Titus, and
Domitian, was the first who formed a regular plan for completing the
conquest, and rendering the acquisition useful to the conquerors. Among
the Britons he introduced the Roman civility and laws; he reconciled
them to the Roman manners and language; he instructed them in learning and the arts; he taught them to know and to covet all the conveniences and delicacies of life; he employed every soothing contrivance
to render their fetters easy, and even fashionable. The inhabitants, taught,
by direful experience, how disproportioned their military strength and
military skill were to the military strength and military skill of the Romans, and lulled by the flattering scenes of ease and elegance, which were
exhibited to their views and wishes, acquiesced in the splendid dominion
of their masters, and were gradually incorporated as a portion of the
mighty empire of Rome.[a]

Agricola disseminated the modes of Roman education among the sons
of the British nobility; and improved them so well, that, in a short time,
those who had most despised the Roman language, applied with ardour,
to the study and the profession of Roman eloquence. An affectation of
the Roman dress was the natural consequence; and the gown was considered in Britain as a splendid distinction. Luxury succeeded splendour
and refinement; and the Britons were Romanised, without reflecting that
the arts and accomplishments which were liberal in a Roman, were, in a
Briton, servile; and that what they viewed as the accompaniments of
politeness, were, in reality, nothing better or nobler than the instruments
of subjection.[b]

* [He showed his frightened back to the Britons he had pursued.]
[a] 1. Guth. Eng. 40.
[b] Tac. Agric. c. 21. — Millar. 16. 17.

The Romans held the possession and the government of the most considerable part of Britain near four hundred years. During that long period, a very frequent and intimate intercommunication of marriages, manners, customs, and laws must have taken place.

In the whole province there are said to have been about one hundred and fifty Roman stations.[e] These were connected by inferiour fortresses, erected at proper distances, and garrisoned by regular troops. Each of those garrisons attracted the neighbouring inhabitants; a town or village was begun; and a settlement was formed indiscriminately by Roman and by native families. As military service was often rewarded with possessions in land, the example of the Roman officers and soldiers must have spread the knowledge and practice of agriculture, while their industry in the management of their estates contributed to beautify and improve the face of the country.

The connexion with Britain, which the soldiers of the Roman army formed by living in the country, was seldom dissolved, even when they were discharged from the service. They had gradually acquired an attachment to the places where they had long resided, and chose to continue that residence where their attachment was now formed. Their offspring became natural inhabitants; and Britain, in this manner, received fresh accessions of Romans, to supply the place of such natives as were drawn from it, in order to recruit the army in other provinces of the empire.

It was the policy of Rome to extend her jurisprudence wherever she had extended her dominion. This policy promoted her influence and her interest among the vanquished people; and, at the same time, established among them tranquillity and order. This policy was peculiarly necessary in Britain, to prevent the private wars, and restrain the mutual acts of violence and outrage, to which the inhabitants were remarkably addicted. The introduction and establishment of the Roman laws was unavoidably, however, a work of time. For a considerable period, the Roman magistrates confined their operations to the publick administration of the province; while the British chiefs were permitted to retain their ancient jurisdiction in matters of private property, and to determine the controversies of their tenants and dependents.

Some writers are of opinion, that this jurisdiction was gradually circumscribed, and, at last, entirely annihilated; and that, during the long government of the Romans, the original laws and customs of the Britons were disused and forgotten. Perhaps the more probable opinion is, that, during this extended succession of time, the two nations became blended together in their laws and customs, as well as by their intermarriages; so as to be neither wholly Roman, nor wholly British. Those laws, in-

[e] Millar. 10.

deed, which related to government and the administration of publick affairs, were, it may be presumed, altogether Roman.

Accordingly, when the exhausted empire was obliged to collect her last expiring efforts around the immediate seat of life and existence; the departure of the Romans from Britain was fatal to all the institutions of government which had been formed, ripened, and established during the long lapse of time, which we have already mentioned. The officers, who directed and managed the administration of the province, and the judges, who, at least in matters relating to publick law, had acquired a complete jurisdiction, retired from a country, abandoned by its master. The courts of justice were shut: government, and the order attendant on government, were dissolved. The rudder of the state knew no hand, which had a right to hold it: the vessel was, therefore, tossed at the pleasure of the winds and waves.

Time, however, and necessity gradually introduced some form of government, though a very simple one. The country was broken into districts, and placed under chiefs. A general of their united forces was appointed. Voltigern was the last, who was promoted to that high dignity.

From the foregoing deduction, it is highly probable, that, at the period to which we have now brought our remarks, the system of law in Britain, if, at that period, any kind of law deserved the name of a system, was a motley mixture of Roman and British institutions. The language, at that time used in Britain, was, as we have every reason to believe, a composition of the Roman and British tongues.

Sir William Blackstone mentions three instances,[d] in which the British jurisprudence bears a great resemblance to some of the modern doctrines of the English law. One is, the very notion itself of an oral unwritten law, delivered down from age to age, by custom and tradition merely. This seems derived from the practice of the Druids, who never committed any of their instructions to writing. This observation suggests a claim, unquestionably, to the notion of a common law subsisting among the Britons. But it, by no means, authorizes an exclusive claim. We have seen that, in the pure times of the Roman commonwealth, a customary law was known and highly respected at Rome. At the time when the Roman law was translated to Britain, it retained its customary qualities in their full vigour and extent.

The second instance mentioned by Sir William Blackstone is, the partible quality of lands by the custom of gavelkind, which still obtains in many parts of England, and, till the reign of Henry the eighth, prevailed universally over Wales. This, says he, is undoubtedly of British original. But the partible quality of lands, if not entirely, yet nearly on the same principles, prevailed among the Romans, as well as among the Britons.

[d] 4. Bl. Com. 401.

Nor was it confined even to those two nations. The Greeks, the Romans, as we are informed in the Commentaries, the Britons, the Saxons, and even originally the feudists divided the lands equally; some among all the children at large, some among the males only.[e]

The third instance, mentioned by Sir William Blackstone as of British original, is, the ancient division of the goods of an intestate between his widow and children, or next of kin; which has since been revived by the statute of distributions. But it is well known, that the statute of distributions is moulded in the form of Roman as well as of ancient British jurisprudence.[f]

Well known is the event of the invitation, which Voltigern gave to a body of the Saxons to aid him against his northern enemies.[g] As it has happened on other occasions, the allies became the masters of those whom they engaged to assist.

We have no complete account of the circumstances which attended the settlement of the Saxons in Britain. From the doleful representations of some early and passionate annalists, our historians, in general, have been led to suppose, that all the Britons, who were not reduced to captivity, were massacred by their barbarous enemies, or, disdaining submission, retreated among the mountains of Wales, or withdrew into the country of Armorica in France; to which country, the name of Bretagne is said to have been derived from those unfortunate refugees. A bold and industrious antiquarian has lately shown, however, that this extraordinary supposition is without any solid foundation. It is, indeed, highly probable, that many of the Britons were subjected to very great hardships, and were obliged even to abandon their native soil. But it appears hard to believe, that the Saxons should be stimulated by barbarity to proceed so far as, contrary to their own interests, to exterminate the ancient inhabitants. There is even complete evidence, that, in some parts of the island, the Britons were so far from being destroyed or obliged to fly their country, that they were permitted to retain a certain proportion of their landed property. This proportion, a third part of the whole, was the same with that allotted to the ancient inhabitants, in some of those provinces on the continent of Europe, which were conquered by the other German tribes.

The language, which spread itself among the Saxons after their settlement in Britain, contained a great proportion of the Latin and British tongues. This large infusion of those different ingredients into the same language, is, of itself, a strong proof, that the inhabitants were compounded of the different nations, by whom those tongues were originally spoken.[h]

[e] 2. Bl. Com. 215.   [f] 2. Bl. Com. 516. 517. Bever. 482.   [g] 2. Whitak. 545.
[h] 2. Whitak. 235. 236.

The victorious Saxons were less civilized than the conquered Britons. The latter gradually communicated to the former a portion of that refinement, which had not been entirely effaced from themselves. At last, after a lapse of near two centuries, the two nations, by habits, treaties, commerce, and intermarriages, were entirely blended together; and their union produced such a compound system of manners and customs, as might be expected to arise from the declining state of one, and the improving state of the other. This blending principle would have its effect upon the laws, as well as upon the manners and habits of both nations. The conquerors and the conquered would be incorporated into one people, and compose, as the antiquarian[1] before mentioned expresses himself, a mingled mass of Saxon Britons and British Saxons.

We are told of three kinds of laws used in England during the government of the Saxons: the Mercian law, which contained the local constitutions of the kingdom of Mercia; the Dane law, which comprised the customs introduced by those, whose name it bore; and the West Saxon law, a system compiled by Alfred the Great; whose elevated and extensive talents were employed, in the most vigorous manner, for the improvement of the laws and constitution of his country.

These three systems of law were different, rather in unessential forms, than in important principles. For this we have the authority of the very learned Spelman. "Our Saxons, though divided into many kingdoms, yet were they all one, in effect, in manners, laws, and language: so that the breaking of their government into many kingdoms, or the reuniting of their kingdoms into a monarchy, wrought little or no change among them, touching laws. For though we talk of the West Saxon law, the Mercian law, and the Dane law, whereby the west parts of England, the middle parts, and those of Suffolk, Norfolk, and the north were severally governed; yet held they all a uniformity of substance, differing rather in their mulcts, than in their canon, that is, in the quantity of fines and amerciaments, than in the course and frame of justice." [j]

These distinct codes were afterwards reduced into one uniform digest, for the use and observance of the whole kingdom. This digest was undertaken and commenced by King Edgar: it was completed by his grandson, King Edward; and has been since well known and distinguished by the appellation of the Confessor's laws. It is conjectured to have been chiefly a revival of the code of the great Alfred, accompanied with such improvements as were suggested by subsequent experience.

We have now brought the history of the common law down to the period of the Norman conquest. We have seen its rise taking place, by slow degrees, in ages very remote, and in nations very different from one another. We have seen it, in its converging progress, run into one

[1] 2. Whitak. 111.   [j] 2. Henry. 277. 278. cites Spel. Rel. p. 49.

uniform system, mellowed by time and improved by experience. In every period of its existence, we find imprinted on it the most distinct and legible characters of a customary law — a law produced, extended, translated, adopted, and moulded by practice and consent.

The period through which we have gone is, indeed, peculiarly interesting. "The whole period of our national history before the conquest," says an English writer, "is the most important and momentous in our annals. It most forcibly lays hold upon the passions by the quick succession and active variety of incidents, and by the decisive greatness of its revolutions. And, what is much more, it is that period of our history, which gives the body and the form to all the succeeding centuries of it. It contains the actual commencement of every part of our publick and private economy." [k]

Here we make a pause in the history of the common law. To pursue it minutely from the Norman conquest to the accession of the Stuart line would be a tedious, a disagreeable, but, fortunately, it is an unnecessary task.

The common law, as now received in America, bears, in its principles, and in many of its more minute particulars, a stronger and a fairer resemblance to the common law as it was improved under the Saxon, than to that law, as it was disfigured under the Norman government. How much it was disfigured, and why we should not receive it in its disfigured state, will appear from the following very interesting part of Sir William Blackstone's Commentaries.

"The last and most important alteration, introduced by the Norman conquest, both in our civil and military polity, was the ingrafting on all landed estates, a few only excepted, the fiction of feodal tenure; which drew after it a numerous and oppressive train of servile fruits and appendages; aids, reliefs, primer seisins, wardships, marriages, escheats, and fines for alienation; the genuine consequences of the maxim then adopted, that all the lands in England were derived from, and holden, mediately or immediately, of the crown.

"The nation, at this period, seems to have groaned under as absolute a slavery, as it was in the power of a warlike, an ambitious, and a politick prince to create. The consciences of men were enslaved by sour ecclesiasticks, devoted to a foreign power, and unconnected with the civil state under which they lived; who now imported from Rome, for the first time, the whole farrago of superstitious novelties, which had been engendered by the blindness and corruption of the times, between the first mission of Augustin, the monk, and the Norman conquest.

"The ancient trial by jury gave way to the impious decision by battle. The forest laws totally restrained all rural pleasures and manly recreations.

[k] 1. Whitak. Pref. 7.

And in cities and towns, the case was no better; all company being obliged to disperse, and fire and candle to be extinguished, by eight at night, at the sound of the melancholy curfew.

"The ultimate property of all lands, and a considerable share of the present profits, were vested in the king, or by him granted out to his Norman favourites; who, by a gradual progression of slavery, were absolute vassals to the crown, and as absolute tyrants to the commons. Unheard of fortfeitures, talliages, aids, and fines were arbitrarily extracted from the pillaged landholders, in pursuance of the new system of tenure. And, to crown all, as a consequence of the tenure by knight service, the king had always ready at his command an army of sixty thousand knights, or *milites;* who were bound, upon pain of confiscating their estates, to attend him in time of invasion, or to quell any domestick insurrection.

"Trade, or foreign merchandise, such as it then was, was carried on by the Jews and Lombards; and the very name of an English fleet, which king Edgar had rendered so formidable, was utterly unknown to Europe: the nation consisting wholly of the clergy, who were also the lawyers; the barons, or great lords of the land; the knights or soldiery, who were the subordinate landholders; and the burghers, or inferiour tradesmen, who, from their insignificancy, happily retained, in their socage and burgage tenure, some points of their ancient freedom. All the rest were villains or bond men.

"From so complete and well concerted a scheme of servility, it has been the work of generations for our ancestors, to redeem themselves and their posterity into that state of liberty, which we now enjoy: and which, therefore, is not to be looked upon as consisting of mere encroachments on the crown, and infringements of the prerogative, as some slavish and narrow minded writers in the last century endeavoured to maintain; but as, in general, a gradual restoration of that ancient constitution, whereof our Saxon forefathers had been unjustly deprived, partly by the policy, and partly by the force, of the Norman." [1]

From the deduction, which we have made, it appears, I think, in a satisfactory manner, that the rich composition of the common law is formed from all the different ingredients, which have been enumerated; yet, when we descend to particular principles and rules, it is very difficult, it is often impossible, to ascertain the particular source, from which such rules and principles have been drawn. That some of our customs have been derived from the Grecians, though probably through the intermediate channel of the Romans; that others of them have been derived immediately from the Romans, others from the Britons, others from the Saxons, and others, in fine, from the Normans, seems to be evinced by the reasonable rules of historical credibility. But to say that

[1] 4. Bl. Com. 411 — 413.

such or such a particular custom has descended to us from such and such a particular origin, would be often to hazard too much upon uncertain conjecture. It may, however, be done sometimes, upon facts and arguments, which are clear and convincing: and whenever it can be done, it will amply repay all the care and trouble of the investigation. As has been already mentioned, the most proper way to teach and to study the common law, is to teach and to study it as a historical science. Under many titles, we shall have an opportunity of pursuing this method.

Besides those particular instances; of which notice will be taken afterwards; there is one pretty general distribution of the common law, according to which, different parts of it may be referred to different nations, by whom, in all probability, they were introduced.

The original frame of the British constitution, different, indeed, in many important points, from what it now is, and bearing, to some of the constitutions which have lately been formed, and established in America, a degree of resemblance, which will strike and surprise those who compare them together — this venerable frame may be considered as of Saxon architecture. To a Saxon origin may also be ascribed much of that part of the common law, which relates to crimes and punishments. One lovely feature, in particular, we have the pleasure to recognise. The ancient Germans, of whom the Saxons composed a part, discriminated punishments, as we are informed by Tacitus,[m] according to the kind, and proportioned them according to the measure of the crime. "Liberty," says the celebrated Montesquieu,[n] "is in its highest perfection, when criminal laws derive each punishment from the particular nature of the crime." With regard to this very interesting part of the law, very wide deviations from Saxon principles have been made in the English criminal code, since the period of the Norman conquest.

The common law, as it respects contracts and personal property, discovers evident traces of the Roman jurisprudence. It has been the opinion of some, that those parts of the common law have been borrowed from the civil law, subsequent to the great legislative era,[o] when the pandects of Justinian were discovered at Amalfi: I suggest, merely for consideration at present, a conjecture, that many of those parts were incorporated into the common law, during the long period of near four centuries, when the Roman jurisprudence predominated in England.

Much of the common law respecting real estates, as it has been received in England since the time of William the Conqueror; and a considerable part of it, as it is still received in that kingdom, particularly the feudal principles and policy, should be referred to a Norman extraction.

Concerning the period, at which the feudal system was introduced into England, there has been long and learned controversy among lawyers and

[m] De mor. Germ. c. 12.   [n] Spir. Laws. b. 12. c. 4.   [o] About the year 1130.

antiquarians. "At the close of the first century," says Whitaker in his History of Manchester, "our tenures in Britain appear undeniably to have been purely military in their design, and absolutely feudal in their essence. The primary institution of feuds is unanimously deduced, by our historical and legal antiquarians, from the northern invaders of the Roman empire; and the primary introduction of them into this island is almost as unanimously referred to the much more recent epocha of the Norman conquest. But they certainly existed among us before, and even formed the primitive establishment of the Britons." "They must have existed coeval with the first plantation of the island. They were plainly the joint result of a colonizing and a military spirit. The former providentially animated the first ages of the Noachidæ, was constantly prosecuted under the discipline of regular order, and the control of regal authority, and had whole regions to partition among the members of the colony. The latter was excited by the frequent migrations of colonists and the numerous invasions of settlements in the same ages, and naturally provided for the security of the colony, by the institution of a military establishment." [p]

From Mr. Whitaker's own account, it appears that he is singular in his sentiments with regard to the antiquity of the feudal system. Indeed, if his sentiments are well founded, that system must have been coeval and coextensive with society itself. But from the account which we have already[q] given of the origin and first principles of society, the inference, we apprehend, may be fairly made, that its first ages were ages of equality, perhaps of some culpable degree of license. The opinion is indeed singular — that rule and subordination in the extreme, in other words, tyranny and slavery, should be necessarily extended with the extension of the human race.

It is remarkable, however, that this very writer makes, with regard to the Saxons, a peculiar exception from this general and almost universal system. "No traces," says he, "of the primitive feuds appear visible among the Saxons; and they seem to have been the only nation of Germany that did not plant them in their conquests." [r] His conjecture, therefore, is, that the Saxons had adopted this improvement from the Britons. He represents the whole Saxon system, in consequence of this adoption, as informed with one strong principle of subordination, which diffused its influence through every part, and formed a scale of dependence from the sovereign to the villain. Thus, one continued chain of subordination was carried regularly from the villain to the monarch; the higher link of the whole being fastened to the foot of the throne, and keeping the whole machine of national power steadily dependent from it.[s]

Others inform us, and apparently on better grounds, that in the early

[p] 1. Whitak. 262. 264.   [q] Ante. p. 240.   [r] 2. Whitak. 153.   [s] Id. 157. 158.

ages of society, estates in land were free; that they were held in propriety, and not by tenure; that they were hereditary as well as free; that such were the real estates of the Greeks, of the Romans, and particularly of the Saxons; that, among the latter, they were alienable likewise at the pleasure of the owner, and devisable by will. The Saxons were absolutely masters of their land; and were not obliged to transmit it to the blood which the donor intended to favour. It was still, however, considered as the property of a citizen; and, therefore, subjected its owner to the general obligation of taking arms in defence of his country.

The differences between estates in land under the Saxon government, and those which were held under that of the conqueror, will be plain and striking by a short enumeration and contrast. Before the conquest, lands were the absolute proprieties of the owners; they could be devised and transferred at pleasure. No wardship or marriage was due or exacted. In all these things, an alteration was made on the introduction of the feudal tenures. Lands could not be alienated without the consent of the superiour: they could not be devised by will. The heir had no right to enter into the inheritance of his ancestor, until he had paid a relief, and had been admitted by his lord. As to landed estates, therefore, the law introduced by the conqueror might well be denominated a new, a Norman law.

At common law, too, all inheritances were estates in fee simple; of different kinds indeed, qualified and conditional, as well as absolute.[t]

"When all estates were fee simple," says my Lord Coke, "then were purchasers sure of their purchases, farmers of their leases, creditors of their debts: and for these, and other like causes, by the wisdom of the common law, all estates of inheritance were fee simple: and what contentions and mischiefs have crept into the quiet of the law by these fettered inheritances, daily experience teacheth us." [u]

"Out of all the books and reports of the common law," says the same very experienced judge, "I have observed, that though sometimes by acts of parliament, and sometimes by invention and contrivance of men, some points of the ancient common law have been diverted from its proper channel; yet, in the revolutions of time, it has been, with much publick satisfaction, and to avoid many great inconveniences, restored to its proper and ancient course. For example, the wisdom of the common law was, that all estates of inheritance should be fee simple, so that one man might safely alien, demise, and contract to and with another. But the statute of Westminster the second created an estate tail, and made a perpetuity by act of parliament, restraining tenant in tail from aliening or demising, but only for his own life. This, in process of time, in-

[t] 2. Ins. 333.   [u] 1. Ins. 19b.

troduced such trouble and mischief, that, after two hundred years, necessity discovered a method, by law, for a tenant in tail to alien.

"In like manner, by the ancient common law, freeholds could not pass from one to another but by matter of record, or solemn livery of seisin. Against this, however, uses were invented, and grew common and almost universal, in destruction of the ancient common law in that point. But, in time, the numerous inconveniences of this being found by experience, the statute of 27. H. VIII. c. 10. was made to restore the ancient common law, in this particular, as expressly appears by the preamble of the statute itself. Of the same truth, an infinity of other examples might be produced; but these shall, at present, suffice." [v]

We have mentioned the common law, as a law which is unwritten. When we assign to it this character, we mean not that it is merely oral, and transmitted from age to age merely by tradition. It has its monuments in writing; and its written monuments are accurate and authentick. But though, in many cases, its *evidence* rests, yet, in all cases, its *authority* rests not, on those written monuments. Its authority rests on reception, approbation, custom, long and established. The same principles, which establish it, change, enlarge, improve, and repeal it. These operations, however, are, for the most part, gradual and imperceptible, partial and successive in a long tract of time.

It is the characteristick of a system of common law, that it be accommodated to the circumstances, the exigencies, and the conveniencies of the people, by whom it is appointed. Now, as these circumstances, and exigencies, and conveniencies insensibly change; a proportioned change, in time and in degree, must take place in the accommodated system. But though the system suffer these partial and successive alterations, yet it continues materially and substantially the same. The ship of the Argonauts became not another vessel, though almost every part of her materials had been altered during the course of her voyage.

Again; we are taught both by observation and by experience, that the farther laws reach from their original institutions, the more extensive and the more numerous they become. In the first association of a community, their prospect is not enlarged, their wants are comparatively few: but as the society increases, their views expand, and their wishes multiply: what is the consequence? New laws and provisions, suited to the growing multitude of successive exigencies, must be made. The system, of course, becomes larger and more complex.

The same principle of accommodation in a system of common law, will adjust its improvement to every grade and species of improvement made by the people, in consequence of practice, commerce, observation,

[v] 3. Rep. Pref. 18.

study, and refinement. As the science of legislation is the most noble, so it is the most slow and difficult of sciences. The jurisprudence of a state, willing to avail itself of experience, receives additional improvement from every new situation, to which it arrives; and, in this manner, attains, in the progress of time, higher and higher degrees of perfection, resulting from the accumulated wisdom of ages. The illustrious legislators, who have illuminated the political world, such as Solon, Numa, Lycurgus, collected the customs which they found already adopted, and disposed them regularly, with the necessary amendments and illustrations.

The same principle of accommodation, which we have already traced in so many directions, may be traced in still one direction more. It silently and gradually introduces; it silently and gradually withdraws its customary laws. Disuse may be justly considered as the repeal of custom. Laws, which are long unobserved in practice, become laws, which are antiquated in theory. "On strong grounds this rule is received, that laws may be abrogated, not only by the express declaration of the legislature, but, through desuetude, by the tacit consent of all." [w] A law ought not, indeed, to be presumed obsolete upon slight pretences; but, on the other hand, a total disuse, for a long period of time, may be justly considered as a sufficient reason for not carrying into effect a disrespected and neglected ordinance.

"It has happened to the law, as to other productions of human invention, particularly those which are closely connected with the transactions of mankind, that the changes wrought by a series of years have been gradually rendering many parts of it obsolete; so that the systems of one age have become the objects of mere historick remembrance in the next. of the numerous volumes that compose a lawyer's library, how many are consigned to oblivion by the revolutions in opinions and practice; and what a small part of those, which are still considered as in use, is necessary for the purposes of common business!" [x]

There are some great eras, when important and very perceptible alterations take place in the situation of men and things: at such eras, the accommodating principle, which we have so often mentioned, will introduce similar and adequate alterations in the rules and practice of the common law. Such considerable changes, together with their extensive influences, diffuse, over many parts of the system, a new air and appearance. At some of those eras, the improvement is as rapid as the change is great. Why should not the present age in America, form one of those happy eras?

During many — very many revolving centuries, the common law has been the peculiar and the deserved favourite of the people of England.

[w] D. l. 1. t. 3. l. 32. p. 1.   [x] 1. Reeve. Pref. 1. Roll. Pref. 3 — 5.

It suffered much, as we have seen, from the violence of the Norman conquest; but it still continued the theme of their warmest praise, and the object of their fondest hopes. Its complete restoration was the burthen of every memorial, and the prayer of every petition. The knowledge of this law formed a considerable part of the little learning of the early and unenlightened ages.

Those, who had received the best education, says Selden, in his dissertation on Fleta,[y] applied themselves assiduously to the study of the ancient English laws and manners, which related to government and the administration of civil affairs. From such characters judges and licensed advocates were selected. These laws and manners were taught in the private families of the most illustrious characters of the kingdom, in monasteries, in colleges, in universities. They had no acquaintance with the Theodosian or Justinian codes. They taught only the manners of our ancestors, and that law, which, even before the period of which we speak, and down to our own times, is known by the name of the common law of England.

The affectionate manner, in which the great and good Lord Chief Justice Hale speaks of this law, recommends it and him with equal warmth. He introduces it — as the common municipal law of the kingdom — as the superintendent of all the particular laws known in any of the courts of justice — as the common rule for the administration of publick affairs in that great kingdom — as the object, of which that great kingdom had been always tender; and with great reason; not only because it is a very just and excellent law in itself; but also because it is singularly accommodated to the frame of the English government, and to the disposition of the English nation. As such, it is by a long experience, incorporated into their very temperament, and has become the constitution of the English commonwealth.[z]

In the natural body, diseases will happen; but a due temperament and a sound constitution will, by degrees, work out those adventitious and accidental diseases, and will restore the body to its just state and situation. So is it in the body politick, whose constitution is animated and invigorated by the common law. When, through the errours, or distempers, or iniquities of men or times, the peace of the nation, or the right order of government have received interruption; the common law has wrought out those errours, distempers, and iniquities; and has reinstated the nation in its natural and peaceful state and temperament.

The best kings of England have been always jealous and vigilant to reform what has, at any time, been found defective in that law; to remove all obstacles, which could obstruct its free course; and to support,

[y] c. 7. s. r.   [z] Hale. Hist. 44.

countenance, and encourage it, as the best, the safest, and the truest rule of justice in all matters, criminal as well as civil.[a]

We have seen how much the common law has been loved and revered by individuals, by families, and by the different seminaries of education throughout England: let us now see how much it has been respected by even the legislative power of the kingdom.

On a petition to parliament for redress, in the thirteenth year of Richard the second, the following remarkable judgment of parliament is entered — It appears to the lords of parliament, that the petition is not a proper petition to parliament; since the matter contained in it ought to be determined by the common law: and, therefore, it was awarded, that the party petitioning should take nothing by his suit in parliament; because he might sue at common law, if he thought proper.[b]

We have viewed, in a number of instances, the accommodating spirit of the common law. In other instances its temper is decided and firm. The means are varied according to times and circumstances; but the great ends of liberty are kept steadily and constantly in view.

Its foundations, laid in the most remote antiquity, have not been overturned by the successive invasions, or migrations, or revolutions which have taken place. The reason has been already hinted at: it contains the common dictates of nature, refined by wisdom and experience, as occasions offer, and cases arise.

In all sciences, says my Lord Bacon,[c] they are the soundest, that keep close to particulars. Indeed a science appears to be best formed into a system, by a number of instances drawn from observation and experience, and reduced gradually into general rules; still subject, however, to the successive improvements, which future observation or experience may suggest to be proper. The natural progress of the human mind, in the acquisition of knowledge, is from particular facts to general principles. This progress is familiar to all in the business of life; it is the only one, by which real discoveries have been made in philosophy; and it is the one, which has directed and superintended the instauration of the common law. In this view, common law, like natural philosophy, when properly studied, is a science founded on experiment. The latter is improved and established by carefully and wisely attending to the phenomena of the material world; the former, by attending, in the same manner, to those of man and society. Hence, in both, the most regular and undeviating principles will be found, on accurate investigation, to guide and control the most diversified and disjointed appearances.

How steadily and how effectually has the spirit of liberty animated the common law, in all the vicissitudes, revolutions, and dangers, to which

[a] Hale. Hist. 44. 45.   [b] Hale. Hist. 46. 47.   [c] 4. Ld. Bac. 5.

that system has been exposed! In matters of a civil nature, that system works itself pure by rules drawn from the fountain of justice: in matters of a political nature, it works itself pure by rules drawn from the fountain of freedom.

It was this spirit, which dictated the frequent and formidable demands on the Norman princes, for the complete restoration of the Saxon jurisprudence: it was this spirit, which, in magna charta, manifested a strict regard to the rights of the commons, as well as to those of the peerage: it was this spirit, which extracted sweetness from all the bitter contentions between the rival houses of Lancaster and York: it was this spirit, which preserved England from the haughtiness of the Tudors, and from the tyranny of the Stuarts: it was this spirit, which rescued the States of America from the oppressive claims, and from all the mighty efforts made to enforce the oppressive claims, of a British parliament.

The common law of England, says my Lord Coke,[a] is a social system of jurisprudence: she receives other laws and systems into a friendly correspondence: she associates to herself those, who can communicate to her information, or give her advice and assistance. Does a question arise before her, which properly ought to be resolved by the law of nations? By the information received from that law, the question will be decided: for the law of nations, is, in its full extent, adopted by the common law, and deemed and treated as a part of the law of the land. Does a mercantile question occur? It is determined by the law of merchants. By that law, controversies concerning bills of exchange, freight, bottomry, and ensurances receive their decision. That law is indeed a part of the law of nations; but it is peculiarly appropriated to the subjects before mentioned. Disputes concerning prizes, shipwrecks, hostages, and ransombills, are, under the auspices of the common law, settled and adjudged by the same universal rule of decision. Does a contract, in litigation, bear a peculiar reference to the local laws of any particular foreign country? By the local laws of that foreign country, the common law will direct the contract to be interpreted and adjusted. Does a cause arise within the jurisdiction of the admiralty? Within that jurisdiction the civil law is allowed its proper energy and extent.

But, while she knows and performs what is due to others, the common law knows also and demands what is due to herself. She receives her guests with hospitality; but she receives them with dignity. She liberally dispenses her kindness and indulgence; — but, at the same time, she sustains, with becoming and unabating firmness, the preeminent character of *gravior lex*.

There is much truth and good sense, though there is some quaintness

[a] Rep. 28. Calvin's Case.

of expression, in the following encomium of the common law, which I take from my Lord Coke.[e] "If all the reason, that is dispersed into so many several heads, were united into one, yet could he not make such a law as the law of England is; because by many successions of ages it has been fined and refined by an infinite number of grave and learned men, and by long experience grown to such a perfection for the government of this realm, as the old rule may be justly verified of it, neminem oportet esse sapientiorem legibus: no man ought to be wiser than the law, which is the perfection of reason." Indeed, what we call human reason, in general, is not so much the knowledge, or experience, or information of any one man, as the knowledge, and experience, and information of many, arising from lights mutually and successively communicated and improved.

To those, who enjoy the advantages of such a law as has been described, I may well address myself in the words of Cicero,[f] "Believe me, a more inestimable inheritance descends to you from the law, than from those who have left, or may leave you fortunes. A farm may be transmitted to me by the will of any one: but it is by the law alone that I can peacefully hold what is already my own. You ought, therefore, to retain the publick patrimony of the law, which you have received from your ancestors, with no less assiduity than you retain your private estates; not only because these are fenced and protected by the law; but for this further reason, because the loss of a private fortune affects only an individual, whereas the loss of the law would be deeply detrimental to the whole commonwealth."

Does this inestimable inheritance follow the person of the citizen; or is it fixed to the spot, on which the citizen first happened to draw the breath of life? On this great question, it will be proper to consider what the law of England, and, also, what the law of reason says. Perhaps both will speak substantially the same language.

By the common law, every man may go out of the realm to carry on trade, or on any other occasion, which he thinks a proper one, without the leave of the king; and for so doing no man shall be punished.[g]

We are told, however, that if the king, by a writ of ne exeat regnum, under his great or privy seal, thinks proper to prohibit any one from

---

[e] 1. Ins. 97. b.

[f] Mihi credite: major hæreditas venit, unicuique vestrum, a jure et a legibus, quam ab iis, a quibus bona sunt. Nam, ut perveniat ad me fundus, testamento alicujus fieri potest: ut retineam quod meum factum sit, sine jure civili non potest. Quapropter non minus diligenter ea, quæ a majoribus accepistis, publica patrimonia juris, quam privatæ rei vestræ, retinere debetis; non solum quod hæc jure civili septa sunt; sed etiam quod patrimonium unius incommodo demittitur; jus amitti non potest sine magno incommodo civitatis. Cic. pro. Caec. c. 26.

[g] F.N.B. 85. Jenk. 88.

going abroad; or sends a writ to any man, when abroad, commanding his return; and, in either case, the subject disobeys; it is a high contempt of the king's prerogative, for which the offender's lands shall be seized, till he return; and then he is liable to fine and imprisonment.[h]

The discussion of this prerogative, and the cases, in which it may be justly and usefully exerted, it is unnecessary, for my present purpose, to undertake or enumerate; because if this prerogative was admitted in the fullest extent, in which it has ever been claimed, it would weaken neither the principles nor the facts, on which my observations shall be grounded.

A citizen may leave the kingdom: an alien may enter it. Does the former lose? — does the latter acquire the rights of citizenship? No. Neither climate, nor soil, nor time entitle one to those rights: neither climate, nor soil, nor time can deprive him of them. Citizens, who emigrate, carry with them, in their emigration, their best and noblest birthright.[i]

It is remarkable, however, that, in the charters of several of the American colonies, there is this declaration, "that the emigrants and their posterity shall still be considered as English subjects." Whether the solicitude of the colonists obtained, or the distrust of the reigning sovereigns imposed this clause, it would be superfluous to inquire; for the clause itself was equally unnecessary and inefficient. It was unnecessary, because, by the common law, they carried with them the rights of Englishmen; it was inefficient; because, if such had not been the operation of the common law, the right of citizenship could not have resulted from any declaration from the crown. A king of England can neither confer nor take away the rights of his subjects. Accordingly, the charter of Pennsylvania, perhaps the most accurate of all the charters, contains no such declaration. When the charter of Massachusetts, soon after the revolution of 1688, was renewed by king William, he was advised by his law council, that such a declaration would be nugatory.[j]

As citizens, who emigrate, carry with them their laws, their best birthright; so, as might be expected, they transmit this best birthright to their posterity. By the statute 25. Edw. III. says my lord Bacon, which, if you believe Hussey, is but a declaration of the common law, all children, born in any part of the world, if they be of English parents, continuing, at that time, as liege subjects to the king, and having done no act to forfeit the benefit of their allegiance, are, ipso facto, naturalized. If divers families of English men and women plant themselves at Lisbon, and have

[h] 1. Bl. Com. 266. Chal. 26. 27.
[i] The law is the birthright of every subject; so wherever subjects go, they carry their laws with them. 2. P. Wms. 75.
[j] Chal. 14. 15.

issue, and their descendants intermarry among themselves, without any intermixture of foreign blood; such descendants are naturalized to all generations; for every generation is still of liege parents, and therefore naturalized; so as you may have whole tribes and lineages of English in foreign countries. And therefore it is utterly untrue that the law of England cannot operate, but only within the bounds of the dominions of England.[k]

This great man, whose keen and comprehensive genius saw and understood so much, seems to have viewed the principles of colonization and the situation of colonists, with his usual penetration and sagacity. It was his sentiment, that the American colonies should be guided and governed by the common law of England.[l]

It has been already observed, that there are some great eras, when important and very perceptible alterations take place in the situation of men and things; and that, at such eras, the accommodating spirit of the common law will introduce, into its practice and rules, corresponding and adequate alterations. To the situation of the American colonists, this observation may be applied with singular propriety and force. The situation, in which they found themselves in America, was, in many important particulars, very different from that, in which they had been before their departure from England. The principles of that law, under whose guidance the emigration was made, taught them, that the system, in its particular parts, must undergo changes proportioned to the changes in their situation. This sentiment was understood clearly and in its full extent. By alterations, which, after their emigration, might be made in England, the obligatory principle of the common law dictated, that they should in no manner be affected; because to such alterations they had now no means of giving their consent. Hence the rule, that acts of parliament, made after the settlement of a colony, have, in that colony, no binding operation.

It is highly requisite, that these great truths should be stated, and supported, and illustrated in all their force and extent.

The emigrants, who in the year 1620 landed near Cape Cod, at a place, which they afterwards called New Plymouth, had the honour of planting the first permanent colony in New England. Before they landed, they entered into a political association, which, on many accounts, deserves to be noticed in the most particular manner. It is in these words. "In the name of God. Amen. We, whose names are hereunder written, the loyal subjects of our dread sovereign lord king James, by the grace of God, of Great Britain, France, and Ireland king, defender of the faith, &c. having undertaken, for the glory of God and advancement of the Christian

[k] 4. Ld. Bac. 192.					[l] 3. Ld. Bac. 581.

faith, and honour of our king and country, a voyage, to plant the first colony in the northern parts of Virginia, do by these presents, solemnly and mutually, in the presence of God and of one another, covenant and combine ourselves together into a civil body politick, for our better ordering and preservation, and furtherance of the ends aforesaid; and by virtue hereof, do enact, constitute, and frame such just and equal laws and ordinances, from time to time, as shall be thought most meet for the general good of the colony, unto which we promise all due subjection and obedience. In witness whereof, we have subscribed our names at Cape Cod, 11th November, 1620." [m]

In this manner was a civil society formed, by an original compact, to which every one consented, and, of consequence, by which every one was bound. During the infancy of the colony, we are told, the legislature consisted of the whole body of the male inhabitants. In the year 1639 they established a house of representatives, composed of deputies from the several towns. These representatives, in the true spirit of the principles, which we have been delineating, determined to make the laws of England the general rule of their government. "To these laws," says their ancient historian, Hubbard, "they were willing to be subject, though in a foreign land; adding some municipal laws of their own, in such cases, where the common and statute laws of England could not well reach, and afford them help in emergent cases." [n] Under the foregoing compact and the principles of legislation, which have been mentioned, this colony long enjoyed all the blessings of a government, in which prudence and vigour went hand in hand.[o]

In Virginia we see the same principles adopted and ratified by practice. In the month of March 1662, the assembly of that ancient dominion met: with the most laudable intentions, it reviewed the whole body of the laws of the colony. In this review, their object was, "to adhere to the excellent and often refined customs of England, as nearly as the capacity of the country would admit." [p]

In Maryland we behold a repetition of the same scene. In the month of April of the same year, the legislature of this colony, with a spirit congenial to that of the common law, declared, that, in all cases where the usages of the province were silent, justice should be administered according to the customs and statutes of England; "so far as the court shall judge them not inconsistent with the condition of the colony." [q]

The foregoing principles were recognised even under the arbitrary government of James the second. When he passed a commission — the legality of which is not the present subject, to carry on a temporary administration in Massachusetts, New Hampshire, Maine, Narraghanset,

[m] Chal. 102. [n] Chal. 87. 88. [o] **Id. 89.** [p] Id. 245. [q] Id. 360.

the commissioners were created a court of record for administering affairs civil and criminal, so that the forms of proceedings and judgments be consonant to the English laws, as near as the circumstances of the colony will admit.[r]

It has been already remarked, that as the rules of the common law are introduced by experience and custom; so they may be withdrawn by discontinuance and disuse. Numerous instances of the conduct of the colonies settled in America evince the force and extent of this remark. Many parts of the common law as received in England, a kingdom populous, ancient, and cultivated, could receive no useful application in the new settlements, inconsiderable in respect both of numbers and improvement.

This principle is fully recognised by the learned Author of the Commentaries on the laws of England. "It hath been held," says he, "that if an uninhabited country be discovered and planted by English subjects; all the English laws then in being, which are the birthright of every subject, are immediately there in force. But this must be understood with very many and very great restrictions. Such colonists carry with them only so much of the English law, as is applicable to their own situation and the condition of an infant colony. The artificial refinements and distinctions incident to the property of a great and commercial people, the laws of police and revenue (such especially as are enforced by penalties) the mode of maintenance for the established clergy, the jurisdiction of spiritual courts, and a multitude of other provisions, are neither necessary nor convenient for them; and, therefore, are not in force." [s]

It has been often a matter of some difficulty to determine what parts of the law of England extended to the colonies, and what parts were so inapplicable to their situation as not to be entitled to reception. On this, as on many other subjects, those who felt had a right to judge. The municipal tribunals in the different colonies decided the question in the controverted instances, which were brought before them; and their decisions and practice were deemed authoritative evidence on the points, to which they related.

The advocates for the legislative power of the British parliament over the American colonies remind us, that the colonists were liable to the *duties* as well as entitled to the *rights* of Englishmen; and that, as Englishmen, they owed obedience to their ancient legislature; according, as it is said, to a principle of universal equity; that he who enjoys the benefit shall submit patiently to all its inconveniences.[t]

It is always proper to guard against verbal equivocation; the source of the grossest errours both in opinion and practice. That it is the duty of some Englishmen to pay obedience to the legislature of England, is

[r] Chal. 417.   [s] 1. Bl. Com. 107.   [t] Chal. 15. 28.

admitted very readily. The principles, on which this obedience is due, have been amply illustrated in a former part of our lectures.[u] Acts of parliament have been shown to be binding, because they are made with the consent or by the authority of those, whom they bind. Such Englishmen, therefore, as have had an opportunity of expressing this consent, or of exercising this authority, are certainly bound to pay obedience to those acts of parliament. But is this the case with all Englishmen? Let us know what is meant by the term. Is it confined to those, who are represented in parliament? In that confined sense, it is conceded that they owe obedience to that legislature. Is it extended to all those, who are entitled to the benefits of the common law of England? In that extended sense, no such concession will or ought to be made: such a concession would destroy the vital principle of all their rights — that of being bound by no human laws, except such as are made with their own consent. It never is the duty of an Englishman, of one entitled to the common law as his inheritance — it never is the duty of such a one to surrender the animating principle of all his rights.

He who enjoys the benefit, it is said, shall submit patiently to all its inconveniences. True: but do Englishmen who are not and cannot be represented in parliament, enjoy the benefit? Unquestionably, they do not. To the inconveniences, then, they are under no obligation of submitting. This the true inference. The opposite inference burthens the colonists with the inconveniences separated from the benefit: it does more — it burthens the colonists with the inconveniences, augmented in consequence of this very separation. When the benefit of representation is lost; the inconveniences will be increased in a dreadful proportion. This reasoning seems to be just in theory. Let us apply to it the touchstone of fact.

In the journals of the house of commons, we find some short notes taken of a parliamentary debate, in the year 1621, concerning tobacco. The result of this debate was a bill, which was afterwards passed into a law, for preventing the inordinate use of tobacco. Among other short notes on this subject, is the following one, very instructive and interesting — "Mr. Solicitor — loveth England better than Virginia."[v] To every claim of obedience to the parliament without representation there, the standing answer and objection ought to be, in reference to the spirit of Mr. Solicitor's honest, and, indeed, natural declaration — the members of parliament love England better than America.

This important subject deserves to be pursued further. Citizens, who emigrate, carry with them their rights and liberties. When to these rights and liberties, duties and obligations are inseparably annexed, the latter

[u] Ante. p. 191.   [v] Chal. 72.

should be performed wherever the former can be enjoyed. But, in some instances, the enjoyment of the former becomes, from the nature and circumstances of things, altogether impracticable. The question, which we now consider, presents to us one of those instances. Obedience to acts of parliament is, as we have seen at large, founded on the principle of consent. That consent is expressed either personally or through the medium of representation. That it cannot be given personally is evident from the case supposed: the citizen has emigrated to another country. The same reason shows, that it cannot be given through the medium of representation. The right of representing is conferred by the act of elect- ing: elections for members of parliament are held within the kingdom: at those elections, the citizen, who has emigrated into another country, cannot vote. The result, then, is unavoidably this: if, by the emigration of the citizen, the enjoyment of his right of representation is necessarily lost; the duty of obedience, the consequence of enjoying that right, can- not possibly arise. When the cause is removed, the effect must cease to operate.

In this plain and simple manner, from the principles, which we have traced and established as the foundation of the obligatory force of law, we prove incontestably, that the colonists, after their emigration, were under no obligations of obedience to the acts of the English or British parliament. Principles, properly and surely laid, are eminently useful both for detecting and confuting errour, and for elucidating and con- firming truth.

The history as well as the principles of this momentous question ought to be fully developed and known. It is an instructive, and it is an interest- ing one. It has engaged the attention of the civilized world. It has em- ployed the treasures and the force of the most respectable nations. Amer- ica, both North and South, almost all the European powers, either as parties or as neutrals, acted or waited in arms for the important and final decision. On one side, it was worth all that it has cost. The auspicious event we have seen and experienced. Its rise, its progress, and its merits, every citizen, certainly every lawyer and statesman, in the United States, should accurately know.

The dependence of the colonies in America on the parliament of Eng- land seems to have been a doctrine altogether unknown and even un- suspected by the colonists who emigrated, and by the princes with whose consent their emigrations were made. It seems not, for a long time, to have been a doctrine known to the parliament itself.

Those, who launched into the unknown deep, in search of new coun- tries and habitations, still considered themselves, it is true, as subjects of the English monarchs, and behaved suitably and unexceptionably in that character; but it no where appears, that they still considered themselves as represented in an English parliament, or that they thought the authority of the English parliament extended over them. They took possession of the country in the king's name: they treated, or made war with the Indians by his authority: they established governments under his prerogative, as it was then understood, or, as it was also then understood, by virtue of his charters. No application, for those purposes, was made to the parliament: no ratification of the charters or letters patent was solicited from that assembly, as is usual in England, with regard to grants and franchises of much less importance.

My Lord Bacon's sentiments on this subject ought to have great weight with us. His immense genius, his universal learning, his deep insight into the laws and constitution of England, are well known and much admired. Besides; he lived at that very time when the settlement and the improvement of the American plantations began to be seriously pursued, and successfully to be carried into execution. Plans for the government and regulation of the colonies were then forming; and it is from the first general idea of those plans that we can best unfold, with precision and accuracy, all the more minute and intricate parts of which they afterwards consisted. "The settlement of colonies," says he, "must proceed from the option of those who will settle them, else it sounds like an exile: they must be raised by the leave and not by the command of the king. At their setting out, they must have their commission or letters patent from the king, that so they may acknowledge their dependency upon the crown of England, and under his protection." "They must still be subjects of the realm." "In order to regulate all the inconveniences, which will insensibly grow upon them," he proposes, that the king should erect a subordinate council in England, whose care and charge shall be, to advise and put in execution all things, which shall be found fit for the good of these new plantations; who, upon all occasions, shall give an account of their proceedings to the king or to the council board, and from them receive such directions as may best agree with the government of that place.[w] It is evident from these quotations, that my Lord Bacon had no conception, that the parliament would or ought to interpose, either in the settlement or in the government of the colonies.

We have seen the original association of the society, who made the first settlement in New England. In that instrument, they acknowledge themselves the loyal subjects of the king; and promise all due subjection and obedience to the colony: but we hear nothing concerning the parliament. Silence is sometimes expressive: it seems to be strongly so in this instance.

About sixty years afterwards, and during the reign of Charles the sec-

[w] 1. Ld. Bac. 725. 726.

ond, the general court of that colony exhibit the following natural account of the principles, on which the first settlement was made. "The first comers here," say they, "having first obtained leave of king James, of happy memory, did adventure, at their own proper costs and charges, through many foreseen and afterwards felt sufferings, to break the ice, and settle the first English plantation in this then uncultivated remote part of your dominions. We have had now near about sixty years lively experience of the good consistency of the order of these churches with civil government and order, together with loyalty to kingly government and authority, and the tranquillity of this colony. May it therefore please your most excellent majesty to favour us with your gracious letters patent for our incorporation into a body politick, with singular the privileges as your majesty has been accustomed to grant to other colonies, so to your majesty's colony of Connecticut." [x] Still no mention is made of parliament: still no application is made to that body. These omissions could not have been owing to accident: they must have been intentional. Before this time, the pretensions of parliament, during the existence of the commonwealth, had been both known and felt; and, at this time, must have been remembered.

By the charter of Rhode Island, granted in the fourteenth year of Charles the second, the king grants and confirms all that part of *his* dominions in New England in America, containing the Narraghanset Bay, and countries and parts adjacent, &c. Here, also, no notice is taken of the parliament.

The following transactions relating to Virginia, exhibit, in a very striking point of view, the sentiments both of the king and of the colonists, concerning the interference of parliament with the business of colonial administration. Sir William Berkely, who, in the year 1639, was appointed governour of that colony, was, among other things, directed to summon the burgesses of all the plantations, who, with the governour and council, should constitute the grand assembly, with power to make acts for the government of the colony, as near as may be to the laws of England.

A discontented party in Virginia contrived, in what particular manner is not mentioned, to have a petition presented, in the name of the assembly to the house of commons, praying a restoration of the ancient patents and corporation government. The governour, the council, and the burgesses no sooner heard of a transaction so contrary to truth and their wishes, than they transmitted an explicit disavowal of it to England; and, at the same time, sent an address to the king, acknowledging his bounty and favour towards them, and earnestly desiring to continue

[x] Chal. 106. 107.

under his immediate protection. In that address, they desired that the king would, under his royal signet, confirm their declaration and protestation against the petition presented, in their names, to the house of commons, and transmit that confirmation to Virginia. The king expresses strong satisfaction with this address; declares that their so earnest desire to continue under his immediate protection is very acceptable to him; and informs them, that he had not before the least intention to consent to the introduction of any company over the colony; but that he was much confirmed in his former resolutions by the address; since he would think it very improper to change a form of government, under which his subjects there received so much content and satisfaction. He transmits to them, under his royal signet, his approbation of their petition and protestation.[y]

In the colony of Massachusetts, the famous navigation act, made by the English parliament, met with a strong and steady opposition. It was not enforced by the governour annually chosen by the people, whose interest it was that it should not be observed. Of consequence, no custom house was established. The colony carried on the greater part of the trade of the plantations to every quarter of the globe: and vessels from every European country, from France, from Spain, from Italy, from Holland, were crowded together in the harbour of Boston. This prosperous situation excited the envy and the jealousy of the mercantile and manufacturing interests in England. These principles produced, from the merchants and manufacturers, a representation to Charles the second; in which they prayed, that the colonies might receive no supplies but from England; and that the subjects of New England might be compelled to trade according to law. When information of these measures was transmitted to Massachusetts by her agents in England; the general court avowed the conduct of the colony; justified that conduct in point of legality; and stated the sacrifice which it was willing to make of its interests, though not of its rights. It acknowledged that no regard had been paid to the laws of navigation. It urged that those laws were an invasion of the rights and privileges of the subjects of his majesty in that colony, they not being represented in the parliament; because, according to the usual sayings of the learned in the law, the laws of England were bounded within the four seas, and did not reach America; but that, as his majesty had signified his pleasure, that those laws should be observed, it had made provision, by an ordinance of the colony, which obliged masters of vessels to yield faithful obedience, and commanded officers to see them strictly observed.[z]

A letter written in the year 1698 from governour Nicholson of Mary-

[y] Chal. 121. 122. 133. 134.   [z] Chal. 400. 407. 408.

land to the board of trade shows that the sentiments of the colony of
Massachusetts, with regard to the authority of acts of parliament, had,
when the letter was written, become general in the colonies. "I have
observed that a great many people in *all* these provinces and colonies,
especially in those under proprietaries, and the two others under Connecticut and Rhode Island, think that no law of England ought to be
in force and binding to them without their own consent: for they
foolishly say they have no representatives sent from themselves to the
parliament of England: and they look upon all laws made in England,
that put any restraint upon them, to be great hardships." [a]

[a] Chal. 442. 443.

XIII

OF THE NATURE AND PHILOSOPHY OF EVIDENCE

Evidence is a subject of vast extensive importance in the study and practice of the law: it is of vast and extensive importance, likewise, in the business and general management of human affairs.

"Experience," says Sir William Blackstone, "will abundantly show, that above a hundred of our law suits arise from disputed facts" — and facts are the objects of evidence — "for one where the law is doubted of. About twenty days in the year are sufficient, in Westminster Hall, to settle, upon solemn argument, every demurrer or other special point of law, that arises throughout the nation. But two months are annually spent in deciding the truth of facts, before six distinct tribunals, in the several circuits of England, exclusive of Middlesex and London, which afford a supply of causes much more than equivalent to any two of the largest circuits." [a]

But evidence is not confined, in its operation and importance, to the courts of justice. Its influence on the human mind, human manners, and human business is great and universal. In perception, in consciousness, in remembrance, belief always forms one ingredient. But belief is governed by evidence. In every action which is performed with an intention to accomplish a particular purpose, there must be a belief that the action is fitted for the accomplishment of the purpose intended. So large a share has belief in our reasonings, in our resolutions, and in our conduct, that it may well be considered as the main spring, which produces and regulates the movements of human life.

In a subject of so great use and extent, it is highly necessary that our first principles be accurate and well founded. It is, however, matter of just and deep regret, that very little has been said, and that still less has been satisfactorily said, concerning the sound and genuine sources and principles of evidence. "An inquiry," says Eden, in his Principles of penal law, "into the general rules and maxims of evidence, is a field still open to investigation. For the considerations of some very ingenious writers on this subject have been too much influenced by their acquiescence in

[a] 3. Bl. Com. 330.

personal authority, and we are furnished rather with sensible and useful histories of what the law of evidence actually is, than with any free and speculative disquisition of what it ought to be." [b] The truth is, I may add, that the philosophy, as well as the law of evidence is a field, which demands and which is susceptible of much cultivation and improvement.

"Evidence, in legal understanding," says my Lord Coke, "doth not only contain matters of record, as letters patent, fines, recoveries, enrollments, and the like; and writings under seal, as charters and deeds; and other writings without seal, as court rolls, accounts, which are called evidences, *instrumenta;* but, in a larger sense, it containeth also *testimonia,* the testimony of witnesses, and other proofs to be produced and given to a jury, for the finding of any issue joined between the parties. And it is called evidence, because thereby the point in issue is to be made evident to the jury. Probationes debent esse evidentes (id est) perspicuæ et faciles intelligi." [c]

The learned Author of the Commentaries on the Laws of England describes evidence as signifying that, which demonstrates, makes clear, or ascertains the truth of the very fact or point in issue, either on the one side or on the other. [d]

When we are informed that it is called evidence, because thereby the point in issue is to be made evident to the jury; we are informed of little, if any thing, more than in identical proposition; and, consequently, are not enabled by it to make any considerable progress in the attainment of science.

To say that evidence demonstrates, makes clear, and ascertains the truth of a fact, is rather to describe its effects than its nature. Its effects, too, are described in a manner, neither very accurate nor precise; as I shall afterwards have occasion to show more particularly.

But the truth is, that evidence is much more easily felt than described. We experience, though it is difficult to explain, its operations and influence. A man may have a good eye, and may make a good use of it, though he cannot unfold the theory of vision.

These reflections naturally lead us to one illustrious source of the propriety of a jury to decide on matters of evidence. "It is much easier," says the Marquis of Beccaria, "to feel the moral certainty of proofs, than to define it exactly. For this reason I think it an excellent law, which establishes assistants to the principal Judge, and those chosen by lot: For that ignorance which judges by its feelings is little subject to errour." [e]

Perhaps there is no more unexceptionable mode of expressing what

[b] Eden 164. 165.
[c] 1. Ins. 283. [Proofs ought to be evident, that is, clear and easily understood.]
[d] 3. Bl. Com. 367.   [e] Bec. c. 14. p. 39.

we feel to be evidence, than to say — it is that which produces belief.

Belief is a simple operation of the mind. It is an operation, too, of its own peculiar kind. It cannot, therefore, be defined or described. The appeal for its nature and existence, must be made to the experience, which every one has of what passes within himself. This experience will, probably, inform him, that belief arises from many different sources, and admits of all possible degrees, from absolute certainty down to doubt and suspicion.

The love of system, and of that unnatural kind of uniformity to which system is so much attached, has done immense mischief in the theory of evidence. It has been long the aim and labour of philosophers to discover some common nature, to which all the different species of evidence might be reduced. This was the great object of the schools in their learned lucubrations concerning the criterion of truth. This criterion they endeavoured to find from a minute and artificial analysis of the several kinds of evidence; by means of which they expected to ascertain and establish some common quality, which might be applied, with equal propriety, to all. Des Cartes placed this criterion of truth in clear and distinct perception,[f] and laid it down as a maxim, that whatever we clearly and distinctly perceive to be true, is true. The meaning, the truth, and the utility of this maxim seem to be all equally problematical.

This criterion of truth was placed by Mr. Locke in a perception of the agreement or disagreement of our ideas. This, indeed, is the grand principle of his philosophy, and he seems to consider it as a very important discovery. "Knowledge," says he, "seems to me to be nothing but the perception of the connexion and agreement, or disagreement and repugnancy of any of our ideas. In this alone it consists. For since the mind, in all its thoughts and reasonings, hath no other immediate object but its own ideas, which it alone does or can contemplate; it is evident, that our knowledge is only conversant about them."[g] "We can have no knowledge farther than we have ideas. We can have no knowledge farther than we have perception of that agreement or disagreement."[h]

In order to perceive whether two ideas agree or disagree, they must be compared together: According to this hypothesis, therefore, all knowledge must arise from the comparison of ideas.

Let us try this hypothesis by applying it minutely and carefully to a principle of knowledge allowed by all philosophers — and the only one allowed by all philosophers — to be sound and unexceptionable: I mean the principle of consciousness: — I mean, farther, the most clear and

[f] We give the name of evidence to a clear and distinct view of things and of their relations. I. Burl. 8.

[g] Locke on Und. b. 4. c. 1.   [h] Id. b. 4. c. 3.

simple appeal, which can possibly be made to that clear and simple principle, *I think.* This has always been admitted to form a principle and a part of knowledge. According to the hypothesis of Mr. Locke, this knowledge must be nothing but the perception of the agreement — for disagreement cannot enter into the question here — between ideas. What are the ideas to be compared, in order that the agreement may be discovered? *I* and *thought?* Let us grant every indulgence, and suppose, for a moment, that existence and thought are nothing more than *ideas;* and then let us see how the comparison of ideas, and how their agreement in consequence of their comparison, will stand.

How is the knowledge of this truth — "I think" — drawn from the perception of any agreement between the idea of *me* and the idea of *thought?* When I think, I am conscious of thinking; and this consciousness is the clearest and most intimate knowledge. But does this consciousness arise from the perception of agreement between the idea of *me* and the idea of *thought?* No. From Mr. Locke's own system, no such knowledge can arise from the perception of any such agreement: because the agreement does not, at all times, take place.

"The mind" says he, "can sensibly put on, at several times, several degrees of thinking, and be sometimes, even in a waking man, so remiss, as to have thoughts dim and obscure to that degree, that they are very little removed from none at all; and, at last, in the dark retirements of sound sleep, loses the sight, perfectly, of all ideas whatsoever.[1] The knowledge, then, of this truth, that *I think,* does not arise from the perception of any agreement between the idea *me* and the idea of *thought;* since, according to Mr. Locke's own account of the matter, that agreement does not always subsist.

Let us try this hypothesis — that knowledge is the perception of the agreement or disagreement of our ideas — by another instance; and let us attend to the result. I perceive a small book in my hand. My faculty of seeing gives me not merely a simple apprehension of the book; it gives me, likewise, a concomitant belief or knowledge of its existence; of its shape, size, and distance. By the perception of the agreement of what ideas, is this knowledge or belief acquired? This belief is inseparably connected with the perception of the book; and does not arise from any perception of agreement between the idea of the book, and the idea of myself.

I remember to have dined a few days ago with a particular company of friends. This remembrance is accompanied with clear and distinct belief or knowledge. How does this belief or knowledge arise? Is it from the perception of agreement between ideas? Between what ideas? Be-

[1] Locke on Und. b. 2. c. 19. s. 4.

tween the idea of *me*, and the idea of my *friends?* This agreement, I presume, would have been the same, whether we had dined together or not. Is it from the agreement between the idea of *me* and the idea of *dining?* But how, from this agreement, will the knowledge of dining with *my friends* arise? On this state of the supposition, I might have dined with strangers or with enemies.

Let us examine the future, as we have examined the past. If a certain degree of cold freezes water now, and has been known to freeze it in all times past; we believe, nay, we rest assured, that the same degree of cold will continue to freeze the water while the cold continues; and returning, will be attended with the same effect, in all times future. But whence does this belief or assurance arise? Does it arise from the comparison of ideas — from the perception of their agreement? When I compare the idea of *cold* with that of *water hardened into a transparent solid body*, I can perceive no connexion between them: no man can show the one to be the necessary effect of the other: no one can give a shadow of reason why nature has conjoined them. But from experience we learn that they have been conjoined in times past; and this experience of the past is attended with a belief and assurance, that those connexions, in nature, which we have observed in times past, will continue and operate in times to come.[j]

We now see, that our knowledge, which proceeds from consciousness, from the senses, from memory, and from anticipation of the future occasioned by experience of the past, arises not from any perception of the agreement or disagreement of our ideas. These are important parts of our knowledge: the evidence, upon which these parts of our knowledge is founded, is an important part of the system of evidence. All, however, rests on principles, very different from that which is assigned by Mr. Locke, as the sole principle of knowledge. We may go farther still, and say, if knowledge consists solely in the perception of the agreement or disagreement of ideas, there can be no knowledge of any proposition, which does not express some agreement or disagreement of ideas; consequently, there can be no knowledge of any proposition, which expresses either the existence, or the attributes, or the relations of things; which are not ideas. If, therefore, the theory of ideas be true, there can be no knowledge of any thing else: if we have knowledge of any thing else, the theory of ideas must be unfounded. For the knowledge of any thing else than ideas must arise from something else than the perception of the agreement or disagreement of ideas.[k]

This principle, assigned by Mr. Locke, that knowledge is nothing but a perception of the agreement or disagreement of our ideas, is founded

[j] Reid's Inq. 437. 438.   [k] Reid's Ess. Int. 552.

upon another — the existence of ideas or images of things in the mind. This theory I have already had an opportunity of considering, and I shall not now repeat what I then delivered at some length. I then showed, I hope, satisfactorily, that this theory has no foundation in reason, in consciousness, or in the other operations of our minds; but that, on the contrary, it is manifestly contradicted by all these, and would, in its necessary consequences, lead to the destruction of all truth, and knowledge, and virtue; though those consequences were, by no means, foreseen by Mr. Locke, and many succeeding philosophers, who have adopted, and still adopt, his theory concerning the existence of ideas or images of things in the mind.

If this theory has, as we have shown it to have, no foundation — if these ideas have, as we have shown them to have, no existence; then Mr. Locke's great principle, which represents knowledge and belief, and consequently evidence, upon which knowledge and belief are grounded, as consisting in the perception of the agreement or disagreement of those ideas, must tumble in ruins, like a superstructure, whose basis has been undermined and removed.

It is nevertheless true, that, in our law books, the general principles of evidence, so far as any notice is taken of general principles on this subject, are referred, for their sole support, to the theory of Mr. Locke. This will appear obvious to any one who is acquainted with that theory, and peruses the first pages of my Lord Chief Baron Gilbert's Treatise upon Evidence. This unfolds the reason why I have employed so much pains to expose and remove the sandy and unsound foundation, on which the principles of the law of evidence have been placed.

Let us now proceed to erect a fabrick on a different and a surer basis — the basis of the human mind.

I am, by no means, attached to numerous and unnecessary distinctions; but, on some occasions, it is proper to recollect the rule, "qui bene distinguit, bene docet." * It is possible to blend, as well as to distinguish, improperly. Nature should always be consulted. We are safe, when we imitate her in her various, as well as when we imitate her in her uniform appearances. By following her as our guide, we can trace evidence to the following fourteen distinct sources.

I. It arises from the external senses: and by each of these, distinct information is conveyed to the mind.

II. It arises from consciousness; or the internal view of what passes within ourselves.

III. It arises from taste; or that power of the human mind, by which we perceive and enjoy the beauties of nature or of art.

* [Who distinguishes well, teaches well.]

IV. It arises from the moral sense; or that faculty of the mind, by which we have the original conceptions of right and wrong in conduct; and the original perceptions, that certain things are right, and that others are wrong.

V. Evidence arises from natural signs: by these we gain our knowledge of the minds, and of the various qualities and operations of the minds, of other men. Their thoughts, and purposes, and dispositions have their natural signs in the features of the countenance, in the tones of the voice, and in the motions and gestures of the body.

VI. Evidence arises from artificial signs; such as have no meaning, except that, which is affixed to them by compact, or agreement, or usage: such is language, which has been employed universally for the purpose of communicating thought.

VII. Evidence arises from human testimony in matters of fact.

VIII. Evidence arises from human authority in matters of opinion.

IX. Evidence arises from memory, or a reference to something which is past.

X. Evidence arises from experience; as when, from facts already known, we make inferences to facts of the *same* kind, unknown.

XI. Evidence arises from analogy; as when, from facts already known, we made inferences to facts of a *similar* kind, not known.

XII. Evidence arises from judgment; by which I here mean that power of the mind, which decides upon truths, that are selfevident.

XIII. Evidence arises from reasoning: by reasoning, I here mean that power of the mind, by which, from one truth, we deduce another, as a conclusion from the first. The evidence, which arises from reasoning, we shall, by and by, see divided into two species — demonstrative and moral.

XIV. Evidence arises from calculations concerning chances. This is a particular application of demonstrative to ascertain the precise force of moral reasoning.

Even this enumeration, though very long, is, perhaps, far from being complete. Among all those different kinds of evidence, it is, I believe, impossible to find any common nature, to which they can be reduced. They agree, indeed, in this one quality — which constitutes them evidence — that they are fitted by nature to produce belief in the human mind.

It will be proper to make some observations concerning each of the enumerated kinds of evidence. In the business of life, and, consequently, in the practice of a lawyer or man of business, they all occur more frequently than those unaccustomed to consider them are apt to imagine.

I. The truths conveyed by the evidence of the external senses are the first principles, from which we judge and reason with regard to the material world, and from which all our knowledge of it is deduced.

The evidence furnished even by any of the several external senses seems to have nothing in common with that furnished by each of the others, excepting that single quality before mentioned. The evidence of one sense may be corroborated, in some instances; and, in some instances, it may be corrected, by that of another sense, when both senses convey information concerning the same object; but still the information conveyed by each is clearly perceived to be separate and distinct. We may be assured that a man is present, by hearing and by seeing him; but the evidence of the eye is nevertheless different from the evidence of the ear.

In the sacred history of the resurrection, a beautiful and emphatical reference is had to this distinct but corresponding and reciprocally corroborating evidence of the senses, by him, by whom our nature was both made and assumed. *"Behold,"* says he, to his trembling and doubting disciples, who supposed they had seen a spirit, *"Behold* my hands and my feet, that it is I myself; *handle* me, and see; for a spirit has not flesh and bones as you see me have: And when he had thus spoken, he showed them his hands and his feet." [1] To the unbelieving Thomas, he is still more particular in his appeal to the evidence of the senses, and in the manner, in which the appeal should be made. "Reach hither thy finger and *behold* my hands; and reach hither thy hand, and *thrust it* into my side; and be not faithless, but believing." [m]

Many philosophers of high sounding fame, deeming it inconsistent with their character to believe, when they could not furnish an argument for belief, have endeavoured, with much learned labour, to suggest proofs for the doctrine — that our senses ought to be trusted. But their proofs are defective, and shrink from the touch of rigid examination. Other philosophers, of no less brilliant renown, have clearly and unanswerably discovered and exposed the fallacy of those pretended proofs: so far they have done well: but very unwisely they have attempted to do more: they have attempted to overturn our belief in the evidence of our senses, because the arguments adduced on the other side to prove its truth were shown to be defective and fallacious. From human nature an equal departure is made on both sides. It appeals not to reason for any argument in support of our belief in the evidence of our senses: but it determines us to believe them.

II. Consciousness furnishes us with the most authentick and the most indubitable evidence of every thing which passes within our own minds. This source of evidence lays open to our view all our perceptions and mental powers; and, consequently, forms a necessary ingredient in all

Luke XXIV. 39. 40.   [m] John XX. 27.

evidence arising from every other source. There can be no evidence of the objects of the senses, without perception of them by the mind: there can be no evidence of the perception of them by the mind, without consciousness of that perception. When we see, and feel, and think, consciousness gives us the most certain information that we thus see, and feel, and think. This, as has been observed on a former occasion, is a kind of evidence, the force and authenticity of which has never been called in question by those, who have been most inclined to dispute every thing else, except the evidence of reasoning.

III. I mentioned taste, or that power of the mind by which we perceive and enjoy the beauties of nature and art, as one of the sources from which evidence arises. This faculty, in its feeling and operations, has something analogous to the impressions and operations of our external senses; from one of which, it has, in our own and in several other languages, derived its metaphorical name.

With the strictest propriety, taste may be called an original sense. It is a power, which furnishes us with many simple perceptions, which, to those who are destitute of it, cannot be conveyed through any other channel of information. Concerning objects of taste, it is vain to reason or discourse with those who possess not the first principles of taste. Again; taste is a power, which as soon as its proper object is exhibited to it, receives its perception from that object, immediately and intuitively. It is not in consequence of a chain of argument, or a deductive process of our reasoning faculties, that we discover and relish the beauties of a poem or a prospect. Both the foregoing characters belong evidently to consciousness and to the external senses. All the three are, therefore, considered, with equal propriety, as distinct and original sources of information and evidence.

That it is fruitless to dispute concerning matters of taste has been so often said, that it has now acquired the authority and notoriety of a proverb; and its suggestions are consequently supposed, by some, to be dictated only by whim and caprice. Nothing, however, can be farther from the truth. The first and general principles of taste are not less uniform, nor less permanent, than are the first and general principles of science and morality. The writings of Cicero present him to us in two very different characters — as a philosopher, and as a man of taste. His philosophical performances are read, and ought to be read, with very considerable grains of allowance; the beauties of his oratory have been the subjects of universal and uninterrupted admiration. The fame of Homer has obtained an undisputed establishment of near three thousand years. Has a reputation equally uniform attended the philosophical doctrines of Aristotle or Plato? The writings of Moses have been admired for their sublimity by those, who never received them as the vehicles of sacred and eternal truth.

The first and most general principles of taste are universal as well as permanent: it is a faculty, in some degree, common to all. With youth, with ignorance, with savageness, its rudiments are found to dwell. It seems not less essential to man to have some discernment of the beauties both of art and nature, than it is to possess, in some measure, the faculties of speech and reason. "Let no one," says Cicero, in his excellent book de oratore, "be surprised that the most uncultivated mind can mark and discern these things: since, in every thing, the energy of nature is great and incredible. Without education or information, every one, by a certain tacit sense, is enabled to judge and decide concerning what is right or wrong in the arts. If this observation is true with regard to pictures, statues, and other performances, in the knowledge of which they have less assistance from nature; it becomes much more evident and striking with regard to the judgments, which they form concerning words, harmony, and pronunciation: for concerning these there is a common sense implanted in all, of which Nature intended that no one should be entirely devoid." [n]

IV. As a fourth source of evidence, I mentioned the moral sense, or that faculty of the mind, by which we have the original conceptions that there is a right and a wrong in conduct; and that some particular actions are right, and others wrong. Without this last power of applying our conceptions to particular actions, and of determining concerning their moral qualities, our general and abstract notions of moral good and evil would be of no service to us in directing the conduct and affairs of human life.

The moral sense is a distinct and original power of the human mind. By this power, and by this power solely, we receive information and evidence of the first principles of right and wrong, of merit and demerit. He, who would know the colour of any particular object, must consult his eye: in vain will he consult every other faculty upon the point. In the same manner, he who would learn the moral qualities of any particular action, must consult his moral sense: no other faculty of the mind can give him the necessary information.

The evidence given by our moral sense, like that given by our external senses, is the evidence of nature; and, in both cases, we have the same grounds for relying on that evidence. The truths given in evidence by the external senses are the first principles from which we reason concerning matter, and from which all our knowledge of the material world is drawn. In the same manner, the truths given in evidence by our moral

[n] Cic. de Orat. l. 3. c. 50.

faculty are the first principles, from which we reason concerning moral subjects, and from which all our knowledge of morality is deduced. The powers, which Nature has kindly bestowed upon us, are the only channels, through which the evidence of truth and knowledge can flow in upon our minds.

Virtuous demeanour is the duty, and should be the aim, of every man: the knowledge and evidence of moral truth is, therefore, placed within the reach of all.

Of right and wrong there are many different degrees; and there are also many different kinds. By the moral faculty we distinguish those kinds and degrees. By the same faculty we compare the different kinds together, and discover numerous moral relations between them.

Our knowledge of moral philosophy, of natural jurisprudence, of the law of nations, must ultimately depend, for its first principles, on the evidence and information of the moral sense. This power furnishes to us the first principles of our most important knowledge. In dignity, it is far superiour to every other power of the human mind.

V. The fifth kind of evidence, of which I took notice, is that, which arises from natural signs. By these, we gain information and knowledge of the minds, and of the thoughts, and qualities, and affections of the minds of men. This kind of evidence is of very great and extensive importance.

We have no immediate perception of what passes in the minds of one another. Nature has not thought it proper to gratify the wish of the philosopher, by placing a window in every bosom, that all interiour transactions may become visible to every spectator. But, although the thoughts, and dispositions, and talents of men are not perceivable by direct and immediate inspection; there are certain external signs, by which those thoughts, and dispositions, and talents are naturally and certainly disclosed and communicated.

The signs, which naturally denote our thoughts, are the different motions of the hand,° the different modulations or tones of the voice, the different gestures and attitudes of the body, and the different looks and features of the countenance, especially what is termed, with singular force and propriety, the expression of the eye. By means of these natural signs, two persons, who never saw one another before, and who possess no knowledge of one common artificial language, can, in some tolerable degree, communicate their thoughts and even their present dispositions to one another: they can ask and give information: they can affirm and deny: they can mutually supplicate and engage fidelity and protection. Of all these we have very picturesque and interesting representations, in

° To this the evidence arising from the similitude of hands may be referred.

the first interviews between Robinson Crusoe and his man Friday; they are interesting, because we immediately perceive them to be natural. Two dumb persons, in their intercourse together, carry the use of these natural signs to a wonderful degree of variety and minuteness.

We acquire information, not only of the thoughts and present dispositions and affections, but also of the qualities, moral and intellectual, of the minds of others, by the means of natural signs. The eloquence or skill of another man cannot, themselves, become the objects of any of our senses, either external or internal. His skill is suggested to us by the signs of it, which appear in his conduct: his eloquence, by those which appear in his speech. In the same manner, and by the same means, we receive evidence concerning his benevolence, his fortitude, and all his other talents and virtues.

This evidence, however, of the thoughts, and dispositions, and passions, and talents, and characters of other men, conveyed to us by natural signs, is neither less satisfactory, nor less decisive upon our conduct in the business and affairs of life, than the evidence of external objects, which we receive by the means of our senses. It is no less a part, nor is it a less important part, of our constitution, that we are enabled and determined to judge of the powers and the characters of men, from the signs of them, which appear in their discourse and conduct, than it is that we are enabled and determined to judge, by our external senses, concerning the various corporeal objects, which we have occasion to view and consider.

The variety, the certainty, and the extent of that evidence, which arises from natural signs, may be conceived from what we discover in the pantomime entertainments on the theatre; in some of which, the whole series of a dramatick tale, and all the passions and emotions to which it gives birth, are represented, with astonishing address, by natural signs. By natural signs, likewise, the painters and statuaries infuse into their pictures and statues the most intelligible, and, sometimes, the most powerful expression of thought, of affections, and even of character.

Among untutored nations, the want of letters is supplied, though imperfectly, by the use of visible and natural signs, which fix the attention, and enliven the remembrance of private or publick transactions. The jurisprudence of the first Romans exhibited the picturesque scenes of the pantomime entertainment. The intimate union of the marriage state was signified by the solemnities attending the celebration of the nuptials. The contracting parties were seated on the same sheep skin; they tasted of the same salted cake of *far* or rice. This last ceremony is well known by the name of *confarreatio*. A wife, divorced, resigned the keys, by the delivery of which she had been installed into the government of domestick affairs. A slave was manumitted by turning him round, and giv-

ing him a gentle stroke on the cheek. By the casting of a stone, a work
was prohibited. By the breaking of a branch, prescription was interrupted. The clenched fist was the emblem of a pledge. The right hand
was the token of faith and confidence. A broken straw figured an indenture of agreement. In every payment, weights and scales were a
necessary formality. In a civil action, the party touched the ear of his
witness; the plaintiff seized his reluctant adversary by the neck, and
implored, by solemn solicitation, the assistance of his fellow citizens.
The two competitors grasped each other's hand, as if they stood prepared for combat, before the tribunal of the pretor. He commanded
them to produce the object of the dispute. They went; they returned,
with measured steps; and a turf was cast at his feet, to represent the field,
for which they contended, and the property of which he was to decide.[p]

In more enlightened ages, however, the use and meaning of these
natural and primitive signs became gradually obliterated. But a libel may
still be expressed by natural signs, as well as by words; and the proof of
the intention may be equally convincing and satisfactory in cases of the
first, as in those of the last kind.

VI. But evidence arises frequently from artificial as well as from natural
signs; from those which are settled by agreement or custom, as well as
from those which are derived immediately from our structure and
constitution. Of these artificial signs there are many different species,
contrived and established to answer the demands and emergencies of
human life. The signals used by fleets at sea, form a very intricate and a
very interesting part of naval tacticks.

But language presents to us the most important, as well as the most
extensive, system of artificial signs, which has been invented for the
purpose of giving information and evidence concerning the thoughts
and designs of men. I mean not that language is altogether an invention
of human art; for I am of opinion, that, if the first principles of language
had not been natural to us, human reason and ingenuity could never
have invented and executed its numerous artificial improvements. But
of every language, at least of every refined language now in use, the
greatest part consists of signs that are purely artificial. The evidence of
language may, therefore, with sufficient propriety, be arranged under
that kind of evidence, which arises from artificial signs.

Natural signs, though, as we have seen, susceptible of very considerable
extent and variety, yet, when compared with the almost boundless
variety and combinations of our conceptions and thoughts, have been
found, in every country, and in every period of society, altogether inadequate to the communication of them in such a degree, as to accom-

[p] Consult Gib. Rom. Emp. c. 44. vol. 8. p. 22. and the authorities cited.

plish, with tolerable conveniency, the necessary ends and purposes of human life. Hence the invention and improvement of language; which, as has been already observed, consists chiefly of artificial signs, contrived, at first, in all probability, only to supply the deficiencies of such signs as were natural; but afterwards, as language became refined and copious, substituted almost entirely in their place.

But even language, however copious and refined, is, on examination and trial, found insufficient for conveying precisely and determinately all our conceptions and designs, consisting of numberless particulars, combined into numberless forms, and related by numberless connexions. Hence the necessity, the use, and the rules of interpretation, which has been introduced into all languages and all laws. A most extensive field now opens before us. But I cannot go into it. I am confined, at present, to the mere outlines of the philosophy of evidence. Let us therefore proceed.

VII. A seventh kind of evidence arises from human testimony in matters of fact.

Human testimony is a source of evidence altogether original, suggested by our constitution, and not acquired, though it is sometimes corroborated, and more frequently corrected, by considerations arising from experience.

"This is very plain," says my Lord Chief Baron Gilbert, "that when we cannot see or hear any thing ourselves, and yet are obliged to make a judgment of it, we must see and hear from report of others; which is one step farther from demonstration, which is founded upon the view of our own senses: and yet there is that faith and credit to be given to the honesty and integrity of credible and disinterested witnesses, attesting any fact under the solemnities and obligation of religion, and the dangers and penalties of perjury, that the mind equally acquiesces therein as in knowledge by demonstration; for it cannot have any more reason to be doubted than if we ourselves had heard or seen it. And this is the original of trials, and all manner of evidence." [q]

I shall not, at present, make any remarks upon the position — that demonstration is founded on the view of our own senses. It will be examined when I come to consider that kind of evidence which arises from reasoning — probable and demonstrative. But, at present, it is material to observe, that, in the sentiments, which the very learned Judge, whose character and talents I hold in the highest estimation, seems to entertain concerning the source of our belief in testimony, the *restraints* which are wisely calculated, by human regulations, to *check*, are mis-

[q] Gilb. Ev. 4.

taken for the *causes* intended to *produce* this belief. The true language of the law, addressed to the native and original sentiments of the human mind concerning testimony, is not to this purport — If you find a witness to be honest and upright, credible and disinterested: if you see him deliver his testimony under all the solemnities and obligations of religion, and all the dangers and penalties of perjury; you must then believe him. Belief in testimony springs not from the precepts of the law, but from the propensity of our nature. This propensity we indulge in every moment of our lives, and in every part of our business, without attending, in the least, to the circumspect precautions prescribed by the law.

Experience has found it necessary and useful, that, at least in legal proceedings, the indulgence of this natural and original propensity should be regulated and restrained. For this purpose, the law has said, that, unless a witness appears, as far as can be known, to be honest and upright, credible and disinterested; and unless he delivers his testimony under all the solemnities and obligations of religion, and all the dangers and penalties of perjury; you shall not — It does not say, you shall not *believe* him. To prevent this act or operation of the mind might be impracticable on hearing the witness: but it says — you shall not *hear* him. Accordingly, every gentleman, in the least conversant about law proceedings, knows very well, that the qualifications and solemnities enumerated by the learned Judge, are requisite to the competency, not to the credibility, of the witness — to the admission, not to the operation, of his testimony.

The proceedings of the common law are founded on long and sound experience; but long and sound experience will not be found to stand in opposition to the original and genuine sentiments of the human mind. The propensity to believe testimony in a natural propensity. It is unnecessary to encourage it; sometimes it is impracticable to restrain it. The law will not order that which is unnecessary: it will not attempt that which is impracticable. In no case, therefore, does it order a witness to be believed; for jurors are triers of the credibility of witnesses, as well as of the truth of facts. The positive testimony of a thousand witnesses is not conclusive as to the verdict. The jury retain an indisputable, unquestionable right to acquit the person accused, if, in their private opinions, they disbelieve the accusers.[r] In no case, likewise, does the law order a witness not to be believed; for belief might be the unavoidable result of his testimony. To prevent that unavoidable, but sometimes improper result, the law orders, that, without the observance of certain precautions, which experience has evinced to be wise and salutary, the witness shall not be

[r] Eden's Pen. Law. 169. 170.

heard. This I apprehend to be the true exposition and meaning of the regulations prescribed by the law, before a witness can be admitted to give his testimony.

It will be pleasing and it will be instructive to trace and explain the harmony, which subsists between those regulations, thus illustrated, and the genuine sentiments of the mind with regard to testimony. To discover an intimate connexion between the doctrines of the law and the just theory of human nature, is peculiarly acceptable to those, who study law as a science founded on the science of man.[s]

In a former part of these lectures,[t] I had occasion to take notice of the quality of veracity, and of the corresponding quality of confidence; and to show the operation and the importance of those qualities in promises, which relate to what is to come. It is material to illustrate the connexion, the importance, and the operation of the same corresponding qualities in testimony, which relates to what is past.

By recalling to our remembrance what we have experienced, we find, that those, with whom we have conversed, were accustomed to express such and such particular things by such and such particular words. But, in strictness, experience conveys to us the knowledge only of what is past: can we be assured, that, in future, those who have it in their power to express different things by the same words, and the same things by different words, will, in neither manner, avail themselves of that power? We act, and we cannot avoid acting, as if we were so assured. On what foundation do we so act? Whence proceeds this belief of the future and voluntary behaviour of those, with whom we converse? Have they come under any engagements to do what we believe they will do? They have not; and if they had, what assurance could engagements convey to those, who possessed no previous reliance on the faith of promises?

There is, in the human mind, an anticipation, an original conviction, that those, with whom we converse, will, when, in future, they express the same sentiments, which they have expressed in time past, convey those sentiments by the same language which, in time past, they have employed to convey them. There is, in the human mind, a farther anticipation and conviction, that those, with whom we converse, will, when they express to us sentiments in the same language, which they have formerly employed to express them, mean, by those sentiments, to convey to us the truth.

The greatest and most important part of our knowledge, we receive by the information of others. We are, accordingly, endowed with the

[s] Parum est jus nosse, says Justinian in his institutes (l. 1. t. 2. s. 12.) si personæ, quarum causa constitutum est, ignorentur. It is to little purpose to know the law, if we are ignorant concerning the persons, for whose sake the law was constituted.
[t] Ante. p. 232.

two corresponding principles, which I have already mentioned, and which are admirably fitted to accomplish the purpose, for which they were intended. The first of them, which is a propensity to speak the truth, and to use language in such a manner as to convey to others the sentiments, which we ourselves entertain, is a principle, degenerate as we are apt to think human nature to be, more uniformly and more universally predominant, than is generally imagined. To speak as we think, and to speak as we have been accustomed to speak, are familiar and easy to us: they require no studied or artificial exertion: a natural impulse is sufficient to produce them. Even the most consummate liar declares truths much more frequently than falsehoods. On some occasions, indeed, there may be inducements to deceive, which will prove too powerful for the natural principle of veracity, unassisted by honour or virtue: but when no such inducements operate, our natural instinct is, to speak the truth. Another instinct, equally natural, is to believe what is spoken to be true. This principle is a proper and a useful counterpart to the former.

A very different theory has been adopted by some philosophers. No species of evidence, it is admitted by them, is more common, more useful, and even more necessary to human life, than that which is derived from testimony. But our reliance, it is contended, on any evidence of this kind is derived from no other principle than our observation of the veracity of human testimony, and of the usual conformity of facts to the reports of witnesses. If it were not discovered by experience, that the memory is tenacious to a certain degree; that men have commonly a principle of probity and an inclination to truth; and that they have a sensibility to shame, when detected in a falsehood — If it were not discovered by experience, that these qualities are inherent in human nature; we should never repose the least confidence in human testimony.[u]

If belief in testimony were the result only of experience; those who have never had experience would never believe; and the most experienced would be the most credulous of men. The fact, however, in both instances, is precisely the reverse; and there are wise reasons, why it should be so. The propensity which children, before they acquire experience, discover to believe every thing that is told to them, is strong and extensive. On the contrary, experience teaches those who are aged, to become cautious and distrustful.

"Oportet discentem credere" * has acquired, and justly, the force and the currency of a proverb. How many things must children learn and believe, before they can try them by the touchstone of experience! The infant mind, conscious, as it should seem, of its want of experience, relies implicitly on whatever is told it; and receives, with assurance, the testi-

[u] 2. Hume's Ess. 119. 120.   * [It is necessary for the learner to believe.]

mony of every one, without attempting and without being able to examine the grounds, upon which that testimony rests. As the mind gradually acquires experience and knowledge, it discovers reasons for suspecting testimony, in some cases, and for rejecting it, in others. But unless some reasons appear for suspicion or disbelief, testimony is, through the whole of life, considered and received as sufficient evidence to form a foundation both of opinion and conduct.

The reasons for suspecting or rejecting testimony may generally be comprised under the following heads. 1. When the witness testifies to something, which appears to us to be improbable or incredible. 2. When he shows himself to be no competent judge of the matter, of which he gives testimony. 3. When, in former instances, we have known him to deliver testimony, which has been false. 4. When, in the present instance, we discover some strong inducement or temptation, which may prevail on him to deceive.

While experience and reflection, on some occasions, diminish the force and influence of testimony, they, on other occasions, give it assistance, and increase its authority. The reputation of the witness, the manner in which he delivers his testimony, the nature of the fact concerning which his testimony is given, the peculiar situation in which he stands with regard to that fact, the occasion on which he is called to produce his testimony, his entire disinterestedness as to the matter in question — each of these taken singly may much augment the force of his evidence — all of these taken jointly may render that force irresistible.

In a number of concurrent testimonies, there is a degree of probability superadded to that, which may be termed the aggregate of all the probabilities of the separate testimonies. This superadded probability arises from the concurrence itself. When, concerning a great number and variety of circumstances, there is an entire agreement in the testimony of many witnesses, without the possibility of a previous collusion between them, the evidence may, in its effect, be equal to that of strict demonstration. That such concurrence should be the result of chance, is as one to infinite; or, to vary the expression, is a moral impossibility.

To this important kind of evidence we are indebted for our knowledge of history, of criticism, and of many parts of jurisprudence; for all that acquaintance with nature and the works of nature, which is not founded on our own personal observations and experience, but on the attested experience and observations of others; and for the greatest part of that information concerning men and things, which is necessary, if not to the mere animal support, yet certainly to the ease, comfort, improvement, and happiness of human life.

In the profession of the law, and in the administration of justice, this kind of evidence acquires an importance very peculiar indeed. To examine, to compare, and to appreciate it, forms much the greatest part of the business and duty of jurors, and a very great part of the business and duty of counsel and judges. It is, therefore, highly interesting to society, that the genuine and unsophisticated principles of this kind of evidence should be generally known and understood. From the very cursory view which we have taken of them, it appears that the rules observed by the common law, in admitting and in refusing testimony, are conformable to the true theory of the human mind, and not to the warped hypotheses of some philosophical systems.

VIII. The eighth source of evidence, which I mentioned, is human authority in matters of opinion.

"Cuilibet in sua arte perito est credendum" * is one of the maxims of the common law. Like many other of its maxims, it is founded in sound sense, and in human nature.

Under the former head we have seen, that the infant mind, inexperienced and unsuspicious, trusts implicitly to testimony in matters of fact. It trusts, in the same implicit manner, to authority in matters of opinion. In proportion as the knowledge of men and things is gradually obtained, the influence of authority as well as of testimony becomes less decisive and indiscriminate. By the most prudent, however, and the most enlightened, it is, at no period of life, suffered to fall into desuetude or disrepute: even in subjects and sciences, which seem the most removed from the sphere of its operations.

Let us suppose, that, in mathematicks, the science in which authority is justly allowed to possess the least weight, one has made a discovery, which he thinks of importance: let us suppose that he has ascertained the truth of this discovery by a regular process of demonstration, in which, after the strictest review, he can find no defect or mistake: will he not feel an inclination to communicate this discovery to the inspection of a mathematical friend, congenial in his studies and pursuits? Will this inclination be prompted merely by the pride or pleasure of making the communication? Will it not arise, in some degree, from a very different principle — a latent but powerful desire to know the sentiments of his friend, not only concerning the merits, but also concerning the certainty of the discovery? Will not the sentiments of his friend, favourable or unfavourable, greatly increase or diminish his confidence in his own judgment? A man must possess an uncommon degree of self-sufficiency, who feels not an increased reliance on the justness of his discoveries, when he finds the truth of them fortified by the sentiments of those, who, with regard to the same subjects, are conspicuous for their penetration and discernment.

The evidence arising from authority, as well as that arising from testi-

* [A man of authority is to be given credence in his own metier.]

mony, other circumstances being equal, becomes strong in proportion to the number of those, on whose voice it rests. An opinion generally received in all countries and all ages, acquires such an accumulation of authority in its favour, as to entitle it to the character of a first principle of human knowledge.

IX. The ninth kind, into which we have distinguished evidence, is that, which arises from memory. The senses and consciousness give us information of those things only which exist at present. The memory conveys to us the knowledge of those things which are past. The evidence of memory, therefore, forms a necessary link in every chain of proof, by which the past is notified. This evidence is not less certain than if it was founded on strict demonstration. No man hesitates concerning it, or will give his assent to any argument brought to invalidate it. On it depends, in part, the testimony of witnesses, and all the knowledge which we possess, concerning every thing which is past.

The memory, as well as other powers of the mind which we have already mentioned, is an original faculty, and an original source of evidence, bestowed on us by the Author of our existence. Of this faculty we can give no other account, but that such, in this particular, is the constitution of our nature. Concerning past events we receive information from our memory; but how it gives this information, it is impossible for us to explain.[v]

"All our other original faculties, as well as memory, are unaccountable. He only, who made them, comprehends fully how they are made, and how they produce in us not only a conception, but a firm belief and assurance of things, which it concerns us to know." [w]

Remembrance, however, is not always accompanied with full assurance. To distinguish by language, those lively impressions of memory, which, produce indubitable conviction, from those fainter traces, which occasion an inferiour degree of assent, or, perhaps, diffidence and suspense, is, we believe, an impracticable attempt. But every one is, in fact, competent to distinguish them in such a manner, as to direct his own judgment and conduct.

X. Evidence arises from experience; as when from facts already known, we make inferences to facts of the *same* kind, unknown.

This branch of our subject is of great extent, of much practical utility, and highly susceptible of curious and instructive investigation. But it cannot, on this occasion, be treated as fully as it deserves to be treated.

The sources, from which experience flows, are — the external senses, consciousness, memory. The senses and consciousness give information to the mind of the existing facts, which are placed within the sphere of their operation. These articles of intelligence, when received, are com-

[v] Reid. Ess. Int. 308.   [w] Reid's Ess. Int. 310.

mitted to the charge of the memory. From all these faculties, however, there results only the knowledge of such facts as have come, or now come under our notice. But, in order to render this knowledge of service to us in directing our own conduct, and in discovering the nature of things, a further process of the mind becomes necessary. From the past, or the present, or from both, inferences must be made to the future: those inferences form that kind of evidence, which arises from experience.

If an object is remembered to have been frequently, still more, if it is remembered to have been constantly, succeeded by certain particular consequences; the conception of the object naturally associates to itself the conception of the consequences; and on the actual appearance of the object, the mind naturally anticipates the appearance of the consequences also. This connexion between the object and the frequent or constant consequences of the object, is the foundation of those inferences, which, as we have observed, form the evidence arising from experience.

If the consequences have followed the object constantly, and the observations of this constant connexion have been sufficiently numerous; the evidence, produced by experience, amounts to a moral certainty. If the connexion has been frequent, but not entirely uniform; the evidence amounts only to probability; and is more or less probable, in proportion as the connexions have been more or less frequent. That cork will float on the surface of water, and that iron will sink in it, are truths, of which we are morally certain; because these inferences are founded on connexions both sufficiently numerous and sufficiently uniform. We are not morally certain whether oak timber will float or sink in water; because, in some circumstances, it sinks, and, in other circumstances, it floats. But, if the circumstances uniformly attending the contrary effects are specified; then, under that specification, we can tell, with moral certainty, whether the timber will sink or swim.

This evidence, by which we infer what the future will be from what the past has been, is the effect of an original principle, implanted in the human mind. This principle appears in our most early infancy. The child, who is burnt, is soon taught to dread the fire. A great and necessary part of our knowledge is drawn from this source, before we are able to exercise the reasoning faculty. It is an instinctive prescience of the operations of nature, very similar to that prescience of human actions, by which we are made to rely upon the testimony of our fellow men. Without the latter, we could not receive information, by the means of language, concerning the sentiments of those, with whom we converse: without the former, we could not, by means of experience, acquire knowledge concerning the operations of nature. When we arrive at the years of discretion and are capable of exercising our reasoning power, this instinctive principle retains in us all its force; but we become more cautious in its application. We observe, with more accuracy, the circumstances attending the appearance of the object and its consequences, and learn to distinguish those which are regularly, from those which are only occasionally, to be discovered.

On this principle is built the whole stupendous fabrick of natural philosophy; and if this principle were removed, that fabrick, solid and strong as it is, would tumble in ruins to the very foundation. "That natural effects of the same kind are produced by the same causes," is a first principle laid down by the great Newton, as one of his laws of philosophizing.

On the same principle depends the science of politicks, which draws its rules from what we know by experience concerning the conduct and character of men. From this experience we conclude, that they will bestow some care and attention on themselves, on their families, and on their friends; that, without some temptation, they will not injure one another; that, on certain occasions, they will discover gratitude, and, on others, resentment. In the science of politicks, we consider not so much what man ought to be, as what he really is; and from thence we make inferences concerning the part which he will probably act, in the different circumstances and situations, in which he may be placed. From such considerations we reason concerning the causes and consequences of different governments, customs, and laws. If man were either better or worse, more perfect or less perfect, than he is, a proportioned difference ought to be adopted in the systems formed, and the provisions made, for the regulation of his conduct.

The same principle is the criterion, at least, if it is not the foundation, of all moral reasoning whatever. It is the basis of prudence in the management of the affairs and business of human life. Scarcely can a plan be formed, whether of a publick or even of a more private nature, which depends solely on the behaviour of him who forms it: it must depend also on the behaviour of others; and must proceed upon the supposition, that those others will, in certain given circumstances, act a certain given part.

XI. Evidence arises from analogy, as well as from experience. The evidence of analogy is, indeed, nothing more than a vague experience, founded on some remote similitude. When the circulation of the blood in one human body was verified by experiment, this was certainly a sufficient evidence, from experience, that, in every other human body, the blood, in like manner, circulates. When we reflect on the strong resemblance which, in many particulars, the bodies of some other animals, quadrupeds, for instance, bear to the human body; and especially on that resemblance, which is discovered in the blood vessels, in the blood itself, and in the pulsation of the heart and arteries; we discover evidence, from analogy, of the circulation of the blood in those other animals; for instance, in quadrupeds. In this application of the experiment, however, the evidence is unquestionably weaker than in that, which is transferred from one to another man. Yet, when the analogies are numerous, and evidence of a closer and more direct application is not to be obtained, the evidence from analogy is far from being without its operation and its use.

Its use, we acknowledge, appears more in answering objections, than in furnishing direct proofs. It may, for this reason, be considered as the defensive rather than the offensive armour of a speaker. It rarely refutes; but it repels refutations: it cannot kill the enemy; but it wards off his blows.

Much of the evidence in natural philosophy rises not higher, than that which is derived from analogy. We learn from experience, that there is a certain gradation in the scale of certain animals: we conclude from analogy, that this gradation extends farther than our experience reaches. Upon the foundation of analogy, the systems of ancient philosophy concerning the material world were entirely built. My Lord Bacon first delineated, and, in some instances, applied the strict and severe method of induction from experiment. Since his time, this has been employed in natural philosophy, with the greatest success.

To the common lawyer, the evidence of analogy is a subject of very great extent and importance.

In speaking of judicial decisions, my Lord Chief Justice Hale distinguishes them into two kinds: one consists of such as have their reasons singly in the laws and customs of the kingdom. In these the law gives an express decision; and the judge is only the instrument, which pronounces it. The other kind consists of decisions, which are framed and deduced, as his Lordship says, by way of deduction and illation upon those laws.

A competition between opposite analogies is the principle, into which a very great number of legal controversies may be justly resolved. When a particular point of law has been once directly adjudged; the adjudication is deemed decisive as to that question, and to every other which, in all its circumstances, corresponds completely with that question. But questions arise, which resemble the decided question only in some parts, in certain circumstances, and in certain indirect aspects; and which, it is contended, bear, in other aspects, in other circumstances, and in other parts, a much closer and stronger resemblance to other cases, which have been likewise adjudged. To stating, to comparing, and to enforcing those opposite analogies, on the opposite sides, much of the business of the bar is appropriated. In discerning the force and extent of the distinctions which are taken; in framing an adjudication in such a manner, as to preserve unimpeached the various former decisions, from which the contending analogies have been drawn; or, if all cannot be so preserved, yet so as that the weaker may be given up to the stronger — in this, much of the wisdom and sagacity of the court are employed and displayed.

The late celebrated dispute concerning literary property will place this subject, and the remarks which have been made concerning it, in a very striking point of view. On one hand, the time which an author employs, the pains which he takes, and the industry which he exerts, in the production of his literary performance, bear the nearest and the most marked resemblance to the industry exerted, to the pains taken, and to the time employed, in the acquisition of property of every other kind. This resemblance, so striking and so strong, between the labour bestowed in this, and the labour bestowed in any other way, justifies the inference and the claim, that he, who bestowed the labour in this way, should be entitled to the same perpetual, assignable, and exclusive right in the production of the labour thus bestowed; and should receive the same protection of the law in the enjoyment of this perpetual, assignable, and exclusive right, as is given and decreed to those who bestow their labour in any other manner. This is the analogy on one side. On the other hand, a book, considered with respect to the author's right in it, has a peculiar resemblance to any other invention of art; the discovery, for instance, of a new medicine, or of a new machine. Now, in these instances, unless an exclusive right is secured to the inventor by a patent, the law permits the machine or medicine to be used or imitated. Why should not the same liberty be enjoyed in the publication and sale of books? This is the analogy on the other side.

XII. Evidence arises from judgment. By judgment I here mean that power of the mind, which decides upon selfevident truths. This is a much more extensive power than is generally imagined. It is, itself, a distinct and original source of evidence; and its jurisdiction is exercised in all the other kinds of evidence, which have been already enumerated.

"There are conceptions, which ought to be referred to the faculty of judgment as their source: because, if we had not that faculty, they could not enter into our minds; and to those who have that faculty, and are capable of reflecting on its operations, they are obvious and familiar.

"Among these, we may reckon the conception of judgment itself; the notions of a proposition, of its subject, predicate, and copula; of affirmation and negation; of true and false; of knowledge, belief, disbelief, opinion, assent, evidence. From no source could we acquire these conceptions, but from reflecting on our judgments. Relations of things make one great class of our notions or ideas; and we cannot have the idea of any relation without some exercise of judgment." [x]

[x] Reid. Ess. Int. 500, 501.

By our senses, we have certain sensations and perceptions. But to furnish us with these, is not the only, nor is it, indeed, the principal office
of our senses. They are powers, by which we judge, as well as feel and
perceive. A man, who has become blind, may, nevertheless, retain very
distinct conceptions of the several colours; but he cannot, any longer,
judge concerning colours; because he has lost the sense, the immediate
operation of which is necessary in order to enable him to form such judgment. By our ears, we have the ideas of sounds of different kinds, such as
acute and grave, soft and loud. But this sense enables us not only to hear,
but to judge of what we hear. We perceive one sound to be loud, another to be soft. When we hear more sounds than one, we perceive and
judge that some are concords, and that others are discords. These are
judgments of the senses.[y]

Judgment exercises its power concerning the evidence of consciousness, as well as concerning the evidence of the senses. The man, who is
conscious of an object, believes that it exists, and is what he is conscious
it is; nor is it in his power to avoid such judgment. Whether judgment
ought to be called a necessary concomitant, or rather an ingredient, of
these operations of the mind, it is not material to inquire; but one thing
is certain; they are accompanied with a determination that something is
true or false, and with a consequent belief. This determination is not
simple apprehension; it is not reasoning; it is a mental affirmation or negation; it may be expressed by a proposition affirmative or negative; and
it is accompanied with the firmest belief. These are the characteristicks of
judgment.[z] This name is sometimes given to every determination of the
mind concerning what is true or what is false.[a] Under this head, I apply
it, and confine it to that degree of judgment, which is commensurate
with what is sometimes called common sense: for, in truth, common
sense means common judgment.[b]

Further; judgment is implied in every operation of taste. When we say
a statue or a poem is beautiful; we affirm something concerning that
poem or statue: but every affirmation or denial expresses judgment. Our
judgment of beauty is not, indeed, dry and uninteresting, like that of a
mathematical truth. It is accompanied with an agreeable feeling or emotion, for which we have no appropriated term. It is called the sense of
beauty.

Judgment is exerted also in the operations of our moral sense. When
we exercise our moral powers concerning our own actions or those of
others, we judge as well as feel. We accuse and excuse; we acquit and
condemn, we assent and dissent; we believe and disbelieve. These are all
acts of judgment.[e]

[y] Reid. Ess. Act. 237, 238.   [z] Reid. Ess. Int. 501, 503.   [a] Id. 504, 533. 534.
[b] Id. 523, 530, 531.   [e] Reid's Ess. Act. 474.

In short, we judge of the qualities of bodies by our external senses; we judge concerning what passes in our minds by our consciousness; we judge concerning beauty and deformity by our taste; we judge concerning virtue and vice by our moral sense: but, in all these cases, we judge; in most of them, our judgment is accompanied by feeling. Judgment accompanied by feeling forms that complex operation of the mind, which is denominated sentiment.

This train of investigation might be carried much farther; but, at present, we stop here.

Judgment, in the sense in which we here use it, is an original and an important source of knowledge, common to all men; and, for this reason, is frequently denominated common sense, as has been already intimated. In different persons, it prevails, indeed, with different degrees of strength; but none, except idiots, have been found originally and totally without it.

The laws, we believe, of every civilized nation distinguish between those who are, and those who are not, endowed with this gift of heaven. This gift is easily discerned by its effects, in the actions, in the discourse, and even in the looks of a man. When it is made a question, whether one is or is not possessed of this power, the courts of justice can usually determine the question with much clearness and certainty.

The same degree of understanding, which enables one to act with common prudence in the business of life, enables him also to discover self-evident truths concerning matters, of which he has distinct apprehension.

Selfevident truths, of every kind, and in every art and science, are the objects of that faculty, which is now under our consideration. Such truths, or axioms, as they are distinguished by way of excellence, are the foundation of all mathematical knowledge. There are axioms, too, in matters of taste. The fundamental rules of poetry, and painting, and eloquence, have always been, and, we may venture to add, always will be the same. The science of morals is also founded on axioms; many of which are accompanied with intuitive evidence, not less strong than that which is discovered in the axioms of mathematicks. Mathematical axioms can never extend their influence beyond the limits of abstract knowledge. But with axioms in other branches of science, the whole business of human life is closely and strongly connected.

XIII. Evidence arises from reasoning.

One observation, which I made concerning judgment, may be made, with the same propriety, concerning reasoning. It is, itself, a distinct and original source of evidence; and its jurisdiction is exercised also in evidence of every other kind. This suggests a very probable account why reason has been considered by many philosophers as the only source and criterion of evidence: for the powers both of judgment and of reasoning have been frequently blended under the name of reason.

As the conception of judgment should be referred to the faculty of judgment; so the conception of reasoning should be referred to the reasoning faculty, as its source. The ideas of demonstration, of probability, and of all the different modes of reasoning, take their origin from the faculty of reason. Without this faculty, we could not be possessed of those ideas.

The power of reasoning is somewhat allied to the power of judging. Reasoning, as well as judgment, must be true or false: both are accompanied with assent or belief. There is, however, a very material distinction between them. Reasoning is the process, by which we pass from one truth to another as a conclusion from it. In all reasoning, there must be a proposition inferred, and one or more, from which the inference is drawn. The proposition inferred is called the conclusion: the name of premises is given to the proposition or propositions, from which the conclusion is inferred. When a chain of reasoning consists of many links, it is easily distinguished from judgment. But when the conclusion is connected with the premises by a single link, the distinction becomes less obvious; and the process is sometimes called by one name; sometimes by the other.

In a series of legitimate reasoning, the evidence of every step should be immediately discernible to those who have a distinct comprehension of the premises and the conclusion.

The evidence, which arises from reasoning, is divided into two species — demonstrative and moral. The nature, the difference, and the uses of these two species of evidence, it is of great importance clearly and fully to understand.

Demonstrative evidence has for its subject abstract and necessary truths, or the unchangeable relations of ideas. Moral evidence has for its subject the real but contingent truths and connexions, which take place among things actually existing. Abstract truths have no respect to time or place; they are universally and eternally the same.

If these observations are just — and they are agreeable to the sentiments of those who have written most accurately on this subject — we may see the impropriety of my Lord Chief Baron Gilbert's remark, when he says, that "all demonstration is founded on the view of a man's proper senses." From hence we may see likewise the inaccuracy of Sir William Blackstone's description of evidence, when he mentions it as demonstrating the very fact in issue. The objects of our senses are objects of moral, but not of demonstrative evidence.

By writers on the civil law, the scientifick distinction, upon this subject, is accurately observed. Truths alone, say they,[a] which depend on abstract principles, are susceptible of demonstrative evidence: truths, that

[a] Encyc. Tit. Jurisprudence. vol. 6. part 2. p. 752. (French.)

depend on matters of fact, however complete may be the evidence by which they are established, can never become demonstrative.

In a series of demonstrative evidence, the inference, in every step, is necessary; for it is impossible that, from the premises, the conclusion should not flow. In a series of moral evidence, the inference drawn in the several steps is not necessary; nor is it impossible that the premises should be true, while the conclusion drawn from them is false.

In demonstrative evidence, there are no degrees: one demonstration may be more easily comprehended, but it cannot be stronger than another. Every necessary truth leaves no possibility of its being false. In moral evidence, we rise, by an insensible gradation, from possibility to probability, and from probability to the highest degree of moral certainty.

In moral evidence, there not only may be, but there generally is, contrariety of proofs: in demonstrative evidence, no such contrariety can take place. If one demonstration can be refuted, it must be by another demonstration: but to suppose that two contrary demonstrations can exist, is to suppose that the same proposition is both true and false: which is manifestly absurd. With regard to moral evidence, there is, for the most part, real evidence on both sides. On both sides, contrary presumptions, contrary testimonies, contrary experiences must be balanced. The probability, on the whole, is, consequently, in the proportion, in which the evidence on one side preponderates over the evidence on the other side.

Demonstrative evidence is simple: in it there is only one coherent series, every part of which depends on what precedes, and suspends what follows. In demonstrative reasoning, therefore, one demonstration is equal to a thousand. To add a second would be a tautology in this kind of evidence. A second, it is true, is sometimes employed; but it is employed as an exercise of ingenuity, not as an additional proof. Moral evidence is generally complicated: it depends not upon any one argument, but upon many independent proofs, which, however, combine their strength, and draw on the same conclusion.

In point of authority, demonstrative evidence is superiour: moral evidence is superiour in point of importance. By the former, the understanding is enlightened, and many of the elegant and useful arts are improved. By the latter, society is supported; and the usual but indispensable affairs of life are regulated. To the acquisitions made by the latter, we owe the knowledge of almost every thing, which distinguishes the man from the child.

XIV. Evidence arises from calculations concerning chances. This kind of evidence does not occur very frequently. I take particular notice of it, because it is of much importance in some commercial transactions; especially in those relating to ensurances.

Chance furnishes materials for calculation, only when we know the remote cause, which will produce some one event of a given number; but know not the immediate cause, which will determine in favour of any one particular event of that given number, in preference to any other particular event. In calculating chances, it is necessary that a great number of instances be taken into consideration; that the greatest exactness and impartiality be used in collecting them on the opposite sides; and that there be no peculiarity in any of them, which would render it improper for becoming a part of the basis of a general conclusion.

I have now finished the long, I will not say, the complete enumeration of the different sources and kinds of evidence. Between several of them something will be found to be analogous. But, upon the most careful review, it will, I think, appear, that no one of them can be resolved into any other. Hence the propriety of considering and treating them separately and distinctly. Much advantage will, I believe, be reaped from acquiring and exercising a habit of considering them in this separate and distinct manner. For this purpose, it will be proper, when a trial of much variety and importance is perused or heard, to digest, at leisure, those things which are given or which appear in evidence, and refer them to their several sources and kinds. After this has been done, it will be of great use carefully to arrange the different sorts and parts of the evidence, and compare them together in point of solidity, clearness, and force. A habit of analyzing, combining, methodising, and balancing evidence, in this manner, will be a constant and a valuable resource in the practice of the law. Every one, who has observed or experienced that practice, must be sensible, that a lawyer's time and attention are more employed, and his talents are more severely tried, by questions and debates on evidence, than by those on all the other titles of the law, various, intricate, and extensive as they are.

To wield the weapons of evidence forms an important article in a lawyer's art. To wield them skilfully evinces a good head: to wield them honestly as well as skilfully evinces, at once, a good head and a good heart; and reflects equal honour on the profession and on the man.

I have, on this occasion, said nothing concerning the artificial rules of evidence, which are framed by the law for convenience in courts of justice. These, unquestionably, ought to be studied and known. Concerning these, much learning may be found in the several law books. Particular rules may be seen, adapted to particular cases. An intimate acquaintance with those rules will be of great practical utility in what I may call the retail business of the law; a kind of business by no means to be neglected; a kind of business, however, which should not be suffered to usurp the place of what is far more essential — the study and the practice too of the law, as a science founded on principle, and on the nature of man. The powers and the operations of the human mind are the native and original fountains of evidence. Gaudy, but scanty and temporary cascades may sometimes be supplied by art. But the natural springs alone can furnish a constant and an abundant supply. He, too, who is in full possession of these, can, with the greatest facility, and to the greatest advantage, display their streams, on proper occasions, in all the forms, and with all the ornaments, suggested and prepared by the most artificial contrivances.

It is generally supposed — and, indeed, our law books, so far as I recollect, go upon the supposition — that the evidence, which influences a court and jury, depends altogether upon what is said by the witnesses, or read from the papers. This, however, is very far from being the case. Much depends on the pleadings of the counsel. His pleadings depend much on a masterly knowledge and management of the principles of evidence. Evidence is the foundation of conviction: conviction is the foundation of persuasion: to convey persuasion is the end of pleading. From the principles of evidence, therefore, must be drawn that train and tenour of reasoning, which will accomplish the aim of the pleader, and produce the perfection of his art.

A rich and an immense prospect opens to my view; but I cannot now attempt to describe it.

PART TWO

I

OF THE CONSTITUTIONS OF THE UNITED STATES AND OF PENNSYLVANIA—OF THE LEGISLATIVE DEPARTMENT

IN my plan, I mentioned, that I would consider our municipal law under two great divisions; that, under the first, I would treat of the law, as it relates to persons; and that, under the second, I would treat of it, as it relates to things. I pursue those two great divisions; and begin with persons.

Persons are divided into two kinds — natural and artificial. Natural persons are formed by the great Author of nature. Artificial persons are the creatures of human sagacity and contrivance; and are framed and intended for the purposes of government and society.

When we contemplate the constitution and the laws of the United States and of the commonwealth of Pennsylvania; the mighty object, which first arrests our attention, is — the people. In the laws of England, as they have been imposed or received during the last seven centuries, the "people" is a title, which has scarcely found a place, or, if it has found a place occasionally, it has attracted but a very disproportionate degree of notice or regard. Of the prerogative of the king, frequent and respectful mention is made: he is considered and represented as the fountain of authority, of honour, of justice, and even of the most important species of property. Of the majesty of the people, little is said in the books of our law. When they are introduced upon the legal stage, they are considered as the body, of which the king is the head, and are viewed as the subjects of his crown and government.

This has not been the case in all countries; it has not been the case in England at all times. It has, indeed, been the case too often and too generally; but the pages of literature will furnish us with a few brilliant exceptions. Of one permit me to take a very particular notice; for of a very particular notice it is highly deserving.

At the mention of Athens, a thousand refined and endearing associations rush immediately into the memory of the scholar, the philosopher, the statesman, and the patriot. When Homer, one of the most correct, as well as the oldest and one of the most respectable, of human authorities, enumerates the other nations of Greece, whose forces acted in the siege of Troy; he arranges them under the names of their different kings: but when he comes to the Athenians, he distinguishes them by the peculiar appellation of "the people" [a] of Athens.

Let it not surprise you, that I cite Homer as a very respectable authority. That celebrated writer was not more remarkable for the elegance and sublimity, than he was for the truth and precision, of his compositions. The geographer, who could not relish the exquisite beauties of his poetry, felt, however, uncommon satisfaction in ascertaining, by the map, the severe accuracy of his geographical descriptions. But let me mention what is still more to my present purpose and justification. From one of the orations of Æschines it appears highly probable,[b] that in the Athenian courts of justice, the poems of Homer, as well as the laws of Athens, were always laid upon the table before the judges; and that the clerk was frequently applied to, by the orator, to read passages from the former, as well as from the latter. On the authority of two lines from Homer's catalogue of the Grecian fleet, was determined a controversy between the Athenians and the inhabitants of Salamis. His immortal poems, like a meteor in the gloom of night, brighten the obscure antiquities of his country.[c]

By some of the most early accounts, which have been transmitted to us concerning Britain, we are informed, that "the people held the helm of government in their own power." [d] This spirit of independence was a ruling principle among the Saxons likewise. Concerning their original, it is both needless and fruitless — I use the expressions of the very learned Selden[e] — to enter the lists; whether they were natives from the northern parts of Germany, or the relicks of the army under Alexander. But their government, adds he, was, in general, so suitable to that of the Grecians, that it cannot be imagined but much of the Grecian wisdom was derived into those parts. The people were a free people, governed by laws which they themselves made; and, for this reason, they were denominated free. This, he subjoins, was like unto the manner of the Athenians.

The Saxons were called freemen, because they were born free from

[a] Δῆμος. Pot. 12. Iliad l. 2. v. 547.   [b] 1. Gill. 26.   [c] 1. Gill. 3.
[d] Bac. on Gov. 2.   [e] Id. 9.

all yoke of arbitrary power, and from all laws of compulsion, except those which were made by their voluntary consent: for all freemen have votes in making and executing the general laws.ᶠ The freedom of a Saxon consisted in the three following particulars. 1. In the ownership of what he had. 2. In voting upon any law, by which his person or property could be affected. 3. In possessing a share in that judiciary power, by which the laws were applied.ᵍ

By this time, we clearly perceive the exquisite propriety, historical as well as political, with which the people appear in the foreground of the national constitution and of that of Pennsylvania. "We, the people of the United States, ordain and establish this constitution for the United States of America." "We, the people of the commonwealth of Pennsylvania, ordain and establish this constitution for its government."

In free states, the people form an artificial person or body politick, the highest and noblest that can be known. They form that moral person, which, in one of my former lectures,ʰ I described as a complete body of free natural persons, united together for their common benefit; as having an understanding and a will; as deliberating, and resolving, and acting; as possessed of interests which it ought to manage; as enjoying rights which it ought to maintain; and as lying under obligations which it ought to perform. To this moral person, we assign, by way of eminence, the dignified appellation of *state*.

In discussing the rights and duties of a state, I observed, that it is its right, and that, generally, it is its duty, to form a constitution, to institute civil government, and to establish laws. The general principles, on which constitutions should be formed, government should be instituted, and laws should be established, were treated at large then, and will not be repeated now. It is my present business to trace the application of those principles, as that application has been practically made by the people of the United States, and, in particular, by the people of Pennsylvania.

I mention the people of Pennsylvania in particular; because, in discussing this system, it is necessary that I should select the constitution, and government, and laws of some one of the states in the Union; and because it is natural, for many reasons, that Pennsylvania should be the state, whose constitution, and government, and laws are selected for this discussion. The observations, however, which I shall have occasion to make with regard to Pennsylvania, will, in the greatest number of instances, apply to her sister states, with an equal degree of propriety. Whenever any very striking difference or coincidence shall occur to me, I shall distinguish it by an especial notice.

The people of the United States must be considered attentively in two

ᶠ Bac. on Gov. 34.　　ᵍ Id. 84.　　ʰ Ante. p. 239.

very different views — as forming one nation, great and united; and as forming, at the same time, a number of separate states, to that nation subordinate, but independent as to their own interiour government. This very important distinction must be continually before our eyes. If it be properly observed, every thing will appear regular and proportioned: if it be neglected, endless confusion and intricacy will unavoidably ensue.

The constitution of the United States is arranged, as we have formerly seen it ought to be, under three great divisions — the legislative department, the executive department, and the judicial department.

The legislative power is divided between two different bodies, a senate, and a house of representatives. The reasons and the importance of this division were explained in a former part of my lectures.[i]

In discoursing farther concerning the legislature of the United States, I shall regulate myself by the following order. I shall treat, I. of the election of its members; II. of their number; III. of the term, for which they are elected; IV. of the laws, and rules, and powers of the two houses; V. of the manner of passing laws, VI. of the powers of congress.

I. I am first to treat concerning the election of members of congress. Many of the remarks, which I shall make on this subject, will be applicable to the election of members of the general assembly of this commonwealth; for the assembly of Pennsylvania, like the congress of the United States, consists of two bodies, a senate and a house of representatives. Some important articles of discrimination will be noticed in their proper places.

The constitution of the United States and that of Pennsylvania rest solely, and in all their parts, on the great democratical principle of a representation of the people; in other words, of the moral person, known by the name of the state. This great principle necessarily draws along with it the consideration of another principle equally great — the principle of free and equal elections. To maintain, in purity and in vigour, this important principle, whose energy should pervade the most distant parts of the government, is the first duty, and ought to be the first care, of every free state. This is the original fountain, from which all the streams of administration flow. If this fountain is poisoned, the deleterious influence will extend to the remotest corners of the state: if this fountain continues pure and salubrious, the benign operation of its waters will diffuse universal health and soundness.

Let me, by the way, be indulged with repeating a remark, which was made and fully illustrated in a former lecture[j] — that government, founded solely on representation, made its first appearance on this, and not on the European side of the Atlantick.

[i] Ante. p. 290 etc.   [j] Ante. p. 311.

Of the science of just and equal government, the progress, as we have formerly seen, has been small and slow. Peculiarly small and slow has it been, in the discovery and improvement of the interesting doctrines of election and representation. If, with regard to other subjects, government may be said, as it has been said, to be still in its infancy; we may, with regard to this subject, consider it as only in its childhood. And yet this is the subject, which must form the basis of every government, that is, at once, efficient, respectable, and free.

The pyramid of government — and a republican government may well receive that beautiful and solid form — should be raised to a dignified altitude: but its foundations must, of consequence, be broad, and strong, and deep. The authority, the interests, and the affections of the people at large are the only foundation, on which a superstructure, proposed to be at once durable and magnificent, can be rationally erected.

Representation is the chain of communication between the people and those, to whom they have committed the exercise of the powers of government. If the materials, which form this chain, are sound and strong, it is unnecessary to be solicitous about the very high degree, to which they are polished. But in order to impart to them the true republican lustre, I know no means more effectual, than to invite and admit the freemen to the right of suffrage, and to enhance, as much as possible, the value of that right. Its value cannot, in truth, be enhanced too highly. It is a right of the greatest import, and of the most improving efficacy. It is a right to choose those, who shall be intrusted with the authority and with the confidence of the people: and who may employ that authority and that confidence for the noblest interests of the commonwealth, without the apprehension of disappointment or control.

This surely must have a powerful tendency to open, to enlighten, to enlarge, and to exalt the mind. I cannot, with sufficient energy, express my own conceptions of the value and the dignity of this right. In real majesty, an independent and unbiassed elector stands superiour to princes, addressed by the proudest titles, attended by the most magnificent retinues, and decorated with the most splendid regalia. Their sovereignty is only derivative, like the pale light of the moon: his is original, like the beaming splendour of the sun.

The benign influences, flowing from the possession and exercise of this right, deserve to be clearly and fully pointed out. I wish it was in my power to do complete justice to the important subject. Hitherto those benign influences have been little understood; they have been less valued; they have been still less experienced. This part of the knowledge and practice of government is yet, as has been observed, in its childhood. Let us, however, nurse and nourish it. In due time, it will repay our care and our labour; for, in due time, it will grow to the strength and stature of a full and perfect man.

The man, who enjoys the right of suffrage, on the extensive scale which is marked by our constitutions, will naturally turn his thoughts to the contemplation of publick men and publick measures. The inquiries he will make, the information he will receive, and his own reflections on both, will afford a beneficial and amusing employment to his mind. I am far from insinuating, that every citizen should be an enthusiast in politicks, or that the interests of himself, his family, and those who depend on him for their comfortable situation in life, should be absorbed in Quixote speculations about the management or the reformation of the state. But there is surely a golden mean in things; and there can be no real incompatibility between the discharge of one's publick, and that of his private duty. Let private industry receive the warmest encouragement; for it is the basis of publick happiness. But must the bow of honest industry be always bent? At no moment shall a little relaxation be allowed? That relaxation, if properly directed, may prove to be instructive as well as agreeable. It may consist in reading a newspaper, or in conversing with a fellow citizen. May not the newspaper convey some interesting intelligence, or contain some useful essay? May not the conversation take a pleasing and an improving turn? Many hours, I believe, are every where spent, in talking about the unimportant occurrences of the day, or in the neighbourhood; and, perhaps, the frailties or the imperfections of a neighbour form, too often, one of the sweet but poisoned ingredients of the discourse. Would it be any great detriment to society or to individuals, if other characters, and with different views, were more frequently brought upon the carpet?

Under our constitutions, a number of important appointments must be made at every election. To make them is, indeed, the business only of a day. But it ought to be the business of much more than a day, to be prepared for making them well. When a citizen elects to office — let me repeat it — he performs an act of the first political consequence. He should be employed, on every convenient occasion, in making researches after proper persons for filling the different departments of power; in discussing, with his neighbours and fellow citizens, the qualities, which ought to be possessed by those, who enjoy places of publick trust; and in acquiring information, with the spirit of manly candour, concerning the manners and characters of those, who are likely to be candidates for the publick choice.

A habit of conversing and reflecting on these subjects, and of governing his actions by the result of his deliberations, would produce, in the mind of the citizen, a uniform, a strong, and a lively sensibility to the interests of his country. The same causes will effectuate a warm and enlightened attachment to those, who are best fitted, and best disposed, to support and promote those interests. By these means and in this manner, pure and genuine patriotism, that kind, which consists in liberal investigation and disinterested conduct, is produced, cherished, and strengthened in the mind: by these means and in this manner, the warm and generous emotion glows and is reflected from breast to breast.

Investigations of this nature are useful and improving, not to their authors only; they are so to their objects likewise. The love of honest and well earned fame is deeply rooted in honest and susceptible minds. Can there be a stronger incentive to the operations of this passion, than the hope of becoming the object of well founded and distinguishing applause? Can there be a more complete gratification of this passion, than the satisfaction of knowing that this applause is given — that it is given upon the most honourable principles, and acquired by the most honourable pursuits? To souls truly ingenuous, indiscriminate praise, misplaced praise, flattering praise, interested praise have no bewitching charms. But when publick approbation is the result of publick discernment, it must be highly pleasing to those who give, and to those who receive it.

If the foregoing remarks and deductions be just; and I believe they are so; the right of suffrage, properly understood, properly valued, and properly exercised, in a free and well constituted government, is an abundant source of the most rational, the most improving, and the most endearing connexion among the citizens.

All power is originally in the people; and should be exercised by them in person, if that could be done with convenience, or even with little difficulty. In some of the small republicks of Greece, and in the first ages of the commonwealth of Rome, the people voted in their aggregate capacity. Among the ancient Germans also, this was done upon great occasions. "De minoribus consultant principes," says Tacitus,[k] "de majoribus omnes:" From their practices, some of the finest principles of modern governments are drawn.

But in large states, the people cannot assemble together. As they cannot, therefore, act by themselves, they must act by their representatives. And, indeed, in point of right, there is no difference between that which is done by the people in their own persons, and that which is done by their deputies, acting agreeably to the powers received from them. In point of utility, there is as little difference; for there is no advantage, which may be not obtained from a free and adequate representation, in as effectual a manner, as if every citizen were to deliberate and vote in person.

[k] De mor. Germ. c. 11. [On matters of lesser importance, the chieftains make decisions; on those of greater weight, the whole people decides.]

To the legitimate energy and weight of true representation, two things are essentially necessary. 1. That the representatives should express the same sentiments, which the represented, if possessed of equal information, would express. 2. That the sentiments of the representatives, thus expressed, should have the same weight and influence, as the sentiments of the constituents would have, if expressed personally.

To accomplish the first object, all elections ought to be free. If a man is under no external bias, when he votes for a representative, he will naturally choose such as, he imagines, will, on the several subjects which may come before them, speak and act in the same manner as himself. Every one, who is not the slave of voluntary errour, supposes that his own opinions and sentiments are right: he must likewise suppose, that the sentiments and opinions of those who think with him are right also. Every other man, equally free from bias, will vote with similar views. When, therefore, the votes generally or unanimously centre in the same representatives, it is a satisfactory proof, that the sentiments of the constituents are generally or altogether in unison, with regard to the matters, which, they think, will be brought under the consideration of their representatives; and also, that the sentiments of the representatives will be, with regard to those matters, in unison with those of all, or of a majority of their constituents.

To accomplish the second object, all elections ought to be equal. Elections are equal, when a given number of citizens, in one part of the state, choose as many representatives, as are chosen by the same number of citizens, in any other part of the state. In this manner, the proportion of the representatives and of the constituents will remain invariably the same.

If both the requisites are established and preserved, such counsels will be given, such resolutions will be taken, and such measures will be pursued, by the representative body, as will receive the concurrence, the approbation, and the support of the community at large.

In a free government, it is of essential importance to ascertain the right of suffrage, and those inhabitants who are entitled to the exercise of that right. To vote for members of a legislature, is to perform an act of original sovereignty. No person unqualified should, therefore, be permitted to assume the exercise of such preeminent power. We are told, that, among the Athenians, exquisitely sensible to all the rights of citizenship, a stranger who interfered in the assemblies of the people, was punished with death. Such dangerous interference was considered as a species of treason against their rights of sovereignty.

A momentous question now occurs — who shall be entitled to suffrage? This darling privilege of freemen should certainly be extended as far as considerations of safety and order will possibly admit. The correct theory and the true principles of liberty require, that every citizen, whose circumstances do not render him necessarily dependent on the will of another, should possess a vote in electing those, by whose conduct his property, his reputation, his liberty, and his life, may be all most materially affected.

By the constitution of the United States,[1] the members of the house of representatives shall be chosen by the people of the several states. The electors, in each state, shall have the qualifications requisite for electors of the most numerous branch of the state legislature.

This regulation is generous and wise. It is generous; for it intrusts to the constitutions or to the legislatures of the several states, the very important power of ascertaining and directing the qualifications of those, who shall be entitled to elect the most numerous branch of the national legislature. This unsuspicious confidence evinces, in the national constitution, the most friendly disposition towards the governments of the several states. For how can such a proper disposition be evinced more strongly, than by providing that its legislature, so far as respects the most numerous branch of it, should stand upon the same foundation with theirs; and by providing farther, that this foundation should be continued or altered by the states themselves?

This regulation is wise as well as generous. An attention to its genuine principle and tendency must have a strong effect, in preventing or destroying the seeds of jealousy, which might otherwise spring up, with regard to the genius and views of the national government. It has embarked itself on the same bottom with the governments of the different states: can a stronger proof be given of its determination to sink or swim with them? Can proof be given of a stronger desire to live in mutual harmony and affection? This is an object of the last importance; for, to adopt an expression used by my Lord Bacon, "the uniting of the hearts and affections of the people is the life and true end of this work." [m]

The remarks which I have made on this subject place, in a clear and striking point of view, the propriety, and indeed the political necessity, of a regulation made in another part of this constitution. In the fourth section of the fourth article it is provided, that, "the United States shall guaranty to every state in this Union a republican form of government." Its own existence, as a government of this description, depends on theirs.

As the doctrine concerning elections and the qualifications of electors is, in every free country, a doctrine of the first magnitude; and as the national constitution has, with regard to this doctrine, rested itself on the governments of the several states; it will be highly proper to take a survey of those provisions, which, on a subject so interesting, have been

[1] Art. 1. s. 2.　　[m] Ld. Bac. 220.

made by the different state constitutions: for every state has justly deemed the subject to be of constitutional importance.

In the constitution of Pennsylvania, the great principle, which animates and governs this subject, is secured by an explicit declaration, that "elections shall be free and equal." [n] This is enumerated among the great points, which are "excepted out of the general powers of government, and shall for ever remain inviolate." [o] The practical operation of this great and inviolable principle is thus specified and directed: "In elections by the citizens, every freeman of the age of twenty one years, having resided in the state two years next before the election, and within that time paid a state or county tax, which shall have been assessed at least six months before the election, shall enjoy the rights of an elector." [p]

It well deserves, in this place, to be remarked, how congenial, upon this great subject, the principles of the constitution of Pennsylvania are to those adopted by the government of the Saxons. The Saxon freemen, as we have already seen, had votes in making their general laws.[q] The freemen of Pennsylvania, as we now see, enjoy the rights of electors. This right, it has been shown, is equivalent, and, in a state of any considerable extent, must, on every principle of order and convenience, be substituted to the other. This is far from being the only instance, in which we shall have the pleasure of finding the old Saxon maxims of government renewed in the American constitutions. Particular attention will be paid to them, as they present themselves.

By the constitution of New Hampshire, "every male inhabitant, with town privileges, of twenty one years of age, paying for himself a poll tax, has a right to vote, in the town or parish wherein he dwells, in the election of representatives." [r]

In Massachussetts, this right is, under the constitution, enjoyed by "every male person, being twenty one years of age, and resident in any particular town in the commonwealth for the space of one year next preceding, having a freehold estate within the same town, of the annual income of three pounds, or any estate of the value of sixty pounds." Every one so qualified may "vote in the choice of a representative for the said town." [s]

The right to choose representatives in Rhode Island is vested in "the freemen of the respective towns or places." This regulation is specified in the charter of Charles the second. The state of Rhode Island and Providence Plantations has not assumed a form of government different from that, which is contained in the abovementioned charter.[t]

[n] Art. 9. s. 5.   [o] Art. 9. s. 26.   [p] Cons. Penn. Art. 3. s. 1.
[q] Bac. on Gov. 34.   [r] Cons. N. H. p. 11. 14.   [s] Cons. Mass. c. 1. s. 3. a. 4.
[t] Char. R. I. p. 41. 51.

The qualifications requisite, in the state of Connecticut, to entitle a person to vote at elections, are, maturity in years, quiet and peaceable behaviour, a civil conversation, and forty shillings freehold, or forty pounds personal estate: if the selectmen of the town certify a person qualified in those respects, he is admitted a freeman, on his taking an oath of fidelity to the state.[u]

It ought to be observed, by the way, that this power to admit persons to be freemen, or to exclude them from being freemen, according to the sentiments which others entertain concerning their conversation and behaviour, is a power of a very extraordinary nature; and is certainly capable of being exercised for very extraordinary purposes.

The constitution of New York ordains, "that every male inhabitant of full age, who shall have personally resided within one of the counties of the state, for six months immediately preceding the day of election, shall, at such election, be entitled to vote for representatives of the said county in assembly; if during the time aforesaid he shall have been a freeholder, possessing a freehold of the value of twenty pounds, within the said county, or have rented a tenement therein of the yearly value of forty shillings; and been rated and actually paid taxes to the state." [v]

"All inhabitants of New Jersey, of full age, who are worth fifty pounds, proclamation money, clear estate within that government, and have resided within the county, in which they shall claim a vote, for twelve months immediately preceding the election, shall be entitled to vote for representatives in assembly." [w]

The right of suffrage is not specified in the constitution of Delaware; but it is provided, that, in the election of members of the legislature, it "shall remain as exercised by law at present." [x]

In Maryland, "all freemen above twenty one years of age, having a freehold of fifty acres of land in the county, in which they offer to vote, and residing therein; and all freemen having property in the state above the value of thirty pounds current money, and having resided in the county, in which they offer to vote, one whole year next preceding the election, shall have a right of suffrage in the election of delegates for such county." [y]

We find, in the constitution of Virginia, no specification of the right of suffrage: it is declared, however, that this right shall remain as it was exercised at the time when that constitution was made.[z]

It is provided by the constitution of North Carolina, "that all freemen of the age of twenty one years, who have been inhabitants of any county within the state twelve months immediately preceding the day of any

[u] Cons. Con. p. 54.　　[v] Cons. N. Y. c. 7. p. 58.　　[w] Cons. N. J. c. 4. p. 70. 71.
[x] Cons. Del. c. 5. p. 95.　　[y] Cons. Mar. c. 2. p. 109.　　[z] Cons. Vir. p. 126.

election, and shall have paid publick taxes, shall be entitled to vote for members of the house of commons, for the county in which they reside." [a]

According to the constitution of South Carolina, "every free white man, of the age of twenty one years, being a citizen of the state, and having resided in it two years previous to the day of election, and who has a freehold of fifty acres of land, or a town lot, of which he hath been legally seized and possessed at least six months before such election, or, not having such freehold or lot, has resided within the election district, in which he offers to give his vote, six months before the election, and has, the preceding year, paid a tax of three shillings sterling towards the support of government, shall have a right to vote for members of the house of representatives for the election district, in which he holds such property, or is so resident." [b]

I am not possessed of the present constitution of Georgia. By its late constitution, it was provided, that "all male white inhabitants, of the age of twenty one years, and possessed, in their own right, of ten pounds value, and liable to pay tax in the state, or being of any mechanick trade, and shall have been a resident six months in the state, shall have a right to vote at all elections for[c] representatives." [d]

[a] Cons. N. C. c. 8. p. 134.   [b] Cons. S. C. art. 1. s. 4.
[c] Cons. Georg. c. 9. p. 158.
[d] Alterations have been made by several of the states in their constitutional provisions on this subject.

According to the present constitution of Delaware, "every white freeman of the age of twenty one years, having resided in the state two years next before the election, and within that time paid a state or county tax, which shall have been assessed at least six months before the election, shall enjoy the right of an elector." Art. 4. s. 1.

By an amendment of the constitution of Maryland, confirmed in the year one thousand eight hundred and two, it is provided that every free white male citizen of the state, and no other, above twenty one years of age, having resided twelve months next preceding the election in the city or county at which he offers to vote, shall have a right of suffrage. Constitutions, p. 174.

The present constitution of Georgia directs that the electors of members of the general assembly shall be citizens and inhabitants of the state, and shall have attained the age of twenty one years, and have paid all publick taxes which may have been required of them, and which they have had an opportunity of paying agreeably to law, for the year preceding the election, and shall have resided six months within the county. Art. 4. s. 1.

In order to complete the view taken of this subject in the text, it will be proper to state the provisions made by the constitutions of the new states admitted into the Union respecting the qualifications of electors.

In Vermont, "every man of the full age of twenty one years, having resided in the state for the space of one whole year next before the election of representatives, and who is of a quiet and peaceable behaviour, and will take the following oath or affirmation, shall be entitled to all the privileges of the state. — 'You do solemnly swear (or affirm) that whenever you give your vote or suffrage, touching any matter that concerns the state of Vermont, you will do it so as in your conscience

From the foregoing enumeration — its length and its minuteness will be justified by its importance — from the foregoing enumeration of the provisions, which have been made, in the several states, concerning the right of suffrage, we are well warranted, I think, in drawing this broad and general inference — that, in the United States, this right is extended to every freeman, who, by his residence, has given evidence of his attachment to the country, who, by having property, or by being in a situation to acquire property, possesses a common interest with his fellow citizens; and who is not in such uncomfortable circumstances, as to render him necessarily dependent, for his subsistence, on the will of others.

By the same enumeration, we are enabled, with conscious pleasure, to view and to display the close approximation, which, on this great subject, the constitutions of the American States have made, to what we have already seen to be the true principles and the correct theory of freedom.

Again; the same enumeration places in the strongest and most striking light, the wisdom and the generous confidence, which rested one of the principal pillars of the national government upon the foundation prepared for it by the governments of the several states.

With this sentiment I began — with this sentiment I conclude my remarks concerning the qualifications required from those, who elect the house of representatives of the United States.

We now proceed to examine the qualifications required from those, who are elected to that dignified trust.

1. A representative must have attained the age of twenty five years.[e]

It is amusing enough to consider the different ages, at which persons have been deemed qualified or disqualified for different purposes, both in private and in publick life.

A woman, as we learn from my Lord Coke and others, has seven ages

---

you shall judge will most conduce to the best good of the same, as established by the constitution, without fear or favour of any man." Cons. Ch. 2. s. 21.

By the constitution of Tennessee, every freeman of the age of twenty one years and upwards, possessing a freehold in the county wherein he may vote, and being an inhabitant of the state, and every freeman, being an inhabitant of any one county in the state six months immediately preceding the day of election, shall be entitled to vote for members of the general assembly, for the county in which he shall reside. Art. 3. s. 1.

The constitution of Kentucky provides, that in all elections for representatives, every free male citizen (negroes, mulattoes, and Indians excepted) who at the time being hath attained to the age of twenty one years, and resided in the state two years, and the county or town in which he offers to vote one year next preceding the election, shall enjoy the right of an elector. Art. 2. s. 8.

In the state of Ohio, the rights of electors are enjoyed by all white male inhabitants above the age of twenty one years, having resided in the state one year next preceding the election, and who have paid or are charged with a state or county tax. Cons. Art. 4. s. 1. *Ed.*

[e] Cons. U. S. art. 1. s. 2.

for several purposes appointed to her by the law. At seven years of age, her father, if a feudal superiour, was entitled to demand from his vassals an aid to marry her: at nine, she may have dower: at twelve, she may consent to marriage: at fourteen, she may choose a guardian: at sixteen, marriage might be tendered to her by her lord: at seventeen, she may act as executrix: at twenty one, she may alienate her lands and goods.[f] A man, also, has different ages assigned to him for different purposes. At twelve years of age, he was formerly obliged to take the oath of allegiance: at fourteen, he can consent to marriage: at the same age he can choose his guardian: at twenty one, he may convey his personal and real estate.[g]

The foregoing are the different ages allowed for different purposes in private life. In publick life, there has, with regard to age, been a similar variety of assignments; the reasons of some of which it is hard to conjecture; for the propriety of others, it is equally hard to account.

In the government of the United States, it is supposed, that no one is fit to be a member of the house of representatives, till he is twenty five years of age; to be a senator, till he is thirty;[h] to be a president, till he is thirty five.[i]

The duration assigned by nature to human life is often complained of as very short: that assigned to it by some politicians is much shorter. For some political purposes, a man cannot breathe before he numbers thirty five years: as to other political purposes, his breath is extinguished the moment he reaches sixty. By the constitution of New York,[j] "the chancellor, the judges of the supreme court, and the first judge of the county court in every county, hold their offices — until they shall respectively have attained the age of sixty years."

How differently is the same object viewed at different times and in different countries! In New York, a man is deemed unfit for the first offices of the state *after* he is sixty: in Sparta, a man was deemed unfit for the first offices of the state *till* he was sixty. Till that age, no one was entitled to a seat in the senate, the highest honour of the chiefs.[k] How convenient it would be, if a politician possessed the power, so finely exercised by the most beautiful of poets! Virgil could, with the greatest ease imaginable, bring Æneas and Dido together; though, in fact, some centuries elapsed between the times, in which they lived. Why cannot some politician, by the same or some similar enchanting art, produce an ancient and a modern government as cotemporaries? The effect would be admirable. The moment that a gentleman of sixty would be disqualified from retaining his seat as a judge of New York, he would be qualified for taking his seat as a senator of Sparta.

[f] 1. Ins. 78. b.   [g] Id. ibid.   [h] Cons. U. S. art. 1. s. 3.   [i] Id. art. 2. s. 1.
[j] C. 24. p. 63.   [k] 1. Gil. c. 3. p. 107. 8. War. Bib. 29.

2. Before one can be a representative, he must have been seven years a citizen of the United States.[1]

Two reasons may be assigned for this provision. 1. That the constituents might have a full and mature opportunity of knowing the character and merit of their representative. 2. That the representative might have a full and mature opportunity of knowing the dispositions and interests of his constituents.

3. The representative must, when elected, be an inhabitant of that state, in which he is chosen.[m]

The qualification of residence we have found to be universally insisted on with regard to those who elect: here the same qualification is insisted on with regard to those who are elected. The same reasons, which operated in favour of the former qualification, operate with equal, indeed, with greater force, in favour of this. A provision, almost literally the same with the present one, was made in England three centuries and a half ago. By a statute made in the first year of Henry the fifth, it was enacted, that "the knights of the shires, which from henceforth shall be chosen in every shire, be not chosen, unless they be resident within the shire where they shall be chosen, the day of the date of the writ of the summons of the parliament" — "And moreover it is ordained and established, that the citizens and burgesses of the cities and boroughs be chosen men, citizens and burgesses, resiant, dwelling, and free in the same cities and boroughs, and no other in any wise." [n] to this moment, this statute continues unrepealed — a melancholy proof, how far degenerate and corrupted manners will overpower the wisest and most wholesome laws. From Sir Bulstrode Whitlocke we learn, that, above a century ago, non-compliance with this statute was "connived at." [o] The statute itself has been long and openly disregarded. The consequences of this disregard may be seen in the present state of the representation in England.

Thus far concerning the election of the house of representatives, and the qualifications of the members and of the electors. It remains to speak concerning the election and the qualifications of the senators.

The senators are chosen by the legislatures of the several states. Every senator must have attained to the age of thirty years; he must have been nine years a citizen of the United States; and he must, when elected, be an inhabitant of that state, for which he shall be chosen.[p]

Some have considered the senators as immediately representing the sovereignty, while the members of the other house immediately represent the people, of the several states. This opinion is founded on a doctrine which I considered and, I believe, refuted very fully in a former lecture:[q]

[1] Cons. U. S. art. 1. s. 2.   [m] Cons. U. S. art. 1. s. 2.
[n] St. 1. Hen. 5. c. 1. Bar. 380.   [o] 1. Whitl. 496.   [p] Cons. U. S. art. 1. s. 3.
[q] Ante. part 1, ch. 5.

the doctrine is this — that the legislative power is the supreme power of the state. The supreme power I showed to reside in the people.

By the constitution of the United States, the people have delegated to the several legislatures the choice of senators, while they have retained in their own hands the choice of representatives. It would be unwise, however, to infer from this, that either the dignity or the importance of the senate is inferiour to the dignity or the importance of the house of representatives. One may intrust to another the management of an equal or even superiour business, while he chooses to transact personally a business of an equal or even an inferiour kind.

Between the senate of the United States, and that of Pennsylvania, there is one remarkable point of difference, of which it will be proper, in this place, to take particular notice. According to the constitution of the United States, two senators are chosen by the legislature of each state: while the members of the house of representatives are chosen by the people. According to the constitution of Pennsylvania,[r] the senators are chosen by the citizens of the state, at the same time, in the same manner, and at the same place where they shall vote for representatives.

To choose the senators by the same persons, by whom the members of the house of representatives are chosen, is, we are told, to lose the material distinction, and, consequently, all the benefits which would result from the material distinction, between the two branches of the legislature.

If this, indeed, should be the necessary consequence of electing both branches by the same persons; the objection, it is confessed, would operate with a force irresistible. But many and strong reasons, we think, may be assigned, why all the advantages, to be expected from two branches of a legislature, may be gained and preserved, though those two branches derive their authority from precisely the same source.

A point of honour will arise between them. The esprit du corps will soon be introduced. The principle, and direction, and aim of this spirit will, we presume, be of the best and purest kind in the two houses. They will be rivals in duty, rivals in fame, rivals for the good graces of their common constituents.

Each house will be cautious, and careful, and circumspect, in those proceedings, which, they know, must undergo the strict and severe criticism of judges, whose inclination will lead them, and whose duty will enjoin them, not to leave a single blemish unnoticed or uncorrected. After all the caution, all the care, and all the circumspection, which can be employed, strict and severe criticism, led by inclination and enjoined by duty, will find something to notice and correct. Hence a double

[r] Art. 1. s. 5.

source of information, precision, and sagacity in planning, digesting, composing, comparing, and finishing the laws, both in form and substance. Every bill will, in some one or more steps of its progress, undergo the keenest scrutiny. Its relations, whether near or more remote, to the principles of freedom, jurisprudence, and the constitution will be accurately examined: and its effects upon the laws already existing will be maturely traced. In this manner, rash measures, violent innovations, crude projects, and partial contrivances will be stifled in the attempt to bring them forth. These effects of mutual watchfulness and mutual control between the two houses, will redound to the honour of each, and to the security and advantage of the state.

The very circumstance of sitting in separate houses will be the cause of emulous and active separate exertion. The era, when the commons of England met in an apartment by themselves, is, with reason, considered, by many writers, as a memorable era in the history of English liberty. "After the formation of the two houses of parliament," says Mr. Millar, in his historical view of the English constitution,[s] "each of them came to be possessed of certain peculiar privileges; which, although probably the objects of little attention in the beginning, have since risen to great political importance. The house of commons obtained the sole power of bringing in money bills." This subject will, by and by, come under our more immediate view.

Rivals for character, as we have seen the two houses to be, they will be rivals in all pursuits, by which character can be acquired, established, and exalted. To these laudable pursuits the crown of success will best be obtained, by vigour and alacrity in the discharge of the business committed to their care.

A difference in the posts assigned to the two houses, and in the number and duration of their members, will produce a difference in their sense of the duties required and expected from them. The house of representatives, for instance, form the grand inquest of the state. They will diligently inquire into grievances, arising both from men and things. Their commissions will commence or be renewed at short distances of time. Their sentiments, and views, and wishes, and even their passions, will have received a deep and recent tincture from the sentiments, and views, and wishes, and passions of their constituents. Into their counsels, and resolutions, and measures, this tincture will be strongly transfused. They will know the evils which exist, and the means of removing them: they will know the advantages already discovered, and the means of increasing them. As the term of their commission and trust will soon expire, they will be desirous, while it lasts, of seeing the publick business

[s] P. 396 (4to.).

put, at least, in a train of accomplishment. From all these causes, a sufficient number of overtures and propositions will originate in the house of representatives. These overtures and propositions will come, in their proper course, before the senate. Those, which shall appear premature, will be postponed till a more convenient season. Those, which shall appear crude, will be properly digested and formed. Those, which shall appear to be calculated upon too narrow a scale, will be enlarged in their operation and extent. Those, which shall appear to be dictated by local views, inconsistent with the general welfare, will be either rejected altogether, or altered in such a manner, as that the interest of the whole shall not be sacrificed, or rendered subservient, to the interest of a part.

Articles of information, detached and seemingly unconnected, introduced by the house of representatives, at different times, from different places, with different motives, and for different purposes, will, in the senate, be collected, compared, methodised, and consolidated. Under their plastick hands, those materials will be employed in forming systems and laws, for the prosperity and happiness of the commonwealth.

If, at any time, the passions or prejudices of the people should be ill directed or too strong; and the house of representatives should meet, too highly charged with the transfusion; it will be the business and the duty of the senate to allay the fervour; and, before it shall give a sanction to the bills or resolutions of the other house, to introduce into them the requisite ingredients of mildness and moderation.

Extremes, on one hand, are often the forerunners of extremes on the other. If a benumbing torpor should appear in the body politick, after the effects of violent convulsions have subsided; and if the contagious apathy should spread itself over the house of representatives; it will then become the business and the duty of the senate, to infuse into the publick councils and publick measures the proper portion of life, activity, and vigour.

In seasons of prosperity, it will become the care of the senate to temper the extravagance, or repress the insolence, of publick joy. In seasons of adversity, the senate will be employed in administering comfort and cure to the publick despondency.

In fine; the senate will consider itself, and will be considered by the people, as the balance wheel in the great machine of government; calculated and designed to retard its movements, when they shall be too rapid, and to accelerate them, when they shall be too slow.

These reflections, which seem to arise naturally from the subject before us, will, we hope, be sufficient to convince you, that the most beneficial purposes may be rationally expected from the senate of Pennsylvania, though the sentators, as well as the members of the house of representatives, be elected immediately by the citizens of the common-wealth.

Another circumstance, not yet mentioned, deserves to be added to this account. The districts for the election of senators, are to be formed by the legislature. In forming those districts, the legislature are empowered to include in them such a number of taxable inhabitants as shall be en-titled to elect four senators.[t] An enlarged and judicious exercise of this power will have a strong tendency to increase the dignity and usefulness of the senate. It may, I believe, be assumed as a general maxim, of no small importance in democratical governments, that the more extensive the district of election is, the choice will be the more wise and enlight-ened. Intrigue and cunning are the bane of elections by the people, who are unsuspicious, because they are undesigning: but intrigue and cun-ning are most dangerous, because they are most successful, in a con-tracted sphere.

II. I am now to consider the number of members of which the legis-lature of the United States consists.

The representatives are apportioned among the several states accord-ing to their numbers. The number of representatives shall not exceed one for every thirty thousand.[u] The senate shall be composed of two senators from each state.[v]

The Union consists now of fourteen, and will soon consist of fifteen states. Of consequence, the senate is composed now of twenty eight, and will be composed soon of thirty members.

A census of the United States has been taken, agreeably to the consti-tution, and the returns of that census are nearly completed. By these it appears, that, allowing one representative for every thirty thousand returned on the census, the house of representatives will consist of one hundred and twelve members.[w]

Every one has heard of the saying of the famous Cardinal de Retz — that every publick assembly, consisting of more than one hundred mem-bers, was a mere mob. It is not improbable, that the Cardinal drew his

---

[t] Cons. Penn. art. i. s. 7.   [u] Cons. U. S. art. i. s. 2.   [v] Id. art. i. s. 3.

[w] After the census mentioned in the text, the representatives were apportioned among the states, by an act of congress passed on the fourteenth day of April, 1792, agreeably to a ratio of one member for every thirty three thousand persons in each state, computed according to the rule prescribed by the constitution. The number of representatives, agreeably to that ratio, amounted to one hundred and five.

A second enumeration was made in the year one thousand eight hundred; and the representatives were, by an act of congress passed on the fourteenth day of January, 1802, apportioned among the states agreeably to the same ratio. Their number amounted to one hundred and forty one. The state of Ohio has since been admitted into the Union, and is entitled to one member. This last apportionment is still in force.

The senate of the United States, at present, consists of thirty four members. *Ed.*

conclusion from what he had seen and experienced. He lived in a turbulent season; and, in that turbulent season, was distinguished as a most turbulent actor. Of consequence, he was much conversant with mere mobs. But surely no good reason can be given, why the number one hundred should form the precise boundary, on one side of which, order may be preserved, and on the other side of which, confusion must unavoidably prevail. The political qualities of publick bodies, it is, in all likelihood, impossible to ascertain and distinguish with such numerical exactness. Besides; the publick bodies, most celebrated for the decency and dignity, as well as for the importance, of their proceedings, have far exceeded, in number, the bounds prescribed by the Cardinal for the existence of those respectable qualities: witness the senate of Rome, and the parliament of Great Britain.

There is, however, with regard to this point, an extreme on one hand, as well as on the other. The number of a deliberative body may be too great, as well as too small. In a great and a growing country, no precise number could, with propriety, be fixed by the constitution. A power, in some measure discretionary, was, therefore, necessarily given to the legislature, to direct that number from time to time. If the spirit of the constitution be observed in other particulars, it will not be violated in this.

III. I proceed, in the third place, to treat of the term, for which the members of the national legislature are chosen.

In the greatest part of the states, the members of the most numerous branch of their legislature are chosen annually; in some, every half year. The members of the least numerous branch are generally chosen for a longer term. By the constitution of the United States,[x] the members of the house of representatives are chosen "every second year."

When we consider the nature and the extent of the general government, we shall be satisfied, I apprehend, that biennial elections are as well proportioned to it, as annual elections are proportioned to the individual states, and half yearly elections to some of the smallest of them.

The senators of the United States are chosen for six years; but are so classed, that the seats of one third part of them are vacated at the expiration of every second year; so that one third part may be chosen every second year.[y]

In Pennsylvania, the senators are chosen for four years; but are so classed, that the seats of one fourth part of them are vacated at the expiration of every year; so that one fourth part may be chosen every year.[z]

The intention, in assigning different limitations to the terms, for which the members of the different houses are chosen, and in establishing a rotation in the senate, is obviously to obtain and secure the different

[x] Art. 1. s. 2.   [y] Cons. U. S. art. 1. s. 3.   [z] Cons. Penn. art. 1. s. 5. 9.

qualities, by which a legislature ought to be distinguished. These qualities are, stability, consistency, and minute information. All these qualities may be expected, in some degree, from each house; but not in equal proportions. For minute information, the principal reliance will be placed on the house of representatives; because that house is the most numerous; and because its members are most frequently chosen. The qualities of stability and consistency will be expected chiefly from the senate; because the senators continue longer in office; and because only a part of them can be changed at any one time.

IV. I proceed to treat concerning the laws, and rules, and powers of the two houses of congress.

The parliament of Great Britain has its peculiar law; a law, says my Lord Coke,[a] with which few are acquainted, but which deserves to be investigated by all. The maxims, however, upon which the parliament proceeds, are not, it seems, defined and ascertained by any particular stated law: they rest entirely in the breast of the parliament itself. The dignity and independence of the two houses, we are told, are preserved, in a great measure, by keeping their privileges indefinite.[b]

Very different is the case with regard to the legislature of the United States, and to that of Pennsylvania. The great maxims, upon which our law of parliament is founded, are defined and ascertained in our constitutions. The arcana of privilege, and the arcana of prerogative, are equally unknown to our system of jurisprudence.

By the constitution of the United States,[c] each house of the legislature shall be the judge of the qualifications and returns, and also of the elections, of its own members. By the constitution of Pennsylvania,[d] each house shall judge of the qualifications of its members: but contested elections shall be determined by a committee to be selected, formed, and regulated in such manner as shall be directed by law. With regard to this subject, the constitution of Pennsylvania has, I think, improved upon that of the United States. Contested elections, when agitated in the house itself, occasion much waste of time, and, too often, a considerable degree of animosity among the members. These inconveniences will be, in a great measure, avoided by the proceedings and decision of a committee, directed and governed by a standing law.

It is proper, in this place, to take notice, that the house of representatives in congress have appointed a standing committee of elections. It is the duty of this committee, to examine the certificates of election, or other credentials of the members returned; to take into their consideration every thing referred to them concerning returns and elections; and to report their opinions and proceedings to the house.[e]

[a] 1. Ins. 11 b.　　[b] 1. Bl. Com. 163. 164.　　[c] Art. 1. s. 5.　　[d] Art. 1. s. 12.
[e] Jour. Rep. 13th April, 1789.

In the United States and in Pennsylvania, the legislature has a right to sit upon its own adjournments: but neither house shall, without the consent of the other, adjourn for more than three days, nor to any other place, than that in which the two houses shall be sitting.[f] In England, the sole right of convening, proroguing, and dissolving the parliament forms a part, and, obviously, a very important part, of the prerogative of the king.[g] Here we discover, in our new constitutions, another renovation of the old Saxon customs. The original meetings of the wittenagemote in England were held regularly at two seasons of the year; at the end of spring, and at the beginning of autumn.[h] Afterwards there came to be two sorts of wittenagemote; one held by custom, and at the stated periods; the other called occasionally,[i] and by a special summons from the king. Under the princes of the Norman and Plantagenet lines, the ancient and regular meetings of the national legislature were more and more disregarded. The consequence was, that, in progress of time, the whole of the parliamentary business was transacted in extraordinary meetings, which were called at the pleasure of the sovereign.[j] *Principiis obsta.*[*] In consequence of acquiring the power to call the parliament together, that of putting a negative upon its meetings, in other words, of proroguing or dissolving it, was, in all cases, vested in the crown.[k]

The constitution of the United States provides,[l] that the senators and representatives shall, in all cases, except treason, felony, and breach of the peace, be privileged from arrest during their attendance at the session of their respective houses, and in going to and returning from them. The constitution of Pennsylvania[m] contains a similar provision, excepting in one particular. The members are not entitled to privilege, if their conduct has been such, as to give reasonable cause of fear that they will break the peace; in the same manner as they are not entitled to it, if, by their conduct, the peace has been actually broken. This necessary privilege has continued substantially the same, since the time of the Saxons. The grand assembly of the wittenagemote, as we are told by Mr. Selden, was holden sacred; and all the members were under the publick faith, both in going and coming, unless the party were *fur probatus.*[†] This privilege of safe pass, being thus ancient and fundamental, and not by any law taken away, resteth still in force.[n]

[f] Cons. U. S. art. 1. s. 5. Cons. Penn. art. 1. s. 16.   [g] 1. Bl. Com. 187. 188.

[h] Bac. on Gov. 36. Millar. 146. 242.

[i] A similar distinction between stated and occasional assemblies was observed by the Athenians. The times of the former were appointed by law: the latter were summoned by those at the head of the civil or of the military department of the government; as emergencies in those different departments arose. 1. Pot. Ant. 91. 92.

[j] Millar. 242. 244.   * [Withstand beginnings; *i.e.* beware the entering wedge.]

[k] Id. 311.   [l] Art. 1. s. 6.   [m] Art. 1. s. 17.   † [A proved thief.]

[n] Bac. on Gov. 38.

The members of the national legislature, and those also of the legislature of Pennsylvania, shall not, for any speech or debate in either house, be questioned in any other place.[o] In England, the freedom of speech is, at the opening of every new parliament, particularly demanded of the king in person, by the speaker of the house of commons.[p] The liberal provision, which is made, by our constitutions, upon this subject, may be justly viewed as a very considerable improvement in the science and the practice of government. In order to enable and encourage a representative of the publick to discharge his publick trust with firmness and success, it is indispensably necessary, that he should enjoy the fullest liberty of speech, and that he should be protected from the resentment of every one, however powerful, to whom the exercise of that liberty may occasion offence.

When it is mentioned, that the members shall not be questioned in any *other* place; the implication is strong, that, for their speeches in either house, they may be questioned and censured by that house, in which they are spoken. Besides; each house, both in the United States and in Pennsylvania, has an express power given it to "punish its members for disorderly behaviour."[q] Under the protection of privilege, to use indecency or licentiousness of language, in the course of debate, is disorderly behaviour, of a kind peculiarly base and ungentlemanly.

Each house may not only punish, but, with the concurrence of two thirds, it may expel a member.[r] This regulation is adopted by the constitution of Pennsylvania:[s] "but," it is added, "not a second time for the same cause." The reason for the addition evidently is — that the member, who has offended, cannot be an object of a second expulsion, unless, since the offence given and punished by the first expulsion, he has been either reelected by his former constituents, or elected by others. In both cases, his election is a proof, that, in the opinion of his constituents, he either has not offended at all, or has been already sufficiently punished for his offence. The language of each opinion is, that he ought not to be expelled again: and the language of the constituents is a law to the house.

Each house may determine the rules of its proceedings. This power is given, in precisely the same terms, by the constitution of the United States, and by that of Pennsylvania.[t] Its propriety is selfevident.

The constitution of the United States directs,[u] that each house shall keep a journal of its proceedings, and, from time to time, publish them, except such parts as may require secrecy: it directs further, that the yeas and nays of the members of either house, on any question, shall, at the

[o] Cons. U. S. art. 1. s. 6. Cons. Penn. art. 1. s. 17.   [p] 1. Bl. Com. 164.
[q] Con. U. S. art. 1. s. 5. Cons. Penn. art. 1. s. 23.   [r] Cons. U. S. art. 1. s. 5.
[s] Art. 1. s. 13.   [t] Cons. U. S. art. 1. s. 5. Cons. Penn. art. 1. s. 13.
[u] Art. 1. s. 5.

desire of one fifth of those present, be entered on the journal. The
constitution of Pennsylvania[v] goes still further upon these points: it
directs, that the journals shall be published weekly; that the yeas and
nays shall be entered on them, at the desire of any two members; and that
the doors of each house, and of committees of the whole, shall be open,
unless when the business shall be such as ought to be kept secret.

That the conduct and proceedings of representatives should be as open
as possible to the inspection of those whom they represent, seems to be,
in republican government, a maxim, of whose truth or importance the
smallest doubt cannot be entertained. That, by a necessary consequence,
every measure, which will facilitate or secure this open communication
of the exercise of delegated power, should be adopted and patronised by
the constitution and laws of every free state, seems to be another maxim,
which is the unavoidable result of the former. For these reasons, I feel
myself necessarily and unavoidably led to consider the additional regulations made, upon this subject, by the constitution of Pennsylvania, as
improvements upon those made by the constitution of the United States.
The regulation — that the doors of each house, and of committees of the
whole, shall be open — I view as an improvement highly beneficial both
in its nature and in its consequences — both to the representatives and
to their constituents. "In the house of commons," says Sir William Blackstone, "the conduct of every member is subject to the future censure of
his constituents, and therefore should be openly submitted to their inspection." [w] But I forbear to enter more largely into this interesting
topick.

The house of representatives in congress shall choose their speaker and
other officers.[x] The like provision is made by the constitution of Pennsylvania,[y] with respect to both houses of the general assembly.

The speaker of the house of commons cannot give his opinion, nor
can he argue any question in the house.[z] From this view of the matter,
one would be apt to imagine, that as the Latins assigned to a grove the
name of *lucus, a non lucendo*,* so the English distinguished the first officer
of the house of commons by the appellation of speaker, because, by the
rules of that house, he could say neither yes nor no. But if we trace
things to their origin, we shall be led to discover the reason of this
denomination.

The first mode of passing a bill through parliament was by a petition
to the king. This petition represented the grievance or inconvenience,
concerning which complaint was made, and requested that it should be
removed. When a petition was offered by the commons, after they
sat in a separate house, it was necessary to appoint some person to

[v] Art. 1. s. 14, 15.   [w] 1. Bl. Com. 181.   [x] Cons. U. S. Art. 1. s. 2.
[y] Art. 1. s. 11.   [z] 1. Bl. Com. 181.   * [A grove, because not shining.]

intimate their views and wishes to the king. This person, chosen by themselves, and approved by the king, whom they would not address by the mouth of a person disagreeable to him, was denominated their speaker.[a]

To discharge this part of his duty in the dignified, and, at the same time, in the respectful manner, in which it ought to be discharged, was frequently considered as a business of a very arduous nature. It will not be unentertaining, to learn, from one of the speakers of the house of commons, the qualities, which, in his opinion, were necessary for the proper performance of the speaker's office.

"Whence," said Serjeant Yelverton, "your unexpected choice of me to be your mouth or speaker should proceed, I am utterly ignorant. Neither from my person nor nature doth this choice arise: for he that supplieth this place ought to be a man big and comely, stately and well spoken, his voice great, his carriage majestical, his nature haughty. But, contrarily, the stature of my body is small, myself not so well spoken, my voice low, my carriage lawyerlike and of the common fashion, my nature soft and bashful. If Demosthenes, being so learned and so eloquent as he was, trembled to speak before Phocion at Athens; how much more shall I, being unlearned and unskilful, supply this place of dignity, to speak before the unspeakable majesty and sacred personage of our dread and dear sovereign, the terrour of whose countenance" (he speaks of Queen Elizabeth) "will appal and abase even the stoutest heart." [b]

All bills for raising revenue shall originate in the house of representatives; but the senate may propose amendments as in other bills. This provision is common to the United States and Pennsylvania.[c]

In a former lecture,[d] this subject was considered under one aspect, under which it then made its appearance. It now claims consideration in other respects: and ought to be examined with a greater degree of minuteness.

In England, all grants of aids by parliament begin in the house of commons. Of that house, this is an ancient,[e] and, now, an indisputable privilege. With regard to it, the commons are so jealous, that, over money bills, they will not suffer the other house to exert any powers, except simply those of concurrence or rejection. From the lords, no alteration or amendment will be received on this delicate subject. The constitutions of the United States and Pennsylvania have, on this head, adopted the parliamentary law of England in part; but they have not adopted it altogether. They have directed, that money bills shall originate in the house of representatives; but they have directed also, that the senate may propose amendments in these, as well as in other bills. It will be proper to

[a] Millar 414.   [b] 4. Parl. Hist. 411, 412.
[c] Cons. U. S. art. 1. s. 7. Cons. Penn. art. 1. s. 20.   [d] Ante. p. 320.
[e] 4. Ins. 29.

424 LECTURES ON LAW

investigate the reasons of each part of the direction. This will best be
done by tracing the matter historically, and attending to the difference
between the institution of the house of lords in England, and that of the
senates of the United States and Pennsylvania.

During a considerable time after the establishment of the house of
commons as a separate branch of the legislature, it appears, that the
members of that house were, with regard to taxes and assessments, governed altogether by the instructions, which they received from their constituents. Each county and borough seems to have directed its representatives, concerning the amount of the rates to which they might give
their assent. By adding together the sums contained in those particular
directions, it was easy to ascertain, in the house of commons, the sum
total, which the commonalty of the kingdom were willing to grant. To
the extent of this sum, the commons conceived themselves empowered
and directed to go; but no farther.

According to this mode of proceeding, the imposition of taxes produced no interchange of communication between the two houses of
parliament. To introduce a money bill, or an amendment to a money
bill, into the house of lords — to deliberate upon the bill or amendment
in that house — after agreeing to it there, to submit it to the deliberation
of the house of commons — all this would have been perfectly nugatory.
Let us suppose, that the bill or amendment had undergone the most full
and careful examination in the house of lords, who, acting only for
themselves, could examine it under every aspect, unfettered by exteriour
direction and control: let us suppose it then transmitted to the house
of commons, for their concurrence: what could the house of commons
do? They could not deliberate upon the bill or the amendment: they
could only compare it with their instructions: if they found it consistent
with them, they could give, if inconsistent, they must refuse, their consent. The only course, therefore, in which this business could be transacted, was, that the commons should begin by mentioning the sum, which
they were empowered to grant, and that what they proposed should be
sent to the house of lords, who, upon all the circumstances, might deliberate and judge for themselves.[f]

In this manner, and for these reasons, the house of commons became
possessed of this important privilege, which is now justly regarded by
them, as one of the strongest pillars of their freedom and power. Once
possessed of this privilege, they were far from relinquishing it, when
the first reasons for its possession had ceased. Other reasons, stronger than
the first, succeeded to them. In the flux of time and things, the revenue
and influence of the crown became so great, and the property of the

[f] Millar. 398.

peerage, considered with relation to the general property of the kingdom, became comparatively so small, that it was judged unwise to permit that body to model, or even to alter, the general system of taxation. This is the aspect, under which this subject was viewed in the lecture, to which I have alluded; and I will not repeat now what was observed then.

From this short historical deduction, it appears, that the provision, which we now consider, is far from being so important here, as it is in England. In the United States and in Pennsylvania, both houses of the legislature draw their authority, either immediately, or, at least, not remotely, from the same common fountain. In England, one of the houses acts entirely in its private and separate right.

But though this regulation is by no means so necessary here, as it is in England; yet it may have its use, so far as it has been adopted into our constitutions. Our houses of representatives are much more numerous than our senates: the members of the former are chosen much more frequently, than are the members of the latter. For these reasons, an information more local and minute may be expected in the houses of representatives, than can be expected in the senates. This minute and local information will be of service, in suggesting and in collecting materials for the laws of revenue. After those materials are collected and prepared, the wisdom and the patriotism of both houses will be employed in forming them into a proper system.

The house of representatives shall have the sole power of impeaching. All impeachments shall be tried by the senate. These regulations are found both in the constitution of the United States[g] and in that of Pennsylvania.[h]

The doctrine of impeachments is of high import in the constitutions of free states. On one hand, the most powerful magistrates should be amenable to the law: on the other hand, elevated characters should not be sacrificed merely on account of their elevation. No one should be secure while he violates the constitution and the laws: every one should be secure while he observes them.

Impeachments were known in Athens. They were prosecuted for great and publick offences, by which the commonwealth was brought into danger. They were not referred to any court of justice, but were prosecuted before the popular assembly, or before the senate of five hundred.[i]

Among the ancient Germans also, we discover the traces of impeachments: for we are informed by Tacitus, in his masterly account of the manners of that people,[j] that it was allowed to present accusations, and to prosecute capital offences, before the general assembly of the nation.

An impeachment is described, by the law of England, to be, a pre-

[g] Art. 1. s. 2, 3.　　[h] Art. 4. s. 1. 2.　　[i] 1. Pot. Ant. 125.　　[j] Ch. 12.

sentment to the most high and supreme court of criminal jurisdiction, by the most solemn grand inquest of the kingdom.[k]

It is evident that, in England, impeachments, according to this description, could not exist before the separation of the two houses of parliament. Previous to that era, the national council was accustomed to inquire into the conduct of the different executive officers, and to punish them for malversation in office, or what are called high misdemeanors. The king himself was not exempted from such inquiry and punishment: for it had not yet become a maxim — that the king can do no wrong.

Prosecutions of this nature were not, like those of ordinary crimes, intrusted to the management of an individual: they were conducted by the national council themselves; who acted, improperly enough, in the double character of accusers and judges. Upon the separation of the two houses, it became an obvious improvement, that the power of trying those high misdemeanors should belong to the house of lords, and that the power of conducting the prosecution should belong to the house of commons. In consequence of this improvement, the inconsistent characters of judge and accuser were no longer acted by the same body.[1]

We find the commons appearing as the grand inquest of the nation, about the latter end of the reign of Edward the third. They then began to exhibit accusations for crimes and misdemeanors, against offenders who were thought to be out of the reach of the ordinary power of the law. In the fiftieth year of that reign, they preferred impeachments against many delinquents. These impeachments were tried by the lords.[m]

In the United States and in Pennsylvania, impeachments are confined to political characters, to political crimes and misdemeanors, and to political punishments. The president, vice president, and all civil officers of the United States; the governour and all other civil officers under this commonwealth, are liable to impeachment; the officers of the United States, for treason, bribery, or other high crimes and misdemeanors; the officers of this commonwealth, for any misdemeanor in office. Under both constitutions, judgments, in cases of impeachment, shall not extend further than to removal from office, and disqualification to hold any office of honour, trust, or profit.[n]

Thus much concerning the laws, and rules, and powers of the two houses of the congress of the United States, and concerning those of the two houses of the general assembly of Pennsylvania.

V. I next consider the manner of passing laws.

To laws properly made, the following things are of indispensable necessity — information — caution — perspicuity — precision — sagacity

---

[k] 2. Hale. P.C. *150. 4. Bl. Com. 256.   [1] Millar. 403.   [m] 2. Reeve. 85.
[n] Cons. U. S. art. 2. s. 4. art. 1. s. 3. Cons. Penn. art. 4. s. 3.

— conciseness. For obtaining those valuable objects, different states have adopted different regulations. It will be worth while to bestow some attention upon the most remarkable among them.

At Athens, laws were made according to the following very deliberate process. When any citizen had conceived any plan, which, he thought, would promote the interests of the commonwealth, he communicated it to certain officers, whose duty it was to receive information of every thing which concerned the publick. These officers laid the plan before the senate. If it appeared to the senate to be pernicious or useless, they rejected it. If otherwise, they agreed to it; and it then became what we may call a bill, or overture. It was written on a white tablet, and fixed up in a publick place, some days before the meeting of the general assembly of the people. This was done, that the citizens might have an opportunity of reading and forming a deliberate judgment, concerning what was to be proposed to them for their determination. When the assembly met, the bill was read to them; and every citizen had a right to speak his sentiments with regard to it. If, after due consultation, it was thought inconvenient or improper, a negative was put upon it: if, on the contrary, the people approved of it, it was passed into a law.

We are informed, that no one, without much caution and a perfect acquaintance with the constitution and former laws, would presume to propose a new regulation; because the danger was very great, if it proved unsuitable to the customs and inclinations of the people.[o]

With all these numerous precautions, so many obscure and contradictory laws were gradually introduced into the Athenian code, that a special commission was established to make a selection among them. The labour even of the special commissioners was, however, fruitless.[p]

Peculiarly rigid was the constitution of the Locrians, with regard to propositions for making a law. The citizen, who proposed one, appeared in the assembly of the people, with a cord round his neck. Encircled by that solemn monitor, he laid before them the reasons, on which his proposal was founded: if those reasons were unsatisfactory, he was instantly strangled.[q]

Among the Romans, legislation, as it might be expected, was considered as a science: it was cultivated with the most assiduous industry, and was enriched with all the treasures of reason and philosophy. The mistress of the world had laws to instruct her how to make laws. In digesting the original plan of a bill, the magistrate, who proposed it, used every possible precaution, that it might come before the people in a form, the most perfect and unexceptionable. He consulted, in private, with his friends, upon its form and matter. The object was, that it might

[o] 1. Pot. Ant. 140.   [p] 2. Anac. 271.   [q] 1. Pot. Ant. 140.

contain no clause contrary to the interests of the commonwealth; no provision inconsistent with former laws, not intended to be repealed or altered; and no regulation, which might produce a partial advantage to the connexions or relations of the proposer, or to the proposer himself.

As unity and simplicity are essential perfections of every good law; every thing foreign to the bill immediately in contemplation was strictly prohibited. By incoherent assemblages, the people might be induced to receive as law what they might dislike; or to reject what they might desire.

A bill, after all the precautions before mentioned, was submitted to the examination of the senate. On being approved there, it was fixed up publickly in some conspicuous part of the forum, that every citizen might understand fully what it contained. A meeting of the "comitia" was appointed by proclamation at the end of twenty seven days. When this time was elapsed, the people assembled. The bill proposed was proclaimed by the publick crier; and the person who proposed it was expected to speak first in its support. After this, any other member of the assembly was at liberty to deliver his sentiments; and, to prevent any improper influence, a private citizen had always the privilege of speaking before a magistrate, except the magistrate who was the proposer of the law.

When the debates concerning the bill were finished, preparation was made for voting upon it. The names of the centuries were thrown promiscuously into an urn, and being blended together by the hand of the presiding magistrate, they were drawn out, one by one. The century first drawn was called the "prerogative century." After these preparatory steps were taken, the magistrate, who proposed the law, commanded proclamation to be made for every one to repair his respective century. The prerogative century was called out first, and afterwards the others, as their lots directed.

In the early times of the republick, the votes were given "viva voce;" but that mode being productive of much confusion, and having a tend-ency to subject the lower orders of citizens to the influence of their superiours, the more secret and independent method by ballot was intro-duced. It is to be remembered, that the citizens voted in their own right, and not by representation. To vote by ballot, in such a situation, was unquestionably a great improvement in a free system of government, such as that of Rome then was; and accordingly we find that Cicero[r] denominates the tablet, "the silent assertor of liberty."

In this solemn, deliberate, circumspect manner, what was called "lex," a law, in its strict and proper sense, was enacted. It was passed at the instance of a senatorial magistrate, by the whole aggregate body of the

[r] De leg. agr. II. 2. De leg. III. 17.

people (senators and patricians, as well as plebians) in whom alone the majesty of the commonwealth resided.[s]

The general preamble to a capitulary of laws made in the reign of Edward the first, gives us an intimation of the course, which, in England, was observed, at that period, in passing laws. It mentions, that, "in the presence of certain reverend fathers, bishops of England, and others of the council of the realm of England, the underwritten constitutions were recited; and afterwards they were heard and published before the king and his council, who all agreed, as well the justices as others, that they should be put into writing for a perpetual memory, and that they should be stedfastly observed."[t]

In Great Britain, laws are now passed in the following manner. All bills, except those of grace, originate in one of the two houses; and all other bills, except those for raising a revenue, may originate in either house of parliament. A bill may be brought in upon motion made to the house; or the house may give directions to bring it in. It is read — suppose in the house of commons — a first, and, at a convenient distance, a second time. After each reading, the speaker opens the substance of it, and puts the question, whether farther proceedings shall be had upon it. When it has had the second reading, it is referred to a selected committee, or to a committee of the whole house. In these committees, paragraph after paragraph is debated, blanks are filled up, and alterations and amendments are made. After the committee have gone through it, they report it with these amendments: the house then consider it again, and the question is put upon every clause and amendment. When it is agreed to by the house, it is then ordered to be engrossed for a third reading. On being engrossed, it is read a third time; amendments are sometimes made to it; and a new clause, which, in this late stage of its progress, is called a rider, is sometimes added. The speaker, again, opens the contents of the bill; and, holding it up in his hand, puts the question — Shall this bill pass? If this is agreed to, the title is then settled; and one of the members is directed to carry it to the lords, and desire their concurrence.

In that house, it passes through the same numerous stages, as in the house of commons. If it is rejected, the rejection passes *sub silentio;* and no communication takes place concerning it, between the two houses. On agreeing to it, the lords send a message, notifying their agreement; and the bill remains with them, if they have made no amendments. If they make amendments, they send them, with the bill, for the concurrence of the house of commons. If the two houses disagree with regard to the amendments; a conference usually takes place between members deputed by them, respectively, for this purpose. In this conference, the

---

[s] Bever. 71–77.   [t] 4. Edw. 1. st. 3.

matters, concerning which the two houses differ in sentiment, are generally adjusted: but if each house continue inflexible, the bill is lost. If the commons agree to the amendments made by the lords to the bill, it is sent back to them with a message communicating their agreement.

Similar forms are observed, when a bill originates in the house of lords.[u]

We see, with what cautious steps, the business proceeds from its commencement to its conclusion. Each house acts repeatedly as a court of review upon itself: each house acts repeatedly as a court of review upon the other also. Could one believe it? — Notwithstanding all these proofs and instances of circumspection and care, which are constantly exhibited by the legislature of Great Britain, when it passes laws, precipitancy in passing them is frequently a well grounded cause of complaint. "Perhaps," says a sensible and humane writer upon the criminal jurisprudence of England, "the great severity of our laws has been, in some degree, owing to their having been made *flagrante ira*, on some sudden occasion, when a combination of atrocious circumstances, attending some particular offence, inflamed the lawgivers." [v]

In the house of representatives in congress, every bill must be introduced by motion for leave, or by an order of the house on the report of a committee: in either case, a committee to prepare the bill shall be appointed. When it is intended to introduce a bill of a general nature by motion for leave, one day's notice, at least, of the motion shall be given: every such motion may be committed.

Every bill must receive three several readings in the house, previous to its passage; and no bill shall be read twice on the same day, without a special order of the house.

The first reading of a bill shall be for information; and, if opposition be made to it, the question shall be, "Shall the bill be rejected?" If no opposition be made, or if the question to reject be determined in the negative, the bill shall go to its second reading without a question.

When a bill is read the second time, the speaker shall state it as ready for commitment or engrossment: if committed, a question shall be, whether to a select committee, or to a committee of the whole house. If the bill be ordered to be engrossed, a day shall be appointed, when it shall receive the third reading. After commitment and report of a bill, it may, notwithstanding, be recommitted, even at any time before its passage.

In forming a committee of the whole house, the speaker shall leave his chair; and a chairman to preside in the committee shall be appointed.

A bill, committed to a committee of the whole house, shall be first read throughout by the clerk, and shall be then read again and debated

[u] 1, Bl. Com. 181, — 184.   [v] 1. Dagge. 274.

by clauses. The body of the bill shall not be defaced or interlined; but all amendments, as they shall be agreed to, shall be duly entered, by the clerk, on a separate paper, noting the page and line, to which they refer; and, in this manner, shall be reported to the house. After being reported, it shall again be subject to be debated and amended by clauses, before a question to engross it be taken.[w]

In the senate of the United States, one day's notice, at least, shall be given of an intended motion for leave to bring in a bill.

Every bill shall receive three readings previous to its being passed: these readings shall be on three different days, unless the senate unanimously direct otherwise: and the president shall give notice at each reading, whether it be the first, or the second, or the third.

No bill shall be committed or amended until it shall have been read twice: it may then be referred to a committee.[x]

The senate never go into a committee of the whole house. A committee of the whole house is composed of every member; and to form it, the speaker leaves the chair, and may sit and debate as any other member of the house. The vice president of the United States is, *ex officio*, president of the senate; but he has no vote, unless they be equally divided.[y] That this high officer might not be placed in a situation in which he could neither preside nor vote, is, I presume, the reason, why the senate do not resolve themselves into a committee of the whole. It is a rule, however, in the senate, that all bills, on a second reading, shall, unless otherwise ordered, be considered in the same manner, as if the senate were in a committee of the whole, before they shall be taken up and proceeded on by the senate, agreeable to the standing rules.[z]

Such, so numerous, and so wise, are the precautions used by our national legislature, before a bill can pass through its two different branches. But all these precautions, wise and numerous as they are, are far from being the only ones directed by the wisdom and care of our national constitution.

After a bill has passed, in both houses, through all the processes, which we have minutely enumerated, still, before it becomes a law, it must be presented to the president of the United States for his scrutiny and revision. If he approve, he signs it; but if not, he returns it, with his objections, to the house, in which it has originated. That house enter the objections, at large, on their journal, and proceed to reconsider the bill. If, after such reconsideration, two thirds of the members agree to pass it, it is sent, with the objections, to the other house, by which also it is reconsidered; and if approved by two thirds of that house, it shall become

[w] Jour. Rep. 7th April, 1789.   [x] Jour. Sen. 1789. p. 15.
[y] Cons. U. S. art. 1. s. 3.   [z] Jour. Sen. 1789. p. 39.

a law. In all such cases, the votes of both houses shall be determined by yeas and nays; and the names of the persons voting for and against the bill shall be entered on the journal of each house respectively.[a]

I have already illustrated,[b] at large, the nature, the political advantages, and the probable consequences, of the qualified negative vested in the president of the United States. I now consider it merely as an excellent regulation, to secure an additional degree of accuracy and circumspection in the manner of passing the laws.

The observations, which I have made on this subject, have a relation to the constitution and legislature of this commonwealth, as close as to those of the national government. A negative, similar to that of the president of the United States, is lodged in the governour of Pennsylvania;[c] and the rules of proceeding, adopted by the two houses which compose the legislature of this state, are substantially the same with the rules framed by the two houses which compose the legislature of the Union. It is, therefore, unnecessary, and it would be tedious, to make, to the former, a formal application of what has been mentioned concerning the latter.

By both constitutions, and in both legislatures, provision has been made, as far as, by human contrivance, it would seem, provision can be made, in order to prevent or to check precipitancy and intemperance, in the exercise of the all-important power of legislation. And yet, after all, there is, perhaps, too much reason to apprehend that the *cacoethes legisferundi** will be but too prevalent in both governments. This is an imperfection — in the present state of things, the very best institutions have their imperfections — this is an imperfection incident to governments, which are free. In such governments, the people, at once subjects and sovereigns, are too often tempted to alleviate or to alter the restraints, which they have imposed upon themselves.

We have already seen, that, in Athens, the number and intricacy of the laws were productive of great inconveniences, and were considered and felt as a grievance of the most uneasy and disagreeable kind. Livy, whose eloquence is marked as conspicuously by its justness as by its splendour, gives us a strong representation of the unwieldiness of Roman laws. He[d] describes them as "immensus aliarum super alias acervatarum legum cumulus" — an immense collection of piles of laws, heaped upon one another in endless confusion. The description of the energetick Tacitus is still more concise and expressive — "legibus laborabatur" — the state staggered under the burthen of her laws.[e] As to Pennsylvania, I will, as it becomes me, simply state the fact. Within the last fifteen

---

[a] Cons. U. S. art. 1. s. 7.   [b] Ante. p. 322.   [c] Cons. Penn. art. 1. s. 22.
* [Incurable urge to make laws.]   [d] L. 3. c. 34.   [e] Tac. Ann. l. 3.

years, she has witnessed and she has sustained an accumulation of acts of legislation, in number eight hundred and seventy one.

Far be it from me to avail myself of the abuse, and to urge it against the enjoyment, of freedom. But while I prize the inestimable blessing highly as I do, I surely ought, in every character which I bear, to suggest, to recommend, and to perform every thing in my power, in order to guard its enjoyment from its abuse.

VI. I come now to the last head, under which I proposed to treat concerning the legislative department: this was, to consider the powers vested in congress by the constitution of the United States.

On this subject, we discover a striking difference between the constitution of the United States and that of Pennsylvania. By the latter,[f] each house of the general assembly is vested with every power necessary for a branch of the legislature of a free state. In the former, no clause of such an extensive and unqualified import is to be found. The reason is plain. The latter institutes a legislature with general, the former, with enumerated, powers. Those enumerated powers are now the subject of our consideration.

One great end [g] of the national government is to "provide for the common defence." Defence presupposes an attack. We all know the instruments by which an attack is made by one nation upon another. We all, likewise, know the instruments necessary for defence when such an attack is made. That nation, which would protect herself from hostilities, or maintain peace, must have it in her power — such is the present situation of things — to declare war. The power of declaring war, and the other powers naturally connected with it, are vested in congress. To provide and maintain a navy — to make rules for its government — to grant letters of marque and reprisal — to make rules concerning captures — to raise and support armies — to establish rules for their regulation — to provide for organizing, arming, and disciplining the militia, and for calling them forth in the service of the Union — all these are powers naturally connected with the power of declaring war. All these powers, therefore, are vested in congress.[h]

As the law is now received in England, the king has the sole prerogative of making war.[i] On this very interesting power, the constitution of the United States renews the principles of government, known in England before the conquest. This indeed, as we are told by a well informed writer,[j] may be accounted the chief difference between the Anglo-Saxon and the Anglo-Norman government. In the former, the power of making peace and war was invariably possessed by the wittenagemote; and was

[f] Art. 1. s. 13.   [g] Cons. U. S. Pream.   [h] Cons. U. S. Art. 1. s. 8.
[i] 1. Bl. Com. 257.   [j] Millar. 30.

regarded as inseparable from the allodial condition of its members. In the latter, it was transferred to the sovereign: and this branch of the feudal system, which was accommodated, perhaps, to the depredations and internal commotions prevalent in that rude period, has remained in subsequent ages, when, from a total change of manners, the circumstances, by which it was recommended, have no longer any existence.

There is a pleasure in reflecting on such important renovations of the ancient constitution of England. We have found, and we shall find, that our national government is recommended by the antiquity, as well as by the excellence, of some of its leading principles.

Another great end of the national government is, "to ensure domestick tranquillity." That it may be enabled to accomplish this end, congress may call forth the militia to suppress insurrections.

Again; the national government is instituted to "establish justice." For this purpose, congress is authorized to erect tribunals inferiour to the supreme court; and to define and punish offences against the law of nations, and piracies and felonies committed on the high seas. These points will be more fully considered under the judicial department.

It is an object of the national government to "form a more perfect union." On this principle, congress is empowered to regulate commerce among the several states, to establish post offices, to fix the standard of weights and measures, to coin and regulate the value of money, and to establish, throughout the United States, a uniform rule of naturalization.

Once more, at this time: the national government was intended to "promote the general welfare." For this reason, congress have power to regulate commerce with the Indians and with foreign nations, and to promote the progress of science and of useful arts, by securing, for a time, to authors and inventors, an exclusive right to their compositions and discoveries.

An exclusive property in places fit for forts, magazines, arsenals, dock yards and other needful buildings; and an exclusive legislation over these places, and also, for a convenient distance, over such district as may become the seat of the national government — such exclusive property, and such exclusive legislation, will be of great publick utility, perhaps, of evident publick necessity. They are, therefore, vested in congress, by the constitution of the United States.

For the exercise of the foregoing powers, and for the accomplishment of the foregoing purposes, a revenue is unquestionably indispensable. That congress may be enabled to exercise and accomplish them, it has power to lay and collect taxes, duties, imposts, and excises.

The powers of congress are, indeed, enumerated; but it was intended that those powers, thus enumerated, should be effectual, and not nugatory. In conformity to this consistent mode of thinking and acting, congress has power to make all laws, which shall be neccessary and proper for carrying into execution every power vested by the constitution in the government of the United States, or in any of its officers or departments.

And thus much concerning the first great division of the national government — its legislative authority. I proceed to its second grand division — its executive authority.

II

—OF THE EXECUTIVE DEPARTMENT

IN a former part of my lectures,[a] it was shown, that the powers of government, whether legislative or executive, ought to be restrained. But there is, it was observed, a remarkable contrast between the proper modes of restraining them; for that the legislature, in order to be restrained, must be divided; whereas the executive power, in order to be restrained, should be one. The reasons of this remarkable contrast were, on that occasion, traced particularly, and investigated fully.

We have seen, in our remarks on the congress of the United States, that it consists of two branches — that it is formed on the principle of a divided legislature. We now see, that, in the executive department, the principle of unity is adopted. "The executive power shall be vested in a president of the United States of America." [b]

In treating of the executive department of the United States, I shall consider, 1. The title of the president. 2. His powers and duties.

1. I am to consider the title of the president of the United States. His title is by election.

The general preference which has been given, by statesmen and writers on government, to a hereditary before an elective title to the first magistracy in a state, was the subject of full discussion in a former lecture.[c] I then, I hope, showed, that this preference, however general, and however favoured, is, in truth and upon the genuine principles of government, ill founded. My remarks on this subject I will not, at this time, repeat.

It will probably occasion surprise, when I state the elective title of our first executive magistrate as a renewal, in this particular, of the ancient English constitution. Without hesitation, however, I state this elective title as such.

Well aware I am, that, with regard to this point, I differ in my opinion from the Author of the Commentaries on the laws of England. He thinks it clearly appears, from the highest authority England is acquainted with, that its crown has ever been a hereditary crown.[d] The best historical evidence, however, speaks, I apprehend, a language very different from that, which Sir William Blackstone considers as the highest authority.

[a] Ante. 1. pp. 293–294. [b] Cons. U. S. art. 2. s. 1. [c] Ante 1. pp. 317–318.
[d] 1. Bl. Com. 210.

A king among the old Saxons, says Selden, was, in probability, a commander in the field, an officer *pro tempore*. His title rested upon the good opinion of the freemen; and it seemeth to be one of the best gems of his crown, for that he was thereby declared to be most worthy of the love and service of the people.[e]

The sheriff, says he, in another place, was chosen by the votes of the freeholders, and, as the king himself, was entitled to his honour by the people's favour.[f] The magistrates, he tells us, in the same spirit, were all choice men; and the king the choicest of the chosen; election being the birth of esteem, and this of merit.[g]

The dignity and office of the king, says Mr. Millar, though higher in degree, was perfectly similar to those of the tithing man, the hundreder, and the earl; and he possessed nearly the same powers over the whole kingdom, which those inferiour officers enjoyed in their particular districts.[h]

King Offa, in an address to his people, speaks of his elective title, and of the great purpose for which he was elected, in the following very remarkable and unequivocal terms — [i] "electus ad liberatatis tuæ tuitionem, non meis meritis, sed sola liberalitate vestra."

It appears from history, says a very accurate inquirer,[j] that all the kings of the Saxon race were elected to their kingly office.

Even the mighty Conqueror, says the learned Selden,[k] stooping under the law of a Saxon king, became a king by leave; wisely foreseeing, that a title gotten by election is more certain than that which is gotten by power. Henry the third brought in with him the first precedent in point, of succession by inheritance in the throne of England.

Sir William Blackstone himself, in one place in his Commentaries, speaking of the Saxon laws, mentions, among others, the election of their magistrates by the people, originally even that of their kings. He adds, indeed, that dear bought experience afterwards evinced the convenience and necessity of establishing a hereditary succession to the crown.[l]

If an elective title is a distemper in the body politick; the history and experience of England would lead us to conclude, that a hereditary title is a remedy still worse than the disease. Henry the third is stated as the first fair instance of a prince ascending the throne by virtue of a hereditary claim. How soon was this claim transmitted, in crimson characters, to his posterity, by the fatal and factious war of the *roses* concerning the right of succession! How long and how destructively did that war rage! How pernicious were its consequences, for ages after its immediate operations

---

[e] Bac. on Gov. 29. 30.   [f] Id. 41.   [g] Id. 70.   [h] Millar. 153.
[i] Sulliv. 244 (4to.) [I have been elected to safeguard your liberty not through any merits of my own, but solely through your liberality.]
[j] Id. 245.   [k] Bac. on Gov. 72.   [l] 4. Bl. Com. 406.

had ceased! How few and how short have been the lucid intervals, during which the madness of a contested claim to the succession or to the enjoyment of the English or the British crown has not disturbed the peace and serenity of the nation!

The intrigues, and cabals, and tumults, and convulsions, which are assumed as necessarily annexed to the election of a first magistrate, are perpetually urged against this mode of establishing a title to the office. It is well worth our while to mark the sedulous attention, with which intrigues, and cabals, and tumults, and convulsions, in the election of our first magistrate, are avoided, nay, we trust, rendered impracticable, by the wise provisions introduced into our national constitution.

To avoid tumults and convulsions, the president of the United States is chosen by electors, equal, in number, to the whole number of sentators and representatives, to which all the states are entitled in congress. These, as we shall find by referring to one part of the constitution, cannot much exceed the number of one for every thirty thousand citizens. These, as we shall find by referring to another part of the constitution, are only equal to the number, which compose the two deliberative bodies of the national legislature. If they are not too numerous to transact, with decency and with tranquillity, the legislative business of the Union, in two places; surely they are not too numerous to perform, with decency and with tranquillity, a single act, in as many places as there are states: for, in their respective states, the electors are obliged to meet.

In the appointment of the electors, there is not reason for the least apprehension of convulsions and tumults. They are to be appointed by each state; and they are to be appointed in such a manner as the legislature of each state shall direct. They will, in all probability, be appointed in one of the two following modes — by the citizens — or by the legislature. If the former; the business will be managed in the same manner as the election of representatives in each state. If the latter; it will be managed by those to whom the different states have intrusted their legislative authority — that kind of authority, the exercise of which requires the greatest degree of coolness and caution. Of either mode, can tumults and convulsions be the apprehended result?

To intrigue and cabal, the election of the president is rendered equally inaccessible, as to convulsions and tumults. Those, who appoint the electors, have a deep interest, or represent such as have a deep interest, in the consequences of the election. This interest will be best promoted by far other arts than those of cabal and intrigue. Such electors, we may, therefore, presume, will be appointed, as will favour and practise those other arts. Some reliance, consequently, may be placed on the characters of the electors.

But this is, by no means, the only circumstance, on which the expectations of the United States rest for candour and impartiality in the election of a president. Other circumstances ensure them. 1. The electors must vote by ballot. Ballot has been called the silent assertor of liberty: with equal justness, it may be called the silent assertor of honesty. 2. The electors must give their votes on the same day throughout the United States. How can cabal and intrigue extend or combine their influence at the same time, in many different places, separated from one another by the distance of hundreds or thousands of miles? 3. Each elector must vote for two persons, without distinguishing which of the two he wishes to be the president. The precise operation of his vote is not known to himself at the time when he gives it. By this regulation, simple but sagacious, cabal and intrigue, could they even be admitted, would be under the necessity of acting blindfold at the election. The sinister plans, formed separately in every part, might and often would be defeated by the joint and unforeseen effect of the whole. For it is the unforeseen effect of the whole, which must finally determine, or furnish materials for finally determining, the election of the president.

His election shall be finally determined in this manner. The person, in whose favour the greatest number of votes is given, provided that number shall be a majority of the whole number of electors, shall be the president. If more than one person have a majority, and, at the same time, an equal number of votes; the house of representatives shall immediately choose one of them for president, by ballot. If no person have a majority of votes of the electors; the house of representatives shall choose, by ballot, a president from the five highest on the list.

After the choice of the president, the person having the greatest number of votes of the electors shall be the vice president. But if there remain two or more having equal votes; the senate shall choose from them the vice president by[m] ballot.[n]

[m] Cons. U. S. art. 2. s. 1.

[n] By an alteration of the constitution recommended by congress in December, 1803, and which, having received the approbation of three fourths of the states in the Union, has now become a part of the constitution, the regulations mentioned in the text have been changed in the following particulars. The electors are directed to name, in their ballots, the person voted for as president, and, in distinct ballots, the person voted for as vice president, and to transmit to the seat of government distinct lists of the persons so voted for. The person having the greatest number of votes for president, shall be the president, if such number be a majority of the whole number of electors appointed; and if no person have such majority, then from the persons having the highest numbers, not exceeding three on the list of those voted for as president, the house of representatives shall choose immediately, by ballot, the president. If the house do not make a choice before the fourth day of March then next following, the vice president shall act as president, as in case of the death or constitutional disability of the president. The person, having the greatest number of votes as vice president, shall be the vice-president, if such number be a majority of the whole number of electors appointed; and if no person have a majority, then from the two highest numbers on the list, the senate shall choose the vice president.

Thus much concerning the title of the president of the United States.
2. I am, in the next place, to consider his powers and duties.[o]

He is to take care that the laws be faithfully executed; he is commander in chief of the army and navy of the United States, and of the
militia, when called into their actual service. In the Saxon government,
the power of the first executive magistrate was also twofold. He had authority to lead the army, as we are informed by Selden, to punish according to demerits and according to laws, and reward according to discretion. The law martial and that of the sea were branches of the positive
law, settled by the general vote in the wittenagemote, and not left to the
will of a lawless general or commander: so tender and uniform were
those times both in their laws and liberties.[p] The person at the head of
the executive department had authority, not to make, or alter, or dispense with the laws, but to execute and act the laws, which were established: and against this power there was no rising up, so long as it gadded
not, like an unfeathered arrow, at random. On the whole, he was no
other than a *primum mobile*, set in a regular motion by laws, which
were established by the whole body of the nation.[q]

The president has power to nominate, and, with the advice and consent of the senate, to appoint ambassadours, judges of the supreme court,
and, in general, all the other officers of the United States. On this subject, there is a very striking and important difference between the constitution of the United States and that of Pennsylvania. By the latter,
the first executive magistrate possesses, uncontrolled by either branch of
the legislature, the power of appointing all officers, whose appointments
are not, in the constitution itself, otherwise provided for.[r] On a former
occasion[s] I noticed a maxim, which is of much consequence in the science
of government — that the legislative and executive powers be preserved
distinct and unmingled in their exercise. This maxim I then considered in
a variety of views: and, in each, found it to be both true and useful. I am
very free to confess, that, with regard to this point, the proper principle
of government is, in my opinion, observed by the constitution of Pennsylvania much more correctly, than it is by the constitution of the United
States. In justice, however, to the latter, it ought to be remarked, that,
though the *appointment* of officers is to be the concurrent act of the
president and senate, yet an indispensable prerequisite — the *nomination*
of them — is vested exclusively in the president.

[Continued in Volume II]

A quorum for the purpose shall consist of two thirds of the whole number of
senators, and a majority of the whole number shall be necessary to a choice. No
person constitutionally ineligible to the office of president, shall be eligible to that
of vice president of the United States. — *Ed.*

[o] Cons. U. S. Art. 2. s. 2, 3.   [p] Bac. on Gov. 40.   [q] Id. 32, 33.
[r] Cons. Penn. art. 2. s. 8.   [s] Ante. p. 298.

Date Due

DEMCO NO. 25-370

APR 15 '69	CANISIUS			
MAY 7 60				
	CANISIUS	JAN 30 '89		
JAN 22 87	CANISIUS			
	JAN 8 '03			
DEC 1 2 1994				